P9-AER-774

400 SAUCES

DIPS, DRESSINGS, SALSAS, JAMS, JELLIES & PICKLES

400 SAUCES

DIPS, DRESSINGS, SALSAS, JAMS, JELLIES & PICKLES

HOW TO ADD SOMETHING SPECIAL TO EVERY DISH FOR EVERY OCCASION, FROM CLASSIC COOKING SAUCES TO FUN PARTY DIPS

Featuring over 400 step-by-step recipes shown in more than
1400 stunning photographs – everything from cordon bleu sauces
to spicy relishes, chutneys or delicious jams and jellies

CATHERINE ATKINSON,
CHRISTINE FRANCE
AND MAGGIE MAYHEW

HERMES
HOUSE

This edition is published by Hermes House

Hermes House is an imprint of Anness Publishing Ltd
Hermes House, 88–89 Blackfriars Road, London SE1 8HA
tel. 020 7401 2077; fax 020 7633 9499
www.hermeshouse.com; www.annesspublishing.com

If you like the images in this book and would like to investigate using them for publishing, promotions or advertising, visit our website www.practicalpictures.com for more information.

Publisher: Joanna Lorenz
Editorial Director: Helen Sudell
Contributing Editor: Bridget Jones
Project Editor: Catherine Stuart
Production Controller: Ben Worley
Page Design: Adelle Morris
Cover Design: Chloe Steers

ETHICAL TRADING POLICY
At Anness Publishing we believe that business should be conducted in an ethical and ecologically sustainable way, with respect for the environment and a proper regard to the replacement of the natural resources we employ.
As a publisher, we use a lot of wood pulp to make high-quality paper for printing, and that wood commonly comes from spruce trees. We are therefore currently growing more than 500,000 trees in two Scottish forest plantations near Aberdeen – Berrymoss (130 hectares/ 320 acres) and West Touxhill (125 hectares/305 acres). The forests we manage contain twice the number of trees employed each year in paper-making for our books.
Because of this ongoing ecological investment programme, you, as our customer, can have the pleasure and reassurance of knowing that a tree is being cultivated on your behalf to naturally replace the materials used to make the book you are holding.
Our forestry programme is run in accordance with the UK Woodland Assurance Scheme (UKWAS) and will be certified by the internationally recognized Forest Stewardship Council (FSC). The FSC is a non-government organization dedicated to promoting responsible management of the world's forests. Certification ensures forests are managed in an environmentally sustainable and socially responsible way. For further information about this scheme, go to www.annesspublishing.com/trees

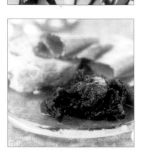

© Anness Publishing Ltd 2006, 2007

All rights reserved. No part of this publication may be reproduced, stored in a retrieval system, or transmitted in any way or by any means, electronic, mechanical, photocopying, recording or otherwise, without the prior written permission of the copyright holder.

A CIP catalogue record for this book is available from the British Library.

Parts of this edition previously appeared in *Sauces* and *The Complete Book of Preserves and Pickles*.

NOTES
Bracketed terms are intended for American readers.
  For all recipes, quantities are given in both metric and imperial measures and, where appropriate, in standard cups and spoons. Follow one set, but not a mixture, because they are not interchangeable.
  Standard spoon and cup measures are level. 1 tsp = 5ml, 1 tbsp = 15ml, 1 cup = 250ml/8fl oz.
  Australian standard tablespoons are 20ml. Australian readers should use 3 tsp in place of 1 tbsp for measuring small quantities of gelatine, flour, salt, etc.
  American pints are 16fl oz/2 cups. American readers should use 20fl oz/2.5 cups in place of 1 pint when measuring liquids.
  Electric oven temperatures in this book are for conventional ovens. When using a fan oven, the temperature will probably need to be reduced by about 10–20°C/20–40°F. Since ovens vary, you should check with your manufacturer's instruction book for guidance.
  Medium (US large) eggs are used unless otherwise stated.
  The nutritional analysis given for each recipe is calculated per portion (i.e. serving or item), unless otherwise stated. If the recipe gives a range, such as Serves 4–6, then the nutritional analysis will be for the smaller portion size, i.e. 6 servings. Measurements for sodium do not include salt added to taste.

CONTENTS

PRESERVES 290

INTRODUCTION

Like the accessory that turns an ordinary outfit into a stunner, or the painting that provides the perfect focal point for a room, a sauce can transform the simplest dish into something unforgettable. It may be integral to the dish, drawing all the elements together into a harmonious whole, or it may be served on the side, providing a complementary or contrasting flavour. The aim may be to offer an alternative texture: a crisp salsa with a salmon steak, for instance, or pickled red cabbage with sausages. Colour has a role to play, too. A simple sweet treat, such as a spoonful of ruby-red plum and cardamom jelly, can look superb alongside a slice of quiche or a portion of deep-fried Camembert. A sauce can also soothe, as when guacamole is offered alongside a fiery chilli, or it can challenge the palate. Think horseradish sauce with roast beef, or wasabi – such an innocent-looking fire-raiser – spooned alongside sushi.

Sauces have been central to culinary tradition for centuries. The word evolved from the Latin *salsus*, which means salted, and they were

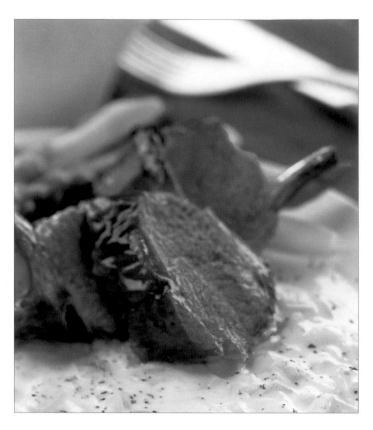

originally conceived by cooks, not to add piquancy to food, but to disguise the fact that the meat or fish that formed the basis of the dish was past its best. To mask suspect flavours, strongly flavoured spice rubs were popular. Subtlety wasn't a strong point until the Italian Renaissance, when inspired chefs at the court of the Medici family began to develop dishes renowned for their fine flavour and flamboyant presentation.

Left: Add herbs such as thyme and bay leaves to sauces and preserves for maximum freshness and flavour.

Above: The classic French white onion sauce is traditionally enjoyed with rare, juicy steak.

When Catherine de Medici travelled to France in 1533 to marry the future King Henry II, she took her personal chefs with her and introduced her hosts to a range of new and delicious dishes, often married with delicate sauces. These were adopted and adapted by the French. Just over a century later, Francois La Varenne developed the roux-based sauce, and for almost three hundred years successive French chefs, including the great

Marie-Antoine Carême, created and classified complex sauces with the kind of energy usually reserved for main course meals!

By the mid-1950s, just as the taste for rich, heavy sauces was declining, Paul Bocuse tossed his chef's hat into the ring and introduced nouvelle cuisine. Sauces became lighter, complementing beautifully presented food made from the finest fresh ingredients.

Cooks have learned that, while classic sauces still have a vital role to play, it is okay to loosen up a little. Sauces can be a simple stock reduction, a fruit coulis, a savoury jelly, a relish made of raw, chopped vegetables. They can be creamy or crisp, hot or cold, sweet or savoury.

Below: Jams and jellies marry up all kinds of fruits and vegetables, and can be savoury or sweet.

They can start out as a marinade or end as a dip. A sauce might be an old favourite, like the apple sauce that always accompanied your grandmother's roast pork, or a more modern blend. Sun-dried tomatoes with radicchio, perhaps, or a Thai-style basil and chilli mixture. Then there are the sauces you store – like chutneys, pickles and other preserves. The art of preserving is as old a tradition as sauce-making, but this too is experiencing a renaissance, thanks to cross-cultural influences and all kinds of new serving ideas. Some classic "spreads" can even work as super-fast sauces: try, for instance, spooning jam or marmalade onto a hot, steamed pudding.

Both reference sections to the book are outstanding, outlining all any cook needs to know about basic ingredients, equipment and

Above: Many preserves are stored using the same, simple methods: tried and tested for centuries!

techniques for making sauces and preserves. Over 400 inspiring recipes are clearly explained, with step-by-step pictures to encourage and inspire. In short, when it comes to classic condiments, this is the only guide you'll ever need.

classic savoury sauces,
salsas and dips, sauces for
main course meat, fish and
vegetable dishes, dressings and
marinades and sweet sauces

SAUCES

SUCCESS WITH SAUCES

A sauce can be many things to many meals – from the simplest aside to accentuate the taste of plain cooking, to the integral part of a more complex dish. Savoury or sweet, fragile or full of punch, the one characteristic shared by all sauces is their liquid content. Unlike dry toppings, spice mixes or rubs, sauces include some form of liquid, even if this is a fat, such as butter, that becomes liquid on heating. There may be hundreds of brands and types to buy but nothing competes with home-made sauce – and it doesn't have to be complicated to be brilliant.

CLASSICAL STANDARDS

Old-school culinary experts still classify sauces by techniques (thickening, reducing or concentrating, or emulsifying methods), uses or colour, highlighting 'mother' or foundation sauces that could be varied to create a range of recipes. While classical methods and combinations

Above: Fresh-tasting salsas combine handfuls of herbs with full, ripe and flavourful fruit and vegetables

are still the essence of many sauces, there is now a much more relaxed approach than this. The basic laws may still apply, but they have given rise to new, exciting interpretations.

FRESH COMBINATIONS

Not only has the approach lightened up, but so have the recipes and sauce partnerships.

Heavy coating sauces and fat-rich liquors that once flooded plates are no longer the norm. New-generation sauces enhance, not mask, good ingredients; gravies bring out the best in meats; and butters moisten rather than render greasy. Light stocks and base liquids, simple reductions, restraint with creams and butter, and fine (rather than heavy) thickening are popular. Marrying sauces with main ingredients has been opened up in simple partnerships that are easy to prepare, and bursting with colour and vitality.

WORLD INFLUENCES

The international food scene has changed sauces and their use dramatically. Whereas previous generations may have introduced the occasional spice to European ingredients with timidity, twenty-first century recipes refine the use of international ingredients to an eclectic art.

Hot or cold, sweet-sour or savoury-sweet, we are all aware of brilliant sauces that transform everyday foods into exciting international meals. Whether based on stock, milk or vegetables, classic methods are now fused with all kinds of cross-cultural influences, and can be enlivened in seconds by an instinctive seasoning twist, or unconventional combinations of ingredients.

Left: There are many delightful twists on the classic tomato sauce, which will work equally well in meat and vegetarian dishes.

COOK IN OR SERVE ON

Many of the recipes in this section of the book concentrate on the integration of a main dish with a complementary sauce. There are variations and suggestions for the different ways in which the sauce can be served, and the ingredients it will suit. As a general rule, 'serve on' sauces added at the very end of the recipe are separated from the main dish in both the listed ingredients and in the method.

Some dishes, such as casseroles and braised dishes, generate their own sauce during cooking, which makes the cook's life a little easier; others involve adding food to a prepared sauce for cooking. While cooking in a sauce is a great way of making full-flavoured dishes that are rounded, with a certain depth and complexity, serve-on sauces can bring different culinary personality.

Cooked in advance and often served with plain cooked foods, sauce accompaniments can be prepared using the cooking residue from roasting, pan-frying or braising. They may be based on a marinade or basting mixture. The simplest flavoured butters or oils can be served as sauces or dressings for cooked foods.

HOT-COLD COMBINATIONS

Cold dressings and fresh, uncooked sauces should not be set aside only for use with salads or as dips – they are also fantastic with hot foods. Oils and vinegars, mayonnaise-based sauces, or yogurt mixtures are all terrific with freshly cooked fish, poultry, meat or vegetables. Smooth purées, finely chopped

salsas or chunky vegetable and fruit mixtures do not have to be cooked to be classed as a sauce. Pepped up with spices, tart with citrus, or aromatic with fresh herbs, all sorts of uncooked sauces are packed with nutrients. They are often low in fat and can be very quick to make.

COOK-AHEAD SIMPLICITY

Making your own sauces does not have to be laborious. Instead of buying mixtures laden with hidden fats, sugars, seasoning and artificial flavourings, pick up a few favourite recipes and some sure-winner tips from the chapters that follow. Use them as your everyday, hassle-free flavour makers. Soon you will gain the confidence to experiment with a whole host of exciting new twists on your culinary repertoire.

The majority of sauces can be made in advance, cooled and chilled in a covered container. Some can be made one or two days in advance, while others can be prepared up to a week ahead. All

Below: Spices such as nutmeg are essential additions to many savoury and sweet sauces.

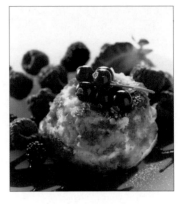

Above: A light, fruity sauce is the perfect accompaniment to all kinds of egg-based puddings.

sorts of sauces freeze well, ready for thawing at the last minute in the microwave. Making a big batch of a favourite simple sauce (tomato or basic white sauce, for example) and freezing it in portions is an excellent way to save time and eat well. Try freezing salsas and dips in little pots.

Seasonal fruit and vegetables can be used for sauces when they are at their best and least expensive. 'Fresh' sauces can be frozen for year-round use. Don't limit yourself to savoury sauces. Fruit purées, chocolate sauces and syrups are all suitable for chilling or freezing.

There is just one simple rule when making sauces ahead, and that's labelling. Always label your pot of sauce with its name, quantity and date. It is also worth stocking up on cook-in bags or containers that can go from freezer to microwave, steamer, double boiler or oven. Creative and cost-effective, successful sauce-making can literally transform your approach to everyday cooking.

a guide to
making sauces

There is no great secret to sauces – it's simply matter of marrying tried and tested techniques with good ingredients, and partnering the right sauce with the main food. A little know-how goes a long way, so it's worth learning the sauce-making basics – when to boil, simmer or barely warm, why some mixtures are whisked hard and others gently stirred, which sauces can be whizzed up in seconds, and when to cook-ahead for last-minute perfection.

FLOURS

There is a wide range of flours and thickening agents on the market. It is important to select the right product, since the choice of flour used for a sauce will determine not only the cooking method used, but the final texture and flavour of the finished sauce. These general guidelines should help remove any mystique involved.

Below from left to right: Brown flour, wholemeal (whole-wheat) flour.

Below: Sauce flour

PLAIN WHITE FLOUR

Also known as all-purpose flour, this is the standard choice for making roux-based sauces and gravies. Its fine, smooth texture combines easily with melted fat for a sauce with a roux base, so that when heated, the starch grains burst and cook, thickening the sauce liquid.

White flour usually contains 70–75 per cent of the wheatgrain. Most of the bran and wheatgerm have been removed during milling, leaving it almost white, so it is excellent for thickening white sauces. White flour is chemically bleached, making it pale in colour and therefore more suitable for white sauces than unbleached, stoneground flours.

Below: Plain (all-purpose) flour.

STRONG AND SOFT FLOURS

These are flours designed for specific baking uses, not for sauces, but could be used in an emergency if you run out of plain flour. Self-raising (self-rising) flour has chemical agents added during milling which react with heat to make cake mixtures rise during cooking. Strong flour, or bread flour, has a higher proportion of gluten, making it most suitable for bread making. Soft flours, or sponge flours, have a lower gluten content, and are designed for cakes, but they also make good thickeners for light sauces.

WHOLEMEAL, WHEATMEAL AND BROWN FLOURS

All of these flours contain more of the bran and wheatgerm, between 80 and 90 per cent of the grain, which gives them a nutty flavour and coarse texture, and a darker colour than white flour. Because of this, they are not usually chosen for making sauces, but if you don't mind the texture and colour, there's no reason why any of these flours should not be used for thickening sauces. The bonus is that they will add a little extra dietary fibre and nutrients to the dish.

SAUCE FLOUR

This flour has been recently introduced, and has a lower protein level than ordinary wheat flour, so that sauces made with it are less likely to go lumpy. It is designed specifically for making cooked white sauces and gravies. It is also a good choice for making low-fat sauces, since it is suitable for use in recipes made by the all-in-one, or blending method, in which no fat is used to mix the flour to a paste.

CORNFLOUR

Also known as cornstarch, this fine maize flour is gluten-free. It is light and smooth, producing velvety-textured sauces, usually made by the blending method. For smooth results it has to be mixed to a smooth paste with a little cold liquid (a technique known as slaking) before adding hot liquid. It is widely used in Chinese sauces, and its light, slightly jellied, texture makes it particularly suitable for sweet sauces and blancmange, or light sauces for coating foods.

POTATO FLOUR

Also known as *farine de fécule*, potato flour is made from pure potato starch. It is very fine and smooth and is bright white in colour. It makes a light, clear thickener for sauces without affecting the flavour. You will need to use slightly less potato flour than ordinary plain flour for thickening. It is most suited to the blending method of sauce making, and is often used as a thickener in Chinese and Asian dishes and stir-fry sauces, so it is easily available from Oriental stores.

ARROWROOT

This is a white, finely ground powder made from the root of a tropical tree, which is grown in Central America. It is used as a thickening agent, in the same way as cornflour, for sauces made by the blending method. Whereas cornflour makes an opaque sauce, arrowroot clears when boiled. It is often used in sweet glazes.

Below, clockwise from top left: Cornflour (cornstarch), custard powder, potato flour, arrowroot.

CUSTARD POWDER

Useful for quick custard sauces, this is an unsweetened cornflour-based mix flavoured with vanilla.

A similar result can be achieved by enriching a cornflour sauce with egg yolks and adding vanilla essence. Make up with milk by the blending method. Sweeten to taste.

STORING FLOUR

Store flour in a cool, dark, dry, airy place, away from steam or damp. Place the flour into a clean tin or a storage jar with a close-fitting lid, and always make sure you wash and dry the container thoroughly before refilling it. Check the "use by" dates, and use up the flour within the recommended pack date, or replace it. Don't add new flour to old in a storage jar – it is always best to use up the older flour first.

Once opened, plain white (all-purpose) flour can be stored under the right conditions for about six months, but

wholemeal (whole-wheat) and brown flours have a higher fat content so these are best used within two months. Like all food, flour is best used while fresh – it develops "off" flavours, ultimately becoming rancid, when old. If stored in damp conditions, it tastes musty, so buy in small quantities.

FATS AND OILS

Fats make sauces palatable, and improve their flavour and texture. The ones usually used in sauces are "yellow" fats, such as butter or margarine, or oils. Many are combined with flour in sauces, for example in a roux, a cooked paste, or in beurre manié, a raw paste. Heating flour with fat allows liquid to be incorporated without forming lumps. The classic emulsified sauces, such as hollandaise or mayonnaise, use either melted butter or liquid oils, beaten with eggs until combined and thickened in an emulsion. The same principle is used in reduced sauces, such as beurre blanc, or in oil-based salad dressings such as vinaigrette, where the fat is whisked into a reduced or well-flavoured liquid base to make a smooth emulsion. In salsas and purées, oil is added for flavour by stirring into, or drizzling over, the other ingredients.

Clockwise from top left: Ghee, clarifed butter, concentrated butter.

TYPES OF FAT

Saturated fats are solid at room temperature, and are the ones that can raise cholesterol levels in the blood. Polyunsaturated fats can help lower cholesterol levels; mono- unsaturated fats, which are beneficial in regulating cholesterol levels, are liquid but can be made solid by a process known as hydrogenation. This is the process used to make margarines and spreads.

butter

A natural product made by churning cream, butter has an 80 per cent fat content, which is saturated fat. Butter is made in two basic types, sweetcream and lactic, and both are available salted, lightly salted or unsalted. The choice will depend largely on flavour, according to whether you are making a sweet or savoury sauce. There are other alternatives, however. Clarified butter, ghee or concentrated butters, which can be made at home, will withstand higher temperatures than untreated butter, and will not burn as easily.

margarine

Soft (tub) margarines, made from a blend of vegetable oils and/or animal oils, have a soft, spreadable texture. Hard (packet) margarines have a firmer texture and are made from animal and vegetable fats. Both types have the same fat content as butter, and can be used as a direct substitute for butter in making sweet and savoury sauces. As the flavour is inferior to butter, margarines are best chosen for more robustly flavoured sauces where their own flavour will not be as noticeable.

Left: Lactic unsalted butter (left), sweetcream salted butter.

spreads

The wide choice of different spreads on the market is confusing to say the least, but as a rough guide, unless they are labelled "low-fat", or "very low-fat", they are generally suitable for sauce-making. After that, choice is very much a matter of personal preference.

Polyunsaturated vegetable oil spreads: Products described in this way are made either from a single vegetable oil or sunflower oil alone, or from a blend of different vegetable oils. They vary in fat content from 61 to 79 per cent.

Monounsaturated vegetable oil spreads: Made from olive oil or rapeseed oil, these vary in fat content from 60 to 75 per cent.

Dairy spreads: These contain cream or buttermilk to retain a buttery flavour and smooth texture, while providing a lower-fat alternative to butter. The fat content varies between 61 and 75 per cent.

Reduced-fat spreads: These products are either made from vegetable oils alone or may also contain some dairy or animal fat. Their fat content is between 50 and 60 per cent.

Low-fat spreads and very low-fat spreads: These spreads, popular with the weight-conscious, contain less than 40 per cent fat, and are often as low as 25 per cent. They are not recommended for cooking, although they can be added to all-in-one method sauces.

STORING FAT

All solid fats should be stored in the refrigerator, below 4°C/39°F. They should be covered or closely wrapped to protect them from light and air. Keep them away from strong-smelling foods as they can absorb other flavours easily. (The section used for storing butter in most refrigerators is in the door, and is not quite so cold as other parts, so the butter should not become too hard.) Oils tend to

Above, from left: Polyunsaturated, olive, dairy, and reduced-fat spreads.

solidify at low temperatures, so are best kept in a cool cupboard with a temperature of 4–12°C/39–54°F. Keep them away from light, which will cause them to become rancid quickly.

OILS

These fats are liquid at room temperature. They are used in emulsion sauces, such as mayonnaise or salad dressings, usually balanced with vinegar or other acids, such as citrus juices. However, they can also be used as a

Below, left to right: Very low-fat and low-fat spreads.

Below: Margarine tub (left) and block.

direct replacement for butter or hard fats in roux or similar flour-thickened sauces, with good results. With the exception of coconut oil and palm oil, they are mostly rich in unsaturated fat, which helps reduce cholesterol levels. The choice of individual oils for a particular sauce depends largely on flavour and personal taste.

Groundnut (peanut) oil: Made from peanuts, this is usually used where a mild flavour is required.

Sesame seed oil: Usually used for flavouring Oriental sauces at the end of cooking, as it has an intense, rich flavour and burns easily when heated. However it can be heated with care, or mixed half and half with another oil, such as groundnut, if necessary.

Soya oil: A mild-flavoured oil

Below, from left: Groundnut (peanut) oil, sunflower oil, soya oil, sesame oil, walnut oil.

which will withstand high temperatures, this keeps well and is economical to use.

Sunflower oil: A little more expensive to use than soya oil, this versatile, light-flavoured oil is good for sauces or dressings, as it does not mask other flavours.

Nut oils: Walnut and hazelnut oils are the most commonly used nut oils for dressings, lending their rich, distinctive flavours to salads. Use in moderation, perhaps combined with a milder oil, as the flavours can be strong.

olive oils

The characteristics and quality of olive oils vary and depend on variety, growing region and method of production. Many are blended, but the best-quality oils are produced on individual estates. For most sauces, including mayonnaise, it's best to choose

virgin or pure olive oil, and keep the more expensive extra virgin ones for salad dressings, or for drizzling directly over foods. It is more economical to buy olive oils in larger quantities.

Extra virgin first pressed or cold pressed olive oils: These oils are made from the first pressing of the olives, with no extra treatment, such as heat or blending. By law, these oils never have more than 1 per cent acidity, ensuring a fine flavour. They have a distinctive flavour and pungent aroma. They are usually a deep green colour and are sometimes cloudy, although both of these factors vary according to the area where the oil was produced.

Virgin olive oil: This is also cold pressed and unrefined, but has a higher acidity content than extra virgin oil, with a maximum level of 1 to 1.5 per cent.

Pure olive oil: This comes from the third or fourth pressing of the olives, and is usually blended. It has a maximum acid content of 2 per cent. It is mild, rather than overpowering, and therefore widely used in cooking.

Light olive oil: This is a product created during the last pressing of the fruit. The term "light" refers to the clear colour and delicate flavour, not the calorie count.

STORE CUPBOARD

A well-stocked store cupboard (pantry) makes every cook's life a lot easier, and when it comes to sauce making, it really makes sense. Just by keeping a few basic ingredients in stock, you will always be able to whip up an impromptu sauce when the occasion demands, transforming a simple dish into something special.

STOCK CUBES AND POWDERS

There is a wide choice of commercial stock (bouillon) cubes and powders, and these vary in flavour and quality. Good-quality products make adequate substitutes for fresh stock, and certainly they are very convenient to use. However, some tend to be quite salty, so allow for this when adding other seasonings. Follow the pack directions for quantities to use. Generally speaking, it is worth paying a little more for good-quality stock cubes or powder, and it is worth choosing one that is made with natural ingredients for a more natural flavour.

Many supermarkets also now sell cartons of basic ready-made fresh stocks on the chilled foods counter, including beef, chicken, fish and vegetable stock. These are a good substitute for home-made if you're short of time.

Canned consommé makes an excellent substitute for a good brown stock in rich savoury sauces, so is well worth keeping handy in the store cupboard. If you need a light stock, the colour of consommé may be too dark to use, but brands do vary widely.

CANNED TOMATOES AND BOILED SAUCES

Since many of the plum tomatoes we buy out of season are lacking in

Above: Consommé
Left: Stock cubes and powder
Below, clockwise from left:
Passata, sugocasa, whole plum
tomatoes, tomato purée, chopped
tomatoes in tomato juice.

flavour, it's a safer bet to go for good-quality canned tomatoes in recipes, either whole or chopped. The best are from Italy, so check the label carefully. Polpa di pomodoro are finely chopped or crushed. Avoid those with added herbs or spices, which are best added fresh.

Crushed or creamed tomatoes: Sold as sugocasa, polpa and passata (bottled strained tomatoes), and usually packed in convenient jars, long-life packs or bottles, these products are invaluable for sauces.

Below, top row from left: Oyster sauce, soy sauce, Worcestershire sauce, fish sauce, hot pepper sauce. Bottom row: Red pesto, green pesto, English mustard.

COOK'S TIP
Chopped canned tomatoes are usually more expensive than whole ones, so you can save valuable pennies by simply chopping them yourself.

Sugocasa and polpa both have a chunky texture, while passata is sieved to a creamy smooth, sauce-like purée.

Tomato purée (paste): This is concentrated, cooked tomato pulp in a strong, thick paste, and is sold in tubes or cans. The strength of different brands varies, so use with care or the flavour can overpower a sauce. Sun-dried tomato paste has a sweet, rich flavour, and is milder than ordinary tomato purée.

COMMERCIAL SAUCES

The huge range of commercially-made flavouring sauces or condiments now available is a boon to the creative cook. The following are some of the most useful to keep in your store cupboard.

Hot pepper sauces: Widely used in West Indian and South American cooking, there are many versions of pepper sauce, the most famous being Tabasco. Use with caution, as they can be fiery hot. These sauces will pep up almost any savoury sauce, marinade or dressing.

Mustards: Ready-made mustards are a blend of ground mustard seeds with flour and salt, often with wine, herbs and other spices. Dijon is often used for classic French sauces and for dressings such as vinaigrette and mayonnaise – it also helps to stabilize the emulsion. Yellow English mustard is a good choice to give colour and bite to cheese sauce or to flavour rich gravies for meat. Milder German mustard is good for a barbecue sauce to serve with chops or sausages. Mild, creamy American mustard is squeezed on hotdogs or burgers. Wholegrain mustard gives a pleasant texture, particularly to creamy savoury sauces and dressings.

Oyster sauce: A thicker-textured

sauce made with the extract of real oysters, this adds a delicious sweet-savoury flavour to sauces for accompanying meat, fish or vegetables (in non-vegetarian dishes).

Pesto: Commercially made pesto is sold in jars, either the traditional green basil pesto, or a red pesto made from sun-dried tomatoes. Use it just as it is as a replacement for fresh pesto sauce to stir into pasta, pepped up with a little freshly grated Parmesan cheese or an extra drizzle of olive oil. You can also add it by the spoonful to enrich and enhance the flavour of tomato sauces, salsas and dressings. Once the jar is opened, this type of product should be treated as fresh and stored in the refrigerator.

Soy sauce: Although this is traditionally used for Chinese and Japanese foods, there is no need to limit its use to Oriental dishes. Use it to flavour and colour all kinds of savoury sauces, marinades and dressings. Light soy sauce is good in light, sweet-and-sour or stir-fry sauces for fish or vegetables, and the richer, sweeter dark soy sauce is best with rich meat sauces, such as satays, or for barbecue sauces.

Thai fish sauce or nam pla: This is a classic Thai sauce made from fermented fish. It has a pungent flavour and is best in cooked sauces. It adds a richness to sauces for both meat and fish.

Worcestershire sauce: This classic English sauce has its origins in India. Its spicy, mellowed, but piquant, flavour enhances savoury sauces, marinades and dressings of any type. It is often used to bring out meaty flavours in gravies and long-cooked casserole sauces.

COCONUT MILK AND CREAM

Coconut milk and cream are used widely in Oriental dishes, particularly those based on spicy and curried sauces. They can be used rather like dairy products, for thickening, enriching and flavouring.

Coconut milk: This is available in cans and long-life packs. It is similar in thickness to single cream.

Coconut cream: This has the thickness of double cream. Creamed coconut is solid and

white; it is sold in solid blocks, so you can cut off just the amount you need and melt it into sauces or in a little hot water.

VINEGARS

These aromatic vinegars are based on malt, wine, beer, cider, rice wine and sugar, and are often used to enhance flavour in sauces or as emulsifiers. Dark, long-matured sherry or balsamic vinegars have intense, powerful flavours and you may only need a few drops.

Below: Red and white wine vinegars and fruit vinegars are useful for salad dressings.

HERBS AND SPICES

Many sauce recipes call for herbs and spices to add flavour and colour, and there's no end to the variety you can buy nowadays, especially in the larger supermarkets and good grocers. Generally speaking, herbs are the leafy tops and stems of an edible plant, and spices are from the berries, seeds, bark and roots.

CULINARY HERBS

It's worth growing a few of the more useful common herbs yourself. Some herbs grown in pots on the kitchen windowsill, will always be handy when you need to snip off a few sprigs. It is considerably cheaper, too, as supermarket fresh herbs, even the ones in pots, have a limited life and can be quite costly. A useful basic selection to grow at home would include parsley, chives, thyme,

mint, oregano, sage, bay and dill.

When cooking with herbs, you don't need to be too precise. Treat the measurements quoted in recipes as a general guide, and add the herbs according to your personal preference.

dried and frozen herbs

Dried herbs are useful to keep in the cupboard for emergencies, but always plump for fresh in preference if you can get them – it will make a noticeable difference to the flavour of the dish. Many of the delicate-leafed herbs, such as basil, coriander or chervil, do not dry successfully, but the ones that are worth buying dried are thyme, rosemary, parsley, mint, oregano,

Above, clockwise from top left: Chopped and frozen herbs – coriander, parsley, chives.

tarragon and dill. Store dried herbs in airtight containers in a cool place away from light, and use them quickly as their flavour is soon lost.

Below, clockwise from bowl: Curry paste, nutmeg, cinnamon sticks, vanilla pods (beans), salt, whole coriander, cumin seeds, black, green, white peppercorns.

Left, clockwise from top: Freeze-dried mint, freeze-dried parsley, freeze-dried dill, freeze-dried tarragon, dried thyme, dried rosemary. Centre: Freeze-dried oregano.

Above, clockwise from left: Mint, bay, thyme.

Frozen herbs, such as parsley, chives and coriander, retain more of the flavour of fresh herbs and can be very useful and convenient – they can be added to a sauce or dressing straight from the freezer.

SALT AND PEPPER

Good-quality sea salt has a more intense flavour than "table" or "cooking" salt. There are different varieties of sea salt with distinctive flavours. Strong black peppercorns, mild white and very mild green are all worth storing.

CULINARY SPICES

Keep a good store of spices in the kitchen. A useful selection includes whole nutmeg, cinnamon sticks, vanilla pods, coriander seeds, cumin seeds and curry paste (curry pastes keep longer than powders).
Cinnamon sticks: These have a sweet, spicy flavour and are widely used in sweet sauces and chutneys. They can be crushed or used whole and removed at the end of cooking.
Coriander: These seeds are valued for seasoning pickles and chutneys; they have a mild sweet flavour.
Cumin: A key ingredient in chutneys and curries, these seeds have a pronounced and slightly bitter taste.
Curry paste: This is sold in a range of strengths and flavours. It keeps for much longer than curry powder.
Vanilla pods (beans): Infuse these dried pods in milk or cream for sweet sauces and custards. Store in a jar of caster sugar to make vanilla sugar.
Whole nutmeg: Freshly grated whole nutmeg is much better than the powdered variety, which quickly loses its flavour.

EXTRACTS AND FLOWER WATERS
Vanilla or other flavouring extracts can be very convenient, but choose carefully, as some are inferior artificial flavourings. Check the label – it should describe the contents as pure vanilla extract or extract of vanilla, not vanilla flavouring.

Flower waters are a delightful way to flavour cold sweet sauces, syrups and creams in particular, but occasionally they are used in Middle Eastern savoury sauces. The best known are rose and orange flower water, and should be used in small amounts – the best quality flower waters are triple-distilled, so just a few drops will add a delicately exotic scent to a creamy sauce.

Right, from left: Flower essences, vanilla extract, almond essence.

DAIRY PRODUCTS

The number of sauces based on dairy products is vast, so it is worth taking the time to understand the different products available. You may be aiming for a rich and creamy sauce, or perhaps you would prefer a lighter, healthier alternative. The following descriptions should help.

MILK

The choice of milk for sauces depends upon the richness desired – for a rich flavour and creamy texture, choose whole milk or Channel Islands milk, but if you're watching fat levels and looking for a lighter sauce, go for skimmed or semi-skimmed (low fat).

Pasteurized: Most milk has been pasteurized, that is heat-treated, to destroy harmful bacteria. This should keep for up to 5 days under refrigeration.

Homogenized: This has been processed to distribute the fat globules evenly throughout the milk, instead of rising to the surface as cream. It has the same keeping quality as ordinary milk.

Sterilized: This is homogenized, bottled and then heat-treated for 20 minutes, so that it keeps without refrigeration until opened.

UHT: This is homogenized then heat-treated to high temperatures for just 1–2 seconds. It has a slightly caramelized flavour, but is useful as a store-cupboard standby as it keeps unopened for about a year without refrigeration.

Condensed: This sweetened or unsweetened milk is canned. It has been boiled until reduced and concentrated. It is very rich and the sweetened type is very sweet, but useful for rich dessert sauces. Lower-fat versions are available.

Evaporated: Unsweetened milk that has had some of the water removed by evaporation, this milk has a concentrated flavour and is slightly caramelized. There are also lighter-fat versions available. It is available either in cans or long-life packs.

Goat's milk: Many people who are allergic to cow's milk can tolerate goat's milk, which is now widely available and can be used as a direct substitute for ordinary milk in cooking. It has a similar flavour, although it is slightly sharper, and is more digestible.

FAT LEVELS IN MILK
• Channel Islands (breakfast milk): 5–8 per cent fat
• Full-fat (whole): 4 per cent fat
• Semi-skimmed (low-fat): 1.7 per cent fat
• Skimmed: 0.1 per cent fat

CREAM

All kinds of creams can be used to enrich and thicken both sweet and savoury sauces, both hot and cold. The following are the main types.

Single (light) cream: This cream has a fat content of just 18 per cent, which is too low for whipping. It will not withstand boiling, but can be stirred into sauces at the end of cooking to enrich the flavour.

Sour cream: In fact, this is really single (light) cream with an added souring culture, which sharpens the

Below, from left: Skimmed milk, semi-skimmed (low fat) milk, full-fat (whole) milk, Channel Islands milk, evaporated milk, condensed milk.

Above, clockwise from left: Single (light) cream, double (heavy) cream, crème fraîche, sour cream, whipping cream. Below-right, from left: Greek (US strained plain) yogurt and low fat yogurt.

flavour and thickens the texture.

Double (heavy) cream: The fat content of double cream is 48 per cent. The cream almost doubles in bulk when whipped. It is especially good in hot sauces, because it can withstand boiling.

Whipping cream: This has 35 per cent fat, and whips up to a light texture, or can be stirred, unwhipped, into hot sauces after cooking without curdling.

COOK'S TIP

When whipping double cream, you can extend the volume by adding 15ml/ 1 tbsp milk to each 150 ml/¼ pint/ ⅔ cup cream. Use a hand whisk instead of an electric one, for more control over the speed.

CRÈME FRAÎCHE

This has a mild, tangy flavour similar to that of soured cream, which makes it great for using in both sweet and savoury sauces and dressings. With a fat content of around 40 per cent, it is more stable than soured cream when heated. You can also buy a half-fat version, which can be successfully added to hot sauces.

STABILIZING YOGURT FOR SAUCES

To prevent yogurt splitting in cooked sauces, allow 5ml/1 tsp cornflour (cornstarch) to each 150ml/¼pint/⅔ cup yogurt. Blend the cornflour and a little yogurt to a smooth paste before adding the rest. Add to the sauce and cook following the recipe.

YOGURT

Yogurt and other lower-fat dairy products, such as fromage frais, make excellent lighter replacements for cream in many sauces, savoury or sweet. In cooking, stabilize yogurt with cornflour (cornstarch).

Greek (US strained plain) yogurt: This may be made from either cow's or sheep's milk. It is richer in flavour and texture than most yogurts, but still only has a fat content of around 8–10 per cent, so it makes a light substitute for cream in sauces.

Low-fat yogurt: Semi-skimmed (low-fat) or skimmed milk are used to make low-fat yogurt. Both types are quite sharp and tangy, which can be refreshing in light sauces. Low-fat yogurt is also used as a base for many dips and dressings.

EGGS

As a general rule, medium eggs are the size to use for recipes, unless the recipe states otherwise, but you may find it useful to have small eggs for using to enrich or thicken modest quantities of sauces.

The freshness of supermarket eggs is easily checked, as most are individually marked with a date stamp on their shells. Fresh eggs should store well for 2 weeks,

Below, clockwise from top:
Parmesan, mascarpone, ricotta,
Cheddar, Gruyère.

Left: Eggs.

providing that the shell is not damaged or dirty. Egg shells are porous, so they are best stored at the bottom of the refrigerator away from strong-smelling foods. As a general rule, before use, eggs should be left at room temperature for about 30 minutes.

SAFETY TIP

Because of the slight risk of contamination in raw eggs, it is recommended that pregnant women, young children, elderly people or anyone weakened by chronic illness should avoid eating raw or lightly cooked eggs.

CHEESES

Many hard cheeses can be grated and melted into sauces.

Strong, hard cheeses: Mature cheeses such as Cheddar, Gruyère and Parmesan will grate easily and melt into hot sauces. Their fine flavour complements pasta sauces or a creamy white sauce to pour over vegetables. Always grate these cheeses freshly as you need them. Once cheese is added to a sauce, heat it gently without boiling, or it will overcook and become stringy.

Soft, fresh cheeses: Those of a creamier consistency such as ricotta or mascarpone are used to enrich sauces and dips, from tomato sauces to fruit purées or custards. Ricotta is light and mild, and makes a good base for dips. Mascarpone is rich, creamy and high in fat, and can be used in the same way as thick cream.

SAUCE-MAKING EQUIPMENT

Making sauces requires very little in the way of specialist items, but a carefully selected set of basic equipment will help make tasks such as boiling, whisking and straining much easier. You may even find that most of these items are already in your kitchen. Shop around for those you still need, as quality varies enormously.

PANS

The rule here is to choose the right pan for the job, which means that your pans do not necessarily have to be a matching set. Some pans may be suitable for more than one task, but you will need a variety of sizes and types. Look for solid, heavy pans that are stable when empty, and have tight-fitting lids and firmly riveted handles. Buying good-quality pans is an investment, as they will last for years, but cheap, thin pans will not only wear out quickly, but also conduct heat unevenly and cause burnt spots. The following examples will cover most culinary requirements.
• Milk pan with high sides and a lip. This may be non-stick, but this is not essential.

• Three pans with lids, ranging in size from about 1 litre/1¾ pints/4 cups to 7 litres/12⅓ pints/30 cups. They should be deep and straight-sided to minimize the amount of evaporation.
• Sauté pan – this is a deep pan with straight sides.
• Double boiler – a useful pan for making delicate creams and custards, and melting ingredients such as chocolate. If you don't have one, you can improvise by placing a heatproof bowl over a pan of gently boiling water.

Top: Double boiler and heatproof bowl placed over pan Right, clockwise from left: Enamelled, anodized aluminium and copper pans.

materials for saucepans

Stainless steel: This is attractive and hard-wearing, and providing they have a thick base with aluminium or copper, the pans will conduct heat evenly and efficiently.

Anodized aluminium: Light and easy to clean, this conducts the heat well and does not corrode. The metal reacts when in contact with acid and alkaline, so food should not be left to stand for too long in these pans.

Copper: These pans are expensive but conduct heat very efficiently and are attractive and durable. Choose pans with a stainless steel lining, which is harder-wearing than tin.

Enamelled cast iron: This is heavy, but conducts the heat well, evenly and slowly. These pans retain the heat for a long time, and are hard-wearing and durable.

WOODEN SPOONS

A good assortment of wooden spoons is essential, and it is a good idea to keep them for individual uses. You might reserve one for spicy sauces, one for creams and custards, and so on; then there is no risk of flavour transfer. A good selection includes a wooden spoon, a wooden corner spoon with an edge to reach into the rims of pans, and a flat-edged wooden spatula.

WHISKS

Balloon whisks and spiral sauce whisks are efficient for blending or whisking. It is useful to have two different sizes.

LADLES

Available in various sizes, ladles are very useful for spooning and

Below, from left: Draining spoon, ladles with variable cup shapes.

Above, from left: Spiral sauce whisks, balloon whisk, wooden spoons.

pouring sauces over foods. Some smaller ones have a useful lip for more precise pouring. Stainless steel ladles are the best. A slotted stainless steel draining spoon is invaluable for skimming and removing small pieces of ingredients from sauces.

Above: Measuring jug and spoons

MEASURING JUG

Choose a solid jug (pitcher) marked with standard measurements. Heatproof glass is ideal, as it is easy to see the liquid level and can take boiling liquids, yet the handle remains cool as it is a poor heat conductor. Stainless steel jugs are attractive and hard-wearing.

MEASURING SPOONS

A set of measuring spoons, either imperial or metric (select the type to correspond to the instructions you prefer to follow) is essential for accurate measuring the small amounts of sauce ingredients. Ordinary table cutlery varies widely in capacity and should not be used for measuring. Spoon measurements given in recipes are always level.

SIEVE AND CHINOIS

A fine-meshed stainless steel sieve is essential for sauce making; look for a double-mesh, hard-wearing sieve. It can also be very useful to have a chinois, a cone-shaped sieve that is used for straining and puréeing. range of ingredients.

Above, from left: Chinois and sieve.

ELECTRICAL EQUIPMENT

Although not essential for making sauces, a blender, food processor, hand blender or whisk can take much of the hard work out of many sauces and dressings. A food processor is brilliant for chopping and slicing. Hand-held electric blenders are perhaps more versatile and convenient than larger machines for sauces, as they can be used to blend or purée mixtures in a pan or jug (pitcher), and are easy to clean by simply swishing in hot soapy water after use. A hand-held electric whisk is also useful for quick beating and whisking.

Left: Hand-held electric whisk.
Below: Hand blender.

STERILIZING AND STORING

Many sauces based on flour, cheese or vegetables will keep for at least two weeks. Store in a sterilized glass jar. Jars can be boiled on top of the stove or heated in the oven.
• Stove-top sterilizing calls for a large deep pan with a wide bottom.
• For oven sterilizing, the jars are arranged on a roasting pan or baking tray, which should be level on the bottom (so the jars do not slide about) and have at least a shallow rim to prevent them from sliding off when lifted.
• Special tongs are available for lifting hot jars.
• Filling jars is easy using a wide-topped jam funnel and a small ladle or small heatproof jug.

storing fresh sauces

A wide variety of fresh sauces can be prepared ahead and chilled or frozen. White sauces, wine sauces and tomato-based sauces are all excellent freezer candidates: make a big batch and freeze useable portions ready for thawing and reheating in the microwave.
• Airtight plastic freezer containers are ideal for chilling or freezing. Remember to allow a little headspace rather than filling the container to the brim.
• Foil freezer bags are brilliant for sauces. They have a gusset and base, so they stand up filling, and the top folds over to seal.
• Alternatively, supporting a freezer bag in a freezerproof bowl or jug to fill and freeze it is a good idea. When the sauce is solid, lift the bag out of the container and place in the freezer for long-term storage.

MAKING BASIC STOCKS

Commercial stock cubes and bouillon powder won't match the flavour of home-made stock; however, they can be useful for enriching a stock that lacks flavour. Heat it until boiling, then stir in a stock cube or a teaspoonful of bouillon powder. Each recipe makes about 1 litre/1¾ pints/4 cups.

BEEF STOCK

INGREDIENTS

675g/1½lb shin (shank) of beef, diced
1 large onion, chopped
1 large carrot, chopped
1 celery stick, chopped
bouquet garni
6 black peppercorns
2.5ml/½ tsp sea salt
1.75 litres/3 pints/7½ cups water

1 Place all the ingredients in a large pan and slowly bring to the boil.

2 Cover the pan and simmer very gently for 4 hours, skimming occasionally to remove scum. Strain the stock and cool.

FISH STOCK

INGREDIENTS

1kg/2¼lb white fish bones and trimmings
1 large onion, sliced
1 large carrot, sliced
1 celery stick, sliced
bouquet garni
6 white peppercorns
2.5ml/½ tsp sea salt
150ml/¼ pint/⅔ cup dry white wine
1 litre/1¾ pints/4 cups water

1 Place the ingredients in a pan and bring to the boil.

2 Skim any scum from the surface, cover the pan and simmer for 20 minutes. Strain and allow to cool.

CHICKEN STOCK

INGREDIENTS

1 chicken carcass
chicken giblets
1 leek, chopped
1 celery stick, chopped
bouquet garni
5ml/1 tsp white peppercorns
2.5ml/½ tsp sea salt
1.75 litres/3 pints/7½ cups water

1 Break up the carcass, place in a pan with the remaining ingredients. Bring to the boil.

2 Reduce the heat, cover and simmer for 2½ hours, skimming off scum occasionally. Strain and cool.

MAKING A BOUQUET GARNI

A traditional bouquet garni usually contains a bay leaf, a sprig of thyme and a few sprigs of parsley, but this can be varied according to taste, and to suit the dish you are making. Other vegetables or herbs you may like to include are a piece of celery for poultry dishes; a rosemary sprig for beef or lamb; a piece of fennel or leek, or a strip of lemon rind, for fish dishes.

Tie the herbs together firmly with fine cotton string, so the bundle is easy to remove from the stock after cooking.

Alternatively, tie the herbs in a clean muslin (cheesecloth) square. Leave a long length of the string to tie to the pan handle.

VEGETABLE STOCK

INGREDIENTS

500g/1¼lb chopped mixed vegetables, such as onions, carrots, celery, leeks
bouquet garni
6 black peppercorns
2.5ml/½ tsp sea salt
1 litre/1¾ pints/4 cups water

1 Place all the ingredients in a large pan and slowly bring to the boil.

2 Skim any scum from the surface, then reduce the heat and cover the pan. Simmer gently for 30 minutes. Strain the stock and allow it to cool before chilling.

KEEPING STOCK CLEAR

For a clear soup it is important to keep the stock clear; avoid boiling the stock but cook it very gently, and skim the top from time to time.

1 Trim any fat from the meat or bones before adding to the stock pan, as excess fat will affect the clarity of the stock.

2 Keep the heat at a low simmer, and skim off any scum as it gathers on the surface during cooking. Most vegetables can be added to stock for flavour, but potatoes tend to break down and make the stock cloudy so it's best to avoid these.

3 Strain the stock through a sieve lined with muslin (cheesecloth), and avoid pressing the solids, as this may spoil the stock's clarity.

REMOVING FAT FROM STOCK

Excess fat should be removed to improve the look and taste; it also helps keep the stock clear.

1 Let the stock stand until the fat surfaces, then skim off the fat with a large, shallow spoon. To absorb more grease, blot the surface with several layers of kitchen paper.

2 Then, drop in a few ice cubes. The fat will set around the ice so it can be simply spooned off.

3 Alternatively, cool then chill until the fat layer rises to the surface and sets. Then the fat can simply be lifted off. Use a large spoon to remove the solidified fat.

HOW TO STORE STOCK

Stock will keep for a week in the refrigerator or freezes well. Reduce it to take up less freezer space.

1 To freeze, pour into airtight containers, allowing 2.5cm/1in headspace for expansion, then seal and freeze for up to 3 months.

2 To freeze stock in convenient portions to add to sauces, pour into ice cube trays for freezing.

COOK'S TIPS

• Do not salt stock: season in later use.
• For a brown stock from beef or veal bones, roast the bones in a hot oven for 40 minutes. Add vegetables halfway through. Deglaze the pan with water and then simmer as usual.
• For concentrated stock, simmer until reduced and syrupy enough to coat the back of a spoon. At its most concentrated it will set to a solid jelly that will richly flavour sauces and soups.

FLOUR-BASED SAUCES

The standard way to adjust the consistency of a sauce is to thicken it with a flour. There are three basic methods for this – roux, blending, or all-in-one.

Many of the classic white sauces are based on a "roux" – a cooked mixture of flour and fat. The most basic white sauce uses milk, but by varying the liquid used, other well-known white sauces can be made. For a classic béchamel sauce, the milk is flavoured with vegetables and herbs. For velouté sauce, the milk is replaced with stock, giving it a more opaque appearance, and the cooked sauce may be enriched with cream. Brown sauces or gravy are made by browning the roux, usually with onions, before adding stock or other liquid such as wine.

BASIC RECIPE FOR WHITE ROUX SAUCES

Using the classic roux method, you can adjust the amount of thickening to create varying consistencies. A pouring sauce is poured directly over foods when serving. The slightly thicker coating sauce is used to make a smooth covering for fish or vegetables.

For a pouring consistency:
15g/½ oz/1 tbsp butter
15g/½ oz/2 tbsp plain (all-purpose) flour
300ml/½ pint/1¼ cups liquid
For a coating consistency:
25g/1oz/2 tbsp butter
25g/1oz/¼ cup plain (all-purpose) flour
300 ml/½ pint/1¼ cups liquid

MAKING A ROUX-BASED WHITE SAUCE

When making a roux, stir the paste over the whole pan base, and add the liquid gradually; heating the liquid first helps to avoid lumps.

1 Melt the butter in a pan, then add the flour. Cook on a low heat and stir for 1–2 minutes. Allow the mixture to bubble until it resembles a honeycomb in texture but does not brown. It is important to cook well at this point, to allow the starch grains to swell and burst, and avoid lumps forming later.

2 Off the heat, gradually stir in the liquid, which may be either hot or cold. Return to the heat and stir until boiling. Reduce the heat and simmer, stirring constantly, for 2 minutes, until the sauce is thickened and smooth.

BLENDING METHOD

Blending-method sauces are usually made with cornflour (cornstarch), arrowroot, potato flour or sauce flour. Cornflour and sauce flour make light, glossy sauces that are good for freezing. If you need a crystal-clear result for glazing, use arrowroot or potato flour. The liquid may be milk, stock, fruit juice or syrup from canned or poached fruit. As a guide, you will need about 20g/¾oz/3 tbsp cornflour or sauce flour to thicken 300ml/½ pint/1¼ cups liquid to a pouring consistency. Arrowroot or potato flour are slightly stronger, so use approximately 15g/½oz to 300ml/½ pint/1¼ cups liquid to obtain the same consistency.

1 Place the flour in a bowl and add just enough liquid to make a smooth, thin paste. Heat the remaining liquid in a pan until almost boiling.

2 Pour a little hot liquid on to the blended mixture, stirring. Pour the mixture back into the pan, whisking, to avoid lumps. Return to the heat and stir until boiling, then simmer gently for 2 minutes, stirring until thickened and smooth.

ALL-IN-ONE METHOD

This uses the same ingredients and proportions as the roux method, but the liquid must be cold. Place the flour, butter and liquid in a pan and whisk over a moderate heat until boiling. Stir for 2 minutes, until thickened and smooth.

USING AN EGG YOLK LIAISON

This is a simple way to lightly thicken milk, stock, cream or reduced liquids. It is good for enriching savoury white or velouté sauces. Two egg yolks enrich and thicken about 300ml/½ pint/1¼ cups liquid. A mixture of egg yolk and cream has the same effect: add it off the heat to avoid curdling.

Stir 30ml/2 tbsp hot liquid or sauce into two yolks in a bowl. Return it to the rest of the sauce. Heat gently, stirring, without boiling.

MAKING BEURRE MANIÉ

Literally translated as "kneaded butter", this is a mixture of flour and butter. It can be stirred into a simmering sauce, poaching liquid or cooked dish to thicken the juices. It's a convenient way to adjust a sauce or dish at the end of cooking, and easy to control as you can add the exact amount required. Any leftover beurre manié can be chilled, covered, for two weeks.

1 Place equal amounts of butter and flour in a bowl and knead together with your fingers or a wooden spoon to make a smooth paste.

2 Drop teaspoonfuls of the beurre manié paste into the simmering sauce, whisking thoroughly to incorporate each spoonful before adding the next, until the sauce is thickened and smooth and the desired consistency is achieved.

INFUSING FLAVOURS

To infuse flavours into milk, stock or other liquids before using in sauces such as béchamel, pour the liquid into a saucepan and add thin slices or dice of onion, carrot and celery, a bouquet garni, peppercorns or a mace blade. Bring the liquid slowly to the boil, then remove the pan from the heat. Cover and leave to stand for about 10 minutes. Strain the milk to remove the flavourings before use.

ADDING FLAVOURINGS TO FLOUR-BASED SAUCES
The follow variations and add variety to a basic sauce.
• Stir 50g/2oz/½ cup grated Cheddar or other strong cheese into a basic white sauce with 5ml/1 tsp wholegrain mustard and a generous dash of Worcestershire sauce.
• Wine livens up the flavour of most stock-based sauces – boil 60ml/4 tbsp red or white wine in a pan until well-reduced, then stir into the finished sauce with a grating of nutmeg or black pepper.
• Add chopped herbs a few minutes before the end of the cooking time.

FIXING A LUMPY SAUCE

If a flour-thickened sauce is lumpy, don't despair – it can be corrected.

1 First, whisk the sauce hard with a light wire whisk to smooth out lumps, then reheat gently, stirring.

2 If the sauce is still not smooth, rub it through a fine sieve, pressing firmly with a wooden spoon. Reheat gently, stirring.

3 Alternatively, process the sauce in a food processor until smooth. Reheat gently, stirring.

KEEPING SAUCES HOT

1 Pour into a heatproof bowl and place over a pan of very gently simmering water.

2 To avoid a skin, place lightly oiled or wetted greaseproof or non-stick baking paper on the sauce.

DEGREASING SAUCES

Remove any fat from a hot sauce or gravy with a flat metal spoon. Drag the flat surface of a piece of kitchen paper over the surface to absorb final traces of grease.

MAKING A ROUX-BASED BROWN SAUCE

The base for many sauces for meat, brown onions and vegetables before adding flour. The fat can be butter and oil, or dripping. Butter alone is unsuitable as it burns easily at high temperatures. Use about 30ml/2 tbsp oil and 25g/1oz/¼ cup flour to 600ml/1 pint/2½ cups brown stock. At the last moment, stir in 15g/½ oz/1 tbsp chilled butter.

1 Melt the fat and fry 1 small, finely chopped onion until soft and brown. Sprinkle on the flour and stir over a low heat for 4–5 minutes, until rich brown.

2 Remove from the heat and gradually stir in the liquid, either hot or cold. Return to the heat and stir until boiling. Simmer gently, stirring, for 2 minutes, until thick and smooth. The sauce may be strained to remove the onions.

DEGLAZING FOR SAUCE

Deglazing means adding a little liquid after roasting or pan-frying to dilute rich juices into sauce. Spoon off excess fat and scrape sediment from the pan as you stir in liquid.

1 Tilt the pan and spoon off excess fat from the surface of the juices.

2 Stir in a few tablespoons of wine, stock or cream.

3 Simmer, stirring and scraping as the sauce boils. Boil rapidly until syrupy, then pour over the food.

MAKING GRAVY

Good gravy should be smooth and glossy, never heavy and floury. It's usually best to use the minimum of thickening, but this can be adjusted to taste. Providing the meat has been roasted to rich brown, the meat juices will have enough colour. If it is pale, a few drops of gravy browning can be stirred in.

1 For thickened gravy, skim off all except about 15ml/1 tbsp fat from the juices in the roasting pan. Gradually stir in about 15ml/1 tbsp flour, scraping sediment and juices.

2 Place the pan on the heat and stir until bubbling. Cook, stirring constantly, for 1–2 minutes until browned and the flour is cooked.

3 Gradually stir in the liquid, until the gravy is the desired thickness. Simmer for 2–3 minutes, stirring, and adjust the seasoning.

IDEAS FOR DEGLAZED SAUCES
Brandy and Peppercorn: deglaze the pan with brandy or sherry, stir in cream and coarsely ground black pepper. Serve with steaks.
Red Wine and Cranberry: deglaze with red wine and stir in cranberry sauce or jelly; good with game or turkey.
Sauce Bercy: deglaze with dry white wine or vermouth, stir in a finely chopped shallot and sauté gently until soft. Add cream, lemon juice and chopped parsley. Excellent with fried or poached fish.

FLAVOUR IN BROWN SAUCE
A well-flavoured brown stock, which has been reduced by between one-third to a half, is the basis of a good brown sauce but it can also be enhanced by these flavourings.
• A handful of chopped fresh basil, chives or flat leaf parsley, stirred into the sauce just before serving, will improve the flavour and look of a basic brown sauce.
• For game or poultry, stir a little curry paste, 2 crushed cloves of garlic and 1 finely chopped onion into the roux and cook for about 5 minutes before adding the stock. Stir in some chopped fresh coriander (cilantro) just before serving.
• Add coarsely grated orange rind to a basic brown sauce for duck or game.

VEGETABLE SAUCES AND SALSAS

Many sauces use vegetables for flavour, colour and texture. There are endless opportunities for different sauces from the basic techniques. Puréed or chopped vegetables are used for cooked sauces or fresh salsas. Vegetable sauces and salsas are often the fresh and light alternatives to classic rich sauces, and they are invariably very easy and quick to make.

BASIC TOMATO SAUCE

Fresh tomatoes must be ripe and plum tomatoes are best. Canned should be plain not flavoured. Peel fresh tomatoes before using and use about 500g/1¼lb tomatoes instead of each 400g/14oz can in these, and other, recipes.

Makes about 450ml/¾ pint/scant 2 cups

INGREDIENTS

1 clove garlic, finely chopped
1 small onion, finely chopped
1 celery stick, finely chopped
15ml/1tbsp olive oil
15g/½ oz/1 tbsp butter
400g/14oz can chopped tomatoes
handful of basil leaves
salt and ground black pepper

1 Cook the onion, garlic and celery in the oil and butter.

2 Continue cooking the onion mixture over low heat, stirring occasionally, for about 15–20 minutes or until the onions soften and are just beginning to colour.

3 Stir in the tomatoes and bring to the boil. Reduce the heat, cover and cook gently for 10–15 minutes, stirring occasionally, until thick.

4 Tear or roughly chop the basil leaves and stir into the sauce. Adjust the seasoning with salt and pepper and serve hot.

COOK'S TIP
A soffritto (Italian), or sofrito (Spanish), is the base of many Mediterranean meat or tomato sauces. Recipes may list "soffritto" as an ingredient. For basic soffritto, finely chopped onion, garlic, green (bell) pepper and celery, perhaps with carrot or pancetta, are sautéed slowly until soft and caramelized.

QUICK SALSA CRUDO

This is literally a "raw sauce" of vegetables or fruits, and it's easy to create your own combinations of flavour. A good basic start for a salsa crudo is chillies, peppers, onions, and garlic. Serve with grilled chicken, pork, lamb or fish.

1 Peel, deseed or trim the vegetables as necessary, then use a sharp knife to cut them into small, even dice. Try to combine texture and colour as well as flavours, and use chillies and other very spicy ingredients sparingly. Put all the diced ingredients into a bowl.

2 Add 15–30ml/1–2 tbsp olive oil and a squeeze of lime or lemon juice and stir in finely chopped fresh basil, coriander (cilantro), flat leaf parsley or mint. Season to taste and toss well before serving.

HOW TO PEEL TOMATOES

Cut crosses in the tomatoes. Add to a pan of boiling water. Turn off the heat and leave for 30 seconds. Transfer to a bowl of cold water. Peel using a small knife.

Alternatively, skewer a tomato firmly on a fork and hold in a gas flame until the skin blisters and splits. When cool enough to handle, peel using a small knife.

GRILLED VEGETABLES FOR PURÉES AND SAUCES

Chargrilled vegetables are used in many sauces or salsas. Rapid grilling on a barbecue gives full flavour, especially with peppers, aubergines (eggplants), tomatoes, garlic or onions, retaining juices while caramelizing the flesh. This is not always practical, so the best alternative is to roast the vegetables on a baking sheet under a grill.

ROAST VEGETABLE SAUCE

Serve with poultry, meat or game. For a sauce with more texture, simply process for a shorter time.

Makes about 300ml/½ pint/1¼ cups

INGREDIENTS

2 red or orange (bell) peppers, halved
1 small onion, halved
1 small aubergine (eggplant), halved
2 tomatoes with skins removed
2 garlic cloves, unpeeled
30–45ml/2–3 tbsp olive oil
15ml/1 tbsp lemon juice
25g/1oz/½ cup fresh white breadcrumbs

1 Place the vegetables and garlic cut-sides down on a baking sheet. Cook under a very hot grill, or in a hot oven, until the skins are black and charred, and the flesh is tender.

2 Remove from the heat and leave until cool enough to handle, then peel the peppers and onions.

3 Scoop the flesh from the aubergines, and squeeze the flesh from the garlic.

4 Place all the vegetables in a blender or food processor and process to a smooth purée, adding oil and lemon juice to taste. If you prefer a very smooth sauce, rub the purée through a fine sieve.

5 To thicken a vegetable purée, stir in a small quantity of fresh breadcrumbs and process for a few seconds. The mixture will thicken further when left to stand, so do not add too much bread.

SAVOURY BUTTER SAUCES

The simplest sauce is melted butter flavoured with lemon juice or herbs. A more refined version uses clarified butter, which has moisture and added ingredients removed. Emulsions of butter with vinegar or other flavourings make rich beurre blanc or hollandaise sauce. Cold flavoured butters flavour and moisten hot foods, and can be shaped prettily for extra garnish.

BLENDER HOLLANDAISE

This rich butter sauce is quick and easy to make in a blender.

Makes 250ml/8fl oz/1 cup

INGREDIENTS

60ml/4 tbsp white wine vinegar
6 peppercorns
1 bay leaf
3 egg yolks
175g/6oz/¾ cup clarified butter
salt and ground black pepper

1 Simmer the vinegar, peppercorns and bay leaf in a small pan until reduced to about 15ml/1 tbsp. Discard the flavourings.

2 Place the egg yolks in a blender and start the motor. Add the reduced liquid through the feeder tube and blend for 10 seconds.

3 Heat the butter until hot. With the motor running, pour the butter through the feeder tube in a thin, steady stream until the sauce is thick and smooth. Season to taste with salt and pepper, and serve warm with poached fish, eggs or vegetables.

CORRECTING CURDLING

If hollandaise sauce is overheated, or if the butter is added too quickly, it may curdle and become slightly granular in texture. If this happens, remove it from the heat immediately, before the sauce separates.

Quickly drop an ice cube into the sauce, then beat hard until the cube melts and cools the sauce. It also helps to stand the base of the pan in a bowl of iced water whilst whisking in the ice cube.

BEURRE BLANC

This is one of the simplest sauces to make. White wine and vinegar are reduced in volume over a high heat to produce an intense flavour. Butter is whisked into the liquid to enrich and thicken it. This is good with poached or grilled fish or chicken.

1 Place 45ml/3 tbsp each of white wine vinegar and dry white wine in a small pan with a finely chopped shallot. Bring to the boil and boil until reduced to about 15ml/1 tbsp.

2 Cut 225g/8oz/1 cup chilled unsalted (sweet) butter into small cubes. On a low heat, gradually whisk in the butter, piece by piece, allowing each piece to melt and be absorbed before adding the next. Season to taste and serve at once.

HOW TO CLARIFY BUTTER

Clarified butter is heated until the moisture evaporates and ingredients other than fat (for example, salt) separate out, leaving clear rich fat. Clarified butter, ghee in Indian cooking, keeps well and can be heated to higher temperatures than ordinary butter without burning. It can be used for sautéing, and in sauces it gives a mild flavour and a high gloss. There are two main methods of clarifying.

Heat the butter in a pan with an equal quantity of water until it melts. Remove from the heat and leave to cool until the butter sets. Carefully lift out the fat, leaving the water and solids behind.

Alternatively, melt the butter over low heat. Cook gently until it stops spitting and a sediment forms. Skim off scum. Strain through a sieve lined with muslin (cheesecloth).

MAKING SAVOURY BUTTERS

Flavoured butters can be shaped or piped decoratively to serve with steaks or poached or grilled fish.

To make a herb-flavoured butter, finely chop your choice of fresh herbs. Beat the butter until softened then stir in the herbs to mix evenly.

MAKING SHAPED SLICES

To make butter slices, chill the softened herb butter lightly. With your hands, roll the butter into a long sausage-shape and wrap in baking parchment or clear film (plastic wrap). Chill and cut off slices of the butter as required.

PIPING BUTTER

Soften the butter before filling the pipe then, using a star nozzle, squeeze on to baking parchment.

MAKING SHAPED BUTTERS

Chill lightly, then roll out the butter between sheets of baking parchment. Chill until firm, then remove the top sheet and stamp out small shapes with a cutter.

FLAVOURINGS FOR SAVOURY BUTTERS

Flavoured butters can be rubbed or spread on meat before roasting, grilling or barbecuing; used on foil-wrapped fish; or used for hot breads instead of garlic butter.
• Finely chopped herbs, such as chives, parsley, dill, mint, thyme or rosemary. Use one herb or a combination and add as much as the butter will comfortably absorb, or to achieve the required flavour.
• Finely grated lemon, lime or orange rind and juice.
• Finely chopped canned anchovy fillets.
• Finely chopped gherkins or capers.
• Crushed, dried chillies or finely chopped fresh chillies.
• Crushed, fresh garlic cloves, or roasted garlic purée.
• Ground coriander seeds, curry spices or paste.

SAVOURY EGG SAUCES

Eggs are widely used for thickening and enriching sauces, or for making an emulsion, such as mayonnaise. Freeze spare egg yolks (left from meringue for sauces: stir in a pinch of salt or sugar before freezing to prevent them from thickening.

MAYONNAISE

Hand-whisked mayonnaise is smooth, glossy and perfect with delicately poached salmon or a chicken salad. The choice of oil depends on taste: extra virgin olive oil is often too strong. It's a good idea to use either light olive oil or half olive oil with half sunflower oil, or another lighter-flavoured oil. All ingredients should be at room temperature for a good sauce and to help avoid curdling.

Makes about 300ml/½ pint/1¼ cups

INGREDIENTS
2 egg yolks
15ml/1 tbsp lemon juice
5ml/1 tsp Dijon mustard
300ml/½ pint/1¼ cups light olive oil
salt and ground black pepper

1 Place the egg yolks, lemon juice, mustard, salt and pepper in a bowl and beat the mixture until smooth and evenly combined.

2 Pouring with one hand and whisking with the other, add the oil gradually, drop by drop, making sure that each drop is whisked in before adding more.

3 Once a thick emulsion has formed, the oil can be poured faster, in a fine, steady stream, whisking until the mixture becomes smooth and thick. Season to taste.

BLENDING MAYONNAISE

A food processor or blender wil speed up the process of making mayonnaise. Use a whole egg instead of the yolks.

Process the egg and flavourings for a few seconds then slowly pour in the oil through the feeder tube in a thin, steady stream with the motor running, until the mixture forms a smooth, creamy texture.

CORRECTING CURDLING

If oil is added too quickly, the mayonnaise will separate; this can be corrected if you stop as soon as the mixture begins to separate. Break a fresh egg yolk into a clean bowl. Gradually whisk in the separated mayonnaise, a small spoonful at a time, whisking constantly until it thickens. Keep going until all the mixture is used.

MAYONNAISE VARIATIONS
• Garlic Mayonnaise: add 3–6 crushed garlic cloves.
• Spicy Mayonnaise: add 15ml/1 tbsp mustard, 7–15ml/1½ tsp–1 tbsp Worcestershire sauce and, if you like, a dash of Tabasco sauce.
• Green Mayonnaise: combine 25g/1oz each of parsley and watercress sprigs in a blender or food processor. Add 3–4 chopped spring onions (scallions) and 1 garlic clove. Blend until finely chopped. Add 120ml/4fl oz mayonnaise and blend until smooth. Season to taste.
• Blue Cheese Dressing: mix 8oz/225g crumbled Danish blue cheese into the mayonnaise.

SWEET EGG SAUCES

Sweet egg sauces are often rich and creamy and include fine pouring or thick and creamy custard. Light and fluffy sabayon can be served on its own or as a luxurious sauce.

CUSTARD SAUCE

Crème anglaise is traditional vanilla pouring custard sauce. It is quite different from custard made with cornflour (cornstarch) or custard powder – thinner, richer and more delicate. As well as being served as a classic sauce, either warm or cold, crème anglaise is often used as the base for creams or ice creams. It may be enriched by using cream instead of milk, or flavoured with liqueurs. This must be heated slowly and gently or it will curdle.

Makes about 400ml/14fl oz/1⅔ cups

INGREDIENTS

300ml/½ pint /1¼ cups milk
1 vanilla pod (bean)
3 egg yolks
15ml/1 tbsp caster (superfine) sugar

1 Heat the milk and vanilla pod until just boiling, then remove from the heat. (To intensify the flavour split the pod lengthways.) Cover and leave to infuse for 10 minutes then strain into a clean pan.

2 Beat the eggs and sugar lightly and pour in the milk, whisking.

3 Heat gently, stirring, until the custard thickens enough to lightly coat a wooden spoon. Remove from the heat and pour into a jug (pitcher) to arrest the cooking.

CORRECTING CURDLING

At first signs of curdling, plunge the pan base into cold water. Whisk in a teaspoonful of cornflour (cornstarch) smoothly, then reheat.

SABAYON SAUCE

1 Whisk 1 egg yolk and 15ml/ 1 tbsp caster (superfine) sugar per portion in a bowl over a pan of simmering water. Whisk in 30ml/ 2 tbsp sweet white wine, liqueur or fruit juice, for each egg yolk. Whisk until frothy and the sauce holds the trail of the whisk. Serve at once or whisk until cool.

BAKED CUSTARD

A classic partner for cooked fruit. Preheat the oven to 180°C/350°F/ Gas 4. Grease an ovenproof dish. Beat 4 large (US extra large) eggs, a few drops of vanilla extract and 15–30ml/1–2 tbsp caster (superfine) sugar. Whisk in 600ml/1 pint/2½ cups hot milk. Strain into the prepared dish. Place in a roasting pan. Pour in warm water to half fill the tin. Bake for 50–60 minutes.

CLASSIC DESSERT SAUCES

As well as the popular custards and flavoured white sauces, quick and easy dessert toppings can be made almost instantly from ready-made ingredients, and these are ideal to serve over scoops of ice cream. They could also be served with pancakes and are particularly popular with children.

HOW TO USE VANILLA

Vanilla pods (beans) are commonly used in sweet dessert sauces, but they are occasionally used to flavour savoury cream sauces.

To flavour sugar, bury a vanilla pod in a jar of caster (superfine) sugar. It can be used as vanilla-flavoured sugar to add to sweet sauces and desserts.

To infuse (steep) milk or cream with vanilla, heat it gently with the vanilla pod over a low heat until almost boiling. Remove, cover and stand for 10 minutes. Remove the pod, rinse and dry; it may be re-used several times in this way.

To get maximum flavour from the pod, use a sharp knife to slit the pod lengthways and open out. Use the tip of the knife to scrape out the sticky black seeds inside and add to the hot sauce.

SPEEDY SAUCES FOR TOPPING ICE CREAM

Lots of store-cupboard ingredients can be quickly transformed into irresistible sauces.

marshmallow melt

Melt 90g/3½oz marshmallows with 30ml/2 tbsp milk or cream in a small pan. Add a little grated nutmeg and spoon over ice cream.

black forest sauce

Drain canned black cherries and blend a little of the syrup with a little arrowroot or cornflour (cornstarch). Add to the remaining syrup in a pan. Heat gently, stirring, until boiling and slightly thick. Add the cherries and a dash of kirsch. Bubble for a few seconds, then use hot, warm or cool.

chocolate-toffee sauce

Chop a Mars bar and heat very gently in a pan, stirring until just melted. Spoon over ice cream and sprinkle with chopped nuts.

marmalade whisky sauce

Heat 60ml/4 tbsp marmalade with 30ml/2 tbsp whisky, until melted and bubbling. Spoon on ice cream.

whisky sauce

Measure 600ml/1 pint/2½ cups milk. Mix 15ml/1 tbsp of the milk with 30ml/2 tbsp cornflour (cornstarch). Bring the remaining milk to the boil and pour a little on the cornflour mixture. Return all to the pan and heat gently, stirring, until thickened. Simmer for 2 minutes. Off the heat, stir in 30ml/2 tbsp sugar and 60–90ml/4–6 tbsp whisky.

PRESENTATION IDEAS

When you've made a delicious sauce for a special dessert, why not make more of it by using it for decoration on the plate, too? Try one of the following simple ideas to make your sauce into a talking point. Individual slices of desserts, cakes or tarts, or a stuffed baked peach, look especially good like this.

MARBLING

Use this technique when you have two contrasting sauces of similar thickness, such as a fruit purée with custard or cream. Spoon alternate spoonfuls of the sauces into a bowl or on to a serving plate, then stir the two sauces lightly together, swirling to create a marbled effect.

YIN-YANG SAUCES

This is ideal for two contrasting colours of purée or coulis, such as a raspberry and a mango fruit coulis. Spoon one sauce on each side of a serving plate and push them together gently with a spoon, swirling one around the other, to make a yin-yang shape.

DRIZZLING

Pour a smooth sauce or coulis into a jug with a fine pouring lip. Drizzle the sauce in droplets or a fine wavy line on to the plate around the food.

PIPING OUTLINES

Spoon a small amount of fruit coulis or chocolate sauce into a piping (pastry) bag fitted with a plain writing nozzle. Pipe the outline of a shape on to a serving plate, then spoon in sauce to fill the inside.

FEATHERING HEARTS

Flood the plate with a smooth sauce, such as chocolate sauce or a fruit purée. Drop in small droplets of pouring (half-and-half) cream from a teaspoon at even intervals. Draw the tip of a small knife through the cream, to drag each drop into a heart.

QUICK SAUCES FOR CRÊPES

rich butterscotch sauce

Melt 75g/3oz/6 tbsp butter, l75g/6oz/1½ cups brown sugar and 30ml/2 tbsp golden (light corn) syrup in a pan over a low heat. Off the heat, add 75ml/5 tbsp double (heavy) cream, stirring until smooth. If you like, add about 50g/2oz/½ cup chopped walnuts. Serve hot with ice cream or crêpes.

orange sauce

Melt 25g/1oz/2 tbsp unsalted (sweet) butter in a heavy pan. Stir in 50g/2oz/¼ cup caster (superfine) sugar and cook until golden. Stir in the juice of 2 oranges and ½ lemon until the caramel has dissolved.

summer berry flambé

Melt 25g/1oz/2 tbsp butter in a frying pan. Add in 50g/2oz/¼ cup caster (superfine) sugar and cook until golden brown. Add the juice of 2 oranges and the grated rind of ½ orange, and cook until syrupy. Add 350g/12oz/3 cups mixed berries and warm through. Add 45ml/3 tbsp of Grand Marnier and set alight in a safe place. When the flames have died, spoon the syrup over the crêpes.

FRUIT SAUCES

From the simplest fresh fruit purée, to a cooked and thickened fruit sauce, there are hundreds of ways to add flavour to puddings, tarts and pies. The addition of a little liqueur or lemon juice can bring out the fruit flavour and prevent discoloration. Some fruit sauces, notably apple and cranberry, also partner meat and poultry, and fresh fruit salsas can cool spicy dishes.

MAKING A FRUIT COULIS

A delicious fruit coulis will add a sophisticated splash of colour and flavour to desserts and ices. It can be made from either fresh or frozen fruit, in any season. Soft fruits and berries such as raspberries, blackcurrants or strawberries, are ideal, and tropical fruit, such as mango and kiwi, can be quickly transformed into aromatic coulis. A few drops of orange flower water or rose water add a scented flavour, but use it with caution – too much will overpower delicate ingredients.

1 Remove any hulls, stems, peel or stones from the fruit.

2 Place the prepared fruit in a blender or food processor and process until smooth.

3 Press the purée through a fine sieve to remove the pips (seeds) or any fibrous parts and create a silk-smooth coulis. Sweeten the coulis to taste with icing (confectioners') sugar, and if necessary add a squeeze of lemon or lime juice to sharpen and intensify the flavour.

COOK'S TIP

For cooked peeled fruit, mash with a potato masher for a coarser purée.

peach sauce

Purée a 400g/14oz can of peaches in light syrup, together with their juice and 1.5ml/¼ tsp of almond essence in a blender or food processor. Transfer to a jug (pitcher) and chill before serving with sponge puddings, tarts, ice creams or mousses. This can be made with other canned fruit.

passion fruit coulis

This coulis is superb with skewered fruit. For example, cut 3 ripe papayas in half and scoop out the seeds. Peel them and cut the flesh into chunks. Thread the chunks on bamboo skewers.

1 Halve eight passion fruit and scoop out the flesh. Purée in a blender for a few seconds.

2 Press the pulp through a sieve and discard the seeds. Add 30ml/ 2 tbsp of lime juice, 30ml/2 tbsp of icing (confectioners') sugar and 30ml/2 tbsp of white rum. Stir well until the sugar has dissolved.

3 Spoon some of the coulis on plates. Place the fruit skewers on top. Drizzle the remaining coulis over the skewers and garnish with a little toasted coconut, if liked.

CHOCOLATE SAUCES

Chocolate sauces are enduringly popular, from simple custards to richly indulgent versions combined with liqueur or cream. They can be served with ice cream and other frozen desserts, but are also delicious with poached pears and a wide range of puddings. Flavoured liqueurs can be chosen to echo the flavour of the dessert, and coffee, brandy and cinnamon all go especially well with chocolate.

The more cocoa solids chocolate contains, the more chocolatey the flavour will be. Plain (semisweet) chocolate may have between 30–70 per cent of cocoa solids. Plain dark (bittersweet) chocolate has around 75 per cent, so if you're aiming at a really rich, dark sauce, this is the best choice. Milk chocolate has 20 per cent cocoa solids. White chocolate contains no cocoa solids, so strictly speaking it is not a chocolate at all, but gets its flavour from cocoa butter.

The best method of melting chocolate is in a double boiler or in a bowl over a pan of hot water. Never allow water or steam to come into contact with the chocolate as this may cause it to stiffen. Overheating will also spoil the flavour and texture.

Plain chocolate should not be heated above 49°C/120°F, and milk or white chocolate not above 43°C/110°F.

For sauce recipes where the chocolate is melted with a quantity of other liquid such as milk or cream, the chocolate may be melted with the liquid in a pan over direct heat, providing there is plenty of liquid. Heat gently, stirring until melted.

Cocoa is ground from the whole cocoa mass after most of the cocoa butter has been extracted.

CREAMY CHOCOLATE SAUCE

Place 120ml/4fl oz/½ cup double (heavy) cream in a pan and add 130g/4½oz chocolate in pieces. Stir over low heat until the chocolate melts. Serve warm or cold.

CHOCOLATE CUSTARD SAUCE

1 Melt 90g/3½oz plain dark (bittersweet) chocolate in a bowl over a pan of hot water.

2 Heat 200ml/7fl oz/scant 1 cup crème anglaise until hot but not boiling and stir in the melted chocolate until evenly mixed. Serve hot or cold.

RICH CHOCOLATE BRANDY SAUCE

Break 115g/4oz plain (semisweet) chocolate into a bowl. Place over a pan of hot water to heat gently until melted. Remove from the heat and add 30ml/2 tbsp brandy and 30ml/2 tbsp melted butter, then stir until smooth. Serve hot.

MAKING MARINADES AND DRESSINGS

Marinades can be savoury or sweet, spicy, fruity or fragrant, to flavour or enhance to all kinds of foods. They're also useful for tenderizing; moistening during cooking; and as the basis of a sauce to serve with the finished dish.

OIL-BASED MARINADES

Choose an oil-based marinade for low-fat foods, such as lean meat, poultry or white fish, which may dry out during cooking. Oil-based marinades are especially useful for grilling and barbecuing, and at their simplest consist of oil with crushed garlic and chopped herbs. Add crushed chillies for a hot and spicy marinade. Do not salt marinades as this draws the juices out of food.

1 Place the marinade ingredients in a measuring jug (pitcher) and beat well with a fork to mix thoroughly. Arrange the food in a single layer in a non-metallic dish and pour the marinade over.

2 Turn the food to coat evenly in the marinade. Cover and leave in the fridge to marinate from 30 minutes to several hours, depending on the recipe. Turn the food occasionally.

3 When ready to cook, remove the food from the marinade. The marinade can be poured into a small pan and simmered for several minutes until thoroughly heated, then served spooned over the cooked food.

WINE- OR VINEGAR-BASED MARINADES

Wine- or vinegar-based mixtures are best with rich foods such as game or oily fish, to add flavour, and to contrast and balance richness. Use herb-flavoured vinegars for oily fish and add chopped fresh herbs, such as tarragon, parsley, coriander (cilantro) and thyme for flavour.

The acid in the wine or vinegar starts the tenderizing process well before cooking. For game, which can have a tendency to be tough, leave in the marinade overnight. Add lemon juice, garlic, black pepper and herbs, and even sherry, cider or orange juice according to your preference.

Yogurt is a good marinade and can be flavoured with crushed garlic, lemon juice, and handfuls of chopped mint, thyme or rosemary for lamb or pork. For fish, use a marinade based on lemon juice with a little oil and lots of black pepper.

1 Measure the ingredients into a jug (pitcher) and beat with a fork.

2 Arrange the food in a wide, non-metallic dish in a single layer and spoon over the marinade. Turn the food to coat evenly. Cover and chill for 30 minutes up to several hours, depending on the recipe.

3 Drain the food of excess marinade before cooking. If the food is to be griddled or grilled (broiled), brush with the marinade during cooking for flavour and to keep it moist.

MAKING A VINAIGRETTE-STYLE DRESSING

A good vinaigrette can do more than dress a salad. It can also be used to baste meat, poultry, seafood or vegetables during cooking. Many classic dressings, such as vinaigrette or French dressing, are based on an oil and acid mixture. The basic proportions are 3 parts oil to 1 part acid beaten together to form an emulsion. This can be done by simply whisking with a fork in a jug (pitcher), or the ingredients can be placed in a screw-topped jar and shaken thoroughly. The oil you choose for a dressing adds character to the flavour, and which one you use for which dressing depends upon your own taste and upon the salad ingredients. A strongly flavoured extra virgin olive oil adds personality to a simple green leaf or potato salad, but can overpower more delicate ingredients. Pure olive oil or sunflower oil adds a lighter flavour. Nut oils, such as walnut or hazelnut, are expensive, but can add a distinctive unusual flavour to a salad when used in small quantities.

The acid in a dressing may be vinegar or lemon juice, and this can define the flavour of the finished salad. Choose from wine, sherry or cider vinegars, herb, chilli or fruit vinegars, to balance or contrast with the salad ingredients and the type of oil. Matured vinegars such as balsamic can be strong

Right: Bottled dressings make pleasing kitchen ornaments and excellent gift ideas.

VARIATIONS
• Use red or white wine vinegar, or use a herb-flavoured vinegar.
• Replace 1 tablespoon of the vinegar with wine.
• Use olive oil, or a mixture of vegetable and olive oils.
• Use 4fl oz/120ml olive oil and 30ml/2 tbsp walnut or hazelnut oil.
• Add 15–30ml/1–2 tbsp Dijon mustard to the vinegar before whisking in the oil.
• Add 15–30ml/1–2 tbsp chopped herbs (parsley, basil, chives, thyme, etc) to the vinaigrette.

in flavour. Balsamic has a strong flavour, because of its ageing in wooden barrels and so the basic proportions of 3 parts oil to 1 of vinegar should be amended to 5 parts oil and 2 of balsamic vinegar.

Lemon juice adds a lively tang. Other fruit juices, such as orange or apple juice can be used for a sweeter, less acid flavour.

classic vinaigrette

To ensure the ingredients blend in a smooth emulsion, they should all be at room temperature.

Put 30ml/2 tbsp vinegar in a bowl with 10ml/2 tsp Dijon mustard, salt and ground black pepper. Add 1.5ml/¼ tsp caster (superfine) sugar if you like. Whisk to combine. Slowly drizzle in 90ml/6 tbsp oil, whisking until the vinaigrette is smooth and well blended. Check the seasoning and adjust if necessary.

creamy orange dressing

This is sufficiently versatile to go with a mixed salad with orange segments and tomatoes; grilled chicken; smoked duck breasts; or chicken kebabs on rice salad.

Serves 4

45ml/3 tbsp half-fat crème fraîche
15ml/1 tbsp white wine vinegar
finely grated rind and juice of 1 small orange
salt and ground black pepper

1 Measure the crème fraîche and wine vinegar into a screw-topped jar with the orange rind and juice.

2 Shake well until evenly combined, then adjust the seasoning to taste as desired.

classic savoury sauces

Hot or cold, cooked or raw, master these influential savoury sauces and you'll have countless variations at your disposal. As well as homely white sauces and gravy, there are lightly whisked sauces, juicy tomato or vegetable concoctions, a speedy technique for making satay sauce and the essential mayonnaise recipe. Use this section as a quick reference for checking technique, finding the right proportions of ingredients and seeking out the right accompaniment.

béchamel sauce

This is a creamy white sauce with an excellent, mellow flavour, which makes it ideal for lasagne as well as a suitable base or accompaniment for many fish, egg and vegetable dishes.

2 Over a gentle heat, melt the butter in a pan, remove from the heat and stir in the flour. Return to the heat and cook for 1–2 minutes, stirring, to make a roux.

3 Reheat the flavoured milk until almost boiling. Strain into a jug (pitcher), pressing the vegetables with a spoon to extract the juices.

Serves four

INGREDIENTS

1 small onion
1 small carrot
1 celery stick
bouquet garni
6 black peppercorns
pinch of freshly grated nutmeg or
  a blade of mace
300ml/½ pint/1¼ cups milk
25g/1oz/2 tbsp butter
25g/1oz/¼ cup plain (all-purpose) flour
30ml/2 tbsp single (light) cream
salt and ground black pepper

1 Peel and finely chop the vegetables. Put the vegetables, flavourings and milk in a pan. Bring to the boil. Remove from the heat

4 Off the heat, gradually add the milk to the roux, stirring constantly until smooth. Return to the heat, bring to the boil and cook gently until the sauce thickens, stirring constantly. Simmer the sauce gently for 3–4 minutes.

5 Remove the pan from the heat. Season the sauce to taste and stir in the cream.

Energy 117kcal/488kJ; Protein 3.4g; Carbohydrate 8.6g, of which sugars 3.8g; Fat 7.9g, of which saturates 5g; Cholesterol 22mg; Calcium 107mg; Fibre 0.2g; Sodium 73mg.

basic white sauce

This white sauce is wonderfully adaptable for all kinds of savoury dishes, but it can be bland so always taste and season carefully.

Serves six

INGREDIENTS

600ml/1 pint/2½ cups milk
25g/1oz/2 tbsp butter
25g/1oz/¼ cup plain (all-purpose) flour
salt and ground black pepper

1 Warm the milk in a pan over a low heat, but do not boil.

2 In a separate pan melt the butter, then stir in the flour and cook gently over low heat for 1–2 minutes to make a roux. Do not allow the roux to brown.

VARIATIONS

This classic white sauce is the "mother" recipe to countless variations, all of which can be prepared by adding one or two ingredients to the base sauce just before it is ready to serve.
• Parsley sauce is traditionally served with bacon, fish or broad (fava) beans. Stir in 30–60ml/2–4 tbsp chopped fresh parsley (to taste) before serving.
• Cheese sauce makes delicious egg and vegetable gratins. Stir in 50g/2oz/½ cup finely grated mature Cheddar and 2.5ml/½ tsp prepared mustard when the sauce has simmered.

3 Remove the pan from the heat, gradually pour in the milk, stirring constantly to make a smooth sauce. Stop adding milk occasionally and stir vigorously to prevent lumps from forming.

4 Return to the heat and bring to the boil slowly, stirring constantly until the sauce thickens.

5 Simmer gently for a further 3–4 minutes until thickened and smooth. Season with salt and ground black pepper to taste.

COOK'S TIPS

• For a thicker, coating sauce, increase the amount of flour to 50g/2oz/½ cup and the butter to 50g/2oz/¼ cup.
• If you aren't using a non-stick pan, use a small whisk to incorporate the flour and milk smoothly.

Energy 91kcal/383kJ; Protein 3.8g; Carbohydrate 8g, of which sugars 4.8g; Fat 5.2g, of which saturates 3.3g; Cholesterol 15mg; Calcium 127mg; Fibre 0.1g; Sodium 68mg.

velouté sauce

This savoury pouring sauce is named after its smooth, velvety texture. It's based on a white stock made from fish, vegetables or meat, so it can easily be adapted to the dish you are serving.

Serves four

INGREDIENTS

600ml/1 pint/2½ cups stock
25g/1oz/2 tbsp butter
25g/1oz/¼ cup plain (all-purpose) flour
30ml/2 tbsp single (light) cream
salt and ground black pepper

1 Heat the stock until almost boiling, but do not boil. In another pan melt the butter and stir in the flour. Cook, stirring, over a moderate heat for 3–4 minutes, or until a pale, straw colour, stirring continuously.

2 Remove the pan from the heat and gradually blend in the hot stock, stirring constantly. Return to the heat and bring to the boil, still stirring constantly, until the sauce thickens.

3 Continue to cook at a very slow simmer, stirring occasionally, until reduced by about a quarter.

4 Skim the surface of the sauce occasionally during cooking to remove any scum, or pour it through a very fine strainer at the end of the simmering time.

5 Just before serving, remove the pan from the heat and stir in the cream. Season to taste.

VARIATIONS

• For a richer flavour in a special dish, replace 30–45ml/2–3 tbsp of the stock with dry white wine or vermouth.
• For a sherry velouté, add 60ml/4 tbsp dry sherry with the stock, reducing the quantity of stock by 60ml/4 tbsp.

Energy 130kcal/538kJ; Protein 1.1g; Carbohydrate 5.2g, of which sugars 0.3g; Fat 11.8g, of which saturates 7.4g; Cholesterol 31mg; Calcium 19mg; Fibre 0.2g; Sodium 130mg.

lemon sauce with tarragon

The sharpness of lemon and the mild aniseed flavour of tarragon transform the delicate flavours of chicken, egg or steamed vegetable dishes.

Serves four

INGREDIENTS

1 lemon
a small bunch of fresh tarragon
1 shallot, finely chopped
90ml/6 tbsp white wine
1 quantity Velouté sauce
45ml/3 tbsp double (heavy) cream
30ml/2 tbsp brandy
salt and ground black pepper

1 Thinly pare the rind from the lemon, taking care not to remove any white pith. Squeeze the juice from the lemon and pour it into a pan. Discard the lemon.

2 Discard the coarse stalks from the tarragon. Chop the leaves and add all but 15ml/1 tbsp to the pan with the lemon rind and shallot.

COOK'S TIP

This sauce goes well with an easy lunch of boiled eggs, or will accompany a range of suitably simple suppers. Try serving with pieces of boned chicken breast, wrapped with streaky (fatty) bacon rashers (strips) and grilled (broiled) or pan-fried.

3 Add the wine and simmer gently until reduced by half. Strain the liquid into a clean pan and return to the hob.

4 Add the Velouté sauce, cream, brandy and reserved tarragon. Heat through, taste and adjust the seasoning if necessary.

Energy 172kcal/713kJ; Protein 1.3g; Carbohydrate 5.6g, of which sugars 0.8g; Fat 12.8g, of which saturates 7.9g; Cholesterol 33mg; Calcium 39mg; Fibre 0.6g; Sodium 46mg.

espagnole sauce

Espagnole is a classic rich brown sauce, ideal for serving with red meat and game. It also makes a delicious, full-flavoured base for other sauces.

2 Gradually stir in the flour and cook for 5–10 minutes over a medium heat until the roux has become a rich brown colour.

3 Remove the pan from the heat and gradually blend in the stock.

4 Slowly bring to the boil, stirring until the sauce thickens. Add the bouquet garni, tomato purée, sherry, if using, and seasoning. Reduce the heat and simmer gently for 1 hour, stirring occasionally.

5 Strain the Espagnole sauce, and gently reheat before serving.

COOK'S TIP

This sauce can be covered and stored in the refrigerator for up to 4 days, or it can be frozen for up to 1 month.

Serves four to six

INGREDIENTS

25g/1oz/2 tbsp butter
50g/2oz bacon, chopped
2 shallots, unpeeled and chopped
1 carrot, chopped
1 celery stick, chopped
mushroom trimmings (if available)
25g/1oz/¼ cup plain (all-purpose) flour
600ml/1 pint/2½ cups hot brown stock
bouquet garni
30ml/2 tbsp tomato purée (paste)
15ml/1 tbsp sherry (optional)
salt and ground black pepper

1 Melt the butter in a heavy pan and fry the bacon for 2–3 minutes. Add the shallots, carrot, celery and mushroom trimmings, if using, and cook the mixture for a further 5–6 minutes, or until golden.

Energy 49kcal/204kJ; Protein 0.8g; Carbohydrate 4g, of which sugars 0.8g; Fat 3.6g, of which saturates 2.2g; Cholesterol 9mg; Calcium 9mg; Fibre 0.3g; Sodium 159mg.

chasseur sauce

This excellent mushroom and wine sauce will transform simple pan-fried or grilled chicken, grilled or roast pork, or rabbit dishes. To give the sauce more flavour use chestnut mushrooms.

Serves three to four

INGREDIENTS

25g/1oz/2 tbsp butter

1 shallot, finely chopped

115g/4oz/2 cups mushrooms, sliced

120ml/4fl oz/½ cup white wine

30ml/2 tbsp brandy

1 quantity Espagnole sauce

15ml/1 tbsp chopped fresh tarragon
  or chervil

3 Pour in the wine and brandy, and simmer over a medium heat until reduced by half.

4 Add the Espagnole sauce and herbs and heat through, stirring occasionally. Serve hot.

1 Melt the butter in a medium or large pan over a medium heat, and fry the shallot, stirring often, until soft but not brown.

2 Add the mushrooms and sauté, stirring occasionally until they just begin to brown.

Energy 166kcal/687kJ; Protein 2g; Carbohydrate 7.5g, of which sugars 2.3g; Fat 10.7g, of which saturates 6.6g; Cholesterol 27mg; Calcium 22mg; Fibre 0.9g; Sodium 279mg.

beurre blanc

This light sauce goes perfectly with poached or grilled salmon or trout.

Makes about 150ml/¼ pint/⅔ cup

INGREDIENTS

3 shallots, very finely chopped

45ml/3 tbsp dry white wine or court-bouillon

45ml/3 tbsp white wine vinegar or tarragon vinegar

115g/4oz/½ cup chilled unsalted (sweet) butter, diced

lemon juice (optional)

salt and ground white pepper

COOK'S TIP

Do use shallots rather than onions if possible. Shallots are sweeter in flavour, particularly when they have began to caramelize over the heat, and work wonderfully well in this simple sauce.

1 Put the shallots in a small pan with the wine or court-bouillon and vinegar. Bring to the boil and cook over a high heat until only about 30ml/2 tbsp liquid remains.

2 Remove the pan from the heat and leave to cool until the reduced liquid is just lukewarm.

3 Whisk in the chilled butter, one piece at a time, to make a pale, creamy sauce. Taste the sauce, then season with salt and pepper and add a little lemon juice to taste.

4 If not serving the sauce at once, keep it warm over a double boiler set over barely simmering water.

Energy 939kcal/3867kJ; Protein 2.5g; Carbohydrate 12.8g, of which sugars 9.4g; Fat 94.8g, of which saturates 59.9g; Cholesterol 245mg; Calcium 62mg; Fibre 2.1g; Sodium 703mg.

hollandaise sauce

This rich, warm sauce goes particularly well with a light supper of poached fish.

Makes about 120ml/4fl oz/½ cup

INGREDIENTS

115g/4oz/½ cup unsalted (sweet) butter

2 egg yolks

15–30ml/1–2 tbsp lemon juice, white wine vinegar or tarragon vinegar

salt and ground white pepper

COOK'S TIP

The barely-cooked egg yolks used in this recipe mean that it is not suitable for young children, pregnant women, the elderly or anyone with a weakened immune system.

1 Melt the butter in a small pan. Meanwhile, put the egg yolks and lemon juice or vinegar in a bowl. Season with the salt and pepper and whisk until the mixture is completely smooth.

2 Pour the melted butter in a steady stream on to the egg yolk mixture, beating vigorously to make a smooth, creamy sauce. Taste the sauce and add more lemon juice or vinegar if necessary.

Energy 978kcal/4023kJ; Protein 6.5g; Carbohydrate 0.7g, of which sugars 0.7g; Fat 105.5g, of which saturates 63g; Cholesterol 648mg; Calcium 68mg; Fibre 0g; Sodium 715mg.

watercress cream

The delicate green colour of this cream sauce looks wonderful against pink-fleshed fish, such as salmon or sea trout. The flavour is complementary, too.

Makes about 250ml/8fl oz/1 cup

INGREDIENTS

2 bunches watercress or rocket (arugula)

25g/1oz/2 tbsp butter

2 shallots, chopped

25g/1oz/¼ cup plain (all-purpose) flour

150ml/¼ pint/⅔ cup hot fish stock

150ml/¼ pint/⅔ cup dry white wine

5ml/1 tsp anchovy extract

150ml/¼ pint/⅔ cup single (light) cream

lemon juice

salt and cayenne pepper

1 Trim the watercress or rocket of any bruised leaves and coarse stalks. Blanch in boiling water for 5 minutes. Drain, refresh under cold running water, and drain again in a sieve or colander.

2 Press the watercress or rocket against the sides of the sieve or colander with a spoon to remove excess moisture. Chop finely and set aside.

3 Melt the butter in a pan and fry the shallots over a medium heat for 3–4 minutes, until soft. Stir in the flour and cook for 1–2 minutes.

4 Remove the pan from the heat and gradually stir in the fish stock and wine. Return the pan to the heat and bring the sauce to the boil, stirring constantly. Reduce the heat and simmer gently for 2–3 minutes, stirring occasionally.

5 Strain the sauce into a clean pan, then stir in the watercress or rocket, with the anchovy extract and cream. Warm over a low heat. Season with salt and cayenne pepper and sharpen with lemon juice to taste. Serve immediately.

Energy 713kcal/2961kJ; Protein 12.6g; Carbohydrate 28.9g, of which sugars 8.5g; Fat 51.1g, of which saturates 31.7g; Cholesterol 139mg; Calcium 387mg; Fibre 3.1g; Sodium 449mg.

mustard mayonnaise

Some people find classic mayonnaise difficult to make, but this version couldn't be easier. The essential thing is to have all the ingredients at room temperature.

Makes about 350ml/12fl oz/1½ cups

INGREDIENTS

1 egg, plus 1 egg yolk

5ml/1 tsp Dijon mustard

juice of 1 large lemon

175ml/6fl oz/¾ cup olive oil

175ml/6fl oz/¾ cup grapeseed, sunflower
or corn oil

salt and ground white pepper

COOK'S TIPS

• Be aware that this recipe contains
raw eggs. If this is a concern, use
bought mayonnaise instead.

• To make the mayonnaise even more
glossy, beat in about 15ml/1 tbsp
boiling water at the end, if you like.

1 Put the whole egg and yolk in a
food processor and process for 20
seconds. Add the mustard, half the
lemon juice and a generous pinch
of salt and pepper. Put on the lid,
then process the mixture for about
30 seconds, until thoroughly mixed.

2 With the motor running, pour in
the oils through the feeder tube in a
thin, steady stream. When the oils
are taken up and the mayonnaise is
pale and thick, taste and add more
lemon juice and seasoning if liked.
Scrape the mayonnaise into a bowl.

Energy 2475kcal/10180kJ; Protein 9.3g; Carbohydrate 0.2g, of which sugars 0.2g; Fat 270.9g, of which saturates 37.3g; Cholesterol 392mg; Calcium 53mg; Fibre 0g; Sodium 138mg.

mustard and dill sauce

Serve this fresh-tasting sauce with any cold, smoked or raw marinated salmon. Note that it contains raw egg yolk, so, as with hollandaise sauce, it is best to avoid serving it to children, pregnant women, the elderly or anyone with a weakened immune system.

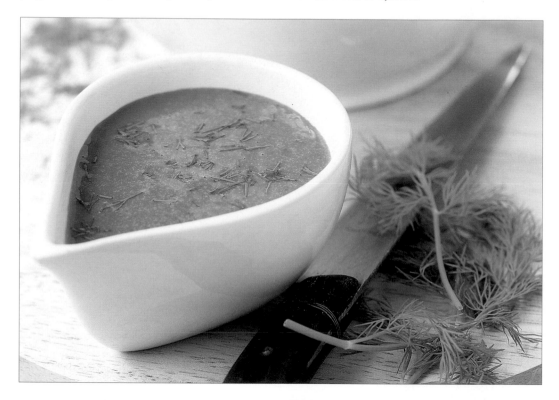

Makes about 120ml/4fl oz/½ cup

INGREDIENTS

1 egg yolk
30ml/2 tbsp brown French mustard
2.5–5ml/½–1 tsp soft dark brown sugar
15ml/1 tbsp white wine vinegar
90ml/6 tbsp sunflower or vegetable oil
30ml/2 tbsp finely chopped fresh dill
salt and ground black pepper

1 Put the egg yolk in a small bowl and add the mustard with a little soft brown sugar to taste. Beat with a wooden spoon until smooth.

2 Stir in the white wine vinegar, then whisk in the oil, drop by drop at first, then in a steady stream. As the oil is added, the dressing will start to thicken and emulsify.

3 When the oil has been completely amalgamated, season the sauce with salt and pepper, then stir in the finely chopped dill. Cover and chill for 1–2 hours before serving.

Energy 716kcal/2950kJ; Protein 5.9g; Carbohydrate 6.3g, of which sugars 5.6g; Fat 74.3g, of which saturates 9.6g; Cholesterol 202mg; Calcium 106mg; Fibre 1.5g; Sodium 904mg.

olive oil, tomato and herb sauce

This aromatic sauce is served warm, rather than hot, with grilled or poached salmon or trout. It tastes so great you'll want to provide plenty of good bread or boiled new potatoes to mop up any sauce remaining on the plate.

Makes about 350ml/12fl oz/1½ cups

INGREDIENTS

225g/8oz tomatoes
15ml/1 tbsp finely chopped shallot
2 garlic cloves, finely sliced
120ml/4fl oz/½ cup extra virgin olive oil
30ml/2 tbsp cold water
15ml/1 tbsp lemon juice
caster (superfine) sugar
15ml/1 tbsp chopped fresh chervil
15ml/1 tbsp chopped fresh chives
30ml/2 tbsp torn fresh basil leaves
salt and ground black pepper

COOK'S TIP

It is essential to the flavour of this sauce that you use the best quality olive oil.

1 Peel and seed the tomatoes, then cut them into fine dice.

2 Place the shallot, garlic and oil in a small pan over a very gentle heat and infuse for a few minutes. The ingredients should warm through, but definitely not fry or cook.

3 Whisk in the cold water and lemon juice. Remove from the heat and stir in the tomatoes. Add a pinch of salt, pepper and caster sugar, then whisk in the chervil and chives. Leave to stand for 10–15 minutes. Reheat gently to warm, then stir in the basil before serving.

Energy 776kcal/3200kJ; Protein 3g; Carbohydrate 9.2g, of which sugars 8.7g; Fat 81.1g, of which saturates 11.7g; Cholesterol 0mg; Calcium 100mg; Fibre 4.5g; Sodium 34mg.

mousseline sauce

A truly luscious sauce, that is subtly flavoured, rich and creamy. Try serving it as a dip for prepared artichokes or artichoke hearts, or with shellfish.

Serves four

INGREDIENTS

2 egg yolks
15ml/1 tbsp lemon juice
75g/3oz/6 tbsp softened butter
90ml/6 tbsp double (heavy) cream
extra lemon juice (optional)
salt and ground black pepper

VARIATION

If you like, substitute the lemon juice in this recipe with an equal amount of freshly squeezed lime juice.

1 To make the sauce, whisk the yolks and lemon juice in a bowl over a pan of barely simmering water, or a double boiler, until very thick and fluffy.

2 Whisk in the butter, a very little at a time, allowing each piece to melt before adding the next, until completely absorbed and the sauce has the consistency of mayonnaise.

3 In a separate bowl, whisk the cream until it forms stiff peaks. Fold the whipped cream into the warm sauce and adjust the seasoning to taste. You can also add a little more lemon juice for extra sharpness, depending on the food the sauce is to accompany.

VARIATION

For a lavish accompaniment to special fish dishes such as lobster or Dover sole, stir in 30–45ml/2–3 tbsp caviar before serving as a Caviar Mousseline.

Energy 282kcal/1159kJ; Protein 1.9g; Carbohydrate 0.5g, of which sugars 0.5g; Fat 30.3g, of which saturates 18.1g; Cholesterol 172mg; Calcium 26mg; Fibre 0g; Sodium 123mg.

béarnaise sauce

For classic, plain meat dishes, this herby butter sauce adds a note of sophistication without swamping grilled or pan-fried steak. It also enhances plain vegetables.

Serves two to three

INGREDIENTS

45ml/3 tbsp white wine vinegar

30ml/2 tbsp water

1 small onion, finely chopped

a few fresh tarragon and chervil sprigs

1 bay leaf

6 crushed black peppercorns

115g/4oz/¹⁄₂ cup butter

2 egg yolks

15ml/1 tbsp chopped fresh herbs, such as tarragon, parsley, chervil

salt and ground black pepper

1 Place the vinegar, water, onion, herb sprigs, bay leaf and peppercorns in a pan. Simmer gently until the liquid is reduced by half. Strain and cool.

2 In a separate bowl, cream the butter until soft.

3 In a bowl over a saucepan of gently simmering water, or a double boiler, whisk the egg yolks and liquid until paler in colour and light and fluffy in texture. Do not allow the water to boil rapidly or overheat the egg mixture or it will cook and curdle.

4 Gradually add the butter, half a teaspoonful at a time. Whisk until all the butter has been incorporated before adding any more.

5 Add the chopped fresh herbs and stir in seasoning to taste.

6 Serve warm, not hot, on the side of a grilled steak or allow a good spoonful to melt over new potatoes.

VARIATION

To make Choron sauce, which is very good with roast or grilled lamb, stir in 15ml/1 tbsp tomato purée (paste) to the sauce at the end of step 1.

Energy 335kcal/1378kJ; Protein 2.6g; Carbohydrate 1.9g, of which sugars 1.5g; Fat 35.3g, of which saturates 21g; Cholesterol 216mg; Calcium 38mg; Fibre 0.5g; Sodium 241mg.

newburg sauce

This creamy Madeira-flavoured sauce originated in America. Its rich flavour will not mask delicate foods and it is ideal for serving with shellfish. It also goes well with pan-fried chicken.

3 Add the cayenne and all but 60ml/4 tbsp of the cream. Leave over the simmering water for 10 minutes to heat through.

4 Stir in the Madeira. Beat the yolks with the remaining cream and stir into the hot sauce. Continue stirring the sauce over barely simmering water until thickened. Season to taste. Serve immediately.

Serves four

INGREDIENTS

15g/½ oz/1 tbsp butter
1 small shallot, finely chopped
pinch of cayenne pepper
300ml/½ pint/1¼ cups double (heavy) cream
60ml/4 tbsp Madeira
3 egg yolks
salt and ground black pepper

1 Melt the butter in a pan then cook the shallot until transparent.

2 Place a heatproof bowl over a pan of simmering water and add the cooked shallot.

VARIATIONS

• For a classic lobster newburg, add 200g/8oz/2 cups lobster meat to the pan with the shallot at the beginning of the recipe and proceed as above.
• For a twist in the tail, add 15–30ml/ 1–2 tbsp pink or black lumpfish roe towards the end of cooking. It will colour the sauce beautifully too.

Energy 469kcal/1930kJ; Protein 3.6g; Carbohydrate 3.4g, of which sugars 3g; Fat 47.5g, of which saturates 28.2g; Cholesterol 262mg; Calcium 60mg; Fibre 0.2g; Sodium 51mg.

rich vegetable sauce

For a full tomato flavour and rich red colour, fresh Italian plum tomatoes are an excellent choice if they are available. This makes a delightful topping for plain-cooked fresh pasta.

Serves four to six

INGREDIENTS

30ml/2 tbsp olive oil

1 large onion, chopped

2 garlic cloves, crushed

1 carrot, finely chopped

1 celery stick, finely chopped

675g/1½lb tomatoes, peeled and chopped

150ml/¼ pint/⅔ cup red wine

150ml/¼ pint/⅔ cup vegetable stock

bouquet garni

2.5–5ml/½–1 tsp sugar

15ml/1 tbsp tomato purée (paste), or to taste

salt and ground black pepper

4 Remove the bouquet garni from the sauce. Taste the sauce and adjust the seasoning, if necessary, adding salt and pepper, and an extra pinch of sugar with a little more tomato purée if the flavour is too weak or slightly sharp.

5 Serve the sauce as it is or, for a smoother texture, press it through a sieve. Alternatively, purée the sauce in a blender or food processor. This is delicious spooned over barely blanched sliced courgettes or cooked whole French (green) beans.

1 Heat the oil in a pan, add the onion and garlic and sauté until soft and pale golden brown. Add the carrot and celery and continue to cook, stirring occasionally, until all the vegetables are golden.

2 Stir in the tomatoes, wine, stock and bouquet garni. Season with salt and ground black pepper to taste.

3 Bring the tomato mixture to the boil. Reduce the heat, cover and simmer gently for 45 minutes, stirring occasionally.

Energy 81kcal/338kJ; Protein 1.2g; Carbohydrate 6.2g, of which sugars 5.9g; Fat 4.1g, of which saturates 0.7g; Cholesterol 0mg; Calcium 18mg; Fibre 1.7g; Sodium 24mg.

cumberland sauce with duck

Orange, redcurrant jelly and red wine make this vibrant sauce perfect with duck. Traditionally it is served with boiled or baked ham, but this classic recipe pairs it with roasted duck.

Serves eight

INGREDIENTS

4 minneolas or oranges, segmented, with rind and juice reserved

2 x 2.25kg/5lb oven-ready ducks, with giblets

salt and ground black pepper

fresh parsley sprig, to garnish

For the Cumberland sauce

30ml/2 tbsp plain (all-purpose) flour

300ml/½ pint/1¼ cups chicken or duck stock

150ml/¼ pint/⅔ cup port or red wine

15ml/1 tbsp redcurrant jelly

1 Preheat the oven to 180°C/350°F/Gas 4. Tie the minneola or orange rind with string and place it inside the cavities of the two ducks.

2 Place the ducks on a rack in one large or two smaller roasting pans, prick the skin well with a fork or a skewer, season with salt and pepper and cook for 30 minutes per every 450g/1lb (about 2½ hours) until the tender and the juices run clear.

3 Halfway through cooking, pour off the fat from the roasting pan(s) into a heatproof bowl.

4 When the ducks are cooked, transfer them to a carving place or board. Cover lightly with foil and leave to rest. Remove the orange rind from the cavities. Finely chop the rind or cut it into fine shreds and set it aside for the sauce.

5 To make the sauce, remove any fat from the roasting pan(s), leaving the sediment and juices. If using two pans, scrape the sediment and juices into one pan. Add the flour and cook gently, stirring, for 2 minutes.

6 Add the reserved rind to the roasting pan with the stock, port or red wine and redcurrant jelly. Stir well to blend, then bring to the boil and simmer, stirring frequently, for about 10 minutes. Strain the sauce into a pan. Add the orange segments with their juices.

7 To carve the ducks, remove the legs and wings, cutting through the joints. Cut the two end joints off the wings and discard them. Cut the breast meat off the carcass in one piece and slice it thinly. Serve with a little of the hot sauce poured over and serve the rest separately.

COOK'S TIP

When the sauce is made to accompany ham or grilled meats, without the roast orange and roasting juices, cook the finely shredded rind of 1 orange in a little boiling water and drain. Make the sauce in a pan, adding the orange.

Energy 244kcal/1028kJ; Protein 31.3g; Carbohydrate 4.3g, of which sugars 1.4g; Fat 10.2g, of which saturates 3.4g; Cholesterol 169mg; Calcium 24mg; Fibre 0.1g; Sodium 176mg.

blue cheese and walnut sauce

This is a very quick but indulgently creamy sauce. The blue cheese melts easily with cream to make a simple sauce to serve with vegetables or pasta for a delicious lunch or supper.

Serves two

INGREDIENTS

50g/2oz/¼ cup butter

50g/2oz/¾ cup button (white) mushrooms, sliced

150g/5oz hard blue cheese, such as Gorgonzola, Stilton or Danish Blue

150ml/¼ pint/⅔ cup sour cream

25g/1oz/⅓ cup grated Pecorino cheese

50g/2oz/⅓ cup broken walnut pieces

salt and ground black pepper

1 Melt the butter in a saucepan, add the mushrooms and cook gently for 3–5 minutes, stirring occasionally until lightly browned.

2 Crumble the blue cheese into a bowl and add the cream. Add seasoning to taste and mash together well using a fork, until thoroughly combined.

3 Stir the cheese cream into the mushroom mixture and heat gently, stirring, until melted.

4 Finally, stir in the Pecorino cheese and the walnut pieces. Remove from the heat. Serve warm.

Energy 828kcal/3420kJ; Protein 26.8g; Carbohydrate 3.9g, of which sugars 3.7g; Fat 78.5g, of which saturates 40.8g; Cholesterol 167mg; Calcium 616mg; Fibre 1.2g; Sodium 1237mg.

quick satay sauce

There are many versions of this tasty peanut sauce. This one is very speedy and it tastes delicious drizzled over grilled or barbecued skewers of chicken. For parties, spear chunks of chicken with cocktail sticks and arrange around a bowl of warm sauce.

3 Add the Worcestershire sauce and a dash of Tabasco, to taste. Pour into a serving bowl.

4 Use a potato peeler to shave thin curls from a piece of fresh coconut, if using. Scatter the coconut over the dish of your choice and serve immediately with the sauce.

Serves four

INGREDIENTS

200ml/7fl oz/scant 1 cup creamed coconut
60ml/4 tbsp crunchy peanut butter
1 tsp Worcestershire sauce
Tabasco sauce, to taste
fresh coconut, to garnish (optional)

1 Pour the coconut cream into a small pan and heat it gently over a low heat, stirring occasionally, for about 2 minutes.

2 Add the peanut butter and stir vigorously until it is blended into the creamed coconut. Continue to heat until the mixture is warm but not boiling hot.

COOK'S TIP

Thick coconut milk can be substituted for creamed coconut, but take care to buy an unsweetened variety for this recipe. Look out for instant coconut milk powder, often available from Asian stores, as it is an excellent and versatile, practical alternative to creams or canned coconut milk.

Energy 108kcal/451kJ; Protein 3.6g; Carbohydrate 5.8g, of which sugars 4.9g; Fat 8g, of which saturates 2.1g; Cholesterol 0mg; Calcium 30mg; Fibre 0.8g; Sodium 150mg.

green peppercorn sauce

This creamy sauce is excellent with pasta, pork or lamb steaks, or grilled chicken. The green peppercorns in brine are a better choice than the dry-packed type because they tend to give this piquant, creamy sauce a more rounded, fuller flavour.

Serves three to four

INGREDIENTS

15ml/1 tbsp green peppercorns in brine, drained
1 small onion, finely chopped
25g/1oz/2 tbsp butter
300ml/½ pint/1¼ cups light stock
juice of ½ lemon
15ml/1 tbsp beurre manié
45ml/3 tbsp double (heavy) cream
5ml/1 tsp Dijon mustard
salt and ground black pepper

3 Whisk in the beurre manié a piece at a time, whisking until the sauce is thick and smooth.

4 Reduce the heat and stir in the peppercorns, cream and mustard. Heat gently without boiling, then season to taste and serve.

VARIATION

For a lighter sauce, use crème fraîche instead of the double (heavy) cream.

COOK'S TIP

For beurre manié, cream equal quantities of butter and plain (all-purpose) flour together. Chill until firm.

1 Dry the peppercorns on kitchen paper, then crush lightly under a knife or in a mortar and pestle.

2 Soften the onion in the butter. Add the stock and lemon juice. Bring to the boil, reduce the heat and simmer for 15 minutes.

Energy 129kcal/533kJ; Protein 0.8g; Carbohydrate 2.5g, of which sugars 1.2g; Fat 13.1g, of which saturates 8.1g; Cholesterol 33mg; Calcium 19mg; Fibre 0.3g; Sodium 86mg.

classic bread sauce

A classic sauce for roast game, chicken or turkey, bread sauce is now reserved almost exclusively for the Christmas turkey. However, in practice it is a versatile white sauce.

Serves six to eight

INGREDIENTS

475ml/16fl oz/2 cups milk

1 small onion, stuck with 4 cloves

1 celery stick, chopped

1 fresh bay leaf, torn in half

6 allspice berries

1 blade of mace

90g/3½oz/1¾ cups day-old breadcrumbs, from a good-quality white loaf

freshly grated nutmeg

30ml/2 tbsp double (heavy) cream

15g/½oz/1 tbsp butter

salt and ground black pepper

1 Place the milk, onion, celery, bay leaf, allspice and mace in a pan and bring to the boil. Take off the heat and half cover the pan. Then set the milk aside to infuse for 30–60 minutes.

2 Strain the milk and place in a blender or food processor. Remove and discard the cloves from the onion and add the onion to the milk with the celery. Process until smooth, then strain the liquid back into the clean pan.

3 Bring back to the boil and stir in the breadcrumbs. Simmer gently, whisking with a small whisk, until the sauce thickens and becomes smooth. Add a little extra milk if the sauce is too thick.

4 Season to taste with salt, pepper and freshly grated nutmeg. Just before serving, whisk in the cream and butter. Serve warm rather than piping hot.

VARIATIONS

The classic bread sauce is at its best for roast poultry left plain, just as it is: it is also good with grilled sausages or pork chops. These subtle variations make versatile use of bread-thickened sauce.

• Add the grated rind of 1 lemon and a good squeeze of lemon juice with the cream and butter. Serve the sauce with poached chicken. Thin it slightly with a little extra milk and serve with baked fish.

• Sherried bread sauce is delicious with grilled (broiled) chicken, served with grilled mushrooms and bacon rolls. Add 45ml/3 tbsp dry sherry with the crumbs, simmer and finish as above.

• Add 15ml/1 tbsp each of finely chopped tarragon and chives, and 30ml/2 tbsp finely chopped parsley.

Energy 100kcal/419kJ; Protein 3.4g; Carbohydrate 11.6g, of which sugars 3.2g; Fat 4.8g, of which saturates 2.9g; Cholesterol 13mg; Calcium 88mg; Fibre 0.3g; Sodium 123mg.

onion gravy

This makes a delicious, dark onion sauce to go with sausages, liver, pork chops or toad-in-the-hole: a mound of creamy mashed potatoes is the essential accompaniment.

Serves four

INGREDIENTS

40g/1½oz/3 tbsp butter or beef dripping
450g/1lb onions, halved and thinly sliced
2.5ml/½tsp brown sugar
45ml/3 tbsp plain (all-purpose) flour
400–500ml/14–17fl oz/1⅔–2 cups hot
  beef or vegetable stock
1 fresh thyme sprig
10ml/2 tsp dark soy sauce
5ml/1 tsp Worcestershire sauce (optional)
salt and ground black pepper

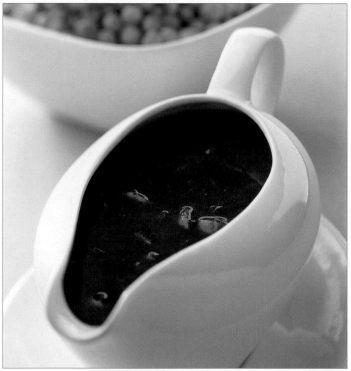

1 Melt the butter or dripping over a gentle heat. Add the onions and fry, stirring occasionally, for 15–20 minutes, until beginning to brown.

2 Add the sugar, increase the heat a little and cook for 20–30 minutes, until the onions are dark brown.

3 Stir in the flour, cook for a few minutes, stirring, then gradually stir in 400ml/14fl oz/1⅔ cups of the hot stock. Simmer, stirring, to make a thickened gravy, adding a little more stock if the gravy is too thick.

4 Add the thyme, season lightly, then cook gently, stirring frequently, for 10–15 minutes.

5 Stir in the soy sauce, and, if using, the Worcestershire sauce. Add more seasoning, if required, and a little more stock if the gravy is too thick. Remove the thyme, and serve immediately.

VARIATIONS

• The onions can be browned in the oven. This is best done in vegetable oil rather than butter or dripping. Place the sliced onions in an ovenproof dish and toss with 45ml/3 tbsp oil. Cook at 190°C/375°F/Gas 5 for 20 minutes, stirring once or twice. Stir in the sugar, then cook at 220°C/425°F/Gas 7 for a further 15–25 minutes, until the onions are dark brown and caramelized.

• Part of the beef or vegetable stock may be replaced with red wine or dark beer. You may need to add a little extra sugar to balance the acidity of the wine or beer.

Energy 636kcal/2648kJ; Protein 10.8g; Carbohydrate 75.8g, of which sugars 3.2g; Fat 34.4g, of which saturates 20.9g; Cholesterol 85mg; Calcium 189mg; Fibre 7.7g; Sodium 2393mg.

peanut sauce

This is based on the famous Indonesian sauce that accompanies grilled pork, chicken or seafood satay. Slightly thinned down with water, it is also used to dress gado-gado, a wonderful salad of mixed raw or cooked vegetables and fruit.

2 Add the shallots, garlic, ginger, most of the sliced chillies and the ground coriander to the oil remaining in the pan, and cook over a low heat, stirring occasionally, for 4–5 minutes, until the shallots are softened but not at all browned.

3 Transfer the spice mixture to a food processor or blender and add the peanuts, lemon grass, 5ml/1 tsp of the sugar, the soy sauce and 105ml/3fl oz of coconut milk and the fish sauce. Blend to form a fairly smooth sauce.

4 Taste and add more fish sauce, tamarind purée, seasoning, lime juice and/or more sugar to taste.

5 Stir in the extra coconut milk and a little water if the sauce seems very thick, but do not let it become too runny.

6 Serve cool or reheat the sauce gently, stirring all the time to prevent it from separating. Garnish with the remaining sliced chilli before serving.

Serves four to six

INGREDIENTS

30ml/2 tbsp peanut oil
75g/3oz/³⁄₄ cup unsalted peanuts, blanched
2 shallots, chopped
2 garlic cloves, chopped
15ml/1 tbsp chopped fresh root ginger
1–2 green chillies, seeded and thinly sliced
5ml/1 tsp ground coriander
1 lemon grass stalk, chopped
5–10ml/1–2 tsp light brown muscovado
  sugar
15ml/1 tbsp dark soy sauce
105–120ml/3–4 fl oz/scant ½ cup
  coconut milk
15–30ml/1–2 tbsp Thai fish sauce (nampla)
15–30ml/1–2 tbsp tamarind purée
lime juice
salt and ground black pepper

1 Heat the oil in a small, heavy frying pan and gently fry the peanuts, stirring frequently, until they are evenly and lightly browned. Use a draining spoon to remove the nuts from the pan and drain thoroughly on kitchen paper. Set aside to cool.

COOK'S TIP

To make tamarind purée, soak 25g/1oz tamarind pulp in 120ml/4fl oz/½ cup boiling water in a non-metallic bowl for about 30 minutes, mashing the pulp occasionally with a fork. Then press the pulp through a stainless steel sieve. This purée will keep for several days in a covered container in the refrigerator.

Energy 123kcal/513kJ; Protein 3.9g; Carbohydrate 5.8g, of which sugars 4.7g; Fat 9.6g, of which saturates 1.6g; Cholesterol 0mg; Calcium 34mg; Fibre 1.3g; Sodium 557mg.

apple sauce

Really more of a condiment than a sauce, this tart purée is usually served warm or cold, rather than hot. It is the classic accompaniment for roast pork, duck or goose, but is also good with grilled sausages, cold meats and savoury pies.

Serves six

INGREDIENTS

225g/8oz tart cooking apples
30ml/2 tbsp water
thin strip of lemon rind
15ml/1 tbsp butter
15–30ml/1–2 tbsp caster (superfine) sugar

1 Peel, quarter, core and thinly slice the apples.

3 Remove and discard the lemon rind. Beat the apples until smooth or press them through a sieve.

4 Stir the butter into the apple sauce and then add sugar to taste.

2 Place the apples in a pan with the water and lemon rind. Cook gently, stirring frequently, until pulpy.

VARIATIONS

• Stir in 15ml/1 tbsp Calvados with the butter and sugar.
• To make a creamy sauce, stir in 30ml/2 tbsp sour cream or crème fraîche at the end of cooking

Energy 42kcal/175kJ; Protein 0.1g; Carbohydrate 6g, of which sugars 6g; Fat 2.1g, of which saturates 1.3g; Cholesterol 5mg; Calcium 3mg; Fibre 0.6g; Sodium 16mg.

salsas and dips

Versatile and eclectic, these brilliant little recipes suit all sorts of occasions. There are classic dips for starters or light meals; punchy mixtures to serve at parties with delicious dunkers; and refreshing blends to transform plain cooked foods into a fusion of flavours. Preparation is often not much more than a whiz in a food processor. Vary ingredients to suit preference and enjoy superlative results every time.

salsa verde

There are many versions of this classic green salsa. Try this one drizzled over chargrilled squid, or with jacket potatoes served with a green salad.

2 Use your fingers to rub the excess salt off the capers. Add them, with the tarragon and parsley, to the food processor and pulse again until the ingredients are quite finely chopped.

3 Transfer the mixture to a bowl. Mix in the lime rind and juice, lemon juice and olive oil, stirring lightly so the citrus juice and oil do not emulsify.

4 Gradually add the Tabasco sauce and black pepper to taste. Chill the salsa, but do not prepare it more than 8 hours in advance.

Serves four

INGREDIENTS

2–4 green chillies, halved
8 spring onions
2 garlic cloves
60ml/4 tbsp salted capers
sprig of fresh tarragon
bunch of fresh parsley
grated rind and juice of 1 lime
juice of 1 lemon
90ml/6 tbsp olive oil
about 15ml/1 tbsp green Tabasco sauce
ground black pepper

1 Halve and seed the chillies and trim the spring onions. Halve the garlic cloves. Place in a food processor and pulse briefly.

COOK'S TIP

Salted capers can be strong and may need rinsing before use. If you prefer, you may use pickled capers instead.

Energy 158kcal/652kJ; Protein 0.9g; Carbohydrate 1.1g, of which sugars 1g; Fat 16.8g, of which saturates 2.4g; Cholesterol 0mg; Calcium 35mg; Fibre 1g; Sodium 6mg.

coriander pesto salsa

This aromatic salsa is delicious over fish, chicken or pasta, or used to dress an avocado and tomato salad. To transform it into a dip, simply mix with a little mayonnaise or sour cream.

Serves four

INGREDIENTS

50g/2oz fresh coriander (cilantro) leaves
15g/½oz fresh parsley
2 red chillies
1 garlic clove
50g/2oz/⅓ cup shelled pistachio nuts
25g/1oz/⅓ cup finely grated Parmesan cheese, plus extra to garnish
90ml/6 tbsp olive oil
juice of 2 limes
salt and ground black pepper

VARIATION

Any number of different herbs or nuts may be used to make a similar salsa to this one – try a mixture of rosemary and parsley, or add a handful of black olives for a Mediterranean flourish.

1 Process the fresh coriander and parsley in a food processor or blender until finely chopped.

2 Halve the chillies lengthways and remove their seeds. Add to the herbs together with the garlic, and process until finely chopped.

3 Add the pistachio nuts to the herb mixture and pulse the power until they are roughly chopped. Stir in the Parmesan cheese, olive oil and lime juice.

4 Add salt and pepper to taste. Spoon the mixture into a serving bowl, then cover and chill until ready to serve. Garnish with a little extra Parmesan.

Energy 263kcal/1083kJ; Protein 5.4g; Carbohydrate 2.5g, of which sugars 1.9g; Fat 25.7g, of which saturates 4.6g; Cholesterol 6mg; Calcium 123mg; Fibre 1.8g; Sodium 140mg.

classic tomato salsa

This is the traditional tomato-based salsa that most people associate with Mexican food. There are innumerable recipes for it, but the basic ingredients of onion, tomato and chilli are common to all. Serve this salsa as a condiment. It goes well with a wide variety of dishes.

Serves six as an accompaniment

INGREDIENTS

3–6 fresh Serrano chillies

1 large white onion

grated rind and juice of
  2 limes, plus strips of lime rind,
  to garnish

8 ripe, firm tomatoes

large bunch of fresh coriander (cilantro)

1.5ml/¼ tsp sugar

salt

VARIATIONS

• Use spring onions (scallions) or mild red onions instead of white onion.
• For a smoky flavour, use chipotle chillies instead of Serrano chillies.

1 Use 3 chillies for a salsa of medium heat; up to 6 if you like it hot. To peel the chillies, spear them on a long-handled metal skewer and roast them over the flame of a gas burner until the skins blister and darken. Do not let the flesh burn. Alternatively, dry-fry them in a griddle pan until the skins are scorched and blackened.

2 Place the roasted chillies in a strong plastic bag and tie the top of the bag to keep the steam in. Set aside for about 20 minutes.

3 Meanwhile, chop the onion finely and put it in a bowl with the lime rind and juice. The lime juice will soften the onion considerably.

4 Remove the chillies from the bag and peel off the skins. Cut off the stalks, then slit the chillies and scrape out the seeds. Chop the flesh and set it aside in a small bowl.

5 Cut a small cross in the base of each tomato. Place in a heatproof bowl and pour over boiling water to cover. Leave for 30 seconds.

6 Lift out the tomatoes and plunge them into a bowl of cold water. Drain well. Remove the skins.

7 Dice the peeled tomatoes and put them in a bowl. Add the chopped onion, which should by now have softened, together with any remaining lime juice and rind. Chop the coriander finely.

8 Add the chopped coriander to the salsa, with the chillies and the sugar. Mix gently until the sugar has dissolved and all the ingredients are coated in lime juice. Cover and chill for 2–3 hours to allow the flavours to blend. Garnish with the extra strips of lime rind just before serving.

Energy 47kcal/199kJ; Protein 1.8g; Carbohydrate 9.1g, of which sugars 7.9g; Fat 0.6g, of which saturates 0.1g; Cholesterol 0mg; Calcium 39mg; Fibre 2.6g; Sodium 16mg.

fragrant tomato and chilli salsa

Roasting the tomatoes gives a greater depth to the flavour of this salsa, which also benefits from the warm, rounded flavour of roasted chillies.

Serves six as an accompaniment

INGREDIENTS

500g/1¼lb tomatoes, preferably beefsteak tomatoes

2 fresh Serrano chillies or other fresh red chillies

1 onion

juice of 1 lime

large bunch of fresh coriander (cilantro)

salt

1 Preheat the oven to 200°C/400°F/ Gas 6. Cut the tomatoes into quarters and place them in a roasting pan. Add the chillies. Roast for 45 minutes to 1 hour, until the tomatoes and chillies are charred and softened.

2 Place the roasted chillies in a strong plastic bag. Tie the top to keep the steam in and set aside for 20 minutes. Leave the tomatoes to cool slightly, then use a small, sharp knife to remove the skins and dice the flesh.

3 Chop the onion finely, then place it in a bowl and add the lime juice and the diced tomatoes. Mix well.

4 Remove the chillies from the bag and peel off the skins. Cut off the stalks, then slit the chillies and scrape out the seeds with a sharp knife. Chop the chillies roughly and mix them into the onion mixture.

5 Chop the coriander and add most of it to the salsa. Add salt to season, cover and chill for at least 1 hour before serving, sprinkled with the remaining chopped coriander. This salsa will keep in the refrigerator for 1 week.

Energy 25kcal/104kJ; Protein 1.1g; Carbohydrate 4.4g, of which sugars 4.1g; Fat 0.4g, of which saturates 0.1g; Cholesterol 0mg; Calcium 26mg; Fibre 1.6g; Sodium 11mg.

smoky tomato salsa

The smoky flavour in this recipe comes from the smoked bacon and the commercial liquid smoke marinade. Served with sour cream, this salsa makes a great baked potato filler.

Serves four

INGREDIENTS

450g/1lb tomatoes

4 rindless smoked streaky (fatty)
  bacon rashers (strips)

15ml/1 tbsp vegetable oil

45ml/3 tbsp chopped fresh coriander
  (cilantro) leaves or parsley

1 garlic clove, finely chopped

15ml/1 tbsp liquid smoke marinade

freshly squeezed juice of 1 lime

salt and ground black pepper

1 Place the tomatoes in a heatproof bowl. Pour over boiling water and leave for 30 seconds. Remove with a slotted spoon, dunk in cold water and then peel. Halve the tomatoes, scoop out and discard the seeds, then finely dice the flesh.

2 Cut the bacon into small pieces. Heat the oil in a frying pan and cook the bacon for 5 minutes, stirring occasionally, until crisp and browned.

3 Remove the cooked bacon from the heat and drain and pat dry on kitchen paper. Leave to cool for a few minutes then place in a bowl.

4 Add the tomatoes and the chopped fresh coriander or parsley to the bacon. Stir in the garlic, then add the liquid smoke and freshly squeezed lime juice. Season the salsa with salt and pepper to taste and mix well, using a wooden spoon or plastic spatula.

5 Spoon the salsa into a serving bowl, cover with clear film (plastic wrap) and chill until ready to serve.

VARIATION

Give this smoky salsa an extra kick by adding a dash of Tabasco sauce or a pinch of dried chilli flakes.

Energy 82kcal/343kJ; Protein 3.1g; Carbohydrate 3.8g, of which sugars 3.8g; Fat 6.2g, of which saturates 1.5g; Cholesterol 8mg; Calcium 31mg; Fibre 1.7g; Sodium 171mg.

fresh tomato and tarragon salsa

Plum tomatoes, garlic, olive oil and balsamic vinegar make for a very Mediterranean salsa – try serving this with grilled lamb cutlets or toss it with freshly cooked pasta.

3 Using a sharp knife, crush or finely chop the garlic.

4 Whisk together the oil, balsamic vinegar and plenty of salt and pepper to make a dressing.

5 Add the chopped fresh tarragon to the dressing and stir lightly.

6 Mix the tomatoes and garlic in a bowl and pour the tarragon dressing over. Leave to infuse (steep) for at least 1 hour before serving at room temperature. Garnish with more shredded tarragon leaves.

Serves four

INGREDIENTS

8 plum tomatoes, or 500g/1¼lb sweet
  cherry tomatoes

1 small garlic clove

60ml/4 tbsp olive oil or sunflower oil

15ml/1 tbsp balsamic vinegar

30ml/2 tbsp chopped fresh tarragon, plus
  extra shredded leaves, to garnish

salt and ground black pepper

1 Plunge the tomatoes into boiling water for 30 seconds. Remove with a slotted spoon; cool in cold water.

2 Use a sharp knife to peel the tomatoes (the skins slip off easily if they have stood in the water long enough) and finely chop the flesh.

COOK'S TIP

Be sure to serve this salsa at room temperature as the tomatoes taste less sweet, and rather acidic, when chilled.

Energy 125kcal/517kJ; Protein 1.3g; Carbohydrate 4.4g, of which sugars 4.1g; Fat 11.5g, of which saturates 1.5g; Cholesterol 0mg; Calcium 29mg; Fibre 1.8g; Sodium 15mg.

grilled corn on the cob salsa

This unusual salsa is full of deliciously sweet vegetables. Use cherry tomatoes for an extra special flavour, and combine them with the ripest and freshest corn on the cob.

Serves four

INGREDIENTS

2 corn on the cob
30ml/2 tbsp melted butter
4 tomatoes
8 spring onions (scallions)
1 garlic clove
30ml/2 tbsp fresh lemon juice
30ml/2 tbsp olive oil
Tabasco sauce, to taste
salt and ground black pepper

1 Remove the husks and silky threads covering the corn on the cob. Brush the cobs with the melted butter and gently barbecue or grill (broil) them for 20–30 minutes, turning occasionally, until tender and tinged brown.

2 To remove the kernels, stand each cob upright on a chopping board and use a large, heavy knife to slice down the length of the cob.

3 Plunge the tomatoes into boiling water for 30 seconds. Remove with a slotted spoon and plunge into cold water to cool. Then peel the tomatoes (the skins should slip off easily) and finely dice the flesh.

4 Place 6 spring onions on a chopping board and chop finely. Crush and chop the garlic, and then mix together with the corn and tomato in a small bowl.

5 Stir the lemon juice and olive oil together, adding Tabasco sauce, salt and pepper to taste.

6 Pour this mixture over the salsa and stir well. Cover the salsa and leave to steep at room temperature for 1–2 hours before serving. Garnish with the remaining spring onions.

COOK'S TIP

Make this salsa in summer when fresh cobs of corn are readily available.

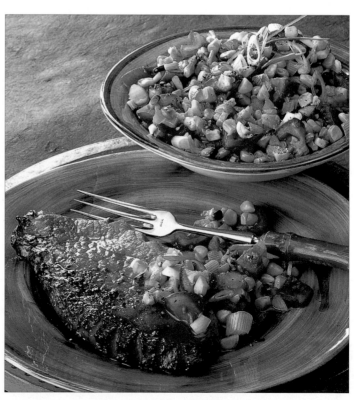

Energy 188kcal/785kJ; Protein 2.6g; Carbohydrate 17.1g, of which sugars 8.5g; Fat 12.7g, of which saturates 4.9g; Cholesterol 16mg; Calcium 18mg; Fibre 2g; Sodium 191mg.

fiery salsa

This is a scorchingly hot salsa for only the very brave! Spread it sparingly on to cooked meats and burgers or add a tiny amount to a curry or pot of chilli.

Serves four to six

INGREDIENTS

6 Scotch bonnet chillies

2 ripe tomatoes

4 standard green jalapeño chillies

30ml/2 tbsp chopped fresh parsley

30ml/2 tbsp olive oil

15ml/1 tbsp balsamic vinegar or sherry vinegar

salt

1 Skin the Scotch bonnet chillies, either by holding them in a gas flame for 3 minutes until the skins blacken and blister, or by plunging them into boiling water. Then, using rubber gloves, rub off the skins from the chillies.

2 Hold each tomato on a fork in a gas flame for 3 minutes until the skin blisters. (Or plunge them into boiling water for 30 seconds, if you prefer.) Once cool enough to touch, remove the skins, halve the tomatoes, and remove the seeds. Chop the flesh very finely.

3 Try not to touch the Scotch bonnet chillies with your bare hands: use a fork to hold them and slice them open with a sharp knife. Scrape out and discard the seeds, then finely chop the flesh.

4 Halve the jalapeño chillies, remove their seeds and finely slice them widthways into tiny strips. Mix both types of chillies, the tomatoes and the chopped parsley in a bowl.

5 In a small bowl, whisk the olive oil with the vinegar and a little salt. Pour this over the salsa and cover the dish. Chill for up to 3 days.

Energy 52kcal/215kJ; Protein 0.8g; Carbohydrate 3.4g, of which sugars 3.2g; Fat 4g, of which saturates 0.6g; Cholesterol 0mg; Calcium 20mg; Fibre 1.3g; Sodium 7mg.

bloody mary salsa

This salsa is perfect for parties – serve it with sticks of crunchy celery or fingers of refreshing cucumber or, on a really special occasion, with freshly shucked oysters.

Serves two

INGREDIENTS

4 ripe tomatoes
1 garlic clove
1 celery stick
2 spring onions (scallions)
45ml/3 tbsp tomato juice
Worcestershire sauce, to taste
Tabasco sauce, to taste
10ml/2 tsp horseradish sauce
15ml/1 tbsp vodka
juice of 1 lemon
salt and ground black pepper

VARIATION

Blend 1–2 seeded, fresh red chillies with the tomatoes, instead of stirring in the Tabasco sauce.

1 Halve the tomatoes, garlic and celery. Trim the spring onions.

2 Put the tomatoes, garlic, celery and spring onions in a blender or food processor. Process until the vegetables are finely chopped, then transfer the mixture to a small serving bowl.

3 Stir in the tomato juice, a little at a time, then add a few drops of Worcestershire sauce and Tabasco sauce to taste. Mix well and set aside for 10–15 minutes.

4 Stir in the horseradish sauce, vodka and lemon juice. Add salt and ground black pepper, to taste. Serve immediately, or cover and chill for 1–2 hours.

Energy 65kcal/275kJ; Protein 2g; Carbohydrate 8.2g, of which sugars 8.1g; Fat 1.1g, of which saturates 0.3g; Cholesterol 1mg; Calcium 29mg; Fibre 2.6g; Sodium 125mg.

sweet pepper salsa

Roasting peppers enhances their sweet flavour; choose red, yellow or orange peppers as the green variety is less ripe and not as sweet. This salsa is delicious served with poached salmon.

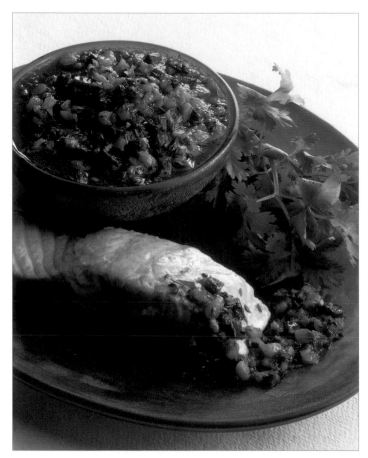

3 Meanwhile, place the cumin seeds in a small frying pan. Heat gently, stirring, until the seeds start to splutter and release their aroma. Remove the pan from the heat, then transfer the seeds to a mortar and crush them lightly with a pestle.

4 When the peppers are cool enough to handle, pierce a hole in the bottom of each and squeeze out all of the juices into a bowl. Peel, core and seed the peppers, and place in a blender or food processor with the chilli, coriander and reserve juice. Process until the ingredients are finely chopped.

Serves four

INGREDIENTS

1 red (bell) pepper

1 yellow (bell) pepper

5ml/1 tsp cumin seeds

1 red chilli, seeded

30ml/2 tbsp chopped fresh coriander (cilantro) leaves, plus extra to garnish

30ml/2 tbsp olive oil

15ml/1 tbsp red wine vinegar

salt and ground black pepper

1 Preheat the grill (broiler) to medium. Place the peppers on a baking sheet and grill them for 8–10 minutes, turning, until they are blackened and blistered.

2 Place the peppers in a bowl and cover with a clean dish towel. Leave the peppers to cool for 5 minutes – the steam helps to lift the skin away from the flesh.

5 Stir in the oil, vinegar and cumin with salt and pepper to taste. Serve the salsa at room temperature, garnished with coriander.

Energy 80kcal/331kJ; Protein 1.1g; Carbohydrate 5.8g, of which sugars 5.5g; Fat 6g, of which saturates 0.9g; Cholesterol 0mg; Calcium 22mg; Fibre 1.8g; Sodium 6mg.

plantain salsa

Here is a summery salsa which is perfect for lazy outdoor eating. Serve with barbecued meat or fish or with potato or vegetable crisps or taco chips for dipping.

Serves four

INGREDIENTS

knob of butter

4 ripe plantains (with blackened skins)

handful of fresh coriander (cilantro) leaves, plus extra to garnish

30ml/2 tbsp olive oil

5ml/1 tsp cayenne pepper

salt and ground black pepper

1 Preheat the oven to 200°C/400°F/Gas 6. Grease four pieces of foil, about 15 x 20cm/ 6 x 8in each, with butter. Make sure the plantains are ripe before cooking, so they are tender sweet.

2 Place a whole plantain on each piece of buttered foil. Carefully fold the pieces of foil over the plantains, sealing them tightly to form four parcels.

3 Bake the plantains for 25 minutes, until tender. Alternatively, they may be cooked in the embers of a charcoal barbecue.

4 Allow the parcels to cool slightly, then remove the plantains, discarding any liquid, and place in a food processor or blender.

5 Process the plantains with the coriander until fairly smooth. Stir in the olive oil, cayenne pepper and salt and pepper to taste.

6 Serve immediately as the salsa will discolour and over-thicken if left to cool for too long. Garnish with torn coriander leaves.

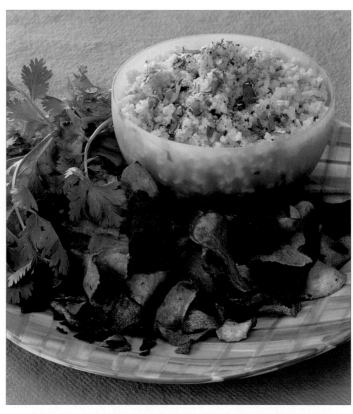

Energy 185kcal/780kJ; Protein 1.1g; Carbohydrate 29.4g, of which sugars 5.7g; Fat 7.9g, of which saturates 2.2g; Cholesterol 5mg; Calcium 10mg; Fibre 1.3g; Sodium 19mg.

chilli and coconut salsa

This fruity sweet-and-sour salsa, spiked with chillies, goes well with grilled or barbecued fish, lamb, pork or sausages. It is also excellent with baked sweet potatoes.

Serves six to eight

INGREDIENTS

1 small coconut
1 small pineapple
2 green Kenyan chillies
5cm/2in piece lemon grass stalk
60ml/4 tbsp natural (plain) yogurt
2.5ml/½ tsp salt
30ml/2 tbsp chopped fresh coriander
  (cilantro)
coriander (cilantro) sprigs, to garnish

1 Puncture two of the coconut eyes with a screwdriver. Drain out the coconut water from inside the shell.

2 Crack the coconut shell, prise away the flesh, and then coarsely grate the pieces of coconut into a mixing bowl.

3 Peel the pineapple and remove the eyes with a potato peeler. Finely chop the flesh and add to the coconut together with any juice.

4 Halve the chillies and remove the stalks, seeds and pith. Chop very finely and stir into the coconut.

5 Finely chop the lemon grass with a very sharp knife. Add to the coconut mixture with the remaining ingredients and stir well. Spoon into a serving dish and garnish with coriander sprigs.

COOK'S TIP

When buying a coconut, check its freshness by shaking gently – you should hear the liquid swishing about inside. If not, it's dried out and stale.

Energy 104kcal/434kJ; Protein 1.4g; Carbohydrate 7.2g, of which sugars 7.2g; Fat 8g, of which saturates 6.7g; Cholesterol 0mg; Calcium 27mg; Fibre 2.5g; Sodium 134mg.

berry salsa

This unusual, richly coloured fruit salsa is the perfect choice for a summer al fresco meal. It tastes terrific with barbecued fish or poultry, or baked gammon (cured or smoked ham).

Serves four

INGREDIENTS

1 fresh jalapeño chilli

½ red onion, finely chopped

2 spring onions (scallions), chopped

1 tomato, finely diced

1 small yellow (bell) pepper, seeded and finely chopped

45ml/3 tbsp chopped fresh coriander (cilantro)

1.5ml/¼ tsp salt

15ml/1 tbsp raspberry vinegar

15ml/1 tbsp fresh orange juice

5ml/1 tsp honey

15ml/1 tbsp olive oil

175g/6oz/1½ cups strawberries, hulled

175g/6oz/1½ cups blueberries or blackberries

200g/7oz/generous 1 cup raspberries

3 In a small bowl, whisk together the salt, vinegar, orange juice, honey and olive oil until thoroughly combined. Pour this dressing over the chilli and pepper mixture and stir well.

4 Coarsely chop the strawberries. Then stir them into the mixture with the blueberries or black berries and the raspberries. Allow to stand at room temperature for 3 hours before serving.

1 Wearing rubber gloves, finely chop the jalapeño chilli (discard the seeds and pith if a less-hot flavour is preferred). Place the pepper in a mixing bowl.

2 Add the red onion, spring onions, tomato, pepper and coriander, and stir until well mixed.

COOK'S TIP

Defrosted frozen berries can be used in the salsa, but the texture will be softer.

Energy 94kcal/392kJ; Protein 2.7g; Carbohydrate 13.7g, of which sugars 13.1g; Fat 3.5g, of which saturates 0.5g; Cholesterol 0mg; Calcium 71mg; Fibre 4.9g; Sodium 14mg.

orange, tomato and chive salsa

*Fresh chives and sweet oranges create a very cheerful combination of flavours in this unusual
salsa that is a very good accompaniment to cheese or meat salads.*

3 Roughly chop the orange
segments and add them to the bowl
with the collected juice. Halve the
tomato and use a teaspoon to
scoop the seeds and soft middle
into the oranges mixture. With a
sharp knife, finely dice the flesh
and add to the mixture in the bowl.

4 Hold the bunch of chives neatly
together and use a pair of kitchen
scissors to snip them into the bowl.

Serves four

INGREDIENTS

2 large, sweet oranges
1 beefsteak tomato or 2 plum tomatoes
bunch of fresh chives
1 garlic clove
30ml/2 tbsp extra virgin olive oil
  or grapeseed oil
sea salt

1 Slice the base off 1 orange so
that it will stand firmly. Using a
sharp knife, remove the peel in
strips by slicing from the top to the
bottom of the orange, cutting just
below the pith. Repeat with the
second orange.

2 Over a bowl, remove the orange
segments: cut to the middle and
close to the membrane on one side
of a segment. Gently twist the knife
and scrape the segment off the
other membrane. Repeat, squeezing
juice from the leftover membrane.

5 Thinly slice the garlic and stir it
into the orange and tomato
mixture. Pour the olive oil into the
salsa, season it to taste with sea
salt and stir well to mix and serve.

VARIATION

It is best to serve the salsa within
2 hours, or it may become too juicy.

Energy 90kcal/376kJ; Protein 1.6g; Carbohydrate 8.3g, of which sugars 8.2g; Fat 5.9g, of which saturates 0.8g; Cholesterol 0mg; Calcium 64mg; Fibre 2.4g; Sodium 13mg.

fiery citrus apple salsa

This very unusual apple salsa is laced with garlic and mint. It makes a fantastic marinade for shellfish, and it is also delicious drizzled over barbecued meat.

Serves four

INGREDIENTS

1 orange
1 green eating apple
2 fresh red chillies, halved and seeded
1 garlic clove
8 fresh mint leaves
juice of 1 lemon
salt and ground black pepper

VARIATION

For a super-fiery flavour, don't seed the chillies: the seeds will make the salsa particularly hot and fierce.

3 Peel the apple, slice it into wedges and remove the core by slicing through the centre.

4 Place the chillies in a blender or food processor with the orange segments and juice, apple wedges, garlic and fresh mint. Process for a few seconds until smooth. Then, with the motor running, slowly pour the lemon juice into the mixture.

5 Season to taste with a little salt and ground black pepper. Pour the salsa mixture into a bowl or small jug (pitcher) and serve immediately.

1 Slice the bottom off the orange so that it will stand firmly on a chopping board. Using a sharp knife, remove the peel by slicing from the top to the bottom of the orange.

2 Hold the orange in one hand over a bowl. Slice towards the middle of the fruit, to one side of a segment, and then gently twist the knife to ease the segment away from the membrane and out of the orange. Remove all the segments. Squeeze any juice from the remaining membrane into the bowl.

Energy 24kcal/104kJ; Protein 1g; Carbohydrate 5.3g, of which sugars 4.2g; Fat 0.1g, of which saturates 0g; Cholesterol 0mg; Calcium 16mg; Fibre 1.1g; Sodium 2mg.

creamy pineapple-passion fruit salsa

Pineapple and aromatic passion fruit create a salsa that's bursting with fruit flavour – great with barbecued pork or baked smoked ham. It also makes a luxurious dessert!

Serves six

INGREDIENTS

1 small pineapple

2 passion fruit

150ml/¼ pint/⅔ cup Greek (US strained plain) yogurt

30ml/2 tbsp light brown muscovado sugar

1 Cut off the top and bottom of the pineapple so that it will stand firmly on a chopping board. Using a large, sharp knife, slice off the peel, working down the fruit.

2 Use a small, sharp knife to carefully cut out the eyes. Slice the peeled pineapple and use a small pastry cutter to cut out the tough core. Finely chop the flesh.

3 Halve the passion fruit and use a spoon to scoop out the seeds and pulp into a bowl.

4 Stir in the chopped pineapple and the Greek yogurt. Cover and chill until required.

5 Stir in the muscovado sugar just before serving the salsa – if you add the sugar too soon, the salsa will become too thin and juicy.

VARIATION

For a spicy twist, add 45ml/3 tbsp finely chopped fresh root ginger to the fruit and leave it to steep for 1 hour. Season the salsa with plenty of ground black pepper and a little freshly grated nutmeg when stirring in the sugar.

Energy 78kcal/328kJ; Protein 2g; Carbohydrate 12.8g, of which sugars 12.8g; Fat 2.7g, of which saturates 1.3g; Cholesterol 0mg; Calcium 53mg; Fibre 1g; Sodium 20mg.

mixed melon salsa

A combination of two very different melons gives this salsa an exciting flavour and texture. Try it with thinly sliced Parma ham or smoked salmon.

Serves ten

INGREDIENTS

1 small orange-fleshed melon,
   such as Charentais

1 large wedge watermelon

2 oranges

1 Quarter the orange-fleshed melon and use a large spoon to scoop out the seeds. Discard them. Use a large, sharp knife to cut off the skin. Dice the melon flesh.

2 Pick out the seeds from the watermelon, then remove the skin. Dice the flesh into small chunks.

3 Use a zester to pare long fine strips of rind from both oranges. Halve the oranges and squeeze out all their juice.

4 Mix both types of the melon and the orange rind and juice together in a bowl. Chill for about 30 minutes and serve.

VARIATION

Other melons can be used for this salsa. Try cantaloupe, Galia or Ogen.

Energy 58kcal/250kJ; Protein 1.1g; Carbohydrate 13.5g, of which sugars 13.5g; Fat 0.4g, of which saturates 0.1g; Cholesterol 0mg; Calcium 30mg; Fibre 0.9g; Sodium 25mg.

mango and red onion salsa

A very simple tropical salsa, which is livened up by the addition of passion fruit pulp. This salsa goes well with salmon and poultry.

3 Score the mango halves deeply in both directions, taking care to avoid cutting through the skin. Carefully turn the skin inside out so the flesh stands out and slice the dice off the skin. Place in the bowl.

4 Place the red onion in the bowl with the mango. Halve the passion fruit, scoop out the pulp, and add to the mango mixture in the bowl.

Serves four

INGREDIENTS

1 large ripe mango
1 red onion, finely chopped
2 passion fruit
6 large fresh basil leaves
juice of 1 lime, to taste
sea salt

1 Holding the mango upright on a chopping board, use a large knife to slice from top to bottom on either side of the large central stone, so that you are left with two sizeable portions of the flesh.

2 Using a smaller knife, trim away any flesh still clinging to the top and bottom of the stone. Peel and dice these trimmings and place in a bowl ready to mix with the rest of the mango flesh for the salsa.

5 Tear the basil leaves coarsely and stir them into the mixture with lime juice and a little sea salt to taste. Mix well and serve the salsa immediately.

VARIATION

Freshly cooked sweetcorn kernels are a delicious addition to this salsa.

Energy 42kcal/178kJ; Protein 1.1g; Carbohydrate 9.7g, of which sugars 8.4g; Fat 0.2g, of which saturates 0.1g; Cholesterol 0mg; Calcium 18mg; Fibre 1.9g; Sodium 4mg.

peach and cucumber salsa

Angostura bitters add an unusual and very pleasing flavour to this salsa. The distinctive, sweet taste of the mint complements chicken and other meat dishes.

Serves four

INGREDIENTS

2 peaches
1 mini cucumber
2.5ml/½ tsp Angostura bitters
15ml/1 tbsp olive oil
10ml/2 tsp fresh lemon juice
30ml/2 tbsp chopped fresh mint
salt and ground black pepper

3 Trim the ends off the cucumber. Slice it lengthways into strips, then finely dice the flesh and stir it into the peaches. Stir the Angostura bitters, olive oil and lemon juice together and then stir this dressing into the peach mixture.

4 Stir in the mint with salt and pepper to taste. Chill and serve within 1 hour.

VARIATION

Use diced mango in place of the peaches for an alternative.

1 Using a small, sharp knife, carefully score a line right around the centre of each peach, taking care to cut just through the skin.

2 Bring a large pan of water to the boil. Add the peaches and blanch them for 1 minute. Drain and briefly refresh in cold water. Peel off and discard the skin. Halve the peaches and remove their stones (pits). Finely dice the flesh and place in a bowl.

COOK'S TIP

The texture of the peach and the crispness of the cucumber will fade fairly rapidly, so try to prepare this salsa as close to serving time as possible.

Energy 49kcal/203kJ; Protein 1.1g; Carbohydrate 4.8g, of which sugars 4.7g; Fat 3g, of which saturates 0.4g; Cholesterol 0mg; Calcium 28mg; Fibre 1.4g; Sodium 5mg.

guacamole

One of the best-loved Mexican salsas, this blend of creamy avocado, tomatoes, chillies, coriander and lime now appears on tables the world over. Bought guacamole usually contains mayonnaise, but this is not an ingredient that you are likely to find in traditional recipes.

Serves six to eight

INGREDIENTS

4 tomatoes

4 ripe avocados, preferably fuerte

juice of 1 lime

½ small onion

2 garlic cloves

small bunch of fresh coriander (cilantro), chopped

3 fresh red fresno chillies

salt

tortilla chips or breadsticks, to serve

COOK'S TIP

To crush a garlic clove, roughly chop it and sprinkle with sea salt, then work in using the side of a large knife blade.

1 Cut a cross in the base of each tomato. Place the tomatoes in a heatproof bowl and pour over boiling water to cover. (If you prefer, add the tomatoes to a pan of boiling water, taking the pan off the heat.)

2 Leave the tomatoes in the water for 30 seconds, then lift them out using a slotted spoon and plunge them into a bowl of cold water. Drain and peel. Cut the tomatoes in half, remove the seeds, then chop the flesh roughly and set it aside.

3 Cut the avocados in half, then remove the stones (pits). Scoop out the flesh and process it in a food processor or blender until almost smooth, then scrape into a bowl and stir in the lime juice.

4 Chop the onion finely, then crush the garlic. Add both to the avocado and mix well. Stir in the coriander.

5 Remove the stalks and seeds from the chillies, then finely chop them and mix them into the avocado mixture, with the tomatoes.

6 Taste the guacamole and add salt if needed. Cover closely with clear film (plastic wrap) and chill for 1 hour. Serve with tortilla chips or breadsticks to dip. If well covered, guacamole will keep in the refrigerator for 2–3 days.

COOK'S TIP

Smooth-skinned fuerte avocados are native to Mexico, so would be ideal for this dip. If they are not available, use any avocados, but make sure they are ripe. To test, gently press the top of the avocado; it should give a little.

Energy 156kcal/645kJ; Protein 2.1g; Carbohydrate 3.7g, of which sugars 2.5g; Fat 14.7g, of which saturates 3.1g; Cholesterol 0mg; Calcium 26mg; Fibre 3.5g; Sodium 11mg.

guacamole with lime

Guacamole is often served as a first course with corn chips for dipping. The chunky texture of this version makes it more versatile and it makes a great accompaniment for grilled fish, poultry or meat, especially steak. It is also very good in baked potatoes or butternut squash.

Serves four

INGREDIENTS

2 large ripe avocados

1 small red onion, very finely chopped

1 red or green chilli, seeded and very finely chopped

½–1 garlic clove, crushed with a little salt

finely shredded rind of ½ lime and juice of 1–1½ limes

pinch of sugar

3 tomatoes, seeded and chopped

30ml/2 tbsp roughly chopped fresh coriander (cilantro)

2.5–5ml/½–1 tsp ground toasted cumin seeds

15ml/1 tbsp olive oil

15–30ml/1–2 tbsp sour cream (optional)

salt and ground black pepper

lime wedges dipped in sea salt, and fresh coriander (cilantro) sprigs, to garnish

1 Cut 1 avocado in half and lift out and discard the stone (pit). Scrape the flesh from both halves into a bowl and mash it to a coarse paste with a fork.

2 Stir in the onion, chilli, garlic, lime rind, sugar, tomatoes and coriander. Add the ground cumin and seasoning to taste, then stir in the olive oil.

3 Halve and stone (pit) the remaining avocado. Dice the flesh and stir it into the guacamole.

4 Squeeze in fresh lime juice to taste, mix well, then cover and leave to stand for 15 minutes so that the flavour develops. Stir in the sour cream, if using. Serve with lime wedges dipped in sea salt, and fresh coriander sprigs.

Energy 189kcal/781kJ; Protein 2.4g; Carbohydrate 5.2g, of which sugars 3.8g; Fat 17.6g, of which saturates 3.6g; Cholesterol 0mg; Calcium 37mg; Fibre 4g; Sodium 15mg.

garlic mayo

This can be as easy to make as stirring crushed garlic into good quality, ready-made mayonnaise; but do make your own mayo if possible – it will make all the difference.

3 When the mayonnaise is as thick as soft butter, stop adding oil. Season the mayonnaise to taste and add more lemon juice or vinegar as required.

4 Crush the garlic with the blade of a knife and stir it into the mayonnaise. For a milder flavour, blanch the garlic cloves twice in boiling water, then purée them before beating into the mayonnaise.

Serves four to six

INGREDIENTS

2 large egg yolks
pinch of dried mustard
up to 300ml/½ pint/1¼ cups mild olive oil
  or olive oil and grapeseed oil, mixed
15–30ml/1–2 tbsp lemon juice
white wine vinegar or warm water
2–4 garlic cloves
salt and ground black pepper

1 Make sure the egg yolks and oil have come to room temperature before you start. Place the yolks in a bowl with the mustard and a pinch of salt, and whisk.

2 Gradually whisk in the oil, drops at a time at first, then in a trickle. As the mayonnaise starts to thicken, thin it down with a few drops of lemon juice or vinegar, or a few teaspoons of warm water.

VARIATIONS

• For Provençal aioli, crush 3–5 garlic cloves with a pinch of salt, then whisk in the egg yolks. Omit the mustard. Continue as above, using all olive oil.
• For spicy garlic mayonnaise, omit the mustard and stir in 2.5ml/½ tsp harissa or red chilli paste and 5ml/1 tsp sundried tomato paste with the garlic.
• Use roasted garlc purée or puréed smoked garlic for a different flavour.
• Beat in 15g/½ oz mixed herbs, such as tarragon, parsley, chervil and chives. Blanch the herbs in boiling water for 20–30 seconds, then drain and dry them on kitchen paper before finely chopping them.

Energy 327kcal/1344kJ; Protein 1.5g; Carbohydrate 1.1g, of which sugars 0.1g; Fat 35.2g, of which saturates 5.3g; Cholesterol 67mg; Calcium 9mg; Fibre 0.3g; Sodium 3mg.

basil and lemon mayo

This fresh mayonnaise is flavoured with lemon and two types of basil. Serve as a dip with potato wedges or crudités, or as an accompaniment to salads and jacket potatoes.

Serves four to six

INGREDIENTS

2 large egg yolks
15ml/1 tbsp lemon juice
150ml/¼ pint/⅔ cup olive oil
150ml/¼ pint/⅔ cup sunflower oil
handful of green basil leaves
handful of dark opal (purple) basil leaves
4 garlic cloves, crushed
salt and ground black pepper
green and dark opal basil leaves and
   sea salt, to garnish

3 Once half the oil has been added, the remainder can be incorporated more quickly. Continue processing the mixture to form a thick and creamy mayonnaise.

4 Tear both types of basil into small pieces and stir into the mayonnaise with the crushed garlic and seasoning. Transfer to a serving dish, cover and chill until ready to serve, garnished with basil leaves and sea salt.

1 Place the egg yolks and lemon juice in a food processor or blender and process them briefly together.

2 In a jug (pitcher), stir the two oils together. With the machine running, pour in the oil very slowly, a drop at a time.

COOK'S TIP

If you can only find green basil leaves, simply use double the amount in the recipe, but it is worth seeking out the dark opal variety. It is quite distinctive in its appearance, with crinkled, dark purple leaves and a richly scented flavour, with a hint of blackcurrants that adds a fruity tang to the mayo.

Energy 329kcal/1355kJ; Protein 1.8g; Carbohydrate 1.3g, of which sugars 0.3g; Fat 35.3g, of which saturates 4.9g; Cholesterol 67mg; Calcium 26mg; Fibre 0.7g; Sodium 6mg.

blue cheese dip

This dip can be made in minutes and it is delicious with pears or vegetable crudités, but its uses don't stop there. In fact, it's thick enough for shaping in little patties to serve as a relish on freshly grilled steak. Add extra yogurt or milk for a thinner salad dressing.

Serves four

INGREDIENTS

150g/5oz blue cheese, such as Stilton or Danish blue

150g/5oz/⅔ cup soft cheese

75ml/5 tbsp Greek (US strained plain) yogurt

salt and ground black pepper

COOK'S TIP

This dip makes a fantastic filling for a sweet-savoury fruit dish. Simply use to stuff apples or pears, fill, and bake.

1 Crumble the blue cheese into a bowl. Using a wooden spoon, beat the cheese to soften it.

2 Add the soft cheese and beat well to blend the two cheeses together.

3 Gradually beat in the Greek-style yogurt, adding enough to give you the consistency you prefer.

4 Season with lots of black pepper and a little salt. Chill the dip until you are ready to serve it.

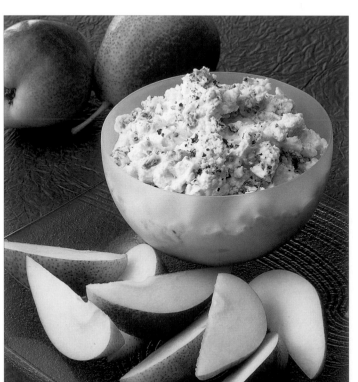

Energy 267kcal/1106kJ; Protein 12.1g; Carbohydrate 0.4g, of which sugars 0.4g; Fat 24.4g, of which saturates 15.4g; Cholesterol 62mg; Calcium 253mg; Fibre 0g; Sodium 595mg.

garlic dip

Two whole heads of garlic may seem like a lot, but roasting transforms the flesh to a tender, sweet and mellow pulp. Serve with crunchy breadsticks and crisps. For a low-fat version, use reduced-fat mayonnaise and low-fat natural yogurt, or try low-fat soft cheese.

Serves four

INGREDIENTS

2 whole garlic heads
15ml/1 tbsp olive oil
60ml/4 tbsp mayonnaise
75ml/5 tbsp Greek (US strained plain) yogurt
5ml/1 tsp wholegrain mustard
salt and ground black pepper

1 Preheat the oven to 200°C/400°F/ Gas 6. Separate the garlic cloves and place them, unpeeled, in a small roasting pan.

4 Place the garlic in a small bowl and stir in the mayonnaise, yogurt and wholegrain mustard.

5 Check and adjust the seasoning, then spoon the dip into a bowl. Cover and chill until ready to serve.

2 Pour the olive oil over the garlic cloves and turn them with a spoon to coat them evenly. Roast them for 20–30 minutes, or until tender and softened. Then set them aside to cool for 5 minutes.

3 Trim off the root end of each roasted garlic clove. Peel the cloves and discard the skins. Place the roasted garlic on a chopping board and sprinkle with salt. Mash with a fork until puréed.

COOK'S TIP

If you are cooking on a barbecue, leave the garlic heads whole and cook until tender, turning occasionally. Peel and mash.

Energy 179kcal/741kJ; Protein 3.6g; Carbohydrate 4.9g, of which sugars 1.1g; Fat 16.5g, of which saturates 3.1g; Cholesterol 11mg; Calcium 38mg; Fibre 1.2g; Sodium 139mg.

saffron dip

Serve this mild dip with fresh vegetable crudités – it is particularly good with florets of cauliflower. It is also superlative with grilled fish or poached eggs and brilliant for dressing small pasta shapes, either freshly cooked or cooled for salad.

2 Beat the fromage frais or soft cheese until smooth, then stir in the infused saffron liquid.

3 Use a pair of scissors to snip the chives into the dip. Tear the basil leaves into small pieces and stir them in.

Serves four

INGREDIENTS

15ml/1 tbsp boiling water

small pinch of saffron threads

200g/7oz/scant 1 cup fromage frais or soft cheese

10 fresh chives

10 fresh basil leaves

salt and ground black pepper

VARIATION

Leave out the saffron and add a squeeze of lemon or lime juice instead. A pinch of turmeric gives a good colour.

1 Pour the boiling water into a small heatproof container and add the saffron strands. Leave to infuse for about 3 minutes.

4 Add salt and pepper to taste. Serve the dip immediately.

Energy 61kcal/253kJ; Protein 3.4g; Carbohydrate 2.6g, of which sugars 2.3g; Fat 4.2g, of which saturates 2.8g; Cholesterol 4mg; Calcium 80mg; Fibre 0.6g; Sodium 22mg.

thousand island dip

This variation on the classic dressing is far removed from the original version, but it can be served in the same way – with grilled king prawns laced on to bamboo skewers for dipping, or with a simple mixed seafood salad.

Serves four

INGREDIENTS

4 sun-dried tomatoes in oil

4 tomatoes

150g/5oz/²⁄₃ cup soft white (farmer's) cheese

60ml/4 tbsp mayonnaise

30ml/2 tbsp tomato purée (paste)

30ml/2 tbsp chopped fresh parsley

grated rind and juice of 1 lemon

Tabasco sauce, to taste

5ml/1 tsp Worcestershire or soy sauce

salt and ground black pepper

1 Drain the sun-dried tomatoes on kitchen paper to remove excess oil, then finely chop them.

2 Skewer each tomato in turn on a metal fork and hold in a gas flame for 1–2 minutes, or until the skin wrinkles and splits. Allow to cool, then slip off and discard the skins. Halve the tomatoes and scoop out the seeds with a teaspoon. Finely chop the tomato flesh and set aside.

3 In a bowl, beat the soft cheese, then gradually beat in the mayonnaise and tomato purée to a smooth mixture.

4 Stir in the chopped parsley and sun-dried tomatoes, then add the chopped tomatoes and their seeds, and mix well.

5 Add the lemon rind and juice and Tabasco sauce to taste. Stir in the Worcestershire or soy sauce, and salt and pepper to taste.

6 Transfer the dip to a serving bowl, cover and chill for about 30 minutes, or until ready to serve.

VARIATION

Stir in cayenne pepper or a chopped fresh chilli for a fiery dip. Garnish with lemon wedges, if liked, so their juice can be squeezed for extra sharpness.

Energy 262kcal/1083kJ; Protein 5.2g; Carbohydrate 6.2g, of which sugars 6.1g; Fat 24.2g, of which saturates 9.2g; Cholesterol 45mg; Calcium 73mg; Fibre 1.9g; Sodium 260mg.

red onion raita

Raita is a traditional Indian side dish served as an accompaniment for hot curries. It is also delicious served with poppadums as a dip.

Serves four

INGREDIENTS

5ml/1 tsp cumin seeds
1 small garlic clove
1 small green chilli
1 large red (Italian) onion
150ml/¼ pint/⅔ cup natural (plain) yogurt
30ml/2 tbsp chopped fresh coriander (cilantro), plus extra to garnish
2.5ml/½ tsp sugar
salt

VARIATION

For an extra tangy raita stir in 15ml/ 1 tbsp lemon juice.

1 Heat a small frying pan and dry-fry the cumin seeds for 1–2 minutes, until they release their aroma and begin to pop.

2 Lightly crush the seeds in a mortar and pestle. Alternatively, try flattening them on a board by using the heel of a heavy-bladed knife, which will crush them slightly.

3 Finely chop the garlic. Remove the fiery seeds from the chilli and chop the flesh finely. Chop the red onion.

4 Place the yogurt in a bowl and add the garlic, chilli and red onion, along with the crushed cumin seeds and fresh coriander. Stir until the ingredients are thoroughly mixed.

5 Add sugar and salt to taste. Spoon the raita into a small bowl and chill until ready to serve. Garnish with extra coriander just before serving.

Energy 32kcal/134kJ; Protein 2.6g; Carbohydrate 4.6g, of which sugars 4g; Fat 0.6g, of which saturates 0.2g; Cholesterol 1mg; Calcium 100mg; Fibre 0.9g; Sodium 36mg.

spicy cajun dip

This piquant dip is fabulous drizzled over crisp potato skins. It can be put to dozens of other uses – try it with burgers, grilled chicken and salad in wraps, or canned tuna tossed with pasta.

Serves two

INGREDIENTS

120ml/4fl oz/½ cup natural (plain) yogurt

1 garlic clove, crushed

5ml/1 tsp tomato purée (paste)

2.5ml/½ tsp green chilli purée or ½ small green chilli, chopped

1.5ml/¼ tsp celery salt

For the potato skins

2 large baking potatoes

vegetable oil, for deep frying

salt and ground black pepper

COOK'S TIP

If you prefer, you can microwave the potatoes to save time. This will take about 10 minutes.

1 For the skins, preheat the oven to 180°C/350°F/Gas 4. Bake the potatoes for 45–50 minutes until tender. Halve and scoop them out, leaving a thin layer in the skins.

2 To make the dip, mix together all the ingredients and chill.

3 Heat a 1cm/½ in layer of oil in a large pan or deep-fat fryer. Cut each potato half in half again, then fry them until crisp and golden on both sides. Drain on kitchen paper, sprinkle with salt and black pepper and serve with a bowl of dip or a dollop of dip in each skin.

Energy 265kcal/1095kJ; Protein 3.8g; Carbohydrate 12.2g, of which sugars 5g; Fat 22.8g, of which saturates 2.9g; Cholesterol 1mg; Calcium 121mg; Fibre 0.8g; Sodium 350mg.

sour cream cooler

This cooling dip makes the perfect accompaniment to hot and spicy Mexican dishes. Alternatively, serve it as a snack with the fieriest tortilla chips you can find.

2 Cut the tomatoes in half, then use a teaspoon to scoop out and discard the seeds. Cut the tomato flesh into tiny dice.

3 Stir the pepper and tomato dice and the chopped parsley into the sour cream and mix well.

4 Spoon the dip into a small bowl and chill for at least 30 minutes. Garnish with grated lemon rind and parsley just before serving.

VARIATIONS

• Use diced avocado or cucumber in place of the pepper or tomato.
• For a zesty green dip, use a green (bell) pepper and kiwi fruit instead of tomatoes; then add lime rind instead of lemon rind. Be sure to dice all the ingredients very finely.

Serves two

INGREDIENTS

1 small yellow (bell) pepper
2 small tomatoes
30ml/2 tbsp chopped fresh parsley, plus extra to garnish
150ml/¼ pint/⅔ cup sour cream
grated lemon rind, to garnish

1 Halve the pepper lengthways. With a sharp knife, remove the core and scoop out the seeds, then cut the flesh into tiny dice.

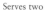

Energy 204kcal/845kJ; Protein 4.2g; Carbohydrate 12g, of which sugars 11.7g; Fat 15.8g, of which saturates 9.6g; Cholesterol 45mg; Calcium 114mg; Fibre 3.2g; Sodium 48mg.

tzatziki

This classic Greek dip is a cooling mix of yogurt, cucumber and mint, perfect for a hot summer's day. Serve it with strips of lightly toasted pitta bread.

Serves four

INGREDIENTS

1 mini cucumber
4 spring onions (scallions)
1 garlic clove
200ml/7fl oz/scant 1 cup Greek (US strained plain) yogurt
45ml/3 tbsp chopped fresh mint
salt and ground black pepper
fresh mint sprig, to garnish (optional)

3 Beat the yogurt until smooth, if necessary, then gently stir in the cucumber, onions, garlic and mint.

4 Add salt and plenty of ground black pepper to taste, then transfer the mixture to a serving bowl. Chill until ready to serve and then garnish with a small mint sprig just before serving.

COOK'S TIP

Choose Greek (US strained plain) yogurt for this dip – it has a higher fat content than most yogurts, but this gives it a deliciously creamy texture.

1 Trim the ends from the cucumber, then cut it into 5mm/¼in dice. Set aside.

2 Trim the roots off the spring onions and peel the garlic. Then chop both very finely and evenly.

Energy 65kcal/269kJ; Protein 3.8g; Carbohydrate 1.9g, of which sugars 1.8g; Fat 5.3g, of which saturates 2.6g; Cholesterol 0mg; Calcium 99mg; Fibre 0.7g; Sodium 40mg.

spiced carrot dip

This is a delicious dip with a sweet and spicy flavour. Serve wheat crackers or fiery tortilla chips as accompaniments for dipping.

Serves four

INGREDIENTS

3 carrots, plus extra to garnish

1 onion, finely chopped

grated rind and juice of 2 oranges

15ml/1 tbsp hot curry paste

150ml/¼ pint/⅔ cup natural (plain) yogurt

handful of fresh basil leaves

15–30ml/1–2 tbsp fresh lemon juice, to taste

Tabasco sauce, to taste

salt and ground black pepper

1 Peel and grate the carrots. Place the onion, carrots, orange rind and juice, and curry paste in a small pan. Bring to the boil, cover and simmer for 10 minutes.

2 Process the mixture in a blender until smooth. Leave to cool.

3 Stir in the yogurt. Tear the basil leaves into small pieces and add most of them to the carrot mixture.

4 Add the lemon juice, Tabasco and seasoning. Serve within a few hours of making (if it is kept too long, the dip becomes runny), at room temperature, garnished with grated carrot and basil.

VARIATION

Greek (US strained plain) yogurt or sour cream may be used in place of the natural (plain) yogurt to make a richer, creamier-textured dip.

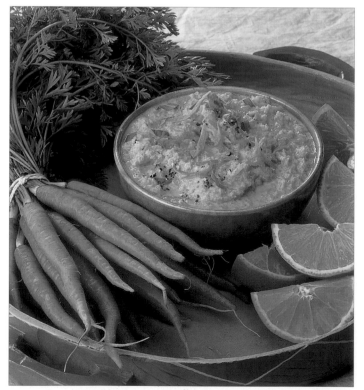

Energy 70kcal/294kJ; Protein 3.1g; Carbohydrate 11.1g, of which sugars 9.4g; Fat 1.9g, of which saturates 0.4g; Cholesterol 1mg; Calcium 130mg; Fibre 3.2g; Sodium 69mg.

squash and parmesan dip

The rich, nutty flavour of butternut squash is enhanced by roasting the roots. Serve this dip with melba toast or cheese straws.

Serves four

INGREDIENTS

1 butternut squash
15g/½ oz/1 tbsp butter
4 garlic cloves, unpeeled
30ml/2 tbsp freshly grated
  Parmesan cheese
45–75ml/3–5 tbsp double (heavy) cream
salt and ground black pepper

1 Preheat the oven to 200°C/400°F/Gas 6.

2 Halve the butternut squash, then scoop out and discard the seeds.

3 Use a small knife to score the flesh deeply in a criss-cross pattern: cut as close to the skin as possible, without cutting through it.

4 Arrange both halves in a small roasting pan and dot them with the butter. Sprinkle the butternut squash with salt and ground black pepper and roast near the top of the oven for 20 minutes.

5 Tuck the unpeeled garlic cloves around the squash and bake for a further 20 minutes, until the squash is tender and softened.

6 Scoop the flesh out of the squash shells and place it in a food processor or blender. Slip the tender garlic cloves out of their skins and add to the squash. Process until smooth.

7 With the motor running, add all but 15ml/1 tbsp of the Parmesan cheese and then the cream. (Alternatively, mash the squash in a bowl using a potato masher, then beat in the cheese and cream with a wooden spoon.) Check the seasoning and spoon the dip into bowl. Scatter the reserved cheese over the top and serve warm.

VARIATION

Try using pumpkin or other types of squash, such as acorn squash or New Zealand kabocha. Adjust the cooking time depending on size.

Energy 145kcal/602kJ; Protein 4.7g; Carbohydrate 4.9g, of which sugars 3.8g; Fat 12g, of which saturates 7.5g; Cholesterol 31mg; Calcium 158mg; Fibre 2.1g; Sodium 107mg.

creamy aubergine dip

Spread this velvet-textured dip thickly on to toasted rounds of bread, then top them with slivers of sun-dried tomato to make wonderful, Italian-style crostini.

Serves four

INGREDIENTS

1 large aubergine (eggplant)
30ml/2 tbsp olive oil
1 small onion, finely chopped
2 garlic cloves, finely chopped
60ml/4 tbsp chopped fresh parsley
75ml/5 tbsp crème fraîche
Red Tabasco sauce, to taste
juice of 1 lemon, to taste
salt and ground black pepper

1 Preheat the grill (broiler) to medium-high. Place the aubergine on a non-stick baking sheet and grill (broil) it for 20–30 minutes, turning, until it is blackened and wrinkled, and soft when squeezed.

2 Remove the aubergine from the oven, cover with a clean dish towel and set aside. It should take around five minutes to cool.

3 Heat the oil in a frying pan and cook the onion and garlic for five minutes, until they are softened, but not browned.

4 Peel the skin from the aubergine. Then mash the flesh with a large fork or potato masher to make a pulpy purée.

5 Stir in the onion and garlic, parsley and crème fraîche. Add Tabasco, lemon juice and salt and pepper to taste.

6 Transfer the dip to a serving bowl and serve warm or leave to cool and serve at room temperature.

COOK'S TIP
The aubergine (eggplant) can also be roasted in the oven at 200°C/400°F/ Gas 6 for 20 minutes or until tender.

Energy 137kcal/566kJ; Protein 1.4g; Carbohydrate 3.1g, of which sugars 2.5g; Fat 13.4g, of which saturates 5.9g; Cholesterol 21mg; Calcium 42mg; Fibre 1.8g; Sodium 9mg.

artichoke and cumin dip

This dip is so easy to make and is unbelievably tasty. Serve with olives, hummus and wedges of pitta bread as an informal summery snack selection.

Serves four

INGREDIENTS

2 x 400g/14oz cans artichoke
  hearts, drained

2 garlic cloves, peeled

2.5ml/½ tsp ground cumin

olive oil

salt and ground black pepper

VARIATION

Grilled (broiled) artichokes bottled in oil have a fabulous flavour and can be used instead of canned artichokes. Try adding a handful of basil leaves to the artichokes before blending.

1 Put the artichoke hearts in a food processor with the garlic and ground cumin, and add a generous drizzle of olive oil. Process to a smooth purée and season with plenty of salt and ground black pepper to taste.

2 Spoon the purée into a serving bowl and serve with an extra drizzle of olive oil swirled on the top and slices of warm pitta bread or wholemeal (whole-wheat) toast fingers and carrot sticks for dipping.

Energy 76kcal/315kJ; Protein 1.6g; Carbohydrate 3.9g, of which sugars 3.5g; Fat 6.2g, of which saturates 1g; Cholesterol 0mg; Calcium 18mg; Fibre 3.5g; Sodium 4mg.

taramasalata

This delicious smoked mullet roe speciality is one of the most famous Greek dips. (Smoked cod's roe is often used as a less-expensive alternative.) It is ideal for a buffet or for handing round with drinks. Fingers of warm pitta bread, breadsticks or crackers are good dippers.

Makes 1 bowl

INGREDIENTS

115g/4oz smoked mullet or cod's roe

2 garlic cloves, crushed

30ml/2 tbsp grated onion

60ml/4 tbsp olive oil

4 slices white bread, crusts removed

juice of 2 lemons

30ml/2 tbsp milk or water

ground black pepper

warm pitta bread, breadsticks or
crackers, to serve

1 Place the smoked roe, garlic, onion, oil, bread and lemon juice in a blender or food processor and process briefly until just smooth.

2 Add the milk or water and process again for a few seconds. (This will give the taramasalata a creamier texture.)

3 Pour the taramasalata into a serving bowl, cover with clear film (plastic wrap) and chill for 1–2 hours in the refrigerator before serving. Sprinkle the dip with freshly ground black pepper just before serving.

Energy 761kcal/3178kJ; Protein 33.7g; Carbohydrate 51.7g, of which sugars 4.3g; Fat 48.1g, of which saturates 6.8g; Cholesterol 380mg; Calcium 130mg; Fibre 1.9g; Sodium 647mg.

hummus

This classic Middle Eastern dish is made from cooked chickpeas, ground to a paste and flavoured with garlic, lemon juice, tahini, olive oil and cumin. It is delicious served with wedges of toasted pitta bread or crudités.

Serves four to six

INGREDIENTS

400g/14oz can chickpeas, drained
60ml/4 tbsp tahini
2–3 garlic cloves, chopped
juice of ½–1 lemon
cayenne pepper
small pinch to 1.5ml/¼ tsp ground cumin, or more to taste
salt and ground black pepper

VARIATION

Process 2 roasted red (bell) peppers with the chickpeas, then continue as above. Serve sprinkled with lightly toasted pine nuts and paprika.

1 Using a potato masher or food processor, coarsely mash the chickpeas. If you prefer a smoother purée, process them in a food processor or blender until smooth and creamy.

2 Mix the tahini into the chickpeas, then stir in the garlic, lemon juice, cayenne, cumin, and salt and pepper to taste. If needed, add a little water. Serve at room temperature.

Energy 142kcal/596kJ; Protein 7.1g; Carbohydrate 11.6g, of which sugars 0.4g; Fat 7.9g, of which saturates 1.1g; Cholesterol 0mg; Calcium 98mg; Fibre 3.7g; Sodium 149mg.

hot chilli bean dip

Make this one as hot as you like – the sour cream helps to balance the heat of the chillies.
Serve it with tortilla chips or vegetable crudités.

2 Add the sea salt and continue simmering for about 30 minutes, or until the beans are tender.

3 Drain the cooked beans, reserving 120ml/4fl oz/½ cup of the liquid. Let the beans cool slightly. Discard the bay leaf.

4 Heat the oil in a non-stick frying pan. Add the onion and garlic and cook over low heat for 8–10 minutes, or until just softened, stirring occasionally.

5 In a food processor or blender, combine the beans, onion mixture, chillies, if using, and the reserved cooking liquid. Process until the mixture is a coarse purée.

6 Transfer to a bowl and stir in the sour cream, cumin, and hot pepper sauce to taste. Stir in the coriander, garnish with sour cream, and serve warm.

Serves four

INGREDIENTS

275g/10oz/1½ cups dried pinto beans, soaked overnight and drained

1 bay leaf

45ml/3 tbsp sea salt

15ml/1 tbsp vegetable oil

1 small onion, sliced

1 garlic clove, minced

2–4 canned hot green chillies (optional)

75ml/5 tbsp sour cream, plus extra to garnish

2.5ml/½ tsp ground cumin

hot pepper sauce, to taste

15ml/1 tbsp chopped fresh coriander (cilantro)

1 Place the soaked and drained beans in a large pan. Add fresh cold water to cover and the bay leaf. Bring to a boil, then cover, and simmer for 30 minutes. Do not add salt at this stage.

VARIATION

To save time, use 2½ x 400g/14oz cans beans instead of the dried beans.

Energy 253kcal/1067kJ; Protein 16g; Carbohydrate 32.3g, of which sugars 3.4g; Fat 7.5g, of which saturates 2.8g; Cholesterol 11mg; Calcium 98mg; Fibre 11.2g; Sodium 22mg.

spicy tuna dip

This piquant dip is so versatile. It's delicious served with breadsticks. Alternatively, you can add more oil to make a thin sauce, less for a mixture to fill hard-boiled eggs or vegetables.

Serves six

INGREDIENTS

90g/3¼oz can tuna in oil
olive oil
3 hard-boiled eggs
75g/3oz/¾ cup pitted green olives
50g/2oz can anchovy fillets, drained
45ml/3 tbsp capers, drained
10ml/2 tsp Dijon mustard
ground black pepper
fresh parsley sprigs, to garnish

3 Reserve a few olives for garnishing, then add the rest to the processor or blender together with the remaining ingredients. Process together until smooth. Season with pepper to taste.

COOK'S TIP

Choose a good quality, light olive oil for this dip – richly flavoured extra virgin oils may dominate the flavour.

4 Spoon the dip into a bowl and garnish with the reserved olives and the parsley.

1 Drain the oil from the can of tuna into a small bowl and make up the quantity to 90ml/6 tbsp with olive oil.

2 Halve the hard-boiled eggs and place the yolks in a food processor or blender. Discard the whites or use in sandwiches or another dish.

Energy 182kcal/752kJ; Protein 7.7g; Carbohydrate 0.4g, of which sugars 0.3g; Fat 16.7g, of which saturates 2.8g; Cholesterol 103mg; Calcium 40mg; Fibre 0.7g; Sodium 411mg.

sauces for pasta

Simple, essential and practical: these meal-makers provide variety for all sorts of occasions, from speedy mid-week suppers to food-sharing to impress. Knocking up a basic tomato sauce is easy and it beats bought alternatives on price, flavour and food value every time. Once you've sampled home-made pesto or an incredibly easy (and healthy) flavoured oil dressing, you will never look back. Many of these sauces can be frozen, and make great use of produce in season.

making pasta dough

Home-made pasta has a wonderfully light, almost silky texture – quite different from the so-called fresh pasta that you buy. If you use egg in the mixture, which is recommended, the dough is easy to make and the initial process is not that different from making bread.

Makes about 500g/1¼ lb

INGREDIENTS

300g/11oz/2¾ cups strong white bread flour or Italian strong flour for pasta

3 eggs

5ml/1 tsp salt

1 Mound the flour on a clean surface and make a large, deep well in the middle. Keep steep sides around the edge so that the eggs will not run out when they are cracked into the well.

2 Crack the eggs into the well and add the salt. With a table knife, or stirring with a fork, mix the eggs and salt together, then gradually incorporate the flour from the sides of the well.

3 As soon as the mixture is no longer runny, sprinkle flour on your fingers and work it into a sticky dough. If the dough is too dry, add a few drops of cold water; too moist, add a sprinkle of flour.

Right: Fresh pasta can be easily rolled into cannelloni tubes.

4 Press the dough into a rough ball and knead it as you would bread. Push it away from you with the heel of your hand, and then fold the dough back on itself so that it faces towards you. Push it out again and continue until the dough is silky smooth.

COOK'S TIP

Don't skimp on the kneading and stick to the recommended time, or you may find that your pasta is not as light and silky as it could be.

5 Continue folding the dough back a little further each time and pushing it out until you have folded it back all the way towards you and all the dough has been kneaded. Give the dough a quarter turn anti-clockwise, then continue kneading, folding and turning for 10 minutes. The dough should be very smooth and elastic.

6 Wrap the dough in clear film (plastic wrap) and leave it to rest for 15–20 minutes at room temperature. Do not chill the dough at this stage or it will become too tough to handle.

7 The dough will be ready to roll when it has relaxed after the kneading – it will be too elastic if you try to roll it out immediately. Simply roll out to around 3mm/¹⁄₈in thickness, cutting into shapes as desired.

Energy 1244kcal/5268kJ; Protein 47g; Carbohydrate 233.1g, of which sugars 4.5g; Fat 20.5g, of which saturates 5.3g; Cholesterol 571mg; Calcium 506mg; Fibre 9.3g; Sodium 2184mg.

italian plum tomato sauce

This tasty sauce uses store-cupboard ingredients, which is time saving if you have an elaborate pasta to make. Here it is served with ravioli filled with prosciutto and cheese. It can also be served with plain pasta or with all sorts of simply cooked fish, poultry or meat.

Serves four to six

INGREDIENTS

500g/1¼lb fresh pasta dough with eggs
60ml/4 tbsp grated fresh Pecorino
cheese, plus extra to serve

For the filling
175g/6oz ricotta cheese
30ml/2 tbsp grated fresh Parmesan
cheese
115g/4oz prosciutto, finely chopped
150g/5oz fresh mozzarella cheese,
drained and finely chopped
1 small egg
15ml/1 tbsp chopped fresh flat leaf
parsley, plus extra to garnish

For the Italian plum tomato sauce
30ml/2 tbsp olive oil
1 onion, finely chopped
400g/14oz can chopped plum tomatoes
15ml/1 tbsp sun-dried tomato purée
(paste)
5–10ml/1–2 tsp dried oregano
salt and ground black pepper

1 To make the sauce, heat the oil in a pan, add the onion and cook, stirring frequently, until softened.

2 Add the tomatoes. Fill the empty can with water, pour it into the pan, then stir in the tomato purée, oregano and seasoning to taste. Bring to the boil and stir well. Then cover the pan and simmer for 30 minutes, stirring occasionally and adding more water if the sauce becomes too thick.

3 Put the filling ingredients in a bowl and season to taste. Mix with a fork, breaking up the ricotta.

4 Using a pasta machine, roll out a quarter of the pasta into a 90–100cm/36–40in strip. Cut the strip into two 45–50cm/18–20in lengths.

5 Using two teaspoons, put little mounds of the filling, 10–12 in total, along one side of one of the pasta strips, spacing them evenly. The filling will be quite moist. Brush a little water around each mound, then fold the plain side of the pasta strip over.

6 Starting from the folded edge, press gently around each mound with your fingertips, pushing the air out at the unfolded edge.

7 Sprinkle lightly with flour. With a fluted pasta wheel, cut first along each long side, then in between each mound, to make small square shapes with the filling sealed in.

8 Put the ravioli on floured dish towels and sprinkle lightly with flour. Allow to dry while filling the remaining pasta, to make 80–96 ravioli altogether.

9 Drop the ravioli into a large pan of boiling, lightly salted water, bring the water back to the boil and boil for 4–5 minutes. Drain well. Spoon a third of the ravioli into a warmed bowl. Sprinkle with 15ml/1 tbsp grated Pecorino and pour over a third of the sauce.

10 Repeat the layers twice, then top with the remaining grated Pecorino. Serve immediately, garnished with chopped parsley.

Below: Meat ravioli topped with Italian plum tomato sauce and a sprinkling of herbs and cheese. This sauce makes a wonderful, understated partner to filled pasta.

Energy 474kcal/1988kJ; Protein 26.4g; Carbohydrate 43.2g, of which sugars 4.8g; Fat 23.1g, of which saturates 11.1g; Cholesterol 180mg; Calcium 369mg; Fibre 2.4g; Sodium 880mg.

tomato and chilli sauce

This is much-loved Italian speciality – the name for the sauce, al arrabbiata, means rabid or angry, and describes the heat that comes from the chilli.

Serves four

INGREDIENTS

300g/11oz dried penne or tortiglioni

For the tomato and chilli sauce

500g/1¼lb sugocasa

2 garlic cloves, crushed

150ml/¼ pint/⅔ cup dry white wine

15ml/1 tbsp sun-dried tomato paste

1 fresh red chilli

30ml/2 tbsp finely chopped fresh flat leaf parsley, plus extra to garnish

salt and ground black pepper

grated fresh Pecorino cheese, to serve

1 Put the sugocasa, garlic, wine, tomato paste and whole chilli in a pan and bring to the boil. Cover and simmer gently.

2 Drop the pasta into a large pan of rapidly boiling salted water and cook for 10–12 minutes, or until *al dente.*

3 Remove the chilli from the sauce and add the parsley. Taste for seasoning. If you prefer a hotter taste, chop some or all of the chilli and return it to the sauce.

4 Drain the pasta and tip into a warmed large bowl. Pour the sauce over the pasta and toss to mix. Serve at once, sprinkled with parsley and grated Pecorino.

COOK'S TIP

Sugocasa literally means "house sauce" and consists of tomatoes, crushed coarsely so that they have a chunky texture.

Energy 304kcal/1295kJ; Protein 10.5g; Carbohydrate 60.3g, of which sugars 7.2g; Fat 1.5g, of which saturates 0.2g; Cholesterol 0mg; Calcium 51mg; Fibre 3.4g; Sodium 303mg.

sun-dried tomato and radicchio sauce

This is a light, modern pasta dish of the kind served in fashionable restaurants. It is the presentation that sets it apart. It is very quick and easy to prepare.

Serves 4

INGREDIENTS

45ml/3 tbsp pine nuts
350g/12oz paglia e fieno pasta
30ml/2 tbsp extra virgin olive oil
4–6 spring onions (scallions), thinly sliced into rings

For the sun-dried tomato and radicchio sauce
15ml/1 tbsp extra virgin olive oil
30ml/2 tbsp sun-dried tomato pureé
40g/1½ oz radicchio leaves, finely shredded
salt and ground black pepper

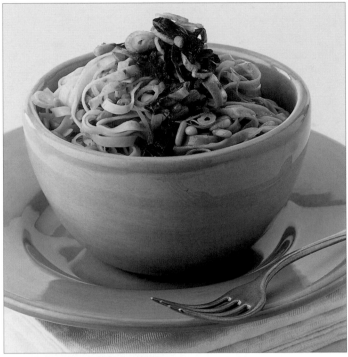

1 Put the pine nuts in a heavy-based frying pan and toss over a medium heat for 1–2 minutes until they are lightly toasted and golden brown. Remove and set aside.

2 Cook the pasta according to the packet instructions, keeping the colours separate by using two pans.

5 Arrange a portion of green and white pasta in each of four warmed bowls, then spoon the sun-dried tomato and radicchio sauce in the centre. Sprinkle the spring onions and toasted pine nuts decoratively over the top and serve immediately. Before eating, each diner should toss the sauce and pasta to mix.

3 To make the sauce, heat the oil in a medium frying pan (or use a pan). Add the sun-dried tomato pureé, then stir in two ladlefuls of pasta cooking water. Simmer until the sauce is slightly reduced, stirring constantly.

4 Stir in the radicchio, and season. Keep on a low heat. Drain the pasta, keeping the colours separate, and return them to their cooking pans. Add 15ml/1 tbsp of oil to each pan and toss over a medium to high heat until the pasta glistens.

COOK'S TIP

If you find the presentation too fussy, you can toss the sun-dried tomato and radicchio mixture with the pasta in one large warmed bowl for everyone to dig into. Sprinkle with spring onions (scallions) and pine nuts before serving.

Energy 460kcal/1938kJ; Protein 12.7g; Carbohydrate 66.8g, of which sugars 4.8g; Fat 17.7g, of which saturates 1.9g; Cholesterol 0mg; Calcium 33mg; Fibre 3.2g; Sodium 22mg.

tomato and aubergine sauce

Full of flavour, this sauce goes well with any short pasta shapes. It can be layered with sheets of pasta and cheese sauce to make lasagne.

2 Remove and discard the chilli. Add the aubergine to the pan. Pour in half the water. Crumble in the stock cube and stir until it is dissolved, then cover and cook, stirring frequently, for about 10 minutes.

3 Add the tomatoes, wine, sugar, saffron and paprika with another handful of parsley, the basil and seasoning. Pour in the remaining water. Stir well, replace the lid and cook for 30–40 minutes, stirring occasionally.

4 About 10 minutes before the sauce is ready, cook the pasta in boiling salted water according to the instructions on the packet until *al dente*.

Serves four to six

INGREDIENTS

350g/12oz dried short pasta shapes

For the tomato and aubergine sauce
30ml/2 tbsp olive oil
1 small fresh red chilli
2 garlic cloves
2 handfuls fresh flat leaf parsley, coarsely chopped, plus extra to serve
450g/1lb aubergine (eggplant), chopped
200ml/7fl oz/scant 1 cup water
1 vegetable stock cube
1 handful fresh basil leaves
8 plum tomatoes, peeled and chopped
60ml/4 tbsp red wine
5ml/1 tsp sugar
1 envelope saffron powder
2.5ml/½ tsp ground paprika
salt and ground black pepper

1 Heat the oil in a large frying pan and add the whole chilli, whole garlic cloves and one handful of chopped parsley. Pound the garlic cloves with a wooden spoon, taking care not to splash hot oil, as this will release their juices. Cover the pan and cook the mixture over a low to medium heat for about 10 minutes, stirring occasionally.

5 Check the sauce for seasoning, then toss with the drained pasta in warmed bowls. Garnish with extra chopped parsley.

VARIATION
Try adding a few chopped anchovies or sun-dried tomatoes about halfway through the cooking time.

Energy 277kcal/1174kJ; Protein 8.8g; Carbohydrate 49.7g, of which sugars 8.3g; Fat 5.5g, of which saturates 0.8g; Cholesterol 0mg; Calcium 45mg; Fibre 4.7g; Sodium 18mg.

two sauces for cannelloni

The combination of tomato sauce and the creamy white sauce makes this cannelloni delicious.
For a special occasion, make it in advance; then add the white sauce and bake on the day.

Serves six

INGREDIENTS

15ml/1 tbsp olive oil
1 small onion, finely chopped
450g/1lb minced (ground) beef
1 garlic clove, finely chopped
5ml/1 tsp dried mixed herbs
120ml/4fl oz/½ cup beef stock
1 egg
75g/3oz cooked ham or Mortadella sausage, finely chopped
45ml/3 tbsp fine fresh white breadcrumbs
115g/4oz/1¼ cups freshly grated Parmesan cheese
18 pre-cooked cannelloni tubes
salt and ground black pepper

For the tomato sauce

30ml/2 tbsp olive oil
1 small onion, finely chopped
½ carrot, finely chopped
1 celery stick, finely chopped
1 garlic clove, crushed
400g/14oz can chopped plum tomatoes
a few sprigs of fresh basil
2.5ml/½ tsp dried oregano

For the white sauce

50g/2oz/¼ cup butter
50g/2oz/½ cup plain (all-purpose) flour
900ml/1½ pints/3¾ cups milk
freshly grated nutmeg

1 Heat the olive oil in a pan and cook the chopped onion over a gentle heat, stirring occasionally, for about 5 minutes, until softened.

2 Add the minced beef and garlic and cook for 10 minutes, stirring and breaking up any lumps with a wooden spoon.

3 Add the herbs, and season to taste, then moisten with half the stock. Cover the pan and allow to simmer for 25 minutes, stirring occasionally and adding more stock as it reduces. Spoon into a bowl and allow to cool.

4 To make the tomato sauce, heat the olive oil in a saucepan, add the vegetables and garlic and cook over a medium heat, stirring frequently, for 10 minutes. Add the tomatoes. Fill the empty can with water, pour it into the pan, then add the herbs, and season to taste. Bring to a boil, lower the heat, cover and simmer for 25–30 minutes, stirring occasionally. Purée the tomato sauce in a blender or food processor.

5 Stir the egg, ham or sausage, breadcrumbs, 90ml/6 tbsp Parmesan and seasoning into the meat. Spread a little tomato sauce in a baking dish.

6 Use a teaspoon to fill the cannelloni with the meat and place in a single layer on the sauce. Pour the remaining tomato sauce over.

7 Preheat the oven to 190°C/375°F/Gas 5. For the white sauce, melt the butter in pan, add the flour and cook for 1–2 minutes. Stir in the milk, then bring to the boil, stirring. Add nutmeg and season.

8 Pour over the cannelloni, then sprinkle with Parmesan. Bake for 40–45 minutes and stand for 10.

green vegetable sauce

This sauce is a simple medley of cooked fresh vegetables, bursting with colour and vitality. Tossed with pasta, it's ideal for a fresh, light lunch or supper dish.

Serves four

INGREDIENTS

450g/1lb dried pasta shapes

For the green vegetable sauce

30ml/2 tbsp butter

45ml/3 tbsp extra virgin olive oil

1 small leek, thinly sliced

2 carrots, diced

2.5ml/½ tsp sugar

1 courgette (zucchini), diced

75g/3oz/generous ½ cup green beans

115g/4oz/1 cup frozen peas

1 handful fresh flat leaf parsley, chopped

2 ripe plum tomatoes, peeled and diced

salt and ground black pepper

fried parsley sprigs, to garnish

1 Melt the butter and oil in a medium frying pan or pan. When the mixture sizzles, add the leek and carrots. Sprinkle the sugar over the vegetables and fry over a medium heat, stirring the mixture frequently, for about 5 minutes.

2 Stir in the courgette, beans and peas, and season. Cover and cook over a low to medium heat for 5–8 minutes, or until the vegetables are tender, stirring occasionally.

3 Meanwhile, cook the pasta according to the instructions on the packet.

4 Stir the parsley and chopped tomatoes into the sauce.

5 Serve the sauce immediately, tossed with freshly cooked pasta and garnished with the sprigs of parsley.

Energy 578kcal/2436kJ; Protein 18g; Carbohydrate 92.6g, of which sugars 9.8g; Fat 17.7g, of which saturates 5.6g; Cholesterol 16mg; Calcium 94mg; Fibre 7.7g; Sodium 65mg.

wild mushroom sauce

This rich mushroom and garlic sauce is delicious with pasta for a main course. Remember to pick wild mushrooms only with expert guidance or buy them from a reliable source.

Serves four

INGREDIENTS

150g/5oz wild mushrooms preserved in olive oil

30ml/2 tbsp butter

150g/5oz fresh wild mushrooms, sliced if large

5ml/1 tsp finely chopped fresh thyme

5ml/1 tsp finely chopped fresh marjoram or oregano, plus extra herbs to serve

4 garlic cloves, crushed

350g/12oz fresh or dried fusilli

200ml/7fl oz/scant 1 cup double (heavy) cream

salt and ground black pepper

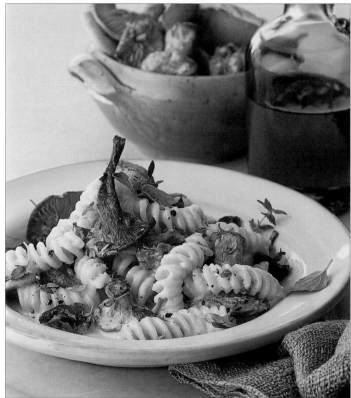

1 Drain about 15ml/1 tbsp of the oil from the mushrooms into a medium pan. Slice or chop the preserved mushrooms into bite-size pieces, if they are large.

2 Add the butter to the oil in the pan and heat over a low heat until sizzling. Add the preserved and the fresh mushrooms, the chopped herbs and garlic. Season to taste.

3 Simmer over a medium heat, stirring frequently, for about 10 minutes or until the fresh mushrooms are soft and tender.

4 Meanwhile, cook the pasta in boiling salted water according to the packet instructions, until *al dente*, tender but with bite.

5 As soon as the mushrooms are cooked, increase the heat to high and toss the mixture with a wooden spoon to boil off any excess liquid. Pour in the cream and bring the mixture to the boil. Season if needed.

6 Drain the pasta and turn it into a warmed bowl. Pour the sauce over and toss well. Serve immediately, sprinkled with chopped fresh herbs.

Energy 662kcal/2769kJ; Protein 12.7g; Carbohydrate 66g, of which sugars 3.9g; Fat 40.5g, of which saturates 21.7g; Cholesterol 85mg; Calcium 52mg; Fibre 3.4g; Sodium 63mg.

carbonara sauce

An all-time favourite sauce that is perfect for spaghetti or tagliatelle. This version has plenty of pancetta or bacon and is not too creamy, but you can vary the amounts.

Serves four

INGREDIENTS

350g/12oz fresh or dried spaghetti

For the carbonara sauce

30ml/2 tbsp olive oil

1 small onion, finely chopped

8 pancetta or lean bacon rashers (strips), cut into 1cm/½ in strips

4 eggs

60ml/4 tbsp crème fraîche

60ml/4 tbsp freshly grated Parmesan cheese, plus extra to serve

salt and ground black pepper

1 Heat the oil in a frying pan, add the onion and cook, stirring, over a low heat, for about 5 minutes or until the onion is transparent and slightly softened.

2 Add the strips of pancetta or bacon to the onion in the pan and cook for about 10 minutes, stirring almost all the time.

3 Meanwhile, cook the pasta in a pan of salted boiling water according to the instructions on the packet, until al dente.

4 Put the eggs, crème fraîche and grated Parmesan in a bowl. Grind in plenty of pepper, then beat the mixture together well.

5 Drain the pasta, turn it into the pan with the pancetta or bacon and toss well to mix.

6 Turn the heat off under the pan. Immediately add the egg mixture and toss vigorously so that it cooks lightly and coats the pasta.

7 Quickly taste for seasoning, then divide among four warmed bowls and sprinkle with black pepper. Serve immediately, with extra grated Parmesan offered separately.

Energy 673kcal/2822kJ; Protein 32.5g; Carbohydrate 66.4g, of which sugars 4.1g; Fat 32.8g, of which saturates 13.2g; Cholesterol 252mg; Calcium 246mg; Fibre 2.8g; Sodium 1106mg.

gorgonzola sauce

This cheese sauce has a strong flavour and so is ideal with potato dumplings (little gnocchi, as here) or plain pasta, like macaroni. Either way, it makes a filling dish ideal for a winter supper.

Serves four

INGREDIENTS

450g/1lb potatoes, unpeeled
1 large egg
115g/4oz/1 cup plain (all-purpose) flour
salt and ground black pepper
fresh thyme sprigs, to garnish
60ml/4 tbsp freshly grated Parmesan
cheese, to serve

For the Gorgonzola sauce

115g/4oz Gorgonzola cheese
60ml/4 tbsp double (heavy) cream
15ml/1 tbsp chopped fresh thyme

1 Cook the potatoes in boiling salted water for about 20 minutes until they are tender. Drain and, when cool enough to handle, remove the skins.

2 Press the potatoes through a sieve, using the back of a spoon, into a mixing bowl. Season, then beat in the egg. Add the flour a little at a time, stirring well with a wooden spoon after each addition until you have a smooth dough. (You may not need all the flour.)

3 Turn the dough out on to a floured surface and knead it for about 3 minutes, adding more flour if you need to, until it is smooth and soft and not at all sticky to the touch.

VARIATION

The Gorgonzola sauce could also be used in a fondue, with croûtons or vegetable pieces to dip.

4 Divide the dough into six pieces. Flour your hands and roll each piece into a log 15–20cm/6–8in long and 2.5cm/1in diameter. Cut each into 2.5cm/1in pieces, then roll in flour. Gently press each piece with a fork to form ridges.

5 To cook, drop the gnocchi into a pan of boiling water about 12 at a time. Once they rise to the surface, after about 2 minutes, cook them for 4–5 minutes more, then drain.

6 To make the sauce, place the Gorgonzola, cream and thyme in a large frying pan and heat gently until the cheese melts to form a sauce with a thick, creamy consistency, then heat through.

7 Add the drained gnocchi to the sauce and toss well to combine. Serve with Parmesan and garnish with thyme.

cream and parmesan sauce

This creamy Parmesan sauce is a perfect accompaniment to home-made spinach and ricotta ravioli but would be just as delicious served with store-bought tortelloni or any other fresh pasta with a stuffing. The addition of nutmeg perfectly complements the cheeses.

Serves eight

INGREDIENTS

500g/1¼ lb fresh pasta dough
grated fresh Parmesan cheese, to serve
salt and ground black pepper

For the filling

45ml/3 tbsp butter
175g/6oz fresh spinach leaves, trimmed, washed and shredded
200g/7oz/scant 1 cup ricotta cheese
25g/1oz/⅓ cup freshly grated Parmesan cheese
freshly grated nutmeg
1 small egg

For the cream and Parmesan sauce

50g/2oz/¼ cup butter
120ml/4fl oz/½ cup double (heavy) cream
50g/2oz/⅔ cup freshly grated Parmesan cheese

2 Tip the spinach into a bowl and set aside until cold, then add the ricotta, grated Parmesan and freshly grated nutmeg to taste. Beat well to mix, taste for seasoning, then add the egg and beat again.

3 Using a pasta machine, roll out a quarter of the pasta dough into a 90–100cm/36–40in strip. Cut the strip with a sharp knife into two 45–50cm/18–20in lengths (you can do this during rolling if the strip gets too long to manage).

1 To make the filling, melt the butter in a pan, add the spinach and salt and pepper to taste and cook over a medium heat for 5–8 minutes, stirring frequently, until the spinach is wilted and tender. Increase the heat to high. Stir until the water boils off and the spinach is quite dry.

4 Using a teaspoon, put 10–12 little mounds of the filling along one side of one of the pasta strips, spacing them evenly. Brush a little water around each mound and fold over the plain side of the pasta.

5 Starting from the folded edge, press down gently with your fingers around each mound of filling, pushing the air out at the unfolded edge. Sprinkle lightly with flour.

6 With a fluted pasta wheel, cut along each long side, then in between each mound.

7 Put the ravioli on floured dish towels, sprinkle lightly with flour and allow to dry while using the rest of the pasta and filling, making 80–96 ravioli altogether.

8 Drop the ravioli into a large pan of boiling salted water, bring to the boil and boil for 4–5 minutes.

9 Meanwhile, make the sauce. Gently heat the butter, cream and Parmesan in a pan until the butter and Parmesan have melted.

10 Increase the heat and simmer for about a minute until the sauce is slightly reduced. Season to taste.

11 Drain the ravioli and divide them equally among eight warmed large bowls. Drizzle the sauce over them and serve sprinkled with Parmesan and ground pepper.

VARIATION

This cheese sauce would also work well with a baked pasta dish, such as macaroni. Sprinkle the top generously with grated Parmesan before baking.

Energy 420kcal/1751kJ; Protein 13.6g; Carbohydrate 30.6g, of which sugars 2g; Fat 28g, of which saturates 16.3g; Cholesterol 161mg; Calcium 226mg; Fibre 1.6g; Sodium 490mg.

classic pesto sauce

Bottled pesto is a useful stand-by, but it bears no resemblance to the heady aroma and flavour of the fresh paste, which is quick and easy to make in a food processor.

Serves four

INGREDIENTS

50g/2oz/1⅓ cups fresh basil leaves, plus fresh basil leaves, to garnish

2–4 garlic cloves

60ml/4 tbsp pine nuts

120ml/4fl oz/½ cup extra virgin olive oil

115g/4oz/1⅓ cups freshly grated Parmesan cheese, plus extra to serve

25g/1oz/⅓ cup freshly grated Pecorino cheese

400g/14oz dried pasta

salt and ground black pepper

COOK'S TIP

Pesto can be made 2–3 days in advance. Transfer it to a bowl and pour a thin film of olive oil over the surface. Cover tightly with clear film (plastic wrap) and keep it in the refrigerator.

1 Put the basil leaves, garlic and pine nuts in a blender or food processor. Add 60ml/4 tbsp of the olive oil. Process until the ingredients are finely chopped, then stop the machine, remove the lid and scrape down the mixture.

2 Turn the machine on again and slowly pour in the remaining oil in a thin, steady stream through the feeder tube. You may need to stop the machine and scrape down the mixture from the sides of the bowl once or twice to make sure everything is evenly mixed

3 Scrape the mixture into a large bowl and beat in the cheeses with a wooden spoon. Taste and add salt and pepper if necessary.

4 Cook the pasta according to the instructions on the packet. Drain it well, then add it to the bowl of pesto and toss well. Serve immediately, garnished with the fresh basil leaves. Hand shaved Parmesan around separately.

Energy 713kcal/2969kJ; Protein 24.1g; Carbohydrate 43.2g, of which sugars 2.7g; Fat 50.5g, of which saturates 11.6g; Cholesterol 35mg; Calcium 468mg; Fibre 2.1g; Sodium 385mg.

deluxe cheese sauce for macaroni

Rich and creamy, this deluxe sauce for macaroni uses Fontina, a slighty sweet and nutty cheese (Taleggio may be used instead). It goes well with tomato and basil salad or a green salad.

Serves four

INGREDIENTS

250g/9oz short-cut macaroni

50g/2oz/¼ cup butter

50g/2oz/½ cup plain (all-purpose) flour

600ml/1 pint/2½ cups milk

100ml/3½fl oz/scant ½ cup panna da cucina or double (heavy) cream

100ml/3½fl oz/scant ½ cup dry white wine

50g/2oz/½ cup grated Gruyère or Emmenthal cheese

50g/2oz Fontina cheese, diced small

50g/2oz Gorgonzola cheese, crumbled

75g/3oz/1 cup freshly grated Parmesan cheese

salt and ground black pepper

1 Preheat the oven to 180°C/350°F/ Gas 4. Cook the pasta according to the instructions on the packet.

2 Meanwhile, gently melt the butter in a pan, add the flour and cook, stirring, for 1–2 minutes. Add the milk a little at a time, whisking vigorously after each addition. Stir in the cream, then the dry white wine. Bring to the boil. Cook, stirring constantly, until the sauce thickens. Remove from the heat.

3 Add the Gruyère or Emmenthal, Fontina, Gorgonzola and about a third of the grated Parmesan to the sauce. Stir well to mix in the cheeses, then taste for seasoning, adding salt and pepper if necessary.

4 Drain the pasta and tip it into a baking dish. Pour the sauce over and mix well, then sprinkle the remaining Parmesan over the top. Bake for 25–30 minutes or until golden brown. Serve hot.

Energy 743kcal/3104kJ; Protein 30.3g; Carbohydrate 52.1g, of which sugars 8.9g; Fat 45.4g, of which saturates 27.8g; Cholesterol 123mg; Calcium 673mg; Fibre 0.4g; Sodium 593mg.

cream and walnut sauce

This walnut and cream pesto is a simplified version of one traditionally served with pansotti in Liguria. The sauce would go equally well with any pasta stuffed with ricotta or spinach, or with plain pasta shells for a less rich alternative.

Serves six to eight

INGREDIENTS

500g/1¼lb herb-flavoured pasta dough with eggs

50g/2oz/¼ cup butter

freshly grated Parmesan cheese, to serve

salt and ground black pepper

For the filling

250g/9oz/generous 1 cup ricotta cheese

115g/4oz/1¼ cups freshly grated Parmesan cheese

1 large handful fresh basil leaves, finely chopped

1 large handful fresh flat leaf parsley, finely chopped

a few sprigs of fresh marjoram or oregano, leaves removed and finely chopped

1 garlic clove, crushed

1 small egg

For the cream and walnut sauce

90g/3½oz/1 cup shelled walnuts

1 garlic clove

60ml/4 tbsp extra virgin olive oil

120ml/4fl oz/½ cup double (heavy) cream

1 To make the filling, put the ricotta cheese, Parmesan cheese, basil, parsley, marjoram or oregano, garlic and egg in a bowl. Season with salt and ground black pepper to taste, and beat well until thoroughly mixed.

COOK'S TIP

To make herb pasta, add chopped fresh oregano, chives and parsley when mixing in the eggs. Take care not to overfill the pansotti, or they will burst open during cooking.

2 To make the sauce, put the walnuts, garlic clove and oil in a food processor and process to a paste, adding up to 120ml/4fl oz/½ cup warm water, through the feeder tube, to thin down the paste.

3 Spoon the mixture into a bowl and add the cream. Beat well to mix, then season to taste.

4 Using a pasta machine, roll out one-quarter of the pasta into a 90–100cm/36–40in strip. Cut the strip with a sharp knife into two 45–50cm/18–20in lengths (you can do this during rolling if the strip gets too long to manage).

5 Using a 5cm/2in square ravioli cutter, cut eight to ten squares from one of the pasta strips.

6 Using a teaspoon, put a mound of filling on each pasta square.

7 Brush a little water around the edge of each square, then fold the square diagonally in half over the filling to make a triangle. Press gently to seal.

8 Spread out the pansotti on clean floured dish towels, sprinkle lightly with flour and set aside to dry, while repeating the process with the remaining dough, to make a total of 64–80 pansotti.

9 Cook the pansotti in a large pan of boiling salted water for 4–5 minutes, until tender.

10 Meanwhile, put the walnut sauce in a large, warmed bowl and add a ladleful of the pasta cooking water to thin it down. Melt the butter in a small pan until sizzling.

11 Drain the pansotti and tip them into the bowl of walnut sauce. Drizzle the butter over them, toss well, then sprinkle with grated Parmesan. Alternatively, toss the pansotti in the melted butter, spoon into warmed individual bowls and drizzle over the sauce. Serve the dish immediately, with extra Parmesan handed round separately.

Energy 535kcal/2228kJ; Protein 17.3g; Carbohydrate 30.9g, of which sugars 2.3g; Fat 39g, of which saturates 16.3g; Cholesterol 157mg; Calcium 271mg; Fibre 1.9g; Sodium 483mg.

butter and herb sauce

You can use just one favourite herb or several for this recipe. The result is the simplest way to dress up pasta but also one of the tastiest.

2 To make the sauce, chop the herbs coarsely or finely, as you prefer.

3 When the pasta is almost *al dente*, melt the butter in a large frying pan or pan. As soon as it sizzles, drain the pasta and add it to the pan, then sprinkle in the herbs with salt and pepper to taste.

4 Toss over a medium heat until the pasta is coated in butter and herbs. Serve immediately in warmed bowls, sprinkled with extra herb leaves and flowers. Pass round some extra grated Parmesan separately.

Serves four

INGREDIENTS

400g/14oz fresh or dried spaghetti alla chitarra

freshly grated Parmesan cheese, to serve

For the butter and herb sauce

2 good handfuls mixed fresh herbs, plus extra herb leaves and flowers to garnish

115g/4oz/½ cup butter

salt and ground black pepper

1 Cook the pasta in boiling, lightly salted water according to the packet instructions, until almost *al dente*.

VARIATION

If you like the flavour of garlic with herbs, add 1–2 crushed garlic cloves when melting the butter.

Energy 562kcal/2362kJ; Protein 12.7g; Carbohydrate 74.8g, of which sugars 3.9g; Fat 25.7g, of which saturates 15.2g; Cholesterol 61mg; Calcium 68mg; Fibre 3.9g; Sodium 184mg.

lemon and oil dressing for spaghetti

This is the dish to make when you rush home for a quick bite to eat and find there's nothing in the house except a lemon, some garlic and what's in the pantry.

Serves four

INGREDIENTS

350g/12oz dried spaghetti
90ml/6 tbsp extra virgin olive oil
juice of 1 large lemon
2 garlic cloves, cut into very thin slivers
salt and ground black pepper

COOK'S TIP

Spaghetti is the best type of pasta for this recipe, because the olive oil and lemon juice cling to its long thin strands.

If you are out of spaghetti, use another dried long pasta shape instead, such as spaghettini, linguine or tagliatelle. Any pasta shape will work in an emergency!

1 Cook the pasta in a pan of lightly salted boiling water for 10–12 minutes, until tender, then drain well and return to the pan.

2 Pour the olive oil and lemon juice over the cooked pasta, sprinkle in the slivers of garlic and add seasoning to taste. Toss the pasta over a medium to high heat for 1–2 minutes. Serve immediately in four warmed bowls.

Energy 448kcal/1886kJ; Protein 10.5g; Carbohydrate 64.9g, of which sugars 3g; Fat 18.1g, of which saturates 2.5g; Cholesterol 0mg; Calcium 22mg; Fibre 2.6g; Sodium 3mg.829mg.

spicy sausage sauce

Serve this heady pasta dish with a robust Sicilian red wine and a crisp, leafy side salad to complement the rich, meaty sauce.

Serves four

INGREDIENTS

300g/11oz dried tortiglioni

salt and ground black pepper

For the spicy sausage sauce

30ml/2 tbsp olive oil

1 onion, finely chopped

1 celery stick, finely chopped

2 large garlic cloves, crushed

1 fresh red chilli, deseeded and chopped

450g/1lb ripe plum tomatoes, peeled and finely chopped

30ml/2 tbsp tomato purée (paste)

150ml/¼ pint/⅔ cup red wine

5ml/1 tsp sugar

175g/6oz spicy salami, rind removed

30ml/2 tbsp chopped parsley, to garnish

freshly grated Parmesan cheese, to serve

1 Heat the oil in a flameproof casserole or large pan, then add the onion, celery, garlic and chilli. Cook gently, stirring frequently, for about 10 minutes, until softened.

COOK'S TIP

Buy the salami for this dish in one piece so that you can chop it into large chunks.

2 Add the tomatoes, tomato purée, wine, sugar and seasoning to taste. Bring to the boil, stirring. Lower the heat, cover and simmer gently, stirring occasionally, for about 20 minutes. Add a little water if the sauce becomes too thick.

3 Meanwhile, cook the pasta in a large pan of rapidly boiling, salted water according to the instructions on the packet, until *al dente*.

4 Chop the salami into bite-size chunks and add to the sauce. Heat through, then taste for seasoning.

5 Drain the pasta, turn it into a bowl, then pour the sauce over and toss to mix. Scatter over the parsley and serve with grated Parmesan.

Energy 561kcal/2357kJ; Protein 19.9g; Carbohydrate 63g, of which sugars 9.5g; Fat 24.5g, of which saturates 7.4g; Cholesterol 36mg; Calcium 64mg; Fibre 4.4g; Sodium 829mg.

bolognese sauce with spaghetti

This recipe will bring back happy memories of flat-sharing and communal eating. While it goes so well with spaghetti or tagliatelle, it tastes good with all sorts of pasta shapes.

Serves four to six

INGREDIENTS

30ml/2 tbsp olive oil

1 onion, finely chopped

1 garlic clove, crushed

5ml/1 tsp dried mixed herbs

1.5ml/¼ tsp cayenne pepper

350–450g/12oz–1lb minced
  (ground) beef

400g/14oz can chopped Italian
  plum tomatoes

45ml/3 tbsp tomato ketchup

15ml/1 tbsp sun-dried tomato pureé
  (paste)

5ml/1 tsp Worcestershire sauce

5ml1 tsp dried oregano

450ml/¾ pint/scant 2 cups beef or
  vegetable stock

45ml/3 tbsp red wine

400–450g/14oz–1lb dried spaghetti

salt and ground black pepper

freshly grated Parmesan cheese, to serve

1 Heat the oil in a medium pan, add the onion and garlic and cook over a low heat, stirring frequently, for about 5 minutes until softened. Stir in the mixed herbs and cayenne and cook for 2–3 minutes more. Add the minced beef and cook gently for about 5 minutes, stirring frequently and breaking up any lumps in the meat.

2 Stir in the canned tomatoes, ketchup, sun-dried tomato paste, Worcestershire sauce, oregano and plenty of black pepper. Pour in the stock and red wine and bring to the boil, stirring. Cover, lower the heat and leave the sauce to simmer for 30 minutes, stirring occasionally.

3 Cook the pasta according to the instructions on the packet. Drain well and divide among warmed bowls. Taste the sauce and add a little salt if necessary, then spoon it on the pasta and sprinkle with a little Parmesan. Serve immediately, with extra Parmesan.

Energy 639kcal/2692kJ; Protein 30.9g; Carbohydrate 83.5g, of which sugars 11.5g; Fat 21.7g, of which saturates 7.1g; Cholesterol 53mg; Calcium 59mg; Fibre 4.2g; Sodium 312mg.

squid sauce

What better partner for a delicious squid sauce than squid ink tagliatelle? The tastes blend perfectly, but the sauce will enhance any plain pasta.

2 Add 30ml/2 tbsp of the parsley to the pan, stir, then add the squid and stir again. Cook for 3–4 minutes, then add wine.

3 Simmer for a few seconds, then add the tomatoes and chilli.

4 Season the mixture. Cover and simmer gently for about 1 hour, until the squid is tender. Add more water if necessary.

5 Cook the pasta in plenty of boiling, salted water, according to the instructions on the packet, until *al dente*. Drain and return the tagliatelle to the pan. Add the squid sauce and mix well.

6 Serve at once, sprinkled with the remaining chopped parsley.

Serves four

INGREDIENTS

450g/1lb squid ink tagliatelle

For the squid sauce

105ml/7 tbsp olive oil

2 shallots, chopped

3 garlic cloves, crushed

45ml/3 tbsp chopped fresh parsley

675g/1½ lb cleaned squid, cut into rings and rinsed

150ml/¼ pint/⅔ cup dry white wine

400g/14oz can chopped plum tomatoes

2.5ml/½ tsp dried chilli flakes or powder

salt and ground black pepper

1 Heat the oil in a pan and add the shallots. Cook until pale golden, then add the garlic and cook for a few more minutes until it colours a little.

Energy 746kcal/3145kJ; Protein 40.8g; Carbohydrate 90.2g, of which sugars 8.1g; Fat 24.6g, of which saturates 3.8g; Cholesterol 380mg; Calcium 87mg; Fibre 5g; Sodium 204mg.

clam and tomato sauce

Clam and tomato sauce is a regular dish in Neopolitan restaurants, where it is often served with vermicelli or spaghetti. Fresh mussels could be substituted for the clams.

Serves four

INGREDIENTS

350g/12oz vermicelli

For the clam and tomato sauce

1kg/2¼ lb fresh hard-shell clams

250ml/8fl oz/1 cup dry white wine

2 garlic cloves, bruised

1 large handful fresh flat leaf parsley

30ml/2 tbsp olive oil

1 small onion, finely chopped

8 ripe plum tomatoes, peeled, deseeded and finely chopped

½–1 fresh red chilli, deseeded and finely chopped

salt and ground black pepper

1 Scrub the clams thoroughly under cold running water and discard any that are open and that do not close when they are sharply tapped against the work surface.

2 Pour the wine into a large pan, add the garlic cloves and half the parsley, then the clams. Cover tightly and bring to the boil over high heat. Cook for about 5 minutes, shaking frequently, until the clams have opened.

3 Tip the clams into a large colander over a bowl to drain. Set aside until cool enough to handle, then remove about two-thirds of them from their shells, pouring the clam liquid into the bowl of cooking liquid. Discard any clams that have failed to open. Set both shelled and unshelled clams aside, keeping the unshelled clams warm in a bowl covered with a lid.

4 Heat the oil in a pan, add the onion and cook gently, stirring frequently, for about 5 minutes until softened and lightly coloured. Add the tomatoes, then strain in the clam cooking liquid. Add the chilli and salt and pepper to taste. Chop the remaining parsley finely and set aside.

5 Bring to the boil, half-cover the pan and allow to simmer gently for 15–20 minutes.

6 Meanwhile, cook the pasta according to the instructions on the packet, until it is *al dente*. Drain the pasta well and tip it into a warmed bowl.

7 Meanwhile, add the shelled clams to the tomato sauce, stir well and heat very gently for 2–3 minutes.

8 Taste the sauce for seasoning, then pour the sauce over the pasta and toss everything together well. Serve garnished with the reserved clams and sprinkled with parsley.

Energy 493kcal/2064kJ; Protein 19.6g; Carbohydrate 77.8g, of which sugars 7.7g; Fat 7g, of which saturates 1.1g; Cholesterol 42mg; Calcium 114mg; Fibre 2.8g; Sodium 782mg.

prawn and vodka sauce

The combination of prawns, vodka and pasta has become a modern classic in Italy. Here the sauce is served with two-coloured pasta, but it also goes well with short shapes such as penne.

Serves four

INGREDIENTS

350g/12oz fresh or dried paglia e fieno

For the prawn and vodka sauce
30ml/2 tbsp olive oil
¼ large onion, finely chopped
1 garlic clove, crushed
15–30ml/1–2 tbsp sun-dried tomato purée (paste)
200ml/7fl oz/scant 1 cup double (heavy) cream
12 large raw prawns (shrimp), peeled and chopped
30ml/2 tbsp vodka
salt and ground black pepper

1 Soften the onion and garlic gently in the oil, stirring, for 5 minutes.

2 Add the tomato purée and stir for 1–2 minutes, then add the cream and bring to the boil, stirring. Season the sauce with salt and pepper to taste, and allow it to bubble gently until it starts to thicken slightly. Then remove the pan from the heat.

3 Cook the pasta according to the packet instructions, until *al dente*. When it is almost ready, add the prawns and vodka to the sauce; toss over a medium heat for 2–3 minutes, until the prawns are pink.

4 Drain the pasta and turn it into a warmed bowl. Pour the sauce over and toss well. Divide among warmed bowls and serve at once.

COOK'S TIP

This sauce is best as soon as it is ready, otherwise the prawns (shrimp) overcook and toughen. Make sure that the pasta is very nearly cooked before adding the prawns to the sauce.

Energy 641kcal/2682kJ; Protein 16.1g; Carbohydrate 67.4g, of which sugars 5.1g; Fat 34.1g, of which saturates 17.7g; Cholesterol 117mg; Calcium 71mg; Fibre 2.9g; Sodium 71mg.

smoked salmon and cream sauce

This modern way of serving pasta is popular all over Italy. The three essential ingredients combine beautifully, and the dish is very quick and easy to make.

Serves four

INGREDIENTS

350g/12oz penne

For the smoked salmon and cream sauce
115g/4oz thinly sliced smoked salmon
2–3 fresh thyme sprigs
30ml/2 tbsp butter
150ml/¼ pint/⅔ cup double (heavy) cream
salt and ground black pepper

1 Cook the pasta in boiling salted water until it is *al dente*.

2 Meanwhile, using kitchen scissors, cut the smoked salmon into thin strips, about 5mm/¼in wide. Strip the leaves from the thyme sprigs.

3 Melt the butter in a large pan. Stir in the cream with a quarter of the salmon and thyme leaves, then season with pepper. Heat gently for 3–4 minutes, stirring constantly. Do not allow to boil. Taste for seasoning.

4 Drain the pasta and toss it in the cream and salmon sauce. Divide among four warmed bowls and top with the remaining salmon and thyme leaves. Serve immediately.

Energy 582kcal/2441kJ; Protein 18.5g; Carbohydrate 65.5g, of which sugars 3.6g; Fat 29.2g, of which saturates 16.8g; Cholesterol 77mg; Calcium 47mg; Fibre 2.6g; Sodium 597mg.

sauces for poultry and meat

These recipes include classic and creative combinations based on flavours from around the world. The sauces are partnered with specific main ingredients so that they can be prepared successfully as part of a complete meal – whether "cooking in" or "pouring on". There are lots of tips and variations, so you can easily marry the sauces with different types of meat, poultry or game. Cooking styles included here range from long simmered to short stir-fried, or rich and fruity to light and spiced.

lemon sauce for chicken

Succulent chicken with a refreshing lemony sauce is a sure winner. The Chinese-style sauce is also excellent with steamed white fish, marinated in sesame oil and sherry before cooking.

Serves four

INGREDIENTS

4 small chicken breast fillets, skinned

5ml/1 tsp sesame oil

15ml/1 tbsp dry sherry

1 egg white, lightly beaten

30ml/2 tbsp cornflour (cornstarch)

15ml/1 tbsp vegetable oil

salt and ground white pepper

chopped coriander (cilantro) leaves,
    spring onions (scallions) and lemon
    wedges, to garnish

For the lemon sauce

45ml/3 tbsp fresh lemon juice

30ml/2 tbsp lime cordial

45ml/3 tbsp caster (superfine) sugar

10ml/2 tsp cornflour

90ml/6 tbsp cold water

1 Place the chicken in a shallow bowl. Mix the sesame oil with the sherry and add 2.5ml/½ tsp salt and 1.5ml/¼ tsp pepper. Pour over the chicken, cover and marinate for 15 minutes.

2 Mix the egg white and cornflour. Add the mixture to the chicken and turn to coat thoroughly. Heat the vegetable oil in a non-stick frying pan or wok and fry the chicken fillets for about 15 minutes, or until the fillets are cooked through and golden brown on both sides.

3 Meanwhile, make the sauce. Combine all the ingredients in a small pan. Add 1.5ml/¼ tsp salt. Bring to the boil over a low heat, stirring constantly until the sauce is smooth and has thickened slightly.

4 Cut the chicken into pieces and arrange on a warm serving plate. Pour the sauce over the chicken, garnish with the coriander leaves, spring onions and lemon wedges and serve.

Energy 282kcal/1194kJ; Protein 36.9g; Carbohydrate 22.3g, of which sugars 14.2g; Fat 5.2g, of which saturates 0.9g; Cholesterol 105mg; Calcium 17mg; Fibre 0g; Sodium 112mg.

orange and mustard sauce for chicken

The beauty of this recipe is its simplicity; the chicken continues to cook in its own juices while you prepare the sauce.

Serves four

INGREDIENTS

2 large oranges

4 chicken breast fillets, skinned

5ml/1 tsp sunflower oil

salt and ground black pepper

new potatoes and sliced courgettes
  (zucchini) tossed in parsley, to serve

For the orange and mustard sauce

10ml/2 tsp cornflour (cornstarch)

150ml/¼ pint/⅔ cup natural
  (plain) yogurt

5ml/1 tsp Dijon mustard

1 Using a sharp knife, cut a slice of peel and pith from each end of the oranges, then cut off all the peel and pith in strips, reserving the juice. Remove any remaining pith. Cut out each segment, leaving the membrane behind. Squeeze the remaining juice from the membrane.

2 Season the chicken with salt and freshly ground black pepper. Heat the oil in a non-stick frying pan and cook the chicken breasts for 5 minutes on each side. Take out of the frying pan and wrap in foil, shiny side inwards: the meat will continue to cook for a short while.

3 To make the sauce, blend together the cornflour with the juice from the oranges. Add the yogurt and mustard. Put into the frying pan used for cooking the chicken and slowly bring to the boil, stirring constantly. Simmer for 1 minute, until thickened.

4 Add the orange segments to the sauce and heat gently. Unwrap the chicken, check that it is cooked through and add any excess juices to the sauce. Slice on the diagonal and serve with the sauce, new potatoes and sliced courgettes tossed in parsley.

Energy 229kcal/970kJ; Protein 39.1g; Carbohydrate 11.8g, of which sugars 9.2g; Fat 3.4g, of which saturates 0.8g; Cholesterol 106mg; Calcium 119mg; Fibre 1.3g; Sodium 126mg.

salsa picante for chicken enchilladas

This "hot" salsa is actually a low-heat version using seeded green chillies, and is also cooled down by the soured cream. It also makes a good side dish with kebabs of chicken or pork.

3 Preheat the oven to 180°C/350°F/ Gas 4 and butter a shallow ovenproof dish. Take one tortilla and sprinkle with a good pinch of cheese and chopped onion, about 40g/1½oz of the chicken and 15ml/ 1 tbsp of salsa picante.

4 Pour over 15ml/1 tbsp of sour cream, roll up and place, seam-side down, in the dish. Make seven more enchilladas.

5 Pour the remaining salsa over the top and sprinkle with cheese and onion. Bake in the oven for 25–30 minutes until golden. Serve with the remaining cream. Garnish with the sliced avocado.

Serves four

INGREDIENTS

8 wheat tortillas

175g/6oz/1½ cups grated Cheddar cheese

1 onion, finely chopped

350g/12oz cooked chicken, cut into small chunks

300ml/½ pint/1¼ cups sour cream

1 avocado, sliced and tossed in lemon juice, to garnish

For the salsa picante

1–2 green chillies

15ml/1 tbsp vegetable oil

1 onion, chopped

1 garlic clove, crushed

400g/14oz can chopped tomatoes

30ml/2 tbsp tomato purée (paste)

salt and ground black pepper

1 To make the salsa picante, cut the chillies in half lengthways and carefully remove the cores and seeds. Slice the chillies very finely. Heat the oil in a frying pan and fry the onion and garlic for about 3–4 minutes until softened. Add the tomatoes, tomato purée and chillies. Simmer gently, uncovered, for 12–15 minutes, stirring the mixture frequently.

2 Pour the sauce into a food processor or blender, and process until smooth. Return to the heat and cook very gently, uncovered, for a further 15 minutes. Season to taste then set aside.

Energy 665kcal/2778kJ; Protein 39.8g; Carbohydrate 39.8g, of which sugars 9.4g; Fat 38.7g, of which saturates 20.6g; Cholesterol 149mg; Calcium 472mg; Fibre 3.7g; Sodium 569mg.

cajun-style tomato sauce for chicken

Sizzling fried chicken served in a hot and tasty tomato sauce is irresistibly good with plain rice mixed with corn and chives. The sauce is also good with pan-fried pork.

Serves four

INGREDIENTS

1 chicken, 1.6kg/3½ lb, cut into 8 pieces

90g/3½ oz/¾ cup plain (all-purpose) flour

250ml/8fl oz/1 cup buttermilk or milk

vegetable oil, for frying

salt and ground black pepper

chopped spring onions (scallions), and
fresh coriander (cilantro) sprigs, to
garnish

For the cajun-style tomato sauce

115g/4oz/½ cup lard or vegetable oil

2 onions, chopped

2–3 celery sticks, chopped

1 large green (bell) pepper, seeded
and chopped

2 garlic cloves, finely chopped

65g/2½ oz/9 tbsp plain (all-purpose) flour

225g/8oz tomatoes

250ml/8fl oz/1 cup passata (bottled
strained tomatoes)

450ml/¾ pint/scant 2 cups red wine or
chicken stock

2 bay leaves

15ml/1 tbsp soft brown sugar

5ml/1 tsp grated orange rind

2.5ml/½ tsp cayenne pepper

1 For the sauce, heat the lard or oil in a large pan. Add the onions, celery, green pepper and garlic and cook, stirring, until softened. Stir in the flour. Cook over a medium heat, stirring for 15–20 minutes.

2 Plunge the tomatoes into boiling water for 30 seconds, then refresh in cold water. Peel and chop the tomatoes, then stir theminto the onion mixture with the remaining sauce ingredients and seasoning. Boil, then simmer gently for 1 hour.

3 Meanwhile, prepare the chicken. Put the flour in a plastic bag and season with salt and pepper. Dip each piece of chicken in buttermilk or milk, then dredge in the flour to coat lightly all over. Shake off the excess flour. Set the chicken aside for 20 minutes to let the coating set before frying.

4 Heat the vegetable oil 2.5cm/1in deep in a large pan until it is very hot and starting to sizzle. Fry the chicken pieces, turning them once, for about 30 minutes, or until deep golden brown all over and cooked through.

5 Drain the chicken on kitchen paper and add them to the sauce. Serve immediately, garnished with a sprinkling of spring onion and coriander sprigs.

Energy 796kcal/3295kJ; Protein 33.2g; Carbohydrate 18.8g, of which sugars 5.9g; Fat 65.7g, of which saturates 12.5g; Cholesterol 160mg; Calcium 57mg; Fibre 2.2g; Sodium 147mg.

sherry and tomato sauce for chicken

In this tasty dish, chicken portions are first fried, then smothered in a rich, herby tomato sauce and baked in the oven. It's also good with pan-fried pork or lamb.

Serves eight

INGREDIENTS

1 chicken, about 1.8kg/4lb cut into 8 pieces, or 8 chicken portions

1.5ml/¼ tsp chopped fresh thyme

40g/1½oz/3 tbsp butter

45ml/3 tbsp vegetable oil

3–4 garlic cloves, crushed

2 onions, finely chopped

salt and ground black pepper

fresh basil and thyme leaves, to garnish

freshly cooked rice, to serve

For the sherry and tomato sauce

120ml/4fl oz/½ cup dry sherry

45ml/3 tbsp tomato purée (paste)

a few fresh basil leaves

30ml/2 tbsp white wine vinegar

generous pinch of granulated sugar

5ml/1 tsp French mustard

400g/14oz can chopped tomatoes

225g/8oz/3 cups mushrooms, sliced

1 Preheat the oven to 180°C/350°F/ Gas 4. Season the chicken with salt, pepper and thyme. In a large frying pan heat the butter and oil, and cook the chicken until golden.

2 Remove the chicken from the pan, place in an ovenproof dish and keep hot. Add the garlic and onions to the pan and cook, stirring, for 2–3 minutes, or until soft.

3 For the sauce, mix together the sherry, tomato purée, salt and pepper, basil, vinegar and sugar. Add the mustard and tomatoes.

4 Pour the sauce mixture into the frying pan and bring to the boil. Reduce the heat and add the mushrooms. Adjust the seasoning with more sugar or vinegar to taste.

5 Pour the tomato sauce over the chicken. Bake in the oven, covered, for 45–60 minutes, or until the chicken is cooked right through. Serve on a bed of rice, garnished with basil and thyme.

VARIATION

Replace the cultivated mushrooms with wild mushrooms, if you like.

Energy 335kcal/1388kJ; Protein 20g; Carbohydrate 5.7g, of which sugars 4.7g; Fat 24.1g, of which saturates 7.7g; Cholesterol 107mg; Calcium 26mg; Fibre 1.5g; Sodium 127mg.

sherried almond sauce for guinea fowl

The Arabs introduced saffron to Spain and this is a Moorish sauce of toasted almonds ground with parsley and several spices, flavoured with precious saffron. Serve with crusty bread.

Serves four

INGREDIENTS

25g/1oz/¼ cup blanched almonds
pinch of saffron threads
120ml/8 tbsp chicken stock
1.2–1.3kg/2½–3lb guinea fowl
60ml/4fl oz/½ cup olive oil
1 thick slice of bread, without crusts
2 garlic cloves, finely chopped
120ml/4fl oz/½ cup fino sherry
1 bay leaf, crumbled
4 thyme sprigs
15ml/1 tbsp finely chopped fresh parsley
pinch of freshly grated nutmeg
pinch of ground cloves
juice of ½ lemon
5ml/1 tsp paprika
salt and ground black pepper

1 Preheat the oven to 150°C/300°F/Gas 2. Spread the almonds on a baking sheet and toast in the oven for about 20 minutes until golden brown.

2 Crumble the saffron with your fingers into a jug (pitcher) or small bowl, pour over 30ml/2 tbsp hot chicken stock and leave to soak.

3 Cut the bird into eight serving pieces, discarding the wing tips, backbone, breastbones and leg tips. This will give you two legs (split them at the joint), two wings with one-third of the breast attached, and two short breast pieces.

4 Heat the olive oil in a shallow flameproof casserole and fry the bread on both sides. Fry the garlic quickly. Transfer both to a blender.

5 Season the fowl and fry until golden all over. Add the remaining stock and sherry, stirring. Add the bay leaf and thyme. Cover and cook gently for 10 minutes.

6 Grind the bread and garlic with the almonds in a food processor. Add the parsley, saffron liquid, nutmeg and cloves, and purée. Stir into the sauce with the lemon juice, paprika and seasoning, and serve.

Energy 534kcal/2221kJ; Protein 45.8g; Carbohydrate 4.5g, of which sugars 1.1g; Fat 33.4g, of which saturates 8.2g; Cholesterol 345mg; Calcium 92mg; Fibre 1.1g; Sodium 145mg.

curried apricot sauce for turkey kebabs

This is a South African way of cooking poultry in a delicious sweet-and-sour spiced sauce.

Serves four

INGREDIENTS

675g/1½lb turkey breast fillet60ml/4 tbsp
crème fraîche

For the curried apricot sauce

15ml/1 tbsp oil
1 onion, finely chopped
1 garlic clove, crushed
2 bay leaves
juice of 1 lemon
30ml/2 tbsp curry powder
60ml/4 tbsp apricot jam
60ml/4 tbsp apple juice
salt

1 Heat the oil in a pan. Add the onion, garlic and bay leaves and cook over low heat until the onions are soft. Add the lemon juice, curry powder, jam, apple juice and salt. Cook for 5 minutes, then cool.

2 Cut the turkey into 2cm/¾in cubes and add to the marinade. Mix well, cover and leave in a cool place to marinate for at least 2 hours or chill overnight.

3 Prepare a barbecue or preheat the grill (broiler). Thread the turkey on to four metal skewers, allowing the marinade to run back into the bowl. Cook the kebabs for 6–8 minutes, turning often, until done.

4 Meanwhile, transfer the marinade to a pan and simmer for 2 minutes. Stir in the crème fraîche and serve.

Energy 411kcal/1733kJ; Protein 60.4g; Carbohydrate 15.4g, of which sugars 13g; Fat 12.5g, of which saturates 5.5g; Cholesterol 142mg; Calcium 72mg; Fibre 1.9g; Sodium 197mg.

sambal kecap for chicken kebabs

A spicy marinade maked tender chicken exotic. The satays can be barbecued or grilled.

Serves four

INGREDIENTS

4 chicken breast fillets, about 175g/6oz
  each, skinned
30ml/2 tbsp deep-fried onion slices

For the sambal kecap

1 fresh red chilli, seeded and finely
  chopped
2 garlic cloves, crushed
60ml/4 tbsp dark soy sauce
20ml/4 tsp lemon juice or 15–25ml/
  1–1½ tbsp tamarind juice
30ml/2 tbsp hot water

1 Soak eight wooden skewers in water for at least 30 minutes. Drain the skewers just before using them – this prevents them from burning during cooking.

2 To make the sambal kecap, mix the chilli, garlic, soy sauce, lemon or tamarind juice and hot water. Leave to stand for 30 minutes.

3 Cut the chicken into 2.5cm/1in cubes and add to the sambal kecap. Mix thoroughly. Cover and leave in a cool place to marinate for 1 hour.

4 Turn the chicken and marinade into a sieve placed over a pan and leave to drain for a few minutes. Set the sieve aside.

5 Add 30ml/2 tbsp hot water to the marinade and bring to the boil. Lower the heat and simmer for 2 minutes, then pour into a bowl and leave to cool. When cool, add the deep-fried onions.

6 Prepare a barbecue or preheat the grill (broiler). Thread the skewers with the chicken and cook for about 10 minutes, turning regularly, until the chicken is golden and cooked through. Serve with the sambal kecap as a dip.

Energy 265kcal/1120kJ; Protein 55.2g; Carbohydrate 3.5g, of which sugars 2g; Fat 3.4g, of which saturates 1g; Cholesterol 158mg; Calcium 19mg; Fibre 0.6g; Sodium 1204mg.

marsala cream for turkey

Marsala and cream make a very rich and opulent sauce. The addition of lemon juice gives it a refreshing tang, which offsets the richness just perfectly.

Serves six

INGREDIENTS

6 turkey breast steaks

45ml/3 tbsp plain (all-purpose) flour

30ml/2 tbsp olive oil

25g/1oz/2 tbsp butter

salt and ground black pepper

For the Marsala cream sauce

175ml/6fl oz/¾ cup dry Marsala

60ml/4 tbsp lemon juice

175ml/6fl oz/¾ cup double (heavy) cream

To serve

lemon wedges and chopped fresh parsley, to garnish

mangetouts (snowpeas) and green beans

1 Put each turkey steak between clear film (plastic wrap) and pound with a rolling pin to flatten out evenly. Cut each steak in half or into quarters, cutting away and discarding any sinew.

2 Spread out the flour in a shallow bowl. Season well with salt and pepper and coat the meat.

COOK'S TIP

To make this sauce without using the pan drippings, omit the oil and heat the butter in a pan before adding the other ingredients.

3 Heat the oil and butter in a wide, heavy pan or frying pan until sizzling. Add as many pieces of turkey as you can, and sauté over a medium heat for about 3 minutes on each side until crispy and tender.

4 Using tongs or a spoon and fork, transfer the turkey to a warmed serving dish and keep hot. Cook the remaining turkey in the same way and remove from the pan. Tent the turkey loosely with foil and keep hot while making the sauce.

5 To make the sauce, mix the Marsala and lemon juice in a jug (pitcher), add to the oil and butter remaining in the pan. Bring to the boil, stirring in the sediment, then add the cream.

6 Heat gently until simmering, then continue to simmer, stirring constantly, until the sauce is reduced and glossy. Taste for seasoning before serving.

7 Spoon the sauce over the turkey, garnish with the lemon wedges and parsley and serve at once.

Energy 391kcal/1625kJ; Protein 29.7g; Carbohydrate 6.8g, of which sugars 1.1g; Fat 23.8g, of which saturates 12.8g; Cholesterol 115mg; Calcium 32mg; Fibre 0.2g; Sodium 93mg.

tarragon and parsley sauce for chicken

The aniseed-like flavour of tarragon has a particular affinity with chicken, especially in creamy sauces. Serve seasonal vegetables and boiled red Camargue rice with the chicken.

Serves four

INGREDIENTS

30ml/2 tbsp light olive oil

4 chicken breast portions (about 250g/9oz each), skinned

3 shallots, finely chopped

2 garlic cloves, finely chopped

115g/4oz/1½ cups wild mushrooms (such as chanterelles or ceps) or shiitake mushrooms, halved

150ml/¼ pint/⅔ cup dry white wine

300ml/½ pint/1¼ cups double (heavy) cream

15g/½oz/¼ cup chopped mixed fresh tarragon and flat leaf parsley

salt and ground black pepper

sprigs of fresh tarragon and flat leaf parsley, to garnish

1 Heat the olive oil in a frying pan and add the chicken, skin side down. Cook for 10 minutes, turning the chicken until it is a golden brown colour on both sides.

2 Reduce the heat and cook the chicken for 10 minutes more, turning occasionally. Remove from the pan and set aside.

3 Add the shallots and garlic to the pan and cook gently, stirring, until the shallots are soft but not brown.

4 Increase the heat, add the mushrooms and stir-fry for 2 minutes. Replace the chicken, then pour in the wine. Simmer for 5–10 minutes, or until most of the wine has evaporated.

5 Add the cream and gently mix the ingredients together. Simmer for 10 minutes, or until the sauce has thickened. Stir the herbs into the sauce and season to taste. Arrange the chicken on warm plates and spoon the sauce over. Garnish with tarragon and parsley.

SAFETY TIP

Unless you're an expert, or know of one who will identify them for you, it's safer not to pick mushrooms in the wild, but buy them instead from a reliable source.

Energy 722kcal/3003kJ; Protein 62.1g; Carbohydrate 2.9g, of which sugars 2.5g; Fat 48.8g, of which saturates 26.6g; Cholesterol 278mg; Calcium 66mg; Fibre 0.7g; Sodium 171mg.

curried yogurt sauce for chicken salad

This spicy yogurt sauce is a contemporary classic – especially with chicken and pasta. It is also delicious with cooked turkey or hard-boiled eggs. The salad is brilliant for lunch or supper.

2 Cook the pasta in a large pan of salted boiling water for 8–10 minutes, or until al dente. Drain and rinse thoroughly.

Serves four

INGREDIENTS

2 chicken breasts, cooked and skinned

175g/6oz green beans

350g/12oz multi-coloured penne

4 firm ripe tomatoes, skinned, seeded and cut in strips

salt and ground black pepper

coriander (cilantro) leaves, to garnish

For the curried yogurt sauce

150ml/¼ pint/⅔ cup low-fat natural (plain) yogurt

5ml/1 tsp mild curry powder

1 garlic clove, crushed

1 green chilli, seeded and finely chopped

30ml/2 tbsp chopped fresh coriander (cilantro)

1 Cut the chicken in strips and set aside. Cut the green beans into 2.5cm/1in lengths and cook them in boiling water for 5 minutes. Drain and rinse under cold water.

3 To make the sauce, mix the yogurt, curry powder, garlic, chilli and chopped coriander together in a bowl. Stir in the chicken pieces and leave to stand for 30 minutes.

4 Transfer the pasta to a bowl and toss with the beans and tomatoes. Spoon over the chicken and sauce. Garnish with coriander leaves.

VARIATION

There is a wide choice of curry pastes and sauces to vary the dish instead of curry powder. Try hot Thai green curry paste or a mild korma-type sauce

Energy 434kcal/1844kJ; Protein 32.4g; Carbohydrate 72.9g, of which sugars 10g; Fat 3.5g, of which saturates 0.7g; Cholesterol 53mg; Calcium 143mg; Fibre 5.2g; Sodium 96mg.

coronation sauce for chicken

A summer favourite, the creamy curry sauce for this dish is sweetened with a little apricot jam and sharpened with lemon juice. It's simple, clever and delicious with a crisp green salad.

Serves eight

INGREDIENTS

½ lemon

1 chicken, about 2.25kg/5lb

1 onion, quartered

1 carrot, quartered

large bouquet garni

8 black peppercorns, crushed

salt

watercress sprigs or parsley, to garnish

For the Coronation sauce

1 small onion, chopped

15g/½oz/1 tbsp butter

15ml/1 tbsp curry paste

15ml/1 tbsp tomato purée (paste)

120ml/4fl oz/½ cup red wine

bay leaf

juice of ½ lemon, or more to taste

10–15ml/2–3 tsp apricot jam

300ml/½ pint/1¼ cups mayonnaise

120ml/4fl oz/½ cup whipping cream

salt and ground black pepper

1 Put the lemon half in the chicken cavity, then place it in a pan in which it fits fairly tightly. Add the vegetables, bouquet garni, peppercorns and salt.

2 Add sufficient water to come two-thirds of the way up the chicken. Bring to the boil, cover and cook gently for 1½ hours, until cooked. The juices should run clear when the thigh meat is pierced.

3 Transfer the chicken to a large bowl, pour over the cooking liquid and leave to cool. Skin, bone, then dice the chicken meat.

4 To make the sauce, cook the onion in the butter until soft. Add the curry paste, tomato purée, wine, bay leaf and lemon juice, then cook for 10 minutes. Add the apricot jam; strain and cool.

5 Beat the sauce into the mayonnaise. Whip the cream and fold it into the sauce. Add seasoning to taste, then stir in the chicken. Serve garnished with watercress or parsley.

Energy 458kcal/1900kJ; Protein 25.1g; Carbohydrate 3.3g, of which sugars 2.5g; Fat 37.3g, of which saturates 9.3g; Cholesterol 118mg; Calcium 33mg; Fibre 0.6g; Sodium 259mg.

cashew nut sauce for chicken

The nut sauce for this chicken dish is deliciously thick and nutty. The sauce is also good with cooked pork or turkey. It is best served with fluffy, plain boiled rice.

Serves four

INGREDIENTS

2 onions

30ml/2 tbsp tomato purée (paste)

50g/2oz/¹⁄₂ cup cashew nuts

7.5ml/1¹⁄₂ tsp garam masala

5ml/1 tsp crushed garlic

5ml/1 tsp chilli powder

15ml/1 tbsp lemon juice

1.5ml/¹⁄₄ tsp ground turmeric

5ml/1 tsp salt

15ml/1 tbsp natural (plain) low-fat yogurt

30ml/2 tbsp corn oil

15ml/1 tbsp chopped fresh
   coriander (cilantro)

15ml/1 tbsp sultanas (golden raisins)

450g/1lb/3¹⁄₄ cups cubed chicken

175g/6oz/2¹⁄₄ cups button (white)
   mushrooms, halved

300ml/¹⁄₂ pint/1¹⁄₄ cups water

chopped fresh coriander (cilantro),
   to garnish

1 Cut the onions into quarters then place them in a food processor or blender and process for about 1 minute, until very finely chopped.

2 Add the tomato purée, cashew nuts, garam masala, garlic, chilli powder, lemon juice, turmeric, salt and yogurt. Process for a further 1–1¹⁄₂ minutes.

3 In a pan, heat the oil, lower the heat to medium and pour in the spice mixture from the food processor. Fry for about 2 minutes, turning down the heat if necessary.

4 Add the fresh coriander, sultanas and cubed chicken and continue to stir-fry for a further 1 minute.

5 Add the mushrooms, pour in the water and bring to a simmer. Cover and cook over a low heat for about 10 minutes, or until the chicken is cooked through and the sauce is thick. Cook for a little longer if necessary.

6 Serve garnished with chopped fresh coriander.

Energy 297kcal/1244kJ; Protein 32g; Carbohydrate 12.5g, of which sugars 9g; Fat 13.6g, of which saturates 2.5g; Cholesterol 79mg; Calcium 51mg; Fibre 2.4g; Sodium 131mg.

orange and pepper sauce for chicken

Orange, ginger, coriander, garlic and black pepper make a deliciously zesty sauce for chicken in this low-fat curry. The sauce is also a good choice for turkey or duck.

Serves four

INGREDIENTS

225g/8oz low-fat fromage frais or
  ricotta cheese

50ml/2fl oz/¼ cup natural (plain)
  low-fat yogurt

120ml/4fl oz/½ cup orange juice

7.5ml/1½ tsp grated fresh root ginger

5ml/1 tsp crushed garlic

5ml/1 tsp freshly ground black pepper

5ml/1 tsp salt

5ml/1 tsp ground coriander

1 chicken, about 675g/1½lb, skinned and
  cut into 8 pieces

15ml/1 tbsp oil

1 bay leaf

1 large onion, chopped

15ml/1 tbsp fresh mint leaves

1 green chilli, seeded and chopped

1 In a small bowl whisk together the fromage frais or ricotta cheese, yogurt, orange juice, ginger, garlic, pepper, salt and coriander.

2 Pour the sauce over the chicken, turn the pieces to coat them evenly, and set aside for 3–4 hours.

3 Heat the oil with the bay leaf in a wok or heavy frying pan and fry the onion until soft.

4 Pour in the chicken mixture and stir-fry for 3–5 minutes over a medium heat. Lower the heat, cover and cook for 7–10 minutes, until the chicken is cooked. Add a little water if the sauce is too thick. Add the mint and chilli, and serve.

COOK'S TIP

If you prefer the taste of curry leaves, you can use them instead of the bay leaf, but you need to double the quantity.

Energy 362kcal/1525kJ; Protein 58.4g; Carbohydrate 13.3g, of which sugars 11.9g; Fat 8.7g, of which saturates 3.1g; Cholesterol 169mg; Calcium 117mg; Fibre 0.3g; Sodium 171mg.

classic korma sauce for chicken

Although kormas are traditionally rich, this recipe uses yogurt instead of cream, which lightens the sauce. To prevent the yogurt from curdling, add it very slowly, stirring until it is mixed.

3 Heat the oil in a large, heavy pan and cook the chicken cubes for 8–10 minutes, or until browned on all sides. Remove the chicken cubes with a slotted spoon and set aside.

4 Add the cardamom pods and fry for 2 minutes. Add the onion and fry for a further 5 minutes.

5 Stir in the garlic and ginger paste, cumin and salt, and cook, stirring, for a further 5 minutes.

6 Add half the yogurt, stirring in a tablespoonful at a time, and cook over a low heat, until it has all been absorbed. Return the chicken to the pan.

7 Cover and simmer over a low heat for 5–6 minutes, or until the chicken is tender. Add the remaining yogurt and simmer for a further 5 minutes. Garnish with toasted flaked almonds, if using, and coriander. Serve with rice.

Serves four

INGREDIENTS

675g/1½lb chicken breast fillet, skinned

2 garlic cloves, crushed

2.5cm/1in piece fresh root ginger, roughly chopped

15ml/1 tbsp oil

3 green cardamom pods

1 onion, finely chopped

10ml/2 tsp ground cumin

1.5ml/¼ tsp salt

300ml/½ pint/1¼ cups natural (plain) low-fat yogurt

toasted flaked (sliced) almonds (optional) and a fresh coriander (cilantro) sprig, to garnish

plain rice, to serve

1 Remove any visible fat from the chicken fillets and cut the meat into 2.5cm/1in cubes.

2 Put the garlic and ginger into a food processor or blender with 30ml/2 tbsp water and process to a smooth, creamy paste.

COOK'S TIP

Traditionally, kormas are spicy dishes with a rich, creamy texture. They are not meant to be very hot curries.

Energy 251kcal/1059kJ; Protein 44.5g; Carbohydrate 6.8g, of which sugars 6.5g; Fat 5.4g, of which saturates 1.3g; Cholesterol 119mg; Calcium 155mg; Fibre 0.2g; Sodium 164mg.

hara masala sauce for chicken

This fruity chicken dish has a creamy sauce, enlivened with a kick of chilli balanced by a twist of mint and coriander flavours. It tastes terrific and looks attractive too.

Serves four

INGREDIENTS

1 crisp green eating apple, peeled, cored and cut into small cubes

60ml/4 tbsp fresh coriander (cilantro) leaves

30ml/2 tbsp fresh mint leaves

120ml/4fl oz/½ cup natural (plain) low-fat yogurt

45ml/3 tbsp low-fat fromage frais or ricotta cheese

2 medium green chillies, seeded and chopped

1 bunch spring onions (scallions), chopped

5ml/1 tsp salt

5ml/1 tsp sugar

5ml/1 tsp crushed garlic

5ml/1 tsp grated fresh root ginger

15ml/1 tbsp oil

225g/8oz chicken breast fillet, skinned and cubed

25g/1oz/2 tbsp sultanas (golden raisins)

1 Process the apple, 45ml/3 tbsp of the coriander, the mint, yogurt, fromage frais or ricotta, chillies, spring onions, salt, sugar, garlic and ginger in a food processor for about 1 minute, pulsing the power.

2 Heat the oil in a frying pan, pour in the yogurt mixture and cook over a low heat for 2 minutes.

3 Next, add the chicken cubes and blend everything together. Cook over a medium-low heat for 12–15 minutes, or until the chicken is fully cooked through.

4 Finally, just before serving the chicken, add the sultanas and the remaining 15ml/1 tbsp fresh coriander leaves. Stir lightly to mix, and serve.

Energy 150kcal/630kJ; Protein 16.8g; Carbohydrate 10.7g, of which sugars 10.5g; Fat 4.8g, of which saturates 1.3g; Cholesterol 41mg; Calcium 111mg; Fibre 1.4g; Sodium 561mg.

pomegranate and nut sauce for duck

This exotic sweet-and-sour sauce originally comes from Iran. Walnuts are nutty but slightly tender when cooked and their mellow flavour is the perfect match for sweet pomegranates.

2 Transfer to a pan, add the walnuts and stock, then season with salt and pepper. Stir, then bring to the boil and simmer the mixture, uncovered, for 20 minutes.

3 Cut the pomegranates in half and scoop out the seeds. Reserve the seeds of one pomegranate. Transfer the remaining seeds to a blender and process to break them up. Strain through a sieve, to extract the juice, and stir in the sugar and lemon juice.

4 Score the skin of the duck breasts in a diamond pattern with a sharp knife. Heat the remaining oil in a frying pan or griddle and place the duck breasts in it, skin-side down.

5 Cook gently for 10 minutes, pouring off the fat, until the skin is dark golden and crisp. Turn the duck breasts over and cook for a further 3–4 minutes. Transfer to a plate and leave to rest. Deglaze the frying pan with the pomegranate juice, then add the walnut and stock mixture and simmer for 15 minutes until thickened.

6 Slice the duck and serve drizzled with a little sauce, and garnished with the reserved pomegranate seeds. Serve the remaining sauce separately.

Serves four

INGREDIENTS

4 duck breasts, about 225g/8oz each

For the pomegranate and nut sauce

30ml/2 tbsp olive oil

2 onions, very thinly sliced

2.5ml/½ tsp ground turmeric

400g/14oz/2½ cups walnuts, roughly chopped

1 litre/1¾ pints/4 cups duck or chicken stock

6 pomegranates

30ml/2 tbsp caster (superfine) sugar

60ml/4 tbsp lemon juice

salt and ground black pepper

1 To make the sauce, heat half the oil in a frying pan. Add the onions and turmeric, and cook gently for a few minutes until soft.

COOK'S TIP

Choose pomegranates with shiny, brightly coloured skins. Only the seeds are used in cooking; pith is discarded.

Energy 1052kcal/4366kJ; Protein 59.6g; Carbohydrate 13.2g, of which sugars 12.2g; Fat 88.7g, of which saturates 9.3g; Cholesterol 248mg; Calcium 131mg; Fibre 4.2g; Sodium 258mg.

spicy plum sauce for duck sausages

These rich duck sausages – which are better baked in their own juices than fried – are perfectly complemented by the spiciness of the plum sauce. Add sweet potato mash for a fabulous meal.

Serves four

INGREDIENTS

8–12 duck sausages

For the sweet potato mash

1.5kg/3¼lb sweet potatoes, cut
  into chunks

25g/1oz/2 tbsp butter

60ml/4 tbsp milk

salt and ground black pepper

For the plum sauce

30ml/2 tbsp olive oil

1 small onion, chopped

1 small red chilli, seeded and chopped

450g/1lb plums, stoned (pitted) and
  chopped

30ml/2 tbsp red wine vinegar

45ml/3 tbsp clear honey

1 Preheat the oven to 190°C/375°F/
Gas 5. Arrange the duck sausages in
a single layer in a large, shallow
ovenproof dish and bake,
uncovered, for 25–30 minutes, until
browned and crisp. Turn the
sausages two or three times during
cooking, to ensure that they brown
and cook evenly.

2 Meanwhile, put the sweet
potatoes in a pan and pour in
enough water to cover them. Bring
to the boil, reduce the heat and
simmer for 20 minutes, or until
tender. Drain and mash, then place
the pan over a low heat. Stir
frequently for about 5 minutes to
dry out the mashed potato. Beat in
the butter and milk, season.

3 Heat the oil in a small pan and
fry the onion and chilli gently for 5
minutes. Stir in the plums, vinegar
and honey, then simmer gently for
10 minutes.

4 Serve the freshly cooked sausages
with the mash and plum sauce.

Energy 1058kcal/4434kJ; Protein 21.9g; Carbohydrate 114.6g, of which sugars 43.6g; Fat 60.3g, of which saturates 22.9g; Cholesterol 85mg; Calcium 190mg; Fibre 11.8g; Sodium 1338mg.

cranberry sauce for venison

Venison steaks are a healthy choice for a special occasion and delicious with this sauce of cranberries, port and ginger. The sauce also complements roast duck, pork, lamb or turkey.

Serves four

INGREDIENTS

30ml/2 tbsp sunflower oil

4 venison steaks

2 shallots, finely chopped

salt and ground black pepper

fresh thyme sprigs, to garnish

creamy mashed potatoes and broccoli,
  to serve

For the cranberry sauce

1 orange

1 lemon

75g/3oz/¾ cup fresh or frozen cranberries

5ml/1 tsp grated fresh root ginger

1 fresh thyme sprig

5ml/1 tsp Dijon mustard

60ml/4 tbsp redcurrant jelly

150ml/¼ pint/⅔ cup ruby port

1 For the sauce, use a vegetable peeler to pare the rind thinly from half the orange and half the lemon, then cut into very fine strips.

2 Blanch the citrus rind strips in a small pan of boiling water for about 5 minutes until tender. Strain the strips and refresh in cold water.

3 Squeeze the juice from the orange and lemon and then pour into a small pan. Add the cranberries, ginger, thyme, mustard, redcurrant jelly and port. Cook over a low heat until the jelly melts.

4 Bring to the boil, stirring occasionally, then cover and cook gently, for about 15 minutes, or until the cranberries are just tender.

5 Heat the oil in a heavy frying pan, add the venison and cook over a high heat for 2–3 minutes.

6 Turn the steaks and add the shallots. Cook for 2–3 minutes, depending on whether you like rare or medium cooked meat.

7 Just before the end of cooking, pour in the sauce and add the citrus strips. Cook for a few seconds to thicken slightly, then remove the thyme and add seasoning to taste.

8 Transfer the venison steaks to warmed plates and spoon over the sauce. Garnish with thyme sprigs and serve accompanied by creamy mashed potatoes and broccoli.

COOK'S TIP

When frying venison, always remember the briefer the better – venison will turn to leather if subjected to fierce heat after it has reached the medium-rare stage. If you dislike any hint of pink, cook it to this stage and then let it rest in a low oven for a few minutes.

Energy 315kcal/1328kJ; Protein 33.7g; Carbohydrate 17.8g, of which sugars 17.8g; Fat 8.9g, of which saturates 1.9g; Cholesterol 75mg; Calcium 16mg; Fibre 0.4g; Sodium 106mg.

redcurrant sauce for lamb burgers

The sweet-sour redcurrant sauce is the perfect complement to the taste of lamb and would go equally well with grilled or roast lamb steaks.

Serves four

INGREDIENTS

500g/1¼lb minced (ground) lean lamb
1 small onion, finely chopped
30ml/2 tbsp finely chopped fresh mint
30ml/2 tbsp finely chopped fresh parsley
115g/4oz mozzarella cheese
30ml/2 tbsp oil, for basting
salt and ground black pepper

For the redcurrant sauce

115g/4oz/1 cup fresh or frozen
  redcurrants
10ml/2 tsp clear honey
5ml/1 tsp balsamic vinegar
30ml/2 tbsp finely chopped mint

1 To make the sauce, place all the ingredients in a bowl and mash them together with a fork. Season with salt and ground black pepper. Set aside at room temperature.

2 Mix the lamb, onion, mint and parsley with plenty of salt and pepper. Divide the mixture into eight and press into a flat rounds.

3 Cut the mozzarella into four chunks. Place a chunk of cheese on half of the lamb rounds. Top each with another round of meat.

4 Press the two rounds of meat together firmly, making four fairly flat burgers. Use your fingers to pinch and blend the edges, and seal in the cheese completely. If the edges are not well sealed, the cheese will flow out as it melts during cooking.

VARIATION

For a store-cupboard (pantry) sauce, melt a jar of redcurrant jelly in a small pan over low heat. Stir in the balsamic vinegar and mint but omit the honey. Add a handful of fresh or frozen rapsberries (if available), lightly crushed.

5 Brush the lamb burgers with olive oil and cook over a moderately hot barbecue for about 15 minutes, or grill for 10 minutes turning once, until golden brown. Serve with the sauce.

Energy 393kcal/1637kJ; Protein 30.1g; Carbohydrate 5.3g, of which sugars 4.9g; Fat 28.2g, of which saturates 12.4g; Cholesterol 113mg; Calcium 172mg; Fibre 1.9g; Sodium 206mg.

cook-in tomato sauce for meatballs

For a quick tomato sauce, passata can be enlivened with a little sugar, bay leaves and onions. This makes an ideal "cook-in" sauce for fish, poultry or meat – little Greek-style meatballs flavour the smooth sauce as they simmer gently in this recipe.

Serves four

INGREDIENTS

50g/2oz/1 cup fresh breadcrumbs
150ml/¼ pint/⅔ cup milk
675g/1½ lb minced (ground) lamb
30ml/2 tbsp grated onion
3 garlic cloves, crushed
10ml/2 tsp ground cumin
30ml/2 tbsp chopped fresh parsley
flour, for dusting
olive oil, for frying
salt and ground black pepper
fresh flat leaf parsley, to garnish

For the tomato sauce

600ml/1 pint/2½ cups passata (bottled
  strained tomatoes)
5ml/1 tsp sugar
2 bay leaves
1 small onion, peeled

1 Mix together the breadcrumbs and milk. Add the lamb, onion, garlic, cumin and parsley and season with salt and pepper.

2 Shape the mixture into little fat sausages, about 5cm/2in long, and roll them in flour. Place on a plate and chill briefly, if possible, so the sausages firm up slightly.

3 Meanwhile, prepare the sauce. Put the passata, sugar, bay leaves and whole onion in a pan. Bring to the boil, reduce the heat and cover the pan. Simmer for 20 minutes.

4 Heat a little olive oil in a frying pan. Fry the sausages for about 8 minutes, turning, until evenly browned. Spoon out any excess fat.

5 Pour the sauce over the sausages and simmer gently for 10 minutes. Serve garnished with parsley.

VARIATION

Lamb is more commonly used in Greece for these sausages, but as an alternative you could try using minced (ground) turkey.

Energy 530kcal/2212kJ; Protein 36.8g; Carbohydrate 19.6g, of which sugars 9.5g; Fat 34.5g, of which saturates 12.4g; Cholesterol 132mg; Calcium 128mg; Fibre 2g; Sodium 576mg.

baked pesto for lamb

The intense aromas of fresh basil and garlic in classic pesto sauce combine irresistibly with lamb, and the pine nuts and Parmesan create a delectable crunchy crust during roasting. This is an unusual way of using the simple sauce that is so good with plain cooked pasta.

Serves six

INGREDIENTS

2.25–2.75kg/5–6lb leg of lamb

For the pesto

90g/3½oz/1¾ cups fresh basil leaves

4 garlic cloves, coarsely chopped

45ml/3 tbsp pine nuts

150ml/¼ pint/⅔ cup olive oil

50g/2oz/⅔ cup freshly grated Parmesan cheese

5ml/1 tsp salt, or to taste

1 To make the pesto, combine the basil, garlic and pine nuts in a food processor, and process until finely chopped. With the motor running, slowly add the oil in a steady stream. Scrape the mixture into a bowl. Stir in the Parmesan and salt.

2 Set the lamb in a roasting dish. Use a small pointed knife to make several slits into the meat. Spoon pesto into each slit.

3 Coat the surface of the lamb in a thick, even layer of the remaining pesto. Cover the meat and leave to stand for 2 hours at room temperature, or chill overnight.

4 Preheat the oven to 180°C/350°F/Gas 4. Place the lamb in the oven and roast, allowing about 20 minutes per 450g/1lb if you like rare meat, or 25 minutes per 450g/1lb if you prefer it medium-rare. Turn the lamb occasionally during roasting.

5 Remove the leg of lamb from the oven, cover it loosely with foil, and let it rest for about 15 minutes before carving and serving.

VARIATION

Lamb steaks or lamb chops could be coated with this delicious pesto. It is also good as a filling for baked butternut squash or potatoes.

Energy 1006kcal/4206kJ; Protein 116.2g; Carbohydrate 0.7g, of which sugars 0.6g; Fat 60g, of which saturates 18.7g; Cholesterol 383mg; Calcium 157mg; Fibre 0.9g; Sodium 332mg.

red onion relish for lamb burgers

A sharp-sweet relish of red onions, ripe little tomatoes and red peppers works well with burgers based on Middle-Eastern style lamb. Serve with pitta bread, fries and a green salad.

Serves four

INGREDIENTS

25g/1oz/3 tbsp bulgur wheat

500g/1¼lb lean minced (ground) lamb

1 small red onion, finely chopped

2 garlic cloves, finely chopped

1 fresh green chilli, seeded and finely chopped

5ml/1 tsp ground toasted cumin seeds

2.5ml/½ tsp ground sumac

15g/½oz fresh flat leaf parsley, chopped

30ml/2 tbsp chopped fresh mint

olive oil, for frying

salt and ground black pepper

For the red onion relish

2 red (Italian) onions, cut into 5mm/¼in thick slices

75ml/5 tbsp extra virgin olive oil

2 red (bell) peppers, halved and seeded

350g/12oz cherry tomatoes, chopped

1 fresh red or green chilli, seeded and finely chopped

30ml/2 tbsp chopped fresh mint

30ml/2 tbsp chopped fresh parsley

15ml/1 tbsp chopped fresh oregano

2.5–5ml/½–1 tsp ground sumac

15ml/1 tbsp lemon juice

sugar, to taste

1 Pour 150ml/¼ pint/⅔ cup hot water over the bulgur wheat in a bowl and leave to stand for 15 minutes, then tip into a sieve lined with a clean dish towel. Drain, then squeeze out the excess moisture.

2 Place the bulgur wheat in a bowl and add the lamb, onion, garlic, chilli, cumin, sumac, parsley and mint. Mix thoroughly together by hand, season with salt and ground black pepper, then mix again.

3 Using your hands, form the mixture into 8 burgers and set aside while you make the relish.

4 For the relish, brush the onions with 15ml/1 tbsp of the oil and grill (broil) for 5 minutes each side, until brown. Cool, then chop. Grill the peppers, skin-side up, until charred. Place in a bowl, cover and leave for 10 minutes. Peel, seed and finely dice the peppers.

5 Mix the onions and peppers in a bowl. Add the tomatoes, chilli, herbs and sumac. Stir in the remaining oil and the lemon juice. Season with salt, pepper and sugar.

7 Heat a heavy frying pan or a ridged, cast-iron grill (broiling) pan over a high heat and grease lightly with olive oil. Cook the burgers for about 5–6 minutes on each side, or until just cooked at the centre.

8 While the burgers are cooking, taste the relish and adjust the seasoning. Serve the burgers freshly cooked, with the relish.

COOK'S TIP

Sumac is a sweet-sour spice made from berries. Substitute grated (shredded) lemon rind, if you prefer.

Energy 514kcal/2135kJ; Protein 27.4g; Carbohydrate 19.1g, of which sugars 13.5g; Fat 37g, of which saturates 10.7g; Cholesterol 96mg; Calcium 96mg; Fibre 4.5g; Sodium 107mg.

onion and caper sauce with bacon

Onions and capers make a piquant sauce that is traditional with boiled mutton, but it is also delicious with boiled bacon or gammon.

Serves six

INGREDIENTS

1.8–2kg/4–4$\frac{1}{2}$lb piece of gammon (smoked ham) or bacon, soaked if necessary

1 onion, quartered, stuck with 4 cloves

1 large carrot, sliced

1 celery stick

1 fresh bay leaf

fresh thyme sprig

30ml/2 tbsp Dijon mustard

45–60ml/3–4 tbsp demerara (raw) sugar

For the onion and caper sauce

50g/2oz/¼ cup butter

225g/8oz onions, chopped

25g/1oz/¼ cup plain (all-purpose) flour

250ml/8fl oz/1 cup milk

1 fresh bay leaf

30ml/2 tbsp small salted capers, rinsed and roughly chopped

30ml/2 tbsp chopped fresh parsley (optional)

15–30ml/1–2 tbsp Dijon mustard

salt and ground black pepper

1 Place the meat in a pan and cover with water. Bring to the boil and simmer for 5 minutes. Drain, rinse, then return to the pan. Cover with water. Add the onion, carrot, celery, bay leaf and thyme. Bring to the boil, then simmer very gently for 25 minutes per 450g/1lb.

2 Preheat the oven 200°C/400°F/ Gas 6. Drain the meat, reserving 475ml/16fl oz/2 cups of the cooking liquid. Place the meat in a roasting pan and strip off and discard the skin, leaving an even layer of fat on the meat. Spread the mustard over the fat and press the sugar all over the mustard.

3 Cook the gammon in the oven for 20–25 minutes, until glazed and browned. Remove from the oven and keep warm, covered loosely in foil, until ready to serve.

4 Start making the sauce just before the meat has finished boiling. Melt 40g/1½oz/3 tbsp of the butter in a pan and cook the onions very gently, half-covered, for about 20 minutes, until they are soft and yellow but not browned. Stir occasionally, to prevent them sticking to the pan.

5 Stir in the flour and cook, stirring constantly, for 2–3 minutes. Gradually stir in 300ml/½ pint/1¼ cups of the hot reserved cooking liquid. Cook until the sauce is thick and smooth, then gradually stir in the milk. Add the bay leaf and cook very gently for 20–25 minutes, stirring frequently.

6 Gradually stir in a little more of the reserved cooking liquid to make a sauce of pouring consistency and cook for a further 5 minutes. Remove the bay leaf.

7 Stir in the chopped capers and parsley, if using. Add 15ml/1 tbsp mustard, then taste for seasoning. Add salt, pepper and more mustard to taste. Stir in the remaining butter and serve immediately with the sliced meat, small new potatoes, tossed a little butter, and garlic, and broad (fava) beans.

Energy 529kcal/2204kJ; Protein 55.2g; Carbohydrate 8.7g, of which sugars 4.6g; Fat 30.5g, of which saturates 12.3g; Cholesterol 89mg; Calcium 106mg; Fibre 1.1g; Sodium 2786mg.

classic white onion sauce

This is the classic French white onion sauce. It is excellent with veal, chicken, pork or lamb –
but also poured over poached eggs and grilled. It can be left chunky with onion, or puréed.

4 Remove and discard the bay leaf
and parsley, then process the sauce
in a blender or food processor if
you want a smooth sauce.

5 Stir in the cream and reheat the
sauce gently, then season to taste
with salt and pepper. Add a little
more milk or stock if the sauce is
very thick. Season with the nutmeg.
before serving.

VARIATIONS

• For leek sauce, substitute leeks for
onions, using the white part of the
leeks. Cook for just 4–5 minutes in the
butter before adding the flour. Omit the
nutmeg and stir in 15ml/1 tbsp Dijon
mustard just before serving.

• Season the sauce with about 30ml/
2 tbsp Dijon mustard at the end of
cooking to make *sauce Robert* – a
classic French sauce traditionally served
with pork chops. It also goes very well
with ham or rabbit.

Serves four

INGREDIENTS

40g/1½oz/3 tbsp butter
350g/12oz onions, chopped
25g/1oz/¼ cup plain (all-purpose) flour
500ml/17fl oz/generous 2 cups hot milk
  or stock, or a mixture of both
1 fresh bay leaf
a few parsley stalks
120ml/4fl oz/½ cup double (heavy) cream
freshly grated nutmeg
salt and ground black pepper

1 Melt the butter in a large heavy
pan. Add the onions and fry gently
over a low heat, stirring, for 10–12
minutes, until they are soft and
golden yellow, but not browned.

2 Stir in the flour and cook gently,
stirring constantly, for 2–3 minutes.

3 Gradually stir in the hot milk,
stock, or milk and stock mixture
and bring to the boil. Add the bay
leaf and parsley. Cook very gently,
stirring often, for 15–20 minutes.

COOKS' TIP

The sauce should be cooked for this
length of time to cook out the raw flour
flavour. A heat diffuser mat is very useful
to keep the heat as low as possible
when cooking delicate sauces.

Energy 334kcal/1384kJ; Protein 6.4g; Carbohydrate 18.2g, of which sugars 11.5g; Fat 26.7g, of which saturates 16.6g; Cholesterol 70mg; Calcium 197mg; Fibre 1.4g; Sodium 124mg.

onion and mustard sauce for pork

The piquant sauce adds punch and flavour to this simple supper dish. Serve favourite creamy potato mash and buttery broccoli or cabbage for the perfect feel-better meal.

Serves four

INGREDIENTS

4 pork loin chops, 2cm/¾in thick
30ml/2 tbsp plain (all-purpose) flour
45ml/3 tbsp olive oil
2 Spanish (Bermuda) onions, thinly sliced
2 garlic cloves, finely chopped
250ml/8fl oz/1 cup dry (hard) cider
150ml/¼ pint/⅔ cup vegetable, chicken
   or pork stock
generous pinch of brown sugar
2 fresh bay leaves
6 fresh thyme sprigs
2 strips lemon rind
120ml/4fl oz/½ cup double (heavy) cream
30–45ml/2–3 tbsp wholegrain mustard
30ml/2 tbsp chopped fresh parsley
salt and ground black pepper

1 Preheat the oven to 200°C/400°F/Gas 6. Trim the chops of excess fat. Season the flour with salt and pepper and use to coat the chops. Heat 30ml/2 tbsp of the oil in a frying pan and brown the chops on both sides, then transfer them to an ovenproof dish.

2 Add the remaining oil to the pan and cook the onions over a fairly gentle heat until they soften and begin to brown. Add the garlic and cook for 2 minutes more.

3 Stir in any left-over flour, then gradually stir in the cider and stock. Season well with salt and pepper and add the brown sugar, bay leaves, thyme sprigs and lemon rind. Bring the sauce to the boil, stirring constantly, then pour over the chops.

4 Cover and cook in the oven for 20 minutes. Reduce the heat to 180°C/350°F/Gas 4 and continue cooking for another 30–40 minutes. Remove the foil for the last 10 minutes of the cooking time.

5 Use a spoon and fork to lift the chops from the sauce and transfer them to a serving dish. Keep warm, covered with foil.

6 Pour the sauce from the roasting dish into a pan. Alternatively, if the dish is flameproof, place it over a direct heat. Discard the herbs and lemon rind, then bring the sauce to the boil, stirring.

7 Add the cream and continue to boil, stirring constantly. Taste for seasoning, adding a pinch more sugar if necessary. Finally, stir in the mustard to taste and pour the sauce over the braised chops. Sprinkle with the chopped parsley and serve immediately.

Energy 541Kcal/2235kJ; Protein 39g; Carbohydrate 19.4g, of which sugars 9g; Fat 32.9g, of which saturates 14.1g; Cholesterol 135mg; Calcium 78mg; Fibre 2g; Sodium 88mg.

cider sauce for pan-fried gammon

Gammon and cider are a delicious combination, with the sweet, tangy flavour of cider complementing the gammon. Serve with mashed potatoes pepped up with a little mustard.

Serves four

INGREDIENTS

4 gammon steaks (smoked or cured ham), about 225g/8oz each

150ml/¼ pint/⅔ cup dry (hard) cider

45ml/3 tbsp double (heavy) cream

30ml/2 tbsp sunflower oil

ground black pepper

COOK'S TIP

The gammon steaks (smoked or cured ham) are usually quite salty, so there is no need to add salt when seasoning the sauce. A good seasoning of black pepper brings out the best in the creamy sauce.

1 Heat the oil in a large frying pan. Snip the rind and fat at intervals all around the gammon to prevent the steaks from curling up during cooking. Lay them in the pan. (You may have to cook them in batches, then replace them all to finish.)

2 Cook the steaks for 3–4 minutes on each side, then pour in the cider. Allow to boil for a couple of minutes, then stir in the cream and cook for 1–2 minutes, or until thickened. Season with pepper, and serve immediately.

Energy 429kcal/1784kJ; Protein 39.6g; Carbohydrate 1.2g, of which sugars 1.2g; Fat 28.4g, of which saturates 10.1g; Cholesterol 67mg; Calcium 24mg; Fibre 0g; Sodium 1985mg.

calvados sauce for pork noisettes

This dish is ideal as part of a formal menu to impress guests. Buttered gnocchi or griddled polenta and red cabbage are suitable accompaniments.

Serves four

INGREDIENTS

30ml/2 tbsp plain (all-purpose) flour

4 noisettes of pork, about 175g/6oz
  each, firmly tied

25g/1oz/2 tbsp butter

4 baby leeks, finely sliced

5ml/1 tsp mustard seeds, coarsely
  crushed

30ml/2 tbsp Calvados

150ml/¼ pint/⅔ cup dry white wine

2 eating apples, peeled, cored
  and sliced

150ml/¼ pint/⅔ cup double (heavy) cream

30ml/2 tbsp chopped fresh parsley

salt and ground black pepper

VARIATION

For a lighter version, use half-fat créme
fraîche instead of the cream.

1 Place the flour in a bowl and add plenty of seasoning. Turn the noisettes in the flour mixture to coat them lightly.

2 Melt the butter in a heavy frying pan and cook the noisettes until golden on both sides. Remove from the pan and set aside.

3 Add the leeks to the fat in the pan and cook for 5 minutes. Stir in the mustard seeds. Pour in the Calvados, then carefully ignite it to burn off the alcohol.

4 When the flames have died down pour in the wine and replace the pork. Cook gently for 10 minutes, turning the pork frequently.

5 Add the apples and cream and simmer for 5 minutes, or until the apples are tender. Taste for seasoning, then stir in the chopped parsley and serve at once.

COOK'S TIP

Calvados is a French apple brandy. For a completely different flavour, Scotch whisky is delicious with lamb noisettes.

Energy 543kcal/2261kJ; Protein 39.9g; Carbohydrate 14.8g, of which sugars 8.8g; Fat 32.7g, of which saturates 18.3g; Cholesterol 175mg; Calcium 60mg; Fibre 2.5g; Sodium 173mg.

sweet and sour sauce for pork

Sweet-and-sour pork must be one of the most popular dishes served in Chinese restaurants and take-aways in the Western world. Unfortunately, it is often spoiled by cooks who use too much tomato ketchup in the sauce. Here is a classic recipe from Canton, the city of its origin.

Serves four

INGREDIENTS

350g/12oz lean boneless pork

1.5ml/¼ tsp salt

2.5ml/½ tsp ground Szechuan peppercorns

15ml/1 tbsp Chinese rice wine or dry sherry

115g/4oz bamboo shoots

30ml/2 tbsp plain (all-purpose) flour

1 egg, lightly beaten

vegetable oil, for deep-frying

For the sweet and sour sauce

15ml/1 tbsp vegetable oil

1 garlic clove, finely chopped

1 spring onion (scallion), cut into short sections

1 small green (bell) pepper, seeded and diced

1 fresh red chilli, seeded and thinly shredded

15ml/1 tbsp light soy sauce

30ml/2 tbsp light brown sugar

30–45ml/2–3 tbsp rice vinegar

15ml/1 tbsp tomato purée (paste)

about 120ml/4fl oz/½ cup chicken or vegetable stock or water

1 Cut the pork into small bite-sized cubes and place in a shallow dish. Add the salt, peppercorns and rice wine or dry sherry. Cover and set aside to marinate at room temperature for 15–20 minutes. Alternatively, chill if leaving for more than about 30 minutes.

2 Drain the bamboo shoots, if canned, and cut them into small cubes the same size as the pork; if they are thinly sliced, cut in half.

3 Dust the pork with flour, dip in the beaten egg and coat with more flour. Heat the oil in a preheated wok and deep-fry the pork in moderately hot oil for 3–4 minutes, stirring to separate the pieces. Remove and drain.

4 Reheat the oil until hot, return the pork to the wok and add the bamboo shoots. Fry for about 1 minute, or until the pork is golden. Remove and drain well.

5 To make the sauce, heat the oil in a clean wok or frying pan and add the garlic, spring onion, green pepper and red chilli. Stir-fry for 30–40 seconds, then add the soy sauce, sugar, rice vinegar, tomato purée and stock or water. Bring to the boil, stirring constantly, then add the pork and bamboo shoots. Heat through and stir to mix, then serve at once.

Energy 336kcal/1403kJ; Protein 22.7g; Carbohydrate 18.6g, of which sugars 12.2g; Fat 19.1g, of which saturates 3.3g; Cholesterol 103mg; Calcium 40mg; Fibre 1.5g; Sodium 359mg.

black bean sauce for beef

This Chinese beef dish is a quick stir-fry with a richly flavoured marinade that bubbles down into a luscious, dark sauce. Broccoli, baby corn and water chestnuts bring colour, flavour and texture. The sauce can also be used for chicken or duck – try boneless skinless breast fillets.

Serves 4

INGREDIENTS

225g/8oz lean fillet (beef tenderloin) or
  rump (round) steak
15ml/1 tbsp sunflower oil
225g/8oz broccoli
115g/4oz baby corn, halved diagonally
45–60ml/3–4 tbsp water
2 leeks, diagonally sliced
225g/8oz can water chestnuts, sliced

For the marinade

15ml/1 tbsp fermented black beans
30ml/2 tbsp dark soy sauce
30ml/2 tbsp Chinese rice vinegar or
  cider vinegar
15ml/1 tbsp sunflower oil
5ml/1 tsp sugar
2 garlic cloves, crushed
2.5cm/1in piece of fresh root ginger,
  peeled and finely chopped

1 For the marinade and sauce base, mash the fermented black beans in a non-metallic bowl. Add the remaining ingredients and stir well.

2 Cut the steak into thin slices across the grain, then add them to the marinade. Stir the steak well to coat it in the marinade. Cover the bowl and leave for several hours.

3 Heat the oil in a large frying pan. Drain the steak (reserving the marinade). When the oil is hot, add the meat and stir-fry for 3–4 minutes. Transfer it to a plate and set aside.

4 Cut the broccoli into small florets. Add the broccoli, corn and water to the pan and bring to the boil. Cover and cook gently for about 5 minutes, until tender

COOK'S TIP

Fermented black beans are cooked, salted and fermented whole soya beans; buy them in Oriental stores.

5 Add the leeks and water chestnuts to the broccoli mixture and toss over the heat for 1–2 minutes. Return the meat to the pan, pour over the reserved marinade and toss briefly over a high heat before serving.

Energy 219kcal/912kJ; Protein 19.5g; Carbohydrate 8.4g, of which sugars 5.8g; Fat 12g, of which saturates 3.1g; Cholesterol 33mg; Calcium 69mg; Fibre 4.5g; Sodium 907mg.

quick chilli sauce for sizzling steak

This Malaysian method of sizzling richly marinated meat on a cast iron grill can be applied with equal success to sliced chicken or pork – all will pair up well with the dipping sauce.

Serves four to six

INGREDIENTS

1 garlic clove, crushed
2.5cm/1in fresh root ginger, chopped
10ml/2 tsp black peppercorns
15ml/1 tbsp sugar
30ml/2 tbsp tamarind sauce
45ml/3 tbsp dark soy sauce
15ml/1 tbsp oyster sauce
4 rump (round) steaks, each 200g/7oz
vegetable oil, for brushing
shredded spring onion (scallion) and carrot, to garnish

For the dipping sauce

75ml/5 tbsp beef stock
30ml/2 tbsp tomato ketchup
5ml/1 tsp chilli sauce
juice of 1 lime

1 Pound together the garlic, ginger, peppercorns, sugar and tamarind sauce in a mortar with a pestle. Mix in the soy sauce and oyster sauce, then spoon over the steaks. Cover and set aside in the refrigerator to marinate for at least 1 hour and up to 8 hours.

2 Heat a cast iron grilling plate over high heat until very hot. Scrape the marinade from the meat and reserve. Brush the meat with oil and grill for 2 minutes on each side for rare and 3–4 minutes on each side for medium, depending on thickness.

3 Meanwhile, make the dipping sauce. Pour the marinade into a pan and add the stock, tomato ketchup, chilli sauce and lime juice. Set over a low heat and simmer to heat through.

4 Arrange the steaks on a serving platter and garnish with a mixture of shredded spring onion and carrot. Serve at once, handing the dipping sauce separately.

Energy 216kcal/908kJ; Protein 29.8g; Carbohydrate 6.2g, of which sugars 5.9g; Fat 8.2g, of which saturates 2.6g; Cholesterol 79mg; Calcium 9mg; Fibre 0.1g; Sodium 777mg.

sweet curry peanut sauce with beef

This Thai curry sauce is deliciously rich and thicker than most other Thai curries. Serve with boiled jasmine rice and salted duck's eggs for an authentic taste of Thai cooking.

Serves four to six

INGREDIENTS

600ml/1 pint/2½ cups coconut milk

45ml/3 tbsp red curry paste

45ml/3 tbsp fish sauce

30ml/2 tbsp palm sugar (jaggery)

2 stalks lemon grass, bruised

450g/1lb rump steak cut into thin strips

75g/3oz roasted ground peanuts

2 red chillies, sliced

5 kaffir lime leaves, torn

salt and freshly ground black pepper

2 salted eggs, to serve

10–15 Thai basil leaves, to garnish

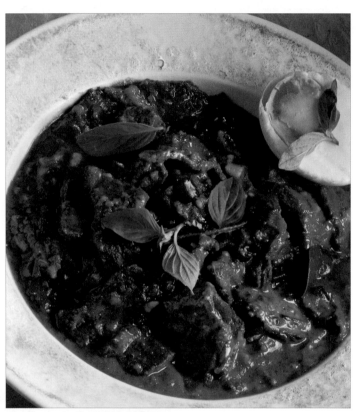

1 Put half the coconut milk into a heavy-bottomed pan and heat, stirring, until it boils and separates.

2 Add the red curry paste and cook until fragrant. Add the fish sauce, palm sugar and lemon grass.

COOK'S TIP

If you don't have the time to make your own red curry paste, you can buy a ready-made Thai curry paste. Most supermarkets now stock a wide range of these.

3 Continue to cook until the colour deepens. Add the rest of the coconut milk, stirring. Bring back to the boil.

4 Add the beef and ground peanuts. Stir to coat the meat thoroughly in the sauce mixture and continue cooking for 8–10 minutes, or until most of the liquid has evaporated.

5 Add the chillies and kaffir lime leaves to the meat mixture. Mix lightly and taste for seasoning, adding a little extra fish sauce to taste, if necessary. Serve at once, with salted eggs and garnish with Thai basil leaves.

Energy 227kcal/953kJ; Protein 21g; Carbohydrate 14.3g, of which sugars 11.5g; Fat 9.9g, of which saturates 2.6g; Cholesterol 44mg; Calcium 92mg; Fibre 2.5g; Sodium 723mg.

roquefort and walnut butter for steak

Make a roll of this savoury cheese-flavoured butter to keep in the refrigerator, ready to top plain steaks or pork chops. It is also delicious with grilled white fish or baked squash.

Serves four

INGREDIENTS

15ml/1 tbsp finely snipped fresh chives

15ml/1 tbsp olive oil or sunflower oil

4 lean rump (round) steaks, about 130g/ 4½oz each

120ml/4fl oz/½ cup dry white wine

30ml/2 tbsp crème fraîche or double (heavy) cream

salt and ground black pepper

fresh chives, to garnish

For the Roquefort and walnut butter

2 shallots, chopped

75g/3oz/6 tbsp butter, slightly softened

150g/5oz Roquefort cheese

30ml/2 tbsp finely chopped walnuts

1 Sauté the shallots in a third of the butter. Turn the mixture into a bowl. Add half the remaining butter, the cheese, walnuts, snipped chives and pepper to taste. Chill lightly, roll in foil to a sausage shape and chill again until firm.

2 Heat the remaining butter and oil and cook the steaks to your liking. Season and remove from the pan.

3 Pour the wine into the pan and stir to incorporate any sediment. Bubble up the liquid for a minute or two, then stir in the crème fraîche or cream. Season with salt and pepper, and pour the sauce over the steaks.

4 Cut pats of the Roquefort butter from the roll and put one on top of each steak. Garnish with chives and serve. Green beans make an ideal accompaniment to this dish.

COOK'S TIP

The butter can also be stored in the freezer, but it is easier to cut it into rounds before freezing, so you can remove just as many as you need, without thawing the rest.

Energy 567kcal/2355kJ; Protein 38g; Carbohydrate 1.2g, of which sugars 1.1g; Fat 43.6g, of which saturates 22.5g; Cholesterol 155mg; Calcium 216mg; Fibre 0.6g; Sodium 655mg.

smoked cheese sauce with veal

Sheep's milk cheese melted with cream makes a simple sauce for serving with pan-fried veal escalopes. The escalopes are used as purchased, not beaten thin.

Serves four

INGREDIENTS

25g/1oz/2 tbsp butter

15ml/1 tbsp extra virgin olive oil

8 small veal escalopes

2 garlic cloves, crushed

250g/9oz/3½ cups button (white) mushrooms or closed-cup mushrooms, sliced

150g/5oz/1¼ cups frozen peas, thawed

60ml/4 tbsp brandy

250ml/8fl oz/1 cup whipping cream

150g/5oz smoked sheep's milk cheese, diced

ground black pepper

sprigs of flat leaf parsley, to garnish

2 Lift the escalopes on to a serving dish and keep hot.

3 Add the remaining butter to the pan. When it melts, stir-fry the garlic and mushrooms for about 3 minutes.

4 Add the peas, pour in the brandy and cook until all the pan juices have been absorbed. Season lightly. Using a slotted spoon, remove the mushrooms and peas and place on top of the escalopes. Pour the cream into the pan.

5 Stir in the diced cheese. Heat gently until the cheese has melted. Season with pepper and pour over the escalopes and vegetables. Serve garnished with flat leaf parsley.

1 Melt half the butter with the oil in a large, heavy-based frying pan. Season the escalopes with plenty of pepper and brown them in batches on each side over a high heat. Reduce the heat and cook for about 5 minutes on each side until just done. The escalopes should feel firm to the touch, with a very light springiness, when tested.

VARIATION

This dish works well with lean pork steaks. Ensure that pork is well cooked, with a slightly longer frying time.

Energy 750kcal/3119kJ; Protein 59.9g; Carbohydrate 6.3g, of which sugars 2.8g; Fat 49.6g, of which saturates 28.9g; Cholesterol 219mg; Calcium 334mg; Fibre 2.5g; Sodium 446mg.

wheat beer sauce for veal

Wheat beers are made in Bavaria, Belgium and northern France, where they are known as bières blanches or white beers. The slight bitterness that the beer gives the sauce in this delectable stew is matched by the sweetness of the caramelized onions and carrots.

Serves four

INGREDIENTS

45ml/3 tbsp plain (all-purpose) flour

900g/2lb boned shoulder or leg of veal, cut into 5cm/2in cubes

65g/2½oz/5 tbsp butter

3 shallots, finely chopped

1 celery stick

fresh parsley sprig

2 fresh bay leaves

5ml/1 tsp caster (superfine) sugar, plus a good pinch

200ml/7fl oz/scant 1 cup wheat beer

450ml/¾ pint/scant 2 cups veal stock

20–25 large silverskin onions or small pickling onions

450g/1lb carrots, thickly sliced

2 large egg yolks

105ml/7 tbsp double (heavy) cream

30ml/2 tbsp chopped fresh parsley

salt and ground black pepper

1 Season the flour and dust the veal in it. Heat 25g/1oz/2 tbsp of the butter in a deep, lidded frying pan, add the veal and quickly seal it on all sides. The veal should be golden but not dark brown. Use a draining spoon to remove the veal from the pan and set aside.

2 Reduce the heat, add another 15g/½oz/1 tbsp butter to the pan and cook the shallots gently for 5–6 minutes, until soft and yellow.

3 Replace the veal. Tie the celery, parsley and 1 bay leaf together in a bundle, then add them to the pan with a good pinch of caster sugar. Increase the heat, pour in the beer and allow to bubble briefly before pouring in the stock. Season, bring to the boil, then cover and simmer gently, stirring once or twice, for 40–50 minutes, or until the veal is cooked and tender.

4 Meanwhile, melt the remaining butter in another frying pan and add the onions, then fry them over a low heat until golden all over. Use a draining spoon to remove the onions from the pan and set aside.

5 Add the carrots and turn to coat them in the butter remaining from the onions. Stir in 5ml/1 tsp caster sugar, a pinch of salt, the remaining bay leaf and enough water to cover the carrots. Bring to the boil and cook uncovered for 10–12 minutes.

6 Return the onions to the pan with the carrots and continue to cook until all but a few tablespoons of the liquid has evaporated and the onions and carrots are slightly caramelized. Keep warm. Transfer the veal to a bowl and discard the celery and herb bundle.

7 Beat the egg yolks and cream together in another bowl, then beat in a ladleful of the hot, but not boiling, carrot liquid. Return this mixture to the pan and cook over a very low heat without boiling, stirring until thickened a little.

8 Add the veal, onions and carrots to the sauce. Reheat and adjust the seasoning, then serve, sprinkled with the parsley.

Energy 660kcal/2752kJ; Protein 52.8g; Carbohydrate 27.8g, of which sugars 16.6g; Fat 37.1g, of which saturates 20.2g; Cholesterol 360mg; Calcium 140mg; Fibre 4.9g; Sodium 399mg.

sauces for fish and shellfish

Fish and shellfish may be delicate but they are also quite distinctive in their flavour. These recipes show just how to combine herbs or spices with the right type of sauce to complement the different strengths of flavour and textures found among fish and shellfish. Spicy and creamy, piquant with horseradish, lively with chilli, or aromatic with Chinese five-spice seasoning, there are plenty of options for producing superb main course meals for all sorts of occasions.

quick parsley sauce for smoked fish

A good, strong, fresh parsley sauce is great with full-flavoured smoked haddock; it is also good with white fish or fish cakes. This recipe is quick to prepare and makes a tasty midweek meal.

Serves four

INGREDIENTS

4 smoked haddock fillets, about
 225g/8oz each

For the quick parsley sauce
75g/3oz/6 tbsp butter, softened
25g/1oz/¼ cup plain (all-purpose) flour
300ml/½ pint/1¼ cups milk
60ml/4 tbsp chopped fresh parsley
salt and ground black pepper
parsley sprigs, to garnish

1 Smear the fish with 50g/2oz/¼ cup butter. Preheat the grill (broiler).

2 Beat the remaining butter and flour together with a wooden spoon to make a smooth, thick paste. Chill the paste to firm it slightly, if necessary, then cut it into lumps.

3 Grill (broil) the fish over a medium high heat for 10–15 minutes, turning when necessary.

4 Meanwhile, heat the milk to just below boiling. Whisk in the lumps of butter and flour. Continue whisking until the sauce boils and thickens. Simmer for 2–3 minutes.

5 Stir in the seasoning and parsley, and serve poured over the fillets, or in a serving jug (pitcher). Serve immediately, garnished with parsley and your choice of vegetables.

Energy 499kcal/2086kJ; Protein 45.6g; Carbohydrate 11.2g, of which sugars 6.4g; Fat 30.6g, of which saturates 18.9g; Cholesterol 157mg; Calcium 228mg; Fibre 0.6g; Sodium 1881mg.

vermouth and chevre sauce for cod

A quick pan sauce of vermouth, creamy goat's cheese, parsley and chervil goes well with chunky cod. Grilled plum tomatoes make the perfect accompaniment.

Serves four

INGREDIENTS

4 pieces cod fillet, about 150g/5oz each, skinned

15ml/2 tbsp olive oil

For the vermouth and chevre sauce

15ml/2 tbsp olive oil

4 spring onions (scallions), chopped

150ml/¼ pint/⅔ cup dry vermouth, preferably Noilly Prat

300ml/½ pint/1¼ cups fish stock

45ml/3 tbsp crème fraîche or double (heavy) cream

65g/2½oz goat's cheese, rind removed, and chopped

30ml/2 tbsp chopped fresh parsley

15ml/1 tbsp chopped fresh chervil

salt and ground black pepper

flat leaf parsley, to garnish

grilled plum tomatoes, to serve

1 Remove any stray bones from the cod. Rinse the fillets under cold running water and pat dry with kitchen paper. Season well.

COOK'S TIP

The sauce will taste delicious with a wide variety of fish, including other types or white fish or salmon. The cooking time may change according to the thickness of the fish fillets.

2 Heat a non-stick frying pan, then add 15ml/1 tbsp of the oil, swirling it around to coat the bottom. Add the fish and cook, without turning or moving the pieces, for 4 minutes, or until browned underneath.

3 Turn the pieces of fish and cook the second sides for 3 minutes, or until just firm. Transfer to a serving plate and keep hot.

4 Heat the remaining oil and stir-fry the spring onions for 1 minute. Add the vermouth and cook until reduced by half. Add the stock and cook again until reduced by half.

5 Stir in the crème fraîche or cream and goat's cheese and simmer for 3 minutes. Add salt and pepper to taste, then stir in the herbs and spoon the sauce over the fish. Garnish with parsley and serve with grilled tomatoes.

Energy 360kcal/1497kJ; Protein 31.7g; Carbohydrate 2.1g, of which sugars 2g; Fat 20.9g, of which saturates 7.7g; Cholesterol 97mg; Calcium 68mg; Fibre 0.7g; Sodium 198mg.

tarragon and mushroom sauce for salmon

Tarragon has a distinctive aniseed flavour that is good with fish and mushrooms, especially in a creamy sauce. Oyster mushrooms have been included for their delicate flavour.

2 Heat the remaining butter in the pan and gently fry the shallot to soften it without letting it colour. Add the mushrooms and cook until the juices begin to flow. Add the stock and simmer for 2–3 minutes.

3 Mix the cornflour and mustard to a smooth paste with 15ml/1 tbsp water. Stir into the sauce and bring to the boil, stirring, until thickened. Add the crème fraîche, tarragon, vinegar, and salt and pepper.

Serves four

INGREDIENTS

50g/2oz/¼ cup unsalted (sweet) butter
4 salmon steaks, about 175g/6oz each
1 shallot, finely chopped
175g/6oz/2½ cups assorted wild and cultivated mushrooms, such as oyster mushrooms, saffron milk-caps, bay boletus or cauliflower fungus, trimmed and sliced
200ml/7fl oz/scant 1 cup chicken or vegetable stock
10ml/2 tsp cornflour (cornstarch)
2.5ml/½ tsp mustard
50ml/3½ tbsp crème fraîche
45ml/3 tbsp chopped fresh tarragon
5ml/1 tsp white wine vinegar
salt and cayenne pepper
new potatoes and a green salad, to serve

1 Melt half the butter in a large, non-stick frying pan. Season the salmon and add to the pan. Cook over a moderate heat for 8 minutes, turning once. (You may have to cook the fish in batches if space in the pan is limited.) Transfer to a plate, cover and keep warm.

4 Spoon the mushrooms over the salmon steaks and serve with new potatoes and a green salad.

COOK'S TIP

Fresh tarragon will bruise and darken quickly after chopping, so prepare the herb just before you use it.

Energy 479kcal/1990kJ; Protein 37g; Carbohydrate 4.4g, of which sugars 1.5g; Fat 35g, of which saturates 13.3g; Cholesterol 128mg; Calcium 76mg; Fibre 1.3g; Sodium 165mg.

spinach and lemon sauce for hake

A light but flavourful sauce of spinach and lemon is the perfect accompaniment to this simple but delicious dish of golden hake sautéed in olive oil.

Serves four

INGREDIENTS

500g/1¼lb fresh spinach, trimmed of thick stalks

4 hake steaks or pieces cod fillet, about 200g/7oz each

30ml/2 tbsp plain (all-purpose) flour

75ml/5 tbsp extra virgin olive oil

175ml/6fl oz/¾ cup white wine

3–4 strips pared lemon rind

salt and ground black pepper

For the egg and lemon sauce

2 large (US extra large) eggs, at room temperature

juice of ½ lemon

2.5ml/½ tsp cornflour (cornstarch)

4 Add the spinach, distributing it evenly around the fish. Let it simmer for 3–4 minutes more, then pull the pan off the heat and let it stand for a few minutes before adding the sauce.

5 To make the sauce, mix the cornflour to a smooth paste with a little water. Beat the eggs. Beat in the lemon juice and the cornflour mixture. Gradually beat in a ladleful of liquid from the fish pan, then beat for 1 minute. Add a second ladleful in the same way, and continue with the rest.

6 Pour the sauce over the fish and spinach, place over very gentle heat and shake to mix the ingredients. If the fish appears too dry, add a little warm water. Allow to cook gently for 2–3 minutes and serve at once.

1 Place the spinach leaves in a large pan with just the water that clings to the leaves after washing. Cover the pan tightly and cook over a medium heat for 5–7 minutes, or until they are cooked. Turn the leaves occasionally using a wooden spoon. Drain and set aside.

2 Dust the fish lightly with the flour and shake off any excess. Heat the olive oil in a large frying pan, add the pieces of fish and sauté gently for 2–3 minutes on each side until the flesh starts to turn golden.

3 Pour in the wine, add the lemon rind and a little seasoning and carefully shake the pan from side to side to blend the flavourings and coat the flesh of the cooking fish. Lower the heat and simmer gently for a few minutes until the wine has reduced a little.

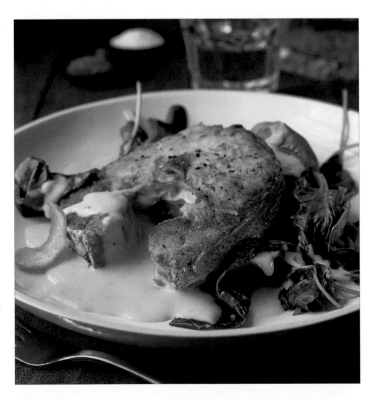

Energy 441kcal/1839kJ; Protein 43.6g; Carbohydrate 10.6g, of which sugars 2.3g; Fat 22.1g, of which saturates 3.5g; Cholesterol 141mg; Calcium 273mg; Fibre 2.9g; Sodium 413mg.

orange and caper sauce for skate

This wonderfully sweet-sour, creamy sauce adds zest to otherwise plain white fish. Slightly peppery and piquant capers are especially good with skate.

Serves four

INGREDIENTS

4 skate wings, about 200g/7oz each
25g/1oz/2 tbsp butter
350ml/12fl oz/1½ cups fish stock

For the orange and caper sauce

25g/1oz/2 tbsp butter
1 onion, chopped
5ml/1 tsp black peppercorns
fish bones and trimmings
300ml/½ pint/1¼ cups dry white wine
2 small oranges
15ml/1 tbsp capers, drained
60ml/4 tbsp crème fraîche
salt and ground white pepper

1 To make the sauce, melt the butter in a non-stick pan and add the onion. Cook, stirring, over a moderate heat for approximately 5 minutes, or until the onion is lightly browned.

2 Add the peppercorns, fish bones and trimmings, and wine. Bring to the boil, reduce the heat and cover. Simmer gently for 30 minutes.

3 Using a serrated knife, peel the oranges, ensuring all the white pith is removed. Ease the segments away from the membrane.

4 Place the skate in a frying pan, add the butter and the fish stock and poach for 10–15 minutes, depending on thickness.

5 Strain the wine sauce into a clean pan. Add the capers and orange segments with any juice, and heat through. Lower the heat and stir in the crème fraîche and seasoning. Serve the skate wings and the sauce, garnished with parsley.

Energy 360kcal/1507kJ; Protein 31.7g; Carbohydrate 8.5g, of which sugars 8.1g; Fat 17.2g, of which saturates 10.6g; Cholesterol 44mg; Calcium 137mg; Fibre 1.5g; Sodium 326mg.

lemon and chive sauce for fishcakes

A fragrant ginger, lemon and chive sauce is an ideal match for these piquant fishcakes.
Flavoured with horseradish and parsley, they are a cut above the rest.

Serves four

INGREDIENTS

350g/12oz potatoes, peeled

75ml/5 tbsp milk

350g/12oz haddock or hoki fillets,
   skinned

15ml/1 tbsp lemon juice

15ml/1 tbsp creamed horseradish

30ml/2 tbsp chopped fresh parsley

flour, for dusting

115g/4oz/2 cups fresh wholemeal
   (whole-wheat) breadcrumbs

salt and ground black pepper

flat leaf parsley sprig, to garnish

mangetouts (snow peas) and a sliced
   tomato and onion salad, to serve

For the lemon and chive sauce

thinly pared rind and juice of ½ small
   lemon

120ml/4fl oz/½ cup dry white wine

2 thin slices fresh root ginger

10ml/2 tsp cornflour (cornstarch)

30ml/2 tbsp chopped fresh chives

1 Cook the potatoes in a large pan of boiling water for 15–20 minutes. Drain and mash with the milk, and season with salt and ground black pepper to taste.

2 Purée the fish together with the lemon juice and horseradish sauce in a food processor or blender. Mix together with the potatoes and parsley.

3 With floured hands, shape the mixture into eight fishcakes and coat with the breadcrumbs. Place on a floured plate, cover with clear film (plastic wrap) and chill in the refrigerator for 30 minutes.

4 Preheated the grill (broiler) to medium and cook the fishcakes for 8 minutes each side, until brown.

5 For the sauce, cut the lemon rind into strips and put in a pan with the lemon juice, wine, ginger and seasoning. Simmer for 6 minutes.

6 Blend 15ml/1 tbsp of cold water into the cornflour. Stir into the sauce, bring to the boil and simmer for 2 minutes. Stir in the chives and serve at once with the fishcakes. Garnish with flat leaf parsley and serve mangetouts and a tomato and onion salad as accompaniments.

Energy 280kcal/1191kJ; Protein 22.5g; Carbohydrate 40.7g, of which sugars 3.8g; Fat 2.1g, of which saturates 0.4g; Cholesterol 33mg; Calcium 102mg; Fibre 2.1g; Sodium 335mg.

orange butter sauce for sea bream

This rich butter sauce, sharpened with tangy orange juice, goes well with the firm white flesh of sea bream served on a bed of fresh mixed salad leaves.

3 Place the orange juice concentrate in a heatproof bowl and heat over a pan of simmering water. Remove the pan from the heat and gradually whisk in the butter until creamy. Season well.

Serves two

INGREDIENTS

2 sea bream, about 350g/12oz each,
  scaled and gutted
10ml/2 tsp Dijon mustard
5ml/1 tsp fennel seeds
30ml/2 tbsp olive oil
50g/2oz watercress
175g/6oz mixed salad leaves

For the orange butter sauce

30ml/2 tbsp frozen orange juice
  concentrate
175g/6oz/¾ cup unsalted (sweet) butter,
  diced
salt and cayenne pepper

1 Slash the fish four times on each side. Mix the mustard and fennel seeds, then spread all over the fish.

2 Preheated the grill (broiler). Brush the fish with olive oil and grill (broil) for 10–12 minutes without burning, turning the fish midway through the cooking time.

4 Dress the watercress and salad leaves with the remaining olive oil, and arrange on two plates. Add the fish to the plates. Spoon the sauce over the fish and serve.

COOK'S TIP

Alternatively, barbecue the bream on a medium-hot barbecue. This is much easier if you use a hinged wire rack that holds the fish firmly and enables you to turn the fish without it breaking up.

Energy 969kcal/4007kJ; Protein 37.1g; Carbohydrate 4.3g, of which sugars 4.3g; Fat 89.5g, of which saturates 47.3g; Cholesterol 263mg; Calcium 166mg; Fibre 1.2g; Sodium 768mg.

tahini sauce for baked fish

This tahini sauce contributes a clever twist of complementary seasoning to this north African recipe that evokes all the colour and rich flavours of Mediterranean cuisine.

Serves four

INGREDIENTS

1 whole fish, about 1.2kg/2½ lb, scaled and cleaned

10ml/2 tsp coriander seeds

4 garlic cloves, sliced

10ml/2 tsp harissa sauce

90ml/6 tbsp olive oil

6 plum tomatoes, sliced

1 mild onion, sliced

3 preserved lemons or 1 fresh lemon

plenty of fresh herbs, such as bay leaves, thyme and rosemary

salt and ground black pepper

extra herbs, to garnish

For the tahini sauce

75ml/2½ fl oz/⅓ cup light tahini

juice of 1 lemon

1 garlic clove, crushed

45ml/3 tbsp finely chopped fresh parsley or coriander (cilantro)

1 Preheat the oven to 200°C/400°F/Gas 6. Grease the base and sides of a large, shallow ovenproof dish.

2 Finely crush the coriander seeds in a mortar, using a pestle. Then add and crush the garlic. Mix in the harissa sauce and stir in about 60ml/4 tbsp of the olive oil until all the ingredients are thoroughly combined in a coarse paste.

3 Slash the fish diagonally on both sides with a sharp knife. Spread a little of the harissa, coriander and garlic paste inside the cavity of the fish. Spread the remainder over each side of the fish, pushing it into the slashes, and set aside.

4 Scatter the tomatoes, onion and preserved or quartered fresh lemon in the greased dish. Sprinkle with the remaining oil, and season. Put the fish on top. Tuck plenty of herbs around it.

5 Bake the fish, uncovered, for about 25 minutes, or until its flesh has turned opaque – test by piercing the thickest part with a knife to ease the flakes apart.

6 Meanwhile, to make the sauce, put the tahini, lemon juice, garlic and parsley or coriander in a small pan. Add 120ml/4fl oz/½ cup cold water and a little salt and ground black pepper. Cook gently, stirring occasionally, until smooth and hot.

7 Garnish the fish with the herbs, and serve the sauce separately.

Energy 423kcal/1755kJ; Protein 33.3g; Carbohydrate 1.5g, of which sugars 0.5g; Fat 31.5g, of which saturates 4.6g; Cholesterol 120mg; Calcium 349mg; Fibre 2.4g; Sodium 112mg.

whisky and cream sauce for salmon

This dish combines two of the finest flavours of Scotland – salmon and whisky. It takes very little time to make, so cook it at the last moment. Serve quite plainly.

Serves four

INGREDIENTS

4 thin pieces salmon fillet, about
   175g/6oz each
5ml/1 tsp chopped fresh thyme leaves
50g/2oz/¼ cup butter

For the whisky and cream sauce
75ml/5 tbsp whisky
150ml/¼ pint/⅔ cup double
   (heavy) cream
juice of ½ lemon (optional)
salt and ground black pepper
fresh dill sprigs, to garnish

VARIATION

Although fresh thyme works particularly
well with this delicious whisky and
cream sauce, you can replace it with
whatever fresh herbs are available.

1 Season the salmon and sprinkle with the thyme. Melt half the butter in a frying pan large enough to hold two pieces of salmon.

2 When the butter is foaming, fry the first two pieces of salmon for 2–3 minutes on each side, until they are golden on the outside and just cooked through.

3 Pour in 30ml/2 tbsp of the whisky and ignite it. When the flames have died down, carefully transfer the salmon to a plate and keep it hot. Heat the remaining butter and repeat with the remaining salmon. Keep hot.

4 Pour the cream into the pan and bring to the boil, stirring constantly and scraping the cooking juices off the pan. Simmer until reduced and slightly thickened. Season and add the last of the whisky and a squeeze of lemon if you like.

5 Place the salmon on warmed plates, pour the sauce over and garnish with dill. New potatoes and green beans are good with this.

Energy 667kcal/2760kJ; Protein 36.1g; Carbohydrate 0.8g, of which sugars 0.8g; Fat 53g, of which saturates 24.5g; Cholesterol 174mg; Calcium 61mg; Fibre 0g; Sodium 164mg.

green peppercorn sauce for salmon

Salmon benefits from being served with a piquant accompaniment. Lemon and lime are the obvious choices, but capers and green peppercorns also serve to counter the rich fish.

Serves four

INGREDIENTS

4 pieces salmon fillet, about
  175g/6oz each
salt and ground black pepper
fresh parsley, to garnish

For the green peppercorn sauce
15g/½oz/1 tbsp butter
2–3 shallots, finely chopped
15ml/1 tbsp brandy (optional)
60ml/4 tbsp white wine
90ml/6 tbsp fish or chicken stock
120ml/4fl oz/½ cup whipping cream
30–45ml/2–3 tbsp green peppercorns
  in brine, rinsed
15–30ml/1–2 tbsp vegetable oil

1 Melt the butter in a heavy pan.
Add the shallots and cook for
1–2 minutes, until just softened.

2 Add the brandy, if using, then
pour in the white wine and stock.
Bring to the boil and reduce by
three-quarters, stirring occasionally.

3 Reduce the heat, then add the
cream and half the peppercorns,
crushing them slightly against the
pan with the back of a spoon.
Cook very gently for 4–5 minutes,
until thickened slightly,

4 Strain the sauce into a clean pan.
Stir in the remaining peppercorns.
Keep the sauce warm over a very
low heat, stirring occasionally,
while you cook the salmon fillets.

5 Heat the oil in a large, heavy
frying pan over medium-high heat.
Lightly season the salmon. Sear the
fillets on both sides, then lower the
heat and cook for 4–6 minutes,
until the flesh is opaque through.
Arrange the fish on warmed plates
and pour over the sauce. Garnish
with parsley and serve.

COOK'S TIP

Green peppercorns are available
pickled in jars or cans for adding to all
kinds of sauces and stews. Rinse the
peppercorns before use.

Energy 497kcal/2063kJ; Protein 36.2g; Carbohydrate 2.1g, of which sugars 1.8g; Fat 37.2g, of which saturates 13.3g; Cholesterol 127mg; Calcium 60mg; Fibre 0.2g; Sodium 110mg.

tomato coulis for marinated monkfish

A light but well-flavoured sauce, this should be made when Italian plum tomatoes are at their ripest. The lime and herb marinade is offset by the sweet tomatoes in the coulis. Serve this delicious dish with a glass of chilled white wine.

Serves four

INGREDIENTS

30ml/2 tbsp olive oil
finely grated rind and juice of 1 lime
30ml/2 tbsp chopped fresh mixed herbs
5ml/1 tsp Dijon mustard
4 skinless, boneless monkfish fillets
salt and ground black pepper
fresh herb sprigs, to garnish

For the tomato coulis

4 plum tomatoes, peeled and chopped
1 garlic clove, chopped
15ml/1 tbsp olive oil
15ml/1 tbsp tomato purée (paste)
30ml/2 tbsp chopped fresh oregano
5ml/1 tsp light soft brown sugar

2 Place the monkfish fillets in a shallow, non-metallic container and pour the lime mixture over. Turn the fish several times in the marinade to coat the pieces evenly. Cover and chill for 1–2 hours.

5 Meanwhile, make the tomato coulis. Place all the coulis ingredients in a food processor or blender and process until smooth. Season to taste, then pour the mixture into a serving dish. Cover and chill until required.

1 Place the oil, lime rind and juice, herbs, mustard, and salt and pepper in a small bowl or jug and whisk together until thoroughly mixed.

3 Preheat the oven to 180°C/350°F/ Gas 4. Cut four pieces of greaseproof (waxed) paper, each large enough to hold a fish fillet. Place the fillets on the papers.

4 Spoon a little marinade over each piece of fish. Gather the paper loosely over the fish and fold over the edges to secure the parcel tightly. Place on a baking sheet. Bake for 20–30 minutes, or until the fish fillets are cooked, tender and just beginning to flake.

6 Carefully unwrap the baked fish parcels and transfer the fish fillets to warm serving plates. Add a little of the chilled coulis and garnish with a few fresh herb sprigs. Serve immediately, offering the remaining coulis separately.

COOK'S TIP

The coulis can be served hot, if you prefer. Simply make as directed in the recipe and heat gently in a pan until almost boiling, just before serving.

VARIATION

Tomato coulis is also delicious seasoned with dill and lemon instead of garlic and oregano. Add the grated rind of 1 lemon, and use dill instead of oregano. Omit the garlic. This is good with fine-textured white fish fillets.

Energy 197kcal/830kJ; Protein 24.5g; Carbohydrate 4.7g, of which sugars 4.7g; Fat 9.2g, of which saturates 1.4g; Cholesterol 21mg; Calcium 21mg; Fibre 1.1g; Sodium 45mg.

tomato-lime sauce for swordfish

This spicy tomato sauce is tempered with crème fraîche, making it a wonderful accompaniment to swordfish. The swordfish can be cooked over the barbecue.

Serves four

INGREDIENTS

4 swordfish steaks, about 225g/8oz each

For the tomato-lime sauce

2 fresh chillies

4 tomatoes

45ml/3 tbsp olive oil

grated rind and juice of 1 lime

2.5ml/½ tsp salt

2.5ml/½ tsp ground black pepper

175ml/6fl oz/¾ cup crème fraîche

fresh flat leaf parsley, to garnish

chargrilled vegetables, to serve

1 Roast the chillies in a dry griddle pan until the skins are blistered. Seal in a plastic bag and leave for 20 minutes. Then peel off the skins, discard the seeds and slice the flesh.

2 Cut a cross in the bases the tomatoes. Place them in a heatproof bowl and pour over boiling water to cover. After 30 seconds, transfer the tomatoes to a bowl of cold water. Drain. The skins will have begun to peel off.

3 Peel the tomatoes, then cut them in half and squeeze out the seeds. Using a serrated knife, chop the tomato flesh into 1cm/½in pieces.

4 Heat 15ml/1 tbsp of the oil in a small pan and add the strips of chilli, with the lime rind and juice. Cook for 2–3 minutes, then stir in the tomatoes. Cook for 10 minutes, stirring the mixture occasionally, until the tomatoes are pulpy.

5 Brush the swordfish steaks with oil and season. Cook on a barbecue or grill (broil) for 3–4 minutes or until just cooked, turning once.

6 Meanwhile, stir the crème fraîche into the sauce, heat it through gently and pour over the swordfish steaks. Garnish with parsley and serve with chargrilled vegetables.

Energy 502kcal/2089kJ; Protein 42.2g; Carbohydrate 4.2g, of which sugars 4g; Fat 35.3g, of which saturates 15.2g; Cholesterol 142mg; Calcium 42mg; Fibre 1g; Sodium 311mg.

sweet chilli sauce for red snapper

This colourful dish combines aromatic bay leaves and olives with fresh green chillies in a rich tomato sauce that tastes terrific with baked fish.

Serves four

INGREDIENTS

4 red snappers, cleaned
juice of 2 limes
4 garlic cloves, crushed
5ml/1 tsp dried oregano
2.5ml/½ tsp salt
drained bottled capers, to garnish
lime wedges, to serve (optional)
lime rind, to garnish

For the sweet chilli sauce

120ml/4fl oz/½ cup olive oil
2 bay leaves
2 garlic cloves, sliced
4 fresh chillies, seeded and cut in strips
1 onion, thinly sliced
450g/1lb fresh tomatoes
75g/3oz/⅓ cup pickled jalapeño chilli slices
15ml/1 tbsp soft dark brown sugar
2.5ml/½ tsp ground cloves
2.5ml/½ tsp ground cinnamon
150g/5oz/1¼ cups green olives stuffed with pimiento

1 Preheat the oven to 180°C/350°F/ Gas 4. Rinse the fish inside and out. Pat dry with kitchen paper. Place in a large roasting pan in a single layer.

2 Mix the lime juice, garlic, oregano and salt. Pour the mixture evenly all over the fish. Bake for about 30 minutes, or until the flesh flakes easily.

3 Make the sauce. Heat the oil in a pan, add the bay leaves, garlic and chilli strips. Cook, stirring frequently, for 3–4 minutes, until the chilli is softened slightly.

4 Add the onion to the pan and cook for a further 3–4 minutes, stirring often, until the onion is softened and translucent. Keep the heat low and stir the onions often so that they do not brown.

5 Cut a cross in the base of each tomato. Place in a heatproof bowl and pour over boiling water to cover. After 30 seconds, lift the tomatoes out on a slotted spoon and plunge them into a bowl of cold water. Drain. The skins will have begun to peel back.

6 Peel the tomatoes, then cut them in half and squeeze out the seeds. Chop the flesh finely and add it to the onion. Cook for 3–4 minutes, until the tomato begins to soften.

7 Add the pickled jalapeños, brown sugar, ground cloves and cinnamon to the sauce. Cook for 10 minutes, stirring frequently. Finally, stir in the olives.

8 Pour a little sauce over each fish. Garnish with the capers and lime rind and serve with lime wedges for squeezing over the fish, if you like. Rice goes well with the fish.

Energy 382kcal/1591kJ; Protein 30.7g; Carbohydrate 8.6g, of which sugars 8.3g; Fat 25.2g, of which saturates 3.9g; Cholesterol 56mg; Calcium 97mg; Fibre 2.4g; Sodium 970mg.

aniseed tomato sauce for fish cutlets

This dish is perfect for a dinner party – the white flesh of the fish contrasts with the striking red sauce and the pastis extends the flavour range. It makes a delicious meal to remember.

Serves four

INGREDIENTS

4 white fish cutlets, about 150g/
  5oz each

150ml/¼ pint/⅔ cup fish stock and/or dry
  white wine, for poaching

1 bay leaf

a few black peppercorns

strip of pared lemon rind

fresh parsley and lemon wedges,
  to garnish

For the tomato sauce

400g/14oz can chopped tomatoes

1 garlic clove

15ml/1 tbsp sun-dried tomato purée
  (paste), or tomato purée (paste)

15ml/1 tbsp pastis or other aniseed
  flavoured liqueur

15ml/1 tbsp drained capers

12–16 black olives, pitted

salt and ground black pepper

1 Make the sauce. Heat the chopped tomatoes in a pan with the garlic. Stir in the sun-dried tomato purée or tomato purée.

2 Measure the pastis or other liqueur into the pan, then add the capers and olives. Season with salt and black pepper. Heat for 5 minutes, stirring occasionally, to blend the flavours.

3 Place the fish, stock and/or wine and flavourings in a frying pan. Cover and simmer for 10 minutes, until the fish flakes easily.

4 Transfer the fish to a heated dish. Strain the stock into the sauce and boil to reduce slightly. Season the sauce and pour it over the fish. Serve immediately, with parsley and lemon wedges.

Energy 183kcal/771kJ; Protein 28.5g; Carbohydrate 3.9g, of which sugars 3.9g; Fat 2.5g, of which saturates 0.4g; Cholesterol 69mg; Calcium 31mg; Fibre 1.4g; Sodium 335mg.

chilli tomato sauce for salmon

This spicy tomato and mustard sauce is delicious served with chargrilled salmon fillets – cook them either on a barbecue or under a hot grill.

Serves four

INGREDIENTS

4 salmon fillets, about 175g/6oz

For the chilli barbecue sauce
10ml/2 tsp butter
1 small red onion, finely chopped
1 garlic clove, finely chopped
6 plum tomatoes, diced
45ml/3 tbsp tomato ketchup
30ml/2 tbsp Dijon mustard
30ml/2 tbsp soft dark brown sugar
15ml/1 tbsp clear honey
5ml/1 tsp ground cayenne pepper
15ml/1 tbsp ancho chilli powder
15ml/1 tbsp ground paprika
15ml/1 tbsp Worcestershire sauce

1 To make the barbecue sauce, melt the butter in a large, heavy pan and gently cook the chopped onion and garlic until tender and translucent.

2 Stir in the tomatoes and simmer for 15 minutes, stirring occasionally to break up the tomato pieces.

3 Add the ketchup, mustard, sugar, honey, cayenne pepper, chilli powder, paprika and Worcestershire sauce. Stir well until thoroughly combined and just about to boil. Reduce the heat and simmer for a further 20 minutes.

4 Cool the sauce a little, then purée it in a blender or food processor until smooth. Leave to cool. Brush the salmon with the cold sauce and chill for at least 2 hours.

5 Barbecue or grill (broil) the salmon for about 2–3 minutes on each side, brushing on the sauce when necessary. Serve drizzled with the remaining sauce.

Energy 431kcal/1802kJ; Protein 37.4g; Carbohydrate 21.1g, of which sugars 20.5g; Fat 22.4g, of which saturates 4.8g; Cholesterol 93mg; Calcium 70mg; Fibre 1.8g; Sodium 558mg.

almond and tomato sauce for prawns

Ground almonds add an interesting texture and delicate nutty taste to the creamy, piquant sauce that accompanies these succulent shellfish.

Serves six

INGREDIENTS

900g/2lb cooked, peeled prawns (shrimp)

For the almond and tomato sauce

1 dried chilli

1 onion

3 garlic cloves

30ml/2 tbsp vegetable oil

8 plum tomatoes

5ml/1 tsp ground cumin

120ml/4fl oz/½ cup chicken stock

130g/4½oz/generous 1 cup ground almonds

175ml/6fl oz/¾ cup crème fraîche

½ lime

salt

fresh coriander (cilantro) and spring onion (scallion) strips, to garnish

cooked rice and warm tortillas, to serve

1 Place the dried chilli in a heatproof bowl and cover with boiling water. Leave to soak for 30 minutes. Drain, remove the stalk, then slit the chilli and scrape out the seeds. Chop the flesh roughly and set it aside.

VARIATION

Try this sauce with other fish. Adding a few prawns (shrimp) and serving it over sole makes a very luxurious dish.

2 Chop the onion finely and then crush the garlic. Heat the oil in a frying pan and fry the onion and garlic over a low heat until soft.

3 Cut a cross in the base of each tomato. Place them in a heatproof bowl and cover with boiling water. After 30 seconds, lift them out with a slotted spoon and plunge them into a bowl of cold water. Drain.

4 Skin and seed the tomatoes. Chop the flesh into 1cm/½ in cubes and stir them into the onion in the frying pan, with the chopped chilli and ground cumin. Cook for 10 minutes, stirring occasionally.

5 Pour the mixture into a food processor or blender. Add the stock and process until smooth.

6 Pour the mixture into a large pan, then add the ground almonds and stir over a low heat for 2–3 minutes. Stir in the crème fraîche until it has been incorporated completely.

7 Squeeze the juice from the lime into the sauce and stir it in. Season with salt to taste, then increase the heat and bring the sauce to simmering point.

8 Add the prawns to the sauce and heat until warmed through. Do not boil or cook for too long once the prawns are added or they will become very tough. Serve on a bed of hot rice garnished with the coriander and spring onion strips. Offer warm tortillas separately.

Energy 416kcal/1732kJ; Protein 32.7g; Carbohydrate 7.1g, of which sugars 6.2g; Fat 28.7g, of which saturates 9.6g; Cholesterol 325mg; Calcium 199mg; Fibre 3.1g; Sodium 307mg.

sorrel sauce for salmon

The sharp, almost lemon-like flavour of the sorrel is delicious with salmon or trout. Young sorrel has the best flavour, so it is worth growing the herb in a large pot or kitchen garden.

Serves four

INGREDIENTS

25g/1oz/2 tbsp butter

4 shallots, finely chopped

90ml/6 tbsp crème fraîche or double (heavy) cream

100g/3½oz fresh sorrel leaves, washed and patted dry

salt and ground black pepper

1 Melt the butter in a heavy pan over a medium heat. Add the shallots and fry for 2–3 minutes, stirring frequently, until just softened.

2 Stir in the crème fraîche or double (heavy) cream. Add the sorrel to the shallots and cook until the leaves are completely wilted, stirring constantly.

3 Spoon the cream and sorrel mixture into a food processor and process for just long enough to chop the sorrel and distribute the pieces evenly throughout the sauce.

4 Return the sauce to the clean pan, season with salt and pepper and heat gently. Serve hot.

VARIATION

If sorrel is not available, use finely chopped watercress instead.

Energy 147kcal/605kJ; Protein 1.5g; Carbohydrate 3g, of which sugars 2.3g; Fat 14.4g, of which saturates 9.4g; Cholesterol 39mg; Calcium 63mg; Fibre 0.9g; Sodium 79mg.

green tartare sauce for seafood pasta

This colourful sauce is good with all kinds of seafood, particularly fresh scallops, and it looks stunning over black, squid ink pasta.

Serves four

INGREDIENTS

350g/12oz black tagliatelle
12 large scallops
60ml/4 tbsp white wine
150ml/¼ pint/⅝ cup fish stock
lime wedges and parsley sprigs,
  to garnish

For the green tartare sauce

120ml/4fl oz/½ cup crème fraîche
10ml/2 tsp wholegrain mustard
2 garlic cloves, crushed
30–45ml/2–3 tbsp fresh lime juice
60ml/4 tbsp chopped fresh parsley
30ml/2 tbsp chopped chives
salt and ground black pepper

4 Put the white wine and fish stock into a pan. Heat to simmering point. Add the scallops and cook very gently for 3–4 minutes (no longer or they will become tough).

5 Remove the scallops from the pan. Boil the wine and stock to reduce by half and add the tartare sauce to the pan. Heat gently to warm the sauce.

6 Replace the scallops and heat for 1 minute. Spoon the sauce over the pasta and garnish with lime wedges and parsley.

COOK'S TIPS

• If you are removing the scallops from the shells yourself, remember to wash them first in plenty of cold water.
• If the scallops are frozen, defrost them before cooking, as they will probably have been glazed with water and will need to be drained well.

VARIATIONS

• This sauce could be made equally well with fresh mussels.
• Instead of serving over pasta, this sauce would go particularly well with fish dishes, such as monkfish, which has a flavour reminiscent of lobster.

1 To make the tartare sauce, blend the crème fraîche, mustard, garlic, lime juice, parsley, chives and seasoning together in a food processor or blender.

2 Cook the pasta in a large pan of boiling, salted water according to the instructions on the packet until *al dente*. Drain thoroughly.

3 Meanwhile, slice the scallops in half, horizontally. Keep any corals whole.

Energy 508kcal/2144kJ; Protein 26.1g; Carbohydrate 68.5g, of which sugars 3.9g; Fat 15.7g, of which saturates 8.6g; Cholesterol 62mg; Calcium 86mg; Fibre 3.1g; Sodium 121mg.

classic tartare sauce for crab cakes

When serving any fried fish, tartare sauce is the traditional accompaniment. Maryland is renowned for its seafood, and these little crab cakes hail from there.

Serves four

INGREDIENTS

675g/1½lb fresh white crab meat

1 egg, beaten

30ml/2 tbsp mayonnaise

15ml/1 tbsp Worcestershire sauce

15ml/1 tbsp sherry

30ml/2 tbsp finely chopped fresh parsley

15ml/1 tbsp finely chopped fresh chives

45ml/3 tbsp olive oil

salt and ground black pepper

For the tartare sauce

1 egg yolk

15ml/1 tbsp white wine vinegar

30ml/2 tbsp Dijon mustard

250ml/8fl oz/1 cup vegetable oil

30ml/2 tbsp lemon juice

45ml/3 tbsp finely chopped spring onion (scallion)

30ml/2 tbsp chopped capers

45ml/3 tbsp finely chopped sour dill pickles

45ml/3 tbsp finely chopped fresh parsley

1 Pick over the crab meat, removing any shell or cartilage. Keep the pieces of crab large.

2 Mix the beaten egg with the mayonnaise, Worcestershire sauce, sherry, herbs and seasoning. Fold in the crab. Divide the mixture into eight and form into an oval cakes.

3 Place the crab cakes on a baking sheet between layers of waxed paper and chill for at least 1 hour.

4 For the sauce, whisk the yolk, vinegar, mustard and seasoning. Whisk in the oil in a slow stream. Mix in the lemon juice, spring onions, capers, dill pickles and parsley. Cover and chill.

5 Preheat the grill (broiler). Brush the surface of the crab cakes with olive oil. Place them on a baking sheet and cook until golden, about 5 minutes each side. Serve hot with the tartare sauce.

Energy 701kcal/2899kJ; Protein 33.4g; Carbohydrate 1.4g, of which sugars 1.3g; Fat 62g, of which saturates 8.1g; Cholesterol 225mg; Calcium 238mg; Fibre 0.4g; Sodium 1029mg.

horseradish sauce for baked cod

Fish keeps moist when baked in a sauce. In this Ukrainian recipe, a creamy horseradish sauce is served alongside, for added flavour.

Serves four

INGREDIENTS

4 thick pieces cod fillet or steaks

15ml/1 tbsp lemon juice

25g/1oz/2 tbsp butter

25g/1oz/¼ cup plain (all-purpose) flour, sifted

150ml/¼ pint/⅔ cup milk

150ml/¼ pint/⅔ cup fish stock

salt and ground black pepper

sprigs of flat leaf parsley, to garnish

potato wedges and fried sliced leeks, to serve

For the horseradish sauce

30ml/2 tbsp tomato purée (paste)

30ml/2 tbsp grated fresh horseradish

150ml/¼ pint/⅔ cup sour cream

1 Preheat the oven to 180°C/350°F/ Gas 4. Place the fish in a buttered ovenproof dish in a single layer. Sprinkle with lemon juice.

2 Melt the butter in a small, heavy pan. Stir in the flour and cook for 3–4 minutes, or until lightly golden. Stir to stop the flour sticking to the pan. Remove from the heat.

3 Gradually whisk the milk, and then the fish stock, into the flour mixture. Season with salt and ground black pepper. Replace the pan on the heat. Bring the sauce back to the boil, stirring, and simmer for 3 minutes, still stirring. The sauce should be smooth and thickened. Taste to check the seasoning when the sauce has finished simmering.

4 Pour the sauce over the fish and bake for 20–25 minutes, depending on the thickness. Check by gently inserting a knife into the thickest part: the flesh should be opaque.

5 Meanwhile, make the horseradish sauce: blend the tomato purée and horseradish with the sour cream in a small pan. Slowly bring the sauce to the boil, stirring to prevent it from sticking to the pan, and then simmer for 1 minute, until thickened. Pour the horseradish sauce into a serving bowl

6 Serve the fish immediately it is cooked, garnished with the parsley sprigs. Serve with the horseradish sauce, potato wedges and fried sliced leeks.

Energy 319kcal/1334kJ; Protein 35.6g; Carbohydrate 10.5g, of which sugars 5.5g; Fat 15.2g, of which saturates 8.6g; Cholesterol 120mg; Calcium 111mg; Fibre 0.6g; Sodium 261mg.

romesco sauce for grilled prawns

This sauce, from the Catalan region of Spain, is served with fish and seafood. Its main ingredients are sweet pepper, tomatoes, garlic and toasted almonds.

Serves four

INGREDIENTS

24 raw king prawns (shrimp)
30–45ml/2–3 tbsp olive oil
fresh flat leaf parsley, to garnish
lemon wedges, to serve

For the romesco sauce

2 well-flavoured tomatoes
60ml/4 tbsp olive oil
1 onion, chopped
4 garlic cloves, chopped
1 canned pimiento, chopped
2.5ml/½ tsp dried chilli flakes or powder
75ml/5 tbsp fish stock
30ml/2 tbsp sherry or white wine
10 blanched almonds
15ml/1 tbsp red wine vinegar
salt

1 To make the sauce, immerse the tomatoes in boiling water for about 30 seconds, remove from the pan with a slotted spoon, then refresh them under cold water. Peel away the skins and roughly chop the flesh.

2 Heat 30ml/2 tbsp of the oil in a pan, add the onion and 3 of the garlic cloves, and cook until soft.

3 Add the pimiento, tomatoes, chilli, fish stock and sherry or wine. Bring to the boil, reduce the heat, then cover and simmer for 30 minutes. Allow to cool slightly.

4 Meanwhile, toast the almonds under the grill until golden.

5 Transfer the almonds to a blender or food processor and grind coarsely.

6 Add the remaining 30ml/2 tbsp of oil, the vinegar and the last garlic clove and process the mixture until it is evenly combined.

7 Carefully add the tomato and pimiento sauce (in batches if necessary) and process until smooth. Season with salt to taste and return to the rinsed pan to keep warm.

8 Remove the heads from the prawns, leaving them otherwise unshelled. With a sharp knife, slit each one down the back and remove the dark vein. Rinse and pat dry on kitchen paper. Preheat the grill (broiler).

9 Toss the prawns in olive oil, then spread out in the grill pan. Grill (broil) for about 2–3 minutes on each side, until pink. Arrange the prawns on a serving platter and garnish with parsley. Serve at once with the lemon wedges, and the sauce in a small bowl.

VARIATION

In Catalonia, romesco sauce is also served with local spicy sausages, grilled fish and poultry dishes. Spoonfuls can also be added to enrich a fish or chicken stew, rather like a rouille is used in French cooking.

Energy 244kcal/1010kJ; Protein 10.7g; Carbohydrate 4.7g, of which sugars 4.2g; Fat 19.9g, of which saturates 2.7g; Cholesterol 98mg; Calcium 62mg; Fibre 1.5g; Sodium 102mg.

tomato and basil salsa for halibut

This fresh-tasting tomato salsa is enlivened with jalapeño pepper and basil. It is ideal with seasoned halibut, grilled or barbecued, and a simple herb garnish.

Serves four

INGREDIENTS

4 halibut fillets, about 175g/6oz each
45ml/3 tbsp olive oil
basil leaves, to garnish

For the salsa

1 tomato, roughly chopped
¼ red onion, finely sliced
1 small jalapeño pepper, chopped
30ml/2 tbsp balsamic vinegar
10 large fresh basil leaves
15ml/1 tbsp olive oil
salt and ground black pepper

1 To make the salsa, mix together the chopped tomato, red onion, jalapeño pepper and balsamic vinegar in a bowl. Slice the fresh basil leaves finely, using a sharp kitchen knife.

2 Stir the basil and the olive oil into the tomato mixture. Season to taste. Cover the bowl with clear film (plastic wrap) and leave to marinate for at least 3 hours.

3 Rub the halibut fillets with oil, and season. Cook under a medium grill (broiler), or on a barbecue, for 8 minutes, basting with oil and turning once. Garnish with basil and serve with the salsa.

COOK'S TIP

It is easy to overcook halibut, making it dry and spoiling its excellent flavour.

Energy 265kcal/1112kJ; Protein 38.1g; Carbohydrate 2g, of which sugars 1.7g; Fat 11.7g, of which saturates 1.7g; Cholesterol 61mg; Calcium 61mg; Fibre 0.6g; Sodium 109mg.

tropical fruit salsa for salmon

Fresh salmon, cooked on the barbecue, is good enough to serve on its own, but tastes even better with this colourful and tasty combination of mango, papaya and chilli.

Serves four

INGREDIENTS

4 salmon steaks or fillets, each about 175g/6oz

finely grated rind and juice of ½ lime

salt and ground black pepper

For the romesco sauce

finely grated rind and juice of ½ lime

1 small, ripe mango

1 small, ripe papaya

1 fresh red chilli

45ml/3 tbsp chopped fresh coriander (cilantro)

salt and ground black pepper

4 Add the chopped fresh coriander to the bowl and mix gently with a large spoon. Stir in the remaining lime rind and juice. Season to taste.

5 Cook the salmon on an oiled barbecue grill over medium-hot coals for 5–8 minutes, turning once. Serve freshly cooked, with the tropical fruit salsa.

COOK'S TIPS

• If fresh chillies are not available, use about 2.5ml/½ tsp of chilli paste from a jar, or add a dash of chilli sauce.

• You may prefer to cook the salmon steaks inside on the griddle, in which case simply add 5ml/1 tsp olive oil to the marinade in step 1.

1 Lay the pieces of salmon in a dish and sprinkle with lime rind and juice. Season well.

2 Remove the stone (pit) from the mango. Finely chop the flesh and put it in a bowl. Halve the papaya, scoop out and discard the seeds and remove the skin. Chop the flesh finely and add it to the mango.

3 Cut the chilli in half lengthways. For a milder flavour, remove the seeds. Leave the seeds to make the salsa hot. Finely chop the chilli and stir it into the chopped fruit.

Energy 376kcal/1573kJ; Protein 36.5g; Carbohydrate 14.4g, of which sugars 14.2g; Fat 19.6g, of which saturates 3.4g; Cholesterol 88mg; Calcium 87mg; Fibre 3.8g; Sodium 88mg.

sauce vierge for grilled halibut

Any thick white fish fillets can be cooked in this versatile dish; turbot, brill and John Dory are especially delicious, but the flavoursome sauce also gives humbler white fish a real lift.

Serves four

INGREDIENTS

2.5ml/½ tsp fennel seeds

2.5ml/½ tsp celery seeds

105ml/7 tbsp olive oil

5ml/1 tsp mixed peppercorns

coarse sea salt

5ml/1 tsp fresh thyme leaves, chopped

5ml/1 tsp fresh rosemary leaves, chopped

5ml/1 tsp fresh oregano or marjoram leaves, chopped

675–800g/1½–1¾lb middle cut of halibut, about 3cm/1¼in thick, cut into 4 pieces

For the sauce vierge

105ml/7 tbsp extra virgin olive oil, plus extra for cooking

juice of 1 lemon

1 garlic clove, finely chopped

2 tomatoes, peeled, seeded and diced

5ml/1 tsp small capers

2 drained canned anchovy fillets, chopped

5ml/1 tsp snipped fresh chives

15ml/1 tbsp shredded fresh basil leaves

15ml/1 tbsp chopped fresh chervil

1 Mix the fennel and celery seeds with the peppercorns in a mortar. Crush with a pestle, and then stir in the coarse sea salt to taste. Spoon the mixture into a shallow dish and stir in the herbs and the olive oil.

2 Heat a ridged grilling pan or preheat the grill (broiler) on high. Brush the grilling pan or grill pan with a little olive oil to prevent the fish from sticking during cooking.

3 Add the halibut pieces to the olive oil mixture, turning them to coat them thoroughly, then arrange them with the dark skin uppermost in the oiled grilling pan or grill pan. Cook for about 6–8 minutes, turning once, until the fish is cooked all the way through and the skin has browned.

4 Combine the sauce ingredients, except the fresh herbs, in a pan and heat gently until warm but not hot. Stir in the chives, basil and chervil.

5 Place the halibut on four warmed plates. Spoon the sauce around and over the fish and serve immediately, with lightly-cooked green cabbage.

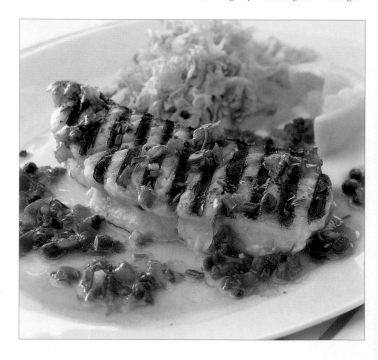

Energy 462kcal/1920kJ; Protein 37.4g; Carbohydrate 1.9g, of which sugars 1.8g; Fat 33.9g, of which saturates 4.9g; Cholesterol 60mg; Calcium 82mg; Fibre 1.1g; Sodium 169mg.

spicy pesto for rolled salmon

This is a great way to serve salmon steaks boneless, as a solid piece of fish. The pesto uses sunflower kernels and chilli as its flavouring rather than the classic basil and pine nuts.

Serves four

INGREDIENTS

4 salmon steaks, about 225g/8oz each
30ml/2 tbsp sunflower oil
finely grated rind and juice of 1 lime
salt and ground black pepper

For the spicy pesto

6 fresh mild red chillies, seeded and
  roughly chopped
2 garlic cloves
30ml/2 tbsp pumpkin or sunflower seeds
finely grated rind and juice of 1 lime
75ml/5 tbsp olive oil

1 Place a salmon steak flat on a board. Insert a very sharp knife close to the top of the bone. Staying close to the bone all the time, cut to the end of the steak to release one side of the steak. Repeat with the other side.

2 Place one piece of salmon skin side down and hold it firmly with one hand. Insert a small sharp knife under the skin and, working away from you, cut the flesh off in a single piece. Repeat with the remaining salmon steaks.

3 Wrap each piece of fish into a circle, with the thinner end wrapped around the fatter end. Tie with string (twine). Place in a shallow bowl.

4 Rub the oil into the boneless fish rounds. Add the lime juice and rind to the bowl. Cover and marinate in the refrigerator for 2 hours.

5 Make the pesto. Process the chillies, garlic, pumpkin or sunflower seeds, lime rind and juice and seasoning in a food processor. until well mixed. With the machine running, gradually add the olive oil. The pesto will slowly thicken and emulsify. Scrape it into a bowl. Preheat the grill (broiler).

6 Drain the salmon and place the rounds in a grill pan. Grill (broil) for 5 minutes on each side or until opaque. Serve with the spicy pesto.

COOK'S TIP

If any small bones remain in the salmon steaks after preparation, remove them with fish tweezers or a pair of new eyebrow tweezers kept for the purpose.

Energy 627kcal/2601kJ; Protein 47.7g; Carbohydrate 1.6g, of which sugars 0.3g; Fat 47.7g, of which saturates 7.3g; Cholesterol 113mg; Calcium 63mg; Fibre 0.5g; Sodium 103mg.

oyster sauce for turbot fillets

This luxurious oyster sauce is perfect for special occasions. It is worth buying a whole turbot and asking the fishmonger to fillet and skin it for you. Keep the head, bones and trimmings for stock. Sole, brill and halibut can all be substituted for the turbot.

Serves four

INGREDIENTS

1 turbot, about 1.8kg/4lb, filleted and skinned

salt and ground white pepper

For the oyster sauce

12 Pacific (rock) oysters

115g/4oz/½ cup butter

2 carrots, cut into julienne strips

200g/7oz celeriac, cut into julienne strips

the white parts of 2 leeks, cut into julienne strips

375ml/13fl oz/generous 1½ cups Champagne or dry white sparkling wine (about ½ bottle)

105ml/7 tbsp whipping cream

salt and ground white pepper

1 Using an oyster knife, open the oysters over a bowl to catch the juices, then carefully remove them from their shells, discarding the shells, and place them in a separate bowl. Set the oysters aside until required.

2 Melt 25g/1oz/2 tbsp of the butter in a pan, add the vegetables and cook gently until tender but not coloured. Add half the Champagne and cook gently until evaporated, without browning the vegetables.

3 Strain the oyster juices into a small pan. Add the cream and remaining Champagne. Place over a medium heat until reduced to the consistency of thin cream. Dice half the remaining butter and whisk it in, a piece at a time. Season. Whizz in a blender until velvet-smooth.

4 Reheat the sauce to just below boiling. Add and poach the oysters for 1 minute, until warm but barely cooked. Keep warm; do not boil.

5 Season the turbot. Heat the rest of the butter in a large frying pan until foaming. Fry the fish over a medium heat for 2–3 minutes each side until cooked and golden.

6 Cut each fillet into three and arrange on warm plates. Pile the vegetables on top, then add the oysters and sauce around the fillets.

Energy 784kcal/3263kJ; Protein 72.9g; Carbohydrate 9.6g, of which sugars 7.5g; Fat 44.8g, of which saturates 24g; Cholesterol 132mg; Calcium 330mg; Fibre 1g; Sodium 630mg.

light curry sauce for john dory fillets

This excellent combination of flavours also works well with other flat fish like turbot, halibut and brill, or more exotic species like mahi-mahi or orange roughy. The curry taste should be very subtle, so use a mild curry powder. Serve the fish with pilau rice and mango chutney.

Serves four

INGREDIENTS

4 John Dory fillets, about 175g/6oz each, skinned

15ml/1 tbsp sunflower oil

25g/1oz/2 tbsp butter

salt and ground black pepper

For the curry sauce

30ml/2 tbsp sunflower oil

1 carrot, chopped

1 onion, chopped

1 celery stick, chopped

white of 1 leek, chopped

2 garlic cloves, crushed

50g/2oz creamed coconut, crumbled

2 tomatoes, peeled, seeded and diced

2.5cm/1in piece fresh root ginger, grated

15ml/1 tbsp tomato purée (paste)

5–10ml/1–2 tsp mild curry powder

500ml/17fl oz/generous 2 cups chicken or fish stock

For the garnish

15ml/1 tbsp fresh coriander (cilantro) leaves

4 banana leaves (optional)

1 small mango, peeled and diced

1 Make the sauce. Heat the oil in a pan. Cook the vegetables and garlic gently until soft but not brown.

2 Add the coconut, tomatoes and ginger. Cook for 1–2 minutes. Stir in the tomato purée, curry powder to taste, stock and seasoning.

3 Bring to the boil, then lower the heat, cover the pan and cook the sauce over the lowest heat for about 50 minutes. Stir once or twice to prevent the sauce from burning. Leave to cool.

4 Purée to a smooth sauce in a blender or food processor. Reheat, adding a little water if too thick.

5 Season the fish fillets with salt and pepper. Heat the oil in a large frying pan, add the butter and heat until sizzling. Put in the fish and fry for about 2–3 minutes on each side, until pale golden and cooked through. Drain on kitchen paper.

6 If you have banana leaves, place these on individual warmed plates and arrange the fillets on top. Pour the sauce around the fish and scatter on the finely diced mango. Garnish with coriander leaves and serve at once.

Energy 398kcal/1657kJ; Protein 34.1g; Carbohydrate 6.5g, of which sugars 5.8g; Fat 26.4g, of which saturates 12.3g; Cholesterol 94mg; Calcium 42mg; Fibre 1.9g; Sodium 170mg.

teriyaki sauce for salmon

Marinating the salmon in this teriyaki sauce makes it so wonderfully tender, it just melts in the mouth, and the crunchy condiment provides an excellent foil.

Serves four

INGREDIENTS

675g/1½lb salmon fillet
30ml/2 tbsp sunflower oil
watercress, to garnish

For the teriyaki sauce

5ml/1 tsp caster (superfine) sugar
5ml/1 tsp dry white wine
5ml/1 tsp sake, rice wine or dry sherry
30ml/2 tbsp dark soy sauce

For the condiment

5cm/2in fresh root ginger, grated
pink food colouring (optional)
50g/2oz mooli, grated

1 For the teriyaki sauce, mix together the sugar, white wine, sake or rice wine or dry sherry and soy sauce, stirring until the sugar dissolves.

2 Remove the skin from the salmon using a very sharp filleting knife. Cut the fillet into strips, then place in a non-metallic dish. Pour over the teriyaki sauce and set aside to marinate for 10–15 minutes.

3 To make the condiment, place the ginger in a bowl and add a little pink food colouring if you wish. Stir in the mooli.

4 Transfer the salmon to a sieve to drain off the teriyaki sauce.

5 Heat a wok, then add and heat the oil. Add the salmon in batches and stir-fry for 3–4 minutes, until it is cooked. Transfer to serving plates. Garnish with the watercress and serve with the mooli and ginger condiment.

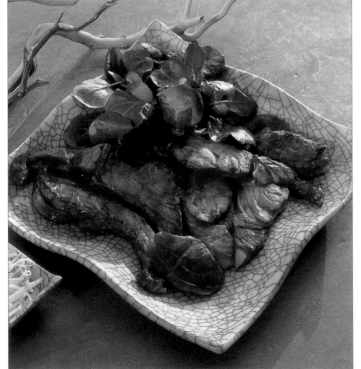

Energy 364kcal/1515kJ; Protein 34.4g; Carbohydrate 1.9g, of which sugars 1.9g; Fat 24.1g, of which saturates 3.9g; Cholesterol 84mg; Calcium 40mg; Fibre 0.1g; Sodium 612mg.

coconut sauce for salmon

Salmon is quite a robust fish, and responds well to being cooked with a sauce of strong flavours, as in this fragrant blend of spices, garlic and chilli.

Serves four

INGREDIENTS

4 salmon steaks, about 175g/6oz each
5ml/1 tsp ground cumin
10ml/2 tsp chilli powder
2.5ml/½ tsp ground turmeric
30ml/2 tbsp white wine vinegar
1.5ml/¼ tsp salt

For the coconut sauce

45ml/3 tbsp oil
1 onion, chopped
2 fresh green chillies, seeded
  and chopped
2 garlic cloves, crushed
2.5cm/1in piece fresh root ginger, grated
5ml/1 tsp ground cumin
5ml/1 tsp ground coriander
175ml/6fl oz/¾ cup coconut milk
fresh coriander (cilantro) sprigs, to garnish
rice with spring onions (scallions), to serve

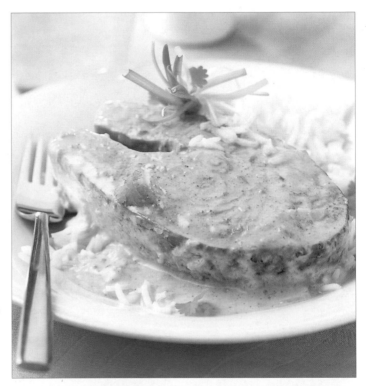

1 Arrange the salmon steaks in a single layer in a shallow glass dish. Put 5ml/1 tsp of ground cumin in a bowl and add the chilli powder, turmeric, vinegar and salt. Rub the paste over the salmon steaks and leave to marinate for about 15 minutes.

2 Heat the oil in a large deep frying pan and fry the onion, chillies, garlic and ginger, stirring frequently, for 5–6 minutes, until the onion is softened. Cool slightly.

3 Transfer the onion mixture to a food processor or blender and process to a smooth paste.

4 Return the onion paste to the pan. Add the remaining cumin, the coriander and coconut milk. Bring to the boil, reduce the heat and simmer the sauce for 5 minutes, stirring occasionally.

5 Add the salmon steaks. Cover and cook for 15 minutes, until the fish is tender. Transfer to a serving dish and garnish with the fresh coriander. Serve with the rice and spring onions.

Energy 416kcal/1729kJ; Protein 36.2g; Carbohydrate 5.2g, of which sugars 4.8g; Fat 27.9g, of which saturates 4.4g; Cholesterol 88mg; Calcium 75mg; Fibre 1.1g; Sodium 132mg.

sweet and sour sauce for baked fish

This sweet and sour sauce is light and slightly piquant, with a hint of red chilli – perfect for whole fish and equally delicious with pan-fried fillets, stir-fried prawns or baked fish steaks.

Serves four

INGREDIENTS

1 whole fish, such as red snapper
   or carp, about 1kg/2¼lb, cleaned

30–45ml/2–3 tbsp cornflour (cornstrach)

oil for frying

salt and ground black pepper

boiled rice, to serve

For the spice paste

2 garlic cloves

2 lemon grass stalks

2.5cm/1in fresh lengkuas

2.5cm/1in fresh root ginger

2cm/¾in fresh turmeric or 2.5ml/
   ½ tsp ground turmeric

5 macadamia nuts or 10 almonds

For the sweet and sour sauce

15ml/1 tbsp brown sugar

45ml/3 tbsp cider vinegar

about 350ml/12fl oz/1½ cups water

2 lime leaves, torn

4 shallots, quartered

3 tomatoes, peeled and cut in wedges

3 spring onions (scallions), finely
   shredded

1 fresh red chilli, seeded and shredded

1 Wash and dry the fish thoroughly and then sprinkle it inside and out with salt. Set aside for 15 minutes.

2 Peel and crush the garlic cloves. Use only the lower white part of the lemon grass stems and slice them thinly. Peel and slice the lengkuas, ginger and fresh turmeric, if using. Grind the nuts, garlic, lemon grass, lengkuas, ginger and turmeric to a fine paste in a food processor or blender, or using a pestle and mortar.

3 Scrape the paste into a bowl. Stir in the brown sugar, cider vinegar, seasoning to taste and water. Add the lime leaves. Set this sauce aside.

4 Dust the fish with the cornflour and fry on both sides in hot oil for about 8–9 minutes or until almost cooked through. Drain the fish on kitchen paper and transfer to a serving dish. Keep warm.

5 Pour off most of the oil and then pour in the sauce. Bring to the boil, stirring. Reduce the heat and cook for 3–4 minutes. Add the shallots and tomatoes, followed a minute later by the spring onions and chilli. Taste and adjust the seasoning if necessary.

6 Pour the sauce over the fish. Serve at once, with plenty of rice.

Energy 280kcal/1176kJ; Protein 32.4g; Carbohydrate 8.4g, of which sugars 7.7g; Fat 13.3g, of which saturates 1.8g; Cholesterol 56mg; Calcium 98mg; Fibre 1.8g; Sodium 125mg.

black bean sauce for stir-fried squid

This dish follows the style of Cantonese cooking and it tastes as good as it looks. Use an authentic full-flavoured fermented black bean sauce rather than a "cook-in" type sauce.

Serves four

INGREDIENTS

350–400g/12–14oz squid

1 medium green (bell) pepper, cored
 and seeded

45–60ml/3–4 tbsp vegetable oil

1 garlic clove, finely chopped

2.5ml/½ tsp finely chopped fresh
 root ginger

15ml/1 tbsp finely chopped spring onion
 (scallion)

5ml/1 tsp salt

15ml/1 tbsp black bean sauce

15ml/1 tbsp Chinese rice wine or
 dry sherry

few drops of sesame oil

3 Cut the green pepper into small triangular pieces. Heat a wok until hot. Add and heat the oil, then add the green pepper and stir-fry for about 1 minute.

4 Add the garlic, ginger, spring onion, salt and squid, then stir for 1 minute. Add the black bean sauce, rice wine or dry sherry and sesame oil and serve.

1 To clean the squid, cut off the tentacles just below the eye. Remove the "quill" from inside the body. Dip your fingers in a little salt, then rub off and discard the mottled skin on the squid. Wash the squid and dry well. Cut open the squid and score the inside in a criss-cross pattern, taking care not to cut right through.

2 Cut the squid into pieces each about the size of an oblong postage stamp. Blanch the squid in a pan of boiling water for a few seconds. Remove and drain. Dry well.

Energy 169kcal/705kJ; Protein 14.3g; Carbohydrate 4.8g, of which sugars 2.9g; Fat 10g, of which saturates 1.6g; Cholesterol 197mg; Calcium 18mg; Fibre 0.9g; Sodium 99mg.

sauces for vegetables

Here is a glorious collection of recipes to bring out the very best in vegetables. There is something so vibrant about them that many cooks simply settle for a hint of butter or a drizzle of olive oil. But for a superlative stand-alone dish, try enhancing them with piquant dressings, braising them in rich wine marinades or combining them with a creamy sauce. Even when flanking a meat or fish course, these fabulous roots, leaves and vegetable-fruits should be given all the special treatment they deserve.

citrus sauce for baby courgettes

This piquant sauce is a refreshingly different accompaniment for green vegetables, but it also complements a variety of ingredients, such as fish or poultry. On its own, it makes a tasty dip for roast potato wedges – why not try a mixture of potatoes and sweet potatoes?

Serves four

INGREDIENTS

350g/12oz baby courgettes (zucchini)

For the citrus sauce

4 spring onions (scallions), finely sliced

2.5cm/1in piece fresh root ginger, grated

30ml/2 tbsp cider vinegar

15ml/1 tbsp light soy sauce

5ml/1 tsp soft light brown sugar

45ml/3 tbsp vegetable stock

finely grated rind and juice of ½ lemon and ½ orange

5ml/1 tsp cornflour (cornstarch)

1 Cook the courgettes in lightly salted, boiling water for 3–4 minutes, or until just tender. Drain well and return them to the pan.

2 Meanwhile, make the sauce. Put all the sauce ingredients, except the cornflour, into a small pan and bring to the boil, stirring occasionally. Simmer for 3 minutes.

3 Blend the cornflour with 10ml/2 tsp cold water and add to the sauce. Bring the sauce to the boil, stirring continuously, until thickened.

4 Pour the sauce over the courgettes and gently heat, shaking the pan to coat evenly. Transfer to a warmed serving dish and serve.

VARIATION

Try this sauce with a mixture of baby vegetables, such as carrots, turnips, baby corn and patty pans.

Energy 30kcal/127kJ; Protein 1.9g; Carbohydrate 4.9g, of which sugars 3.6g; Fat 0.4g, of which saturates 0.1g; Cholesterol 0mg; Calcium 28mg; Fibre 1g; Sodium 270mg.

parsley sauce for baked marrow

This parsley sauce turns a simple and modest vegetable into a glorious treat. Try to find a small, firm and unblemished marrow for this recipe, as the flavour will be sweet, fresh and delicate. Young marrows do not need peeling; more mature ones do.

Serves four

INGREDIENTS

1 small young marrow (large zucchini), about 900g/2lb

30ml/2 tbsp olive oil

15g/½ oz/1 tbsp butter

1 onion, chopped

15ml/1 tbsp plain (all-purpose) flour

300ml/½ pint/1¼ cups milk and single light cream, mixed

30ml/2 tbsp chopped fresh parsley

salt and ground black pepper

1 Preheat the oven to 180°C/350°F/ Gas 4 and cut the marrow into pieces measuring about 5 x 2.5cm/ 2 x 1in.

2 Heat the oil and butter in a flameproof casserole that can be used in the oven. Fry the onion over a gentle heat until very soft.

3 Add the marrow and sauté for 1–2 minutes and then stir in the flour. Cook for a few minutes.

4 Gradually pour the milk and cream into the vegetable mixture, stirring to incorporate it smoothly with the flour.

5 Add the parsley and seasoning to taste, and stir well.

6 Cover and cook in the oven for 30–35 minutes. If liked, uncover for the final 5 minutes of cooking to brown the top. Alternatively, serve the marrow in its rich, but pale, sauce.

VARIATION

For a subtle change to accent, use chopped fresh basil, or a mixture of basil and chervil or tarragon, instead of the parsley.

Energy 228kcal/944kJ; Protein 7.4g; Carbohydrate 11g, of which sugars 7.5g; Fat 17.5g, of which saturates 7.9g; Cholesterol 31mg; Calcium 159mg; Fibre 2.7g; Sodium 55mg.

roast pepper sauce for spinach malfatti

A smoky pepper and tomato sauce adds the finishing touch to spinach and ricotta dumplings. The Italians call these malfatti (badly made) because of their uneven shape.

Serves four

INGREDIENTS

500g/1¼lb young leaf spinach
1 onion, finely chopped
1 garlic clove, crushed
15ml/1 tbsp extra virgin olive oil
350g/12 oz/1½ cups ricotta cheese
3 eggs, beaten
50g/2oz/scant 1 cup undyed
  dried breadcrumbs
50g/2oz/½ cup plain (all-purpose) flour
50g/2 oz/⅔ cup freshly grated
  Parmesan cheese
freshly grated nutmeg
25g/1oz/2 tbsp butter, melted

For the roast pepper sauce

2 red (bell) peppers, seeded and
  quartered
30ml/2 tbsp extra virgin olive oil
1 onion, chopped
400g/14oz can chopped tomatoes
salt and ground black pepper

1 Make the sauce. Preheat the grill (broiler) and roast the pepper quarters skin-side up until they blister and blacken. Place in a plastic bag to cool slightly, then peel and chop the flesh.

2 Heat the oil in a pan and lightly sauté the onion and peppers for 5 minutes.

3 Add the tomatoes and stir in 150ml/¼ pint/⅔ cup water, with salt and pepper to taste. Bring to the boil, lower the heat and simmer gently for 15 minutes.

4 Purée the mixture in a food processor or blender, in batches if necessary, then return to the clean pan and set aside.

5 Trim any thick stalks from the spinach, wash it well if necessary, then blanch in a pan of boiling water for about 1 minute. Drain, refresh under cold water and drain again. Squeeze the spinach dry, then chop it finely.

6 Put the finely chopped onion, garlic, olive oil, ricotta, eggs and breadcrumbs in a bowl. Add the spinach and mix well. Stir in the flour and 5ml/1 tsp salt with half the Parmesan, then season to taste with pepper and nutmeg.

7 Roll the mixture into 16 small logs and chill lightly.

8 Bring a large pan of water to the boil. Carefully drop in the malfatti in batches and cook them for 5 minutes. Remove with a fish slice and toss with the melted butter.

9 To serve, reheat the sauce and divide it among four plates. Arrange four malfatti on each and sprinkle the remaining Parmesan over. Serve at once.

Energy 563kcal/2345kJ; Protein 25.8g; Carbohydrate 35.2g, of which sugars 15.3g; Fat 36.4g, of which saturates 16.5g; Cholesterol 205mg; Calcium 440mg; Fibre 6.1g; Sodium 511mg.

peanut sauce for vegetable salad

This spicy sauce is based on the classic Indonesian sauce served with satay, but is equally delicious served with this main-course salad which mixes steamed and raw vegetables.

Serves two to four

INGREDIENTS

8 new potatoes

225g/8oz broccoli, cut into small florets

200g/7oz/1⅓ cups fine green beans

2 carrots, cut into thin ribbons with a
  vegetable peeler

50g/2oz/¼ cup beansprouts

1 red (bell) pepper, seeded and cut into
  strips

sprigs of watercress, to garnish

For the peanut sauce

15ml/1 tbsp sunflower oil

1 bird's eye chilli, seeded and sliced

1 garlic clove, crushed

5ml/1 tsp ground coriander

5ml/1 tsp ground cumin

60ml/4 tbsp crunchy peanut butter

75ml/5 tbsp water

15ml/1 tbsp dark soy sauce

1cm/½ in piece fresh root ginger,
  finely grated

5ml/1 tsp soft dark brown sugar

15ml/1 tbsp lime juice

60ml/4 tbsp coconut milk

1 First make the peanut sauce. Heat the oil in a pan, add the chilli and garlic, and cook for 1 minute, or until softened. Add the spices and cook for 1 minute.

2 Stir in the peanut butter and water, then cook for 2 minutes, or until combined, stirring constantly.

3 Add the soy sauce, ginger, sugar, lime juice and coconut milk, then cook over a low heat until smooth and heated through, stirring frequently. Transfer to a bowl.

4 Bring a pan of lightly salted water to the boil, add the potatoes and bring back to the boil. Reduce the heat if necessary and boil for 10–15 minutes, until tender. Drain, then halve or thickly slice the potatoes, depending on their size.

5 Meanwhile, steam the broccoli and green beans for 4–5 minutes, or until tender but still crisp. Add the carrots 2 minutes before the end of the cooking time.

6 Arrange the cooked vegetables on a platter with the beansprouts and pepper. Garnish with watercress and serve with the peanut sauce.

COOK'S TIP

Adjust the dipping consistency by adding slightly less water than recommended; you can always stir in a little more at the last minute. Serve the sauce either warm or cold.

Energy 253kcal/1057kJ; Protein 9.6g; Carbohydrate 28.3g, of which sugars 11.4g; Fat 11.9g, of which saturates 2.6g; Cholesterol 0mg; Calcium 79mg; Fibre 5.9g; Sodium 360mg.

light tomato sauce for aubergine rolls

The tomato sauce in this recipe is light and perfect with rich or creamy ingredients. Here it is just right with a rich cheese and rice filling in little rolls of aubergine.

Serves four

INGREDIENTS

2 aubergines (eggplants)

olive oil, or sunflower oil for shallow frying

75g/3oz/scant ½ cup ricotta cheese

75g/3oz/scant ½ cup soft goat's cheese

225g/8oz/2 cups cooked long grain white
  rice

15ml/1 tbsp chopped fresh basil

5ml/1 tsp chopped fresh mint, plus mint
  sprigs, to garnish

salt and ground black pepper

For the tomato sauce

15ml/1 tbsp olive oil

1 red onion, finely chopped

1 garlic clove, crushed

400g/14oz can chopped tomatoes

120ml/4fl oz/½ cup vegetable stock or
  white wine or a mixture

15ml/1 tbsp chopped fresh parsley

1 Make the tomato sauce. Heat the oil in a small pan. Fry the onion and garlic for 3–4 minutes until softened. Add the tomatoes, vegetable stock and/or wine, and parsley. Season well. Bring to the boil, then lower the heat and simmer for 10–12 minutes until slightly thick, stirring occasionally.

2 Preheat the oven to 190°C/375°F/ Gas 5. Slice the aubergines lengthways. Heat the oil in a large frying pan and fry the aubergine slices until they are golden brown on both sides. Drain on kitchen paper. Mix the ricotta, goat's cheese, rice, basil and mint in a bowl. Season well.

3 Place a generous spoonful of the cheese and rice mixture at one end of each aubergine slice and roll up. Arrange the rolls side by side in a shallow ovenproof dish. Pour the tomato sauce over the top and bake for 10–15 minutes until heated through. Garnish with the mint sprigs and serve.

Energy 233kcal/980kJ; Protein 8.9g; Carbohydrate 24.6g, of which sugars 6.7g; Fat 11.8g, of which saturates 5.8g; Cholesterol 25mg; Calcium 56mg; Fibre 3.3g; Sodium 125mg.

quick tomato sauce on cheese polenta

This quick tomato sauce can be prepared from store-cupboard ingredients. Adding tomato purée enriches its flavour, making it ideal for plain vegetables or baked polenta, as here.

Serves four

INGREDIENTS

5ml/1 tsp salt
250g/9oz/2¼ cups quick-cook polenta
5ml/1 tsp paprika
2.5ml/½ tsp ground nutmeg
75g/3oz/¾ cup grated Gruyère cheese

For the rich tomato sauce
30ml/2 tbsp olive oil
1 large onion, finely chopped
2 garlic cloves, crushed
30ml/2 tbsp brandy or medium sherry
2 x 400g/14oz cans chopped tomatoes
60ml/4 tbsp tomato purée (paste)
5ml/1 tsp sugar
salt and ground black pepper

1 Line a 28 x 18cm/11 x 7in baking tin with clear film (plastic wrap. Bring 1 litre/1¾ pints/4 cups water to the boil with the salt.

2 Add the polenta in a thin stream. Cook, stirring, for 5 minutes. Beat in the paprika and nutmeg. Spread in the tin, smoothing the top. Cool.

3 To make the rich tomato sauce, heat the oil in a pan. Cook the onion and garlic until soft. Add the brandy or sherry, tomatoes, tomato purée and sugar. Bring to the boil. Reduce the heat, season and cover, then simmer gently for 20 minutes. Taste for seasoning and set aside.

4 Preheat the oven to 200°C/400°F/ Gas 6. Turn out the polenta on to a board, and cut into 5cm/2in squares. Place half the squares in a greased ovenproof dish. Spoon over half the tomato sauce, and sprinkle with half the cheese. Repeat the layers. Bake for 25 minutes.

Energy 492kcal/2052kJ; Protein 20g; Carbohydrate 55.8g, of which sugars 8.4g; Fat 20.3g, of which saturates 8.8g; Cholesterol 37mg; Calcium 394mg; Fibre 3.6g; Sodium 861mg.

wild mushroom sauce for polenta

The flavour of wild mushrooms combines well with mascarpone in this sauce to heighten the taste of the polenta. It also makes a delicious topping for baked potatoes.

Serves four to six

INGREDIENTS

900ml/1½ pints/3¾ cups milk
900ml/1½ pints/3¾ cups water
5ml/1 tsp salt
300g/11oz/2¾ cups polenta
50g/2oz/¼ cup butter
115g/4oz Gorgonzola cheese
fresh thyme sprigs, to garnish

For the wild mushroom sauce

40g/1½ oz/scant 1 cup dried porcini mushrooms
150ml/¼ pint/⅔ cup hot water
25g/1oz/2 tbsp butter
115g/4oz/1½ cups button (white) mushrooms, chopped
60ml/4 tbsp dry white wine
generous pinch of dried thyme
60ml/4 tbsp mascarpone
salt and ground black pepper

1 Pour the milk and water into a large, heavy pan. Add the salt and bring to the boil. Using a long-handled spoon, stir the liquid briskly with one hand while drizzling in the polenta with the other. When the mixture is thick and smooth, lower the heat to a gentle simmer and cook for about 20 minutes, stirring occasionally.

2 Remove from the heat and stir in the butter and Gorgonzola. Spoon the polenta mixture into a shallow dish and level the surface.

3 Let the polenta set until solid, then cut it into wedges.

4 Meanwhile, make the sauce. Soak the porcini in the hot water for 15 minutes. Drain, reserving the liquid. Finely chop the porcini and strain the soaking liquid through a sieve lined with kitchen paper. Discard the kitchen paper.

5 Melt half the butter in a small pan. Sauté the chopped fresh mushrooms for about 5 minutes. Add the wine, porcini and strained soaking liquid, with the dried thyme. Season to taste. Cook for a further 2 minutes. Stir in the mascarpone and simmer for a few minutes, until reduced by a third. Set aside to cool.

6 Heat a ridged griddle pan or grill (broiler), and grill (broil) the polenta until crisp. Brush with melted butter and serve hot with the sauce. Garnish with thyme.

COOK'S TIP

If fresh porcini mushrooms are available, use this nutty-tasting variety instead of the dried mushrooms. You will not need to soak them beforehand. You would need about 175g/6oz fresh porcini for this recipe. They are also sold under the name ceps.

Energy 478kcal/1992kJ; Protein 15.9g; Carbohydrate 47.7g, of which sugars 7.5g; Fat 24.8g, of which saturates 12.7g; Cholesterol 56mg; Calcium 283mg; Fibre 1.4g; Sodium 412mg.

mornay sauce for two-veg gratin

This nursery favourite is enjoying a revival. The secret of a good cheese sauce is not to make it too thick and to stir in the cheese off the heat so that it melts gently.

Serves four to six

INGREDIENTS

1 medium cauliflower

2 heads of broccoli

1 onion, sliced

3 hard-boiled eggs, quartered

6 cherry tomatoes, halved (optional)

30–45ml/2–3 tbsp natural-coloured
dried breadcrumbs

For the mornay sauce

40g/1½oz/3 tbsp butter

40g/1½oz/⅓ cup plain (all-purpose) flour

600ml/1 pint/2½ cups milk or a mixture
of milk and vegetable water

150g/5oz/1¼ cups grated mature
Cheddar cheese

freshly grated nutmeg

salt and ground black pepper

1 Trim the cauliflower and broccoli and cut them into even-size florets, slicing the thinner parts of the stalks if you prefer.

2 Bring a large pan of lightly salted water to the boil and cook the cauliflower, broccoli and onion slices for 5–7 minutes or until just tender. Do not over-cook.

3 Drain the cauliflower and broccoli, reserving some of the vegetable water if you intend using it for the sauce. Arrange the vegetables in a shallow flameproof dish and add the quartered eggs.

4 To make the sauce, melt the butter in a pan and stir in the flour. Cook gently for 1 minute, stirring occasionally, and taking care not to brown the flour.

5 Gradually add the milk, or milk and vegetable water, whisking constantly. Bring to the boil, whisking until smooth and thick. Lower the heat and simmer for 2 minutes. Whisk in three-quarters of the cheese and season with nutmeg, salt and pepper.

6 Preheat the grill (broiler). Pour the sauce over the vegetables and dot with the tomato halves, if using. Mix the remaining cheese with the dried breadcrumbs. Sprinkle the cheese and breadcrumb mixture over the vegetables, and grill (broil) until bubbling and golden brown. Serve immediately.

VARIATION

The sauce can also be used for macaroni cheese. Cook 200g/7oz/ 1¾ cups dried macaroni or pasta shapes according to the package instructions. Drain and mix with the sauce, quartered hard-boiled eggs and tomato halves.

Energy 336kcal/1404kJ; Protein 20.9g; Carbohydrate 18.6g, of which sugars 8.9g; Fat 19.8g, of which saturates 11.1g; Cholesterol 139mg; Calcium 403mg; Fibre 4.1g; Sodium 352mg.

tamarind sauce for stuffed aubergines

The traditional way of cooking with tamarind is in a terracotta dish, which brings out the full fruity tartness of the tamarind. This spicy dish of stuffed aubergines in a tart tamarind sauce will add a refreshing tang to any meal.

Serves four

INGREDIENTS

12 baby aubergines (eggplants)

For the stuffing

15ml/1 tbsp vegetable oil

1 small onion, chopped

10ml/2 tsp grated fresh root ginger

10ml/2 tsp crushed garlic

5ml/1 tsp coriander seeds

5ml/1 tsp cumin seeds

10ml/2 tsp white poppy seeds

10ml/2 tsp sesame seeds

10ml/2 tsp desiccated (dry unsweetened shredded) coconut

105ml/7tbsp warm water

15ml/1 tbsp dry-roasted skinned peanuts

2.5–5ml/½–1 tsp chilli powder

5ml/1 tsp salt

For the tamarind sauce

15ml/1 tbsp vegetable oil

6–8 curry leaves

1–2 dried red chillies, chopped

2.5ml/½ tsp concentrated tamarind paste

105ml/7tbsp hot water

COOK'S TIP

Some food processors are too big for grinding spices for sauces, or simply do not have the requisite small blade and bowl attachment. There are alternatives: many cooks keep a coffee grinder especially for grinding spices. Grind spices in small batches and wipe the grinder out with paper after use. Japanese-style ridged mortars are brilliant for grinding spices, particularly moist pastes. They are partnered by special pestles made from very hard wood.

1 Make three deep slits lengthways in each aubergine, without cutting through, then soak in salted water for 20 minutes.

2 Heat 15ml/1 tbsp oil in a pan and sauté the onion for 3–4 minutes. Add the ginger and garlic and cook for 30 seconds.

3 Add the coriander and cumin seeds and sauté for 30 seconds, then add the poppy seeds, sesame seeds and coconut. Sauté for 1 minute, stirring constantly. Allow to cool slightly, then grind the spices in a food processor, adding 105ml/7 tbsp warm water. This mixture is the base for the stuffing and it should form a thick, slightly coarse paste.

4 Mix the peanuts, chilli powder and salt into the spice paste. Drain the aubergines and dry on kitchen paper. Stuff each of the slits with the spice paste and reserve any remaining paste.

5 For the sauce, heat the remaining oil in a wok or large pan over a medium heat. Add the curry leaves and chillies. Let the chillies blacken, then add the aubergines and the tamarind blended with 105ml/7 tbsp hot water. Stir, adding any remaining spice paste.

6 Cover the pan and simmer gently for 15–20 minutes or until the aubergines are tender. Serve with chapatis and a meat or poultry dish, if you like.

Energy 132kcal/549kJ; Protein 2.9g; Carbohydrate 4.7g, of which sugars 3.8g; Fat 11.5g, of which saturates 3.3g; Cholesterol 0mg; Calcium 36mg; Fibre 3.7g; Sodium 5mg.

egg and lemon sauce for asparagus

Eggs and lemons are often found in dishes from Greece, Turkey and the Middle East. This sauce has a fresh, tangy taste and brings out the best in asparagus.

2 Blend the cornflour with the cooled, reserved cooking liquid and place in a small pan. Bring to the boil, stirring constantly, and cook over a low heat until the sauce thickens slightly. Stir in 10ml/2 tsp sugar, then remove the pan from the heat and leave to cool slightly.

3 Beat the egg yolks thoroughly with the lemon juice and then stir gradually into the cooled sauce. Cook over a very low heat, stirring constantly, until the sauce is fairly thick. Be careful not to overheat the sauce or it may curdle.

4 As soon as the sauce has thickened, remove the pan from the heat and continue stirring for 1 minute. Taste and add salt or sugar as necessary. Leave the sauce to cool slightly.

5 Stir the cooled sauce, then pour a little over the asparagus. Cover and chill for at least 2 hours before serving with the rest of the sauce.

Serves four

INGREDIENTS

675g/1½lb asparagus, tough ends
  removed, and tied in a bundle

For the egg and lemon sauce

15ml/1 tbsp cornflour (cornstarch)

about 10ml/2 tsp sugar

2 egg yolks

juice of 1½ lemons

salt

VARIATION

This sauce goes very well with young vegetables. Try it with baby leeks, cooked whole or chopped.

1 Cook the bundle of asparagus in salted boiling water for 7–10 minutes. Drain well and arrange the asparagus in a serving dish. Reserve 200ml/7fl oz/scant 1 cup of the cooking liquid.

COOK'S TIP

Use only the tiny asparagus spears for a light, elegant first course.

Energy 96kcal/399kJ; Protein 6.4g; Carbohydrate 9.5g, of which sugars 5.8g; Fat 3.8g, of which saturates 1g; Cholesterol 101mg; Calcium 59mg; Fibre 2.9g; Sodium 8mg.

fruity red wine sauce for braised leeks

Fragrant oregano and strong dark vinegar give a distinctive flavour to this dish of braised leeks and fruity wine sauce. Serve it as part of a mixed meze or as a partner for baked white fish.

Serves six

INGREDIENTS

12 baby leeks or 6 thick leeks
15ml/1 tbsp coriander seeds, lightly crushed
5cm/2in piece of cinnamon stick
120ml/4fl oz/½ cup olive oil
3 fresh bay leaves
2 strips pared orange rind
5 or 6 fresh or dried oregano sprigs
5ml/1 tsp sugar
150ml/¼ pint/⅔ cup fruity red wine
10ml/2 tsp balsamic or sherry vinegar
30ml/2 tbsp coarsely chopped fresh oregano or marjoram
salt and ground black pepper

1 If using baby leeks, simply trim the ends, but leave them whole. Cut thick leeks into 5–7.5cm/2–3in lengths.

2 Place the coriander seeds and cinnamon in a pan wide enough to take all the leeks in a single layer. Cook over a medium heat for 2–3 minutes, or until the spices give off a fragrant aroma, then stir in the olive oil, bay leaves, orange rind, oregano, sugar, wine and balsamic or sherry vinegar. Bring to the boil and simmer for 5 minutes.

3 Add the leeks to the pan. Bring back to the boil, reduce the heat and cover the pan. Cook the leeks gently for 5 minutes. Uncover and simmer gently for another 5–8 minutes, or until the leeks are just tender when tested with the tip of a sharp knife.

4 Use a slotted spoon to transfer the leeks to a serving dish. Boil the pan juices rapidly until reduced to about 75–90ml/5–6 tbsp. Add salt and pepper to taste and pour the liquid over the leeks. Set aside and leave to cool.

5 The leeks can be left to stand for several hours. If you chill them, bring them back to room temperature again before serving. Sprinkle the chopped herbs over the leeks just before serving.

COOK'S TIP

Balsamic vinegar is ideal for this dish. It has a high sugar content and wonderfully strong bouquet. It is a very dark brown colour and has a deep, rich flavour with hints of herbs and port. It is expensive, but the flavour is so rich that you only need to use a little.

Energy 151Kcal/621kJ; Protein 1.1g; Carbohydrate 1.7g, of which sugars 1.3g; Fat 13.7g, of which saturates 2g; Cholesterol 0mg; Calcium 29mg; Fibre 1.5g; Sodium 5mg.

tomato and ginger sauce for tofu rosti

In this recipe, the tofu is marinated in a mixture of tamari, honey and oil, flavoured with garlic and ginger. This marinade is then added to the fresh tomatoes to make a thick, creamy tomato sauce with a delicious tang, and the method ensures the tofu is infused with the same flavours.

Serves four

INGREDIENTS

425g/15oz tofu, cut into 1cm/½in cubes
4 large potatoes, about 900g/2lb total
  weight, peeled
sunflower oil, for frying
salt and ground black pepper
30ml/2 tsp sesame seeds, toasted

For the tomato and ginger sauce

30ml/2 tbsp tamari or dark soy sauce
15ml/1 tbsp clear honey
2 garlic cloves, crushed
4cm/1½in piece fresh root ginger, grated
5ml/1 tsp toasted sesame oil
15ml/1 tbsp olive oil
8 tomatoes, halved, seeded and chopped

1 For the sauce, mix together the tamari or dark soy sauce, clear honey, garlic, root ginger and toasted sesame oil in a large shallow dish.

2 Add the tofu, then spoon the liquid over the tofu and leave to marinate in the fridge for at least 1 hour. Turn the tofu occasionally in the marinade to allow the flavours to infuse.

3 To make the rösti, par-boil the potatoes for 10–15 minutes until almost tender. Leave to cool, then grate coarsely. Season well with salt and freshly ground black pepper.

4 Preheat the oven to 200°C/400°F/Gas 6. Using a slotted spoon, remove the tofu from the marinade and reserve the marinade on one side. Spread out the tofu on a baking tray and bake for about 20 minutes, turning occasionally, until the tofu squares are golden and crisp on all sides.

5 Divide the potato mixture into four equal portions. Take a quarter and shape it into a rough cake by hand. Repeat with the remaining three portions of mixture.

6 Heat a frying pan and pour in just enough oil to cover the base. Heat the oil. Place the cakes in the frying pan and flatten the mixture, using your hands (taking care not to touch the pan) or a metal spatula or palette knife to form rounds about 1cm/½in thick.

7 Cook for about 6 minutes, or until golden and crisp underneath. Carefully turn the rösti over and cook for a further 6 minutes, or until golden brown on both sides.

8 Meanwhile, complete the sauce. Heat the oil in a pan, add the reserved marinade and then the tomatoes and cook for 2 minutes, stirring continuously.

9 Reduce the heat and simmer, covered, for 10 minutes, stirring occasionally, until the tomatoes break down. Press the mixture through a sieve to make a thick, smooth sauce.

10 To serve, place a rösti on each of four warm plates. Scatter the tofu on top and spoon over the tomato sauce. Sprinkle with sesame seeds and serve at once.

COOK'S TIPS

• Tamari is a thick, mellow soy sauce, which is sold in Japanese food shops and some larger health-food stores.
• Tofu can be rather bland so allow it to marinate for 2–3 hours if possible.

Energy 523kcal/2184kJ; Protein 15.2g; Carbohydrate 46.1g, of which sugars 12.4g; Fat 32.1g, of which saturates 4.6g; Cholesterol 0mg; Calcium 620mg; Fibre 4.9g; Sodium 49mg.

walnut and garlic sauce for vegetables

This sauce, which boasts several versions throughout the Mediterranean, is excellent with roast steamed cauliflower or potatoes, or poached chicken. It can also be a dip served with bread.

Serves four

INGREDIENTS

2 x 1cm/½in slices good white bread, crusts removed

60ml/4 tbsp milk

150g/5oz/1¼ cups shelled walnuts

4 garlic cloves, chopped

120ml/4fl oz/½ cup mild olive oil

15–30ml/1–2 tbsp walnut oil (optional)

juice of 1 lemon

salt and ground black pepper

walnut or olive oil, for drizzling

paprika, for dusting (optional)

1 Soak the slices of white bread in the milk for about 5 minutes, then process with the walnuts and chopped garlic in a food processor or blender, to make a rough paste.

2 Gradually add the olive oil to the paste with the motor still running, until the mixture forms a smooth thick sauce. Blend in the walnut oil, if using.

3 Scoop the sauce into a bowl and squeeze in lemon juice to taste. Season with salt and pepper and beat well.

4 Transfer the sauce to a serving bowl, drizzle over a little more walnut or olive oil, then dust lightly with paprika, if using.

COOK'S TIP

Once opened, walnut oil has a fairly short shelf life. Buy it in small bottles and keep it in a cool, dark place. It is delicious in many salad dressings.

VARIATION

For an Italian salsa di noci for pasta, process 90g/3½oz/scant 1 cup walnuts with 2 garlic cloves and 15g/½oz flat leaf parsley. Blend in 1 slice white bread (crusts removed), soaked in milk, and 120ml/4fl oz/½ cup fruity olive oil as above. Season with salt, pepper and lemon juice. Thin with more milk or single (light) cream if very thick.

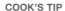

Energy 474kcal/1958kJ; Protein 7.1g; Carbohydrate 8.1g, of which sugars 2g; Fat 46.2g, of which saturates 5.1g; Cholesterol 1mg; Calcium 67mg; Fibre 1.5g; Sodium 74mg.

garlic sauce for roasted beetroot

In Greece, beetroot is a favourite winter vegetable, either served solo as a salad or with a layer of the flavourful garlic sauce, known as skordalia, on top.

Serves four

INGREDIENTS

675g/1½lb medium or small beetroot (beets)

75–90ml/5–6 tbsp extra virgin olive oil

salt

For the garlic sauce

4 medium slices of bread, crusts removed, soaked in water for 10 minutes

2 or 3 garlic cloves, chopped

15ml/1 tbsp white wine vinegar

60ml/4 tbsp extra virgin olive oil

1 Preheat the oven to 180°C/350°F/Gas 4. Rinse the beetroot under cold running water and rub off any grit, but be careful not to pierce the skin or the colour will run. If the leaves are still on the beetroot, cut them off leaving short lengths of stalks in place.

2 Line a roasting pan with a large sheet of foil and place the beetroot on top. Drizzle a little of the olive oil over them, sprinkle lightly with salt and fold over both edges of the foil to enclose the beetroot completely. Bake for about 1½ hours until perfectly soft.

3 Meanwhile, make the garlic sauce. Squeeze most of the water out of the soaked bread, but leave it quite moist.

4 Place the bread in a blender or food processor. Add the garlic and vinegar, with salt to taste, and blend until smooth. Scrape the mixture down in the bowl.

5 While the blender or food processor is running, drizzle in the extra virgin olive oil through the lid or feeder tube. The sauce should absorb the oil and become creamy, not runny. Taste the sauce for seasoning. Spoon it into a serving bowl and set it aside.

6 Remove the beetroot from the foil package. When they are cool enough to handle, carefully peel them. Cut them into thin, round slices and arrange these on a flat platter or individual plates.

7 Drizzle with the remaining oil. Either spread a thin layer of garlic sauce on top, or hand it around separately. Serve with fresh bread, if you like.

Energy 342kcal//1425kJ; Protein 5g; Carbohydrate 25.2g, of which sugars 12.5g; Fat 25.4g, of which saturates 3.6g; Cholesterol 0mg; Calcium 61mg; Fibre 3.6g; Sodium 242mg.

classic dressings and marinades

Whereas a dressing was once set aside for tossing into a salad and a marinade seen simply as a seasoned wine for soaking meat, in contemporary cooking they are viewed as exciting and flavourful infusions. Dressings now enhance hot as well as cold dishes, including fish, meat, game and leafy combinations. Herbs, seasonings, citrus fruits and spices come together with oils and vinegars, wine, cider, yogurt or creams in these most eclectic of light meal recipes.

hot 'n' sweet tofu for cucumber

This recipe for a hot, sweet-and-sour dressing is a versatile one – it works well as a marinade for raw ingredients or as a punchy dressing for cold salads, or grilled or pan-fried foods.

2 Cut the tofu into cubes. Heat a little oil in a pan and fry the tofu until golden brown all over. Take care to avoid breaking the tofu cubes. Drain on kitchen paper.

Serves four to six

INGREDIENTS

1 small cucumber
115g/4oz square tofu
oil, for frying
115g/4oz/½ cup beansprouts
salt
celery leaves, to garnish

Hot 'n' sweet dressing

1 small onion, grated
2 garlic cloves, crushed
5–7.5ml/1–1½ tsp chilli sauce
30–45ml/2–3 tbsp dark soy sauce
15–30ml/1–2 tbsp rice wine vinegar
10ml/2 tsp dark brown sugar

1 Cut the cucumber into neat cubes. Place on a plate and sprinkle with salt to extract excess liquid. Set aside, while preparing the remaining ingredients for the salad and the dressing.

3 To make the dressing, place together the onion, garlic and chilli sauce in a screw-top jar. Shake well. Then add the soy sauce, vinegar, sugar and salt to taste. Shake again until the ingredients are thoroughly mixed.

4 Just before serving, rinse the cucumber under cold running water. Drain and dry thoroughly. Toss the cucumber, tofu and beansprouts together in a serving bowl and pour over the dressing. Garnish with the celery leaves and serve the salad at once.

Energy 69kcal/287kJ; Protein 2.7g; Carbohydrate 4.4g, of which sugars 3.7g; Fat 4.6g, of which saturates 0.6g; Cholesterol 0mg; Calcium 114mg; Fibre 0.7g; Sodium 182mg.

raspberry dressing for asparagus

Raspberry vinegar gives this quick dressing a refreshing, tangy fruit flavour. It is an ideal accompaniment to asparagus and also delicious with warm, freshly cooked beetroot.

Serves four

INGREDIENTS

675g/1½ lb thin asparagus spears

115g/4oz/1½ cups fresh raspberries,
  to garnish

For the creamy raspberry dressing

30ml/2 tbsp raspberry vinegar

2.5ml/½ tsp salt

5ml/1 tsp Dijon-style mustard

60ml/4 tbsp crème fraîche or
  natural (plain) yogurt

ground white pepper

1 Pour water into a pan to a depth of about 10cm/4in and bring to the boil. Trim the tough ends off the asparagus spears.

2 Tie the asparagus spears into two bundles. Lower the bundles into the boiling water and cook for 3–5 minutes, or until just tender.

3 Remove the asparagus and immerse it in cold water to stop the cooking. Drain and untie the bundles. Pat dry. Chill for 1 hour.

4 To make the dressing, mix the vinegar and salt in a bowl and stir with a fork until dissolved. Stir in the mustard, crème fraîche or yogurt. Add pepper to taste. Place the asparagus on individual plates and drizzle the dressing across the middle of the spears. Garnish with fresh raspberries.

Energy 112kcal/462kJ; Protein 6g; Carbohydrate 5.3g, of which sugars 4.9g; Fat 7.7g, of which saturates 4.3g; Cholesterol 17mg; Calcium 66mg; Fibre 3.6g; Sodium 6mg.

balsamic-basil dressing for hot avocado

If you make the basil oil ahead of time, or buy a ready prepared basil oil, this is an ultra-simple dish that can be made in a flash. It makes an eye-catching first course.

Serves six

INGREDIENTS

3 ready-to-eat avocados, ideally Hass
  for flavour

105ml/7 tbsp balsamic vinegar

For the basil oil

40g/1½oz/1½ cups fresh basil leaves,
  stalks removed

200ml/7fl oz/scant 1 cup olive oil

1 To make the basil oil, place the leaves in a bowl and pour boiling water over. Leave for 30 seconds. Drain, refresh under cold water and drain again. Squeeze dry and pat with kitchen paper to remove as much moisture as possible. Place in a food processor with the oil and process to a purée. Put into a bowl, cover and chill overnight.

2 Line a sieve with muslin (cheesecloth), set it over a deep bowl and pour in the basil purée. Leave undisturbed for 1 hour, or until all the oil has filtered into the bowl. Discard the solids and pour into a bottle, then chill.

3 Prepare the barbecue. Cut each avocado in half and prize out the stone (pit). Brush with a little of the oil. Heat the balsamic vinegar gently in a pan on the stove or on the barbecue. When the vinegar starts to boil, simmer for 1 minute, or until it is just beginning to turn slightly syrupy.

4 Once the flames have died down, position a grill (broiling) rack over the coals to heat. When the coals are hot, or with a light coating of ash, heat a griddle until a few drops of water sprinkled on to the surface evaporate instantly.

5 Lower the heat a little, place the avocado halves cut-side down and cook for 30–60 seconds until branded with grill marks. Serve hot with the vinegar and extra oil drizzled over.

Energy 222kcal/916kJ; Protein 1g; Carbohydrate 1g, of which sugars 0.3g; Fat 23.8g, of which saturates 4.1g; Cholesterol 0mg; Calcium 6mg; Fibre 1.7g; Sodium 3mg.

sweet-and-sour salsa for artichoke

A sweet-and-sour minty sauce, poured over lightly cooked summer vegetables, works perfectly in this delicious salad – perfect for a summer's evening.

Serves four

INGREDIENTS

6 small globe artichokes

juice of 1 lemon

30ml/2 tbsp olive oil

2 onions, roughly chopped

175g/6oz/1½ cups fresh or frozen broad (fava) beans (shelled weight)

175g/6oz/1½ cups fresh or frozen peas (shelled weight)

salt and ground black pepper

fresh mint leaves, to garnish

For the sweet-and-sour sauce

120ml/4fl oz/½ cup white wine vinegar

15ml/1 tbsp caster (superfine) sugar

handful of fresh mint leaves, roughly torn

1 Peel the outer leaves from the artichokes and discard. Cut the artichokes into quarters and place them in a bowl of water with the lemon juice.

2 Heat the olive oil in a large pan and add the onions. Cook until the onions are golden. Add the beans and stir, then drain the artichokes and add to the pan. Pour in about 300ml/½ pint/1¼ cups water and cook, covered, for a further 10–15 minutes.

3 Add the peas, season with salt and pepper and cook for a further 5 minutes, stirring from time to time, until the vegetables are tender. Strain through a sieve or colander and place all the vegetables in a bowl. Leave to cool, then cover and chill.

4 To make the sweet-and-sour sauce, mix all the ingredients in a pan. Heat gently for 2–3 minutes, until the sugar has dissolved. Simmer gently for 5 minutes, stirring occasionally. Leave to cool. To serve, drizzle the sauce over the vegetables and garnish with mint.

Energy 148kcal/616kJ; Protein 7.2g; Carbohydrate 15.8g, of which sugars 7g; Fat 6.7g, of which saturates 1g; Cholesterol 0mg; Calcium 80mg; Fibre 6.2g; Sodium 65mg.

parsley-balsamic dressing for red onions

This dressing marries a fine mix of flavours. On its own, this is a good vegetarian salad, but it is also delicious with grilled meat. Combine as many different onions as you wish: from the fat pink variety sold in West Indian markets to the pink banana shallot and white spring onions.

Serves four to six

INGREDIENTS

6 red spring onions (scallions), trimmed

6 green salad onions, trimmed and split lengthways

250g/9oz small or baby (pearl) onions, peeled and left whole

2 pink onions, sliced horizontally into 5mm/¼in rounds

2 red onions, sliced into wedges

2 small yellow onions, sliced into wedges

4 banana shallots, halved lengthways

200g/7oz shallots, preferably Thai

For the parsley and balsamic dressing

45ml/3 tbsp olive oil, plus extra for drizzling

juice of 1 lemon

45ml/3 tbsp chopped fresh flat leaf parsley

30ml/2 tbsp balsamic vinegar

salt and ground black pepper

kuchai flowers (optional), to garnish

1 Prepare the barbecue. Spread out the onions and shallots in a large flat dish.

2 Whisk the oil and lemon juice together and pour over the mixture. Turn the onions and shallots in the dressing to coat, and season.

3 Once the flames have died down, position a grill (broiling) rack over the coals to heat. When the coals are medium-hot, or covered in a moderate coating of ash, place a griddle or perforated metal vegetable basket on the grill rack to heat, rather than cook on the rack and risk losing onions through the gaps in the rack. Grill (broil) the onions in batches, for 5–7 minutes, turning them occasionally.

4 As each batch of onions is cooked, lift them on to a platter and keep hot. Just before serving, finish the dressing process by adding the parsley to the cooked onions, and gently toss to mix. Then drizzle over the balsamic vinegar and extra olive oil.

5 Garnish with a few kuchai flowers, if you like, and serve with warmed pitta bread.

Energy 117kcal/485kJ; Protein 2.7g; Carbohydrate 14g, of which sugars 10.1g; Fat 6g, of which saturates 0.8g; Cholesterol 0mg; Calcium 66mg; Fibre 3.1g; Sodium 9mg.

chive flower dressing for grilled potato

There is something very enjoyable about using edible flowering plants and herbs from the garden. Grabbing a handful of this herb or that flower is all part of the creativity of cooking, and can produce really exciting and unexpected results in the simplest dressings or marinades.

Serves four to six

INGREDIENTS

900g/2lb salad potatoes, such as
  charlottes, Jersey royals or French ratte

For the chive flower dressing
15ml/1 tbsp champagne vinegar
105ml/7 tbsp olive oil
45ml/3 tbsp chopped chives
about 10 chive flowers
4–6 small bunches yellow cherry
  tomatoes on the vine
salt and ground black pepper

1 Prepare the barbecue. Boil the potatoes in a pan of salted water for 10 minutes, or until tender.

2 Make the dressing: whisk the vinegar with 75ml/5 tbsp of the oil, then stir in the chives and flowers. Drain and halve the potatoes.

3 Position a grill (broiling) rack over the coals. When the coals are medium-hot, or with a moderate coating of ash, toss the potatoes in the remaining oil and lay them on the grill rack. Leave for 5 minutes, then press down lightly so that they are imprinted with grill marks.

4 Turn the potatoes over and cook the second side for about 3 minutes. Place the potatoes in a bowl, pour over the dressing and toss lightly to mix. Serve hot or set aside to cool until warm, or cold.

5 Grill (broil) the tomatoes for 3 minutes, or until they are just beginning to blister. Serve the tomatoes with the potatoes.

Energy 232kcal/970kJ; Protein 3g; Carbohydrate 26.2g, of which sugars 4g; Fat 13.5g, of which saturates 2.1g; Cholesterol 0mg; Calcium 14mg; Fibre 2.2g; Sodium 23mg.

balsamic dressing for fennel and orange

This balsamic dressing is laced with garlic, zesty orange, delicate fennel and peppery rocket.

Serves four

INGREDIENTS

2 oranges, such as Jaffa, Shamouti or
blood oranges

1 fennel bulb

115g/4oz rocket (arugula) leaves

50g/2oz/⅓ cup black olives

For the dressing

30ml/2 tbsp extra virgin olive oil

15ml/1 tbsp balsamic vinegar

1 small garlic clove, crushed

salt and ground black pepper

VARIATION

If you aren't a fan of garlic, you can
leave it out of this dressing.

1 With a vegetable peeler, cut strips of rind from the oranges, without pith, and cut into thin julienne strips. Cook in boiling water for a few minutes. Drain and set aside. Peel the oranges, removing all pith. Slice them thinly and discard seeds.

2 Trim the fennel bulb, then cut in half lengthways and slice it across as thinly as possible, preferably in a food processor fitted with a slicing disc or using a mandolin.

3 Combine the slices of orange and fennel in a serving bowl and toss with the rocket leaves.

4 To make the dressing, mix together the oil, vinegar, garlic and seasoning. Pour over the salad, toss together well and leave to stand for a few minutes. Sprinkle with the black olives and julienne strips of orange. Serve.

Energy 105kcal/434kJ; Protein 2.3g; Carbohydrate 8g, of which sugars 7.7g; Fat 7.3g, of which saturates 1g; Cholesterol 0mg; Calcium 104mg; Fibre 3.5g; Sodium 331mg.

lemon, caper and olive dressing

Lemons subtly underline the flavours of vegetables while capers add a touch of a piquancy.

Serves four

INGREDIENTS

1 large aubergine (eggplant), weighing
about 675g/1½lb

60ml/4 tbsp olive oil

grated rind and juice of 1 lemon

30ml/2 tbsp capers, rinsed

12 green olives, pitted

30ml/2 tbsp chopped fresh flat
leaf parsley

salt and ground black pepper

COOK'S TIP

This salad tastes best when made a
day ahead. It will keep well, covered, in
the refrigerator, for up to 4 days. Return
it to room temperature before serving.

1 Cut the aubergine into 2.5cm/1in cubes. Heat the olive oil in a large, heavy frying pan and cook the aubergine for about 10 minutes, tossing frequently, until golden and softened. Drain on kitchen paper; sprinkle with salt.

2 For the dressing, mix the lemon rind and juice, capers, olives and parsley with seasoning. Place the aubergine cubes in a large serving bowl, add the dressing and mix well to coat the aubergine. Serve at room temperature.

Energy 140kcal/580kJ; Protein 1.9g; Carbohydrate 4g, of which sugars 3.6g; Fat 13.2g, of which saturates 2g; Cholesterol 0mg; Calcium 42mg; Fibre 4.2g; Sodium 288mg.

lime dressing for stir-fried vegetables

There is nothing quite like crisp, sweet, young vegetables. They are finished to perfection with a zesty dressing – when dressings are bursting with flavour a small quantity goes a long way.

3 Add the sugar-snap peas, asparagus, spring onions and cherry tomatoes, and stir-fry for a further 1–2 minutes. Use two wooden spoons or chopsticks to toss the ingredients, so that they cook evenly on all sides.

4 To make the dressing, mix the lime juice, honey, soy sauce and sesame oil in a small bowl, and stir until thoroughly combined. Add the dressing to the frying pan or wok and stir through.

5 Cover the pan or wok and cook the vegetables for 2–3 minutes more, or until they are just tender but still crisp. Transfer to individual bowls or plates and serve immediately.

Serves four

INGREDIENTS

15ml/1 tbsp groundnut (peanut) oil

1 garlic clove, sliced

2.5cm/1in piece fresh root ginger, peeled and finely chopped

115g/4oz baby carrots

115g/4oz patty pan squash

115g/4oz baby corn

115g/4oz green beans, trimmed

115g/4oz sugar-snap peas, trimmed

115g/4oz young asparagus, cut into 7.5cm/3in pieces

8 spring onions (scallions), cut into 5cm/2in pieces

115g/4oz cherry tomatoes

For the lime dressing

juice of 2 limes

15ml/1 tbsp clear honey

15ml/1 tbsp soy sauce

5ml/1 tsp sesame oil

1 Heat the groundnut oil in a large frying pan or wok. Add the garlic and chopped root ginger and stir-fry over a high heat for 1 minute, until the ingredients are aromatic.

2 Add the baby carrots, patty pan squash, baby corn and green beans and stir-fry for another 3–4 minutes, until the vegetables are beginning to cook.

COOK'S TIP

Stir-fries cook quickly and the trick for success is to have all the ingredients prepared and ready to go before you begin. The preparation can be done in advance, and everything kept covered and chilled. Stir-frying is a pan-to-plate method – last-minute cooking means the dish will be crisp and fresh.

Energy 115kcal/479kJ; Protein 5.9g; Carbohydrate 12.7g, of which sugars 9.4g; Fat 4.9g, of which saturates 0.7g; Cholesterol 0mg; Calcium 93mg; Fibre 4.8g; Sodium 647mg.

coriander dressing for chicken salad

Serve this salad warm to make the most of the wonderful flavour of barbecued chicken basted with a marinade of coriander, sesame and mustard, and finished with a matching dressing.

Serves six

INGREDIENTS

4 boneless chicken breasts, skinned

225g/8oz mangetouts (snow peas)

2 heads lettuce, such as lollo rosso or frisée lettuce

3 carrots, cut into matchstick strips

175g/6oz/2¼ cups button mushrooms, sliced

6 bacon rashers (strips), fried and chopped

15ml/1 tbsp chopped fresh coriander (cilantro), to garnish

For the coriander dressing

120ml/4fl oz/½ cup lemon juice

30ml/2 tbsp wholegrain mustard

5ml/1 tsp coriander seeds, crushed

250ml/8fl oz/1 cup olive oil

75ml/5 tbsp sesame oil

3 Cook the mangetouts for about 2 minutes in boiling water, then drain and refresh in cold water.

4 Preheat the grill (broiler) or prepare the barbecue. Tear the lettuces into small pieces and mix with all the carrots, mushrooms and bacon. Divide the salad among six individual bowls.

5 Cook the chicken breasts on a medium barbecue or under the grill (broiler) for 10–15 minutes, basting with the marinade and turning once, until cooked through.

6 Slice the chicken on the diagonal into thin pieces. Divide among the bowls of salad and add some of the reserved dressing to each. Combine quickly and scatter some fresh coriander over each bowl.

1 To make the coriander dressing, whisk the lemon juice with the mustard and coriander seeds in a bowl. Whisk in the olive and sesame oils.

2 Place the chicken breasts in a dish and pour over half the dressing. Marinate overnight in the refrigerator. Chill the remaining dressing ready for finishing the cooked chicken and salad

Energy 555kcal/2300kJ; Protein 31.3g; Carbohydrate 7.1g, of which sugars 6.4g; Fat 44.8g, of which saturates 7.5g; Cholesterol 83mg; Calcium 68mg; Fibre 3.4g; Sodium 544mg.

ginger and lime marinade for prawns

This fragrant marinade will guarantee a mouth-watering aroma from the barbecue, and is as delicious with chicken or pork as it is with prawns – or salmon.

Serves four

INGREDIENTS

225g/8oz peeled raw tiger prawns (shrimp)

½ cucumber

15ml/1 tbsp sunflower oil

15ml/1 tbsp sesame seed oil

175g/6oz mangetouts (snow peas)

4 spring onons (scallions), sliced

a little chopped fresh coriander (cilantro)

For the ginger and lime marinade

15ml/1 tbsp clear honey

15ml/1 tbsp light soy sauce

15ml/1 tbsp dry sherry

2 garlic cloves, crushed

small piece fresh root ginger, peeled and finely chopped

juice of 1 lime

VARIATION

This marinade is also a good one to use with larger pieces of fish for grilling, such as salmon, trout or tuna.

1 To make the marinade, mix the honey, soy sauce and sherry in a bowl. Stir in the garlic, ginger and lime juice. Add the prawns and turn them in the marinade until they are completely coated. Cover and leave to marinate in the refrigerator for 1-2 hours.

2 Prepare the cucumber. Slice it in half lengthways, scoop out the seeds, then slice each half neatly into crescents. Set aside.

3 Heat the sunflower and sesame oils in a large, heavy frying pan or wok. Drain the prawns (reserving the marinade) and stir-fry over a high heat for 4 minutes, or until they begin to turn pink. Add the mangetouts and cucumber and stir-fry for 2 minutes more.

4 Stir in the reserved marinade and heat through until it is boiling. Finally, stir in the spring onions and cook for a few seconds until they are bright green, but not soft.

5 Remove the pan from the heat and sprinkle with chopped fresh coriander. Divide the stir-fry among four warm serving bowls and serve immediately.

Energy 198kcal/831kJ; Protein 12g; Carbohydrate 24.4g, of which sugars 24g; Fat 6g, of which saturates 0.8g; Cholesterol 110mg; Calcium 74mg; Fibre 1.3g; Sodium 113mg.

peppered citrus marinade for monkfish

Monkfish is a firm, meaty fish that cooks well on the barbecue. Its flavour is delicate but not weak and is enhanced by a pepper and uplifting citrus marinade. Serve with a green salad.

Serves four

INGREDIENTS

2 monkfish tails, about 350g/12oz each

1 lime

1 lemon

2 oranges

handful of fresh thyme sprigs

30ml/2 tbsp olive oil

15ml/1 tbsp mixed peppercorns, roughly crushed

salt and ground black pepper

1 Using a sharp kitchen knife, remove any membrane from the monkfish tails. Cut the fish carefully down one side of the backbone, sliding the knife between the bone and flesh, to remove the fillet from one side.

2 Turn the fish and repeat on the other side to remove the second fillet. Repeat on the second tail. Place the four fillets flat on a chopping board.

3 Cut two fine slices from each of the citrus fruit and arrange them over two of the fillets. The tops of the fillets should be covered by the two slices each of lime, lemon and orange, overlapped neatly to fit.

4 Add a few sprigs of fresh thyme, and sprinkle with plenty of salt and ground black pepper. Finely grate the rind from the remaining fruit and sprinkle it over the fish. Press on about half the peppercorns.

5 Lay the other two fillets on top and tie firmly. Place in a dish.

6 Squeeze the juice from the citrus fruits and mix with the olive oil and seasoning. Spoon over the fish. Cover with clear film (plastic wrap) and chill for about 1 hour, spooning the marinade over the fish once or twice.

7 Drain the monkfish, reserving the marinade. Sprinkle the peppercorns over and cook on a medium-hot grill (broiler) for 15–20 minutes, basting with marinade.

Energy 179kcal/753kJ; Protein 31g; Carbohydrate 0g, of which sugars 0g; Fat 6.3g, of which saturates 1g; Cholesterol 28mg; Calcium 32mg; Fibre 0g; Sodium 37mg.

orange-peppercorn marinade for bass

This is an excellent light marinade for whole fish – sea bass here, but salmon trout or sea bream would also be delicious cooked this way. The cooked fish, in the aromatic and delicate marinade, needs only a sprinkling of fresh herbs as a garnish.

Serves four

INGREDIENTS

1 medium whole sea bass, cleaned

For the peppercorn marinade

1 red onion
2 small oranges
90ml/6 tbsp light olive oil
30ml/2 tbsp cider vinegar
30ml/2 tbsp green peppercorns in brine, drained
30ml/2 tbsp chopped fresh parsley
salt and sugar, to taste

COOK'S TIP

If you do not have an ovenproof dish large enough to hold the fish, place it in a serving dish for marinating and transfer it to a baking sheet or roasting pan for cooking.

1 Note the weight of the fish. With a sharp knife, slash the bass three or four times on both sides.

2 Line an ovenproof dish with foil. Peel and slice the onion and oranges. Place half the onion and oranges in the dish, place the fish on top, and cover with the remaining onion and orange.

3 Mix the remaining marinade ingredients and pour over the fish. Fold up the foil to enclose the fish completely and stand for 4 hours.

4 Preheat the oven to 180°C/350°F/ Gas 4. Make sure the foil over the fish is folded to seal in juices. Bake for 15 minutes per 450g/1lb, plus 15 minutes. Serve with the juices.

Energy 329kcal/1369kJ; Protein 34g; Carbohydrate 1.2g, of which sugars 0.9g; Fat 20.9g, of which saturates 3.1g; Cholesterol 140mg; Calcium 231mg; Fibre 0.2g; Sodium 121mg.

summer herb marinade for salmon

Make the best use of summer herbs in this marinade – vary the mixture according to whatever you have available, remembering to use more of the delicate herbs and less of those with a stronger flavour. The marinade is also excellent for veal, chicken, pork or lamb.

Serves four

INGREDIENTS

4 salmon steaks or fillets, about 175g/6oz each

For the herb marinade

large handful of fresh herb sprigs, such as chervil, thyme, parsley, sage, chives rosemary, oregano

90ml/6 tbsp olive oil

45ml/3 tbsp tarragon vinegar

1 garlic clove, crushed

2 spring onions (scallions), chopped

salt and ground black pepper

COOK'S TIP

For a smoked herb flavour, keep the herb stalks to throw on to the barbecue coals when you cook the fish that way. Thyme and rosemary stalks are ideal.

1 Discard any coarse stalks or damaged leaves from the herbs, then chop them very finely, especially slightly tough rosemary.

2 Mix the oil, tarragon vinegar, garlic and spring onions in a bowl. Add the chopped herbs and stir to mix thoroughly.

3 Place the salmon in a dish and spoon the marinade over. Cover and leave to marinate in the refrigerator for 4–6 hours.

4 Preheat a grill (broiler) barbecue. Drain the fish and grill for 2–3 minutes each side, brushing with the leftover marinade occasionally.

Energy 383kcal/1593kJ; Protein 34.6g; Carbohydrate 0.5g, of which sugars 0.4g; Fat 27g, of which saturates 4.4g; Cholesterol 84mg; Calcium 63mg; Fibre 0.7g; Sodium 81mg.

tandoori-style marinade for chicken

A marinade or sauce that recreates the flavours of tandoori cooking is a must in any cook's collection. This marinade is terrifically versatile – delicious with chicken or turkey, and also good with lamb. A chilli onion salad, or kachumbar, makes a refreshing accompaniment.

Serves six

INGREDIENTS

12 small chicken drumsticks, skinned

naan breads and lemon wedges, to serve

For the tandoori marinade

3 garlic cloves, crushed

150ml/¼ pint/⅔ cup Greek (US strained plain) yogurt

10ml/2 tsp ground coriander

5ml/1 tsp ground cumin

5ml/1 tsp ground turmeric

1.5ml/¼ tsp cayenne pepper

2.5ml/½ tsp garam masala

15ml/1 tbsp curry paste

juice of ½ lemon

For the kachumbar

2 pink onions, halved and thinly sliced

10ml/2 tsp salt

4cm/1½in piece of fresh root ginger, finely shredded

2 fresh long green chillies, seeded and finely chopped

20ml/4 tsp sugar, preferably palm sugar (jaggery)

juice of ½ lemon

60ml/4 tbsp chopped fresh coriander (cilantro)

1 Using a sharp knife, score each drumstick around the flesh that attaches itself to the tip of the bone and remove the end of the chunky knuckle. (Alternatively, this can be done after marinating.) Place the drumsticks in a non-metallic bowl.

2 For the marinade, whizz the garlic, yogurt, spices, curry paste and lemon juice in a blender or food processor until smooth. Pour the marinade over the drumsticks and turn them to coat them evenly. Cover and chill overnight.

3 Make the kachumbar 2 hours before serving. Put the onions in a bowl, sprinkle with the salt, cover and leave for 1 hour. Drain the onions into a sieve, rinse well under cold water, then drain and pat dry. Roughly chop the slices and put them in a serving bowl. Mix in the remaining ingredients. Cover and set aside until ready to serve.

4 About 30 minutes before cooking, add salt (to taste) to the drumsticks in their marinade, and turn to season them evenly.

5 Prepare the barbecue. When the flames have died down, position a lightly oiled grill rack over the coals to heat. The barbecue is ready when the coals are medium-hot, or with a moderate coating of ash. Alternatively, if not cooking on a barbecue, preheat a grill (broiler) and oil a rack in a grill pan.

6 Carefully lift the drumsticks out of the marinade. To cook on the barbecue, wrap the tips with foil to prevent them from burning. Place the drumsticks to one side of the rack so that they are not directly over the hottest coals. Cover with a lid or tented foil. If using a grill, place the pan well away from the heat source. Cook for 5 minutes, turning often. Brush the drumsticks with marinade and cook for a further 5–7 minutes, until well browned and cooked. Pierce the meat with a knife to check that there are no signs of blood.

7 Serve the tandoori drumsticks hot, with the kachumbar, warmed naan breads and wedges of lemon for extra juice, if required.

Energy 155kcal/654kJ; Protein 23g; Carbohydrate 6.4g, of which sugars 6.1g; Fat 4.5g, of which saturates 1.3g; Cholesterol 108mg; Calcium 81mg; Fibre 0.6g; Sodium 160mg.

basil and chilli marinade for sea trout

Sea trout is similar to wild salmon in texture and flavour. This Thai-style marinade is an ideal seasoning, with chillies and lime to complement and cut the richness of the fish.

Serves six

INGREDIENTS

6 sea trout cutlets, about 115g/4oz each, or wild or farmed salmon

For the basil and chilli marinade

2 garlic cloves, chopped

1 fresh long red chilli, seeded and chopped

45ml/3 tbsp chopped Thai basil

15ml/1 tbsp palm sugar (jaggery) or granulated sugar

3 limes

400ml/14fl oz/1¾ cups coconut milk

15ml/1 tbsp Thai fish sauce

1 Place the sea trout cutlets in a single layer in a large shallow dish.

2 Using a pestle, pound the garlic and chilli in a large mortar to break it up roughly. Then add 30ml/2 tbsp of the Thai basil with the sugar and continue to pound until reduced to a rough paste.

3 Grate the rind from 1 lime and squeeze the juice. Mix the rind and juice into the chilli paste, with the coconut milk. Pour the mixture over the fish cutlets, cover and chill them for about 1 hour. Cut the remaining limes into wedges.

4 Prepare the barbecue. Once the flames have died down, position a lightly oiled grill rack over the coals to heat. The barbecue is ready when the coals are cool to medium-hot, or with a thick to moderate coating of ash. Alternatively, if not cooking the fish on a barbecue, preheat the grill (broiler).

5 Remove the fish from the refrigerator before cooking so that it returns to room temperature. Transfer the cutlets to an oiled, hinged wire fish basket, or directly to the grill rack, reserving the marinade. If cooking indoors, place them on an oiled rack in a grill pan. Cook the fish for 4 minutes on each side. Do not move the cutlets too soon as they tend to stick to the rack until they firm up.

6 Strain the remaining marinade into a pan, reserving the contents of the sieve. Bring the marinade to the boil, simmer gently for 5 minutes, then stir in the contents of the sieve and continue to simmer for 1 minute more. Add the Thai fish sauce and the remaining Thai basil. Lift each fish cutlet on to a plate, pour over the sauce and serve with the lime wedges.

Energy 157kcal/662kJ; Protein 23.1g; Carbohydrate 5.9g, of which sugars 5.9g; Fat 4.7g, of which saturates 0.1g; Cholesterol 0mg; Calcium 46mg; Fibre 0.4g; Sodium 141mg.

soy and star anise marinade for chicken

Chicken cooks quickly and benefits from being marinated first. Aromatic star anise brings clear, punchy flavour to this uncomplicated marinade of soy sauce and olive oil.

Serves four

INGREDIENTS

4 skinless chicken breast fillets
2 whole star anise
45ml/3 tbsp olive oil
30ml/2 tbsp soy sauce
ground black pepper

VARIATION

If you prefer, cook on a barbecue. When the coals are dusted with ash, spread them out evenly. Remove the chicken breasts from the marinade and cook for 8 minutes on each side, spooning over the marinade from time to time, until the chicken is cooked through.

1 Put the chicken breast fillets in a shallow, non-metallic dish and add the star anise.

2 In a small bowl, whisk together the oil and soy sauce and season with black pepper to make the base for marinade.

3 Pour the mixture over the chicken and turn chicken fillets to coat them all over. Cover the dish with clear film (plastic wrap) and set aside for as much time as you have. If you are able to prepare ahead, leave the chicken in the marinade overnight or for about 6–8 hours as the flavour will be improved. Place the covered dish in the refrigerator.

4 Preheat the grill (broiler). Lift the chicken from the marinade and place on a rack in a grill pan. Cook, turning occasionally, for about 8 minutes on each side. Serve immediately.

Energy 206kcal/868kJ; Protein 36g; Carbohydrate 0g, of which sugars 0g; Fat 6.9g, of which saturates 1.2g; Cholesterol 105mg; Calcium 8mg; Fibre 0g; Sodium 90mg.

aromatic marinade for duck

This aromatic marinade makes a delicious alternative to the classic plum sauce that is so often served with duck and pancakes. It takes a long time to prepare but is well worth the effort.

Serves six to eight

INGREDIENTS

1.75–2.25kg/4–5¼lb oven-ready duck

10ml/2 tsp salt

5–6 whole star anise

15ml/1 tbsp Szechuan peppercorns

5ml/1 tsp cloves

2–3 cinnamon sticks

3–4 spring onions (scallions)

3–4 slices fresh root ginger, unpeeled

75–90ml/5–6 tbsp Chinese rice wine
or dry sherry

vegetable oil, for deep-frying

To serve

20–24 thin Chinese pancakes

120ml/4fl oz/½ cup duck sauce or
plum sauce

6–8 spring onions (scallions), thinly
shredded

½ cucumber, thinly shredded

1 Remove the wings from the duck. Split the body in half down the backbone. The best way to do this is using a meat cleaver: if you are nervous about using a chopping technique, use a rolling pin to tap the cleaver through the duck.

2 Rub salt all over the two duck halves, taking care to rub it well in.

3 Place the duck in a dish with the star anise, peppercorns, cloves, cinnamon, spring onions, ginger and rice wine or dry sherry. Cover and set aside to marinate for at least 4–6 hours.

4 Place the duck with the marinade in a steamer positioned in a wok partly filled with boiling water and steam vigorously for 3–4 hours (longer if possible). Remove the duck from the cooking liquid and leave to cool for at least 5–6 hours. The duck must be completely cold and dry or the skin will not crisp.

5 Heat the oil in a preheated wok until smoking, place the duck pieces in the oil, skin side down, and deep-fry for 5–6 minutes or until crisp and brown, turning just once at the very last moment.

6 Drain the duck well. Take the meat off the bone and pile it, with the skin, on lettuce. Serve with the accompaniments: pancakes spread with a little sauce to wrap a portion of the duck meat, plus the shredded spring onion and cucumber. Eat with your fingers.

Energy 337kcal/1411kJ; Protein 18.1g; Carbohydrate 27.2g, of which sugars 5.1g; Fat 17.8g, of which saturates 4.6g; Cholesterol 66mg; Calcium 59mg; Fibre 1.3g; Sodium 438mg.

spicy yogurt marinade for chicken

Plan this dish well in advance; the extra-long marinating time is necessary to develop a really mellow spicy flavour. Use a little less onion if you'd prefer this aspect to be slightly milder.

Serves six

INGREDIENTS

6 chicken pieces
juice of 1 lemon
5ml/1 tsp salt
fresh mint, lemon and lime, to garnish

For the yogurt marinade

5ml/1 tsp coriander seeds
10ml/2 tsp cumin seeds
6 cloves
2 bay leaves
1 onion, quartered
2 garlic cloves
5cm/2in piece fresh root ginger, peeled and roughly chopped
2.5ml/½ tsp chilli powder
5ml/1 tsp turmeric
150ml/¼ pint/⅔ cup natural (plain) yogurt

1 Skin the chicken joints and make deep slashes in the fleshiest parts with a sharp knife. Sprinkle the lemon juice and salt over the chicken, and rub in well.

2 Make the marinade. Spread the coriander and cumin seeds, cloves and bay leaves in the bottom of a large frying pan and dry-fry over a moderate heat until the bay leaves are crispy.

3 Allow the spice mixture to cool, then grind it coarsely in a mortar and pestle.

4 Finely mince the onion, garlic and ginger in a food processor or blender with the ground spices, chilli, turmeric and yogurt. Strain in the lemon from the chicken.

5 Arrange the chicken in a single layer in a roasting pan. Pour the marinade over, then cover and chill for 24–36 hours, turning the chicken pieces occasionally.

6 Preheat the oven to 200°C/400°F/ Gas 6. Cook the chicken for 45 minutes, or until the juices run clear when the meat is pierced. Serve the chicken hot or cold, garnished with fresh mint and slices of lemon or lime.

VARIATION

This marinade will also work well brushed over skewers of lamb or pork fillet prior to grilling or barbecuing.

Energy 156kcal/660kJ; Protein 32.9g; Carbohydrate 2.2g, of which sugars 1.5g; Fat 1.8g, of which saturates 0.5g; Cholesterol 94mg; Calcium 44mg; Fibre 0.5g; Sodium 98mg.

five-spice marinade for quail

This marinade is a Chinese classic. Although the quail is a relatively small bird it is surprisingly meaty. One bird is usually quite sufficient for one serving.

Serves four

INGREDIENTS

4 oven-ready quails

For the five-spice marinade

2 pieces star anise

10ml/2 tsp ground cinnamon

10ml/2 tsp fennel seeds

10ml/2 tsp ground Szechuan or Chinese pepper

pinch of ground cloves

1 small onion, finely chopped

1 garlic clove, crushed

60ml/4 tbsp clear honey

30ml/2 tbsp dark soy sauce

To garnish

2 spring onions (scallions), roughly chopped

1 mandarin orange or satsuma, finely shredded

radish and carrot flowers

banana leaves, to serve

1 Remove the backbones from the quails by cutting down either side with a pair of kitchen scissors.

2 Flatten the birds with the palm of your hand and secure each one with two bamboo skewers.

COOK'S TIP

If you prefer, or if quails are not available, you could use other small poultry such as poussins. Poussins will take around 25–30 minutes to cook.

3 Grind together the star anise, cinnamon, fennel seeds, pepper and cloves in a mortar with a pestle. Add the onion, garlic, honey and soy sauce and combine well.

4 Place the quails on a flat dish, cover with the spice mixture and cover the dish. Set aside to marinate for at least 8 hours.

5 Cook the quails under a preheated grill (broiler) or on a barbecue for 7–8 minutes on each side, basting from time to time with the marinade.

6 Arrange the quails on a bed of banana leaves and garnish with the spring onion, orange rind and radish and carrot "flowers", and serve immediately.

Energy 159kcal/664kJ; Protein 13.2g; Carbohydrate 5.6g, of which sugars 5.6g; Fat 9.5g, of which saturates 2.6g; Cholesterol 68mg; Calcium 7mg; Fibre 0.1g; Sodium 404mg.

lavender balsamic marinade for lamb

Lavender is an unusual flavour to use with meat, but its heady, summery scent works well with barbecued lamb. Use the flower heads for a garnish.

Serves four

INGREDIENTS

4 racks of lamb, with 3–4 cutlets each
lavender flowers, to garnish

For the balsamic marinade

1 shallot, finely chopped
45ml/3 tbsp chopped fresh lavender
15ml/1 tbsp balsamic vinegar
30ml/2 tbsp olive oil
15ml/1 tbsp lemon juice
handful of lavender sprigs
salt and ground black pepper

1 Place the racks of lamb in a large mixing bowl or wide dish and sprinkle the chopped shallot over.
2 Sprinkle the chopped fresh

lavender over the lamb in the bowl. Then rub the lavender into the meat, especially into the the fat.

3 Beat together the vinegar, olive oil and lemon juice and pour them over the lamb. Season well with salt and ground black pepper and then turn the meat to coat evenly.

4 Scatter a few lavender sprigs over the coals of a medium-hot barbecue. Alternatively, preheat a grill (broiler) and have a grill pan with a rack in it ready for cooking the lamb.

5 Cook the lamb for 15–20 minutes, turning once and basting with any remaining marinade, until golden outside and slightly pink in the centre. Keep the lamb well away from the source of heat under a grill. Just before serving, garnish with lavender flower heads.

Energy 565kcal/2333kJ; Protein 31.4g; Carbohydrate 1.2g, of which sugars 0.9g; Fat 48.3g, of which saturates 21.5g; Cholesterol 135mg; Calcium 26mg; Fibre 0.2g; Sodium 111mg.

red wine and juniper marinade for lamb

Juniper berries have a pungent flavour which is ideal for lamb. It is also a classic spice for game and it goes very well with gammon steaks or baked ham.

2 Remove the lamb and vegetables and set aside. Strain the marinade into a jug (pitcher).

3 Preheat the oven to 160°C/325°F/ Gas 3. Heat the oil in a pan and fry the meat and vegetables in batches until lightly browned. Transfer to a casserole and pour over the reserved marinade and stock. Cover and cook in the oven for 2 hours.

Serves four to six

INGREDIENTS

675g/1½lb boned leg of lamb, trimmed
   and cut into 2.5cm/1in cubes

2 carrots, cut into batons

225g/8oz baby onions or shallots

115g/4oz/1½ cups button (white)
   mushrooms

30ml/2 tbsp vegetable oil

150ml/¼ pint/⅔ cup stock

30ml/2 tbsp beurre manié

salt and ground black pepper

For the red wine and juniper marinade

4 rosemary sprigs

8 dried juniper berries, lightly crushed

8 black peppercorns, lightly crushed

300ml/½ pint/1¼ cups red wine

1 Place the meat in a bowl. Add the vegetables, rosemary, berries and peppercorns, then pour over the wine. Cover the bowl and leave the meat in a cool place for 4–5 hours, stirring once or twice during this time.

4 Twenty minutes before the end of cooking, stir in the beurre manié, then cover and return to the oven. Season to taste before serving.

COOK'S TIP

Beurre manié is made of equal parts of butter and flour blended together. It is used as a thickening agent and should be added a small piece at a time.

Energy 289kcal/1204kJ; Protein 23g; Carbohydrate 4.1g, of which sugars 3.2g; Fat 16.5g, of which saturates 6.3g; Cholesterol 86mg; Calcium 26mg; Fibre 1g; Sodium 106mg.

lemon and rosemary marinade for lamb

Marinate the leg of lamb overnight in the refrigerator so that the flavours of this delicate white wine marinade have plenty of time to penetrate the meat fully.

Serves six

INGREDIENTS

1.3–1.6kg/3–3½lb leg of lamb

2 garlic cloves, sliced

15ml/1 tbsp cornflour (cornstarch)

For the lemon and rosemary marinade

1 lemon, sliced

6 rosemary sprigs

4 lemon thyme sprigs

300ml/½ pint/1¼ cups dry white wine

60ml/4 tbsp olive oil

salt and ground black pepper

3 Mix the wine, oil and seasoning and pour over the lamb. Cover and leave in a cool place for 4–6 hours, turning occasionally.

4 Preheat the oven to 180°C/350°F/Gas 4, then roast the lamb for 25 minutes per 450g/1lb plus 25 minutes. Baste with the marinade occasionally during roasting.

VARIATION

You can also use lemon and rosemary marinade for chicken pieces, but you must roast the meat without the marinade or it will become tough. Use the marinade for making gravy.

5 When the lamb is cooked, transfer to a warmed plate to rest. Drain the excess fat from the pan. Blend the cornflour with a little cold water and stir into the juices. Stir over a moderate heat for 2–3 minutes, then adjust the seasoning.

1 Make small cuts at intervals over the lamb surface. Insert a piece of garlic in each cut.

2 Place the lamb in a roasting pan. Scatter the lemon slices and herbs over the top.

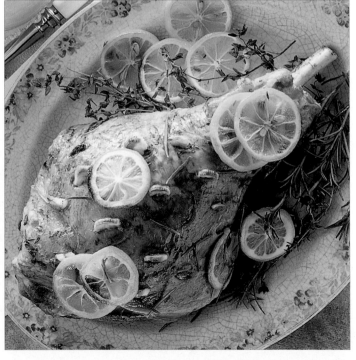

Energy 435kcal/1812kJ; Protein 46g; Carbohydrate 0.2g, of which sugars 0.2g; Fat 26g, of which saturates 11.1g; Cholesterol 178mg; Calcium 13mg; Fibre 0g; Sodium 103mg.

chinese sesame marinade for beef

Toasted sesame seeds bring their distinctive smoky aroma to this Oriental marinade.
It's delicious with lean pork or lamb as well as the beef used in this recipe.

Serves four

INGREDIENTS

450g/1lb rump (round) steak

30ml/2 tbsp sesame seeds

15ml/1 tbsp sesame oil

30ml/2 tbsp vegetable oil

115g/4oz/1½ cups small mushrooms, quartered

1 green (bell) pepper, seeded and diced

4 spring onions (scallions), chopped

For the Chinese sesame marinade

10ml/2 tsp cornflour (cornstarch)

30ml/2 tbsp rice wine or sherry

15ml/1 tbsp lemon juice

15ml/1 tbsp soy sauce

few drops Tabasco sauce

2.5cm/1in piece fresh root ginger, peeled and grated

1 garlic clove, crushed

1 To make the marinade, blend the cornflour with the rice wine or sherry. Add the other marinade ingredients.

2 Trim the steak and cut it into thin strips about 1 x 5cm/½ x 2in. Stir into the marinade, cover and leave in a cool place for 3–4 hours.

3 Place the sesame seeds in a large frying pan or wok. Cook dry over a moderate heat, shaking the pan until the seeds are golden: do not overcook. Set aside.

4 Heat the oils in the frying pan. Drain the beef, reserving the marinade, and brown a few pieces at a time. Remove the meat with a slotted spoon.

5 Add the mushrooms and pepper and fry for 2–3 minutes, stirring continuously. Add the spring onions and cook for about a further minute.

6 Replace the beef and reserved marinade, and stir over a moderate heat for 2 minutes, or until the strips of beef are evenly coated with the glaze. Sprinkle with the toasted sesame seeds, and serve.

VARIATION

This marinade would also be good with lean pork fillet or chicken breast. Instead of the Tabasco, a seeded and diced red chilli may be added with the mushrooms and bell pepper to bring a little chilli heat to the dish.

Energy 290kcal/1208kJ; Protein 27.4g; Carbohydrate 5.8g, of which sugars 3.2g; Fat 17.6g, of which saturates 3.7g; Cholesterol 66mg; Calcium 65mg; Fibre 1.8g; Sodium 252mg.

winter-spiced ale marinade for beef

This marinade can also be used as a flavouring base for a casserole of beef or lamb pieces. It will imbue the meat with a rich malty flavour.

Serves six

INGREDIENTS

1.3kg/3lb top rump beef

For the winter-spiced ale marinade

1 onion, sliced

2 carrots, sliced

2 celery sticks, sliced

2–3 parsley stalks, lightly crushed

large fresh thyme sprig

2 bay leaves

6 cloves, lightly crushed

1 cinnamon stick

8 black peppercorns

300ml/½ pint/1¼ cups brown ale

45ml/3 tbsp vegetable oil

30ml/2 tbsp beurre manié

salt and ground black pepper

1 Put the meat in a polythene bag placed inside a large, deep bowl. For the marinade, add the vegetables, herbs and spices, then pour the ale over the meat in the bag. Gather up the bag and tie or close the end to seal the meat in the marinade. Leave in a cool place for at least 5–6 hours.

2 Remove the beef and set aside. Strain the marinade into a bowl, reserving the vegetables and liquid.

3 Heat the oil in a flameproof casserole. Fry the vegetables until lightly browned, then remove with a slotted spoon and set aside. Brown the beef all over in the remaining oil.

4 Preheat the oven to 160°C/325°F/ Gas 3. Return the vegetables to the casserole and pour the reserved marinade over the beef.

5 Cover the casserole and cook in the oven for 2½ hours. Turn the beef two or three times in the marinade during cooking so that it cooks evenly.

6 To serve, remove and slice the beef. Arrange on plates with the vegetables. Bring the liquor to the boil. Gradually stir in the beurre manié and simmer for 3 minutes. Taste the sauce and adjust the seasoning. Serve with the meat.

Energy 380kcal/1590kJ; Protein 48.4g; Carbohydrate 5.3g, of which sugars 3.8g; Fat 15.8g, of which saturates 5.2g; Cholesterol 131mg; Calcium 27mg; Fibre 0.3g; Sodium 155mg.

sauces for
sweet dishes

*Dessert sauces are the ultimate sweet treat,
loved by adults and children alike. Fruit
sauces bursting with flavour are divine
served on understated dairy desserts;
lusciously dark chocolate sauces bring bittersweet intrigue to simple ice creams, while
zesty citrus infusions transform crisp waffles
into an exotic sweet course. There are also
delicate creams and pastes – perfect for
toppings or fillings – plus custards, syrups
and caramels. Something for every
heart's desire.*

berry sauce for baked ricotta cakes

This fabulously fragrant, fruity sauce complements ice creams, custards, sponge puddings and cheesecakes – especially these honey and vanilla-flavoured baked ricotta cheesecakes.

Serves four

INGREDIENTS

250g/9oz/generous 1 cup ricotta cheese
2 egg whites
about 60ml/4 tbsp clear honey
few drops of vanilla extract
fresh mint leaves, to decorate (optional)

For the red berry sauce

450g/1lb/4 cups mixed fresh or frozen fruit, such as strawberries, raspberries, blackberries and cherries

COOK'S TIPS

• The sauce can be made a day ahead. Chill until ready to use.
• Frozen fruit doesn't need extra water, as there will be ice crystals clinging to the berries.

1 Preheat the oven to 180°C/350°F/ Gas 4. Grease four ramekins.

2 Place the ricotta cheese in a bowl and break it up with a wooden spoon. Lightly whisk the egg whites with a fork to break them up a little, then mix into the cheese with the honey and vanilla until thoroughly combined and smooth.

3 Spoon the ricotta mixture into the prepared ramekins and level the tops. Bake for 20 minutes or until risen and golden.

4 Meanwhile, make the berry sauce. Reserve about a quarter of the fruit for decoration. Place the rest of the fruit in a pan, with a little water if the fruit is fresh, and heat gently until softened. Cool slightly, removing any cherry stones (pits), if necessary.

5 Press the fruit through a sieve, then taste and sweeten with honey if it is too tart. Serve the sauce, warm or cold, with the ricotta cakes. Decorate with the reserved berries and mint leaves, if using.

Energy 186kcal/782kJ; Protein 8.7g; Carbohydrate 18g, of which sugars 18g; Fat 9.4g, of which saturates 5.8g; Cholesterol 26mg; Calcium 27mg; Fibre 2.5g; Sodium 35mg.

papaya sauce for grilled pineapple

This papaya sauce partners slightly tart fruit perfectly – pineapple, redcurrants or gooseberries. It is also excellent with grilled chicken, game birds, pork or lamb.

Serves six

INGREDIENTS

1 sweet pineapple

melted butter, for greasing and brushing

2 pieces drained stem ginger in syrup, cut into fine matchstick pieces

30ml/2 tbsp demerara (raw) sugar

pinch of ground cinnamon

30ml/2 tbsp stem ginger syrup

fresh mint sprigs, to decorate

For the papaya sauce

1 ripe papaya, peeled and seeded

175ml/6fl oz/¾ cup apple juice

VARIATIONS

Try papaya nectar in the sauce, using it half and half with the apple juice.

Try grilled bananas instead of pineapple, adding the grated rind and juice of 1 lime and omitting the ginger.

1 Cut the leaves and stalk end off the pineapple. Peel it and cut out the eyes by removing spiral wedges around the fruit. Then slice it across into six slices, each about 2.5cm/1in thick.

2 Line a baking tray with a sheet of foil, rolling up the edges to make a rim. Grease the foil with melted butter. Preheat the grill (broiler).

3 To make the sauce, cut a few slices from the papaya and set them aside. Then purée the rest with the apple juice in a food processor or blender. Press the purée through a fine sieve and set aside.

4 Arrange the pineapple slices on the foil. Brush with butter, then top with the ginger and sprinkle with the sugar and cinnamon. Drizzle over the ginger syrup. Grill (broil) for 5–7 minutes, or until the slices are lightly charred.

5 Arrange the pineapple slices on warm plates. Stir any cooking juices into the papaya sauce and drizzle a little on each plate. Decorate with the reserved papaya slices and the mint sprigs.

Energy 110kcal/469kJ; Protein 0.9g; Carbohydrate 27.5g, of which sugars 27.5g; Fat 0.4g, of which saturates 0g; Cholesterol 0mg; Calcium 44mg; Fibre 3.1g; Sodium 7mg.

strawberry sauce for lemon hearts

This speedy sweet sauce makes a delicious accompaniment for these delicate lemon and cheese hearts. Strawberry sauce is also irresistible with ice cream or with chilled rice pudding.

Serves four

INGREDIENTS

175g/6oz/¾ cup ricotta cheese

150ml/¼ pint/⅔ cup natural (plain) yogurt

15ml/1 tbsp sugar

finely grated rind of ½ lemon

30ml/2 tbsp lemon juice

10ml/2 tsp powdered gelatine

2 egg whites

oil, for greasing

For the strawberry sauce

225g/8oz/2 cups fresh or frozen and
  thawed strawberries, plus extra
  to decorate

15ml/1 tbsp lemon juice

1 Beat the ricotta cheese until smooth. Stir in the yogurt, sugar and lemon rind. Lightly oil four individual heart-shaped moulds, preferably using sweet almond oil.

2 Place the lemon juice in a small bowl and sprinkle the gelatine over it. Allow to stand for about 1 minute. Dissolve the gelatine over a pan of hot water, stirring often.

3 Whisk the egg whites until they form soft peaks. Quickly stir the gelatine into the ricotta cheese mixture, mixing it in evenly, then immediately fold in the whisked egg whites.

4 Spoon the ricotta mixture into the prepared moulds. Cover and chill for a few hours, until set.

5 Meanwhile, make the strawberry sauce. Place the strawberries and lemon juice in a food processor or blender and process until smooth.

6 To serve, pour the sauce on to plates. Turn out the lemon hearts on to a board and use a metal slice to transfer them to the plates. Decorate with strawberries.

VARIATION

Add a dash of Cointreau or Grand Marnier liqueur to the strawberry sauce.

Energy 134kcal/563kJ; Protein 8.2g; Carbohydrate 10.7g, of which sugars 10.7g; Fat 6.9g, of which saturates 4.2g; Cholesterol 19mg; Calcium 88mg; Fibre 1.4g; Sodium 64mg.

raspberry sauce for baked peaches

Peaches and raspberries are classic partners – a combination that's hard to beat for a
sophisticated summer dessert. Try this sauce with a cool slice of melon for a summer starter.

Serves six

INGREDIENTS

45ml/3 tbsp unsalted (sweet) butter, at
room temperature

50g/2oz/¼ cup caster (superfine) sugar

1 egg, beaten

50g/2oz/½ cup ground almonds

6 ripe peaches

For the raspberry sauce

175g/6oz/1 cup raspberries

15ml/1 tbsp icing (confectioner's) sugar

15ml/1 tbsp fruit-flavoured brandy
(optional)

1 Preheat the oven to 180°C/350°F/
Gas 4. Beat the butter with the
sugar until pale, soft and fluffy.
Lightly beat in the egg – do not
overbeat the mixture or it may
become grainy. Add the ground
almonds and beat until just
combined.

2 Halve the peaches and remove
the stones (pits). With a spoon,
scrape out some of the flesh from
each peach half – just enough to
enlarge the hollow left by the stone
slightly. Reserve the scooped-out
peach flesh to use in the sauce.

3 Place the peach halves on a
baking sheet, supporting them on
crumpled foil to keep them steady.
Spoon the butter and almond
mixture into the peach halves.

4 Bake the peaches for about 30
minutes, or until the almond filling
is puffed and golden and the
peaches are very tender.

5 For the sauce, combine all the
ingredients in a food processor or
blender. Add the reserved peach
flesh. Process until smooth and
then press the sauce through a sieve
to remove fibres and seeds.

6 Let the peaches cool. Place two
halves on each plate and spoon
the sauce over. Serve immediately.

Energy 240kcal/1005kJ; Protein 4.4g; Carbohydrate 26.3g, of which sugars 24.4g; Fat 13.8g, of which saturates 5.6g; Cholesterol 54mg; Calcium 43mg; Fibre 2.4g; Sodium 88mg.

passion fruit coulis for fruit sundae

Frozen yogurt pairs up delightfully with a luxurious fruit coulis, and this coulis is very simple to make. Fresh summer strawberries are unlikely to need much sweetening.

Serves four

INGREDIENTS

175g/6oz/1½ cups strawberries, hulled and halved

2 ripe peaches, stoned (pitted) and chopped

8 scoops (about 350g/12oz) vanilla or strawberry frozen yogurt

For the passion fruit coulis

175g/6oz/1½ cups strawberries, hulled and halved

1 passion fruit

10ml/2 tsp icing (confectioners') sugar (optional)

1 To make the coulis, purée the strawberries in a food processor or blender until smooth. Scoop out the passion fruit pulp and add it to the coulis. Taste the coulis and sweeten it with icing sugar if necessary.

2 Spoon half the remaining strawberries and half the chopped peaches into four tall sundae glasses.

3 Add a scoop of frozen yogurt to each glass. Set aside a few choice pieces of fruit for decoration, and use the rest in another layer on each sundae. Top each with a scoop of frozen yogurt.

4 Pour the passion fruit coulis over, and decorate the sundaes with the reserved strawberries and pieces of peach. Serve immediately.

Energy 137kcal/581kJ; Protein 4.8g; Carbohydrate 24.8g, of which sugars 23.8g; Fat 2.8g, of which saturates 1.8g; Cholesterol 3mg; Calcium 125mg; Fibre 1.8g; Sodium 57mg.

hazelnut dip for sweet summer fruits

Fresh fruit is always a good choice for a colourful, simple dessert, and this recipe makes it complete, with a delicious sauce for dipping. Choose any fruit that can be served raw.

Serves two

INGREDIENTS

selection of fresh fruits, such as satsumas, kiwi fruit, grapes, physalis and whole strawberries

For the hazelnut dip

50g/2oz/¼ cup soft cheese

150ml/¼ pint/⅔ cup hazelnut yogurt

5ml/1 tsp vanilla extract

5ml/1 tsp caster (superfine) sugar

50g/2oz/⅓ cup shelled hazelnuts, chopped

COOK'S TIP

You can use any soft cheese, but Italian ricotta is to be recommended.

1 First prepare the fruits according to type: peel and segment the satsumas. Peel the kiwi fruit and cut into wedges. Wash the grapes and peel the physalis by piercing the papery casing and pulling back.

2 To make the dip, beat the soft cheese with the hazelnut yogurt, vanilla essence and sugar in a bowl. Stir in three-quarters of the chopped hazelnuts.

3 Spoon the hazelnuts into a glass serving dish and place this on a platter. Alternatively, serve the dip in small dishes on individual plates. Scatter the remaining hazelnuts over the dip.

4 Arrange the prepared fruits around the bowl – or bowls – of dip and serve immediately.

Energy 365kcal/1521kJ; Protein 10.9g; Carbohydrate 32.7g, of which sugars 31.3g; Fat 22g, of which saturates 5g; Cholesterol 13mg; Calcium 168mg; Fibre 4.4g; Sodium 60mg.

lemon and lime sauce for pancakes

This tangy, refreshing sauce is the perfect foil for pancakes. It is also good with fruit fritters – especially banana fritters – or a lively accompaniment for steamed sponge pudding.

2 Place the rind in a pan with enough water to cover. Bring to the boil, drain and set aside, discarding the water.

3 Mix a little sugar with the arrowroot and stir in enough of the water to give a smooth paste. Heat the remaining water until hot but not boiling. Stir in the paste and bring to the boil, stirring. Remove from the heat at once. Stir in the remaining sugar, citrus juice and reserved rind. Keep the sauce hot but do not boil.

4 For the pancakes, sift the flour into a bowl and make a well in the middle. Add the egg and a little milk, then beat together drawing in flour and gradually adding the rest of the milk for a smooth batter.

5 Heat a little oil in a frying pan. Add a thin layer of batter and cook until set. Turn the pancake and lightly brown the other side. Turn out on to a plate and keep warm while you repeat the method with the rest of the batter. To serve, fold the pancakes, drizzle with sauce and decorate with mint.

Serves four

INGREDIENTS

90g/3½oz/scant 1 cup plain (all-purpose) flour

1 egg

300ml/½ pint/1¼ cups milk

vegetable oil, for frying

mint or lemon balm, to decorate

For the lemon and lime sauce

1 lemon

2 limes

300ml/½ pint/1¼ cups water

50g/2oz/¼ cup caster (superfine) sugar

25ml/1½ tbsp arrowroot

1 First, make the sauce. Using a citrus zester, remove the rind in fine shreds from the lemon and limes, taking care not to cut into the pith. Squeeze the juice from the fruit into a single bowl and and set it aside while you make the pancakes.

Energy 181kcal/770kJ; Protein 6.3g; Carbohydrate 34.7g, of which sugars 11.7g; Fat 3g, of which saturates 1.2g; Cholesterol 52mg; Calcium 133mg; Fibre 0.7g; Sodium 51mg.

butterscotch sauce for waffles

This is a deliciously sweet sauce which will be loved by everyone. It is a classic with waffles but also ice cream. Be sure to use dark muscovado for rich success.

Serves four to six

INGREDIENTS

1 pack ready-made waffles
vanilla ice cream, to serve

For the butterscotch sauce

75g/3oz/6 tbsp butter
175g/6oz/¾ cup dark muscovado
(molasses) sugar
175ml/6fl oz/¾ cup evaporated milk
50g/2oz/⅓ cup hazelnuts

1 Warm the waffles in a preheated oven, according to the packet instructions, while you make the butterscotch sauce.

2 Melt the butter and sugar in a heavy-based pan, bring to the boil and simmer for 2 minutes. Cool for 5 minutes.

3 Heat the evaporated milk to just below boiling point, then gradually stir into the sugar mixture. Cook over a low heat for 2 minutes, stirring the sauce frequently.

VARIATION

Substitute any nut for the hazelnuts. You could also add plump raisins and a dash of rum instead of the nuts.

4 Spread the hazelnuts on a baking sheet and toast under a hot grill until golden brown. Tip on to a clean dish towel and rub briskly to remove the skins.

5 Chop the nuts roughly and stir into the sauce. Serve the sauce hot, poured over scoops of vanilla ice cream and the warm waffles.

Energy 405kcal/1694kJ; Protein 6.6g; Carbohydrate 47.3g, of which sugars 35.1g; Fat 22.3g, of which saturates 7.6g; Cholesterol 32mg; Calcium 192mg; Fibre 1.1g; Sodium 305mg.

orange sauce for crêpes

This is one of the best-known French desserts and is easy to do at home. You can make the crêpes in advance, and then coat them in the tangy orange sauce at the last minute.

Serves six

INGREDIENTS

115g/4oz/1 cup plain (all-purpose) flour

1.5ml/¼ tsp salt

25g/1oz/2 tbsp caster (superfine) sugar

2 eggs, lightly beaten

about 250ml/8fl oz/1 cup milk

about 60ml/4 tbsp water

30ml/2 tbsp orange flower water,
    Cointreau or orange liqueur

25g/1oz/2 tbsp unsalted (sweet) butter,
    melted, plus extra for frying

For the orange sauce

75g/3oz/6 tbsp unsalted (sweet) butter

50g/2oz/¼ cup caster (superfine) sugar

grated rind and juice of 1 large orange,
    such as Jaffa

grated rind and juice of 1 lemon

150ml/¼ pint/⅔ cup freshly squeezed
    orange juice

60ml/4 tbsp Cointreau or orange liqueur,
    plus more for flaming (optional)

brandy, for flaming (optional)

orange segments, to decorate

COOK'S TIP

Cointreau is the world's leading brand of orange liqueur. It is colourless and flavoured with a mixture of bitter orange peel and sweet oranges.

1 Sift the flour, salt and sugar into a large bowl. Make a well in the centre and pour in the eggs. Beat the eggs, gradually incorporating the flour.

2 Whisk in the milk, water and orange flower water or liqueur to make a very smooth batter. Strain into a jug (pitcher) and set aside for 20–30 minutes.

3 Heat an 18–20cm/7–8in crêpe pan (preferably non-stick) over a medium heat. If the crêpe batter has thickened, add a little more water or milk to thin it. Stir the melted butter into the batter.

4 Brush the hot pan with a little extra melted butter and pour in about 30ml/2 tbsp of batter. Quickly tilt and rotate the pan to cover the base evenly with a thin layer of batter. Cook for about 1 minute, or until the top is set and the base is golden. With a metal spatula, lift the edge to check the colour, then carefully turn over the crêpe and cook for 20–30 seconds, just to set. Tip out on to a plate.

5 Continue cooking the crêpes, stirring the batter occasionally and brushing the pan with a little more melted butter as and when necessary. Place a sheet of clear film (plastic wrap) or baking parchment between each crêpe as they are stacked to prevent them from sticking. (The crêpes can be prepared ahead to this point – put them in a plastic bag and chill until ready to use.)

6 To make the sauce, melt the butter in a large frying pan over a medium-low heat, then stir in the sugar, orange and lemon rind and juice, the additional orange juice and the orange liqueur.

7 Place a crêpe in the pan browned-side down, swirling gently to coat with the sauce. Fold it in half, then in half again to form a triangle, and push to the side of the pan. Continue until all the crêpes are covered with the sauce.

8 To flame, heat 30–45ml/2–3 tbsp each of orange liqueur and brandy in a small pan over a medium heat. Remove from the heat, carefully ignite the liquid with a match then pour evenly over the crêpes. Top with the orange segments and serve.

Energy 316kcal/1323kJ; Protein 5.6g; Carbohydrate 34.2g, of which sugars 19.6g; Fat 17.2g, of which saturates 10.1g; Cholesterol 103mg; Calcium 100mg; Fibre 0.6g; Sodium 152mg.

caramel sauce for oranges

The appeal of this tasty dessert is the contrast between sweet caramel and tangy oranges. Make it in advance for convenient entertaining – try caramel with pineapple for a classy alternative.

Serves six

INGREDIENTS

6 large seedless oranges, such
as Navelina, well-scrubbed
90g/3½oz/½ cup sugar

1 With a vegetable peeler, remove
wide strips of rind from two of the
oranges. Stack two or three strips
at a time and cut into very thin
julienne strips.

2 Using a sharp knife, cut a thin
slice of peel and pith from both
ends of each orange. Place cut-side
down on a plate and cut off the
peel and pith in strips down the
side of the fruit. Remove any
remaining pith. Slice the peeled
fruit crossways into thick rounds
about 1cm/½in thick. Put the
orange slices in a serving bowl and
pour over any juice.

3 Half-fill a large bowl with cold
water and set aside. Place the sugar
and 45ml/3 tbsp water in a small,
heavy pan without a non-stick
coating and bring to the boil over a
high heat, swirling the pan to
dissolve the sugar.

4 Continue to boil, without
stirring, until the mixture turns a
dark caramel colour. Remove the
pan from the heat and, standing
well back, dip the base of the pan
into the cold water to stop the
cooking process.

5 Add about 30ml/2 tbsp water to
the caramel, pouring it down the
sides of the pan, swirling to mix.

6 Add the strips of orange rind and
return the pan to the heat. Simmer
gently over a medium-low heat,
stirring occasionally, for 8–10
minutes, or until the strips are
slightly translucent. Remove the
pan from the heat.

7 Pour the caramel and rind over
the oranges, turn gently to mix and
cool, then chill for at least 1 hour
before serving.

Energy 96kcal/410kJ; Protein 1.2g; Carbohydrate 24.2g, of which sugars 24.2g; Fat 0.1g, of which saturates 0g; Cholesterol 0mg; Calcium 55mg; Fibre 1.7g; Sodium 6mg.

hot plum sauce for meringue islands

The plum sauce can be made in advance, then reheated just before you cook the meringues. This makes an unusual and healthy pudding that is simpler to make than it looks.

Serves four

INGREDIENTS

2 egg whites

30ml/2 tbsp concentrated apple juice syrup

freshly grated nutmeg

For the hot plum sauce

450g/1lb red plums

300ml/½ pint/1¼ cups apple juice

1 To make the plum sauce, halve the plums and remove, and discard, the stones (pits). Place the plum halves in a wide pan and pour in the apple juice.

2 Bring to the boil and then cover the pan. Reduce the heat and leave the fruit to simmer very gently for 15–20 minutes, or until the plums are tender.

3 Meanwhile, whisk the egg whites into firm, soft peaks. Gradually whisk in the apple juice syrup, and continue whisking until the meringue is stiff and glossy.

COOK'S TIP

Concentrated apple juice or apple juice syrup is available from health food shops. Golden (light corn) syrup may be used instead.

4 Use two spoons to scoop the meringue in ovals and add them to the gently simmering sauce. (If the pan is not big enough, do this in two batches.)

5 Cover and simmer gently for 2–3 minutes, until the meringues are just firm and set. Serve the meringues on the sauce as soon as they are all cooked. Sprinkled with a little nutmeg.

Energy 81kcal/347kJ; Protein 2.2g; Carbohydrate 18.8g, of which sugars 18.8g; Fat 0.2g, of which saturates 0g; Cholesterol 0mg; Calcium 22mg; Fibre 1.8g; Sodium 35mg.

lime sabayon for ice cream

Sabayon is a light, foamy sauce. This tangy version is irresistible with chocolate ice cream or it can be served with vanilla or tropical fruit ice cream.

2 Whisk the mixture over a pan of simmering water until the sabayon is smooth and thick, and the mixture leaves a ribbon trail when the whisk is lifted from the bowl.

3 Lightly whisk in the cream. Remove the bowl from the pan and cover with a lid or plate.

4 Working quickly, place scoops of the chocolate ice cream into four chilled sundae glasses or individual serving dishes. Spoon the warm lime sabayon sauce over the ice cream, sprinkle with the strips of lime rind to decorate and serve immediately.

Serves four

INGREDIENTS

2 egg yolks
65g/2½oz/5 tbsp caster (superfine) sugar
finely grated rind and juice of 2 limes
60ml/4 tbsp white wine or apple juice
45ml/3 tbsp single (light) cream
500ml/17fl oz/2¼ cups chocolate
  ice cream
thinly pared strips of lime rind, to decorate

COOK'S TIP

For a special occasion, serve the ice cream in frosted glass. Rub the rim of the glasses with a lime wedge, then dip in a saucer of caster (superfine) sugar. Leave to dry before carefully adding the scoops of ice cream.

1 Put the egg yolks and caster sugar in a heatproof bowl and beat well until thoroughly combined. Beat in the lime rind and juice, then the white wine or apple juice.

VARIATIONS

• You can substitute other citrus fruit for the limes in the sabayon sauce. Orange sabayon, using the rind and juice of one orange, would also go well with chocolate ice cream, while lemon sabayon sauce complements peach sorbet (sherbet).
• For a completely different dessert serve the lime sabayon with fresh strawberries or sliced bananas piled on hot waffles.

Energy 343kcal/1440kJ; Protein 6.4g; Carbohydrate 43.5g, of which sugars 42.1g; Fat 15.7g, of which saturates 9.8g; Cholesterol 137mg; Calcium 157mg; Fibre 0g; Sodium 84mg.

lime and cardamom sauce for bananas

Aromatic cardamom and fresh lime give an exotic hint to the flaked almonds in this delicious sauce for pouring over bananas.

Serves four

INGREDIENTS

6 small bananas

50g/2oz/¼ cup butter

50g/2oz/½ cup flaked (sliced) almonds

seeds from 4 cardamom pods, crushed

thinly pared rind and juice of 2 limes

50g/2oz/¼ cup light muscovado
  (molasses) sugar

30ml/2 tbsp dark rum

vanilla ice cream, to serve

VARIATIONS

• If you prefer not to use alcohol in your cooking, replace the rum with a fruit juice of your choice, such as orange or even pineapple juice.

• The sauce is equally good poured over folded crêpes.

1 Peel the bananas and cut them in half lengthways. Heat half the butter in a large frying pan. Add half the bananas, and cook until golden. Turn carefully and cook the second side until golden.

2 As they cook, transfer the bananas to a heatproof serving dish. Cook the remaining bananas in the same way.

3 Melt the remaining butter, then add the almonds and cardamom seeds. Cook, stirring until golden.

4 Stir in the lime rind and juice, then the sugar. Cook, stirring, until the mixture is smooth, bubbling and slightly reduced. Stir in the rum. Pour the sauce over the bananas and serve immediately, with vanilla ice cream.

Energy 347kcal/1452kJ; Protein 4.2g; Carbohydrate 41.3g, of which sugars 38.2g; Fat 17.6g, of which saturates 7.2g; Cholesterol 27mg; Calcium 46mg; Fibre 2.2g; Sodium 80mg.

kumquat sauce for apple sponges

The intense flavour of kumquats makes these dainty puddings special. Served with more kumquats in a creamy sauce, this is a dessert that is sure to please.

Serves eight

INGREDIENTS

150g/5oz/10 tbsp butter, at room temperature, plus extra for greasing

175g/6oz cooking apples, peeled and thinly sliced

75g/3oz kumquats, thinly sliced

150g/5oz/¾ cup golden caster (superfine) sugar

2 eggs

115g/4oz/1 cup self-raising (self-rising) flour

For the sauce

75g/3oz kumquats, thinly sliced

75g/3oz/6 tbsp caster (superfine) sugar

250ml/8fl oz/1 cup water

150ml/¼ pint/⅔ cup crème fraîche

5ml/1 tsp cornflour (cornstarch) mixed with 10ml/2 tsp water

lemon juice to taste

1 Prepare a steamer. Butter eight 150ml/¼ pint/⅔ cup dariole moulds or ramekins and put a disc of buttered baking parchment on the base of each.

2 Melt 25g/1oz/2 tbsp butter in a frying pan. Add the apples, kumquats and 25g/1oz/2 tbsp sugar and cook over medium heat for 5–8 minutes, or until the apples start to soften and the sugar begins to caramelize. Leave to cool.

3 Cream the remaining butter with the remaining sugar until pale and fluffy. Add the eggs, one at a time, beating after each addition. Fold in the flour.

4 Divide the apple and kumquat mixture among the moulds. Top with the sponge mixture. Cover and steam for 45 minutes.

5 Make the sauce. Bring the kumquats, sugar and water to the boil, stirring to dissolve the sugar. Simmer for 5 minutes.

6 Stir in the crème fraîche and bring back to the boil, stirring. Remove the pan from the heat and gradually whisk in the cornflour mixture. Return the pan to the heat and simmer very gently for 2 minutes, stirring constantly. Add lemon juice to taste.

7 Turn out the puddings and serve hot, with the sauce spooned over and around the sponges.

Energy 402kcal/1680kJ; Protein 3.7g; Carbohydrate 44.4g, of which sugars 33.7g; Fat 24.5g, of which saturates 15.3g; Cholesterol 109mg; Calcium 93mg; Fibre 1g; Sodium 190mg.

malted chocolate and banana dip

Chocolate and banana combine irresistibly in this rich dip, served with fresh fruit in season. For a creamier dip, stir in some lightly whipped cream just before serving.

Serves four

INGREDIENTS

50g/2oz plain (semisweet) chocolate

2 large ripe bananas

15ml/1 tbsp malt extract

mixed fresh fruit, such as strawberries, peaches and kiwi fruit, halved or sliced, to serve

1 Break the chocolate into pieces and place in a small, heatproof bowl. Stand the bowl over a pan of gently simmering water and stir the chocolate occasionally until it melts. Allow to cool slightly.

2 Break the bananas into pieces and place in a food processor or blender. Pulse the power until the bananas are finely chopped.

3 With the motor running, pour in the malt extract, and continue processing the mixture until it is thick and frothy.

4 Drizzle in the chocolate in a steady stream and process until well blended. Serve immediately, with the prepared fruit alongside.

Energy 144kcal/607kJ; Protein 2.1g; Carbohydrate 27.1g, of which sugars 26.1g; Fat 3.7g, of which saturates 2.2g; Cholesterol 1mg; Calcium 27mg; Fibre 2.1g; Sodium 19mg.

mexican hot fudge sauce for sundaes

Definitely not one for dieters, this fantastic fudge sauce is best kept for those special, indulgent days! It's superlative with warmed doughnuts for a truly naughty treat.

2 Remove from the heat and stir in the chocolate. When melted and smooth, stir in the cream and liqueur, if using. Let the sauce cool just to lukewarm. Alternatively, if made ahead, reheat the sauce gently while assembling the sundaes.

3 Using an ice-cream scoop, fill the sundae dishes with 1 scoop each of vanilla and coffee ice cream.

4 Arrange the bananas on the top of the ice creams. Pour the warm sauce over the bananas.

5 Top each sundae with a generous swirl of whipped cream. Sprinkle the sundaes with the toasted almonds and serve immediately, before the ice cream melts or the sauce cools.

Serves four

INGREDIENTS

600ml/1 pint/2½ cups vanilla ice cream
600ml/1 pint/2½ cups coffee ice cream
2 large ripe bananas, sliced
whipped cream
toasted sliced almonds

For the hot fudge sauce

60ml/4 tbsp light muscovado brown sugar
115g/4oz/⅓ cup golden (light corn) syrup
45ml/3 tbsp strong black coffee
5ml/1 tsp ground cinnamon
150g/5oz plain dark (bittersweet) chocolate, broken up
75ml/5 tbsp whipping cream
45ml/3 tbsp coffee liqueur (optional)

1 To make the sauce, combine the sugar, golden syrup, coffee and cinnamon in a heavy pan. Bring to the boil, stirring. Turn down the heat a little and continue to simmer the mixture, stirring constantly, for about 5 minutes.

Energy 1010kcal/4238kJ; Protein 14.1g; Carbohydrate 139.5g, of which sugars 134.2g; Fat 44.1g, of which saturates 29.4g; Cholesterol 95mg; Calcium 340mg; Fibre 1.8g; Sodium 266mg.

rich chocolate sauce for profiteroles

A real treat if you're not counting calories, this classic sauce is so versatile – it's good with scoops of vanilla ice cream, fabulous with fruit and delectable with pancakes or waffles.

Serves six

INGREDIENTS

65g/2½ oz/9 tbsp plain (all-purpose) flour

50g/2oz/¼ cup butter

150ml/¼ pint/⅔ cup water

2 eggs, lightly beaten

150ml/¼ pint/⅔ cup whipping cream, whipped

For the chocolate sauce

150ml/¼ pint/⅔ cup double (heavy) cream

50g/2oz/¼ cup butter

50g/2oz/¼ cup vanilla sugar

175g/6oz plain (semisweet) chocolate

30ml/2 tbsp brandy

VARIATION

White chocolate and orange sauce

40g/1½ oz/3 tbsp caster (superfine) sugar, to replace vanilla sugar

finely grated rind of 1 orange

175g/6oz white chocolate, to replace plain (semisweet) chocolate

30ml/2 tbsp orange liqueur, to replace brandy

1 Make the chocolate sauce. Place the cream, butter and vanilla sugar in a heatproof bowl. Stand the bowl over a pan of hot, not boiling, water. Stir until smooth.

2 Break the chocolate into pieces and add to the cream. Turn the heat off under the pan – remove the pan from the heat, if necessary. Stir until the chocolate has melted and thoroughly mixed with the sauce.

3 Stir in the brandy a little at a time, then leave the sauce to cool to room temperature.

4 If making the white chocolate and orange sauce (variation), heat the cream and butter with the caster sugar and orange rind in a heatproop bowl over hot water until the butter has melted. Add the white chocolate and, when it has melted, stir in the orange liqueur.

5 To make the profiteroles, preheat the oven to 200°C/400°F/Gas 6. Sift the flour on to a plate. Melt the butter and water in a pan and bring to the boil.

6 Add the flour all at once, stir and remove the pan from the heat. Stir until the mixture comes away from

the pan in a smooth ball. Do not beat. Cool for about 5 minutes, then gradually beat in the eggs, adding enough to make a paste with a piping consistency. Beat until smooth and glossy. Pipe small balls of the mixture on to dampened baking sheets.

7 Bake for 15–20 minutes, or until crisp. Make a slit in the sides and cool on a wire rack.

8 Fill a piping (pastry) bag with cream and pipe some into each profiterole. Pile on to a plate, topped with a little sauce. Serve the remaining sauce separately.

Energy 597kcal/2481kJ; Protein 5.6g; Carbohydrate 36.9g, of which sugars 28.3g; Fat 47.4g, of which saturates 28.8g; Cholesterol 161mg; Calcium 69mg; Fibre 1.1g; Sodium 139mg.

sabayon sauce

This frothy sauce is very versatile and can be served alone with light dessert biscuits or hot over cake, fruit or even ice cream. Never let the sauce stand before serving, as it will collapse.

Serves four to six

INGREDIENTS

2 egg yolks

75g/3oz/scant ½ cup caster (superfine) sugar

150ml/¼ pint/⅔ cup Marsala or other sweet white wine

finely grated rind and juice of 1 lemon

dessert biscuits, to serve

COOK'S TIP

A generous pinch of arrowroot, whisked with the yolks, will help to prevent the sauce from collapsing too quickly.

1 Whisk the egg yolks and sugar in a large heatproof bowl until they are pale and thick. A hand whisk is ideal but you may want to start at this stage with an electric beater.

2 Stand the bowl over a pan of hot, but not boiling, water. Gradually add the Marsala or white wine and lemon juice, a little at a time, whisking vigorously.

3 Continue whisking until the mixture is thick enough to hold a trail when the whisk is lifted. The sabayon can be served freshly prepared, in which case, stir in the lemon rind. Divide the sabayon among glasses and serve at once.

4 To serve the sabayon cold, place the bowl of mixture over a bowl of iced water and continue whisking until it is cool and chilled. Add the finely grated lemon rind and stir in. Pour into small glasses and serve at once, with the dessert biscuits.

Energy 59kcal/248kJ; Protein 2.1g; Carbohydrate 2.4g, of which sugars 2.4g; Fat 2.8g, of which saturates 0.8g; Cholesterol 99mg; Calcium 17mg; Fibre 0g; Sodium 18mg.

red fruit sauce for boyer cream

This creamy soft cheese mousse is fluffy and light. Scented with rose water and flavoured with an exuberant sauce of red soft fruit, it is a glorious summer treat.

Serves four to six

INGREDIENTS

225g/8oz/1 cup full-fat soft white
  (farmer's) cheese
75ml/5 tbsp sour cream
2 eggs, separated
50g/2oz/¾ cup vanilla sugar

For the red fruit sauce
115g/4oz/⅔ cup raspberries
115g/4oz/1 cup strawberries
icing (confectioners') sugar, sifted,
  to taste
15ml/1 tbsp rose water
halved strawberries, mint leaves and
  small pink roses, to decorate

COOK'S TIP

This dessert looks beautiful served on saucers decorated with strawberries, rosebuds and mint leaves.

1 Beat the cheese in a bowl with the sour cream and egg yolks until the cheese has thoroughly softened. Stir in half of the sugar.

2 Whisk the egg whites in another bowl until they are stiff, then whisk in the remaining sugar. Fold the egg whites into the cheese mixture and set aside to chill.

3 To make the red fruit sauce, purée the raspberries and strawberries in a blender. Press through a sieve (strainer) to remove pips (seeds) and add icing sugar, to taste.

4 Swirl 4–6 glass dishes with a little rose water and divide three-quarters of the red fruit sauce among the dishes.

VARIATION

Try different berries and fruit to vary the sauce. Serve the sauce with ice creams, sundaes or cheesecakes.

5 Top the sauce with the cheese mixture, spreading it evenly. Add the remaining sauce in a thin stream from a small jug (pitcher), using the point of a knife to swirl.

Energy 210kcal/875kJ; Protein 6.1g; Carbohydrate 11.2g, of which sugars 11.2g; Fat 16g, of which saturates 9.4g; Cholesterol 105mg; Calcium 75mg; Fibre 0.7g; Sodium 155mg.

sticky toffee sauce for sponge pudding

Forget the main course because this is gooey and gorgeous for a sweet-course-only meal! The sauce is also fabulous with ice cream or, for a complete change, try it with apple pie or tart.

Serves six

INGREDIENTS

115g/4oz/1 cup walnuts, chopped
175g/6oz/¾ cup butter
175g/6oz/scant 1 cup soft brown sugar
60ml/4 tbsp double (heavy) cream
30ml/2 tbsp lemon juice
2 eggs, beaten
115g/4oz/1 cup self-raising
 (self-rising) flour

1 Toast the walnuts by dry-frying in an ungreased pan. Remove from the heat as soon as they begin to brown. Next, grease a 900ml/1½ pint/¾ cup heatproof bowl. Place half the nuts in the bowl.

2 To make the sauce, heat 50g/2oz/ 4 tbsp of the butter with 50g/2oz/ 4 tbsp of the sugar, the cream and 15ml/1 tbsp lemon juice in a small pan, stirring until smooth. Pour half over the nuts, then swirl the bowl to part-coat the sides.

3 For the pudding, beat the remaining butter and sugar until fluffy, then beat in the eggs. Fold in the flour, remaining nuts and lemon juice and spoon into the bowl.

4 Cover with greaseproof (waxed) paper with a pleat folded across the middle, then tie securely with string. Steam the pudding for about 1¼ hours, until risen, springy and set in the centre.

6 Just before serving, gently warm the remaining sauce. Unmould the pudding on to a warm plate and pour over the warm sauce.

Energy 606Kcal/2523kJ; Protein 7.5g; Carbohydrate 46g, of which sugars 31.6g; Fat 44.9g, of which saturates 20.3g; Cholesterol 152mg; Calcium 122mg; Fibre 1.3g; Sodium 279mg.

real custard

Adding cornflour helps to prevent custard from curdling. This recipe uses enough cornflour for sure success – simple to make and seriously good with all sorts of heartwarming hot puddings.

Serves four to six

INGREDIENTS

450ml/¾ pint/scant 2 cups milk

few drops of vanilla extract

2 eggs plus 1 egg yolk

15–30ml/1–2 tbsp caster (superfine)
  sugar)

15ml/1 tbsp cornflour (cornstarch)

30ml/2 tbsp water

COOK'S TIP

If you are not serving the custard immediately, cover the surface of the sauce with clear film (plastic wrap) to prevent a skin from forming and keep warm in a heatproof bowl over a pan of hot water.

1 In a pan heat the milk with the vanilla extract and remove from the heat just as the milk comes to the boil.

3 Strain the egg and milk mixture back into the pan and heat gently, stirring constantly. Take care not to overheat the mixture or the eggs will curdle.

4 Continue stirring until the custard thickens sufficiently to coat the back of a wooden spoon. Do not allow to boil or it will curdle. Serve immediately.

2 Whisk the eggs and yolk in a bowl with the caster sugar until well combined but not frothy. In a separate bowl, blend together the cornflour with the water and mix into the eggs. Whisk in a little of the hot milk, then mix in all the remaining milk.

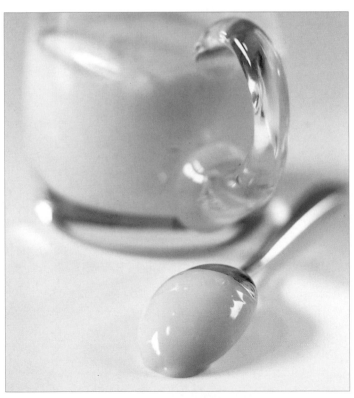

Energy 156Kcal/656kJ; Protein 8g; Carbohydrate 17.9g, of which sugars 11g; Fat 6.5g, of which saturates 2.4g; Cholesterol 170mg; Calcium 147mg; Fibre 0g; Sodium 92mg.

orange-almond paste for baked apricots

Take advantage of the short apricot season by making this charming apricot and almond dessert, delicately scented with lemon juice and orange flower water.

Serves six

INGREDIENTS

75g/3oz/6 tbsp caster (superfine) sugar

30ml/2 tbsp lemon juice

300ml/½ pint/1¼ cups water

115g/4oz/1 cup ground almonds

50g/2oz/½ cup icing (confectioners') sugar

a little orange flower water

25g/1oz/2 tbsp unsalted (sweet) butter, melted

2.5ml/½ tsp almond extract

900g/2lb fresh apricots

fresh mint sprigs, to decorate

1 Preheat the oven to 180°C/350°F/ Gas 4. Place the sugar, lemon juice and water in a small pan and bring to the boil, stirring occasionally until the sugar has all dissolved. Simmer gently for 5–10 minutes to make a thin syrup.

COOK'S TIP

Always use a heavy pan when making syrup and stir constantly until the sugar has completely dissolved. Do not let liquid come to the boil before it has dissolved, or the result will be grainy.

2 Place the ground almonds, icing sugar, orange flower water, butter and almond extract in a large bowl and blend together to make a smooth paste.

3 Wash the apricots and then make a slit in the flesh and ease out the stone (pit). Take small pieces of the almond paste, roll into balls and press one into each of the apricots.

4 Arrange the stuffed apricots in a shallow ovenproof dish and carefully pour the sugar syrup around them. Cover with foil and bake in the oven for 25–30 minutes.

5 Serve the apricots with a little of the syrup, and decorated with sprigs of fresh mint.

Energy 277kcal/1164kJ; Protein 5.5g; Carbohydrate 33.9g, of which sugars 33.4g; Fat 14.3g, of which saturates 3g; Cholesterol 9mg; Calcium 80mg; Fibre 4g; Sodium 32mg.

lime cheese for lemon grass skewers

Grilled fruits make a fine finale. Lemon grass skewers and bay leaves add delicate flavour.
Lime cheese is the perfect accompaniment – it is also good with any fresh fruit, grilled or raw.

Serves four

INGREDIENTS

4 long fresh lemon grass stalks

1 mango, peeled, stoned (pitted) and
   cut into chunks

1 papaya, peeled, seeded and cut
   into chunks

1 star fruit (carambola), cut into chunks

8 fresh bay leaves

oil, for greasing

a little nutmeg

60ml/4 tbsp maple syrup

50g/2oz/¼ cup demerara (raw) sugar

For the lime cheese

150g/5oz/⅔ cup curd (farmer's) cheese
   or low-fat soft cheese

120ml/4fl oz/½ cup double (heavy) cream

grated rind and juice of ½ lime

30ml/2 tbsp icing (confectioners') sugar

1 Prepare the barbecue or preheat
the grill (broiler). Cut the top of
each lemon grass stalk into a point
with a sharp knife. Discard the
outer leaves, then use the back of
the knife to bruise the length of
each stalk to release the oils.

2 Thread each lemon grass stalk,
skewer-style, with a selection of the
fruit pieces and two bay leaves.

3 Support a piece of foil on a
baking sheet and roll up the edges
to make a rim. Grease the foil, lay
the kebabs on top and grate a little
nutmeg over each. Drizzle the
maple syrup over and dust liberally
with the demerara sugar. Grill
(broil) or barbecue for 5 minutes,
until the kebabs are lightly charred.

4 Meanwhile, make the lime cheese.
Mix together the cheese, cream,
grated lime rind and juice, and icing
sugar in a bowl. Serve at once with
the lightly charred fruit kebabs.

COOK'S TIP

The lime cheese can be made in
advance and chilled. It makes a great
dip for strawberries, apple wedges or
chunks of banana.

Energy 390kcal/1634kJ; Protein 7.1g; Carbohydrate 51.3g, of which sugars 51.2g; Fat 19.3g, of which saturates 12g; Cholesterol 50mg; Calcium 102mg; Fibre 3.7g; Sodium 219mg.

rose petal cream for fruit shortcakes

Rose petal cream and fresh raspberries fill this delectable and luxurious dessert. Although they look impressive, these shortcakes are easy to make and are ideal for a dinner party. Offer the rose-flavoured cream as an accompaniment for all sorts of desserts, from ices to hot fruit pies.

Serves six

INGREDIENTS

115g/4oz/½ cup unsalted (sweet) butter, softened

50g/2oz/¼ cup caster (superfine) sugar

½ vanilla pod (bean), split and seeds reserved

115g/4oz/1 cup plain (all-purpose) flour, plus extra for dusting

50g/2oz/⅓ cup semolina

For the filling

300ml/½ pint/1¼ cups double (heavy) cream

15ml/1 tbsp icing (confectioners') sugar, plus extra for dusting

2.5ml/½ tsp rose water

450g/1lb/2⅔ cups raspberries

For the decoration

12 miniature roses, unsprayed

6 mint sprigs

1 egg white, beaten

caster (superfine) sugar, for dusting

COOK'S TIPS

• For best results, serve the shortcakes as soon as possible after assembling them. Otherwise, they are likely to turn soggy from the raspberries' liquid.

• If necessary, ground rice can be substituted for the semolina used for making the shortcakes.

• For the best-flavoured shortcakes, always use butter and not margarine.

1 Cream the butter, sugar and vanilla seeds together in a bowl until the mixture is pale and fluffy. Sift the flour and semolina together, then gradually work the dry ingredients into the creamed mixture to make a dough.

2 Gently knead the dough on a lightly floured surface until smooth. Roll out quite thinly and prick all over with a fork. Using a 7.5cm/3in fluted cutter, cut out 12 rounds. Place these on a baking sheet and then chill them in the refrigerator for 30 minutes.

3 Meanwhile, make the rose petal cream. Whisk the double cream with the icing sugar until soft peaks form. Gently fold the rose water into the mixture. Cover and then chill until required.

4 Preheat the oven to 180°C/350°F/Gas 4. Paint the roses and mint sprigs with the beaten egg white. Dust with sugar; place on a wire rack to dry.

5 Bake the shortcakes in the preheated oven for 15 minutes, or until they are lightly golden. Lift them off the baking sheet with a metal fish slice (spatula) and transfer to a wire rack to cool.

6 To assemble the shortcakes, spoon the rose water cream on to half the shortcakes. Arrange a layer of raspberries on top of the cream, then top with a second shortcake.

7 Dust the filled shortcakes with icing sugar. Decorate with the frosted roses and mint sprigs.

VARIATIONS

Other soft, red summer berries, such as mulberries, loganberries and tayberries, would be equally good in this dessert.

Energy 547kcal/2273kJ; Protein 4.7g; Carbohydrate 37.1g, of which sugars 16g; Fat 43.2g, of which saturates 26.8g; Cholesterol 109mg; Calcium 81mg; Fibre 2.7g; Sodium 132mg.

preserved sauces, chutneys, relishes, pickles, preserved fruits, savoury and sweet jellies, jams, marmalades and butters

PRESERVES

PERFECTING PRESERVES

Modern preserving has evolved from ancient methods of keeping summer produce edible for winter months. Drying was the earliest method of preserving, relying on summer sun or by using fire and smoking food. Salt, vinegar and alcohol followed as mediums for preventing the growth of micro-organisms and putrification. Sugar followed later as a preservative, once it was sourced from sugar beet. Preserving developed as a culinary "craft", a country pastime, during the eighteenth century.

Above: Stone fruits, such as plums, figs and cherries, can be pickled whole in wine or cider vinegar.

GROWING POPULARITY

From simple methods, rich products evolved. Vegetables, fruit and spices were combined with vinegar and sugar in complex concoctions, bursting with flavour. The pickled vegetables, store sauces or ketchups, chutneys and mixed pickles of tradition became condiments for plain foods. Sweet or sour, smooth or chunky, chutneys or pickles, and tart, piquant relishes epitomize European savoury preserves. They

are fabulous served with cold pies or cheese, with grilled meats, or with cold and hot roasts.

The same principles are used for capturing the fresh flavour of fruit and vegetables in different countries. Pickled lemons or limes may be rich with the oils and spices of Indian cooking or salted and aromatic for flavouring Middle-Eastern dishes. There are fiery Indian chutneys or sweet-sour combinations that can be used in Chinese cooking.

SWEET PRESERVES

Every culture has its sweet preserves, including jams, jellies and conserves. Some set, some gently flowing, but all packed with fruit flavour captured in syrup or cooked with sugar. Sweet, fruity and sparkling jellies are classic accompaniments for rich poultry or

Left: A simple addition such as citrus rind may add as much flavour as the fruit itself.

game. Fruit pickled in sweetened vinegars become plump and juicy asides for savoury dishes.

Alcohol and sugar together act as potent preservatives and they can be used to prevent whole pieces of fruit from decaying when preserved in sauces and syrups. Flowers and fruit rind are also popular in sweet preserves. Spices often enhance flavours, making them richer or warmer. Herbs can also be preserved in fruit jellies for sumptuous sweet-savoury condiments.

SELECTING THE BEST

Only the best ingredients are worth preserving. Vegetables and fruit should be in their prime: well developed and just ripe, at their peak of flavour. They should be perfect, neither bruised nor damaged, neither under- nor over-ripe. Some fruit have a high pectin content, an ingredient that reacts with acid and sugar to make liquids set: this is the foundation of classic jams, jellies and marmalades. Not all fruit are rich in pectin and those that are have most when they are slightly under-ripe, so they are usually combined with fruit that is just peaked for a perfect flavour and set combination.

SIMPLE YET SO GOOD

It is often the chutneys and sauces with sophisticated, quite complex flavours that are easiest to make. Vinegar and sugar together form a formidable preservation partnership that protects sauces, chutneys, pickles and relishes for long-term keeping with the minimum of fuss. As long as the sugar is not added too soon, there is no secret technique for perfect results with these savoury condiments. Spices and flavouring ingredients generally require nothing more critical than long simmering. For sure success all you need is perfectly clean pots and equipment, good lids, and all the time in the world to eat up the rewards of your work – these vinegary preserves will usually keep for at least a year or so.

VERSATILITY

Home-made preserves are far superior to most commercial alternatives. There really is no comparison. The vinegar, sugar and spices in savoury preserves are better. Many are useful for

Right: Who can resist the chunky texture and piquant flavours of a fruity chutney?

enriching gravies and sauces, acting as marinades, or enhancing salad dressings and dips.

Sweet fruit preserves usually have more fruit. As long as the concentration of sugar is high enough and the fruit is fantastic, worrying over the perfect set is not essential because the flavour will always be quite luxurious. When sweet preserves are so fruity, they become hugely versatile. With yogurt or soft, fresh cheeses they become brilliant desserts; thinned with a little brandy, sherry or liqueur they make instant, superior sauces for crêpes or other desserts.

Left: The addition of sugar and a tightly-lidded jar are two essentials for successful storage.

PRACTICALITIES

It is also worth remembering that you do not have to embark on a Victorian-style preserving marathon. Row upon row of glistening pots might have suited country house kitchens catering for large families and regular weekend parties but they may be too much for a typical household. The recipes in these chapters are practical for modern cooks and they reflect realistic servings. Seriously good, spicy relishes and fiery sauces are welcome in most households, so you can present your best efforts as gifts for friends and family.

The microwave can be used for cooking small amounts of preserves, especially relishes, and the freezer can be used for storing sweet or savoury preserves. If finding a cool, dark cupboard for storage is a problem, it is worth remembering the garage, where a clean cupboard can be ideal.

a guide to preserving

Preserves are little powerhouses of concentrated flavour, capturing and retaining the essence of seasonal produce at its very best. Whether savoury, sweet, spicy or piquant, making them does not have to be difficult – it simply involves a planned window of time. Potted or bottled, labelled, stored and matured, these inspired recipes work as condiments to main meals and many will also make highly original gifts for friends and family.

PRESERVING INGREDIENTS

A few special ingredients are essential when making preserves, because they contribute to the keeping quality of the final jam, jelly or pickle. The four main preservatives are sugar, vinegar, salt and alcohol. These all help to prolong the life of the other ingredients used in the preserve by creating an environment in which micro-organisms such as moulds and bacteria cannot grow.

SUGAR

This is the key preservative used in jams, jellies, marmalades, curds and many preserved fruits. A high proportion of sugar is needed and if the sugar content is less than 60 per cent of the total weight of the preserve (for example, in low-sugar

jams), this will affect the keeping quality of the preserve. These low-sugar jams and fruit preserves should be used within a few months or kept in the refrigerator to prevent the growth of mould.

Sugar also plays an important role in the setting of jams, jellies and marmalades. To achieve a good set, sugar should make up between 55 and 70 per cent of the total weight of the preserve. (High acid content in the fruit will also aid the setting of sweet preserves.)

white sugars

Use these refined sugars to produce clarity in sweet, set preserves.

Preserving sugar: This has quite large, irregular crystals and is ideal for jams, jellies and marmalades. The large crystals allow water to percolate between them, which helps to prevent the preserve burning and reduces the need for stirring (which is important to avoid breaking up fruit too much). Use this sugar for the clearest preserves. If preserving sugar is unavailable, granulated sugar can be used instead.

Preserving sugar with pectin: Also known as jam sugar, this sugar is used with low-pectin fruit. The sugar contains natural pectin and citric acid to help overcome setting problems. Preserves made with this sugar tend to have a shorter shelf-life and should be stored for no longer than six months.

Left: White and golden sugars are a key ingredient used in sweet fruit preserves, jams and jellies.

Granulated sugar: This is coarser than caster (superfine) sugar, less expensive and gives a clear result.

Cube sugar: Made from white granulated sugar that has been moistened, moulded into blocks, dried and cubed, this gives the same results as preserving sugar.

brown sugars

These sugars give a pronounced flavour and darker colour to both sweet and savoury preserves.

Demerara/raw sugar: A pale golden sugar with a mild caramel flavour. Traditionally an unrefined sugar with a low molasses content, it may also be made from refined white sugar with molasses added.

Golden granulated sugar: This may be refined or unrefined. It can be used instead of white sugar for a hint of flavour and colour.

Soft brown sugar: Moist, with fine grains and a rich flavour, it may be light or dark in colour and is usually made from refined white sugar with molasses added.

Muscovado/molasses sugar: This may be light or dark and is usually made from unrefined cane sugar. It has a deeper, more pronounced taste than soft brown sugar.

Palm sugar: Made from the sap of palms, this has a fragrant flavour. Sold pressed into blocks, it needs to be chopped before use. Light muscovado (brown) sugar is a good alternative.

Jaggery: This raw sugar from India has a distinctive taste. It must be chopped before use. Use a mixture of light brown muscovado and demerara sugar as an alternative.

Right: Raspberry and white wine vinegar are used both to preserve ingredients and to add a sharp, tangy flavour.

VINEGARS

The word vinegar comes from the French *vin aigre*, meaning sour wine. Vinegar is made by exposing fruit or grain-based alcohol to air; a bacterial reaction then turns the alcohol into acetic acid and it is this acid that helps to prevent the growth of micro-organisms in pickles and preserves. Vinegar used for pickling must have an acetic acid content of at least 5 per cent.

Malt vinegar: Made from a type of beer, this usually has an acetic acid content of 8 per cent, which allows it to be safely diluted by moisture and juices from fruit and vegetables. Malt vinegar usually contains caramel, which turns it a dark brown colour. Its strong flavour makes it ideal for pickles, chutneys and bottled sauces.

Pickling vinegar: Simply malt vinegar flavoured with spices.

Distilled malt vinegar: This has the same strong flavour as ordinary malt vinegar but is colourless and therefore suitable for making clear pickles and light preserves.

Wine vinegar: May be red or white, depending on the colour of the original wine. Most wine vinegars contain about 6 per cent acetic acid. White wine vinegar is mild and better for delicate preserves; red wine vinegar is slightly more robust and good for spiced fruits.

Raspberry vinegar: Made by steeping the fruit in wine vinegar, this is excellent for pickled fruits.

Balsamic vinegar: Has a smooth, mellow flavour. Its low acidity makes it unsuitable for use on its own, but it can be used as a flavouring for mild preserves, stirred in at the end of cooking.

Sherry vinegar: Slightly sweet with a fairly strong flavour.

Cider vinegar: Has a slightly sharp taste and a fruity flavour. It is excellent for fruit preserves.

Rice vinegar: Colourless, mild rice vinegar is made from rice wine and is often used for pickling ginger.

SALT

This is used in preserving both as a seasoning and as a dehydrator. It is often used in a process called brining to draw out moisture from vegetables such as cucumber and marrow, making them crisp while preventing the dilution of the preserve, which would reduce its keeping quality. Ordinary table and cooking salt is fine for this process, but use pure crystal salt, also known as kosher salt, or preserving or rock salt for clear pickles as ordinary table and cooking salts contain anti-caking ingredients that contribute to the clouding of preserves.

ALCOHOL

Spirits, such as brandy and rum, and liqueurs, which are at least 40 per cent ABV (alcohol by volume), can be used. Fortified wine, wine, beer and cider have a lower alcohol content so are not effective alone and should be either heat treated or combined with sugar.

ACIDS

These help to set jams and jellies and prevent discoloration.

Lemon juice: This adds pectin, prevents fruits from turning brown and enhances both flavour and colour. Use either freshly squeezed or bottled lemon juice.

Citric acid is sold as fine white crystals and can be used instead of lemon juice in preserves.

Tamarind: This is a brown, dense spice used both for its acid flavour and its character.

Below: Many different kinds of salt can be used for pickling, from coarse sea salt, prized for its ability to draw out flavour, to preserving, or "kosher", salt.

HERBS AND FLOWERS

Flavourings are an essential part of most preserves and using the right amount is as important as selecting the correct one. In some preserves a subtle hint is all that is needed; in others the flavouring is one of the main ingredients.

HERBS

Fresh and dried herbs are invaluable in savoury preserves, and are included occasionally in sweet ones. They can be added during the initial cooking, then removed, or finely chopped and stirred in towards the end of cooking. If dried herbs are used instead of fresh, then reduce the quantity by a third to half.

Below: Oregano has a lovely, aromatic flavour that is very good with summer squashes.

tender herbs

Herbs with fragile leaves need careful handling to avoid bruising. Once picked, they should be used within a few days. Tie the whole herb stalks in muslin (cheesecloth) and add to the simmering preserve, or stir chopped leaves into the preserve at the end of cooking.
Basil: This highly aromatic herb bruises and discolours easily, so rather than adding it to a preserve, it can be steeped in vinegar until it imparts its flavour, then removed.
Chervil: Use these tiny, soft and lacy leaves soon after picking. They have a flavour similar to parsley with a hint of aniseed, which goes well with mild, delicate vegetables.
Mint: The many varieties of this aromatic herb include peppermint, spearmint, apple mint, lemon mint and pineapple mint. It adds a fresh flavour to preserves, but should be used sparingly.
Parsley: Curly and flat leaf varieties are available. It is an essential herb in a bouquet garni.
Tarragon: This herb is excellent for flavouring vinegars but is rarely used in its fresh form because it darkens and discolours on heating.

robust herbs

Often woody, with pungent leaves, these herbs are added to preserves during cooking to extract and mellow their flavour.
Bay leaf: Essential in bouquet garni, these dark green glossy leaves should be dried for a few days before use. They add a slightly spicy flavour to preserves.

Above: Parsley has a mild flavour and is often used with other herbs.

Marjoram and oregano: Popular in tomato preserves, these herbs are also good with marrow (large zucchini). They should be added towards the end of cooking.
Rosemary: Powerfully aromatic, fresh or dried rosemary should be used in small quantities. It goes very well with citrus fruits.
Sage: A strong herb that often partners garlic and tomatoes.
Thyme: This robust herb works well with preserves made from roasted vegetables and beans.

aromatic and spicy herbs

Some herbs have aromatic citrus flavours, others aniseed tones; a few have a warm, spicy pungency.
Coriander/cilantro Every part of this aromatic herb can be used – from its delicate leaves and sturdier stalks to its hard brown seeds. Also known as Chinese parsley, the leaves resemble slightly rounded

flat leaf parsley. They have a warm, spicy taste and add pungency to Middle Eastern, Asian and Indian chutneys and fresh, Mexican-style relishes.

Dill: This delicate herb has dark green, feathery leaves and has a subtle aniseed taste. It is an excellent flavouring for mild-tasting courgette (zucchini) and cucumber relishes and pickles.

Fennel: Part of the same family as dill, with a similar, but stronger flavour, it is particularly good for flavouring vinegars.

Kaffir lime leaf: This strong-tasting, aromatic leaf is used to flavour Thai and Malaysian preserves.

Lemon grass: A tall hard grass, with a distinctive lemony aroma and taste, lemon grass is often used in Thai preserves and should be bruised to release the flavour.

Lovage Similar to celery leaves with a peppery flavour, lovage is good with root vegetables and in mixed vegetable chutneys.

FLOWERS

Many types of edible flowers and their leaves can be used to add fragrance and flavour to preserves, including the flowers of herbs such as rosemary, thyme, marjoram, fennel and chives.

Borage: The tiny, brilliant blue or purple flowers of this plant can be candied or used to decorate jellies. Borage leaves have a fresh cucumber-like taste and can be used to flavour jellies.

Geranium leaves: These give jams and jellies a subtle flavour. There are several different varieties with apple, rose or lemon aromas.

Lavender: Intensely fragrant, sprigs of lavender can be used to flavour sugar, jams and jellies. The sprigs also look very pretty suspended in jelly: dip them in boiling water first, then shake off the excess before putting them in the jar and pouring over the hot jelly.

Rose: Scented red, pink or yellow petals make wonderful jams and jellies. They are often combined with fruit juice, such as grape, and with added pectin, so that the preserve sets quickly without destroying the aroma of the petals. Be sure to use unsprayed roses.

Left: Tender-leafed basil has a fragrant, peppery flavour that goes particularly well with tomato-based preserves.

MAKING A BOUQUET GARNI
This is a bunch of aromatic herbs, tied with a piece of string or in a square of muslin (cheesecloth). A bouquet garni can be added to preserves and simmered until the flavours have infused (steeped) into the mixture, giving a subtle taste and aroma. Fresh herbs will give the best flavour.

1 For jellies or sauces that will be strained after cooking, tie together a sprig of parsley, a sprig of thyme, and a bay leaf with a piece of string. Suspend the bunch of herbs in the preserve, tying it to the pan handle for easy removal.

2 For chutneys and relishes, tie the herbs loosely in a piece of fine muslin (cheesecloth), about 15cm/6in square, so that the liquid can bubble through and extract the herbs' flavour.

SPICES

These can be hot and spicy or warm and fragrant and are used in all kinds of preserves both for flavour and decoration. Store spices in a cool, dark place: ground ones will keep for up to six months, whole spices for a year.

HOT SPICES

These spices are used to add heat to preserves, and can be mild and subtle or exceedingly fiery.

Cayenne: Made from ground dried chillies, cayenne is extremely hot and should be used sparingly.

Chillies: Fresh chillies may be cooked in preserves to add heat, or added whole or chopped to clear pickles when bottling.

Below: Sweet, mild paprika is used to add both flavour and colour to chutneys and relishes.

Chilli powder: This hot spice is made from ground dried chillies. Mild chilli powder and chilli seasoning are both blends of ground chilli and milder spices such as cumin, oregano and garlic.

Galangal: Related to ginger, with pink-tinged flesh, galangal is often used in Malasian- and Thai-style preserves. Ginger may be used as a substitute.

Ginger: Good in both sweet and savoury preserves, root ginger may be used fresh, dried or ground. Preserved stem ginger can be added to conserves and marmalades.

Mustard There are three types of mustard seed: white, brown and black; the latter is the hottest. The taste and aroma develops when the seeds are crushed or mixed with liquid. Whole mustard seeds are often included in pickles and ground mustard powder in relishes. The intensity diminishes with long simmering, so mustard powder is often added towards the end of cooking. Salt and vinegar also reduce its pungency.

Paprika: This rich, red spice is sold ground and used for its colour and flavour, which ranges from mild and sweet to strong and pungent.

Peppercorns: Often added whole to pickles, these tiny round berries may be green, black or white. Green ones are unripe and mildly flavoured, black ones are hot and pungent. White peppercorns have a mild aromatic flavour.

Turmeric: Although yellow turmeric has a distinctive warm, spicy taste, it is often used simply for its colour as a cheap alternative to saffron in pickles and relishes.

Above: Fresh root ginger adds warmth and a lively fresh flavour to all kinds of preserves.

SEED SPICES

Some plants such as coriander and dill are cultivated for both their leaves and seeds; others, including caraway and cumin, are grown for their seeds alone.

Caraway seeds: These are mildly pungent and feature in many northern European preserves, notably sauerkraut. The seeds need long soaking or cooking to soften them and release the flavour.

Cumin seeds: Tiny light brown seeds with a distinctive warm flavour, cumin is used in Indian, Mexican, North African and Middle Eastern preserves. Cumin seeds are widely available both whole and ground.

GRINDING WHOLE SPICES

Spices may be bought ready-ground but most are best when freshly ground because, once ground, they quickly lose their flavour and aroma. Grind spices by hand using a mortar and pestle, or use a spice mill or coffee grinder reserved solely for this purpose.

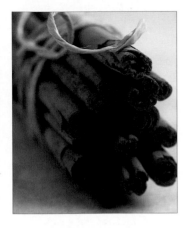

Above: Whole cinnamon sticks are often used to flavour sweet syrups for preserving fruits.

Coriander seeds: These small round seeds have a mild orange flavour. They are usually included in pickling spice.

Dill seeds: Small oval seeds with a similar flavour to caraway.Often used with cucumber pickles.

Left: Golden saffron threads can be used to impart a subtle flavour and glorious colour.

FRAGRANT SPICES

Spices with a warm, fragrant flavour are good used in both fruity and sweet preserves.

Allspice: With an aroma and flavour that is reminiscent of cloves, cinnamon and nutmeg, this is good used with orchard fruits.

Cassia and cinnamon: The bark of evergreen trees, these are available ground or in sticks. The sticks are best used whole for flavouring pale or clear preserves.

Cloves: These tiny dried flower buds, sold whole or ground, have a distinctive taste that goes well with apples and citrus fruit.

Juniper: Used to give gin its distinctive flavour, blue-black juniper berries may be used fresh, but are more usually dried.

Nutmeg and mace: Nutmeg has a warm nutty flavour. It is best bought whole and grated fresh. Mace is the orange-coloured lacy outer covering of the nutmeg; it is sold as blades.

Saffron: Made from the dried stigmas of the *Crocus sativus*, saffron is the most expensive of all spices. Only a few threads are needed to produce a golden colour and impart a bitter-sweet flavour.

Star anise: This star-shaped, aniseed-flavoured spice looks wonderful in pickles and bottled preserves. It can also be used sparingly in chutneys.

Tamarind: This dark brown pulp from the pod of the tamarind tree adds a unique sour flavour to preserves and pickles.

Vanilla: Used to flavour bottled fruits and occasionally jams and jellies, long, dark brown vanilla pods (beans) have a sweet, warm, aromatic flavour.

PICKLING SPICES

Various blends of pickling spices are available, or you can make your own. Typical mixtures include allspice, bay leaf, cardamom, coriander and mustard seeds, cassia or cinnamon, dried chillies, whole cloves, dried root ginger and peppercorns. Add 5–15ml/1–3 tsp of pickling spices to each 600ml/1 pint/2½ cups vinegar and simmer for 5–15 minutes, then cool and strain. Alternatively, tie the spices in muslin (cheesecloth), cook in the preserve, then remove.

Below: Vanilla, star anise, ground ginger and cinnamon sticks are all widely used in preserves.

PRESERVING EQUIPMENT

While very few specialist items are essential for preserving, having the correct equipment for the job will make the whole process easier and helps to ensure success. You will probably have most of the basic items such as a large heavy pan, weighing scales or calibrated measuring cups, wooden spoons, a chopping board and a few sharp knives. However, a few specific items such as a jam funnel for potting preserves and a jelly bag for straining fruit juices will prove invaluable. The following is a brief outline of the more useful items, all of which are readily available from large department stores and specialist kitchen equipment stores.

PRESERVING PAN

A preserving pan or large, heavy pan is essential. It must be of a sufficient size to allow rapid boiling without bubbling over (a capacity of about 9 litres/ 16 pints/8 quarts is ideal); wide enough to allow rapid evaporation of liquid, so that setting point is reached quickly; and have a thick heavy base to protect the preserve from burning. Preserving pans are fitted with a pair of short-looped handles, or a carrying handle over the top. A non-corrosive preserving pan such as one made of stainless steel is the best choice for making all types of preserves, especially for pickles, chutneys and relishes that contain a high concentration of acid. Traditional copper preserving pans, usually very wide at the top and sloping to a narrow base, are intended only for jam- and jelly-

making and are unsuitable for preserves containing vinegar or lemon juice, or for acidic or red fruit, as both the flavour and colour will be spoilt. Enamel pans do not conduct heat fast enough for preserving and they burn easily.

SUGAR THERMOMETER

Invaluable for cooking preserves to the exact temperature needed for a perfect set. Choose a thermometer that goes up to at least 110°C/ 230°F, and has a clip or a handle that can be attached to the pan, so that it does not slip into the boiling preserve.

JELLY BAG

Used to strain fruit juices from cooked fruit pulp for jelly-making, jelly bags are made from calico, cotton flannel or nylon. The close weave allows only the fruit juice to flow through, leaving the pulp behind. Some jelly bags have their own stands; others have loops with which to suspend the bag.

MUSLIN/CHEESECLOTH

Used for making spice and herb bags, muslin is also useful for tying together pips and peel, particularly when making marmalade. It can also be used instead of a jelly bag. To do this, layer three or four squares of muslin together and tie lengths of strong string (twine) securely to each corner. Either knot the ends together to hang from a single support, or make four loops so the bag can be suspended on the legs of an upturned stool or chair. Alternatively, line a large strainer with the muslin squares and place over a bowl to catch the juices.

JARS AND BOTTLES

When making preserves, a selection of containers is needed. Clear glass is ideal because it is non-corrosive, you can easily check for trapped air bubbles when potting preserves, and it looks very pretty when filled. As well as ordinary jam jars and bottles, there are specialist preserving jars that are designed to be heated to a high temperature. Non-corrosive seals are essential, particularly when potting acidic preserves and pickles.

Be sure to choose appropriately shaped and sized containers. Wide-necked jars are essential for recipes using whole or large pieces of fruit or vegetables, but for most preserves it is better to use several smaller jars than one or two large

Left: A jelly bag with its own stand can make an easy job of straining jellies.

ones. Preserves stored in very large jars are likely to deteriorate more quickly once the seal is broken; the preserve is not consumed as quickly and the contents are exposed to the air for longer than a preserve stored in a small jar.

PRESERVE COVERS

The cheapest way to cover jams, jellies and marmalades is to use a waxed paper disc and cellophane cover, secured by an elastic band. The paper discs should be pressed down very lightly over the contents of the jar once filled; they will form a seal to keep out air and moisture. Cellophane covers are available to fit both 450g/1lb and 900g/2lb jars. Do note, however, that paper and cellophane are not vinegar-proof so are unsuitable for preserves containing vinegar. Pot in preserving jars with acid-resistant seals, or use jam jars with plastic-lined lids.

FUNNELS

These make potting preserves considerably easier. A jam funnel with a wide tube (10–13cm/4–5in diameter) that fits into the top of the jar or container can make quick, clean work of filling jars.

An ordinary funnel with a slimmer tube is useful for adding liquid to jars of pickles or fruit as well as for bottling smooth sauces and jellies. Choose funnels made of heat-proof plastic or stainless steel.

HYDROMETER

Also known as a *pese syrop*, a hydrometer measures the density of sugar syrup and is sometimes used when bottling fruit and for jam- and jelly-making. The tube is marked from 0 to 40 and measures the point to which the weighted tube sinks. The more sugar a syrup contains, the higher the hydrometer will float in it.

Above: A jam funnel can prove to be a real time-saver when potting jellies, jams and conserves.

SALOMETER

This works in the same way as a hydrometer but is used to measure the amount of salt dissolved in brine. Salometers are marked from 0 to 100, where 1°S is about 0.26% salt by weight, as fully satured brine contains about 26% salt.

Below: A selection of jars with either clamp-top, screw-top or two-piece screw-band lids are perfect for preserving.

BOWLS

Several non-corrosive bowls in different sizes are essential for salting, soaking and mixing.

CHOPPING BOARDS

Plastic chopping boards are considered more hygienic than wooden ones because they are easier to clean properly. However, a wooden board comes into its own during potting and is an ideal surface to stand jars on when they are cooling; placing hot jars on cold or damp surfaces can sometimes cause the jars to crack.

SIEVES AND COLANDERS

Use nylon, plastic or stainless steel sieves and colanders when straining acidic fruit or preserves. Some metals may spoil the colour and give a faint metallic taste to the finished preserve.

WOODEN SPOONS

Choose long-handled spoons to keep your hand at a safe distance from hot simmering preserves. If possible, keep separate spoons for sweet and savoury recipes. Avoid metal spoons as these conduct heat and may discolour the preserve.

SLOTTED SPOONS AND SKIMMERS

These are useful for lifting and draining solid ingredients and packing them into jars. A fine-mesh skimmer may be used for skimming jams and jellies to keep them clear.

LADLES

A large deep-bowled ladle is useful for transferring preserves to jars. Some ladles have pointed lips for easy pouring. Stainless steel ladles are best for this purpose.

Below: Fixed and swivel-blade vegetable peelers are good for peeling both fruits and vegetables.

Below: A corer is useful for preparing orchard fruits such as apples and pears.

VEGETABLE PEELERS

There are a number of different types of vegetable peeler available. Those with a swivel action follow the contours of the fruit or vegetable closely and allow peel to be pared very thinly. Some peelers have a bean slicer attachment on the handle.

CORERS

When pickling or preserving whole fruits such as pears and apples, a corer can be used to cut out and remove the cores neatly without damaging the fruit. When coring halved fruits, a melon baller or teaspoon are the best tools to use.

Left: Slotted skimmers and spoons are good for skimming jellies.

STONERS

It can be fiddly to stone (pit) small fruit such as cherries with a knife and almost impossible to keep the fruit whole. There are different types of stoners for different sized fruits. The fruit is placed in a holder, and the handles are squeezed together, which causes a prong to push through the fruit and pop out the stone.

ZESTERS

The cutting edge of a zester has five little holes, which, when pulled firmly across the fruit, remove fine strands of citrus rind, leaving the white pith behind.

CANELLE KNIVES

These have a v-shaped tooth that pares 6mm/¼in strips of peel from fruit and vegetables leaving grooves and creating a striped effect. If the fruit is then cut into slices, these will have attractively notched edges. A mushroom fluter is a similar tool for creating a pattern on mushroom caps.

Above: A canelle knife and zester are excellent for paring off thin strips of citrus rind.

Below: A cherry stoner effortlessly removes the stones from fiddly fruit.

MANDOLINS

Firm fruits and vegetables such as apples, beetroot (beet) and turnips can be sliced or shredded finely and evenly using a mandolin. Most mandolins have adjustable cutting blades and supporting struts that hold the mandolin at the desired angle. Choose one with a safety guard to hold the food being sliced because the blades are extremely sharp and it would otherwise be very easy to cut yourself.

GRATERS

Box graters usually have a choice of at least three different surfaces, from fine (for nutmeg and lemon rind) to coarse (for hard fruits and vegetables). They often have slicing blades for vegetables such as cucumbers. Most have a handle to hold them steady during use. Flat graters take up less space and are easier to clean, but usually have only one or two different-size grating surfaces.

MINCERS AND FOOD MILLS

Both hand and electric mincers can save a good deal of time and energy when processing large quantities of fruit or vegetables. Rotary food mills are especially useful when making fruit butters and smooth sauces because they reduce cooked fruit to a purée, leaving the skins and stones (pits) behind. Pressing the mixture through a fine sieve using the back of a wooden spoon or metal ladle is just as effective, although it may take a little more time and effort.

GRINDERS

The traditional mortar and pestle is perfect for coarsely grinding small quantities of spices. For larger amounts or when a fine powder is required, use a spice mill or coffee grinder kept solely for that purpose.

Left: A box grater with several different cutting surfaces is useful for preparing fruits, vegetables and spices.

POTTING AND COVERING PRESERVES

Make sure you have enough jars and bottles, and the correct sterilizing equipment before you start to make any preserve. Preparing, covering and storing preserves correctly helps to ensure the preserve retains its colour, flavour and texture.

CHOOSING CONTAINERS

To make the most of preserves, always pot them in the right type of container. Pickles made from whole or large pieces of fruit or vegetables should be packed into medium or large jars or bottles with a wide neck. Smooth, pourable sauces or relishes can be stored in narrow-necked bottles, but thicker, spoonable preserves should be packed in jars. It is generally better to pack preserves into several smaller containers rather than one large one, especially those that need to be consumed soon after opening.

STERILIZING JARS AND BOTTLES

Before potting, it is essential to sterilize jars and bottles to destroy any micro-organisms in containers. An unsterilized jar or bottle may contain contamination that could cause the preserve to deteriorate or become inedible. Sterilizing is important for all containers, but you should take particular care when re-using jars and bottles.

Check jars and bottles for cracks or damage, then wash thoroughly in hot, soapy water, rinse well and turn upside-down to drain. Jars and bottles may be sterilized in five different ways: by heating in a low oven, immersing in boiling water, heating in a microwave, hot-washing in a dishwasher, or using sterilizing tablets.

Below: Medium, wide-necked jars with plastic-coated screw-top lids are ideal for most preserves.

oven method

Stand the containers, spaced slightly apart, on a baking sheet lined with kitchen paper. Rest any lids on top. Place in a cold oven, then heat to 110°C/225°F/Gas ¼ and bake for 30 minutes. Leave to cool slightly before filling. (If the jars or bottles are not used immediately, cover with a clean cloth and warm again before use.)

boiling water method

1 Place the containers, open-end up, in a deep pan that is wide enough to hold them in one layer.

2 Pour enough hot water into the pan to cover the containers. (Do not use boiling water because this can crack glass.) Bring the water to the boil and boil for 10 minutes.

3 Leave the containers in the pan until the water stops bubbling, then carefully remove and drain upside-down on a clean dishtowel. Turn the containers upright and leave to air-dry for a few minutes.

4 Immerse lids, seals and corks in simmering water for 20 seconds. (Only ever use corks once.)

microwave method

This method is particularly useful when sterilizing only a few jars for potting a small amount of preserve. Follow the microwave manufacturer's instructions and only use for jars that hold less than 450g/1lb and short squat bottles.

1 Half fill the clean jars or bottles with water and heat on full power until the water has boiled for at least 1 minute.

2 Using oven gloves, remove the jars or bottles from the microwave. Carefully swirl the water inside them, then pour it away. Drain upside-down on a clean dishtowel, then turn upright and leave to dry.

dishwasher method

This is the simplest way to clean and sterilize a large number of containers at the same time. Put the containers and lids in a dishwasher and run it on its hottest setting, including drying. If the jars are already washed and clean, you can run the cycle without adding detergent.

sterilizing tablet method

This method is not suitable for delicately flavoured preserves because the tablets may leave a slight taste. However, it is fine for robustly flavoured preserves such as chutneys and relishes. Following the instructions on the packet, dissolve the tablets and soak the containers in the sterilizing solution. Drain and dry before use.

FILLING JARS AND BOTTLES

Most preserves should be potted into hot containers as soon as they are ready, particularly jellies and fruit preserves with a high pectin content; a jam funnel can make quick work of this. Whole fruit jams, marmalades with peel, and jellies with added ingredients such as fresh herbs should be left to cool for 10 minutes until a thin skin forms on the surface. The preserve should then be stirred to distribute the ingredients and prevent them sinking once potted.

Some preserves such as fruits bottled in alcohol or vegetables preserved in vinegar are potted when cold rather than hot. The ingredients may be cooked, or simply washed, then packed into jars and cold alcohol or vinegar poured over them.

SEALING JARS

Different types of preserves need to be covered and sealed in different ways. Jams, conserves, jellies, marmalades and fruit cheeses can be covered with a waxed paper disc and the jar covered with cellophane held in place with an elastic band. Or, the jar can be sealed with a screw-top lid. (Waxed discs and cellophane covers should not be used together with a screw-top lid.)

Bottled fruits and pickled vegetables must be sealed in jars with new rubber seals and vacuum or clamp top lids. Chutneys and pickles should be sealed with vinegar-proof lids; the acid in the vinegar will corrode metal lids.

using waxed discs and cellophane covers

1 Using a heat-resistant ladle or jug (pitcher) and a jam funnel, carefully fill the jars with hot jam, almost to the top. Leave a small space of no more than 1cm/½in.

2 Using a clean, damp cloth, wipe the rim of the jar, making sure there are no dribbles of jam.

3 Place a waxed paper disc (waxed side down) on top of the preserve and smooth it down to form a good fit over the hot preserve.

4 Moisten a cellophane disc with a damp cloth and place on the jar, moist side up, then secure with an elastic band. Do this either when the preserve is very hot, or leave it to cool completely. (If sealed while warm, mould will grow on the surface.) As it dries, the cellophane will shrink, creating a tight seal.

using lidded jars

There are a number of different types of lidded jars available – from ordinary screw-top jars to large jars with clamped lids. Different types of jars are suitable for different types of preserves.

Screw-top lidded jars: These are suitable for most sweet preserves, but uncoated metal lids should be avoided when potting acidic preserves containing vinegar because the metal lid may corrode and rust when it comes in contact with the acid.

Two-piece lidded jars: Also known as lid and screw-band jars, they consist of a flat rubber- or plastic-coated lid that fits exactly over the top of the jar and a ring that screws on to the neck of the jar to hold the lid in place.

To use, fill the sterilized jar, wipe the rim and cover with the sterilized rubber-coated lid. Holding the jar steady with a cloth, position the metal ring over the lid and screw down tightly.

If the potted preserve needs to be heat-treated, release the lid by a quarter turn, or according to the manufacturer's instructions. (The glass expands during heating and may crack if the metal ring is too tight.)

Clamp-top jars: These can be used for any kind of preserve from jams and jellies to bottled fruits and pickles. To use, fit the sterilized rubber ring on to the lid before filling the jar to within 1cm/½in of the top, or to the manufacturer's mark on the jar. Holding the jar steady with a cloth, clamp the lid shut. An airtight vacuum will form as the preserve cools.

sealing with paraffin wax

The surface of preserves can also be sealed with paraffin wax, which is available from hardware stores.

1 Break the wax into small pieces and heat in a bowl set over a pan of hot water until just melted. (If the wax becomes too hot, it will shrink away from the sides of the jar as it cools, breaking the seal.)

2 Pour a very thin layer of wax over the hot preserve. Using a wooden cocktail stick (toothpick), prick any air bubbles, then leave the wax to set.

3 When the wax has set, pour on a second layer to make the seal about 3mm/⅛in thick. As the wax sets it will become opaque and dip slightly. To use the preserve, break and remove the wax seal. Re-cover with clear film (plastic wrap) and store in the refrigerator.

FILLING AND SEALING BOTTLES

Bottles are perfect for storing sauces and pourable relishes. They can be stoppered with a sterilized cork, then dipped in wax to seal.

1 Using a ladle and funnel, fill the hot sterilized bottles to within 2.5cm/1in of the top. Wipe the bottle rim clean with a damp cloth.

2 Soak the corks in very hot water for 3–4 minutes, then push into the tops of the bottles as far as they will go. Gently tap the cork into the bottle using a rolling pin or wooden mallet until the cork is within 5mm/¼in of the top of the bottle. Leave the bottles until cold.

3 To seal, tap down the corks as far as possible, then dip the top of each bottle in melted candle or sealing wax to coat. Leave to set, then dip a second time.

PRESENTATION, LABELLING AND STORING

Left: Preserves stored in clamp-top and two-piece lidded jars make very attractive gifts.

STORING PRESERVES

Although they look very attractive arranged on a sunny kitchen shelf, preserves should always be kept in a cool, dark, dry place because warmth and light will affect their colour and flavour, and shorten their shelf-life. Many pickles, chutneys and bottled fruits need time to mature before using.

The way in which a preserve is packaged, labelled and stored is almost as important as the way it is made.

PRESENTATION

Glass jars and bottles look very pretty because they allow you to see the preserve inside. Preserving jars are practical and attractive for savoury preserves, while shaped or decorative jars with fluted and embossed designs are good for sweet preserves. Small jars, no larger than 350g/12oz capacity, look very pretty and are perfect for preserves that have a short shelf-life once opened. Glazed earthenware pots are good for storing chutneys and mustards.

No matter how much care you take, jars and bottles usually become sticky when filling. While still warm, wipe the outside of the containers with a damp cloth and a little detergent. When the preserve is cold and set, the jars may be polished with a little methylated spirit (denatured alcohol).

You can use cellophane covers or new plastic or coloured lids in place of old lids to seal jars. Pretty fabric, or coloured or brown paper can be placed over plain lids. Cut these at least 4cm/1½in bigger than the lid and secure with an elastic band, then tie with ribbon.

LABELLING PRESERVES

All preserves should be clearly labelled, especially if they are to be offered as gifts. Self-adhesive, cardboard, wooden or metal labels may be used. Always write the date, the name of the preserve and any special notes on the label. It is a good idea to add an "eat-by" if giving as a gift.

STORAGE TIMES

Most preserves will keep for a year if packed and stored properly. Once opened, they should be eaten within 3 months. Some preserves have a shorter shelf-life:

Fruit curds, butters and cheeses can be stored in the refrigerator for 2–3 months and, once opened, should be used within 4 weeks.

Relishes with a low proportion of vinegar and sugar and a short cooking time can be stored for up to 4 months. Once opened, they should be stored in the refrigerator and used within 4 weeks.

Low-sugar jams and similar specialist preserves rely on sterilizing for their keeping qualities. They are usually processed commercially. Home-made versions are made in small quantities for short keeping in the refrigerator.

JAMS, JELLIES AND MARMALADES

These are made from fruit boiled with sugar until setting point is reached. They rely on pectin, sugar and acid for a good set. Pectin is a natural, gum-like substance, which is essential in jam-, jelly- and marmalade-making. Found in the cores, pips (seeds), pith and skins of fruits, it reacts with sugar and acid to form the gel that helps to set jams, jellies and marmalades.

TESTING PECTIN CONTENT

Pectin content can vary according to the variety of fruit, when it is picked, and growing conditions. It is best to test for pectin content at an early stage in jam-making and add extra pectin if necessary.

1 To test for pectin content, cook the fruit until soft, then spoon 5ml/1 tsp of the juices into a glass. Add 15ml/1 tbsp methylated spirits (denatured alcohol) and shake.

2 After 1 minute a clot should form: one large jelly-like clot indicates high pectin content; two or three small clots indicate the pectin content is medium and should achieve a set; lots of small clots, or no clots at all indicate low pectin content and that extra pectin will be needed for a set.

3 If the pectin content is medium, add 15ml/1 tbsp lemon juice for every 450g/1lb fruit. If the pectin content is low, add 75–90ml/ 5–6 tbsp pectin stock for every 450g/1lb fruit. Alternatively, add pectin powder or liquid, or use sugar containing pectin.

MAKING PECTIN STOCK

Home-made pectin stock is very easy to make and can be stirred into low-pectin fruit jams and jellies to improve their set. Stir in after the initial cooking of the fruit and before the sugar is added. A teaspoon of the juices can be taken from the pan at this stage and tested for pectin content.

1 Roughly chop 900g/2lb cooking apples, including the cores, peel and pips. Place in a large heavy pan and pour over cold water to cover. Bring to the boil, then reduce the heat, cover and simmer for 40 minutes, or until very soft.

2 Pour the mixture into a sterilized jelly bag suspended over a bowl. Leave to drain for at least 2 hours.

3 Pour the drained juices into the cleaned pan and boil for about 20 minutes, or until the volume is reduced by one-third.

4 Pour the pectin stock into 150ml/¼ pint/⅔ cup sterilized containers and store in the refrigerator for up to 1 week or freeze for up to 4 months.

5 To use frozen pectin stock, defrost at room temperature, or overnight in the refrigerator, then stir into the preserve.

TESTING FOR A SET
Some preserves reach setting point quickly, so check early in the cooking time.

Wrinkle test: Remove the preserve from the heat and spoon a little preserve on to a chilled plate. Leave to cool for 1 minute, then push the preserve with a finger; the top should wrinkle. If it wrinkles only slightly, return the preserve to the heat and cook for 2 minutes more, then test again.

Flake test: Coat a spoon in the preserve; cool for a few seconds, then hold the spoon horizontally. When shaken, the jam should run off the side in one flat flake.

Thermometer test: Briefly stir the preserve, dip a jam thermometer into very hot water, then place in the preserve. Move it around, but do touch the pan base. Jams and marmalades reach setting point at 105°C/220°F; jellies and conserves a degree lower.

MAKING JAM

Usually made with whole or cut fruit, jam should have distinct flavour, bright colour and soft set.

making summer fruit jam

Use sound, slightly under-ripe fruit; over-ripe fruit contains less pectin and will not set well.

Makes about 1.6kg/3½lb

INGREDIENTS
900g/2lb mixed fruits, such as cherries, raspberries, strawberries, gooseberries, blackcurrants and redcurrants
2.5–20ml/½–4 tsp lemon juice
900g/2lb/4½ cups preserving or granulated (white) sugar

1 Weigh each type of fruit, then prepare. Rinse and drain cherries, gooseberries, blackcurrants and redcurrants; wash raspberries and strawberries only if necessary; remove any stems and leaves and cut off any damaged parts.

2 Put the lemon juice in a large heavy pan: strawberries and cherries are low in pectin, so add 10ml/2 tsp lemon juice for each 450g/1lb fruit; add 2.5ml/½ tsp for each 450g/1lb raspberries; and add no lemon juice for high-pectin gooseberries and currants.

3 Put the prepared gooseberries, blackcurrants and redcurrants in the pan with 60ml/4 tbsp water and cook over a low heat for 5 minutes until the skins soften.

4 Add the raspberries, cherries and strawberries to the pan. (If using only these fruits, do not add any water.) Cook for 10 minutes until all the fruit is just tender.

5 Using the back of a spoon, crush one-third of the fruit to release the pectin. If using a high proportion of strawberries or cherries, do a pectin test at this stage.

6 Add the sugar to the pan and stir over a low heat until it has dissolved completely. Increase the heat and bring to the boil. Continue to boil rapidly for about 10 minutes, stirring occasionally, until setting point is reached (105°C/220°F). Skim off any froth that rises to the surface.

IS IT A JAM, CONSERVE OR SPREAD?
Understanding the labels on store-bought preserves can be difficult. Here's a brief guide:
Jam: This contains a minimum of 30g/1¼oz fruit and 60g/2¼oz/generous ¼ cup sugar per 100g/3¾oz jam. It may contain colourings, preservatives and gelling agents.
Extra jam: This must contain at least 45g/1¾oz whole fruit per 100g/3¾oz jam. It contains no colourings, preservatives or flavourings.
Reduced-sugar jam: This has a minimum of 35g/1½oz fruit and 30–55g/1¼–2¼oz sugar per 100g/3¾oz jam.
Conserve: This implies a quality jam with a high fruit content, but check the label. Usually, the fruit is whole and steeped in sugar before cooking, giving a softer set.
Fruit spreads: These are made from fruit pulps sweetened with fruit juice.

7 Remove the pan from the heat and leave to stand for 5 minutes. If necessary, skim off any froth, then stir to distribute larger pieces of fruit. Pot, seal and label.

making seedless raspberry jam

Some fruits, notably raspberries and blackberries, contain a large number of pips (seeds), which result in a very "pippy" jam or conserve. If you prefer a smooth jam without pips, they can be removed after initial cooking by pressing the fruit through a nylon or stainless steel sieve.

Makes about 750g/1⅔lb

INGREDIENTS

450g/1lb/2⅔ cups raspberries

about 450g/1lb/2¼ cups preserving or granulated (white) sugar

1 Use a mixture of just-ripe and a few slightly underripe berries to ensure a good set. Put the fruit in a large heavy pan and gently crush to release the juices using the back of a wooden spoon.

2 Gently heat the fruit mixture to boiling point, then simmer for about 10 minutes, stirring now and then, until the fruit is really soft.

3 Tip the mixture into a fine nylon or stainless steel sieve (sifter) placed over a bowl and push through the fruit purée using the back of the wooden spoon. Discard the pips left in the sieve.

4 Measure the fruit pulp into the cleaned pan, adding 450g/1lb/2¼ cups sugar for each 600ml/1 pint/2½ cups purée. Heat gently, stirring, until the sugar dissolves, then boil rapidly until setting point is reached (105°C/220°F).

5 Using a slotted spoon, skim any froth from the surface, then pot the jam, cover and seal.

making cherry jam with commercial pectin

Fruits with a low pectin content require additional pectin to achieve a good set. Adding commercial pectin is an easy way to do this. Jams made in this way need only short boiling and require little or no water and a smaller proportion of fruit to sugar.

Makes about 1.8kg/4lb

INGREDIENTS

1.2kg/2½lb/6 cups pitted cherries

150ml/¼ pint/⅔ cup water

45ml/3 tbsp lemon juice

1.3kg/3lb/generous 6¼ cups granulated (white) sugar

250ml/8fl oz/1 cup liquid pectin

1 Put the cherries, water and lemon juice in a large pan. Cover and cook for 15 minutes, stirring, until the cherries are tender.

2 Add the sugar to the pan and stir over a low heat until dissolved completely. Bring to the boil and boil rapidly for 1 minute.

3 Stir the liquid pectin into the jam, return to the boil and cook for 1 minute.

4 Remove the pan from the heat and, using a slotted spoon, skim off any froth from the surface. Set the jam aside and leave to stand for 5 minutes.

5 Stir the jam briefly to distribute the fruit evenly, then pot and seal. Use within 6 months.

PECTIN CONTENT OF FRUIT

Although the pectin content of fruits can vary depending on variety, growing conditions and when the fruits were picked, the list below can be used as a good basic guide to the set that will be achieved.

High: Apples, blackcurrants, cranberries, damsons, gooseberries, grapefruit, lemons, limes, loganberries, redcurrants, quinces

Medium: Apricots (fresh), apples (eating), bilberries, blackberries (early), grapes, greengages, mulberries, peaches, plums, raspberries

Low: Bananas, blackberries (late), cherries, elderberries, figs, guavas, japonica, melons, nectarines, pears, pineapples, rhubarb, strawberries

MAKING CONSERVES

These are very similar to jams, but they have a slightly softer set and contain whole or large pieces of fruit. The fruit is first mixed with sugar and sometimes a little liquid, then allowed to stand for several hours or even days. The sugar draws out the juices from the fruit, making it firmer and minimizing the cooking time needed. The fruit should be just ripe and even in size. Not all fruit is suitable for making conserves; tough fruit skins do not soften when sugar is added, so fruit such as gooseberries are no good for making conserves.

making strawberry conserve

This preserve takes several days to make, so be sure to leave plenty of time for preparation.

Makes about 1.3kg/3lb

INGREDIENTS

1.3kg/3lb small or medium strawberries, hulled

1.3kg/3lb/generous 6¾ cups granulated (white) sugar

1 Layer the hulled strawberries in a large bowl with the sugar. Cover with clear film (plastic wrap) and chill for 24 hours.

2 Transfer the strawberries, sugar and juices to a large heavy pan. Heat gently, stirring occasionally, until the sugar has dissolved. Bring to the boil and cook steadily (not rapidly) for 5 minutes.

3 Leave the mixture to cool, then place in a bowl, cover with clear film and chill for 2 days.

4 Pour the strawberry mixture into a large pan, bring to the boil and cook steadily for 10 minutes, then remove from the heat and set aside for 10 minutes. Stir, then ladle into warmed sterilized jars and seal.

flavouring conserves

Conserves are more luxurious than jams and often include dried fruit, nuts and spirits or liqueurs. These extra ingredients should be added after setting point is reached.

When adding dried fruit or nuts, chop them evenly and allow about 50g/2oz/½ cup fruit or nuts per 750g/1¾lb conserve.

Choose spirits or liqueurs that complement the flavour of the chosen fruit. For example, add apricot brandy or amaretto liqueur to apricot conserve, kirsch to cherry conserve and ginger wine to melon conserve; allow 30ml/2 tbsp to every 750g/1¾lb conserve.

TOP TIPS FOR SUCCESSFUL JAM-MAKING

• Always use the freshest fruit possible and avoid overripe fruit.

• If you wash the fruit, dry it well and use promptly because it will deteriorate on standing.

• Cook the fruit very slowly at first over a low heat to extract the maximum amount of juice and pectin. Stir the fruit frequently until very tender, but do not overcook. (Fruit skins toughen once sugar is added.)

• Warm the sugar in a low oven for about 10 minutes before adding it to the fruit. This will help it to dissolve.

• Stir the preserve to ensure the sugar is completely dissolved before boiling.

• Do not stir frequently when boiling. This lowers the temperature and delays reaching setting point.

• It is wasteful to remove scum too often. To help prevent scum from forming, add a small amount of unsalted (sweet) butter (about 15g/½oz/1 tbsp for every 450g/1lb fruit) when you add the sugar.

• Do not move freshly potted preserves until they are cool and have set completely.

MAKING JELLIES

Jellies are made using the juice strained from simmered fruit, which is then boiled with sugar to setting point. There is very little preparation of fruit, other than giving it a quick rinse and roughly chopping larger fruit, but you do need to allow plenty of time to make the jelly itself. The secret to a beautifully clear jelly lies in straining the fruit pulp through a jelly bag, drip by drip, which takes several hours.

The basic principles of jelly-making are the same as those for jam and the same three substances – pectin, sugar and acid – are needed for the jelly to set. A perfectly set jelly should retain its shape and quiver when spooned out of the jar. Fruits that are low in pectin such as strawberries, cherries and pears are not suitable on their own for making jellies, so are usually combined with high-pectin fruit.

Because the fruit pulp is discarded in jelly-making, the yield is not as large as in jam-making. For this reason many jelly recipes have evolved to make the most of wild fruits, which are free, or gluts of home-grown fruit.

Jellies can be served both as sweet and savoury preserves. Some, such as redcurrant, rowan and cranberry jellies, are classic accompaniments for hot or cold roasted meat or game, or are added to gravy for flavour and give an attractive glossy finish. Savoury jellies often contain chopped herbs and sometimes wine vinegar or cider vinegar to give it a sharper flavour. Sweet jellies may be eaten as a spread.

yield of jelly

The final yield of jelly depends on how juicy the fruit is, and this can vary depending on the time of the year, the weather during growth and its ripeness when harvested. Because of this, the juice, rather than the fruit, is measured and the amount of sugar is calculated accordingly. As a general rule, 450g/1lb/2¼ cups sugar is added for each 600ml/1 pint/2½ cups juice. (If the fruit is very rich in pectin, the recipe may suggest adding slightly less sugar.) As a rough guide, recipes containing 450g/1lb/2¼ cups sugar will make about 675–800g/1½–1¾lb jelly.

making redcurrant jelly

Makes about 1.3kg/3lb

INGREDIENTS

1.3kg/3lb just-ripe redcurrants
600ml/1 pint/2½ cups water
about 900g/2lb/4½ cups preserving or granulated (white) sugar

1 Check the fruit is clean. If necessary, rinse in cold water and use a little less water in the recipe.

2 Remove the currants from the stalks. There is no need to top and tail the fruit.

3 Place the redcurrants in a large heavy pan with the water and simmer gently for about 30 minutes, or until the fruit is very soft and pulpy. Stir occasionally during cooking to prevent the fruit from catching and burning.

4 Pour the cooked fruit and juices into a sterilized jelly bag suspended over a large bowl. Leave to drain for about 4 hours, or until the juice stops dripping. (Do not press or squeeze the fruit in the bag because this will result in a cloudy jelly.)

5 Discard the pulp remaining in the bag (unless you plan to boil the pulp a second time – see page 316). Pour the juice into the cleaned pan and add 450g/1lb/2¼ cups warmed sugar for each 600ml/1 pint/2½ cups of juice. (When making jellies with low-pectin fruit or vegetables, stir in a little lemon juice or vinegar to improve the set. This will also help to offset the sweetness of the jelly.)

6 Heat the mixture gently, stirring frequently, until the sugar has completely dissolved, then increase the heat and bring to the boil.

7 Boil the jelly rapidly for about 10 minutes, or until setting point is reached. You can check this using the flake test or wrinkle test, or you can use a jam thermometer. The jelly should be heated to 105°C/220°F.

8 Remove the pan from the heat, then skim any froth from the surface of the jelly using a slotted spoon.

9 Carefully remove the last traces of froth using a piece of kitchen paper. Pot the jelly immediately because it will start to set fairly quickly.

10 Cover and seal the jelly while it is hot, then leave to cool completely. (Do not move or tilt the jars until the jelly is completely cold and set.) Label the jars and store in a cool, dark place.

USING A JELLY BAG

Jelly bags, which are made from heavy-duty calico, cotton flannel or close-weave nylon, allow only the juice from the fruit to flow through, leaving the skins, pulp and pips (seeds) inside the bag. The fruit pulp and juices are very heavy, so strong tape or loops are positioned on the corners for hanging the bag securely on a stand, upturned stool or chair.

1 Before use, sterilize the jelly bag by scalding in boiling water. This process also helps the juices to run through the bag, rather than being absorbed into it.

2 If you don't have a jelly bag, you can use three or four layers of sterilized muslin (cheesecloth) or a piece of fine linen cloth instead. Simply line a large nylon or stainless-steel sieve with the muslin or linen.

3 Carefully suspend the jelly bag or lined sieve over a large bowl to catch the juice. Make sure the bag or sieve is secure before spooning some of the simmered fruit and juices into it. (Don't add too much to start with.)

4 Leave the fruit to drain for a while, then spoon in more fruit. Continue gradually adding fruit in this way until it has all been placed in the bag or sieve, then leave to drain until it stops dripping completely. Some fruits will take 2–3 hours to release all their juice, while others may take as long as 12 hours.

5 Immediately after use, wash the jelly bag thoroughly, then rinse several times to remove all traces of detergent. Ensure the bag is completely dry before storing. The jelly bag may be reused many times, but be sure to sterilize it before every use.

boiling fruit twice

Rather than discarding the fruit pulp from the jelly bag after draining, you can boil it again to extract more liquid and flavour. This should be done only with pectin-rich fruits such as sharp apples, damsons or currants. The resulting jelly may have a slightly less concentrated flavour than jelly made from juice obtained from fruit that has been boiled once.

To boil the fruit a second time, return the fruit pulp to the pan and add just enough cold water to cover, using no more than half the amount of water used for the first boiling. Simmer the fruit gently for about 20 minutes, then drain through the jelly bag as before. Add the juice to the first batch.

flavouring jelly

Savoury jellies are often flavoured with fresh herbs such as thyme, mint, sage and rosemary. In some, such as mint jelly, the herb is most important and the fruit provides a base in which to suspend the herb; in others, herbs are used in small quantities to impart a subtle flavour.

1 To simply add flavour, add sprigs of herbs at the beginning of cooking. Woody herbs should be removed before draining because stems may damage the jelly bag.

2 When adding finely chopped herbs to the finished jelly, even distribution can be difficult and, if the jelly is too hot, the pieces may float to the top. To overcome this problem, put the herbs in a sieve and sprinkle with a little water to dampen them.

3 Leave the jelly to stand until it just starts to form a thin skin on top, then quickly stir in the chopped herbs. Pot straight away in very warm, but not hot, sterilized jars and seal. Cool before labelling.

4 Herb sprigs and aromatic leaves, such as lemon verbena or geranium leaves, can look stunning set in jelly. Pour the jelly into sterilized jars, then leave until semi-set and insert the herb sprigs or leaves.

TOP TIPS FOR SUCCESSFUL JELLY-MAKING

• There is no need to peel or stone (pit) fruit before cooking because all the debris will be removed during straining. However, it is important to discard any bruised or mouldy parts of the fruit because these will spoil the flavour. Rinse the fruit only if dusty or dirty.

• If using fruits such as apples that require longer cooking, chop the fruit very finely to reduce the cooking time required. Cooking the fruit for a shorter time also helps to give the jelly an intense, fresh flavour.

• Simmer the fruit very gently to extract the maximum amount of pectin and to avoid evaporating too much liquid. When cooking hard fruits that take a long time to soften, cover the pan for the first half of the cooking time to reduce the amount of liquid lost.

• Some fruits such as redcurrants or blackcurrants can be cooked in the oven to make highly flavoured jellies. Place the fruit in an oven-proof dish with about 75ml/5 tbsp water, cover tightly and cook at 140°C/275°F/Gas 1 for about 50 minutes, stirring occasionally, until pulpy. Drain through a jelly bag, then add 425g/15oz/generous 2 cups sugar for every 600ml/ 1 pint/2½ cups strained juice.

• Jellies set very quickly, so pot immediately. Warm a stainless steel funnel in the oven, or rinse a plastic one under hot water and dry it, then use to pot the jelly. If the jelly starts to set in the pan, warm it briefly until liquid again.

• Gently tap the jars as you fill with jelly to remove air bubbles.

• Although you can add a little butter to jam to disperse any scum, do not do this with jelly – it will make it cloudy.

MAKING MARMALADE

This preserve consists of a jelly base, usually with small pieces of fruit suspended in it. The name marmalade is derived from the Portuguese word *marmelo*, meaning quince, and it was from this fruit that marmalades were first made.

Modern marmalades are usually made from citrus fruits, or citrus fruits combined with other fruits such as pineapple, or flavoured with aromatic spices. Marmalades can range from thick and dark to light and translucent.

The citrus peel is shredded and cooked with the fruit juices and water until soft and tender, then boiled with sugar to make the marmalade. Citrus peel requires long, slow cooking in a large amount of water to become soft. The pith of Seville (Temple) oranges, lemons and grapefruits becomes clear when cooked, but that of sweet oranges does not, so the pith should be scraped off the rind before shredding and cooking.

As well as classic marmalade, there is also jelly marmalade. This is perfect for people who enjoy the flavour of marmalade but do not like the peel that is suspended in the jelly. Rather than adding the shredded rind to the juices and water in the pan, the rind is tied in a muslin (cheesecloth) bag to keep it separate. The juices are then strained and boiled to setting point. The jelly may be left plain and potted as it is, or a little of the shredded rind can be stirred into the jelly just before potting. As with any jelly, it is difficult to give an exact yield for jelly marmalade.

making seville orange marmalade

Bitter Seville (Temple) oranges are popular for marmalade-making.

Makes about 2.5kg/5½lb

INGREDIENTS

900g/2lb Seville (Temple) oranges
1 large lemon
2.4 litres/4 pints/2 quarts water
1.8kg/4lb/generous 9 cups preserving or granulated (white) sugar

1 Wash and dry the fruits. If you are using waxed oranges and lemons, scrub the skins gently.

2 Halve the fruits and squeeze out the juice and pips (seeds), then pour into a muslin- (cheesecloth-) lined sieve set over a bowl.

3 Remove some of the pith from the citrus peels and reserve, then cut the peel into narrow strips.

4 Add the reserved pith to the pips in the muslin and tie together to make a loose bag. Allow plenty of room so that the water can bubble through the bag and extract the pectin from the pith and pips.

5 Place the shredded peel, juices and the muslin bag in a large preserving pan and pour in the water. Using a clean ruler, measure the depth of the contents in the pan and make a note of it.

6 Slowly bring the mixture to the boil and simmer for 1½–2 hours, or until the peel is very soft and the contents have reduced by about half their depth.

COOK'S TIPS

• To save time, shred the citrus peel in a food processor rather than by hand. Use either the fine or coarse cutting attachment.

• If you can't find Seville oranges, use Temple oranges instead.

7 To check that the peel is cooked, remove a piece from the pan and leave for a few minutes to cool. Once cooled, press the peel between finger and thumb; it should feel very soft.

8 Using a slotted spoon, remove the muslin bag from the pan and set it aside until cool enough to handle. Squeeze as much liquid as possible back into the pan to extract all the pectin from the pips and pith.

9 Add the sugar to the pan and stir over a low heat until the sugar has completely dissolved.

10 Bring the marmalade to the boil, then boil rapidly for about 10 minutes until setting point is reached (105°C/220°F). You may also use the flake or wrinkle test to check the set.

11 Using a slotted spoon, remove any scum from the surface of the marmalade, then leave to cool until a thin skin starts to form on the surface of the preserve.

12 Leave the marmalade to stand for about 5 minutes, then stir gently to distribute the peel evenly. Ladle into hot sterilized jars, then cover and seal.

making orange jelly marmalade

This recipe uses Seville (Temple) oranges, and may be made as a plain jelly marmalade, or a few fine shreds of peel can be added before potting, which can look very pretty and adds an interesting texture. Any marmalade can be made in the same way; use exactly the same ingredients listed in the recipe but use the method below.

Makes about 2kg/4½lb

INGREDIENTS

450g/1lb Seville (Temple) oranges
1.75 litres/3 pints/7½ cups water
1.3kg/3lb/generous 6¾ cups preserving or granulated (white) sugar
60ml/4 tbsp lemon juice

1 Wash and dry the oranges; gently scrub them with a soft brush if they have waxed skins.

2 If you want to add a little peel to the jelly marmalade, thinly pare and finely shred the rind from 2 or 3 of the oranges. Place the shreds in a square of muslin (cheesecloth) and tie it into a neat bag.

3 Halve the oranges and squeeze out the juice and pips (seeds), then tip the juice and pips into a large preserving pan.

4 Roughly chop the orange peel, including all the pith, and add it to the pan. Add the bag of shredded rind, if using, and pour over the water. Cover the pan with a lid and leave to soak for at least 4 hours, or overnight.

5 Bring the mixture to the boil, then reduce the heat and simmer gently for 1½ hours. Using a slotted spoon, remove the bag of peel, and carefully remove a piece of peel to check that it is tender. If not, re-tie the bag and simmer for a further 15–20 minutes. Remove the bag of peel and set aside.

6 Line a large nylon or stainless steel sieve with a double layer of muslin and place over a large bowl. Pour boiling water through the muslin to scald it. Discard the scalding water from the bowl. Alternatively, use a scalded jelly bag suspended over a bowl instead of the muslin-lined sieve.

7 Pour the fruit and juices into the sieve or jelly bag and leave to drain for at least 1 hour. Pour the juices into the cleaned pan.

8 Add the sugar, lemon juice and shredded orange rind, if using, to the pan. Stir over a low heat until the sugar has dissolved, then bring to the boil and boil rapidly for about 10 minutes until setting point is reached (105°C/220°F).

9 Remove any scum from the surface. Leave to cool until a thin skin starts to form on the surface. Stir, then pot, cover and seal.

TOP TIPS FOR SUCCESSFUL MARMALADE-MAKING

• Always wash citrus fruit well. Most citrus fruits have a wax coating that helps to prolong the life of the fruit, which should be removed before making the fruit into marmalade. Alternatively, buy unwaxed fruit, but always rinse before use.

• When shredding peel, always slice it slightly thinner than required in the finished preserve because the rind will swell slightly during cooking.

• Coarse-cut peel will take longer to soften than finely shredded peel. To reduce cooking time, soak the peel for a few hours in the water and juices before cooking.

• If the fruit needs to be peeled, put it in a bowl of boiling water and leave to stand for a couple of minutes. This will help to loosen the skins and make peeling easier. The rind's flavour will leach into the water, so use the soaking water in place of some of the measured water.

• If using small, thin-skinned fruit such as limes, cut the fruit into quarters lengthways, then slice flesh and rind into thin or thick shreds. If using larger, thick-skinned fruit such as grapefruit, pare off the peel, including some white pith, and shred. Cut the fruit into quarters, remove the remaining white pith and roughly chop the flesh.

• To make a coarse-cut preserve, boil the whole fruit for 2 hours until soft; pierce with a skewer to test. Lift out the fruit, halve, prise out the pips, then tie them loosely in muslin (cheesecloth) and add to the hot water. Boil rapidly for 10 minutes, then remove the bag. Slice the fruit and return to the pan. Stir in the sugar until dissolved, then boil to setting point.

• Shredded peel should be simmered gently; fierce cooking can give a tough result. Check that the peel is really soft before adding the sugar because it will not tenderize further after this.

• For easy removal, tie the muslin bag of pith and pips with string and attach it to the pan handle. It can then be lifted out of the boiling mixture easily.

• If the fruit contains a lot of pith, put only a small amount in the muslin bag with the pips (seeds). Put the remaining pith in a small pan, cover with water and boil for 10 minutes. Strain the liquid and use in place of some of the measured water for the recipe.

• To flavour marmalade with liqueur or spirits, add 15–30ml/ 1–2 tbsp for every 450g/1lb/ 2¼ cups sugar – stir it in just before potting. Unsweetened apple juice or dry (hard) cider may be used to replace up to half the water to add flavour to marmalades made with sharper fruits such as kumquats.

FRUIT CURDS, BUTTERS AND CHEESES

These rich, creamy preserves were once the highlight of an English tea during Edwardian and Victorian times. Curds and butters are delicious spread on slices of fresh bread and butter, or used as fillings for cakes; firmer fruit cheeses are usually sliced and can be enjoyed in similar ways. Fruit cheeses and butters are also very good served with roast meat, game or cheese.

Curds are made from fruit juice or purée cooked with eggs and butter. They have a soft texture and short keeping qualities. Fruit butters and cheeses are made from fruit purée boiled with sugar and are good if you have a glut of fruit because they require a relatively high proportion of fruit. Butters are lower in sugar and cooked for a shorter time, producing a soft, fruity preserve with a short shelf-life. Cheeses have a firm texture and may be set in moulds and turned out to serve.

MAKING FRUIT CURDS

Fruit curds are usually made with the juice of citrus fruits, but other acidic fruits such as passion fruit may be used. Smooth purées made from, for example, cooking apples or gooseberries can also be used.

The juice or purée is heated with eggs, butter and sugar until thick. The mixture is always cooked in a double boiler or a bowl set over a pan of simmering water to prevent the eggs curdling. Whole eggs are generally used, but if there is a lot of juice, egg yolks or a combination of whole eggs and yolks give a thicker result.

making lime curd

Makes about 675g/1½lb

INGREDIENTS

5 large, ripe juicy limes

115g/4oz/½ cup butter, cubed, at room temperature

350g/12oz/scant 1¾ cups caster (superfine) sugar

4 eggs, at room temperature

1 Finely grate the lime rind, ensuring you do not include any of the bitter white pith. Halve the limes and squeeze out the juice.

2 Place the lime rind in a large heatproof bowl set over a pan of barely simmering water, then strain in the lime juice to remove any bits of fruit or pips (seeds).

3 Add the cubed butter and the sugar to the bowl. Heat gently, stirring frequently, until the butter melts; the mixture should be barely warm, not hot.

4 Lightly beat the eggs with a fork, then strain through a fine sieve into the warm fruit mixture.

5 Keeping the water at a very gentle simmer, stir the fruit mixture continuously until the curd is thick enough to coat the back of a wooden spoon. Do not overcook because the curd will thicken on cooling.

6 Spoon the curd into warmed sterilized jars, then cover and seal when cold. Store in a cool, dark place, ideally in the refrigerator. Use within 2 months.

MAKING FRUIT BUTTERS

Smoother and thicker than jam, fruit butters have a spreadable quality not unlike dairy butter. Many recipes also contain a small amount of butter.

making apricot butter

Makes about 1.3kg/3lb

INGREDIENTS

1.3kg/3lb fresh ripe apricots

1 large orange

about 450ml/¾ pint/scant 2 cups water

about 675g/1½lb/scant 3½ cups caster (superfine) sugar

15g/½oz/1 tbsp butter (optional)

1 Rinse the apricots, then halve, stone (pit) and roughly chop. Remove the skins, unless you are going to purée the fruit by pressing through a sieve.

2 Scrub the orange and thinly pare 2–3 large strips of rind, avoiding any pith. Squeeze out the juice and put the apricots and the orange rind and juice in a large heavy pan.

3 Pour over enough of the water to cover the fruit. Bring to the boil, half-cover, then reduce the heat and simmer for 45 minutes.

4 Remove the orange rind, then blend the apricot mixture in a food processor until very smooth. Alternatively, press through a fine nylon or stainless steel sieve.

5 Measure the apricot purée and return it to the cleaned pan, adding 375g/13oz/1¾ cups sugar for each 600ml/1 pint/2½ cups purée.

6 Heat the mixture gently, stirring, until the sugar has dissolved, then bring to the boil and boil for about 20 minutes, stirring frequently, until thick and creamy. Remove the pan from the heat.

7 If using, stir the butter into the mixture until melted. (The butter gives a glossy finish.) Spoon into warmed sterilized jars and cover. Store in the refrigerator and use within 6 months.

MAKING FRUIT CHEESES

These sweet, firm preserves are known as cheeses because they are stiff enough to be cut into slices or wedges rather like their dairy counterparts. This name is particularly appropriate when the cheeses are set in moulds and turned out. They may be made either from fresh fruit, or from the pulp left from making jellies.

making cranberry and apple cheese

Makes about 900g/2lb

INGREDIENTS
450g/1lb/4 cups fresh cranberries
225g/8oz cooking apples
600ml/1 pint/2½ cups water
10ml/2 tsp lemon juice
about 450g/1lb/2¼ cups
  granulated (white) sugar
glycerine, for greasing (optional)

1 Rinse the cranberries and place in a large heavy pan. Wash the apples and cut into small pieces (there is no need to peel or core). Add the water and lemon juice.

2 Cover the pan with a lid and bring the mixture to the boil; do not lift the lid until the cranberries stop popping because they often jump out of the pan and can be very hot. Simmer gently for 1 hour, or until the fruit is soft and pulpy.

3 Press the cranberry and apple mixture through a fine nylon or stainless steel sieve into a bowl.

4 Weigh the purée, then return it to the cleaned pan, adding 450g/1lb/ 2¼ cups sugar for every 450g/1lb purée. Gently heat the mixture over a low heat, stirring, until the sugar has dissolved completely.

5 Increase the heat a little and simmer the mixture until it is so thick that the spoon leaves a clean line through the mixture when drawn across the pan. It may take as long as 30 minutes to reduce the purée to this consistency. Stir frequently to stop the mixture burning on the base of the pan.

6 Spoon the fruit cheese into warmed sterilized jars and seal. Alternatively, spoon the mixture into moulds or jars greased with a little glycerine and cover with clear film (plastic wrap) when cool. In sealed jars, the cheese will keep for up to 1 year; in covered moulds, it should be kept in the refrigerator until you are ready to turn it out; eat within 1 month of making.

USING LEFTOVER PULP
The fruit pulp left from jelly-making is perfect for making into fruit cheeses. Remove the pulp from the jelly bag, stir in enough hot water to make a soft purée, then push through a sieve. Place the purée in a clean pan, adding 450g/1lb/2¼ cups sugar for every 450g/1lb purée and cook following the instructions for making fruit cheese above.

MODERN PRESERVING TECHNIQUES

With the advent of new kitchen equipment such as microwaves, pressure cookers and freezers, new ways to make fruit preserves have developed. The increased concern over healthy eating has also led to new types of preserves such as reduced-sugar jams.

PRESERVING IN A MICROWAVE

Preserves can be made using a microwave, but only using specific recipes intended for the appliance. It is difficult to adapt conventional recipes because many rely on the evaporation of liquid to achieve a set or to thicken the preserve.

Make sure the ingredients are at room temperature; if they are not, it will affect cooking times. Frozen fruit and vegetables can be used to make microwave preserves, but they must be defrosted first.

Chop fruit and vegetables into equal-size pieces so that they cook at the same speed, and stir the preserve frequently during cooking to distribute the heat evenly and avoid hot spots. Use a suitable microwave-proof bowl that will withstand very hot temperatures, and that is large enough to hold twice the volume of the ingredients.

When the preserve has finished cooking, leave it to stand for several minutes until it has stopped bubbling. It is essential to protect your hands with oven gloves when lifting the bowl; take care not to place it on a cold surface because this may cause the glass to crack – a wooden board is ideal for protecting the surface and bowl.

making microwave lemon curd

This recipe is based on an 800 watt microwave. For microwaves with a different wattage, adjust cooking times as follows – for a 900 watt oven: subtract 10 seconds per minute; for a 850 watt oven: subtract 5 seconds per minute; for a 750 watt oven: add 5 seconds per minute; for a 700 watt oven: add 10 seconds per minute.

Makes about 450g/1lb

INGREDIENTS
115g/4oz/½ cup butter, cubed
finely grated rind and juice
  of 3 large lemons
225g/8oz/generous 1 cup caster
  (superfine) sugar
3 eggs plus 1 egg yolk

1 Put the butter, lemon rind and juice in a large microwave-proof bowl. Cook on high for 3 minutes.

2 Add the sugar and stir until it has almost dissolved. Return to the microwave and cook on full power for 2 minutes, stirring after 1 minute.

3 Beat the eggs and the yolk together, then whisk into the lemon mixture, a little at a time.

4 Cook on 40% power, for 10–12 minutes, whisking every 2 minutes, until the curd thickens. Ladle into hot sterilized jars, cover and seal. When cool, store in the refrigerator. Use within 2 months.

PRESERVING IN A PRESSURE COOKER

Preserves can be made very quickly using a pressure cooker. They are particularly useful for marmalades and for softening whole or hard fruits. Never fill the pan more than half full and always check the manufacturer's instructions.

making pressure-cooker orange marmalade

Makes about 2.5kg/5½lb

INGREDIENTS
900g/2lb Seville (Temple) oranges
1 large lemon
1.2 litres/2 pints/5 cups water
1.8kg/4lb/generous 9 cups preserving
  or granulated (white) sugar

1 Scrub the fruit, then halve and squeeze out the juice. Quarter the oranges, scrape off the pulp and membranes and tie in a piece of muslin (cheesecloth) with the lemon halves and any pips.

2 Place the orange peel in the pressure cooker with the muslin bag and 900ml/1½ pints/3¾ cups of the water. Bring to medium (4.5kg/10lb) pressure and cook for 10 minutes.

3 Reduce the pressure and leave until the fruit is cool enough to handle. Remove the muslin bag and squeeze it over the pan.

4 Cut the orange peel into fine shreds and return to the pan with the remaining water and the fruit juice. Add the sugar and heat gently until the sugar has dissolved. Bring to the boil, then boil rapidly for about 10 minutes until setting point is reached (105°C/220°F).

5 Remove any scum from the surface using a slotted spoon, then leave the marmalade to cool until a thin skin starts to form on the surface. Stir gently to distribute the peel evenly, then ladle into hot sterilized jars, cover and seal.

MAKING FREEZER JAMS

This type of jam is not cooked, so it has a fresher, fruitier flavour and a brighter colour than cooked jam. Once thawed, it does not keep as well as traditional jam. Commercial pectin is used as a setting agent.

making strawberry freezer jam

Makes about 1.3kg/3lb

INGREDIENTS

800g/1¾lb/7 cups strawberries
900g/2lb/4½ cups caster (superfine) sugar
30ml/2 tbsp lemon juice
120ml/4fl oz/½ cup commercial liquid pectin

1 Wipe the fruit. (Only wash if necessary, then pat dry on kitchen paper.) Hull and cut into quarters, then put in a bowl with the sugar.

2 Lightly mash the fruit with a fork, leaving plenty of lumps of fruit. Cover and leave to stand for 1 hour, stirring once or twice.

3 Add the lemon juice and pectin to the fruit and stir for 4 minutes until thoroughly combined. Ladle the jam into small freezer-proof containers, cover and leave to stand for about 4 hours.

4 Put the jam in the refrigerator and chill for 24–48 hours, or until the jam sets. Freeze the jam for up to 6 months, or until ready to use.

5 To serve, remove the jam from the freezer and leave at room temperature for about 1 hour, or until defrosted. Keep any leftover defrosted jam in the refrigerator and use quickly.

MAKING REDUCED-SUGAR PRESERVES

Sugar is the vital preserving agent in sweet fruit preserves. It helps to prevent fermentation and spoilage, as well as adding sweetness and flavour, and improving the set. The proportion of sugar required for this is about 60 per cent of the final weight of preserve. Although it is possible to make reduced-sugar preserves, the yield is smaller and they will not keep for as long. In most recipes, the sugar content can be reduced by up to half. The jam should be stored in the refrigerator and used within 4 months.

USING FROZEN FRUIT
Freezing is a quick and convenient way to preserve fruit when it is at its best and cheapest. It is especially useful for fruit with a very short season, such as Seville or Temple oranges. Freezing does destroy some of the pectin content, so to compensate for this, an extra 10 per cent of fruit should be used in the recipe. Do a pectin test during cooking to check the set.

BOTTLED FRUITS

Bottling is a traditional method of preserving fruit in syrup. The jars or bottles of fruit and syrup are heated to destroy micro-organisms. Although superseded by freezing, bottling is more suitable for some fruits such as peaches, pears, grapes and oranges; the method is less suitable for preserving soft berries such as raspberries.

MAKING BOTTLED FRESH FRUIT SALAD

Makes about 1.8kg/4lb

INGREDIENTS

250g/9oz/generous 1¼ cups
  granulated (white) sugar

350ml/12fl oz/1½ cups water

1 lemon

450g/1lb each eating apples, pears,
  peaches or nectarines

350g/12oz seedless green grapes

4 oranges

1 Put the sugar and water in a pan. Pare off a small strip of lemon rind, avoiding the pith, and add to the pan. Heat gently, stirring, until the sugar has dissolved. Bring to the boil and simmer for 1 minute. Cover and leave to stand.

2 Halve the lemon, then squeeze out the juice and strain.

3 Prepare the fruit, allowing 275g/10oz fruit for each 450g/1lb jar. Peel, core and slice the apples and pears and toss in lemon juice. Peel, halve, stone (pit) and slice the peaches or nectarines; halve the grapes; and segment the oranges.

4 Rinse hot sterilized jars with boiling water. Pack the fruit into the jars tightly, pressing down gently with a wooden spoon.

5 Strain the syrup through a fine sieve and return it to the cleaned pan. Bring to the boil, then pour over the fruit, filling the jars to within 1cm/½in of the top. Cover and heat-treat.

MAKING POACHED PEARS

Fruit is often poached in syrup until just tender before bottling.

Makes about 1.8kg/4lb

INGREDIENTS

225g/8oz/scant 1¼ cups
  granulated (white) sugar

1.2 litres/2 pints/5 cups water

1 orange

1 cinnamon stick

2kg/4½lb cooking pears

1 Put the sugar and water in a large, wide pan and add a thinly pared strip of orange rind and the cinnamon. Heat gently until the sugar has dissolved, then bring to the boil and simmer for 1 minute.

2 Squeeze the juice from the orange, then strain. Peel and core the pears, then toss in lemon juice as soon as each one is prepared.

3 Add the pears to the syrup in a single layer. Place greaseproof (waxed) paper over the pears to keep them immersed. Poach for 15 minutes until just tender and slightly transluscent; the syrup should hardly bubble so that the fruit holds its shape. Once cooked, bottle and heat-treat.

MAKING SUGAR SYRUPS

Poach whole and slightly hard fruits such as pears and plums in a light syrup; poach figs, peaches, nectarines and apricots in a medium syrup; and poach soft fruits such as strawberries and raspberries in a heavy syrup.

To make a light syrup, use 115g/4oz/generous ½ cup sugar to 600ml/1 pint/2½ cups water; to make a medium syrup, use 175g/6oz/scant 1 cup sugar to 600ml/1 pint/2½ cups water; to make a heavy syrup, use 350g/12oz/1¾ cups sugar to 600ml/1 pint/2½ cups water.

Put the sugar and water in a pan and heat gently, stirring, until the sugar has dissolved. Bring to the boil and simmer for 1 minute. Use hot or cool.

HEAT TREATMENTS

There are several ways to heat-treat bottled fruit. The filled jars may be heated in hot water, in the oven, or in a pressure cooker. As the fruit cools, a vacuum is created.

Use jars specifically designed for heat treatment. Preserving jars with clamp tops should be sealed once filled; the clamps expand slightly to allow steam to escape. Screw tops on preserving jars should not be tightened until after heating because the steam will not be able to escape and the jars may burst. Heat-treated preserves may be kept for up to 2 years.

water bath method

This is suitable for fruits bottled in either hot or cold syrup; the latter will take a little longer to process.

1 Wrap folded newspaper or cloth around each filled container, then stand them on a metal trivet or a thick layer of paper or cloth in a large heavy pan. (Containers placed directly on the pan may crack.)

2 Pour tepid water around the jars, right up to the neck, then cover the pan. Bring slowly to the boil (this should take 25–30 minutes), then simmer for the required time.

3 Turn off the heat and ladle out some of the hot water. Using tongs or oven gloves, lift the containers out of the pan and place on a wooden board. If they have screw-band lids, tighten immediately.

4 Leave the containers to cool for 24 hours, then remove the screw bands or clips. Holding the rim of the lid, carefully lift the container; it should hold its own weight. Containers with one-piece lids should have a very slight dip in the lid to indicate that they are sealed. If a jar is not sealed properly, it should be stored in the refrigerator and used as soon as possible.

HEATING TIMES FOR THE WATER BATH METHOD
The following times are for fruit packed in hot syrup after boiling. Allow 5 minutes more for fruit packed in cold syrup.

Fruit	Minutes
Soft berries and	
redcurrants	2
Blackcurrants,	
gooseberries, rhubarb,	
cherries, apricots	
and plums	10
Peaches and nectarines	20
Figs and pears	35

---

moderate oven method

This is only suitable for fruits covered with hot syrup; cold-filled jars may crack in the warm oven.

1 Preheat the oven to 150°C/300°F/Gas 2. Put the rubber rings and lids on the filled jars, but do not seal. Place in a roasting pan lined with newspaper or cloth, spacing the jars about 5cm/2in apart. Pour 1cm/½in boiling water into the pan.

2 Place the pan in the middle of the oven. Cook 500–600ml/17–20fl oz jars for 30–35 minutes and 1 litre/1¾ pint jars for 35–55 minutes. If there are more than four jars, allow a little extra time.

3 Remove from the oven and seal the lids immediately. Cool on a wooden board. Test the seals as for the water bath method.

pressure cooker method

If using clip-top jars, move the clips slightly to the side of the lid to reduce the pressure. Check the instructions for the pressure cooker.

1 Stand the jars on the trivet in the pressure cooker, ensuring they do not touch each other or the pan.

2 Pour in 600ml/1 pint/2½ cups hot water. Put on the lid with a low (2.25kg/5lb) weight and slowly bring to pressure. Maintain this pressure for 4 minutes. Leave to stand until the pressure drops.

3 Transfer the jars to a board and seal. Leave for 12 hours, then test as for the water bath method.

PICKLES

These can be sharp or sweet or a combination of the two. They are made by preserving raw or lightly cooked fruit or vegetables in spiced vinegar. They may be eaten alone or as a condiment with cheese or cold meat. There are two types of pickles: clear pickles or sweet pickles. To make clear pickles such as pickled onions, salt or brine is used to extract water from the vegetables to give them a crisp texture before they are bottled in vinegar. To make sweet pickles, fruit or vegetables are usually cooked until tender, then bottled in a sweet vinegar syrup.

Fruit and vegetables used for pickling should be firm and young. Small varieties such as baby (pearl) onions, beetroot (beets), gherkins, plums and cherries, which can be pickled whole, are particularly good. Large vegetables such as cucumbers, marrows (large zucchini), cabbage and cauliflower should be sliced or chopped.

Most pickles have to be matured in a cool dark place for a minimum of 3 weeks and preferably for at least 2 months to develop and mellow their flavour before eating. Pickled cabbage loses its crisp texture after 2–3 months, so it should be eaten within 2 months of making.

Take care when packing the fruit or vegetables into jars – they should be well packed, but not too tightly because the vinegar must surround each piece. It is important to fill jars to the brim and avoid trapping air in the pickles because this will cause discoloration and may encourage the growth of bacteria and moulds.

Large, wide-necked jars are recommended for pickling. Screw-top jars with lids that have plastic-coated linings such as those used for commercial pickles are an ideal choice. Vinegar reacts with metal, causing it to corrode and flavour the pickle, so metal tops should always be avoided when pickling.

MAKING CLEAR PICKLES

When making clear pickles, the ingredients are usually prepared first by soaking them in a brine. The salt draws out the moisture from the vegetables, making them more receptive to vinegar and preventing vegetable juices from diluting the preserving vinegar. Pure or kosher salt should always be used because iodized salt will taint the pickle with an iodine flavour and the additives in table salt will make it cloudy. There are two types of brine: dry brine, where the salt is sprinkled over the vegetables; and wet brine, where the salt is dissolved in water first.

making pickled peppers using dry brine

For this method, salt is rubbed into the vegetables or, more simply, sprinkled between layers of vegetables to draw out the juices. This then produces a brine. Salting vegetables makes them firmer and crunchier. It is particularly suitable for vegetables with a high water content such as (bell) peppers. Other vegetables that suit this method include cucumbers and courgettes (zucchini).

Makes about 1.8kg/4lb

INGREDIENTS

1.3kg/3lb red and yellow (bell) peppers
60ml/4 tbsp salt
750ml/1¼ pints/3 cups distilled malt vinegar
2 fresh bay leaves
2 thyme sprigs
5ml/1 tsp black peppercorns

1 Wash the peppers and pat them dry on kitchen paper. Cut each one into quarters lengthways, remove the seeds and cores, then cut each quarter in half to make long wide strips. If the peppers are very large, cut each quarter into three strips rather than two.

2 Layer the peppers in a large, non-corrosive bowl, fleshy side up, lightly sprinkling salt between each layer. Cover the bowl with clear film (plastic wrap) and leave to stand in a cool place for 8 hours or overnight to extract the moisture. If the weather is warm, place the bowl in the refrigerator.

3 Tip the peppers into a colander or large sieve and rinse thoroughly in cold water to remove the salt. The easiest way to check for salt is to taste one of the peppers: if it is too salty, rinse again.

4 Drain the peppers well and pat dry with kitchen paper. This is important because excess water will dilute the vinegar.

5 Pour the vinegar into a pan and add the herbs and peppercorns. Slowly bring to the boil, then simmer for 2 minutes.

6 Meanwhile, pack the peppers into hot sterilized jars. Remove the herbs from the pickling vinegar and tuck them into the jars.

7 Pour the vinegar and peppercorns over the peppers, filling the jars almost up to the brim. (To make an even crunchier pickle, allow the vinegar to cool first.)

8 Gently tap the jars on the work surface to release any trapped air bubbles, then seal with vinegar-proof lids. Store in a cool, dark place for 4 weeks before eating. Use within 1 year.

making vegetable pickle using wet brine

For this method, salt is mixed with water to make a brine solution. The ingredients are then immersed in the brine, sometimes for several days before pickling in vinegar. Wet brine may be used hot but it is more often used cold. For most pickles, a 10 per cent salt solution is used; this requires 50g/2oz/¼ cup salt to every 600ml/1 pint/2½ cups water. In some preserves where vinegar is used with sugar, this may be reduced to a 5 per cent solution.

Pickling using wet brine is suitable for ingredients with a very dense texture or thick skin such as whole lemons, watermelon rind and green walnuts, or where a softer result is required.

Makes about 1.3kg/3lb

INGREDIENTS
1.3kg/3lb mixed vegetables such as baby (pearl) onions, carrots, cauliflower and green beans
175g/6oz/¾ cup salt
1.75 litres/3 pints/7½ cups water
2 bay leaves
0.75–1 litre/1¼–1¾ pints/3–4 cups spiced vinegar

1 Prepare the vegetables: skin, peel, and trim as necessary. Leave the onions whole, thickly slice the carrots, break the cauliflower into small florets and cut the beans into 2.5cm/1in lengths. Place the vegetables in a large glass bowl.

2 Put the salt and water in a large pan and warm over a low heat until the salt has dissolved completely. Leave to cool, then pour enough over the prepared vegetables to cover completely.

3 Place a plate, slightly smaller than the diameter of the bowl, on top of the vegetables to keep them submerged in the brine. Leave to stand for 24 hours.

4 Tip the vegetables into a colander or sieve to drain, then rinse well in cold water to remove the excess brine. Drain again and pat dry using kitchen paper.

5 Put the bay leaves and vinegar in a pan and slowly bring to the boil over a low heat.

6 Meanwhile, pack the brined vegetables into hot sterilized jars. Tuck in the bay leaves and pour in the hot vinegar, filling the jars almost to the top.

7 Gently tap the jars to release any trapped air bubbles, cover and seal. Store the vegetables in a cool, dark place for 4 weeks before eating. Use within 1 year.

making unbrined pickled mushrooms

Not all clear pickles are brined before bottling in vinegar. The moisture can be removed from mushrooms by simmering them gently in water with a little salt until just tender. This method is also suitable for beetroot (beets).

Makes about 450g/1lb

INGREDIENTS

1 small onion
1 garlic clove
300ml/½ pint/1¼ cups
   white wine vinegar
6 black peppercorns
sprig of fresh thyme
275g/10oz/3¼ cups small button
   (white) mushrooms
600ml/1 pint/2½ cups water
10ml/2 tsp salt

1 Thinly slice the onion and bruise the garlic clove and place in a pan with the vinegar, peppercorns and thyme. Bring the mixture slowly to the boil over a low heat, then half cover the pan with a lid. Simmer for 15 minutes. Remove from the heat, cover completely with the lid and leave to cool.

2 Meanwhile, wipe the mushrooms clean with damp kitchen paper and trim the stems if necessary.

3 Place the mushrooms in a pan with the water and salt. Bring to the boil and simmer for 1 minute. Remove from the heat, cover and leave to cool for 4 minutes, stirring a couple of times, so that all sides of the mushrooms are immersed in the hot water.

4 Tip the mushrooms into a colander or sieve, leave to drain, then pat dry using kitchen paper.

5 Pack the mushrooms into clean sterilized jars, then strain the vinegar mixture into the jars, covering the mushrooms and filling the jars almost to the top.

6 Seal the jars and store in a cool dark place for at least 3 weeks before eating. Use within 1 year.

> ### PICKLING GREEN VEGETABLES
> The colour of green vegetables tends to be lost if stored for more than a few months, although their flavour remains the same. Blanching them in boiling water mixed with 5ml/ 1 tsp bicarbonate of soda (baking soda) for 30 seconds helps to retain their colour, but destroys the vitamin C content.

MAKING SPICED PICKLING VINEGAR

Ready-spiced pickling vinegar and jars or packets of mixed pickling spices are readily available from supermarkets. However, you can make your own, adapting the combination of spices according to personal preference and the ingredients to be preserved. You can use any variety of vinegar, but make sure that it has an acetic acid content of at least 5 per cent.

making basic spiced pickling vinegar

Makes 1.2 litres/2 pints/5 cups

INGREDIENTS

15ml/1 tbsp allspice berries
15ml/1 tbsp cloves
5cm/2in piece fresh root ginger, peeled
   and sliced
1 cinnamon stick
12 whole black peppercorns
1.2 litres/2 pints/5 cups vinegar

1 Put all the spices in a jar and pour over the vinegar. Cover the jar and leave to steep for 1–2 months, shaking occasionally.

2 After this time, strain the vinegar and return it to the cleaned jar and store it in a cool dark place until ready to use.

COOK'S TIP

To make quick pickling vinegar for immediate use, put all the ingredients in a pan and heat gently to boiling point. Simmer for about 1 minute, then remove from the heat, cover and leave to infuse (steep) for 1 hour. Strain and use.

MAKING SWEET PICKLES

For these pickles, fruit and some vegetables such as cucumbers are preserved in sweetened vinegar. They are excellent served as an accompaniment to cold meats, poultry and cheeses. Pickled apples or pears are also delicious served with hot baked ham or grilled (broiled) meat such as lamb chops. Sweet pickles are always made with distilled malt, wine or cider vinegar rather than brown malt vinegar, which would overpower the flavour and affect the colour of the fruit.

To offset the sharpness of the vinegar, a fairly large amount of sugar is added, usually between 350g/12oz/scant 1¾ cups and 450g/1lb/2¼ cups to every 300ml/ ½ pint/1¼ cups vinegar. Unlike vegetables, fruits do not need to be brined before pickling. Fruits that are pickled whole such as plums and cherries should be pricked before the initial cooking to allow the vinegar syrup to penetrate the skin and stop the fruit shrivelling. Some fruits such as berries become very soft when pickled and are therefore better preserved in sugar syrup or alcohol.

Spices and flavourings add zest to sweet pickles. They are best infused in the vinegar at the start of cooking, but also look attractive added to the bottle when packing the preserve. Use whole spices such as cinnamon, cloves, allspice, ginger, nutmeg and mace; ground spices will make the pickle murky. Citrus rind and vanilla pods (beans) also add a wonderful taste and aroma. Robustly flavoured herbs such as rosemary and bay leaves work well in sweet pickles.

making pickled apples

Makes about 1.3kg/3lb

INGREDIENTS

750ml/1¼ pints/3 cups raspberry, cider or white wine vinegar

1 cinnamon stick

5cm/2in piece fresh root ginger, peeled and sliced

6 whole cloves

1.3kg/3lb eating apples, peeled, cored and halved

800g/1¾lb/4 cups granulated (white) sugar

1 Put the vinegar in a stainless steel pan with the cinnamon, ginger and cloves, and bring to the boil. Reduce the heat and simmer gently for about 5 minutes.

2 Add the apples to the vinegar and simmer for 5–10 minutes until they are almost tender. Be careful not to overcook the fruit; it will continue to cook in the hot syrup and should still be firm when packed into the jars.

3 Using a slotted spoon, lift the apples out of the vinegar and pack them into hot sterilized jars, adding the cloves and the cinnamon stick, if you like.

4 Add the sugar to the vinegar and heat gently over a low heat, stirring until dissolved completely.

5 Increase the heat and boil the syrup rapidly for 5 minutes, or until the syrup has reduced and thickened slightly.

6 Strain the syrup through a sieve into a jug (pitcher), then pour it over the apples to cover them completely. Seal and label. Store the jars in a cool dark place and use within 1 year.

RASPBERRY VINEGAR

Fruit vinegars are perfect for making sweet pickles and are very easy to make at home.

To make about 750ml/ 1¼ pints/3 cups raspberry vinegar, put 450g/1lb/generous 2½ cups fresh raspberries in a bowl with 600ml/1 pint/ 2½ cups white wine or cider vinegar. Cover the bowl with a cloth and leave in a cool place for 4–5 days, stirring each day.

Strain the vinegar through a nylon or stainless-steel sieve and discard the raspberries. Pour the liquid into a jelly bag suspended over a large bowl or jug (pitcher). Leave to drain, then pour the vinegar into sterilized bottles and seal. Store in a cool dark place and use within 1 year.

PICKLING DRIED FRUITS

All sorts of dried fruits can be made into excellent pickles. The fruits soak up the pickling syrup, becoming soft, succulent and juicy. Dried apricots, peaches, pears, figs, prunes and mango slices are all perfect for pickling.

Pickles made with dried fruit do not need as much sugar as pickles made with fresh fruit; dried fruits are already packed with sugar. A small amount of liquid such as apple juice or water may be used to rehydrate the fruit before pickling. This prevents the fruit soaking up too much vinegar and the flavour becoming overpowering.

When pickling light-coloured dried fruits such as apricots, pears or apples, use light-coloured sugars and vinegars. Dark-coloured fruits such as figs and prunes can be pickled using malt or red wine vinegar and darker sugars.

SWEET PICKLING VINEGAR

When choosing vinegar for sweet pickles, it is important to think about the colour as well as the flavour of the vinegar. For green fruits such as green figs or red fruits such as plums, choose a light-coloured vinegar and spices or flavourings that won't alter the colour. Using a dark vinegar will turn the fruits a sludgy brown colour. Yellow fruits such as nectarines and apricots, and white or creamy fruits such as pears look stunning pickled in a coloured vinegar such as raspberry.

making pickled prunes

Makes about 1.3kg/3lb

INGREDIENTS

675g/1½lb/3 cups prunes
150ml/¼ pint/⅔ cup clear apple juice
750ml/1¼ pints/3 cups pickling malt vinegar
strip of pared orange rind
350g/12oz/1½ cups light muscovado (brown) sugar

1 Put the prunes in a non-corrosive pan, pour over the apple juice and cover. Leave to soak for 2 hours, or until the prunes have absorbed most of the juice.

2 Uncover the pan, add the vinegar and orange rind and bring slowly to the boil over a gentle heat. Reduce the heat and simmer gently for 10–15 minutes until the prunes are plump and juicy.

3 Remove the strip of orange rind from the pan and discard. Using a slotted spoon, lift the prunes out of the vinegar and pack well into hot sterilized jars.

4 Add the sugar to the vinegar and heat gently, stirring, until the sugar has dissolved completely. Bring the mixture to a rapid boil and cook for about 5 minutes, or until slightly reduced and thickened.

5 Carefully pour the hot vinegar syrup over the prunes and seal. Store in a cool dark place for at least 2 weeks before eating. Use within 1 year.

USING DRIED FRUITS IN PRESERVES

Dried fruits can be used in many types of preserve. They absorb liquid readily, so are often added to chutneys to help thicken the mixture. Raisins and sultanas (golden raisins) are particularly popular for this. Chopped dried apricots, peaches, dates and figs can also be used and contribute a substantial texture as well as a lovely sweet flavour.

Dried fruit is widely used to impart a full, fruity flavour to cooked relishes and savoury preserves made with mildly flavoured vegetables such as pumpkin, squash and green (unripe) tomatoes.

When choosing dried fruit for pickling, select the fully dried type, rather than the softer ready-to-eat variety that is popular for general cooking. The former has a better texture when soaked for a long time in pickling vinegar.

FRUITS PRESERVED IN ALCOHOL

Fruits preserved in alcohol make luxurious instant desserts, served with crème fraîche or ice cream. One of the best-known fruit and alcohol preserves is German *rumtopf*, which means rum pot. It consists of summer and early autumn fruits bottled in alcohol, usually rum, but not always, with a little sugar. Traditionally, this preserve is made in a large jar with a wide neck and tight-fitting lid.

Pure alcohol is the best preservative because bacteria and moulds are unable to grow in it. Clear liqueurs, such as eau de vie, orange liqueur, Kirsch and amaretto, or spirits such as brandy, rum and vodka, which are at least 40 per cent ABV, may be used.

The alcohol content of table wine and dry (hard) cider is too low and so these are not effective preservatives on their own unless the bottles are heat-treated. Fruits preserved in wine or cider should be stored in the refrigerator and used within 1 month of making.

When using alcohol to preserve, it is usually best to combine it with sugar syrup because high-alcohol liqueurs and spirits tend to shrink the fruit. Most fruits are first simmered in syrup, which helps to tenderize the fruit and kills the bad enzymes.

The type of syrup used for preserving fruits in alcohol varies depending on the sweetness and juiciness of the fruit, as well as the desired result. A typical syrup would be 600ml/1 pint/2½ cups alcohol, blended with a syrup of 150ml/¼ pint/⅔ cup water and 150g/5oz/¾ cup sugar.

MAKING NECTARINES IN BRANDY SYRUP

For extra flavour, you can add whole spices such as vanilla or cinnamon to the syrup.

Makes about 900g/2lb

INGREDIENTS
350g/12oz/1¾ cups preserving or granulated (white) sugar
150ml/¼ pint/⅔ cup water
450g/1lb firm, ripe nectarines
2 bay leaves
150ml/¼ pint/⅔ cup brandy

1 Put the sugar in a large heavy pan with the water and heat gently, stirring until dissolved completely. Bring to the boil, then reduce the heat and simmer for 10 minutes.

2 Halve and stone (pit) the nectarines. (If liked, you may also peel them.) Add them to the syrup.

3 Reduce the heat so that the syrup is barely simmering and poach the nectarines until almost tender. Add the bay leaves 1 minute before the end of the cooking. Turn off the heat and leave them to stand for 5 minutes; they will cook a little more as it cools.

4 Using a slotted spoon, lift the fruit out of the pan and pack into hot sterilized jars.

5 Bring the syrup to a rapid boil and cook for 3–4 minutes. Leave to cool for a few minutes, then stir in the brandy. (Do not add the brandy to the boiling syrup because the alcohol will evaporate and the syrup will lose its preserving qualities.) Pour the syrup into the jars, covering the fruit completely. Tap the jars to release any air and seal. Store in a cool dark place and use within 1 year.

CHUTNEYS

These are made from finely cut ingredients, cooked slowly with vinegar, a sweetener and frequently spices or other flavourings to make a thick, savoury jam-like mixture. Onions and apples are popular, but almost any fruits and vegetables can be used. Chutneys should be matured in a cool dark place for at least 2 months before eating.

MAKING TOMATO CHUTNEY

Makes about 2.25kg/5lb

INGREDIENTS
450g/1lb onions, chopped
900ml/1½ pints/3¾ cups malt vinegar
50g/2oz whole pickling spices, such as peppercorns, allspice berries, dried chillies, dried ginger and celery seeds
1kg/2¼lb ripe tomatoes, skinned and chopped
450g/1lb cooking apples, peeled, cored and chopped
350g/12oz/1½ cups soft light brown sugar
10ml/2 tsp salt
225g/8oz/1 cup sultanas (golden raisins)

1 Put the onions and vinegar in a large pan. Tie the pickling spices in a muslin (cheesecloth) bag and add to the pan. Bring slowly to the boil, then simmer gently for 30 minutes until the onions are almost tender.

2 Add the tomatoes and apples to the pan, and simmer for 10 minutes until the fruit is softened and starts to break down slightly.

3 Add the sugar and salt to the pan, and stir over a low heat until the sugar has dissolved completely, then stir in the sultanas.

4 Gently simmer the chutney for 1½–2 hours, stirring occasionally to prevent the mixture sticking. The chutney is ready when it is thick and there is no liquid on the surface. Draw a wooden spoon across the base of the pan: it should leave a clear line in the mixture.

5 Remove the pan from the heat and leave to cool for 5 minutes. Remove the spice bag and discard. Stir the mixture to ensure the chutney is evenly mixed, then spoon into warmed, sterilized jars.

6 Use the handle of a wooden spoon to release any trapped air bubbles and ensure the chutney is packed down well. Seal the jars immediately and leave to cool. Store the chutney in a cool, dark place and leave to mature for at least 1 month before eating. Use within 2 years.

TOP TIPS FOR SUCCESSFUL CHUTNEY-MAKING

• Use malt vinegar for its intense flavour. Wine vinegar or cider vinegar are better for preserving colourful or light-coloured vegetables because they will not spoil the colour of the vegetables.

• The choice of sugar will affect the end result: brown sugar gives the richest flavour and colour; demerara (raw) sugar and golden granulated sugar give a caramel flavour; and white sugar helps to retain the colour of light ingredients.

• Never cover the pan when making chutney. Cooking the preserve uncovered allows the liquid to evaporate and the chutney to thicken. Towards the end, stir the chutney frequently to prevent it from catching and burning on the base of the pan.

• Always store chutney in a cool dark place: warmth can cause it to ferment, and bright sunlight can affect the colour.

RELISHES

These are similar to chutneys, but cooked for less time to give a fresher result. The fruits and vegetables are usually cut into smaller, neater pieces, and wine or cider vinegar is more frequently used than malt vinegar. Relishes contain a low proportion of vinegar and sugar, so do not keep for long. They can be eaten immediately or chilled and used within 2–3 months.

MAKING HOT PEPPER RELISH

Makes about 1.3kg/3lb

INGREDIENTS

900g/2lb red (bell) peppers, quartered, cored and seeded
10ml/2 tsp salt
4 fresh red chillies, seeded
450g/1lb red (Italian) onions, finely chopped
400ml/14fl oz/1⅔ cups red wine vinegar
5ml/1 tsp celery seeds
6 black peppercorns
200g/7oz/1 cup granulated (white) sugar

1 Cut the peppers into 1cm/½in pieces and layer them in a colander or sieve placed over a large bowl, sprinkling salt between each layer. Leave the peppers to drain for at least 30 minutes.

2 Tip the red peppers into a large heavy pan and add the chillies, onions and vinegar.

3 Tie the celery seeds and black peppercorns in a square of muslin (cheesecloth) and add to the pan. Slowly bring to the boil over a low heat. Reduce the heat and simmer for about 25 minutes, or until the peppers are just tender.

4 Add the sugar and stir over a low heat until dissolved. Bring to the boil and simmer for 15 minutes, or until the relish is thick.

5 Remove the spice bag from the pan and discard. Spoon the relish into warmed, sterilized jars and seal. Store in the refrigerator and use within 3 months.

RELISHES WITH THICKENED SAUCES

Some relishes have a sauce base thickened with flour or cornflour (cornstarch). Mustard or turmeric may be added to the relish to give it a yellow colour. Corn relish, piccalilli and chow-chow are examples. The vegetables should retain their shape and be slightly crunchy, rather than soft.

making mustard relish

Makes about 1.3kg/3lb

INGREDIENTS

900g/2lb mixed vegetables, such as cauliflower, green beans, courgettes (zucchini), carrots, (bell) peppers and green (unripe) tomatoes
225g/8oz shallots, finely sliced
750ml/1¼ pints/3 cups malt vinegar
1 garlic clove, crushed
50g/2oz/½ cup plain (all-purpose) flour
25g/1oz/¼ cup English mustard powder
200g/7oz/1 cup caster (superfine) sugar
2.5ml/½ tsp ground coriander
5ml/1 tsp salt

1 Break the cauliflower into small florets, cut the beans into 2.5cm/1in lengths and dice the courgettes, carrots, peppers and tomatoes.

2 Put the shallots in a large heavy pan with 600ml/1 pint/2½ cups of the vinegar. Simmer, uncovered, for 10 minutes. Add the vegetables and garlic and simmer for 10 minutes.

3 Mix together the flour, mustard, sugar, coriander, salt and remaining vinegar to make a smooth paste, then stir into the vegetables. Simmer for 10 minutes, stirring. Pot and store for 2 weeks before eating. Use within 6 months.

SALSAS

These fresh sauces and relishes originated in Mexico. They are made from fresh raw fruit and vegetables and usually flavoured with spices such as chilli and aromatic herbs such as coriander (cilantro). They may be hot and fiery or cool and refreshing.

Many salsas are meant to be eaten on the day of making. Some, however, are lightly cooked and will keep for a short time in the refrigerator. They can also be frozen and stored in the freezer for up to 2 months.

Vinegar and sugar may be included in salsas, but only as flavouring ingredients and not as preservatives. Like relishes, they are ready for eating immediately.

MAKING SWEET PEPPER AND TOMATO SALSA

This light and refreshing salsa uses similar ingredients to a relish, but the result is completely different due to the very short cooking time.

Makes about 900g/2lb

INGREDIENTS

450g/1lb firm ripe tomatoes

7.5ml/1½ tsp salt

675g/1½lb red, yellow and green (bell) peppers, quartered and seeded

1 onion

2 large fresh green chillies, seeded

1 garlic clove, crushed

45ml/3 tbsp olive oil

30ml/2 tbsp red wine vinegar

5ml/1 tsp caster (superfine) sugar

30ml/2 tbsp chopped fresh coriander (cilantro)

1 Cut a small cross in the base of each tomato and place in a large, heatproof bowl. Pour over boiling water to cover, then leave to stand for about 30 seconds. Drain the tomatoes and peel off the skins.

2 Cut the tomatoes into quarters and use a teaspoon to scoop out the seeds. (This gives a more attractive result and prevents the salsa becoming too wet.)

3 Cut the tomato flesh into 5mm/ ¼in pieces and layer them up in a nylon or stainless-steel sieve set over a bowl, sprinkling a little salt between each layer. Leave to drain for about 20 minutes.

4 Meanwhile, cut the peppers and onion into 5mm/¼in pieces and finely slice the chillies, ensuring all the white membrane has been discarded. Put in a large pan.

5 Add the chopped tomatoes to the pan and add the crushed garlic, olive oil, vinegar, sugar and fresh coriander. Bring the mixture to the boil and simmer for 5 minutes, stirring frequently.

6 If you are going to use the salsa quickly, spoon into clean jars, packing it down well, then seal. Store in the refrigerator and use within 2–3 days.

7 Alternatively, pack the salsa into freezerproof containers and freeze for up to 2 months. Before serving, remove the salsa from the freezer and place in the refrigerator. Leave to defrost overnight.

COOK'S TIPS

• It is important to lightly cook all the ingredients, including the coriander, because this kills enzymes that would otherwise cause the salsa to deteriorate more quickly.

• The oily substance, capsaicin, which is found in chillies, can cause intense irritation to the skin and eyes. Always wash your hands with soap and water immediately after handling chillies. Alternatively, protect your hands by wearing a pair of rubber (latex) gloves when chopping the chillies.

BOTTLED SAUCES

Made with similar ingredients to chutneys, sauces have a thinner consistency and are sieved to a smooth purée. Those made with vegetables low in acid must either be stored in the refrigerator and consumed quickly, or heat-treated.

MAKING SIMPLE KETCHUP

Makes about 600ml/1 pint/2½ cups

INGREDIENTS

900g/2lb ripe tomatoes
225g/8oz shallots, peeled
2cm/¾in piece fresh root ginger, peeled
2 garlic cloves, peeled
150ml/¼ pint/⅔ cup cider vinegar
about 40g/1½oz/scant ¼ cup granulated
   (white) or soft light brown sugar
5ml/1 tsp paprika
5ml/1 tsp salt

1 Roughly chop the tomatoes, shallots, ginger and garlic. Make the pieces fairly small, so that the mixture cooks quickly and retains its fresh flavour.

2 Put the chopped vegetables in a large heavy pan and slowly bring to the boil, stirring frequently until the juices start to run. Reduce the heat, cover and simmer for about 20 minutes, stirring frequently, until the shallots are tender.

3 Spoon the tomato mixture into a sieve placed over a clean pan and press through using the back of a spoon. Alternatively, push the mixture through a food mill.

4 Bring the tomato purée to the boil, then reduce the heat and simmer gently for 45 minutes, or until reduced by half.

5 Add the vinegar, sugar, paprika and salt to the pan and stir to combine. Simmer the sauce for a further 45 minutes, stirring frequently, until well reduced and thickened. (The hot sauce should be a slightly thinner consistency at this stage than is required for the final ketchup; it will thicken as it cools.)

6 Using a funnel, carefully pour the hot sauce into hot sterilized bottles, then seal with corks and heat-treat. (If the bottles are not going to be heat-treated, plastic screw caps can be used instead of corks.)

7 Store the ketchup in a cool dark place, preferably the refrigerator. If it has been heat-treated, it will keep for up to 2 years; if it has simply been bottled, it will keep for up to 2 months in the refrigerator.

HEAT-TREATING BOTTLES

When sterilizing bottles, use those with a ridge on the neck to secure the cork with string.

1 Press a cork into the neck of a filled bottle and make a shallow cut across the top of the cork. Cut a 40cm/16in length of string. Keeping one end about 20cm/8in longer than the other, wedge the string into the cut.

2 Loop the longest end of string around the bottle neck, then pull the end through the front of the loop. Pull both ends down to tighten. Securely tie the loose ends of the string on the top of the cork. Repeat with the other bottles.

3 Wrap cloth around each bottle, then stand on a thick layer of cloth in a deep pan. Pour water up to the bottle necks and heat for 20 minutes for 600ml/1 pint/2½ cup hot-packed bottles; 25 minutes for 1 litre/1¾ pint/4 cup hot-packed and 600ml/1 pint/2½ cup cold-packed bottles; and 30 minutes for 1 litre/1¾ pint/4 cup cold-packed bottles.

DRIED FRUITS AND VEGETABLES

Removing moisture from foods is one of the oldest methods of preserving. Traditional techniques depend on the correct proportions of sunlight, heat and humidity for successful results. If food is dried too fast, moisture can get trapped and spoil it; if it is dried too slowly, micro-organisms may start to grow. Most commercially dried fruits and vegetables, such as apricots, figs and tomatoes, which are high both in sugar and acid, are still wind- and sun-dried in the way they have been for centuries.

To re-create these conditions, an airy place with a steady temperature is needed. A very warm room or cupboard may be used if the temperature is constant, but the most efficient way is to use an oven on the lowest setting.

A fan oven is ideal because of the constant circulation of air. If using a conventional oven, leave the door open with the tiniest possible gap, or open frequently during the drying process to let steam escape. Be careful that the temperature does not become too high, or the fruit or vegetables will cook and shrivel. If necessary, turn off the oven occasionally and leave it to cool down.

Choose firm, fresh and ripe fruit and vegetables for drying. Citrus fruits and melons consist mainly of water, so do not dry well, nor do berry fruits because they discolour and become very seedy. To help preserve the dried fruit and prevent discoloration, the prepared pieces should be dipped into a very weak brine solution, or acidulated water, before drying.

making dried apple rings

INGREDIENTS

15ml/1 tbsp salt, or 90ml/6 tbsp lemon juice, or 30ml/2 tbsp ascorbic acid (vitamin C) powder

1.2 litres/2 pints/5 cups water

900g/2lb firm, ripe apples

1 Put the salt, lemon juice or ascorbic acid powder in a large bowl and pour in the water. Stir until dissolved.

2 Peel and core the apples, then cut into rings slightly thicker than 5mm/¼in. As soon as each apple is cut, put the rings in the bowl of water and leave for 1 minute before lifting out. Pat the rings dry using kitchen paper.

3 Thread the apple rings on to wooden skewers, leaving a small space between each ring, or spread the apple rings out on wire racks. (Baking sheets are not suitable because air needs to circulate around the fruit.)

4 If using skewers, rest them on the oven shelves, allowing the apple rings to hang between the gaps. If using wire racks, simply place the racks in the oven. Leave the door very slightly ajar.

5 Dry the apples at 110°C/225°F/Gas ¼ for about 5 hours, or until the apple rings resemble soft, pliable leather.

6 Remove the fruit from the oven and leave to cool completely. Very crisp fruits and vegetables should be stored in airtight containers, but leathery, pliable fruits are better stored in paper bags or cardboard boxes; storing them in plastic bags may make them go mouldy.

7 To reconstitute the dried apple slices, put them in a bowl and pour over boiling water. Leave to soak for at least 5 minutes, then place in a pan and gently cook in the soaking liquid.

COOK'S TIPS

• Dried apple slices make a healthy snack and are popular with children.
• They are also good chopped and added to desserts and bakes.

PREPARING FRUITS AND VEGETABLES FOR DRYING

The time taken for fruit and vegetables to dry depends greatly on their size, so cut them into equal-size pieces.

Apples and pears: Peel and core. Cut apples into 5mm/¼in slices; halve or quarter pears, depending on size.

Apricots, plums and figs: These may be dried whole, but are better if halved and stoned (pitted). Place on the racks with the cut sides uppermost, so that the juices do not run out. If the oven has a lower setting, dry on this for 1 hour, before turning up to 110°C/225°C/Gas ¼, to prevent the skins from bursting.

Grapes: Use seedless grapes. These can be dried whole: prick a tiny hole in each one to stop the skins bursting.

Onions and leeks: Slice thinly crossways. The pieces may fall through wire racks, so cover the racks with muslin (cheesecloth) first.

Mushrooms and chillies: Tie these up on to fine string or cotton thread and hang up to air-dry in the sun or in an airy room for 2–3 weeks until dry and shrivelled. The dried strings of mushrooms and chillies can look very pretty hung in the kitchen.

Plum tomatoes: Split these lengthways and arrange cut side up. Sprinkle lightly with salt before placing in the oven to dry out.

FRUIT LEATHER

This unusual delicacy is made from slightly sweetened fruit pulp that has been spread out thinly and dried. The final result is a sweet, chewy fruit "leather" that can be eaten as confectionery or a snack. Most ripe fruits can be used; mangoes, peaches and apricots work particularly well and produce an intensely flavoured, orange-coloured confection.

making apricot leather

Makes about 115g/4oz

INGREDIENTS

900g/2lb ripe apricots
10ml/2 tsp lemon juice
45ml/3 tbsp caster (superfine) sugar

1 Put the apricots in a bowl and pour over boiling water. Leave to stand for about 30 seconds, then drain and peel off the skins. Halve the fruits and remove the stones (pits). Using a sharp knife, roughly chop the flesh.

2 Put the chopped apricots, lemon juice and sugar in a food processor or blender and process for about 3 minutes, or until the fruit has formed a smooth purée.

3 Line a large baking sheet with a piece of baking parchment. Pour the purée on to the middle of the baking parchment, then, using a palette knife (metal spatula), spread the purée out to a thickness of 5mm/¼in, leaving a 2cm/¾in margin. Tap the baking sheet on the work surface to level the purée.

4 Put the baking sheet in the oven, leaving the door slightly ajar, and dry at 110°C/225°F/Gas ¼ for about 8 hours, or until the purée is dry, but still pliable.

5 Leave the apricot leather to cool on the baking sheet, then roll it up, still on the baking parchment, and store in an airtight container for up to 3 months.

6 To eat, carefully unroll the fruit leather and cut into squares or 5cm/2in lengths while still on the baking parchment, then peel off the baking parchment.

CANDIED FRUIT

Sugar is an excellent preservative. Candying is a method by which fruit or citrus peel is preserved by steeping in syrup. The fruit or peel becomes so saturated in sugar that natural deterioration is virtually halted. The process works by gradually replacing the fruit's moisture with a saturated sugar solution. This has to be done slowly and takes at least 15 days, but is well worth it. Candied fruit is expensive to buy and, although you need to plan ahead when making candied fruit or peel, it requires only a little time each day.

making candied fruit

You can candy as much or as little fruit as you like, working with the basic proportions of fruit to sugar given in the recipe below. Always candy different fruits separately, so that each type retains its own flavour. Choose firm, fresh fruits that are free of blemishes.

INGREDIENTS

fresh, firm, just-ripe fruit, such as
   pineapples, peaches, pears, apples,
   plums, apricots, kiwi fruit or cherries
granulated (white) sugar
caster (superfine) sugar, for sprinkling

Day 1

1 Prepare the fruit. Thickly peel and core pineapples, then slice into rings; peel, stone (pit) or core peaches, pears and apples, then halve or cut into thick slices; plums and apricots can be left whole (prick them all over with a fine skewer) or halve and stone; skin and quarter kiwi fruit, or thickly slice; stone cherries.

2 Weigh the fruit, then put in a pan and just cover with water. Bring to the boil and simmer until just tender. Do not overcook because the flavour and shape will be lost; do not undercook because the fruit will be tough when candied.

3 Using a slotted spoon, lift the cooked fruit into a large wide bowl; avoid piling the fruit up high. Retain the cooking liquid.

4 For every 450g/1lb prepared (uncooked) fruit, use 300ml/½ pint/1¼ cups of the cooking liquid and 175g/6oz/scant 1 cup sugar. Gently heat the sugar and liquid in a pan, stirring, until the sugar has dissolved, then bring to the boil.

5 Pour the boiling syrup over the fruit, making sure that the fruit is completely immersed. Cover and leave to stand for 24 hours.

Day 2

1 Drain the syrup from the fruit back into a pan, being careful not to damage the fruit as you do so. Return the fruit to the bowl.

2 Add 50g/2oz/¼ cup granulated sugar to the syrup and heat gently, stirring until dissolved completely, then bring to the boil.

3 Pour the hot syrup over the fruit. Allow to cool, then cover and leave to stand for 24 hours.

Days 3–7

Repeat the instructions for day 2 every day for the next 5 days. The concentration of sugar will become much stronger.

Days 8–9

1 Drain the syrup from the fruit into a large wide pan and add 90g/3½oz/½ cup sugar. Heat gently, stirring, until dissolved.

2 Carefully add the fruit to the syrup and simmer gently for about 3 minutes. Return the fruit and syrup to the bowl, cool, then cover and leave to stand for 48 hours.

Days 10–13

Repeat the instructions for days 8–9, leaving the fruit to soak for 4 days rather than 2.

COOK'S TIP

The final soaking stage from days 10–13 can be extended another 6 days, if you like – to a total of 10 days. The longer the fruit is left to soak in the syrup, the sweeter and more intense its flavour will become.

Days 14–15

1 Drain the fruit, discarding the syrup. Carefully spread the fruit out, spacing each piece slightly apart, on a wire rack placed over a baking sheet.

2 Cut a sheet of baking parchment or foil slightly larger than the baking sheet. Using a fine skewer, prick about 12 tiny holes at equal intervals in the sheet.

3 Cover the fruit with the baking parchment or foil, being very careful not to touch the fruit. The parchment or foil is simply to keep off any dust; air should still be able to circulate around the fruit.

4 Leave the fruit in a warm place such as a sunny windowsill or airing cupboard for 2 days, turning each piece of fruit occasionally until all the fruit is thoroughly dry.

5 Sprinkle the fruit with a little caster sugar, then store in an airtight container in single layers between sheets of baking parchment. Eat within 1 year.

COOK'S TIP
Candied fruits are very pretty, retaining the colour of the original fruits. They make great sweetmeats for serving after a meal, particularly at Christmas.

making candied peel

Citrus peel contains less moisture than the fruit, making candying simpler and less time-consuming.

INGREDIENTS
5 small oranges, 6 lemons or 7 limes, or a combination
granulated (white) sugar
caster (superfine) sugar, for sprinkling

1 Scrub the fruit. Remove the peel in quarters, scraping away the pith. Place in a pan, cover with cold water and simmer for 1¼–1½ hours. Drain, reserving 300ml/½ pint/1¼ cups of the cooking water.

2 Pour the reserved water into the pan and add 200g/7oz/1 cup sugar. Heat gently, stirring until dissolved, then bring to the boil. Add the peel and simmer for 1 minute. Leave to cool, tip into a bowl, cover and leave for 48 hours.

3 Remove the peel and tip the syrup back into the pan. Add 150g/5oz/¾ cup sugar and heat gently, stirring until dissolved. Add the peel, bring to the boil, then simmer until transparent. Cool, tip into a bowl, cover and leave for 2 weeks.

4 Drain the peel, then dry, sprinkle and store in the same way as candied fruit.

making glacé fruit

Glacé, or crystallized, fruit is made from candied fruit, dipped in heavy syrup to give it a glossy coating.

INGREDIENTS
candied fruit
400g/14oz/2 cups granulated (white) sugar
120ml/4fl oz/½ cup water

1 Make sure the candied fruit is dry and dust off any sugar coating. Put the sugar and water in a pan and heat gently, stirring, until the sugar has dissolved. Bring to the boil and simmer for 2 minutes.

2 Pour one-third of the syrup into a small bowl. Fill a second bowl with boiling water. Using a slotted spoon or fork, first dip the fruit into the boiling water for 15 seconds, then shake and dip into the syrup for 15 seconds. Place on a wire rack.

3 Repeat with the remaining fruit, topping up the bowl of syrup when necessary (return the syrup to the boil before doing this).

4 Dry the fruit on wire racks placed over baking sheets in a very warm place for 2–3 days, turning the fruit occasionally. Store in the same way as candied fruit.

preserved sauces and mustards

Also known as "store sauces" these long-keeping sauces are condiments rather than pouring sauces. Often serving up a spicy punch, they are accompaniments for poultry, meat or game, and also pep up gravies and deglazed juices. They can also be whisked into a salad dressing or marinade, or introduced to a basting sauce, especially for a piquant, sweet-sour and caramelized result. The mustards are delicious with plain-cooked sausages and meats, and smoked fish.

sherried plum sauce

Here, plums are cooked with their skins, then strained to make a smooth sauce. Sharp cooking plums, damsons or bullaces – globular, fleshy, black-skinned berry fruits – give the best flavour and help counteract the sweetness of the sauce. Wonderful served with roast duck or goose.

2 Roughly chop the flesh and put in a large, heavy pan. If you're using damsons or bullaces, you may find it easier simply to chop them, leaving in the stones. Stir in the sherry and vinegar.

3 Slowly bring the mixture to the boil, then cover and cook over a gentle heat for about 10 minutes, or until the plums are very soft. Push the fruit through a food mill or sieve to remove the skins.

4 Return the plum purée to the pan and add the sugar, garlic, salt and ginger. Stir until the sugar has dissolved, then bring back to the boil and simmer uncovered for about 15 minutes, until thickened.

Makes about 400ml/14fl oz/1⅔ cups

INGREDIENTS

450g/1lb dark plums or damsons
120ml/4fl oz/½ cup dry sherry, plus extra
30ml/2 tbsp sherry vinegar
175g/6oz/scant 1 cup light muscovado (brown) sugar
1 garlic clove, crushed
1.5ml/¼ tsp salt
2.5cm/1in piece fresh root ginger, finely chopped
3–4 drops of Tabasco sauce

1 Cut each plum in half, then twist apart and remove the stone (pit).

5 Remove the pan from the heat and stir in the Tabasco sauce. Ladle the sauce into hot sterilized jars. Add 5–10ml/1–2 tsp sherry to the top of each jar, then cover and seal. The sauce will keep for several weeks in the refrigerator or, if heat treated, for 6 months. Once opened, store in the refrigerator and use within 3 weeks.

Energy 996kcal/4237kJ; Protein 4.2g; Carbohydrate 225g, of which sugars 224.2g; Fat 0.5g, of which saturates 0g; Cholesterol 0mg; Calcium 161mg; Fibre 7.4g; Sodium 1014mg.

cumberland sauce

This sauce is thought to have been named after the Duke of Cumberland who became ruler of Hanover at a time when fruit sauces were served with meat and game in Germany. It goes well with cold cuts, pâtés and terrines, and Christmas or Thanksgiving turkey.

Makes about 750ml/1¼ pints/3 cups

INGREDIENTS

4 oranges
2 lemons
450g/1lb redcurrant or rowan jelly
150ml/¼ pint/⅔ cup port
20ml/4 tsp cornflour (cornstarch)
pinch of ground ginger

1 Scrub the oranges and lemons, then remove the rind thinly, paring away any white pith.

2 Cut the orange and lemon rind into very thin matchstick strips. Put the strips in a heavy pan, cover them with cold water and bring the water to the boil.

3 Simmer the rind for 2 minutes, then drain, cover with cold water, bring to the boil and simmer for about 3 minutes. Drain well and return the rind to the pan.

4 Squeeze the juice from the fruits, then add it to the pan with the redcurrant or rowan jelly. Reserve 30ml/2 tbsp of the port and add the rest to the pan.

5 Slowly bring the mixture to the boil, stirring until the jelly has melted. Simmer for 10 minutes until slightly thickened. Blend the cornflour and ginger with the reserved port and stir into the sauce. Cook over a low heat, stirring until the sauce thickens and boils. Simmer for 2 minutes.

6 Leave the sauce to cool for about 5 minutes, then stir again briefly. Pour into warmed sterilized wide-necked bottles or jars, cover and seal. The sauce will keep for several weeks in the refrigerator or, if heat treated, for 6 months. Once opened, store in the refrigerator and use within 3 weeks.

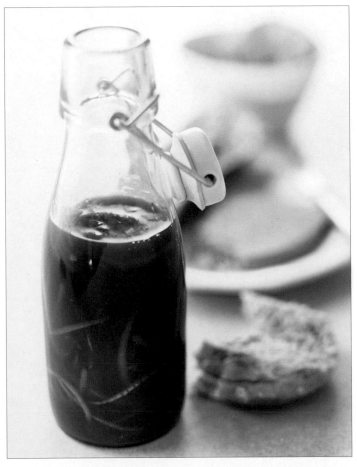

Energy 1481kcal/6297kJ; Protein 3g; Carbohydrate 346.9g, of which sugars 328.5g; Fat 0.1g, of which saturates 0g; Cholesterol 0mg; Calcium 63mg; Fibre 0g; Sodium 147mg.

mint sauce

The fresh, tart, astringent flavour of mint sauce makes it the perfect foil to rich, strongly flavoured lamb. It is very simple to make and is infinitely preferable to ready-made varieties.

Makes about 250ml/8fl oz/1cup

INGREDIENTS

1 large bunch mint
105ml/7 tbsp boiling water
150ml/¼ pint/⅔ cup wine vinegar
30ml/2 tbsp granulated (white) sugar

COOK'S TIP

To make a quick Indian raita for serving with crispy poppadums, simply stir a little mint sauce into a small bowl of natural (US strained plain) yogurt. Serve the raita alongside a bowl of tangy mango chutney.

1 Using a sharp knife, chop the mint very finely and place it in a 600ml/1 pint/2½ cup jug (pitcher). Pour the boiling water over the mint and leave to infuse for about 10 minutes.

2 When the mint infusion has cooled and is lukewarm, stir in the wine vinegar and sugar. Continue stirring (but do not mash up the mint leaves) until the sugar has dissolved completely.

3 Pour the mint sauce into a sterilized bottle or jar, seal and store in the refrigerator.

COOK'S TIP

This mint sauce can keep for up to 6 months stored in the refrigerator, but is best used within 3 weeks.

Energy 161kcal/685kJ; Protein 3.9g; Carbohydrate 36.6g, of which sugars 31.4g; Fat 0.7g, of which saturates 0g; Cholesterol 0mg; Calcium 226mg; Fibre 0g; Sodium 17mg.

traditional horseradish sauce

Fiery, peppery horseradish sauce is without doubt the essential accompaniment to roast beef and is also delicious served with smoked salmon.

Makes about 200ml/7fl oz/scant 1 cup

INGREDIENTS

45ml/3 tbsp freshly grated
  horseradish root
15ml/1 tbsp white wine vinegar
5ml/1 tsp granulated (white) sugar
pinch of salt
150ml/¼ pint/⅔ cup thick double
  (heavy) cream, for serving

COOK'S TIP

To counteract the potent fumes of the horseradish, keep the root submerged in water while you chop and peel it. Use a food processor to do the fine chopping or grating, and avert your head when removing the lid.

1 Place the grated horseradish in a bowl, then add the white wine vinegar, granulated sugar and just a pinch of salt.

2 Stir the ingredients together until thoroughly combined.

3 Pour the mixture into a sterilized jar. It will keep in the refrigerator for up to 6 months.

4 A few hours before serving, stir the cream into the horseradish and leave to infuse (steep).

Energy 774kcal/3190kJ; Protein 2.8g; Carbohydrate 9.9g, of which sugars 9.8g; Fat 80.7g, of which saturates 50.1g; Cholesterol 206mg; Calcium 98mg; Fibre 1.1g; Sodium 40mg.

tomato ketchup

Sweet, tangy, spicy tomato ketchup is perfect for serving with barbecued or grilled burgers and sausages. This home-made variety is so much better than store-bought tomato ketchup.

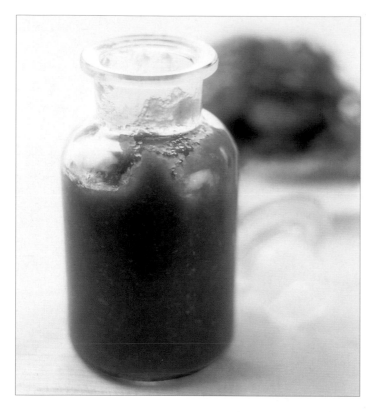

2 Tie the onion with the allspice, peppercorns, rosemary and ginger into a double layer of muslin (cheesecloth) and add to the pan. Chop the celery, plus the leaves, and add to the pan with the sugar, raspberry vinegar, garlic and salt.

3 Bring the mixture to the boil over a fairly high heat, stirring occasionally. Reduce the heat and simmer for 1½–2 hours, stirring regularly, until reduced by half. Purée the mixture in a food processor, then return to the pan, bring to the boil and simmer for 15 minutes. Bottle in clean, sterilized jars and store in the refrigerator. Use within 2 weeks.

Makes about 1.3kg/3lb

INGREDIENTS

2.25kg/5lb very ripe tomatoes
1 onion
6 cloves
4 allspice berries
6 black peppercorns
1 fresh rosemary sprig
25g/1oz fresh root ginger, sliced
1 celery heart
30ml/2 tbsp soft light brown sugar
65ml/4½ tbsp raspberry vinegar
3 garlic cloves, peeled
15ml/1 tbsp salt

1 Carefully peel and seed the ripe tomatoes, then chop and place in a large pan. Peel the onion, leaving the tip and root intact and stud it with the cloves.

Energy 543kcal/2327kJ; Protein 18.1g; Carbohydrate 108.5g, of which sugars 107.2g; Fat 7.5g, of which saturates 2.3g; Cholesterol 0mg; Calcium 313mg; Fibre 26.6g; Sodium 6281mg.

barbecue sauce

As well as enlivening burgers and other food cooked on the barbecue, this sauce is also good for all manner of grilled meats and savoury pastries.

Makes about 900ml/1½ pints/3¾ cups

INGREDIENTS

30ml/2 tbsp olive oil

1 large onion, chopped

1 garlic clove, crushed

1 fresh red chilli, seeded and sliced

2 celery sticks, sliced

1 large carrot, sliced

1 medium cooking apple, quartered, cored, peeled and chopped

450g/1lb ripe tomatoes, quartered

2.5ml/½ tsp ground ginger

150ml/¼ pint/⅔ cup malt vinegar

1 bay leaf

4 whole cloves

4 black peppercorns

50g/2oz/¼ cup soft light brown sugar

10ml/2 tsp English mustard

2.5ml/½ tsp salt

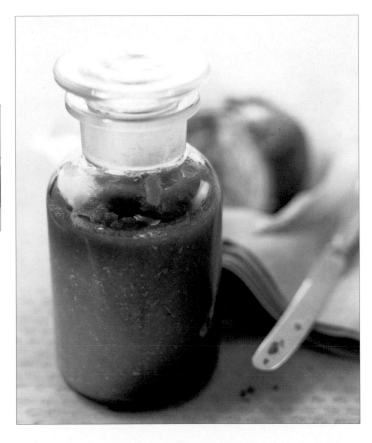

1 Heat the oil in a large heavy pan. Add the onion and cook over a low heat for 5 minutes.

2 Stir in the garlic, chilli, celery and carrot into the onions and cook for 5 minutes, stirring frequently, until the onion just begins to colour.

3 Add the apple, tomatoes, ground ginger and malt vinegar to the pan and stir to combine.

4 Put the bay leaf, cloves and peppercorns on a square of muslin (cheesecloth) and tie into a bag with fine string. Add to the pan and bring to the boil. Reduce the heat, cover and simmer for about 45 minutes, stirring occasionally.

5 Add the sugar, mustard and salt to the pan and stir until the sugar dissolves. Simmer for 5 minutes. Leave to cool for 10 minutes, then remove the bag and discard.

6 Press the mixture through a sieve and return to the cleaned pan. Simmer for 10 minutes, or until thickened. Adjust the seasoning.

7 Pour the sauce into hot sterilized bottles or jars, then seal. Heat process, cool and, if using cork-topped bottles, dip the corks in wax. Store in a cool, dark place and use within 1 year. Once opened, store in the refrigerator and use within 2 months.

Energy 561kcal/2359kJ; Protein 5.8g; Carbohydrate 84.3g, of which sugars 82.4g; Fat 24.7g, of which saturates 3.7g; Cholesterol 0mg; Calcium 126mg; Fibre 8.9g; Sodium 396mg.

roasted red pepper and chilli ketchup

Roasting the peppers gives this ketchup a richer, smoky flavour. You can add fewer or more chillies according to taste. Once opened, store in the refrigerator and use within 3 months.

Makes about 600ml/1 pint/2½ cups

INGREDIENTS

900g/2lb red (bell) peppers

225g/8oz shallots

1 tart cooking apple, quartered, cored and roughly chopped

4 fresh red chillies, seeded and chopped

1 large sprig each thyme and parsley

1 bay leaf

5ml/1 tsp coriander seeds

5ml/1 tsp black peppercorns

600ml/1 pint/2½ cups water

350ml/12fl oz/1½ cups red wine vinegar

50g/2oz/scant ¼ cup granulated (white) sugar

5ml/1 tsp salt

7.5ml/1½ tsp arrowroot

1 Preheat the grill (broiler). Place the peppers on a baking sheet and grill for 10–12 minutes, turning regularly, until the skins have blackened. Put the peppers in a plastic bag and leave for 5 minutes.

2 When the peppers are cool enough to handle, peel away the skin, then quarter the peppers and remove the seeds. Roughly chop the flesh and place in a large pan.

3 Put the shallots in a bowl, pour over boiling water and leave to stand for 3 minutes. Drain, then rinse under cold water and peel. Chop the shallots and add to the pan with the apple and chillies.

4 Tie the thyme, parsley, bay leaf, coriander and peppercorns together in a square of muslin (cheesecloth).

5 Add the bag of herbs and the water to the pan and bring to the boil. Reduce the heat, cover and simmer for 30 minutes. Leave to cool for 15 minutes, then remove and discard the muslin bag.

6 Purée the mixture in a food processor, then press through a sieve and return the purée to the cleaned pan. Reserve 15ml/1 tbsp of the vinegar and add the rest to the pan with the sugar and salt.

7 Bring to the boil, stirring until the sugar has dissolved, then simmer for 45 minutes, or until the sauce is well reduced. Blend the arrowroot with the reserved vinegar, stir into the sauce, then simmer for a 2–3 minutes, or until slightly thickened.

8 Pour the sauce into hot sterilized bottles, then seal, heat process and store in a cool, dark place and use within 18 months.

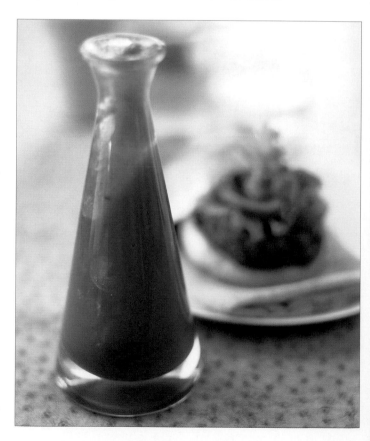

Energy 553kcal/2341kJ; Protein 12.8g; Carbohydrate 123.2g, of which sugars 120.5g; Fat 4.1g, of which saturates 0.9g; Cholesterol 0mg; Calcium 155mg; Fibre 18.6g; Sodium 1045mg.

aromatic mustard powder

This pungent condiment has the added flavour of herbs and spices and should be served in small quantities with meats and cheese. To serve, simply mix it with a little water.

Makes about 200g/7oz/1⅔ cups

INGREDIENTS

115g/4oz/1 cup mustard powder

25ml/1½ tbsp ground sea salt

5ml/1 tsp dried thyme

5ml/1 tsp dried tarragon

5ml/1 tsp mixed spice (apple pie spice)

2.5ml/½ tsp ground black pepper

2.5ml/½ tsp garlic powder (optional)

1 Put the mustard powder and salt in a small bowl and stir together until evenly blended.

2 Add the dried thyme and tarragon to the mustard with the mixed spice, ground black pepper and garlic powder, if using. Stir until thoroughly mixed.

3 Spoon the mustard powder into small clean, dry jars, then seal tightly. Store it in a cool, dark place and use within 6 months. (Although the mustard powder won't go off, the potency of the herbs and spices will fade with age and the final mustard will not have the same lovely, strong flavour.)

4 To serve, combine the mustard powder with an equal amount of cold water 10 minutes before needed. Mix well until smooth.

COOK'S TIPS

• The mustard is best when freshly made, so mix up small quantities as and when you need it.

• To sharpen the flavour when serving the mustard with rich meats, use about a third cider or tarragon vinegar and two-thirds water. It can also be blended with sherry, white or red wine or port; the latter two will give the mustard a darker colour.

• The mustard powder is also great added to sauces and salad dressings to give extra flavour.

Energy 520kcal/2167kJ; Protein 33.2g; Carbohydrate 23.8g, of which sugars 0g; Fat 51.9g, of which saturates 1.7g; Cholesterol 5mg; Calcium 381mg; Fibre 0g; Sodium 5901mg.

moutarde aux fines herbes

This classic, fragrant mustard may be used either as a delicious condiment or for coating meats such as chicken and pork, or oily fish such as mackerel, before cooking.

Makes about 300ml/½ pint/1¼ cups

INGREDIENTS

75g/3oz/scant ½ cup white mustard seeds

50g/2oz/¼ cup soft light brown sugar

5ml/1 tsp salt

5ml/1 tsp whole peppercorns

2.5ml/½ tsp ground turmeric

200ml/7fl oz/scant 1 cup distilled malt vinegar

60ml/4 tbsp chopped fresh mixed herbs, such as parsley, sage, thyme and rosemary

COOK'S TIP

Stir a spoonful of this fragrant mustard into creamy savoury sauces and salad dressings to enhance their flavour.

1 Put the mustard seeds, sugar, salt, whole peppercorns and ground turmeric into a food processor or blender and process for about 1 minute, or until the peppercorns are coarsely chopped.

2 Gradually add the vinegar to the mustard mixture, 15ml/1 tbsp at a time, processing well between each addition, then continue processing until a coarse paste forms.

3 Add the chopped fresh herbs to the mustard and mix well, then leave to stand for 10–15 minutes until the mustard thickens slightly.

4 Spoon the mustard into a 300ml/ ½ pint/1¼ cup sterilized jar. Cover the surface of the mustard with a waxed disc, then seal with a screw-top lid or a cork, and label. Store in a cool, dark place.

Energy 553kcal/2324kJ; Protein 23.4g; Carbohydrate 69.1g, of which sugars 53.4g; Fat 34.5g, of which saturates 1.1g; Cholesterol 3mg; Calcium 374mg; Fibre 2.5g; Sodium 23mg.

honey mustard

Delicious home-made mustards mature to make the most aromatic of condiments. This honey mustard is richly flavoured and is wonderful served with meats and cheeses or stirred into sauces and salad dressings to give an extra, peppery bite.

Makes about 500g/1¼lb

INGREDIENTS

225g/8oz/1 cup mustard seeds

15ml/1 tbsp ground cinnamon

2.5ml/½ tsp ground ginger

300ml/½ pint/1¼ cups white wine vinegar

90ml/6 tbsp dark clear honey

COOK'S TIP

Make sure you use well-flavoured clear honey for this recipe. Set (crystallized) honey does not have the right consistency and will not work well.

1 Put the mustard seeds in a bowl with the spices and pour over the vinegar. Stir well to mix, then leave to soak overnight.

2 The next day, put the mustard mixture in a mortar and pound with a pestle, adding the honey very gradually.

3 Continue pounding and mixing until the mustard resembles a stiff paste. If the mixture is too stiff, add a little extra vinegar to achieve the desired consistency.

4 Spoon the mustard into four sterilized jars, seal and label, then store in the refrigerator and use within 4 weeks.

COOK'S TIP

This sweet, spicy mustard is perfect for adding extra flavour to cheese tarts or quiches. Spread a very thin layer of mustard across the base of the pastry case before adding the filling, then bake according to the recipe. The mustard will really complement the cheese, giving a mouth-watering result.

Energy 1276kcal/5345kJ; Protein 65.4g; Carbohydrate 115.3g, of which sugars 68.8g; Fat 101.5g, of which saturates 3.4g; Cholesterol 9mg; Calcium 747mg; Fibre 0g; Sodium 21mg.

tarragon and champagne mustard

This mild-tasting mustard goes particularly well with cold chicken, fish and shellfish.

Makes about 250g/9oz

INGREDIENTS

30ml/2 tbsp mustard seeds
75ml/5 tbsp champagne vinegar
115g/4oz/1 cup mustard powder
115g/4oz/½ cup soft light brown sugar
2.5ml/½ tsp salt
50ml/3½ tbsp virgin olive oil
60ml/4 tbsp chopped fresh tarragon

COOK'S TIP

Champagne vinegar has a lovely flavour but can sometimes be hard to find. Look in specialist delicatessens and food stores, or large supermarkets that stock a good range of gourmet foods.

1 Put the mustard seeds and vinegar in a bowl and leave to soak overnight.

2 The next day, tip the mustard seeds and vinegar into a food processor and add the mustard powder, sugar and salt.

3 Blend the mustard mixture until smooth, then slowly add the oil while continuing to blend.

4 Tip the mustard into a bowl, stir in the tarragon, then spoon into sterilized jars, seal and store in a cool, dark place.

Energy 1405kcal/5885kJ; Protein 42.5g; Carbohydrate 150.2g, of which sugars 120.2g; Fat 98.4g, of which saturates 6.9g; Cholesterol 6mg; Calcium 539mg; Fibre 0g; Sodium 14mg.

horseradish mustard

This tangy mustard has a wonderfully creamy, peppery taste and is the ideal condiment for cold meats, smoked fish or cheese. It also makes a lovely spread for cold roast beef sandwiches.

Makes about 400g/14oz

INGREDIENTS

25ml/1½ tbsp mustard seeds
250ml/8fl oz/1 cup boiling water
115g/4oz/1 cup mustard powder
115g/4oz/scant ½ cup granulated (white) sugar
120ml/4fl oz/½ cup white wine or cider vinegar
50ml/2fl oz/¼ cup olive oil
5ml/1 tsp lemon juice
30ml/2 tbsp horseradish sauce

1 Put the mustard seeds in a bowl and pour over the boiling water. Set aside and leave to soak for at least 1 hour.

2 Drain the mustard seeds and discard the soaking liquid, then tip the seeds into a food processor or blender.

3 Add the mustard powder, sugar, white wine or cider vinegar, olive oil, lemon juice and horseradish sauce to the mustard seeds in the food processor or blender.

4 Process the ingredients into a smooth paste, then spoon the mustard into sterilized jars. Store the mustard in the refrigerator and use within 3 months.

Energy 1428kcal/5982kJ; Protein 41.8g; Carbohydrate 154.5g, of which sugars 124.7g; Fat 98.6g, of which saturates 7.1g; Cholesterol 10mg; Calcium 536mg; Fibre 0.8g; Sodium 287mg.

spiced tamarind mustard

Tamarind has a distinctive sweet and sour flavour, a dark brown colour and sticky texture. Combined with spices and ground mustard seeds, it makes a wonderful condiment.

Makes about 200g/7oz

INGREDIENTS

115g/4oz tamarind block

150ml/¼ pint/⅔ cup warm water

50g/2oz/¼ cup yellow mustard seeds

25ml/1½ tbsp black or brown mustard seeds

10ml/2 tsp clear honey

pinch of ground cardamom

pinch of salt

COOK'S TIP

The mustard will be ready to eat in 3–4 days. It should be stored in a cool, dark place and used within 4 months.

1 Put the tamarind in a small bowl and pour over the water. Leave to soak for 30 minutes. Mash to a pulp with a fork, then strain through a fine sieve into a bowl.

2 Grind the mustard seeds in a spice mill or coffee grinder and add to the tamarind with the remaining ingredients. Spoon into sterilized jars, cover and seal.

Energy 376kcal/1570kJ; Protein 22.3g; Carbohydrate 24.2g, of which sugars 8.7g; Fat 34.1g, of which saturates 1.1g; Cholesterol 3mg; Calcium 295mg; Fibre 1.3g; Sodium 74mg.

clove-spiced mustard

This spicy mustard is the perfect accompaniment to robust red meats such as sausages and steaks, particularly when they are cooked on the barbecue.

Makes about 300ml/½ pint/1¼ cups

INGREDIENTS

75g/3oz/scant ½ cup white mustard seeds

50g/2oz/¼ cup soft light brown sugar

5ml/1 tsp salt

5ml/1 tsp black peppercorns

5ml/1 tsp cloves

5ml/1 tsp turmeric

200ml/7fl oz/scant 1 cup distilled malt vinegar

COOK'S TIP

Cloves add a lovely, warming taste to this mustard. Make sure you use whole cloves in this mustard – ground cloves tend to have less flavour.

1 Put all the ingredients except the malt vinegar into a food processor or blender and process. Gradually add the vinegar, 15ml/1 tbsp at a time, processing well between each addition. Continue processing the mustard until it forms a fairly thick, coarse paste.

2 Leave the mustard to stand for 10–15 minutes to thicken slightly. Spoon into a 300ml/½ pint/1¼ cup sterilized jar or several smaller jars, using a funnel. Cover the surface with a waxed paper disc, then seal with a screw-top lid or a cork, and label.

Energy 536kcal/2254kJ; Protein 21.9g; Carbohydrate 67.8g, of which sugars 52.3g; Fat 33.8g, of which saturates 1.1g; Cholesterol 3mg; Calcium 275mg; Fibre 0g; Sodium 1972mg.

chutneys and relishes

*Familiar and easy to make, these are classic
condiments for "feel-good" cooking sessions.
If you grow your own vegetables, or simply
have a few tomato plants in a pot, you will
probably have a glut of produce at some
time or other. Otherwise, explore farm shops
and markets for the best, freshest produce.
Many of these glorious savoury fusions will
make a substantial amount to squirrel away
and enjoy gradually; others should be served
fairly soon after preparation, as sandwich
fillers, dips or dressings.*

green tomato chutney

This is a classic chutney for using the last tomatoes of summer that just never seem to ripen. Apples and onions contribute essential flavour, which is enhanced by the addition of spice.

Makes about 2.5kg/5½lb

INGREDIENTS

1.8kg/4lb green (unripe) tomatoes, roughly chopped

450g/1lb cooking apples, peeled, cored and chopped

450g/1lb onions, chopped

2 large garlic cloves, crushed

15ml/1 tbsp salt

45ml/3 tbsp pickling spice

600ml/1 pint/2½ cups cider vinegar

450g/1lb/2¼ cups granulated (white) sugar

COOK'S TIP

Allow the chutney to mature for at least 1 month before using.

1 Place the tomatoes, apples, onions and garlic in a large pan and add the salt.

2 Tie the pickling spice in a piece of muslin (cheesecloth) and add to the ingredients in the pan.

3 Add half the vinegar to the pan and bring to the boil. Reduce the heat and simmer for 1 hour, or until the chutney is reduced and thick, stirring frequently.

4 Put the sugar and remaining vinegar in a pan and heat gently until the sugar has dissolved, then add to the chutney. Simmer for 1½ hours until the chutney is thick, stirring it occasionally.

5 Remove the muslin bag from the chutney, then spoon the hot chutney into warmed sterilized jars. Cover and seal immediately.

COOK'S TIPS

• To avoid spillages and speed up the process of potting preserves, use a wide-necked jam funnel to transfer the chutney into the jars. Wipe the jars immediately, then label them when cold.

• Use a long-handled teaspoon to press and poke the chutney right down into the pots to exclude any trapped air pockets.

• Press wax discs on the surface of the chutney before sealing the jar.

Energy 2399kcal/10233kJ; Protein 21.6g; Carbohydrate 601.6g, of which sugars 591.3g; Fat 6.8g, of which saturates 1.8g; Cholesterol 0mg; Calcium 496mg; Fibre 31.5g; Sodium 2177mg.

classic tomato chutney

This spicy and dark, sweet-sour chutney is delicious served with a selection of well-flavoured cheeses and biscuits or bread, or with cold roast meats such as ham, turkey, tongue or lamb.

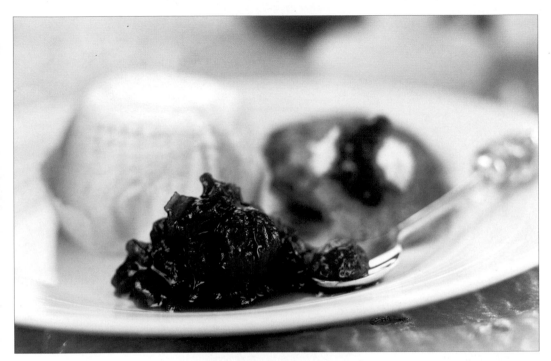

Makes about 1.8kg/4lb

INGREDIENTS

900g/2lb tomatoes, skinned
225g/8oz/1½ cups raisins
225g/8oz onions, chopped
225g/8oz/generous 1 cup caster (superfine) sugar
600ml/1 pint/2½ cups malt vinegar

VARIATION

Dried dates may be used in place of the raisins, and red wine or sherry vinegar may be used in place of the malt vinegar. Stone (pit) and chop the dates, or buy stoned cooking dates that have been compressed in a block and chop them finely.

1 Chop the tomatoes roughly and place in a preserving pan. Add the raisins, onions and caster sugar.

2 Pour the vinegar into the pan and bring the mixture to the boil. Simmer for 2 hours, uncovered, until soft and thickened.

3 Transfer the chutney to warmed sterilized jars. Top with waxed discs and lids. Store in a cool, dark place and leave to mature for 1 month. The chutney will keep unopened for up to 1 year. Once the jars have been opened, store them in the refrigerator.

Energy 1733kcal/7385kJ; Protein 14.9g; Carbohydrate 436.7g, of which sugars 431.6g; Fat 4.1g, of which saturates 0.9g; Cholesterol 0mg; Calcium 342mg; Fibre 16.6g; Sodium 236mg.

mediterranean chutney

Reminiscent of the warm Mediterranean climate, this mixed vegetable chutney is colourful, mild and warm in flavour and goes particularly well with grilled meats and sausages. For a hotter, spicier flavour, add a little cayenne pepper with the paprika.

Makes about 1.8kg/4lb

INGREDIENTS

450g/1lb Spanish (Bermuda) onions, chopped

900g/2lb ripe tomatoes, skinned and chopped

1 aubergine (eggplant), weighing about 350g/12oz, trimmed and cut into 1cm/½in cubes

450g/1lb courgettes (zucchini), sliced

1 yellow (bell) pepper, quartered, seeded and sliced

1 red (bell) pepper, quartered, seeded and sliced

3 garlic cloves, crushed

1 small sprig of rosemary

1 small sprig of thyme

2 bay leaves

15ml/1 tbsp salt

15ml/1 tbsp paprika

300ml/½ pint/1¼ cups malt vinegar

400g/14oz/2 cups granulated sugar

1 Put the chopped onions, tomatoes, aubergine, courgettes, peppers and garlic in a preserving pan. Cover the pan with a lid and cook gently over a very low heat, stirring occasionally, for about 15 minutes, or until the juices start to run.

2 Tie the rosemary, thyme and bay leaves in a piece of muslin (cheesecloth). Add to the pan with the salt, paprika and half the malt vinegar. Simmer, uncovered, for 25 minutes, or until the vegetables are tender and the juices reduced.

3 Add the remaining vinegar and sugar to the pan and stir over a low heat until the sugar has dissolved. Simmer for 30 minutes, stirring the chutney frequently towards the end of cooking time.

4 When the chutney is reduced to a thick consistency and no excess liquid remains, discard the herbs, then spoon the chutney into warmed sterilized jars. Set aside until cool, then cover and seal with vinegar-proof lids.

5 Store the chutney in a cool, dark place and allow to mature for at least 2 months before eating. Use the chutney within 2 years. Once opened, store in the refrigerator and use within 2 months.

Energy 2114kcal/8986kJ; Protein 27.1g; Carbohydrate 516.4g, of which sugars 504.1g; Fat 7.6g, of which saturates 1.9g; Cholesterol 0mg; Calcium 550mg; Fibre 29g; Sodium 6036mg.

confit of slow-cooked onions

This jam of slow-cooked, caramelized onions in sweet-sour balsamic vinegar will keep for several days in a sealed jar in the refrigerator. You can make it with red, white or yellow onions, but yellow onions will produce the sweetest result.

Makes about 500g/1¼lb

INGREDIENTS

30ml/2 tbsp olive oil

15g/½oz/1 tbsp butter

500g/1¼lb onions, sliced

3–5 fresh thyme sprigs

1 fresh bay leaf

30ml/2 tbsp light muscovado (brown) sugar, plus a little extra

50g/2oz/¼ cup ready-to-eat prunes, chopped

30ml/2 tbsp balsamic vinegar, plus a little extra

120ml/4fl oz/½ cup red wine

salt and ground black pepper

3 Add the prunes, vinegar, wine and 60ml/4 tbsp water to the pan and cook over a low heat, stirring frequently, for 20 minutes, or until most of the liquid has evaporated. Add a little more water and reduce the heat if it looks dry. Remove from the heat.

4 Adjust the seasoning if necessary, adding more sugar and/or vinegar to taste. Leave the confit to cool then stir in the remaining 5ml/ 1 tsp olive oil and serve.

VARIATION

Gently brown 500g/1¼lb peeled pickling (pearl) onions in 60ml/4 tbsp olive oil. Sprinkle in 45ml/3 tbsp brown sugar and caramelize a little, then add 7.5ml/1½ tsp crushed coriander seeds, 250ml/8fl oz/1 cup red wine, 2 bay leaves, a few thyme sprigs, 3 strips orange rind, 45ml/3 tbsp tomato purée (paste) and the juice of 1 orange. Cook gently, covered, for 1 hour, stirring occasionally. Uncover for the last 20 minutes. Sharpen with 15–30ml/ 1–2 tbsp sherry vinegar.

1 Reserve 5ml/1 tsp of the oil, then heat the remaining oil with the butter in a large pan. Add the onions, cover and cook gently over a low heat for about 15 minutes, stirring occasionally.

2 Season the onions with salt and ground black pepper, then add the thyme, bay leaf and sugar. Cook slowly, uncovered, for a further 15–20 minutes until the onions are very soft and dark. Stir the onions occasionally during cooking to prevent them sticking or burning.

Energy 678kcal/2827kJ; Protein 7.5g; Carbohydrate 87.9g, of which sugars 76.4g; Fat 35.5g, of which saturates 11g; Cholesterol 32mg; Calcium 161mg; Fibre 9.8g; Sodium 113mg.

kashmir chutney

In the true tradition of the Kashmiri country store, this is a typical family recipe passed down from generation to generation. It is wonderful served with plain or spicy grilled sausages.

Makes about 2.75kg/6lb

INGREDIENTS

1kg/2¼lb green eating apples
15g/½oz garlic cloves
1 litre/1¾ pints/4 cups malt vinegar
450g/1lb dates
115g/4oz preserved stem ginger
450g/1lb/3 cups raisins
450g/1lb/2 cups soft light brown sugar
2.5ml/½ tsp cayenne pepper
30ml/2 tbsp salt

COOK'S TIP

This sweet, chunky, spicy chutney is perfect served with cold meats for an informal buffet lunch.

1 Quarter the apples, remove the cores and chop coarsely. Peel and chop the garlic.

2 Place the apple and garlic in a pan with enough vinegar to cover. Bring to the boil and boil for 10 minutes.

3 Chop the dates and ginger and add them to the pan, together with the rest of the ingredients. Cook gently for 45 minutes.

4 Spoon the mixture into warmed sterilized jars and seal immediately.

Energy 3920kcal/16737kJ; Protein 22.6g; Carbohydrate 1014.4g, of which sugars 1012.2g; Fat 3.3g, of which saturates 0g; Cholesterol 0mg; Calcium 599mg; Fibre 33.7g; Sodium 12139mg.

fiery bengal chutney

Not for timid tastebuds, this fiery chutney is the perfect choice for lovers of hot and spicy food. Although it can be eaten a month after making, it is better matured for longer.

Makes about 2kg/4½lb

INGREDIENTS

115g/4oz fresh root ginger

1kg/2¼lb cooking apples

675g/1½lb onions

6 garlic cloves, finely chopped

225g/8oz/1½ cups raisins

450ml/¾ pint/scant 2 cups malt vinegar

400g/14oz/1¾ cups demerara
  (raw) sugar

2 fresh red chillies

2 fresh green chillies

15ml/1 tbsp salt

5ml/1 tsp turmeric

1 Peel and finely shred the fresh root ginger. Peel, core and roughly chop the apples. Peel and quarter the onions, then slice as thinly as possible. Place in a preserving pan with the garlic, raisins and vinegar.

2 Bring to the boil, then simmer steadily for 15–20 minutes, stirring occasionally, until the apples and onions are thoroughly softened. Add the sugar and stir over a low heat until the sugar has dissolved. Simmer the mixture for about 40 minutes, or until thick and pulpy, stirring frequently towards the end of the cooking time.

3 Halve the chillies and remove the seeds, then slice them finely. (Always wash your hands with soapy water immediately after handling chillies.)

4 Add the chillies to the pan and cook for a further 5–10 minutes, or until no excess liquid remains. Stir in the salt and turmeric.

5 Spoon the chutney into warmed sterilized jars, cover and seal them immediately, then label when cool.

6 Store the chutney in a cool, dark place and leave to mature for at least 2 months before eating. Use within 2 years of making. Once opened, store in the refrigerator and use within 1 month.

Energy 2789kcal/11889kJ; Protein 18.4g; Carbohydrate 717.3g, of which sugars 701.8g; Fat 3.5g, of which saturates 0g; Cholesterol 0mg; Calcium 573mg; Fibre 31.2g; Sodium 6163mg.

butternut, apricot and almond chutney

Coriander seeds and turmeric add a slightly spicy touch to this rich golden chutney. It is delicious in little canapés or with cubes of mozzarella cheese; it is also good in sandwiches.

Makes about 1.8kg/4lb

INGREDIENTS

1 small butternut squash, weighing about 800g/1¾lb

400g/14oz/2 cups golden granulated sugar

600ml/1 pint/2½ cups cider vinegar

2 onions, chopped

225g/8oz/1 cup ready-to-eat dried apricots, quartered

finely grated rind and juice of 1 orange

2.5ml/½ tsp turmeric

15ml/1 tbsp coriander seeds

15ml/1 tbsp salt

115g/4oz/1 cup flaked (sliced) almonds

1 Halve the butternut squash lengthways and scoop out the seeds. Peel off the skin, then cut the flesh into 2cm/¾in cubes.

2 Put the sugar and vinegar in a preserving pan and heat gently, stirring occasionally, until the sugar has dissolved.

3 Add the squash, onions, apricots, orange rind and juice, turmeric, coriander seeds and salt to the preserving pan. Bring the mixture slowly to the boil.

4 Reduce the heat and simmer gently for 45–50 minutes, stirring frequently towards the end of the cooking time, until the chutney is reduced to a thick consistency and no excess liquid remains. Stir in the flaked almonds.

5 Spoon the chutney into warmed sterilized jars, cover and seal. Store in a cool, dark place and allow to mature for at least 1 month before eating. Use within 2 years. Once opened, store in the refrigerator and use within 2 months.

VARIATION

If butternut squash is unavailable, use a wedge of pumpkin weighing about 500g/1¼lb instead.

Energy 2847kcal/12045kJ; Protein 44.5g; Carbohydrate 549.4g, of which sugars 535.4g; Fat 67.7g, of which saturates 5.9g; Cholesterol 0mg; Calcium 959mg; Fibre 34.9g; Sodium 81mg.

sweet and hot dried fruit chutney

*This rich, thick and slightly sticky preserve of spiced dried fruit is a wonderful way to
enliven cold roast turkey left over from Christmas or Thanksgiving dinners.*

Makes about 1.5kg/3lb 6oz

INGREDIENTS

350g/12oz/1½ cups ready-to-eat
  dried apricots

225g/8oz/1¼ cups dried dates,
  stoned (pitted)

225g/8oz/1¼ cups dried figs

50g/2oz/⅓ cup glacé (candied)
  citrus peel

150g/5oz/1 cup raisins

50g/2oz/½ cup dried cranberries

120ml/4fl oz/½ cup cranberry juice

400ml/14fl oz/1¾ cups cider vinegar

225g/8oz/1 cup demerara (raw) sugar

finely grated rind and juice of 1 lemon

5ml/1 tsp mixed spice (apple pie spice)

5ml/1 tsp ground coriander

5ml/1 tsp cayenne pepper

5ml/1 tsp salt

1 Roughly chop the dried apricots,
dates, figs and citrus peel, then put
all the dried fruit in a preserving
pan. Pour over the cranberry juice,
stir, then cover and leave to soak
for 2 hours, or until the fruit has
absorbed most of the juice.

2 Add the cider vinegar and sugar
to the pan. Stir over a low heat
until the sugar has dissolved.

3 Bring the mixture to the boil,
then reduce the heat and simmer for
about 30 minutes, or until the fruit
is soft and the chutney fairly thick.
Stir occasionally during cooking.

4 Stir in the lemon rind and juice,
mixed spice, coriander, cayenne
pepper and salt. Simmer for a
further 15 minutes, stirring
frequently towards the end of the
cooking, until the chutney is thick
and no excess liquid remains.

VARIATIONS

If you prefer, substitute dried sour
cherries for the dried cranberries.
Apple juice can be used instead
of the cranberry juice.

5 Spoon the chutney into warmed
sterilized jars, cover and seal. Store
in a cool, dark place and allow to
mature for at least 1 month before
eating. Use within 1 year. Once
opened, store in the refrigerator
and use within 2 months.

Energy 2998kcal/12789kJ; Protein 31.9g; Carbohydrate 746.7g, of which sugars 729.4g; Fat 7.2g, of which saturates 0g; Cholesterol 0mg; Calcium 1157mg; Fibre 51.4g; Sodium 458mg.

pickled peach and chilli chutney

This is a spicy, rich chutney with a succulent texture. It is great served traditional-style, with cold roast meats such as ham, pork or turkey; it is also good with pan-fried chicken served in warm wraps. Try it with ricotta cheese as a filling for pitta bread.

Makes about 450g/1lb

INGREDIENTS

475ml/16fl oz/2 cups cider vinegar

275g/10oz/1¼ cups light muscovado (brown) sugar

225g/8oz/1⅓ cups dried dates, stoned (pitted) and finely chopped

5ml/1 tsp ground allspice

5ml/1 tsp ground mace

450g/1lb ripe peaches, stoned and cut into small chunks

3 onions, thinly sliced

4 fresh red chillies, seeded and finely chopped

4 garlic cloves, crushed

5cm/2in piece fresh root ginger, peeled and finely grated

5ml/1 tsp salt

1 Place the vinegar, sugar, dates, allspice and mace in a large pan and heat gently, stirring, until the sugar has dissolved. Bring to the boil, stirring occasionally.

2 Add the peaches, sliced onions, chopped chillies, crushed garlic, grated ginger and salt, and bring the mixture back to the boil, stirring occasionally.

3 Reduce the heat and simmer for 40–50 minutes, or until the chutney has thickened. Stir frequently to prevent the mixture sticking to the bottom of the pan.

4 Spoon the hot cooked chutney into warmed sterilized jars and seal immediately. When cold, store the jars in a cool, dark place and leave the chutney to mature for at least 2 weeks before eating. Use within 6 months.

COOK'S TIP

To test the consistency of the chutney before bottling, spoon a little of the mixture on to a plate; the chutney should hold its shape.

Energy 2039kcal/8684kJ; Protein 20.9g; Carbohydrate 517.3g, of which sugars 502.9g; Fat 2g, of which saturates 0.2g; Cholesterol 0mg; Calcium 407mg; Fibre 23.6g; Sodium 59mg.

hot yellow plum chutney

It is well worth seeking out yellow plums to make this hot, fragrant chutney. They give it a slightly tart flavour and make it the perfect accompaniment to deep-fried Asian-style snacks such as spring rolls and wontons, or battered vegetables and shellfish.

Makes 1.3kg/3lb

INGREDIENTS

900g/2lb yellow plums, halved and stoned (pitted)

1 onion, finely chopped

7.5cm/3in piece fresh root ginger, peeled and grated

3 whole star anise

350ml/12fl oz/1½ cups white wine vinegar

225g/8oz/1 cup soft light brown sugar

5 celery sticks, thinly sliced

3 green chillies, seeded and finely sliced

2 garlic cloves, crushed

1 Put the halved plums, onion, ginger and star anise in a large pan and pour over half the white wine vinegar. Bring to the boil and simmer gently over a low heat for about 30 minutes, or until the plums have softened.

2 Stir the remaining vinegar, sugar, sliced celery, chillies and crushed garlic into the plum mixture. Cook very gently over a low heat, stirring frequently, until the sugar has completely dissolved.

3 Bring the mixture to the boil, then simmer for 45–50 minutes, until there is no excess liquid. Stir frequently during the final stages to prevent the chutney sticking.

4 Spoon the plum chutney into warmed sterilized jars, then cover and seal immediately.

5 Store the chutney in a cool, dark place and allow to mature for at least 1 month before using. Use within 2 years.

COOK'S TIPS

• Once opened, store the chutney in the refrigerator and use within 3 months.

• Be sure to use jars with non-metallic lids to store the chutney.

Energy 1243kcal/5312kJ; Protein 8g; Carbohydrate 320.4g, of which sugars 319g; Fat 1.3g, of which saturates 0g; Cholesterol 0mg; Calcium 313mg; Fibre 16.9g; Sodium 123mg.

mango chutney

No Indian meal would be complete without this classic chutney. Its gloriously sweet, tangy flavour complements the warm taste of Indian spices perfectly, but it is equally good scooped up on crispy fried poppadums. Mango chutney is also great served with chargrilled chicken, turkey or duck breasts; with potato wedges and sour cream; or spread on cheese on toast.

Makes about 1kg/2¼lb

INGREDIENTS

900g/2lb mangoes, halved; peeled and stoned

2.5ml/½ tsp salt

225g/8oz cooking apples, peeled

300ml/½ pint/1¼ cups distilled malt vinegar

200g/7oz/scant 1 cup demerara (raw) sugar

1 onion, chopped

1 garlic clove, crushed

10ml/2 tsp ground ginger

COOK'S TIPS

• Once opened, store the chutney in the refrigerator and use within 3 months.

• When serving mango chutney with crispy poppadums, also offer a selection of other condiments such as salty lime pickle, finely chopped fresh onion salad and minty yogurt.

1 Using a sharp knife, slice the mango flesh into chunks and place in a large, non-metallic bowl. Sprinkle with salt and set aside while you prepare the apples.

2 Using a sharp knife, cut the apples into quarters, then remove and discard the cores and peel. Chop the flesh roughly.

3 Put the malt vinegar and sugar in a preserving pan and heat very gently, stirring occasionally, until the sugar has dissolved completely.

4 Add the mangoes, apple, onion, garlic and ginger to the pan and slowly bring the mixture to the boil, stirring occasionally.

5 Reduce the heat and simmer gently for about 1 hour, stirring frequently towards the end of the cooking time, until the chutney is reduced to a thick consistency and no excess liquid remains.

6 Spoon the chutney into warmed sterilized jars, cover and seal. Store in a cool, dark place and allow to mature for at least 2 weeks before eating. Use within 1 year of making.

VARIATION

To make a chutney with a fiery, spicy kick to serve with cheeses and cold meats, seed and finely slice two green chillies and stir into the chutney with the garlic and ginger.

Energy 1401kcal/5997kJ; Protein 8.7g; Carbohydrate 360.7g, of which sugars 356.6g; Fat 2.1g, of which saturates 0.9g; Cholesterol 0mg; Calcium 238mg; Fibre 27.8g; Sodium 1019mg.

chunky pear and walnut chutney

This chutney recipe is ideal for using up hard windfall pears. Its mellow flavour is excellent with cheese and also good with grains such as in pilaff or with tabbouleh.

Makes about 1.8kg/4lb

INGREDIENTS

1.2kg/2½lb firm pears

225g/8oz tart cooking apples

225g/8oz onions

450ml/¾ pint/scant 2 cups cider vinegar

175g/6oz/generous 1 cup sultanas (golden raisins)

finely grated rind and juice of 1 orange

400g/14oz/2 cups granulated (white) sugar

115g/4oz/1 cup walnuts, roughly chopped

2.5ml/½ tsp ground cinnamon

1 Peel and core the fruit, then chop into 2.5cm/1in chunks. Peel and quarter the onions, then chop into pieces the same size. Place in a preserving pan with the vinegar.

2 Slowly bring to the boil, then reduce the heat and simmer for 40 minutes, until the apples, pears and onions are tender, stirring the mixture occasionally.

3 Meanwhile, put the sultanas in a small bowl, pour over the orange juice and leave to soak.

4 Add the sugar, sultanas, and orange rind and juice to the pan. Gently heat until the sugar has dissolved, then simmer for 30–40 minutes, or until the chutney is thick and no excess liquid remains. Stir frequently towards the end of cooking to prevent the chutney sticking on the bottom of the pan.

5 Gently toast the walnuts in a non-stick pan over a low heat for 5 minutes, stirring frequently, until lightly coloured. Stir the nuts into the chutney with the cinnamon.

6 Spoon the chutney into warmed sterilized jars, cover and seal. Store in a cool, dark place and leave to mature for at least 1 month. Use within 1 year.

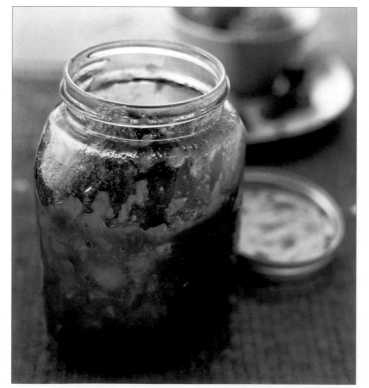

Energy 3501kcal/14797kJ; Protein 29.8g; Carbohydrate 705.3g, of which sugars 699.3g; Fat 81.4g, of which saturates 6.4g; Cholesterol 0mg; Calcium 603mg; Fibre 40.7g; Sodium 189mg.

green grape chutney

A hint of lime heightens the fragrant grape flavour and complements the sweetness of this chutney. It is delicious warmed with a knob of butter and served with roast pork.

Makes 1.2kg/2½lb

INGREDIENTS

900g/2lb/6 cups seedless green grapes

900g/2lb tart cooking apples

450g/1lb/2¼ cups granulated (white) sugar

450ml/¾ pint/scant 2 cups white wine vinegar

finely grated rind and juice of 1 lime

1.5ml/¼ tsp salt

COOK'S TIP

Once opened, store the chutney in the refrigerator and use within 1 month.

1 Halve the grapes if large, then peel, core and finely chop the apples. Put the fruit in a preserving pan with the sugar and vinegar and slowly bring to the boil.

2 Reduce the heat and simmer the chutney for about 45 minutes, or until the fruit is tender and the chutney fairly thick.

3 Stir the lime rind and juice and salt into the chutney and simmer for 15 minutes until the chutney is thick and no excess liquid remains.

4 Spoon the chutney into warmed sterilized jars, cover and seal. Store in a cool, dark place and leave to mature for at least 1 month before eating. Use within 18 months.

Energy 2628kcal/11237kJ; Protein 8.6g; Carbohydrate 689g, of which sugars 689g; Fat 1.8g, of which saturates 0g; Cholesterol 0mg; Calcium 392mg; Fibre 20.7g; Sodium 63mg.

christmas chutney

This savoury mixture of spices and dried fruit takes its inspiration from mincemeat, and makes a delicious traditional addition to a Chirstmas buffet. Serve with cold meats.

Makes about 1–1.6kg/2¼–3½ lb

INGREDIENTS

450g/1lb cooking apples, peeled, cored and chopped

500g/1¼ lb/3⅓ cups luxury mixed dried fruit

grated rind of 1 orange

30ml/2 tbsp mixed spice

150ml/¼ pint/⅔ cup cider vinegar

350g/12oz/1½ cups light muscovado (brown)sugar

COOK'S TIP

If possible, prepare this seasonal speciality several months before the festive period to allow it to fully mature.

1 Place the chopped apples, dried fruit and grated orange rind in a large, heavy pan. Stir in the mixed spice, cider vinegar and sugar. Heat the ingredients gently, stirring until all the sugar has dissolved.

2 Bring to the boil, then lower the heat and simmer the mixture for 40–45 minutes, stirring occasionally, until thick.

3 Ladle into warm, sterilized jars, cover and seal. Keep for 1 month before using.

COOK'S TIPS

• Watch the chutney carefully towards the end of the cooking time, as it has a tendency to catch on the bottom of the pan. Stir frequently at this stage.

• Once a jar is opened, store it in the refrigerator until finished.

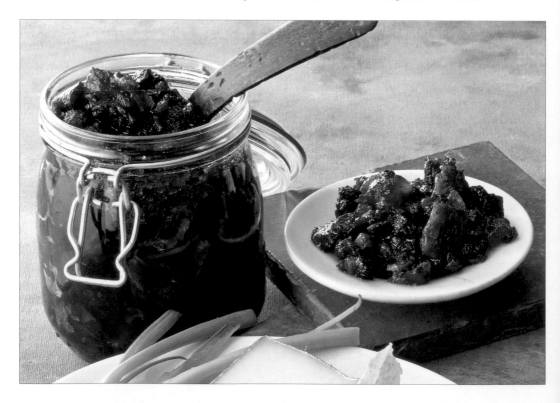

Energy 2877kcal/12283kJ; Protein 14.6g; Carbohydrate 746.3g, of which sugars 746.3g; Fat 2.5g, of which saturates 0g; Cholesterol 0mg; Calcium 569mg; Fibre 18.2g; Sodium 270mg.

apple and tomato chutney

This mellow spicy chutney transforms an ordinary lunch of cheese or cooked meat into a real treat. It's brilliant in sandwiches. Any type of tomatoes can be used successfully in this recipe.

Makes 1.8kg/4lb

INGREDIENTS

1.3kg/3lb cooking apples
1.3kg/3lb tomatoes
2 large onions
2 garlic cloves
250g/9oz pitted dates
2 red (bell) peppers
3 dried chillies
15ml/1 tbsp black peppercorns
4 cardamom pods
15ml/1 tbsp coriander seeds
10ml/2 tsp cumin seeds
10ml/2 tsp ground turmeric
15ml/1tbsp salt
1kg/2¼lb/4½ cups sugar
600ml/1 pint/2½ cups distilled malt
  vinegar

1 Peel and chop the apples. Peel and chop the tomatoes, onions and garlic. Quarter the dates. Core and seed the peppers, then cut into chunky pieces. Put all the prepared ingredients, except the red peppers, into a preserving pan.

2 Slit the chillies. Put the pepper-corns and remaining spices into a mortar and roughly crush with a pestle. Add the chillies, spices and salt to the pan.

3 Add the sugar and vinegar and simmer for 30 minutes, stirring often. Add the red pepper. Cook for 30 minutes, stirring until thickened.

4 Spoon into a warm, dry sterilized jars. Immediately top with a circle of waxed paper and cover tightly. Leave to cool.

Energy 5583kcal/23819kJ; Protein 35.8g; Carbohydrate 1432.9g, of which sugars 1420.3g; Fat 8.1g, of which saturates 1.9g; Cholesterol 0mg; Calcium 940mg; Fibre 56.4g; Sodium 6152mg.

beetroot and orange preserve

With its vibrant red colour and rich earthy flavour, this distinctive chutney is good with salads as well as full-flavoured cheeses, such as mature Cheddar, Stilton or Gorgonzola. You might also like to try it with cream cheese in baked potatoes.

Makes about 1.4kg/3lb

INGREDIENTS

350g/12oz raw beetroot (beets)

350g/12oz eating apples

300ml/½ pint/1¼ cups malt vinegar

200g/7oz/1 cup sugar

225g/8oz red (Italian) onions, finely chopped

1 garlic clove, crushed

finely grated rind and juice of 2 oranges

5ml/1 tsp ground allspice

5ml/1 tsp salt

1 Scrub and thinly peel the beetroot, then cut into 1cm/½in pieces. Peel, quarter and core the apples and cut into 1cm/½in pieces.

2 Put the vinegar and sugar in a preserving pan and heat gently, stirring occasionally, until the sugar has dissolved.

3 Add the beetroot, apples, onions, garlic, orange rind and juice, ground allspice and salt to the pan. Bring to the boil, reduce the heat, then simmer for 40 minutes.

4 Increase the heat slightly and boil for 10 minutes, or until the chutney is thick and no excess liquid remains. Stir frequently to prevent the chutney catching on the base of the pan.

5 Spoon the chutney into warmed sterilized jars, cover and seal. Store in a cool, dark place and allow to mature for at least 2 weeks before eating. Use within 6 months of making. Refrigerate once opened and use within 1 month.

COOK'S TIP

For speedy preparation and a fine-textured chutney, put the peeled beetroot through the coarse grating blade of a food processor.

Energy 1055kcal/4506kJ; Protein 8.3g; Carbohydrate 271.2g, of which sugars 269.1g; Fat 0.8g, of which saturates 0g; Cholesterol 0mg; Calcium 195mg; Fibre 12.3g; Sodium 255mg.

rhubarb and tangerine chutney

*The rhubarb in this soft-textured chutney is added part way through the cooking, so that
it retains its attractive colour and shape. It works especially well when partnered with
Chinese-style roast duck, or with cold meats such as ham or gammon.*

Makes about 1.3kg/3lb

INGREDIENTS

1 large onion, finely chopped

300ml/½ pint/1¼ cups distilled
 malt vinegar

4 whole cloves

7.5cm/3in cinnamon stick

1 tangerine

400g/14oz/2 cups sugar

150g/5oz/1 cup sultanas (golden raisins)

1kg/2¼lb rhubarb, cut into
 2.5cm/1in lengths

1 Put the onion in a preserving
pan with the vinegar, whole cloves
and cinnamon stick. Bring to the
boil, then reduce the heat and
simmer for 10 minutes, or until
the onions are just tender.

2 Meanwhile, thinly pare the rind
from the tangerine. (It is often
easier to peel the fruit first, then
slice the white pith from the rind.)
Finely shred the rind.

3 Add the tangerine rind, sugar
and sultanas to the pan. Stir until
all the sugar has dissolved, then
simmer for 10 minutes, or until the
syrup is thick.

4 Add the rhubarb to the pan.
Cook gently for about 15 minutes,
stirring carefully from time to
time, until the rhubarb is soft but
still retains its shape, and just a
little spare liquid remains.

5 Remove the pan from the heat
and leave to cool for 10 minutes,
then stir gently to distribute the
fruit. Spoon the chutney into
warmed sterilized jars, cover and
seal. Store in a cool, dark place
and allow to mature for at least
1 month. Use within 1 year. Once
opened, store in the refrigerator
and use within 2 months.

COOK'S TIP

The finely shredded rind of half an
orange may be used in place of the
shredded tangerine rind.

Energy 2215kcal/9455kJ; Protein 20.2g; Carbohydrate 564.6g, of which sugars 555.4g; Fat 2.4g, of which saturates 0g; Cholesterol 0mg; Calcium 1354mg; Fibre 23.1g; Sodium 95mg.

tart tomato relish

Adding lime to this relish gives it a wonderfully tart, tangy flavour and a pleasantly sour after-taste. It is particularly good served with grilled or roast meats, such as pork or lamb.

Makes about 500g/1¼lb

INGREDIENTS

2 pieces preserved stem ginger

1 lime

450g/1lb cherry tomatoes

115g/4oz/½ cup muscovado
(molasses) sugar

120ml/4fl oz/½ cup white wine vinegar

5ml/1 tsp salt

VARIATION

Use chopped tomatoes in place of
the cherry tomatoes, if you prefer.

1 Coarsely chop the preserved
stem ginger. Slice the lime thinly,
including the rind, then chop the
slices into small pieces.

2 Place the cherry tomatoes, sugar,
vinegar, salt, ginger and lime in a
large heavy pan.

3 Bring the mixture to the boil,
stirring until the sugar dissolves,
then simmer rapidly for about
45 minutes. Stir frequently until
the liquid has evaporated and the
relish is thick and pulpy.

4 Leave the relish to cool for
about 5 minutes, then spoon into
sterilized jars. Leave to cool, then
cover and store in the refrigerator
for up to 1 month.

COOK'S TIP

There is always discussion between
preserving enthusiasts as to the best
choice of covering for chutneys and
pickles. While cellophane covers are
vinegarproof, they are difficult to secure
for a good airtight seal, and not very
good once opened. Screw-top lids
with a plastic coating inside are best:
put them on as soon as the piping
hot preserve is potted and they will
provide a hygienic, air-tight seal. New
lids can be purchased for standard-
size glass jars.

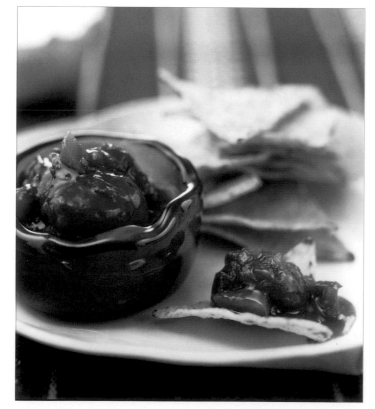

Energy 530kcal/2262kJ; Protein 3.7g; Carbohydrate 134.1g, of which sugars 134.1g; Fat 1.4g, of which saturates 0.5g; Cholesterol 0mg; Calcium 93mg; Fibre 4.5g; Sodium 2012mg.

red hot relish

Make this relish during the summer months when tomatoes and peppers are plentiful.
It enhances simple, plain dishes such as a cheese or mushroom omelette.

Makes about 1.3kg/3lb

INGREDIENTS

800g/1¾lb ripe tomatoes, peeled
  and quartered

450g/1lb red (Italian) onions, chopped

3 red (bell) peppers, seeded
  and chopped

3 fresh red chillies, seeded
  and finely sliced

200g/7oz/1 cup sugar

200ml/7fl oz/scant 1 cup red
  wine vinegar

30ml/2 tbsp mustard seeds

10ml/2 tsp celery seeds

15ml/1 tbsp paprika

5ml/1 tsp salt

1 Put the chopped tomatoes, onions, peppers and chillies in a preserving pan, cover with a lid and cook over a very low heat for about 10 minutes, stirring once or twice, until the tomato juices start to run.

2 Add the sugar and vinegar to the tomato mixture and slowly bring to the boil, stirring occasionally until the sugar has dissolved completely. Add the mustard seeds, celery seeds, paprika and salt, and stir well to combine.

3 Increase the heat under the pan slightly and cook the relish, uncovered, for about 30 minutes, or until most of the liquid has evaporated and the mixture has a thick, but moist consistency. Stir frequently towards the end of cooking time to prevent the mixture sticking to the pan.

4 Spoon the relish into warmed sterilized jars, cover and seal. Store in a cool, dark place and leave to mature for at least 2 weeks before eating. Use the relish within 1 year of making.

COOK'S TIP
Once opened, store the relish in the refrigerator and use within 2 months.

Energy 1270kcal/5392kJ; Protein 17.8g; Carbohydrate 306.2g, of which sugars 294.1g; Fat 5.6g, of which saturates 1.4g; Cholesterol 0mg; Calcium 321mg; Fibre 23.5g; Sodium 121mg.

bloody mary relish

This fresh-tasting relish with contrasting textures of tomatoes, celery and cucumber is perfect for al fresco *summer eating. For a special occasion, serve it with freshly shucked oysters.*

Makes about 1.3kg/3lb

INGREDIENTS

1.3kg/3lb ripe well-flavoured tomatoes
1 large cucumber
30–45ml/2–3 tbsp salt
2 celery sticks, chopped
2 garlic cloves, peeled and crushed
175ml/6fl oz/¾ cup white wine vinegar
15ml/1 tbsp sugar
60ml/4 tbsp vodka
5ml/1 tsp Tabasco sauce
10ml/2 tsp Worcestershire sauce

COOK'S TIP

To peel the tomatoes, plunge them in a bowl of just-boiled water for 30 seconds. The skins will split and will be easy to peel off.

1 Peel and chop the tomatoes. Peel the cucumber and slice the flesh from around the seeds. Discard the seeds and chop the flesh. Layer the vegetables in a colander placed over a bowl, lightly sprinkling each layer with salt. Cover, put in the refrigerator and leave to drain overnight.

2 The next day, rinse the tomatoes and cucumber thoroughly under cold running water to remove as much salt as possible. Drain well, then place in a pan. (Discard the salty vegetable juices in the bowl.)

3 Add the celery, garlic, vinegar and sugar to the pan and slowly bring to the boil over a low heat.

4 Cook the vegetables, uncovered, for about 30 minutes, stirring occasionally, until the vegetables have softened and most of the liquid has evaporated.

5 Remove the pan from the heat and leave to cool for about 5 minutes. Add the vodka, and Tabasco and Worcestershire sauces and stir well to combine.

6 Spoon the hot relish into warmed sterilized jars, cool, cover and seal. Store in the refrigerator for at least 1 week.

COOK'S TIP

Use the relish within 3 months. Once opened, store it in the refrigerator and use within 1 month.

Energy 430kcal/1814kJ; Protein 13.1g; Carbohydrate 65.6g, of which sugars 65g; Fat 4.5g, of which saturates 1.3g; Cholesterol 0mg; Calcium 233mg; Fibre 16.7g; Sodium 289mg.

yellow pepper and coriander relish

Fresh relishes are quick and easy to make although they do not have a long shelf life. Try this relish with mild, creamy cheeses or with grilled tuna or other firm fish, poultry or meat.

Serves four

INGREDIENTS

1 large yellow (bell) pepper
45ml/3 tbsp sesame oil
1 large mild fresh red chilli
small handful of fresh coriander (cilantro)
salt

1 Seed and coarsely chop the yellow pepper. Heat the oil in a pan, add the pepper and cook, stirring frequently, for 8–10 minutes, until lightly coloured.

2 Meanwhile, seed the chilli, slice it very thinly and set aside. Transfer the pepper to a food processor and process until chopped, but not puréed. Transfer half the pepper to a bowl, leaving the rest in the food processor.

3 Using a sharp knife, chop the fresh coriander, then add it to the mixture in the food processor and process briefly to combine. Tip the mixture into the bowl with the rest of the pepper, add the sliced chilli and stir well to combine.

4 Season the relish with salt to taste and stir well to combine. Cover the bowl with clear film (plastic wrap) and chill in the refrigerator until ready to serve.

COOK'S TIPS

• Red and orange sweet peppers work just as well as yellow, though green peppers are unsuitable as they are not sweet enough in flavour.

• This relish does not keep well, so use within 3 or 4 days of making.

• If you find the flavour of chilli too hot, use only half a chilli and chop into tiny pieces.

Energy 91kcal/374kJ; Protein 0.8g; Carbohydrate 2.9g, of which sugars 2.8g; Fat 8.5g, of which saturates 1.3g; Cholesterol 0mg; Calcium 8mg; Fibre 0.7g; Sodium 3mg.

tomato and red pepper relish

This spicy relish will keep for at least a week in the refrigerator. It is particularly good with sausages and burgers, but also makes a great accompaniment for a full-flavoured hard cheese.

Serves eight

INGREDIENTS

6 tomatoes

1 onion

1 red (bell) pepper, seeded

2 garlic cloves

30ml/2 tbsp extra virgin olive oil or sunflower oil

5ml/1 tsp ground cinnamon

about 5ml/1 tsp chilli flakes

5ml/1 tsp ground ginger

5ml/1 tsp salt

2.5ml/½ tsp ground black pepper

75g/3oz/⅓ cup light brown sugar, or other dark sugar

75ml/5 tbsp cider vinegar

handful of fresh basil leaves

1 Put the tomatoes in a heatproof bowl. Boil some water in a kettle or pan and then pour it over the tomatoes. Leave for 30 seconds. Remove the tomatoes with a slotted spoon and cool in cold water. Drain well.

2 Using a small, sharp knife, scrape and peel off the skins from each tomato in turn. They should slip off fairly easily, but you may need to slice off the skin if it sticks. Chop the tomatoes.

3 Chop the onion, pepper and garlic. Gently heat the oil in a pan. Add the onion, pepper and garlic to the pan.

4 Cook gently for 5–8 minutes, until the pepper has softened, but still retains its shape. Add the chopped tomatoes. Cover and cook for 5 minutes, stirring often, until the tomatoes release their juices.

5 Stir in the cinnamon, chilli flakes, ginger, salt, pepper, sugar and vinegar. Cook the relish gently over a low heat, stirring constantly until all the sugar has dissolved and the mixture does not feel gritty. Then bring the relish to the boil, stirring occasionally. Reduce the heat so that the relish simmers steadily, not too rapidly.

6 Simmer the relish mixture, uncovered, for 20 minutes, until it becomes pulpy. Stir in the basil leaves and check the seasoning.

7 Allow the relish to cool completely, then transfer it to a glass jar or a plastic container with a tightly fitting lid. Cover tightly, label if necessary and store in the refrigerator.

COOK'S TIPS

• This relish thickens slightly on cooling so do not worry if the mixture seems a little thin after simmering.

• The precise amount of chilli flakes added depends upon personal taste. Chillies can be omitted entirely for a relish with a milder flavour or more flakes can be added to intensify the chilli flavour.

Energy 84kcal/355kJ; Protein 0.9g; Carbohydrate 14.1g, of which sugars 13.9g; Fat 3.1g, of which saturates 0.4g; Cholesterol 0mg; Calcium 14mg; Fibre 1.2g; Sodium 254mg.

sweet piccalilli

Undoubtedly one of the most popular relishes, piccalilli can be eaten with grilled sausages, ham or chops, cold meats or a strong, well-flavoured cheese such as Cheddar. It should contain a good selection of fresh crunchy vegetables in a smooth, mustard sauce.

Makes about 1.8kg/4lb

INGREDIENTS

1 large cauliflower

450g/1lb pickling (pearl) onions

900g/2lb mixed vegetables, such as marrow (large zucchini), cucumber, French (green) beans

225g/8oz/1 cup salt

2.4 litres/4 pints/10 cups cold water

200g/7oz/1 cup sugar

2 garlic cloves, peeled and crushed

10ml/2 tsp mustard powder

5ml/1 tsp ground ginger

1 litre/1¾ pints/4 cups distilled (white) vinegar

25g/1oz/¼ cup plain (all-purpose) flour

15ml/1 tbsp turmeric

1 Prepare the vegetables. Divide the cauliflower into small florets; peel and quarter the pickling onions; seed and finely dice the marrow and cucumber; top and tail the French beans, then cut them into 2.5cm/1in lengths.

2 Layer the vegetables in a large glass or stainless steel bowl, generously sprinkling each layer with salt. Pour over the water, cover the bowl with clear film (plastic wrap) and leave to soak for about 24 hours.

3 Drain the soaked vegetables, and discard the brine. Rinse well in several changes of cold water to remove as much salt as possible, then drain them thoroughly.

4 Put the sugar, garlic, mustard, ginger and 900ml/1½ pints/3¾ cups of the vinegar in a preserving pan. Heat gently, stirring occasionally, until the sugar has dissolved.

5 Add the vegetables to the pan, bring to the boil, reduce the heat and simmer for 10–15 minutes, or until they are almost tender.

6 Mix the flour and turmeric with the remaining vinegar and stir into the vegetables. Bring to the boil, stirring, and simmer for 5 minutes, until the piccalilli is thick.

7 Spoon the piccalilli into warmed sterilized jars, cover and seal. Store in a cool, dark place for at least 2 weeks. Use within 1 year.

Energy 1358kcal/5757kJ; Protein 34.1g; Carbohydrate 300.8g, of which sugars 266g; Fat 12g, of which saturates 1.2g; Cholesterol 0mg; Calcium 555mg; Fibre 20.6g; Sodium 4011mg.

corn relish

When golden corn cobs are in season, try preserving their kernels in this delicious relish. It has a lovely crunchy texture and a wonderfully bright, appetizing appearance.

Makes about 1kg/2¼lb

INGREDIENTS

6 large fresh corn on the cob

½ small white cabbage, weighing about 275g/10oz, very finely shredded

2 small onions, halved and very finely sliced

475ml/16fl oz/2 cups distilled malt vinegar

200g/7oz/1 cup golden granulated sugar

1 red (bell) pepper, seeded and finely chopped

5ml/1 tsp salt

15ml/1 tbsp plain (all-purpose) flour

5ml/1 tsp mustard powder

2.5ml/½ tsp turmeric

1 Put the corn cob in a pan of boiling water and cook for 2 minutes. Drain and, when cool enough to handle, use a sharp knife to slice the kernels from the cobs.

2 Put the corn kernels in a pan with the cabbage and onions. Reserve 30ml/2 tbsp of the vinegar, then add the rest to the pan with the sugar. Slowly bring to the boil, stirring occasionally until the sugar dissolves. Simmer for 15 minutes. Add the red pepper and simmer for a further 10 minutes.

3 Blend the salt, flour, mustard and turmeric with the reserved vinegar to make a smooth paste.

4 Stir the paste into the vegetable mixture and bring back to the boil. Simmer for 5 minutes, until the mixture has thickened.

5 Spoon the relish into warmed sterilized jars, cover and seal. Store in a cool dark place. Use within 6 months of making. Once opened, store in the refrigerator and use within 2 months.

COOK'S TIP

This tangy relish is the perfect barbecue preserve. It is perfect for enlivening barbecued meats such as chicken, sausages and burgers.

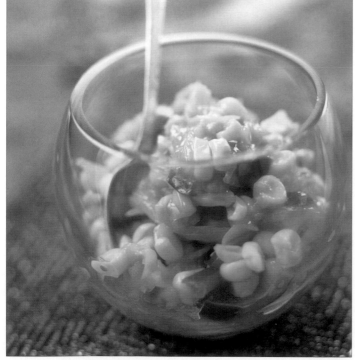

Energy 1479kcal/6291kJ; Protein 20.3g; Carbohydrate 356.7g, of which sugars 275.1g; Fat 6.4g, of which saturates 1g; Cholesterol 0mg; Calcium 307mg; Fibre 15.5g; Sodium 3086mg.

pineapple relish

This fruity sweet-and-sour relish is excellent with grilled chicken, gammon, sausages or bacon. It is not a long-keeping preserve but a clever 'fresh' relish made with canned pineapple.

Serves four

INGREDIENTS

400g/14oz can crushed pineapple in natural juice

30ml/2 tbsp light muscovado (brown) sugar

30ml/2 tbsp wine vinegar

1 garlic clove, finely chopped

4 spring onions (scallions), finely chopped

2 red chillies, seeded and chopped

10 fresh basil leaves, finely shredded

salt and ground black pepper

VARIATION

This relish can be made with fresh pineapple: remove the leafy top, peel and eyes, and cut out the core. Then chop the fruit, reserving all juices.

1 Drain the pineapple and reserve 60ml/4 tbsp of the juice.

2 Place the juice in a small pan with the sugar and vinegar. Heat gently, stirring, until the sugar dissolves. Remove from the heat and season with salt and pepper.

3 Place the pineapple, garlic, spring onions and chillies in a bowl. Mix well and stir in the juice. Allow to cool for at least 5 minutes.

4 Taste the relish for seasoning when cool. Stir in the basil just before serving.

Energy 83kcal/351kJ; Protein 1g; Carbohydrate 20.6g, of which sugars 20.6g; Fat 0.2g, of which saturates 0g; Cholesterol 0mg; Calcium 22mg; Fibre 0.7g; Sodium 4mg.

toffee onion relish

Slow, gentle cooking reduces onions to a soft, caramelized golden brown in this recipe. This sweet relish complements mature cheese, savoury tarts or quiches, and will keep for a week.

Serves four

INGREDIENTS

3 large onions

50g/2oz/¼ cup butter

30ml/2 tbsp olive oil

30ml/2 tbsp light muscovado (brown) sugar

30ml/2 tbsp pickled capers

30ml/2 tbsp chopped fresh parsley

salt and ground black pepper

COOK'S TIP

Choose a heavy pan that does not burn easily to cook the relish – this is essential for an evenly browned toffee mixture that does not begin to burn.

1 Peel the onions and cut them in half vertically, down through the core, then slice them thinly. Keep the slices as even as possible – they will cook and brown evenly, and the relish will have a good texture.

2 Heat the butter and oil together in a large, heavy-based saucepan. Add the sliced onions and sugar. Then cook very gently for about 30 minutes over a low heat, stirring occasionally, until the onions are reduced to a soft rich-brown, toffee-like mixture.

3 Roughly chop the capers and stir into the browned onion mixture. Allow to cool completely and transfer to a bowl.

4 Stir in the chopped parsley and add salt and freshly ground black pepper to taste. Cover and chill until ready to serve.

VARIATION

Make this recipe with red (Italian) onions or shallots for a subtly different flavour.

Energy 239kcal/992kJ; Protein 2.6g; Carbohydrate 22.1g, of which sugars 18g; Fat 16.3g, of which saturates 7.3g; Cholesterol 27mg; Calcium 75mg; Fibre 3.1g; Sodium 86mg.

cool cucumber and green tomato relish

This is a great way to use up those green tomatoes that seem as though they're never going to ripen. Combined with cucumber, they make a pale green relish that is good for barbecues.

Makes about 1.6kg/3½lb

INGREDIENTS

2 cucumbers

900g/2lb green (unripe) tomatoes

4 onions

7.5ml/1½ tsp salt

350ml/12fl oz/1½ cups distilled
 (white) vinegar

150g/5oz/scant ¾ cup demerara (raw) sugar

200g/7oz/1 cup sugar

15ml/1 tbsp plain (all-purpose) flour

2.5ml/½ tsp mustard powder

1 Wash the cucumbers and green tomatoes. Cut into 1cm/½in cubes. Peel and finely chop the onions.

2 Layer the vegetables in a strainer or colander placed over a bowl, lightly sprinkling each layer with salt, then cover and leave to drain for at least 6 hours, or overnight.

3 Discard the salty liquid and tip the salted vegetables into a large heavy pan. Reserve 30ml/2 tbsp of the vinegar and add the rest to the pan with the demerara and granulated sugars.

4 Slowly bring the vegetable mixture to the boil, stirring occasionally until the sugar has dissolved completely. Reduce the heat slightly and cook, uncovered, for about 30 minutes, or until the vegetables are tender.

5 In a small bowl, blend the flour and mustard to a paste with the reserved vinegar. Stir the mixture into the relish and simmer for about 20 minutes, or until the mixture is very thick.

6 Spoon the relish into warmed sterilized jars, cover and seal. Store in a cool, dark place for at least 1 week. Use the relish within 6 months. Once opened, keep in the refrigerator and use within 2 months.

Energy 1803kcal/7668kJ; Protein 18.3g; Carbohydrate 450.8g, of which sugars 427.5g; Fat 4.3g, of which saturates 0.9g; Cholesterol 0mg; Calcium 467mg; Fibre 18.9g; Sodium 129mg.

malay mixed vegetable relish

This traditional, full-flavoured relish, with its crunchy texture and spicy kick, is known as acar kuning *in Malaysia. It is served in very generous portions, almost like a side salad.*

Makes about 900g/2lb

INGREDIENTS

12 small pickling (pearl) onions, quartered

225g/8oz French (green) beans, cut into 2.5cm/1in lengths

225g/8oz carrots, cut into 2.5cm/1in long thin sticks

225g/8oz cauliflower, cut into small florets

5ml/1 tsp mustard powder

5ml/1 tsp salt

10ml/2 tsp sugar

60ml/4 tbsp sesame seeds

For the spice paste

2 shallots, finely chopped

2 garlic cloves, crushed

2 fresh green chillies, seeded and finely chopped

115g/4oz/1 cup dry-roasted peanuts

5ml/1 tsp turmeric

5ml/1 tsp chilli powder

60ml/4 tbsp distilled (white) vinegar

30ml/2 tbsp vegetable oil

175ml/6fl oz/¾ cup boiling water

1 Make the spice paste. Put the shallots, garlic, chillies, peanuts, turmeric, chilli powder, vinegar and oil in a food processor or blender and process to a fairly smooth paste.

2 Transfer the mixture to a large heavy pan and slowly bring to the boil. Reduce the heat and simmer gently for 2 minutes, stirring all the time. Gradually stir in the water and simmer the mixture for a further 3 minutes.

3 Add the onions to the pan, cover and simmer for 5 minutes, then add the beans and carrots. Cover the pan again and cook for a further 3 minutes.

4 Finally, add the cauliflower, mustard, salt and sugar to the pan and simmer, uncovered, for about 5 minutes, or until the vegetables are tender and have absorbed most of the sauce. Remove the pan from the heat and set aside to cool for a few minutes.

5 Meanwhile, toast the sesame seeds in a non-stick pan over a medium heat until golden, stirring frequently. Stir the seeds into the vegetable mixture.

6 Spoon the relish into warmed sterilized jars, cover and seal. Leave until completely cold, then store in the refrigerator.

COOK'S TIP
The relish can be served immediately and should be used within 4 weeks.

Energy 1200kcal/4978kJ; Protein 48g; Carbohydrate 77.7g, of which sugars 57.8g; Fat 79.6g, of which saturates 13.5g; Cholesterol 0mg; Calcium 348mg; Fibre 27.4g; Sodium 92mg.

carrot and almond relish

This is a Middle Eastern classic, usually made with long fine strands of carrot, available from many supermarkets. Alternatively, grate large carrots lengthways on a medium grater.

2 Put the lemon juice, vinegar, water, honey and salt in a jug (pitcher) and stir until the salt has dissolved. Pour over the carrot mixture. Mix well, cover and leave in the refrigerator for 4 hours.

3 Transfer the chilled mixture to a preserving pan. Slowly bring to the boil, then reduce the heat and simmer for 15 minutes until the carrots and ginger are tender.

4 Increase the heat and boil for 15 minutes, or until most of the liquid has evaporated and the mixture is thick. Stir frequently towards the end of the cooking time to prevent the mixture from sticking to the pan.

Makes about 675g/1½lb

INGREDIENTS

15ml/1 tbsp coriander seeds
500g/1¼lb carrots, grated
50g/2oz fresh root ginger,
   finely shredded
200g/7oz/1 cup caster (superfine) sugar
finely grated rind and juice
   of 1 lemon
120ml/4fl oz/½ cup white wine vinegar
75ml/5 tbsp water
30ml/2 tbsp clear honey
7.5ml/1½ tsp salt
50g/2oz/½ cup flaked (sliced) almonds

1 Crush the coriander seeds using a mortar and pestle. Put them in a bowl with the carrots, ginger, sugar and lemon rind and mix together well to combine.

5 Put the almonds in a frying pan and toast over a low heat until just beginning to colour. Gently stir into the relish, taking care not to break the almonds.

6 Spoon the relish into warmed sterilized jars, cover and seal. Leave for at least 1 month and use within 18 months. Once opened, store in the refrigerator.

Energy 1359kcal/5743kJ; Protein 14.9g; Carbohydrate 275.3g, of which sugars 271.5g; Fat 29.5g, of which saturates 2.7g; Cholesterol 0mg; Calcium 374mg; Fibre 16.3g; Sodium 3125mg.

lemon and garlic relish

This powerful relish is flavoured with North African spices and punchy preserved lemons, which are widely available in Middle Eastern stores. It is great served with Moroccan tagines.

Serves six

INGREDIENTS

45ml/3 tbsp olive oil

3 large red onions, sliced

2 heads of garlic, separated into cloves and peeled

10ml/2 tsp coriander seeds, crushed

10ml/2 tsp light muscovado (brown) sugar, plus a little extra

pinch of saffron threads

5cm/2in piece cinnamon stick

2–3 small whole dried red chillies (optional)

2 fresh bay leaves

30–45ml/2–3 tbsp sherry vinegar

juice of ½ small orange

30ml/2 tbsp chopped preserved lemon

salt and ground black pepper

1 Gently heat the oil in a large heavy pan. Add the onions and stir, then cover and cook on the lowest setting for 10–15 minutes, stirring occasionally, until soft.

2 Add the garlic cloves and the coriander seeds. Cover and cook for 5–8 minutes, until soft.

3 Add a pinch of salt, lots of ground black pepper and the sugar to the onions and cook, uncovered, for a further 5 minutes.

4 Soak the saffron threads in about 45ml/3 tbsp warm water for 5 minutes, then add to the onions, with the soaking water. Add the cinnamon stick, dried chillies, if using, and bay leaves. Stir in 30ml/2 tbsp of the sherry vinegar and the orange juice.

5 Cook very gently, uncovered, until the onions are very soft and most of the liquid evaporated. Stir in the preserved lemon and cook gently for 5 minutes.

6 Taste the relish and adjust the seasoning, adding more salt, sugar and/or vinegar to taste.

7 Serve warm or cold (not hot or chilled). The relish tastes best if left to stand for 24 hours.

COOK'S TIP

You can store the relish in a tightly covered bowl or jar for up to a week in the refrigerator. Allow it to stand at room temperature for about an hour before serving.

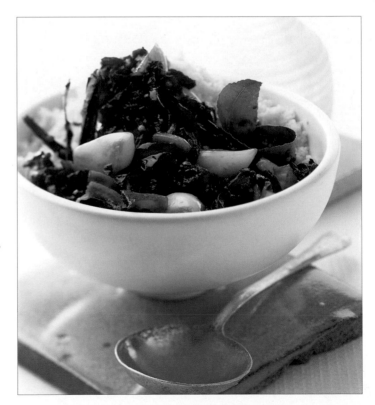

Energy 102kcal/422kJ; Protein 1.9g; Carbohydrate 11.4g, of which sugars 7.8g; Fat 5.8g, of which saturates 0.8g; Cholesterol 0mg; Calcium 28mg; Fibre 1.8g; Sodium 4mg.

papaya and lemon relish

This chunky relish is best made with a firm, unripe papaya. Leave for a week before eating to allow all the flavours to mellow. Serve with roast meats or with a robust cheese and crackers.

2 Bring the liquid to the boil, then immediately lower the heat and allow to simmer for 10 minutes.

3 Add all the remaining ingredients to the pan and bring to the boil, stirring all the time. Check that all the sugar has dissolved, then lower the heat and simmer for 50–60 minutes, or until the relish is thick and syrupy.

Makes about 450g/1lb

INGREDIENTS

1 large unripe papaya
1 onion, thinly sliced
40g/1½ oz/⅓ cup raisins
250ml/8fl oz/1 cup red wine vinegar
juice of 2 lemons
150ml/¼ pint/⅔ cup elderflower cordial
150g/5oz/¾ cup golden granulated sugar
1 cinnamon stick
1 fresh bay leaf
2.5ml/½ tsp hot paprika
2.5ml/½ tsp salt

1 Peel the papaya and cut in half lengthways. Remove the seeds with a teaspoon. Use a sharp knife to cut the flesh into small chunks and place them in a saucepan. Add the onion slices and raisins, then stir in the red wine vinegar.

4 Remove and discard the bay leaf. Ladle the relish into hot, sterilized jars. Seal and label, and store in a cool, dark place for 1 week before using. Keep the relish chilled after opening.

COOK'S TIP

The seeds of papaya have a peppery taste and are good in a salad dressing.

Energy 1069kcal/4559kJ; Protein 5g; Carbohydrate 277.9g, of which sugars 276.5g; Fat 0.8g, of which saturates 0g; Cholesterol 0mg; Calcium 241mg; Fibre 12.6g; Sodium 72mg.

mango and papaya relish

Brightly coloured pieces of dried papaya add flavour and texture to this anise-spiced mango preserve. The fruit is cooked for only a short time to retain its juicy texture and fresh flavour.

Makes about 800g/1¾lb

INGREDIENTS

115g/4oz/½ cup dried papaya

30ml/2 tbsp orange or
  apple juice

2 large slightly under-ripe mangoes

2 shallots, very finely sliced

4cm/1½in piece fresh root
  ginger, grated

1 garlic clove, crushed

2 whole star anise

150ml/¼ pint/⅔ cup cider vinegar

75g/3oz/scant ½ cup light muscovado
  (brown) sugar

1.5ml/¼ tsp salt

1 Using a sharp knife or scissors, roughly chop the papaya and place in a small bowl. Sprinkle over the orange or apple juice and leave to soak for at least 10 minutes.

2 Meanwhile, peel and slice the mangoes, cutting the flesh away from the stone (pit) in large slices. Cut into 1cm/½in chunks, then set the flesh aside.

3 Put the sliced shallots, ginger, garlic and star anise in a large pan. Pour over the vinegar. Slowly bring to the boil, then reduce the heat, cover and simmer for 5 minutes, or until the shallots are just beginning to soften.

4 Add the sugar and salt to the pan and stir over a low heat until dissolved. When the mixture is simmering, add the papaya and mango and cook for a further 20 minutes, or until the fruit is just tender and the relish mixture has reduced and thickened.

5 Allow the relish to cool for about 5 minutes, then spoon into warmed sterilized jars. Allow to cool completely before covering and sealing. Store in a cool, dark place and use within 3 months of making. Once opened, keep the jars in the refrigerator and use within 1 month.

Energy 621kcal/2654kJ; Protein 4.6g; Carbohydrate 158.5g, of which sugars 157.6g; Fat 1g, of which saturates 0.3g; Cholesterol 0mg; Calcium 171mg; Fibre 16.6g; Sodium 623mg.

cranberry and red onion relish

This wine-enriched relish is perfect for serving with hot roast turkey at Christmas or Thanksgiving. It can be made several months in advance of the festive season.

Makes about 900g/2lb

INGREDIENTS

450g/1lb small red (Italian) onions

30ml/2 tbsp olive oil

225g/8oz/1 cup soft light
   brown sugar

450g/1lb/4 cups fresh or
   frozen cranberries

120ml/4fl oz/½ cup red wine vinegar

120ml/4fl oz/½ cup red wine

15ml/1 tbsp mustard seeds

2.5ml/½ tsp ground ginger

30ml/2 tbsp orange liqueur or port

salt and ground black pepper

1 Halve and thinly slice the red onions. Heat the oil in a large pan, add the onions and cook gently for about 15 minutes, stirring often, until softened. Add 30ml/2 tbsp of the sugar. Cook for 5 minutes, or until the onions are caramelized.

2 Meanwhile, put the cranberries in a pan with the remaining sugar, and the vinegar, red wine, mustard seeds and ginger. Heat gently until the sugar has dissolved. Bring to the boil, reduce the heat and cover.

3 Simmer the relish mixture for 12–15 minutes, until the berries have burst and are tender, then stir in the caramelized onions.

4 Increase the heat slightly and cook uncovered for a further 10 minutes, stirring the mixture frequently until it is well reduced and thickened. Remove the pan from the heat, then season with salt and pepper to taste.

5 Transfer the relish to warmed sterilized jars. Spoon a little of the orange liqueur or port over the top of each, then cover and seal. Store in a cool place for up to 6 months. Store in the refrigerator once opened and use within 1 month.

COOK'S TIP

It is important to cover the pan when cooking the cranberries because they can sometimes pop out of the pan during cooking and are very hot.

VARIATION

Redcurrants work well instead of cranberries – they produce a relish with a slightly less tart flavour and a very pretty colour.

Energy 1532kcal/6486kJ; Protein 8g; Carbohydrate 314.6g, of which sugars 304.2g; Fat 23.3g, of which saturates 3.1g; Cholesterol 0mg; Calcium 259mg; Fibre 13.5g; Sodium 46mg.

sweet and sour pineapple relish

This simple preserve is an excellent condiment for perking up grilled chicken or bacon chops. Using canned pineapple means it can be made mainly from store-cupboard ingredients.

Makes about 675g/1½lb

INGREDIENTS

2 x 400g/14oz cans pineapple rings
  or pieces in natural juice

1 lemon

115g/4oz/½ cup sugar

45m/3 tbsp white wine vinegar

6 spring onions (scallions),
  finely chopped

2 fresh red chillies, seeded and
  finely chopped

salt and ground black pepper

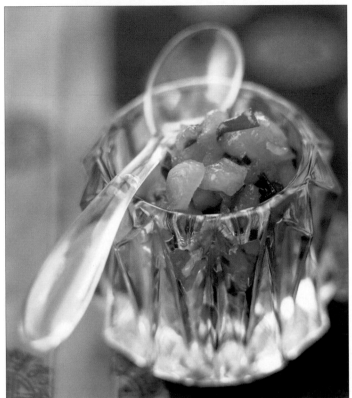

1 Drain the pineapple, reserving 120ml/4fl oz/½ cup of the juice. Pour the juice into a preserving pan. Finely chop the pineapple, if necessary, and place in a sieve (strainer) set over a bowl.

2 Pare a strip of rind from the lemon. Squeeze the lemon juice and add to the pan with the lemon rind, sugar and vinegar.

3 Heat over a low heat, stirring occasionally, until the sugar has dissolved, then bring to the boil. Cook, uncovered, over a medium heat for about 10 minutes, or until the sauce has thickened slightly.

4 Add the chopped onions and chillies to the pan, together with any juice that has been drained from the chopped pineapple.

5 Cook the sauce for 5 minutes, until thick and syrupy, stirring frequently towards the end of the cooking time.

6 Increase the heat slightly, add the pineapple and cook for about 4 minutes, or until most of the liquid has evaporated. Season.

7 Spoon the relish into warmed sterilized jars, cover and seal. Store in the refrigerator and eat within 3 months of making.

Energy 859kcal/3659kJ; Protein 4.7g; Carbohydrate 222.8g, of which sugars 222.5g; Fat 0.5g, of which saturates 0.1g; Cholesterol 0mg; Calcium 152mg; Fibre 5.7g; Sodium 21mg.

plum and cherry relish

This luxurious sweet-sour fruity relish complements rich poultry, game or meat, including roast duck or grilled duck breasts. Sieve a few spoonfuls into a sauce or gravy to add fruity zest and flavour, as well as for uplifting colour when a sauce looks a little dull.

Makes about 350g/12oz

INGREDIENTS

350g/12oz dark-skinned red plums
350g/12oz/2 cups cherries
2 shallots, finely chopped
15ml/1 tbsp olive oil
30ml/2 tbsp dry sherry
60ml/4 tbsp red wine vinegar
15ml/1 tbsp balsamic vinegar
1 bay leaf
90g/3½oz/scant ½ cup demerara (raw) sugar

1 Halve and stone (pit) the plums, then roughly chop the flesh. Stone all the cherries.

2 Cook the shallots gently in the oil for 5 minutes, or until soft. Add the fruit, sherry, vinegars, bay leaf and sugar.

3 Slowly bring the mixture to the boil, stirring until the sugar has dissolved completely. Increase the heat and cook briskly for about 15 minutes, or until the relish is very thick and the fruit tender.

4 Remove the bay leaf and spoon the relish into warmed sterilized jars. Cover and seal. Store the relish in the refrigerator and use within 3 months.

Energy 804kcal/3407kJ; Protein 6.5g; Carbohydrate 170.3g, of which sugars 168.9g; Fat 11.8g, of which saturates 1.6g; Cholesterol 0mg; Calcium 156mg; Fibre 9.6g; Sodium 21mg.

nectarine relish

This sweet and tangy fruit relish goes very well with hot roast meats such as pork and game birds such as guinea fowl and pheasant. Make it while nectarines are plentiful and keep tightly covered in the refrigerator to serve for Christmas, or even to give as a seasonal gift.

Makes about 450g/1lb

INGREDIENTS

45ml/3 tbsp olive oil

2 Spanish (Bermuda) onions, thinly sliced

1 fresh green chilli, seeded and finely chopped

5ml/1 tsp finely chopped fresh rosemary

2 bay leaves

450g/1lb nectarines, stoned (pitted) and cut into chunks

150g/5oz/1 cup raisins

10ml/2 tsp crushed coriander seeds

350g/12oz/1½ cups demerara (raw) sugar

200ml/7fl oz/scant 1 cup red wine vinegar

1 Heat the oil in a large pan. Add the onions, chilli, rosemary and bay leaves. Cook, stirring frequently, for about 15 minutes, or until the onions are soft.

COOK'S TIP

Pots of this relish make lovely gifts. Store it in pretty jars and add colourful labels identifying the relish, and reminding the recipient that it should be stored in the refrigerator, and when it should be used by.

2 Add the nectarines, raisins, coriander seeds, sugar and vinegar to the pan, then slowly bring to the boil, stirring frequently.

3 Reduce the heat under the pan and simmer gently for 1 hour, or until the relish is thick and sticky. Stir occasionally during cooking, and more frequently towards the end of cooking time to prevent the relish sticking to the pan.

4 Spoon the relish into warmed, sterilized jars and seal. Leave the jars to cool completely, then store in the refrigerator. The relish will keep well in the refrigerator for up to 5 months.

Energy 2408kcal/10211kJ; Protein 16g; Carbohydrate 541.8g, of which sugars 532.6g; Fat 34.8g, of which saturates 4.7g; Cholesterol 0mg; Calcium 386mg; Fibre 14g; Sodium 128mg.

pickles and preserved fruits

Pickles are king of the preserves, and this selection of savoury and sweet items draws on culinary traditions from all over the world. There are sweet-sour fruits to enhance hot or cold meats or cheese, or spiced fruit and vegetables to complement Asian or Middle-Eastern main courses. Italian-style pickled vegetables make appetizing first courses, plus you have the classics: pickled cucumbers, sweet onions, dill pickles, and delicious fruits preserved in alcohol.

dill pickles

Redolent of garlic and piquant with fresh chilli, salty dill pickles can be supple and succulent or crisp and crunchy. Every pickle aficionado has a favourite type.

Makes about 900g/2lb

INGREDIENTS

20 small, ridged or knobbly pickling (small) cucumbers
2 litres/3½ pints/8 cups water
175g/6oz/¾ cup coarse sea salt
15–20 garlic cloves, unpeeled
2 bunches fresh dill
15ml/1 tbsp dill seeds
30ml/2 tbsp mixed pickling spice
1 or 2 hot fresh chillies

1 Scrub the cucumbers and rinse well in cold water. Leave to dry.

2 Put the measured water and salt in a large pan and bring to the boil. Turn off the heat and leave to cool to room temperature.

3 Using the flat side of a knife blade or a wooden mallet, lightly crush each garlic clove, breaking the papery skin.

4 Pack the cucumbers tightly into one or two wide-necked, sterilized jars, layering them with the garlic, fresh dill, dill seeds and pickling spice. Add one chilli to each jar. Pour over the cooled brine, making sure that the cucumbers are completely covered. Tap the jars on the work surface to dispel any trapped air bubbles.

5 Cover the jars with lids and then leave to stand at room temperature for 4–7 days before serving. Store in the refrigerator.

COOK'S TIP

If you cannot find ridged or knobbly pickling (small) cucumbers, use any kind of small cucumbers instead.

Energy 45kcal/180kJ; Protein 3.1g; Carbohydrate 6.8g, of which sugars 6.3g; Fat 0.5g, of which saturates 0g; Cholesterol 0mg; Calcium 83mg; Fibre 2.7g; Sodium 5909mg.

pickled mushrooms with garlic

This method of preserving mushrooms is popular throughout Europe. The pickle is good made with cultivated mushrooms, but it is worth including a couple of sliced ceps for their flavour.

Makes about 900g/2lb

INGREDIENTS

500g/1¼lb/8 cups mixed mushrooms, such as small ceps, chestnut mushrooms, shiitake and girolles

300ml/½ pint/1¼ cups white wine vinegar or cider vinegar

15ml/1 tbsp sea salt

5ml/1 tsp caster (superfine) sugar

300ml/½ pint/1¼ cups water

4–5 fresh bay leaves

8 large fresh thyme sprigs

15 garlic cloves, peeled, halved, with any green shoots removed

1 small red (Italian) onion, halved and thinly sliced

2–3 small dried red chillies

5ml/1 tsp coriander seeds, lightly crushed

5ml/1 tsp black peppercorns

a few strips of lemon rind

250–350ml/8–12fl oz/1–1½ cups extra virgin olive oil

1 Trim and wipe the mushrooms and cut any large ones in half.

2 Put the vinegar, salt, sugar and water in a pan and bring to the boil. Add the bay leaves, thyme, garlic, onion, chillies, coriander seeds, peppercorns and lemon rind and simmer for 2 minutes.

3 Add the mushrooms to the pan and simmer for 3–4 minutes. Drain the mushrooms through a seive, retaining all the herbs and spices, then set aside for a few minutes more until the mushrooms are thoroughly drained.

4 Fill one large or two small cool sterilized jars with the mushrooms. Distribute the garlic, onion, herbs and spices evenly among the layers of mushrooms, then add enough olive oil to cover by at least 1cm/½in. You may need to use extra oil if you are making two jars.

5 Leave the pickle to settle, then tap the jars on the work surface to dispel any air bubbles. Seal the jars, then store in the refrigerator. Use within 2 weeks.

Energy 579kcal/2392kJ; Protein 9g; Carbohydrate 7.2g, of which sugars 6.2g; Fat 57.4g, of which saturates 8.4g; Cholesterol 0mg; Calcium 33mg; Fibre 5.5g; Sodium 25mg.

pickled red cabbage

This delicately spiced and vibrant-coloured pickle is an old-fashioned favourite to serve with bread and cheese for an informal lunch, or to use to accompany cold ham, duck or goose.

Makes about 1–1.6kg/2¼–3½lb

INGREDIENTS

675g/1½lb/6 cups red cabbage, shredded

1 large Spanish onion, sliced

30ml/2 tbsp sea salt

600ml/1 pint/2½ cups red wine vinegar

75g/3oz/6 tbsp light muscovado (brown) sugar

15ml/1 tbsp coriander seeds

3 cloves

2.5cm/1in piece fresh root ginger

1 whole star anise

2 bay leaves

4 eating apples

1 Put the cabbage and onion in a bowl, add the salt and mix well until thoroughly combined. Tip the mixture into a colander over a bowl and leave to drain overnight.

2 The next day, rinse the salted vegetables, drain well and pat dry using kitchen paper.

3 Pour the vinegar into a pan, add the sugar, spices and bay leaves and bring to the boil. Remove from the heat and leave to cool.

4 Core and chop the apples, then layer with the cabbage and onions in sterilized preserving jars. Pour over the cooled spiced vinegar. (If you prefer a milder pickle, strain out the spices first). Seal the jars and store for 1 week before eating. Eat within 2 months. Once opened, store in the refrigerator.

Energy 674kcal/2869kJ; Protein 12g; Carbohydrate 161.4g, of which sugars 159.3g; Fat 2g, of which saturates 0g; Cholesterol 0mg; Calcium 406mg; Fibre 23g; Sodium 64mg.

pickled turnips and beetroot

This delicious pickle is a Middle Eastern speciality. The turnips turn a rich red in their beetroot-spiked brine and look gorgeous stacked on shelves in the storecupboard.

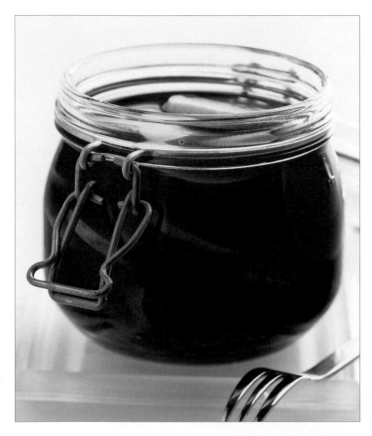

2 Put the salt and water in a bowl, stir and leave to stand until the salt has completely dissolved.

3 Sprinkle the beetroot with lemon juice and place in the bottom of four 1.2 litre/2 pint sterilized jars. Top with sliced turnip, packing them in very tightly, then pour over the brine, making sure that the vegetables are covered.

4 Seal the jars and leave in a cool place for 7 days before serving.

Makes about 1.6kg/3½lb

INGREDIENTS

1kg/2¼lb young turnips
3–4 raw beetroot (beets)
about 45ml/3 tbsp coarse sea salt
about 1.5 litres/2½ pints/6¼ cups water
juice of 1 lemon

COOK'S TIP

Be careful when preparing the beetroot because their bright red juice can stain clothing.

1 Wash the turnips and beetroot, but do not peel them, then cut into slices about 5mm/¼in thick.

Energy 338kcal/1442kJ; Protein 14.1g; Carbohydrate 69.8g, of which sugars 66g; Fat 3.3g, of which saturates 0g; Cholesterol 0mg; Calcium 541mg; Fibre 29.7g; Sodium 4278mg.

shallots in balsamic vinegar

These whole shallots, cooked in balsamic vinegar and herbs, are a modern variation on traditional pickled onions. They have a much more gentle, smooth flavour and are delicious served with cold meats or robustly flavoured hard cheeses.

Makes one large jar

INGREDIENTS

500g/1¼lb shallots

30ml/2 tbsp muscovado (molasses) sugar

several bay leaves and/or fresh thyme sprigs

300ml/½ pint/1¼ cups balsamic vinegar

VARIATION

Use other robust herbs in place of the thyme sprigs. Rosemary, oregano or marjoram are all good choices.

1 Put the unpeeled shallots in a bowl. Pour over boiling water and leave to stand for 2 minutes to loosen the skins. Drain and peel the shallots, leaving them whole.

2 Put the sugar, bay leaves and/or thyme and vinegar in a large heavy pan and bring to the boil. Add the shallots, cover and simmer gently for about 40 minutes, or until the shallots are just tender.

3 Transfer the shallots and vinegar mixture to a warmed sterilized jar, packing the shallots down well. Seal and label the jar, then store in a cool, dark place for about 1 month before eating.

Energy 298kcal/1254kJ; Protein 6.2g; Carbohydrate 70.8g, of which sugars 59.4g; Fat 1g, of which saturates 0g; Cholesterol 0mg; Calcium 141mg; Fibre 7g; Sodium 17mg.

hot thai pickled shallots

Although they may be quite difficult to find and require lengthy preparation, Thai pink shallots look and taste exquisite in this spiced pickle. The shallots taste good finely sliced, and served as a condiment with a wide range of South-east Asian meals.

Makes about three jars

INGREDIENTS

5–6 fresh red or green bird's eye chillies, halved and seeded if liked

500g/1¼lb Thai pink shallots, peeled

2 large garlic cloves, peeled, halved and green shoots removed

600ml/1 pint/2½ cups cider vinegar

45ml/3 tbsp granulated (white) sugar

10ml/2 tsp salt

5cm/2in piece fresh root ginger, sliced

15ml/1 tbsp coriander seeds

2 lemon grass stalks, cut in half lengthways

4 kaffir lime leaves or strips of lime rind

15ml/1 tbsp chopped fresh coriander (cilantro)

1 If leaving the chillies whole (they will be hotter), prick several times with a cocktail stick (toothpick).

2 Bring a large pan of water to the boil. Blanch the chillies, shallots and garlic for 1–2 minutes, then drain. Rinse the vegetables under cold water and leave to drain.

VARIATION

Ordinary shallots and pickling (pearl) onions are widely available and can be preserved in the same way.

3 To prepare the vinegar, put the cider vinegar, sugar, salt, ginger, coriander seeds, lemon grass and lime leaves or lime rind in a large pan and bring to the boil. Simmer over a low heat for 3–4 minutes, then remove from the heat and set aside to cool.

4 Using a slotted spoon, remove the sliced ginger from the pan and discard. Return the vinegar to the boil, then add the fresh coriander, garlic and chillies, and cook for about 1 minute.

5 Pack the shallots, spices and aromatics into warmed sterilized jars and pour over the hot vinegar. Cool, then seal. Leave in a dark place for 2 months before eating.

Energy 127kcal/536kJ; Protein 2.3g; Carbohydrate 30.4g, of which sugars 26.5g; Fat 0.4g, of which saturates 0g; Cholesterol 0mg; Calcium 52mg; Fibre 2.7g; Sodium 7mg.

english pickled onions

These powerful pickles are traditionally served with a plate of cold meats and bread and cheese. They should be made with malt vinegar and stored for at least 6 weeks before eating.

Makes about four jars

INGREDIENTS

1kg/2¼lb pickling onions
115g/4oz/½ cup salt
750ml/1¼ pints/3 cups malt vinegar
15ml/1 tbsp sugar
2–3 dried red chillies
5ml/1 tsp brown mustard seeds
15ml/1 tbsp coriander seeds
5ml/1 tsp allspice berries
5ml/1 tsp black peppercorns
5cm/2in piece fresh root ginger, sliced
2–3 blades mace
2–3 fresh bay leaves

1 To peel the onions, trim off the root ends, but leave the onion layers attached. Cut a thin slice off the top (neck) end of the onion. Place the onions in a bowl, then cover with boiling water. Leave to stand for about 4 minutes, then drain. The skin should then be easy to peel using a small, sharp knife.

2 Place the peeled onions in a bowl and cover with cold water, then drain the water into a large pan. Add the salt and heat slightly to dissolve it, then cool before pouring the brine over the onions.

3 Place a plate inside the top of the bowl and weigh it down slightly so that it keeps all the onions submerged in the brine. Leave to stand for 24 hours.

4 Meanwhile, place the vinegar in a large pan. Wrap all the remaining ingredients, except the bay leaves, in a piece of muslin (cheesecloth). Bring to the boil, simmer for about 5 minutes, then remove the pan from the heat. Set aside and leave to infuse overnight.

5 The next day, drain the onions, rinse and pat dry. Pack them into sterilized 450g/1lb jars. Add some or all of the spice from the vinegar, except the ginger slices. The pickle will become hotter if you add the chillies. Pour the vinegar over to cover and add the bay leaves. (Store leftover vinegar in a bottle for another batch of pickles.)

6 Seal the jars with non-metallic lids and store in a cool, dark place for at least 6 weeks before eating.

Energy 105kcal/438kJ; Protein 3g; Carbohydrate 23.7g, of which sugars 17.9g; Fat 0.5g, of which saturates 0g; Cholesterol 0mg; Calcium 65mg; Fibre 3.5g; Sodium 8mg.

instant pickle of mixed vegetables

This fresh, salad-style pickle doesn't need lengthy storing so makes the perfect choice if you need a bowl of pickle immediately. However, it does not have good storing properties.

Makes about 450g/1lb

INGREDIENTS

½ cauliflower head, cut into florets

2 carrots, sliced

2 celery sticks, thinly sliced

¼–½ white cabbage, thinly sliced

115g/4oz/scant 1 cup runner (green) beans, cut into bitesize pieces

6 garlic cloves, sliced

1–4 fresh chillies, whole or sliced

5cm/2in piece fresh root ginger, sliced

1 red (bell) pepper, sliced

2.5ml/½ tsp turmeric

105ml/7 tbsp white wine vinegar

15–30ml/1–2 tbsp granulated (white) sugar

60–90ml/4–6 tbsp olive oil

juice of 2 lemons

salt

1 Toss the cauliflower, carrots, celery, cabbage, beans, garlic, chillies, ginger and pepper with salt and leave them to stand in a colander over a bowl for 4 hours.

2 Shake the vegetables well to remove any excess juices.

3 Transfer the salted vegetables to a bowl. Add the turmeric, vinegar, sugar to taste, oil and lemon juice. Toss to combine, then add enough water to distribute the flavours. Cover the bowl and leave to chill for at least 1 hour, or until you are ready to serve.

Energy 776kcal/3211kJ; Protein 19.1g; Carbohydrate 42.5g, of which sugars 38.3g; Fat 59.6g, of which saturates 8.7g; Cholesterol 0mg; Calcium 302mg; Fibre 17.8g; Sodium 109mg.

stuffed baby aubergines

This Middle Eastern fermented pickle makes a succulent and spicy accompaniment to cold meats, but is equally good served with a few salad leaves and bread as a simple appetizer.

Makes about three jars

INGREDIENTS

1kg/2¼lb baby aubergines (eggplants)
2 fresh red chillies, halved lengthways
2 green chillies, halved lengthways
2 celery sticks, cut into matchstick strips
2 carrots, cut into matchstick strips
4 garlic cloves, peeled and finely chopped
20ml/4 tsp salt
4 small fresh vine leaves (optional)
750ml/1¼ pints/3 cups cooled boiled water
45ml/3 tbsp white wine vinegar

1 Trim the aubergine stems, but do not remove them completely. Cut a slit lengthways along each aubergine, almost through to the other side, to make a pocket.

2 Steam the slit aubergines for 5–6 minutes or until they are just tender when tested with the tip of a sharp knife.

3 Put the aubergines in a colander set over a bowl, then place a plate on top. Place a few weights on the plate to press it down gently and leave for 4 hours to squeeze out the moisture from the vegetables.

6 Pour the water into a jug (pitcher) and add the remaining 15ml/1 tbsp salt and the vinegar. Stir together until the salt has dissolved. Pour enough brine into the jar to cover the aubergines, then weigh down the top.

7 Cover the jar with a clean dishtowel and leave in a warm, well-ventilated place to ferment. The brine will turn cloudy as fermentation starts, but will clear after 1–2 weeks when the pickle has finished fermenting. As soon as this happens, cover and seal the jar and store in the refrigerator. Eat the pickle within 2 months.

COOK'S TIPS

• Aubergines come in a multitude of colours from a deep purple-black to yellow and creamy white. Whichever type you use, choose ones with taut, glossy skins.
• Steam the aubergines as soon as you have slit them open because their flesh discolours rapidly when exposed to air.

4 Finely chop two red and two green chilli halves and place in a bowl. Add the celery and carrots to the chillies with the garlic and 5ml/1 tsp of the salt. Mix and use to stuff the aubergine pockets.

5 Tightly pack the aubergines, remaining chillies and vine leaves, if using, into a large sterilized jar.

Energy 71kcal/301kJ; Protein 3.6g; Carbohydrate 11.6g, of which sugars 10.7g; Fat 1.6g, of which saturates 0.4g; Cholesterol 0mg; Calcium 50mg; Fibre 8g; Sodium 26mg.

preserved lemons

These richly flavoured fruits are widely used in Middle Eastern cooking. Only the rind, which contains the essential flavour of the lemon is used in recipes. Traditionally whole lemons are preserved, but this recipe uses wedges, which can be packed into jars more easily.

2 Pack the salted lemon wedges into two 1.2 litre/2 pint/5 cup warmed sterilized jars. To each jar, add 30–45ml/2–3 tbsp sea salt and half the lemon juice, then top up with boiling water to cover the lemon wedges. Seal the jars and leave to stand for 2–4 weeks before using.

3 To use, rinse the preserved lemons well to remove some of the salty flavour, then pull off and discard the flesh. Cut the lemon rind into strips or leave in chunks and use as desired.

Makes about two jars

INGREDIENTS

10 unwaxed lemons

about 200ml/7fl oz/scant 1 cup fresh lemon juice or a combination of fresh and preserved juice

boiling water

sea salt

COOK'S TIP

The salty, well-flavoured juice that is used to preserve the lemons can be used to flavour salad dressings or added to hot sauces.

1 Wash the lemons well and cut each into six to eight wedges. Press a generous amount of salt on to the cut surface of each wedge.

Energy 95kcal/395kJ; Protein 5g; Carbohydrate 16g, of which sugars 16g; Fat 1.5g, of which saturates 0.5g; Cholesterol 0mg; Calcium 425mg; Fibre 0g; Sodium 25mg.

pickled limes

This hot, pungent pickle comes from the Punjab in India. Salting softens the rind and intensifies the flavour of the limes, while they mature in the first month or two of storage. Pickled limes are extremely salty so are best served with slightly under-seasoned dishes.

Makes about 1kg/2¼lb

INGREDIENTS

1kg/2¼lb unwaxed limes
75g/3oz/⅓ cup salt
seeds from 6 green cardamom pods
6 whole cloves
5ml/1 tsp cumin seeds
4 fresh red chillies, seeded
  and sliced
5cm/2in piece fresh root ginger, peeled
  and finely shredded
450g/1lb/2¼ cups preserving or
  granulated (white) sugar

1 Put the limes in a large bowl and pour over cold water to cover. Leave to soak for 8 hours, or overnight, if preferred.

2 The next day, remove the limes from the water. Using a sharp knife, cut each lime in half from end to end, then cut each half into 5mm/¼in-thick slices.

3 Place the lime slices in the bowl, sprinkling the salt between the layers. Cover and leave to stand for a further 8 hours.

4 Drain the limes, catching the juices in a preserving pan. Crush the cardamom seeds with the cumin seeds. Add to the pan with the chillies, ginger and sugar. Bring to the boil, stirring until the sugar dissolves. Simmer for 2 minutes and leave to cool.

5 Mix the limes in the syrup. Pack into sterilized jars, cover and seal. Store in a cool, dark place for at least 1 month before eating. Use within 1 year.

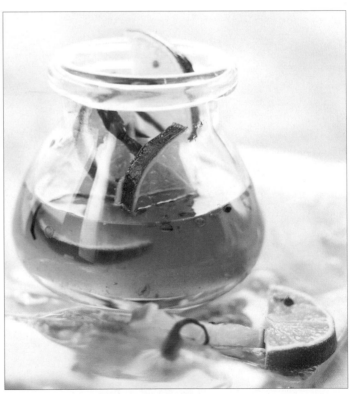

Energy 1963kcal/8355kJ; Protein 12.3g; Carbohydrate 502.3g, of which sugars 502.3g; Fat 3g, of which saturates 1g; Cholesterol 0mg; Calcium 1089mg; Fibre 0g; Sodium 2042mg.

striped spiced oranges

These delightful sweet-sour spiced orange slices have a wonderfully warming flavour and look very pretty. Serve them with baked ham, rich terrines and gamey pâtés. They are also delicious with roasted red peppers and grilled halloumi cheese.

Makes about 1.2kg/2½lb

INGREDIENTS

6 small or medium oranges

750ml/1¼ pints/3 cups white wine vinegar

900g/2lb/4½ cups preserving or granulated (white) sugar

7.5cm/3in cinnamon stick

5ml/1 tsp whole allspice

8 whole cloves

45ml/3 tbsp brandy (optional)

COOK'S TIP

These preserved oranges, with their bright colour and warming flavour, make them a perfect accompaniment during the festive season – delicious with leftover turkey or wafer thin slices of festive ham.

1 Scrub the oranges well, then cut strips of rind from each one using a canelle knife (zester) to achieve a striped effect. Reserve the strips of rind.

2 Using a sharp knife, cut the oranges across into slices slightly thicker than 5mm/¼in. Remove and discard any pips (seeds).

3 Put the orange slices into a preserving pan and pour over just enough cold water to cover the fruit. Bring to the boil, then reduce the heat and simmer gently for about 5 minutes, or until the oranges are tender. Using a slotted spoon, transfer the orange slices to a large bowl and discard the cooking liquid.

4 Put the vinegar and sugar in the cleaned pan. Tie the cinnamon, whole allspice and orange rind together in muslin (cheesecloth) and add to the pan. Slowly bring to the boil, stirring, until the sugar has dissolved. Simmer for 1 minute.

5 Return the oranges slices to the pan and cook gently for about 30 minutes, or until the rind is translucent and the orange slices look glazed. Remove from the heat and discard the spice bag.

6 Using a slotted spoon, transfer the orange slices to hot sterilized jars, adding the cloves between the layers. Bring the syrup to a rapid boil and boil for about 10 minutes, or until slightly thickened.

7 Allow the syrup to cool for a few minutes, then stir in the brandy, if using. Pour the syrup into the jars, making sure that the fruit is completely immersed. Gently tap the jars on the work surface to release any air bubbles, then cover and seal. Store for at least 2 weeks before using. Use within 6 months.

Energy 3768kcal/16077kJ; Protein 11.1g; Carbohydrate 991.5g, of which sugars 991.5g; Fat 0.6g, of which saturates 0g; Cholesterol 0mg; Calcium 759mg; Fibre 10.2g; Sodium 84mg.

pickled plums

This preserve is popular in Central Europe and works well for all varieties of plums, from small wild bullaces and astringent damsons to the more delicately flavoured yellow or red-flushed mirabelle. Plums soften easily, so make sure that you choose very firm fruit.

Makes about 900g/2lb

INGREDIENTS

900g/2lb firm plums

150ml/¼ pint/⅔ cup clear apple juice

450ml/¾ pint/scant 2 cups cider vinegar

2.5ml/½ tsp salt

8 allspice berries

2.5cm/1in piece fresh root ginger, peeled and cut into matchstick strips

4 bay leaves

675g/1½lb/scant 3½ cups preserving or granulated (white) sugar

VARIATION

Juniper berries can be used instead of the allspice berries.

1 Wash the plums, then prick them once or twice using a wooden cocktail stick (toothpick). Put the apple juice, vinegar, salt, allspice berries, ginger and bay leaves in a preserving pan.

2 Add the plums to the pan and slowly bring to the boil. Reduce the heat and simmer gently for 10 minutes, or until the plums are just tender. Remove the plums with a slotted spoon and pack them into hot sterilized jars.

3 Add the sugar to the pan and stir over a low heat until dissolved. Boil steadily for 10 minutes, or until the mixture is syrupy.

4 Leave the syrup to cool for a few minutes, then pour over the plums. Cover and seal. Store for at least 1 month before using and use within 1 year of making.

Energy 3041kcal/12988kJ; Protein 8.9g; Carbohydrate 799.4g, of which sugars 799.4g; Fat 1.1g, of which saturates 0g; Cholesterol 0mg; Calcium 485mg; Fibre 14.4g; Sodium 62mg.

italian mustard fruit pickles

*This traditional and popular Italian preserve is made from late summer and autumn fruits,
and then left to mature in time for Christmas when it is served with Italian steamed sausage.
The fruits can be mixed together, or arranged in layers in the jars for a stunning effect.*

Makes about 1.2kg/2½lb

INGREDIENTS

450ml/¾ pint/scant 2 cups white
  wine vinegar

30ml/2 tbsp mustard seeds

1kg/2¼lb mixed fruit, such as peaches,
  nectarines, apricots, plums, melon,
  figs and cherries

675g/1½lb/scant 3½ cups preserving
  or granulated (white) sugar

VARIATION

If you prefer a slightly less tangy
pickle, use cider vinegar instead of
the white wine vinegar used here.

1 Put the vinegar and mustard
seeds in a pan, bring to the boil,
then simmer for 5 minutes.
Remove from the heat, cover and
leave to infuse for 1 hour. Strain
the vinegar into a clean pan and
discard the mustard seeds.

2 Prepare the fruit. Wash and
pat dry the peaches, nectarines,
apricots and plums, then stone
(pit) and thickly slice or halve.
Cut the melon in half, discard the
seeds (pips), then slice into 1cm/
½in pieces or scoop into balls using
a melon baller. Cut the figs into
quarters and remove the stalks
from the cherries.

3 Add the sugar to the mustard
vinegar and heat gently, stirring
occasionally, until the sugar has
dissolved completely. Bring to the
boil, reduce the heat and simmer
for 5 minutes, or until syrupy.

4 Add the fruit to the syrup and
poach it over a gentle heat for
5–10 minutes. Some fruit will be
ready sooner than others, so lift
out as soon as each variety is
tender, using a slotted spoon.

5 Pack the fruit into hot sterilized
jars. Ladle the hot mustard syrup
over the fruit. Cover and seal.
Allow the pickles to mature for at
least 1 month before eating. Use
within 6 months.

Energy 3140kcal/13399kJ; Protein 20.2g; Carbohydrate 813.4g, of which sugars 813.4g; Fat 1.2g, of which saturates 0g; Cholesterol 0mg; Calcium 442mg; Fibre 14.4g; Sodium 53mg.

sweet pickled watermelon rind

This unusual pickle has a slightly aromatic melon flavour and a crunchy texture. It's the perfect way to use up the part of the fruit that is normally discarded.

Makes about 900g/2lb

INGREDIENTS

900g/2lb watermelon rind
(from 1 large fruit)
50g/2oz/¼ cup salt
900ml/1½ pints/3¾ cups water
450g/1lb/2¼ cups preserving or
granulated (white) sugar
300ml/½ pint/1¼ cups white wine vinegar
6 whole cloves
7.5cm/3in cinnamon stick

COOK'S TIP

Leave the watermelon rind to mature for at least 4 weeks before eating. This really helps the flavours to develop.

1 Remove the dark green skin from the watermelon rind, leaving a thin layer, no more than 3mm/⅛in thick, of the pink fruit. Cut the rind into slices about 5cm × 5mm/2 × ¼in thick, and place in a large bowl.

2 Dissolve the salt in 600ml/1 pint/2½ cups of the water. Pour over the watermelon rind, cover and leave for at least 6 hours or overnight.

3 Drain the watermelon rind and rinse under cold water. Put the rind in a pan and cover with fresh water. Bring the boil, reduce the heat and simmer for 10–15 minutes until just tender. Drain well.

4 Put the sugar, vinegar and remaining water in a clean pan. Tie the cloves and cinnamon in muslin (cheesecloth) and add to the pan. Heat gently, stirring occasionally, until the sugar has dissolved, then bring to the boil and simmer for 10 minutes. Turn off the heat. Add the rind, cover and leave to stand for about 2 hours.

5 Slowly bring the mixture back to the boil, then reduce the heat and simmer gently for 20 minutes, or until the rind has a translucent appearance. Remove and discard the spice bag. Place the rind in hot sterilized jars. Pour over the hot syrup, tapping the jar to release any trapped air. Cover and seal.

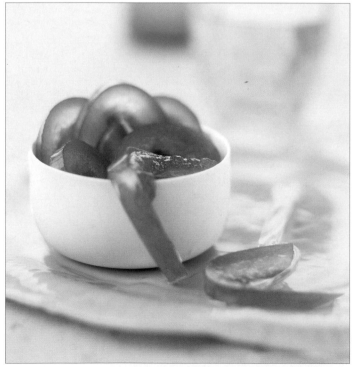

Energy 1836kcal/7835kJ; Protein 6.8g; Carbohydrate 478.4g, of which sugars 478.4g; Fat 1.8g, of which saturates 0g; Cholesterol 0mg; Calcium 608mg; Fibre 9.9g; Sodium 567mg.

blushing pears

As this pickle matures, the fruits absorb the colour of the vinegar, giving them a glorious pink hue. They're especially good served with cold turkey, game pie, well-flavoured cheese or pâté.

Makes about 1.3kg/3lb

INGREDIENTS

1 small lemon

450g/1lb/2¼ cups golden granulated sugar

475ml/16fl oz/2 cups raspberry vinegar

7.5cm/3in cinnamon stick

6 whole cloves

6 allspice berries

150ml/¼ pint/⅔ cup water

900g/2lb firm pears

1 Using a sharp knife, thinly pare a few strips of rind from the lemon. Squeeze out 30ml/2 tbsp of the juice and put it in a large pan with the strips of rind.

2 Add the sugar, vinegar, spices and water to the pan. Heat gently, stirring occasionally, until the sugar has completely dissolved, then slowly bring to the boil.

VARIATION

Nectarines and peaches may be pickled using the same method. Blanch and skin the fruits, then halve and stone (pit). Add a strip of orange rind to the syrup instead of lemon rind.

3 Meanwhile, prepare the pears. Peel and halve the pears, then scoop out the cores using a melon baller or small teaspoon. If the pears are very large, cut them into quarters rather than halves.

4 Add the pears to the pan and simmer very gently for about 20 minutes, or until tender and translucent but still whole. Check the pears frequently towards the end of the cooking time. Using a slotted spoon, remove the pears from the pan and pack into hot sterilized jars, adding the spices and strips of lemon rind.

5 Boil the syrup for 5 minutes, or until slightly reduced. Skim off any scum, then ladle the syrup over the pears. Cover and seal. Store for at least 1 month before eating.

Energy 2133kcal/9086kJ; Protein 5g; Carbohydrate 560.3g, of which sugars 560.3g; Fat 0.9g, of which saturates 0g; Cholesterol 0mg; Calcium 338mg; Fibre 19.8g; Sodium 54mg.

mulled pears

These pretty pears in a warming spiced syrup make a tempting dessert, particularly during the cold winter months. Serve them with crème fraîche or vanilla ice cream, or in open tarts.

Makes about 1.3kg/3lb

INGREDIENTS

1.8kg/4lb small firm pears

1 orange

1 lemon

2 cinnamon sticks, halved

12 whole cloves

5cm/2in piece fresh root ginger, peeled and sliced

300g/11oz/1½ cups granulated (white) sugar

1 bottle fruity light red wine

COOK'S TIP

Pears have a delicate flavour, so use a light, fruity wine such as Beaujolais or Merlot to make the syrup.

1 Peel the pears leaving the stalks intact. Peel very thin strips of rind from the orange and lemon, using a vegetable peeler. Pack the pears and citrus rind into large sterilized preserving jars, dividing the spices evenly between the jars.

2 Preheat the oven to 120°C/250°F/Gas ½. Put the sugar and wine in a large pan and heat gently, stirring, until the sugar has completely dissolved. Bring the mixture to the boil, then cook for 5 minutes.

3 Pour the wine syrup over the pears, making sure that there are no air pockets and that the fruits are completely covered with the syrup.

4 Cover the jars with their lids, but do not seal. Place them in the oven and cook for 2½–3 hours.

5 Carefully remove the jars from the oven, place on a dry dishtowel and seal. Leave the jars to cool completely, then label and store in a cool, dark place.

COOK'S TIP

To check that jars are properly sealed, leave them to cool for 24 hours, then loosen the clasp. Very carefully, try lifting the jar by the lid alone: if the jar is sealed properly, the lid should be fixed firmly enough to take the weight of the pot. Replace the clasp and store until ready to use.

Energy 2412kcal/10208kJ; Protein 7.7g; Carbohydrate 495g, of which sugars 495g; Fat 1.8g, of which saturates 0g; Cholesterol 0mg; Calcium 410mg; Fibre 39.6g; Sodium 125mg.

poached spiced plums in brandy

Bottling plums in a spicy syrup is a great way to preserve the flavours of autumn and provide a store of instant desserts during the winter months. Serve them with whipped cream.

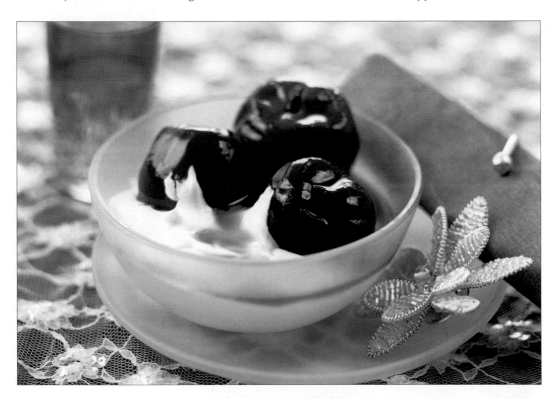

Makes about 900g/2lb

INGREDIENTS

600ml/1 pint/2½ cups brandy
rind of 1 lemon, peeled in a long strip
350g/12oz/1¾ cups caster
 (superfine) sugar
1 cinnamon stick
900g/2lb plums

VARIATION

Any member of the plum family can be preserved using this recipe. Try bottling damsons or wild yellow plums as a delicious alternative. Cherries will also work very well.

1 Put the brandy, lemon rind, sugar and cinnamon in a large pan and heat gently until the sugar dissolves. Add the plums and poach for 15 minutes until soft. Remove the fruit and pack in sterilized jars.

2 Boil the syrup rapidly until reduced by a third, then strain over the plums to cover. Seal the jars tightly. Label when cold and store for up to 6 months in a cool, dark place.

Energy 3035kcal/12793kJ; Protein 7.2g; Carbohydrate 444.9g, of which sugars 444.9g; Fat 0.9g, of which saturates 0g; Cholesterol 0mg; Calcium 303mg; Fibre 14.4g; Sodium 39mg.

apricots in amaretto syrup

Amaretto brings out the delicious flavour of apricots. Try serving the drained fruit on top of a tart filled with crème patissière, using some of the amaretto syrup to glaze the apricots.

2 Add the apricots to the syrup and bring almost to the boil. Cover and simmer gently for 5 minutes. Remove the apricots with a slotted spoon and drain in a colander.

3 Add the remaining sugar to the pan and heat gently, stirring until the sugar has dissolved, then boil rapidly until the syrup reaches 104°C/219°F. Cool slightly, then remove the vanilla pod and stir in the amaretto.

4 Pack the apricots loosely in large, warmed sterilized jars. Pour the syrup over, twisting and tapping the jars to expel any air. Seal and store in a cool, dark place for 2 weeks before eating.

Makes about 900g/2lb

INGREDIENTS

1.3kg/3lb firm apricots

1 litre/1¾ pints/4 cups water

800g/1¾lb/4 cups granulated (white) sugar

1 vanilla pod (bean)

175ml/6fl oz/¾ cup amaretto liqueur

1 Cut a slit in each apricot and remove the stone (pit), keeping the fruit intact. Put the water, half the sugar and the vanilla pod in a large pan, heat gently, stirring, until the sugar dissolves. Increase the heat and simmer for 5 minutes.

COOK'S TIP

For the best results, make this preserve when apricots are in season. Choose firm, unblemished fruits blushed with pink, that give slightly when squeezed gently in the palm of the hand.

Energy 3890kcal/16577kJ; Protein 12.1g; Carbohydrate 958.2g, of which sugars 958.2g; Fat 0.9g, of which saturates 0g; Cholesterol 0mg; Calcium 568mg; Fibre 15.3g; Sodium 87mg.

figs infused with earl grey

The aromatic flavour of Earl Grey tea in this syrup permeates the figs to create a sweet and intriguing flavour. They are delicious spooned over creamy Greek yogurt.

Makes about 1.8kg/4lb

INGREDIENTS

900g/2lb ready-to-eat dried figs
1.2 litres/2 pints/5 cups Earl Grey tea
pared rind of 1 orange
1 cinnamon stick
275g/10oz/1⅓ cups granulated (white) sugar
250ml/8fl oz/1 cup brandy

VARIATION

Use Grand Marnier or Cointreau instead of brandy to emphasize the flavour of zesty orange in the syrup.

1 Put the figs in a pan and add the tea, orange rind and cinnamon stick. Bring to the boil, cover and simmer for 10–15 minutes, or until the figs are tender.

2 Using a slotted spoon, remove the figs from the pan and leave to drain. Add the sugar to the tea and heat gently, stirring, until the sugar has dissolved. Boil rapidly for 2 minutes until syrupy.

3 Remove the pan from the heat, then stir in the brandy. Pack the figs and orange rind into warmed sterilized jars and pour in the hot syrup to cover. Twist and gently tap the jars to expel any air bubbles, then seal and store in a cool, dark place for 1 month.

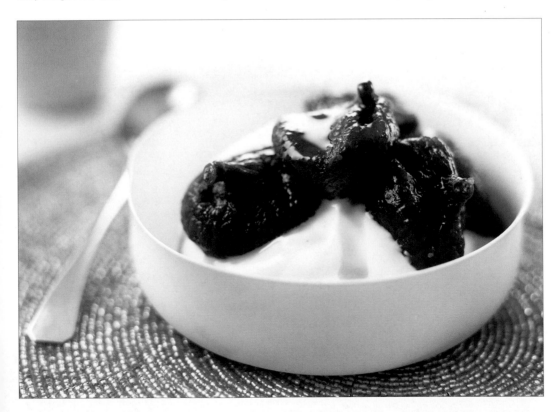

Energy 3520kcal/14921kJ; Protein 31.1g; Carbohydrate 724.8g, of which sugars 724.8g; Fat 13.5g, of which saturates 0g; Cholesterol 0mg; Calcium 2216mg; Fibre 62.1g; Sodium 530mg.

peaches in peach schnapps

The fragrant taste of peaches is complemented and intensified by the addition of the schnapps. Serve with whipped cream flavoured with some of the syrup and a squeeze of lemon juice.

Makes about 1.3kg/3lb

INGREDIENTS

1.3kg/3lb firm peaches

1 litre/1¾ pints/4 cups water

900g/2lb/4½ cups granulated (white) sugar

8 green cardamom pods

50g/2oz/½ cup whole blanched almonds, toasted

120ml/4fl oz/½ cup peach schnapps

VARIATION

Amaretto can be used instead of peach schnapps.

1 Put the peaches in a bowl and pour over boiling water. Drain immediately and peel, then halve and remove the stones (pits).

2 Put the water and half the sugar in a large pan and heat gently until the sugar has dissolved. Increase the heat and boil for 5 minutes.

3 Add the peaches to the syrup and return to the boil. Reduce the heat, cover and simmer gently for 5–10 minutes, or until tender but not too soft. Using a slotted spoon, remove the peaches and set aside to drain.

4 Put the cardamom pods and almonds in a large pan, then add 900ml/1½ pints/3¾ cups of the syrup and the remaining sugar.

5 Gently heat the syrup, stirring until the sugar has dissolved. Bring to the boil and boil until the syrup reaches 104°C/219°F. Leave to cool slightly, remove the cardamom pods, then stir in the schnapps.

6 Pack the peaches loosely in warmed sterilized jars. Pour the syrup and almonds over the fruit, twisting and gently tapping the jars to release any air bubbles. Seal and store in a cool, dark place for 2 weeks before eating.

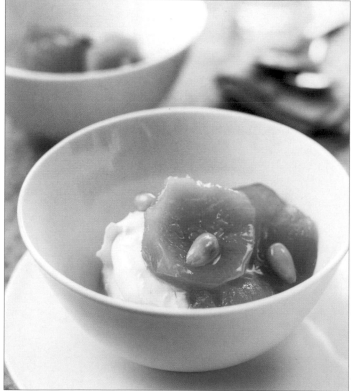

Energy 4595kcal/19561kJ; Protein 28.1g; Carbohydrate 1082.1g, of which sugars 1080.8g; Fat 29.2g, of which saturates 2.2g; Cholesterol 0mg; Calcium 694mg; Fibre 23.2g; Sodium 88mg.

pineapple in coconut rum

The tropical flavour of pineapple is enhanced by the addition of coconut rum. For a really special treat, serve topped with whipped cream and grated bitter chocolate.

Makes about 900g/2lb

INGREDIENTS

1 orange
1.2 litres/2 pints/5 cups water
900g/2lb/4½ cups granulated (white)
  sugar
2 pineapples, peeled, cored and cut
  into small chunks
300ml/½ pint/1¼ cups coconut rum

COOK'S TIP

Choose plump pineapples that feel heavy for their size, with fresh, stiff plumes. To test for ripeness, gently pull out one of the bottom leaves; it should come out easily.

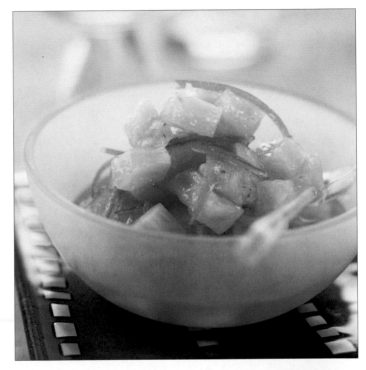

1 Thinly pare strips of rind from the orange, then slice into thin matchsticks. Put the water and half the sugar in a large pan with the orange rind and heat gently until the sugar has dissolved. Increase the heat and boil for 5 minutes.

2 Carefully add the pineapple pieces to the syrup and return to the boil. Reduce the heat and simmer gently for 10 minutes. Using a slotted spoon, remove the pineapple from the pan and set aside to drain.

3 Add the remaining sugar to the syrup and heat, stirring, until the sugar has dissolved completely. Bring to the boil and boil for about 10 minutes, or until the syrup has thickened. Remove from the heat and set aside to cool slightly, then stir in the coconut rum.

4 Pack the drained pineapple loosely into warmed sterilized jars. Pour in the syrup until the fruit is completely covered, tapping and twisting the jars to release any air bubbles before sealing. Seal, label and store in a cool, dark place for 2 weeks before eating.

Energy 4660kcal/19834kJ; Protein 7.7g; Carbohydrate 1119.7g, of which sugars 1119.7g; Fat 1.6g, of which saturates 0g; Cholesterol 0mg; Calcium 636mg; Fibre 9.6g; Sodium 106mg.

clementines in juniper syrup

These are lovely served with a spoonful of mascarpone, or can be added to trifles.

Makes about 1.3kg/3lb

INGREDIENTS

5cm/2in piece fresh root ginger, sliced

6 whole cloves, plus extra for the jars

5ml/1 tsp juniper berries, crushed, plus extra for the jars

900g/2lb/4½ cups granulated (white) sugar

1.2 litres/2 pints/5 cups water

1.3kg/3lb clementines, peeled

COOK'S TIPS

• These clementines look fabulous packed in jars and make an excellent Christmas gift for friends and family.
• When peeling the clementines, try to remove as much of the white pith from the fruit as possible.

1 Tie the ginger, cloves and juniper berries together in a small muslin (cheesecloth) bag.

2 Put the sugar and water in a large pan and heat gently, stirring, until the sugar has dissolved. Add the spice bag to the pan, bring to the boil and cook for 5 minutes.

3 Add the clementines to the pan and simmer for 8–10 minutes, or until tender. Using a slotted spoon, remove the fruit from the syrup and drain well.

4 Pack the hot fruit into warmed sterilized jars and add a few cloves and juniper berries to each jar. Pour off any excess liquid.

5 Return the syrup to the boil and boil rapidly for 10 minutes. Leave the syrup to cool slightly, then pour over the fruit to cover completely. Twist and gently tap the jars to release any trapped air bubbles, then seal and store in a cool, dark place.

Energy 4027kcal/17183kJ; Protein 16.2g; Carbohydrate 1053.6g, of which sugars 1053.6g; Fat 1.3g, of which saturates 0g; Cholesterol 0mg; Calcium 880mg; Fibre 15.6g; Sodium 106mg.

kumquats and limequats in brandy syrup

These yellow and green fruits are highly decorative and taste very good indeed. For a really indulgent dessert, serve these fruit pickles with good quality ice cream or baked custard.

Makes about 900g/2lb

INGREDIENTS

450g/1lb kumquats and limequats

175g/6oz/scant 1 cup granulated (white) sugar

600ml/1 pint/2½ cups water

150ml/¼ pint/⅔ cup brandy

15ml/1 tbsp orange flower water

COOK'S TIP

Kumquats and limequats are unusual among the citrus family because they are eaten whole and do not need to be peeled.

1 Using a cocktail stick (toothpick), prick each individual kumquat and limequat several times.

2 Put the sugar and water in a large pan and heat, stirring, until the sugar has dissolved. Bring to the boil, add the fruit and simmer for 25 minutes, or until tender. Using a slotted spoon, remove the fruit to warmed, sterilized jars.

3 The syrup should be fairly thick: if not, boil for a few minutes, then leave to cool very slightly.

4 Stir the brandy and orange flower water into the syrup, then pour over the fruit and seal immediately. Store in a cool, dark place and use within 6 months.

Energy 1189kcal/5031kJ; Protein 4.9g; Carbohydrate 222g, of which sugars 222g; Fat 0.5g, of which saturates 0g; Cholesterol 0mg; Calcium 232mg; Fibre 5.4g; Sodium 29mg.

forest berries in kirsch

This preserve captures the essence of the season in its rich, dark colour and flavour. Adding the sweet cherry liqueur Kirsch to the syrup intensifies the flavour of the bottled fruit.

Makes about 1.3kg/3lb

INGREDIENTS

1.3kg/3lb/12 cups mixed prepared
summer berries, such as blackberries,
raspberries, strawberries, redcurrants
and cherries

225g/8oz/generous 1 cup
granulated sugar

600ml/1 pint/2½ cups water

120ml/4fl oz/½ cup Kirsch

COOK'S TIP

Be careful not to overcook the fruits because they will lose their beautiful colour and fresh flavour.

1 Preheat the oven to 120°C/ 250°F/Gas ½. Pack the prepared fruit loosely into sterilized jars. Cover without sealing and place in the oven for 50–60 minutes, or until the juices start to run.

2 Meanwhile, put the sugar and water in a large pan and heat gently, stirring, until the sugar has dissolved. Increase the heat, bring to the boil and boil for 5 minutes. Stir in the Kirsch and set aside.

3 Carefully remove the jars from the oven and place on a dishtowel. Use the fruit from one of the jars to top up the rest.

4 Pour the boiling syrup into each jar, twisting and tapping each one to ensure that no air bubbles have been trapped. Seal, then store in a cool, dark place.

Energy 1518kcal/6487kJ; Protein 19.3g; Carbohydrate 334g, of which sugars 334g; Fat 3.9g, of which saturates 1.3g; Cholesterol 0mg; Calcium 444mg; Fibre 32.5g; Sodium 53mg.

cherries in eau de vie

These potent cherries should be consumed with respect as they pack quite an alcoholic punch. Serve them with rich, dark chocolate torte or as a wicked topping for creamy rice pudding.

2 Spoon the sugar over the fruit, then pour in the eau de vie to cover and seal tightly.

3 Store for at least 1 month before serving, shaking the bottle now and then to help dissolve the sugar.

COOK'S TIP

Eau de vie actually refers to all spirits distilled from fermented fruits. Eau de vie is always colourless, with a high alcohol content (sometimes 45% ABV) and a clean, pure scent and the flavour of the founding fruit. Popular eaux de vie are made from cherries and strawberries.

Makes about 1.3kg/3lb

INGREDIENTS

450g/1lb/generous 3 cups ripe cherries
8 blanched almonds
75g/3oz/6 tbsp granulated (white) sugar
500ml/17fl oz/scant 2¼ cups eau de vie

VARIATIONS

Strawberries, raspberries and blackcurrants are all excellent preserved in eau de vie. They will all produce fine fruity liqueurs as well as the macerated fruit.

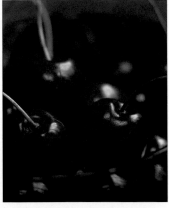

1 Wash and stone (pit) the cherries then pack them into a sterilized, wide-necked bottle along with the blanched almonds.

Energy 1479kcal/6142kJ; Protein 9.3g; Carbohydrate 53.5g, of which sugars 52.8g; Fat 14.4g, of which saturates 1.1g; Cholesterol 0mg; Calcium 119mg; Fibre 5.9g; Sodium 8mg.

blackcurrant brandy

Spoon a little of the brandy into a wine glass and top up with chilled white wine or champagne.

Makes about 1 litre/1¾ pints/4 cups

INGREDIENTS

900g/2lb/8 cups blackcurrants, washed
600ml/1 pint/2½ cups brandy
350g/12oz/1¾ cups granulated (white)
  sugar

COOK'S TIP

When you have strained off the brandy, reserve the blackcurrants and freeze for later use. They are great added to fruit salads and trifles, or make a delicious richly flavoured ice cream topping. Be careful though, because they pack quite a boozy punch.

1 Strip the blackcurrants off their stems and pack the fruit into a sterilized 1.5 litre/2½ pint/6¼ cup preserving jar. Using the back of a wooden spoon, crush the blackcurrants lightly.

2 Add the brandy and sugar to the jar, ensuring the fruit is completely covered by the brandy. Twist and gently tap the jar to ensure there are no trapped air bubbles.

3 Seal the jar, then store in a cool, dark place for about 2 months, shaking the jar occasionally.

4 Pour the liquor through a sieve lined with a double layer of muslin (cheesecloth) into a sterilized jug (pitcher). Pour into sterilized bottles, seal, label and store in a cool, dark place.

Energy 2963kcal/12487kJ; Protein 9.8g; Carbohydrate 425.1g, of which sugars 425.1g; Fat 0g, of which saturates 0g; Cholesterol 0mg; Calcium 726mg; Fibre 32.4g; Sodium 48mg.

blueberries in gin syrup

This syrup turns a fabulous blue colour and the distinctive flavour of the gin complements, rather than masks, the essence of the blueberries.

Makes about 1.8kg/4lb

INGREDIENTS

1.3kg/3lb/12 cups blueberries
225g/8oz/1 cup granulated (white) sugar
600ml/1 pint/2½ cups water
120ml/4fl oz/½ cup gin

1 Preheat the oven to 120°C/250°F/Gas ½. Pack the blueberries into sterilized jars and cover, without sealing. Put the jars in the oven and bake for 50–60 minutes until the juices start to run.

2 Meanwhile, put the sugar and water in a pan and gently heat, stirring continuously, until the sugar has dissolved completely. Increase the heat and boil for 5 minutes. Stir in the gin.

3 Carefully remove the jars from the oven and place on a dry dishtowel. Use the fruit from one of the jars to top up the others.

4 Carefully pour the boiling gin syrup into the jars to completely cover the fruit. Twist and gently tap the jars to ensure that no air bubbles have been trapped.

5 Seal, then store in a cool, dark place until ready to serve.

Energy 1478kcal/6237kJ; Protein 12.8g; Carbohydrate 301.4g, of which sugars 301.4g; Fat 2.6g, of which saturates 0g; Cholesterol 0mg; Calcium 652mg; Fibre 40.3g; Sodium 40mg.

rumtopf

This fruit preserve originated in Germany, where special earthenware rumtopf pots are traditionally filled with fruits as they come into season. It is not necessary to use the specific pot; you can use a large preserving jar instead. Store in a cool, dark place.

Makes about 3 litres/5 pints/12½ cups

INGREDIENTS

900g/2lb fruit, such as strawberries, blackberries, blackcurrants, redcurrants, peaches, apricots, cherries and plums

250g/9oz/1¼ cups granulated (white) sugar

1 litre/1¾ pints/4 cups white rum

1 Prepare the fruit: remove stems, skins, cores and stones (pits) and cut larger fruit into pieces. Put the fruit and sugar in a bowl, cover and leave to stand for 30 minutes.

2 Spoon the fruit and juices into a sterilized 3 litre/5 pint/12½ cup preserving or earthenware jar and pour in the white rum to cover.

3 Cover the jar with clear film (plastic wrap), then seal and store in a cool, dark place.

4 As space allows, and as different fruits come into season, add more fruit, sugar and rum in appropriate proportions, as described above.

5 When the jar is full, store in a cool, dark place for 2 months. Serve the fruit spooned over ice cream or other desserts and enjoy the rum in glasses as a liqueur.

Energy 3448kcal/14410kJ; Protein 8.4g; Carbohydrate 315.3g, of which sugars 315.3g; Fat 0.9g, of which saturates 0g; Cholesterol 0mg; Calcium 277mg; Fibre 9.9g; Sodium 69mg.

spiced apple mincemeat

This fruity mincemeat is traditionally used to fill little pies at Christmas but it is great at any time. Try it as a filling for large tarts finished with a lattice top and served with custard. To make a lighter mincemeat, add some extra grated apple just before using.

Makes about 1.8kg/4lb

INGREDIENTS

500g/1¼lb tart cooking apples, peeled, cored and finely diced

115g/4oz/½ cup ready-to-eat dried apricots, coarsely chopped

900g/2lb/5⅓ cups luxury dried mixed fruit

115g/4oz/1 cup whole blanched almonds, chopped

175g/6oz/1 cup shredded beef or vegetarian suet (chilled, grated shortening)

225g/8oz/generous 1 cup dark muscovado (molasses) sugar

grated rind and juice of 1 orange

grated rind and juice of 1 lemon

5ml/1 tsp ground cinnamon

2.5ml/½ tsp grated nutmeg

2.5ml/½ tsp ground ginger

120ml/4fl oz/½ cup brandy

1 Put the apples, apricots, dried fruit, almonds, suet and sugar in a large non-metallic bowl and stir together until thoroughly combined.

2 Add the orange and lemon rind and juice, cinnamon, nutmeg, ginger and brandy and mix well. Cover the bowl with a clean dishtowel and leave to stand in a cool place for 2 days, stirring occasionally.

3 Spoon the mincemeat into cool sterilized jars, pressing down well, and being very careful not to trap any air bubbles. Cover and seal.

4 Store the jars in a cool, dark place for at least 4 weeks before using. Once opened, store in the refrigerator and use within 4 weeks. Unopened, the mincemeat will keep for 1 year.

COOK'S TIP

If, when opened, the mincemeat seems dry, pour a little extra brandy or orange juice into the jar and gently stir in. You may need to remove a spoonful or two of the mincemeat from the jar to do this.

Energy 6071kcal/25579kJ; Protein 52.2g; Carbohydrate 963.6g, of which sugars 939.7g; Fat 227.3g, of which saturates 92.4g; Cholesterol 144mg; Calcium 1156mg; Fibre 44.4g; Sodium 488mg.

savoury and sweet jellies

Jellies are sumptuously slow preserves, not to be rushed in the preparation, but to gently drip their juicy yield through old-fashioned jelly bags. Then a miraculous transformation turns the cloudy, dull and tart liquid into a bright, exciting firm fruit gem as sugar is added. As well as sweet fruit, herbs and spices bring glorious flavour to savoury jellies. They may be sharp with citrus or with vinegar, can also be added to sauces and gravies, or used to glaze fruity fillings in tarts and pastries.

lemon grass and ginger jelly

This aromatic jelly is delicious with Asian-style roast meat and poultry such as Chinese crispy duck. It is also the perfect foil for rich fish, especially cold smoked trout or mackerel.

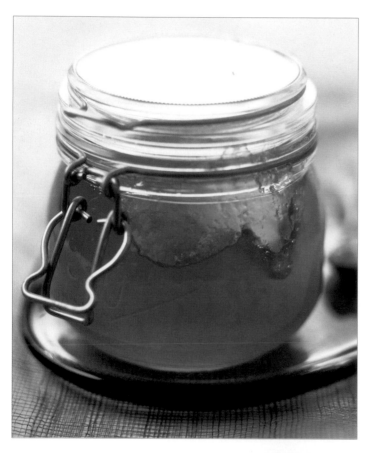

2 Put the chopped lemon grass in a preserving pan and pour over the water. Add the lemons and ginger. Bring to the boil, then reduce the heat, cover and simmer for 1 hour, or until the lemons are pulpy.

3 Pour the fruit and juices into a sterilized jelly bag suspended over a large bowl. Leave to drain for at least 3 hours, or until the juice stops dripping.

4 Measure the juice into the cleaned preserving pan, adding 450g/1lb/2¼ cups sugar for every 600ml/1 pint/2½ cups juice.

5 Heat the mixture gently, stirring occasionally, until the sugar has dissolved completely. Boil rapidly for about 10 minutes until the jelly reaches setting point (105°C/220°F). Remove from the heat.

6 Skim any scum off the surface using a slotted spoon, then pour the jelly into warmed sterilized jars, cover and seal. Store in a cool, dark place and use within 1 year. Once opened, keep in the refrigerator. Eat within 3 months.

Makes about 900g/2lb

INGREDIENTS

2 lemon grass stalks

1.5 litres/2½ pints/6¼ cups water

1.3kg/3lb lemons, washed and cut into small pieces

50g/2oz fresh root ginger, unpeeled, thinly sliced

about 450g/1lb/2¼ cups preserving or granulated (white) sugar

1 Using a rolling pin, bruise the lemon grass, then chop roughly.

Energy 1715kcal/7304kJ; Protein 27.4g; Carbohydrate 417.1g, of which sugars 231.8g; Fat 4.5g, of which saturates 0.7g; Cholesterol 0mg; Calcium 63mg; Fibre 14.4g; Sodium 41mg.

roasted red pepper and chilli jelly

The hint of chilli in this glowing red jelly makes it ideal for spicing up hot or cold roast meat, sausages or hamburgers. The jelly is also good stirred into sauces or used as a glaze for poultry.

Makes about 900g/2lb

INGREDIENTS

8 red (bell) peppers, quartered
  and seeded
4 fresh red chillies, halved and seeded
1 onion, roughly chopped
2 garlic cloves, roughly chopped
250ml/8fl oz/1 cup water
250ml/8fl oz/1 cup white wine vinegar
7.5ml/1½ tsp salt
450g/1lb/2¼ cups preserving
  or granulated (white) sugar
25ml/1½ tbsp powdered pectin

4 Scrape the purée into a large stainless steel pan, then stir in the white wine vinegar and salt.

5 In a bowl, combine the sugar and pectin, then stir it into the pepper mixture. Heat gently, stirring, until the sugar and pectin have dissolved completely, then bring to a rolling boil. Cook the jelly, stirring frequently, for exactly 4 minutes, then remove the pan from the heat.

6 Pour the jelly into warmed, sterilized jars. Leave to cool and set, then cover, label and store.

1 Arrange the peppers, skin side up, on a rack in a grill (broiling) pan and grill (broil) until the skins blister and blacken.

2 Put the peppers in a polythene bag until they are cool enough to handle, then remove the skins.

3 Put the skinned peppers, chillies, onion, garlic and water in a food processor or blender and process to a purée. Press the purée through a nylon sieve set over a bowl, pressing hard with a wooden spoon, to extract as much juice as possible. There should be about 750ml/1¼ pints/3 cups.

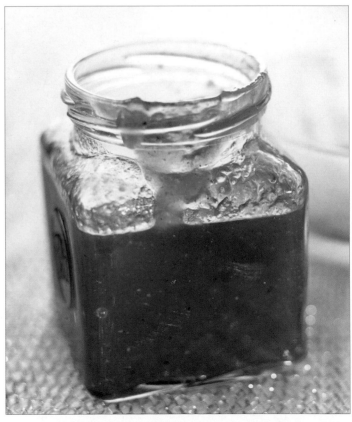

Energy 2275kcal/9665kJ; Protein 18g; Carbohydrate 571g, of which sugars 565.1g; Fat 6.1g, of which saturates 1.5g; Cholesterol 0mg; Calcium 374mg; Fibre 24.8g; Sodium 89mg.

tomato and herb jelly

This dark golden jelly is delicious served with roast and grilled meats, especially lamb. It is also great for enlivening tomato-based pasta sauces: stirring a couple of teaspoons of the jelly into sauces helps to heighten their flavour and counteract acidity.

Makes about 1.3kg/3lb

INGREDIENTS

1.8kg/4lb tomatoes

2 lemons

2 bay leaves

300ml/½ pint/1¼ cups cold water

250ml/8fl oz/1 cup malt vinegar

bunch of fresh herbs such as rosemary, thyme, parsley and mint, plus a few extra sprigs for the jars

about 900g/2lb/4½ cups preserving or granulated (white) sugar

COOK'S TIP

Once you have opened a jar of this jelly, store it in the refrigerator and use within 3 months.

1 Wash the tomatoes and lemons well, then cut the tomatoes into quarters and the lemons into small pieces. Put the chopped tomatoes and lemons in a large heavy pan with the bay leaves and pour over the water and vinegar.

2 Add the herbs, either one herb or a mixture if preferred. (If you are using pungent woody herbs such as rosemary and thyme, use about six sprigs; if you are using milder leafy herbs such as parsley or mint, add about 12 large sprigs.)

3 Bring the mixture to the boil, then reduce the heat. Cover the pan with a lid and simmer for about 40 minutes, or until the tomatoes are very soft.

4 Pour the tomato mixture and all the juices into a sterilized jelly bag suspended over a large bowl. Leave to drain for about 3 hours, or until the juices stop dripping.

5 Measure the juice into the cleaned pan, adding 450g/1lb/2¼ cups sugar for every 600ml/1 pint/2½ cups juice. Heat gently, stirring, until the sugar dissolves. Boil rapidly for 10 minutes, to setting point (105°C/220°F), then remove from the heat. Skim off any scum.

6 Leave the jelly for a few minutes until a skin forms. Place a herb sprig in each warmed sterilized jar, then pour in the jelly. Cover and seal when cold. Store in a cool, dark place and use within 1 year.

Energy 3767kcal/16078kJ; Protein 13.6g; Carbohydrate 980.8g, of which sugars 980.8g; Fat 3.9g, of which saturates 1.3g; Cholesterol 0mg; Calcium 568mg; Fibre 13g; Sodium 171mg.

citrus thyme jelly

You can vary the sharpness of this jelly by altering the proportions of fruit. Use more oranges and fewer lemons and limes to obtain a milder, sweeter-tasting jelly.

Makes about 1.3kg/3lb

INGREDIENTS

675g/1½lb lemons
675g/1½lb limes
450g/1lb oranges
2 bay leaves
2 litres/3½ pints/8¾ cups water
about 800g/1¾lb/4 cups preserving or granulated (white) sugar
60ml/4 tbsp fresh thyme leaves

COOK'S TIP

It is important to stir the jelly before potting to re-distribute the herbs.

1 Wash all the fruit, then cut into small pieces. Place in a large heavy pan with the bay leaves and pour over the water.

2 Bring the mixture to the boil, then reduce the heat, cover and simmer for 1 hour, or until pulpy. Discard the bay leaves, then pour the fruit and juices into a sterilized jelly bag suspended over a large bowl. Leave to drain for 3 hours, or until the juices stop dripping.

3 Measure the juice into the cleaned pan, adding 450g/1lb/ 2¼ cups sugar for every 600ml/ 1 pint/2½ cups juice. Heat gently until the sugar has dissolved. Bring to the boil, then boil rapidly for about 10 minutes, or until setting point is reached (105°C/220°F). Remove the pan from the heat.

4 Skim any scum off the surface, then stir in the thyme leaves. Leave to cool for a few minutes until a thin skin forms, then gently stir again to make sure the thyme is evenly distributed.

5 Pour the jelly into warmed sterilized jars. Cover and seal when cold. Store in a cool, dark place and use within 1 year. Once opened, store in the refrigerator and eat within 3 months.

Energy 3154kcal/13455kJ; Protein 4.2g; Carbohydrate 836.1g, of which sugars 836.1g; Fat 0.1g, of which saturates 0g; Cholesterol 0mg; Calcium 434mg; Fibre 0.3g; Sodium 50mg.

bitter lime and juniper jelly

In this sharp, aromatic jelly the distinctive taste of zesty lime and the rich, resinous flavour of juniper berries is enhanced with a hint of aniseed from the splash of Pernod.

Makes about 1.6kg/3½lb

INGREDIENTS

6 limes
1.3kg/3lb tart cooking apples
6 juniper berries, crushed
1.75 litres/3 pints/7½ cups water
about 800g/1¾lb/4 cups preserving
  or granulated (white) sugar
45ml/3 tbsp Pernod (optional)

1 Wash the limes and apples, then cut them into small pieces. Put them in a large heavy pan with the juniper berries. Pour over the water, then bring to the boil and simmer for about 1 hour, or until the fruit is very tender and pulpy.

2 Pour the fruit and juices into a sterilized jelly bag suspended over a large bowl. Leave the fruit to drain for at least 3 hours, until the juices stop dripping.

3 Measure the juice into the cleaned pan, adding 450g/1lb/ 2¼ cups sugar for every 600ml/ 1 pint/2½ cups juice. Heat gently, stirring occasionally, until the sugar has dissolved. Boil rapidly for about 10 minutes, to setting point (105°C/220°F), then remove the pan from the heat.

4 Skim any scum off the surface using a slotted spoon, then stir in the Pernod, if using. Pour the jelly into warmed sterilized jars, cover and seal immediately.

5 Store the jelly in a cool, dark place and use within 1 year. Once opened, keep in the refrigerator and eat within 3 months.

COOK'S TIP

When using citrus fruits for preserves, try to use unwaxed ones. If they are unavailable, scrub waxed fruits well.

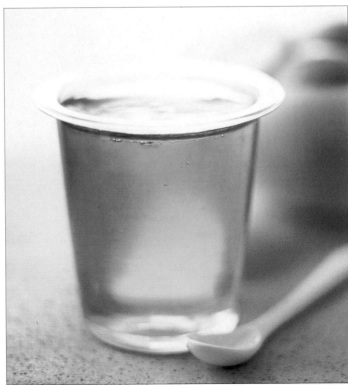

Energy 3152kcal/13448kJ; Protein 4g; Carbohydrate 836g, of which sugars 836g; Fat 0g, of which saturates 0g; Cholesterol 0mg; Calcium 424mg; Fibre 0g; Sodium 48mg.

apple, orange and cider jelly

A spoonful or two of this tangy amber jelly adds a real sparkle to a plate of cold meats, especially ham and pork or rich game pâtés. Tart cooking apples make the best-flavoured jelly, while the addition of cloves gives it a wonderfully warm, spicy taste and aroma.

Makes about 1.8kg/4lb

INGREDIENTS

1.3kg/3lb tart cooking apples

4 oranges

4 whole cloves

1.2 litres/2 pints/5 cups sweet cider

about 600ml/1 pint/2½ cups cold water

about 800g/1¾lb/4 cups preserving
  or granulated (white) sugar

VARIATION

Replace some of the apples with crab apples for a more distinctive taste.

1 Wash and chop the apples and oranges, then put in a preserving pan with the cloves, cider and water to barely cover the fruit.

2 Bring the mixture to the boil, cover and simmer gently for 1 hour, stirring occasionally.

3 Pour the fruit and juices into a sterilized jelly bag suspended over a large bowl. Leave to drain for at least 4 hours, or overnight, until the juices stop dripping.

4 Measure the juice into the cleaned preserving pan, adding 450g/1lb/2¼ cups sugar for every 600ml/1 pint/2½ cups juice.

5 Heat the mixture gently stirring, until the sugar has dissolved. Boil rapidly for about 10 minutes until setting point is reached (105°C/ 220°F). Remove from the heat.

6 Skim any scum off the surface, then pour the jelly into warmed sterilized jars. Cover and seal. Store in a cool, dark place and use within 18 months. Once opened, store in the refrigerator and eat within 3 months.

Energy 3442kcal/14691kJ; Protein 10.4g; Carbohydrate 905.2g, of which sugars 905.2g; Fat 0.8g, of which saturates 0g; Cholesterol 0mg; Calcium 671mg; Fibre 13.3g; Sodium 79mg.

quince and rosemary jelly

The amount of water needed for this jelly varies according to the ripeness of the fruit. For a good set, hard under-ripe quinces should be used as they contain the most pectin. If the fruit is soft and ripe, add a little lemon juice along with the water.

Makes about 900g/2lb

INGREDIENTS

900g/2lb quinces, cut into small pieces, with bruised parts removed

900ml–1.2 litres/1½–2 pints/ 3¾–5 cups water

lemon juice (optional)

4 large sprigs of fresh rosemary

about 900g/2lb/4½ cups preserving or granulated (white) sugar

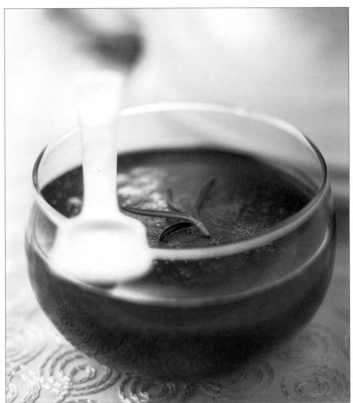

1 Put the chopped quinces in a large heavy pan with the water, using the smaller volume if the fruit is ripe and the larger volume plus lemon juice if it is hard.

2 Reserve a few small sprigs of rosemary, then add the rest to the pan. Bring to the boil, reduce the heat, cover with a lid and simmer gently until the fruit becomes pulpy.

3 Remove and discard all the rosemary sprigs. (Don't worry about any tiny leaves that have fallen off during cooking). Pour the fruit and juices into a sterilized jelly bag suspended over a large bowl. Leave for 3 hours, or until the juices stop dripping.

4 Measure the drained juice into the cleaned pan, adding 450g/1lb/ 2¼ cups sugar for every 600ml/ 1 pint/2½ cups juice.

5 Heat the mixture gently over a low heat, stirring occasionally, until the sugar has dissolved completely. Bring to the boil, then boil rapidly for about 10 minutes until the jelly reaches setting point (105°C/220°F). Remove the pan from the heat.

6 Skim any scum from the surface using a slotted spoon, then leave the jelly to cool for a few minutes until a thin skin begins to form on the surface.

7 Place a sprig of rosemary in each warmed sterilized jar, then pour in the jelly. Cover and seal when cold. Store in a cool, dark place and use within 1 year. Once the jelly is opened, keep it in the refrigerator and use within 3 months.

Energy 3666kcal/15636kJ; Protein 5.4g; Carbohydrate 970.5g, of which sugars 970.5g; Fat 0.3g, of which saturates 0g; Cholesterol 0mg; Calcium 510mg; Fibre 6.6g; Sodium 63mg.

minted gooseberry jelly

The colour of this tart jelly is often a surprise as the gooseberry juice turns pink during cooking.

Makes about 1.2kg/2½lb

INGREDIENTS

1.3kg/3lb/12 cups gooseberries

1 bunch fresh mint

750ml/1¼ pints/3 cups cold water

400ml/14fl oz/1⅔ cups white wine vinegar

about 900g/2lb/4½ cups preserving or
  granulated (white) sugar

45ml/3 tbsp chopped fresh mint

1 Place the gooseberries, mint and water in a preserving pan. Bring to the boil, reduce the heat, cover and simmer for about 30 minutes, until the gooseberries are soft. Add the vinegar and simmer uncovered for a further 10 minutes.

2 Pour the fruit and juices into a sterilized jelly bag suspended over a large bowl. Leave to drain for at least 3 hours, or until the juices stop dripping, then measure the strained juices back into the cleaned preserving pan.

3 Add 450g/1lb/2½ cups sugar for every 600ml/1 pint/2½ cups juice, then heat gently, stirring, until the sugar has dissolved. Bring to the boil and cook for 15 minutes, or to setting point (105°C/220°F). Remove the pan from the heat.

4 Skim any scum from the surface. Leave to cool until a thin skin forms, then stir in the mint.

5 Pour the jelly into warmed sterilized jars, cover and seal. Store and use within 1 year. Once opened, store in the refrigerator and eat within 3 months.

Energy 3641kcal/15534kJ; Protein 10g; Carbohydrate 955.5g, of which sugars 955.5g; Fat 2g, of which saturates 0g; Cholesterol 0mg; Calcium 617mg; Fibre 12g; Sodium 64mg.

plum and apple jelly

This sweet jelly complements savoury dishes such as rich roast meats like lamb and pork.

Makes about 1.3kg/3lb

INGREDIENTS

900g/2lb plums

450g/1lb tart cooking apples

150ml/¼ pint/⅔ cup cider vinegar

750ml/1¼ pints/3 cups water

about 675g/1½lb/scant 3½ cups
  preserving or granulated (white) sugar

COOK'S TIPS

• Use dark red cooking plums, damsons or wild plums to offset the sweetness of this jelly.

• It can be stored for up to 2 years. However, once opened, it should be stored in the refrigerator and eaten within 3 months.

1 Cut the plums in half along the crease, twist the two halves apart, then remove the stones (pits) and roughly chop the flesh. Chop the apples, including the cores and skins. Put the fruit in a large heavy pan with the vinegar and water.

2 Bring the mixture to the boil, reduce the heat, cover and simmer for 30 minutes or until the fruit is soft and pulpy.

3 Pour the fruit and juices into a sterilized jelly bag suspended over a large bowl. Leave to drain for at least 3 hours, or until the fruit juices stop dripping.

4 Measure the juice into the cleaned pan, adding 450g/1lb/2¼ cups sugar for every 600ml/1 pint/2½ cups juice.

5 Bring the mixture to the boil, stirring occasionally, until the sugar has dissolved, then boil rapidly for about 10 minutes, or until the jelly reaches setting point (105°C/220°F). Remove the pan from the heat.

6 Skim any scum from from the surface, then pour the jelly into warmed sterilized jars. Cover and seal while hot. Store in a cool, dark place and use within 2 years.

Energy 2803kcal/11963kJ; Protein 5.5g; Carbohydrate 740.7g, of which sugars 740.7g; Fat 0.4g, of which saturates 0g; Cholesterol 0mg; Calcium 401mg; Fibre 6.4g; Sodium 49mg.

blackberry and sloe gin jelly

Although they have a wonderful flavour, blackberries are full of pips, so turning them into a deep-coloured jelly is a good way to make the most of this full-flavoured hedgerow harvest. This preserve is delicious served with richly flavoured roast meats such as lamb.

Makes about 1.3kg/3lb

INGREDIENTS

450g/1lb sloes (black plums)
600ml/1 pint/2½ cups cold water
1.8kg/4lb/16 cups blackberries
juice of 1 lemon
about 900g/2lb/4½ cups preserving
  or granulated (white) sugar
45ml/3 tbsp gin

VARIATION

Sloes (black plums) are much harder to come by than blackberries and you will usually need to find them growing in the wild. If you can't find sloes, use extra blackberries in their place.

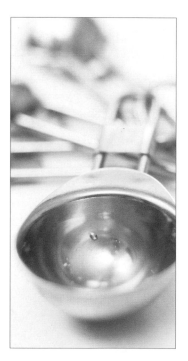

1 Wash the sloes and prick with a fine skewer. Put them in a large heavy pan with the water and bring to the boil. Reduce the heat, cover and simmer for 5 minutes.

2 Briefly rinse the blackberries in cold water and add them to the pan with the lemon juice.

3 Bring the fruit mixture back to a simmer and cook gently for about 20 minutes, or until the sloes are tender and the blackberries very soft, stirring once or twice.

4 Pour the fruit and juices into a sterilized jelly bag suspended over a large bowl. Leave to drain for at least 4 hours or overnight, until the juices have stopped dripping.

5 Measure the fruit juice into the cleaned preserving pan, adding 450g/1lb/2¼ cups sugar for every 600ml/1 pint/2½ cups juice.

6 Heat the mixture gently, stirring occasionally, until the sugar has dissolved completely. Bring to the boil, then boil rapidly for about 10 minutes until the jelly reaches setting point (105°C/220°F). Remove the pan from the heat.

7 Skim off any scum from the surface of the jelly using a slotted spoon, then stir in the gin.

8 Pour the jelly into warmed sterilized jars, cover and seal. Store in a cool, dark place and use within 2 years. Once opened, keep the jelly in the refrigerator and eat within 3 months.

COOK'S TIP

Sloes (black plums) bring a good level of pectin to the jelly. If all blackberries are used without sloes, select some under-ripe fruit and use preserving sugar with added pectin.

Energy 3750kcal/15986kJ; Protein 10.8g; Carbohydrate 984.3g, of which sugars 984.3g; Fat 1.3g, of which saturates 0g; Cholesterol 0mg; Calcium 743mg; Fibre 21g; Sodium 69mg.

cranberry and claret jelly

The slight sharpness of cranberries makes this a superb jelly for serving with rich meats such as lamb or game. Together with claret, the cranberries give the jelly a beautiful deep red colour.

Makes about 1.2kg/2½lb

INGREDIENTS

900g/2lb/8 cups fresh or
  frozen cranberries

350ml/12fl oz/1½ cups water

about 900g//2lb/4½ cups preserving
  or granulated (white) sugar

250ml/8fl oz/1 cup claret

COOK'S TIP

When simmering the cranberries, keep the pan covered until they stop "popping", as they can occasionally explode and jump out of the pan.

1 Wash the cranberries, if fresh, and put them in a large heavy pan with the water. Cover the pan and bring to the boil.

2 Reduce the heat under the pan and simmer for about 20 minutes, or until the cranberries are soft.

3 Pour the fruit and juices into a sterilized jelly bag suspended over a large bowl. Leave to drain for at least 3 hours or overnight, until the juices stop dripping.

4 Measure the juice and wine into the cleaned preserving pan, adding 400g/14oz/2 cups preserving or granulated sugar for every 600ml/ 1 pint/2½ cups liquid.

5 Heat the mixture gently, stirring occasionally, until the sugar has dissolved, then bring to the boil and boil rapidly for 10 minutes until the jelly reaches setting point (105°C/220°F). Remove the pan from the heat.

6 Skim any scum from the surface using a slotted spoon and pour the jelly into warmed sterilized jars. Cover and seal. Store in a cool, dark place and use within 2 years. Once opened, keep the jelly in the refrigerator and eat within 3 months.

Energy 3821kcal/16290kJ; Protein 5.7g; Carbohydrate 967.7g, of which sugars 967.7g; Fat 0.3g, of which saturates 0g; Cholesterol 0mg; Calcium 507mg; Fibre 4.8g; Sodium 78mg.

red grape, plum and cardamom jelly

Enhance the flavour of roast beef and steaks with a spoonful of deep ruby-coloured jelly.
You may need to add a little pectin to the jelly to ensure you achieve a really good set.

Makes about 1.3kg/3lb

INGREDIENTS

1.8kg/4lb plums
450g/1lb/3 cups red grapes
15ml/1 tbsp cardamom pods
600ml/1 pint/2½ cups cold water
350–450ml/12fl oz–¾ pint/1½ cups–
  scant 2 cups pectin stock (optional)
about 1kg/2¼lb/5 cups preserving
  or granulated (white) sugar

1 Cut the plums in half, then twist the two halves apart and remove the stone (pit). Roughly chop the flesh and halve the grapes. Remove the cardamom seeds from the pods and crush them in a mortar.

2 Put the fruit and cardamom seeds in a large heavy pan and pour over the water. Slowly bring to the boil, then simmer for about 30 minutes, or until very tender.

3 Check the pectin content of the fruit (see below); if it is low, stir the pectin stock into the fruit mixture and simmer for 5 minutes.

COOK'S TIP

To check the pectin content of the fruit, spoon 5ml/1 tsp of the juices into a glass. Add 15ml/1 tbsp of methylated spirits (denatured alcohol) and shake gently. After about a minute a clot should form. If the clot is large and jelly-like or if two or three smaller clots form, the pectin content should be sufficient for a set. If there are lots of small clots, or none at all, the pectin content is low and additional pectin will be needed.

4 Pour the fruit into a sterilized jelly bag suspended over a large bowl. Leave to drain for 3 hours, or until the juices stop dripping. Measure the juice into a clean pan, adding 450g/1lb/2¼ cups sugar for every 600ml/1 pint/2½ cups juice.

5 Heat the mixture gently, stirring occasionally, until the sugar has completely dissolved.

6 Bring the mixture to the boil, then boil rapidly for 10 minutes until setting point is reached (105°C/220°F). Remove the pan from the heat.

7 Skim off any scum from the surface, then pour the jelly into warmed sterilized jars, cover and seal. Store in a cool, dark place and use within 2 years. Keep in the refrigerator once opened, and eat within 3 months.

Energy 4246kcal/18126kJ; Protein 9.2g; Carbohydrate 1120.9g, of which sugars 1120.9g; Fat 0.8g, of which saturates 0g; Cholesterol 0mg; Calcium 628mg; Fibre 10.7g; Sodium 75mg.

pear and pomegranate jelly

This delicate jelly has a faintly exotic perfume. Pears are not naturally rich in pectin so liquid pectin needs to be added to the jelly during cooking to help it achieve a good set.

4 While the pears are simmering, cut the pomegranates in half horizontally, and use a lemon squeezer to extract all the juice: there should be about 250ml/ 8fl oz/1 cup.

5 Add the pomegranate juice to the pan and bring back to the boil. Reduce the heat and simmer for 2 minutes. Pour the fruit and juices into a sterilized jelly bag suspended over a large bowl. Leave to drip for at least 3 hours.

6 Measure the strained juice into the cleaned pan, adding 450g/1lb/ 2¼ cups sugar for every 600ml/ 1 pint/2½ cups juice.

Makes about 1.2kg/2½lb

INGREDIENTS

900g/2lb pears
pared rind and juice of 2 lemons
1 cinnamon stick
750ml/1¼ pints/3 cups water
900g/2lb red pomegranates
about 900g/2lb/4½ cups preserving or
   granulated (white) sugar
250ml/8fl oz/1 cup liquid pectin
15ml/1 tbsp rose water (optional)

COOK'S TIP

Once opened, store the jelly in the refrigerator and use within 3 months.

1 Wash and remove the stalks from the pears and chop the fruit roughly. Put the chopped fruit in a large heavy pan with the lemon rind and juice, cinnamon stick and measured water.

2 Bring the mixture to the boil, then reduce the heat to low, cover with a lid and simmer gently for about 15 minutes.

3 Remove the lid from the pan, stir the fruit mixture, then leave to simmer, uncovered, for a further 15 minutes.

7 Heat gently, stirring occasionally, until the sugar has dissolved. Bring to the boil, then boil rapidly for 3 minutes. Remove the pan from the heat and stir in the liquid pectin.

8 Skim any scum from the surface, then stir in the rose water, if using. Pour the jelly into warmed sterilized jars. Cover and seal. Store in a cool, dark place and use within 18 months.

Energy 3756kcal/16022kJ; Protein 6g; Carbohydrate 993.6g, of which sugars 993.6g; Fat 0.4g, of which saturates 0g; Cholesterol 0mg; Calcium 530mg; Fibre 7.6g; Sodium 66mg.

guava jelly

Fragrant guava makes an aromatic, pale rust-coloured jelly with a soft set and a slightly sweet-sour flavour that is enhanced by lime juice. Guava jelly goes well with goat's cheese.

Makes about 900g/2lb

INGREDIENTS

900g/2lb guavas

juice of 2–3 limes

about 600ml/1 pint/2½ cups cold water

about 500g/1¼lb/2½ cups preserving or granulated (white) sugar

4 Measure the juice into the cleaned preserving pan, adding 400g/14oz/2 cups sugar and 15ml/ 1 tbsp lime juice for every 600ml/ 1 pint/2½ cups guava juice.

5 Heat gently, stirring occasionally, until the sugar has dissolved. Boil rapidly for about 10 minutes. When the jelly reaches setting point, remove the pan from the heat.

6 Skim any scum from the surface of the jelly using a slotted spoon, then pour the jelly into warmed sterilized jars. Cover and seal.

7 Store the jelly in a cool, dark place and use within 1 year. Once opened, keep in the refrigerator and eat within 3 months.

1 Thinly peel and halve the guavas. Using a spoon, scoop out the seeds (pips) from the centre of the fruit and discard them.

2 Place halved guavas in a large heavy pan with 15ml/1 tbsp lime juice and the water – there should be just enough to cover the fruit. Bring the mixture to the boil, then reduce the heat, cover with a lid and simmer for 30 minutes, or until the fruit is tender.

3 Pour the fruit and juices into a sterilized jelly bag suspended over a large bowl. Leave to drain for at least 3 hours.

COOK'S TIP

Do not be tempted to squeeze the jelly bag while the fruit juices are draining from it; this will result in a cloudy jelly.

Energy 2090kcal/8912kJ; Protein 3.4g; Carbohydrate 552.5g, of which sugars 552.5g; Fat 0.3g, of which saturates 0g; Cholesterol 0mg; Calcium 298mg; Fibre 6.6g; Sodium 39mg.

hedgerow jelly

In the autumn, hedgerows are laden with damsons, blackberries and elderberries and it is well worth spending an afternoon in the countryside picking fruit to make into this delightful jelly.

2 Mash the fruit and leave to cool slightly. Pour into a scalded jelly bag suspended over a non-metallic bowl and leave to drain overnight.

3 Measure the strained juice into a preserving pan. Add 450g/1lb/ 2¼ cups sugar for every 600ml/ 1 pint/2½ cups strained fruit juice.

4 Heat the mixture, stirring, over a low heat until the sugar has dissolved. Increase the heat and boil rapidly without stirring for 10–15 minutes, or until the jelly reaches setting point (105°C/220°F).

Makes about 1.3kg/3lb

INGREDIENTS

450g/1lb damsons, washed
450g/1lb/4 cups blackberries, washed
225g/8oz/2 cups raspberries
225g/8oz/2 cups elderberries, washed
juice and pips (seeds) of 2 large lemons
about 1.3kg/3lb/6½ cups preserving
  or granulated (white) sugar, warmed

COOK'S TIP

If you do not have enough of one fruit, you can vary the quantities as long as the total weight of fruit is the same.

1 Put the fruit, lemon juice and pips in a large pan. Pour over just enough water to cover. Put a lid on the pan and simmer for 1 hour.

5 Remove the pan from the heat and skim off any scum using a slotted spoon. Ladle into warmed, sterilized jars and seal. Leave to cool, then label and store.

Energy 5229kcal/22307kJ; Protein 9.3g; Carbohydrate 1382.9g, of which sugars 1382.9g; Fat 0.4g, of which saturates 0.1g; Cholesterol 0mg; Calcium 799mg; Fibre 8.6g; Sodium 86mg.

mulberry jelly

Deep red mulberries are not often available but if you have access to a tree you will find they make the most wonderful jellies and jams. For a good set, pick the fruits when they are red.

Makes about 900g/2lb

INGREDIENTS

900g/2lb/8 cups unripe red mulberries
grated rind and juice of 1 lemon
600ml/1 pint/2½ cups water
about 900g/2lb/4½ cups preserving
  or granulated (white) sugar, warmed

1 Put the mulberries in a pan with the lemon rind and juice and the water. Bring to the boil, cover and simmer for 1 hour, then remove from the heat and leave to cool.

2 Pour the fruit into a scalded jelly bag suspended over a non-metallic bowl and leave to drain overnight.

3 Measure the strained juice into a preserving pan. Add 450g/1lb/ 2¼ cups sugar for every 600ml/ 1 pint/2½ cups fruit juice.

4 Heat the mixture over a low heat, stirring, until the sugar has completely dissolved. Increase the heat and boil rapidly, without stirring, for 5–10 minutes, or to setting point (105°C/220°F).

5 Skim off any scum from the surface of the jelly using a slotted spoon. Ladle into warmed, sterilized jars, cover and seal. When the jars are completely cool, label, then store in a cool, dark place.

COOK'S TIPS

• To test for the set, spoon a little jelly on to a chilled saucer. Chill for about 3 minutes, then gently push the jelly with your finger; if the surface wrinkles, the jelly has reached setting point and it is ready to bottle.

• To make redcurrant jelly using the method here, measure the same quantity of fruit, but add slightly less sugar to the strained juice: 450g/ 1lb/1¼ cups sugar for every 600ml/ 1 pint/2½ cups juice.

Energy 3621kcal/15456kJ; Protein 8.7g; Carbohydrate 954.3g, of which sugars 954.3g; Fat 0.9g, of which saturates 0.3g; Cholesterol 0mg; Calcium 552mg; Fibre 7.5g; Sodium 63mg.

cranberry jelly

This clear, well-flavoured preserve has a tart flavour and is absolutely delicious served with freshly baked scones, toasted tea cakes and crumpets, or as a glaze for fruit tarts. It can also be served at Christmas with a festive roast turkey, pheasant or guinea fowl.

Makes about 900g/2lb

INGREDIENTS

900g/2lb/8 cups cranberries

450g/1lb sweet eating apples, washed and chopped with skins and cores intact

grated rind and juice of 1 orange

600ml/1 pint/2½ cups water

about 900g/2lb/4½ cups preserving or granulated (white) sugar, warmed

COOK'S TIP

Do not be tempted to squeeze the jelly bag while it is draining or the jelly will become cloudy.

1 Put the cranberries and apples in a pan with the orange rind, juice and water. Bring to the boil then cover and simmer for 1 hour.

2 Remove the pan from the heat and set aside to cool slightly. Pour the fruit and juices into a scalded jelly bag suspended over a non-metallic bowl and leave to drain overnight.

3 Measure the strained juice into a preserving pan. Add 450g/1lb/2¼ cups sugar for every 600ml/1 pint/2½ cups strained juice.

4 Heat, stirring, over a low heat until the sugar has dissolved completely. Increase the heat and boil rapidly, without stirring, for 5–10 minutes, or until the jelly reaches setting point (105°C/220°F).

5 Remove the pan from the heat and skim off any scum from the surface using a slotted spoon. Ladle into warmed, sterilized jars, cover and seal. Leave to cool, then label and store in a cool, dark place.

Energy 3721kcal/15884kJ; Protein 6g; Carbohydrate 985g, of which sugars 985g; Fat 0.5g, of which saturates 0g; Cholesterol 0mg; Calcium 497mg; Fibre 8g; Sodium 64mg.

red plum and cardamom jelly

The fragrance of warm, spicy cardamom combines wonderfully with all varieties of plum – red plums with a good tart flavour are perfect for making into this sweet, fruity, aromatic jelly. Serve it with plain rich ice creams and custards or spread it on toast for breakfast.

Makes about 1.8kg/4lb

INGREDIENTS

1.8kg/4lb red plums, stoned (pitted)

10ml/2 tsp crushed green
  cardamom pods

600ml/1 pint/2½ cups red grape juice

150ml/¼ pint/⅔ cup water

about 1.3kg/3lb/6½ cups preserving
  or granulated (white) sugar, warmed

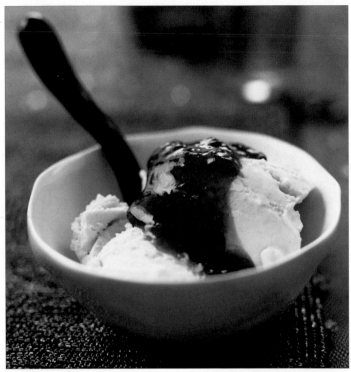

1 Put the plums, cardamom pods, grape juice and water in a large pan. Bring to the boil, then cover and simmer gently for 1 hour. Leave to cool slightly, then pour into a scalded jelly bag suspended over a non-metallic bowl and leave to drain overnight.

2 Measure the strained juice into a preserving pan. Add 450g/1lb/ 2¼ cups sugar for every 600ml/ 1 pint/2½ cups strained juice.

3 Heat the mixture over a low heat, stirring constantly until the sugar has dissolved completely. Increase the heat and boil, without stirring, for 10–15 minutes, or until the jelly reaches setting point (105°C/220°F).

4 Remove the pan from the heat and skim off any scum. Spoon the jelly into warmed sterilized jars, cover and seal. When cool, label and store in a cool, dark place.

Energy 5338kcal/22783kJ; Protein 10.1g; Carbohydrate 1411.3g, of which sugars 1411.3g; Fat 0.6g, of which saturates 0g; Cholesterol 0mg; Calcium 767mg; Fibre 9.6g; Sodium 90mg.

rhubarb and mint jelly

The speckling of this jelly with tiny pieces of chopped fresh mint makes it a very pretty gift.

Makes about 2kg/4½lb

INGREDIENTS

1kg/2¼lb rhubarb

about 1.3kg/3lb/6½ cups preserving
  or granulated (white) sugar, warmed

large bunch fresh mint

30ml/2 tbsp finely chopped
  fresh mint

COOK'S TIPS

• This recipe is a good way to use
up older dark red or green-stemmed
rhubarb, which is usually too tough to
use for desserts.

• As well as serving as a delightful
sweet preserve, this jelly is also very
good served with fatty roast meats
such as lamb and goose.

1 Using a sharp knife, cut the
rhubarb into chunks and place in
a large, heavy pan. Pour in just
enough water to cover, cover the
pan with a lid and cook until the
rhubarb is soft.

2 Remove the pan from the heat
and leave to cool slightly. Pour the
stewed fruit and juices into a
scalded jelly bag suspended over
a non-metallic bowl and leave to
drain overnight.

3 Measure the strained juice into
a preserving pan and add 450g/
1lb/2¼ cups warmed sugar for
each 600ml/1 pint/2½ cups
strained juice.

4 Add the bunch of mint to the
pan. Bring to the boil, stirring
until the sugar has dissolved. Boil
to setting point (105°C/220°F).
Remove the mint.

5 Leave to stand for 10 minutes,
stir in the chopped mint, then pot
and seal. Label when cold.

Energy 5165kcal/22040kJ; Protein 11.1g; Carbohydrate 1363.6g, of which sugars 1360.9g; Fat 0.6g, of which saturates 0g; Cholesterol 0mg; Calcium 1073mg; Fibre 4.2g; Sodium 95mg.

red gooseberry jelly

*This delicious jelly is perfect for spreading on toast at any time of the day. Choose small dark
red gooseberries to produce a jelly with the best colour and flavour.*

Makes about 2kg/4½lb

INGREDIENTS

1.3kg/3lb/12 cups red gooseberries

2 red-skinned eating apples, washed
  and chopped with skins and cores intact

2.5cm/1in piece fresh root ginger, sliced

about 1.3kg/3lb/6½ cups preserving
  or granulated (white) sugar, warmed

COOK'S TIPS

The amount of pectin in gooseberries
diminishes as the fruit ripens so select
firm, just ripe fruit when making this jelly
to achieve a really good set.

1 Put the fruit and ginger in a pan
and pour over just enough water
to cover the fruit. Cover and
simmer for 45 minutes.

2 Remove from the heat, cool
slightly, then pour the fruit and
juices into a scalded jelly bag
suspended over a non-metallic
bowl and leave to drain overnight.

3 Measure the strained juice into
a preserving pan and add 450g/1lb/
2¼ cups warmed sugar for every
600ml/1 pint/2½ cups juice.

4 Stir over a low heat until the
sugar has dissolved. Boil for about
10 minutes, or to setting point
(105°C/220°F). Skim off any scum,
then pot, seal and label.

Energy 5233kcal/22327kJ; Protein 11.8g; Carbohydrate 1378.3g, of which sugars 1378.3g; Fat 1.9g, of which saturates 0g; Cholesterol 0mg; Calcium 820mg; Fibre 12.1g; Sodium 89mg.

rosehip and apple jelly

This economical jelly is made with windfall apples and wild rosehips. It is still rich in vitamin C, full of flavour, and excellent spread on freshly toasted crumpets or scones.

Makes about 2kg/4½lb

INGREDIENTS

1kg/2¼lb windfall apples, peeled, trimmed and quartered

450g/1lb firm, ripe rosehips

about 1.3kg/3lb/6½ cups preserving or granulated (white) sugar, warmed

1 Place the quartered apples in a large pan with just enough water to cover, plus 300ml/½ pint/ 1¼ cups of extra water.

COOK'S TIP

There is no need to remove all the peel from the apples: simply cut out any bruised, damaged or bad areas.

2 Bring the mixture to the boil and cook gently until the apples soften and turn to a pulp. Meanwhile, chop the rosehips coarsely. Add the rosehips to the pan with the apple and simmer for 10 minutes.

3 Remove from the heat and stand for 10 minutes, then pour the mixture into a scalded jelly bag suspended over a non-metallic bowl and leave to drain overnight.

4 Measure the juice into a preserving pan and bring to the boil. Add 400g/14oz/2 cups warmed sugar for each 600ml/ 1 pint/2½ cups of liquid. Stir until the sugar has completely dissolved. Boil to setting point (105°C/220°F).

5 Pour the jelly into warmed, sterilized jars and seal. Label and store when completely cold.

Energy 5684kcal/24259kJ; Protein 8.4g; Carbohydrate 1505.7g, of which sugars 1505.7g; Fat 0.5g, of which saturates 0g; Cholesterol 0mg; Calcium 761mg; Fibre 7.7g; Sodium 94mg.

spiced cider and apple jelly

This wonderful spicy jelly has a rich, warming flavour, making it ideal to serve during the cold winter months. Serve as a spread or use it to sweeten apple pies and desserts.

Makes about 1.3kg/3lb

INGREDIENTS

900g/2lb tart cooking apples, washed and coarsely chopped with skins and cores intact

900ml/1¼ pints/3¾ cups sweet (hard) cider

juice and pips (seeds) of 2 oranges

1 cinnamon stick

6 whole cloves

150ml/¼ pint/⅔ cup water

about 900g/2lb/4½ cups preserving or granulated (white) sugar, warmed

2 Leave to cool slightly, then pour the fruit into a scalded jelly bag suspended over a non-metallic bowl and leave to drain overnight.

3 Measure the strained juice into a preserving pan. Add 450g/1lb/2¼ cups warmed sugar for every 600ml/1 pint/2½ cups juice.

4 Heat, stirring, over a low heat until the sugar has dissolved. Increase the heat and boil, without stirring, for 10 minutes, or until the jelly reaches setting point (105°C/220°F).

5 Remove from the heat and skim off any scum. Ladle into warmed sterilized jars. Cover, seal and label.

1 Put the apples, cider, juice and pips, cinnamon, cloves and water in a large pan. Bring to the boil, cover and simmer for about 1 hour.

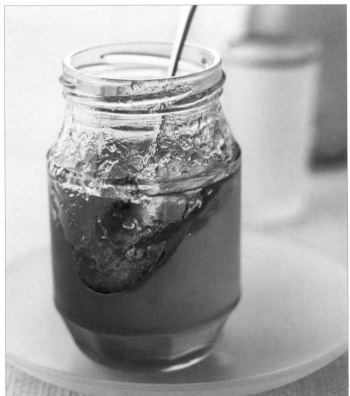

Energy 3975kcal/16950kJ; Protein 5.4g; Carbohydrate 990.6g, of which sugars 990.6g; Fat 0.3g, of which saturates 0g; Cholesterol 0mg; Calcium 561mg; Fibre 4.8g; Sodium 123mg.

quince and coriander jelly

*When raw, quinces are inedible but once cooked and sweetened they become aromatic and have
a wonderful flavour, which is enhanced here by the addition of warm, spicy coriander seeds.*

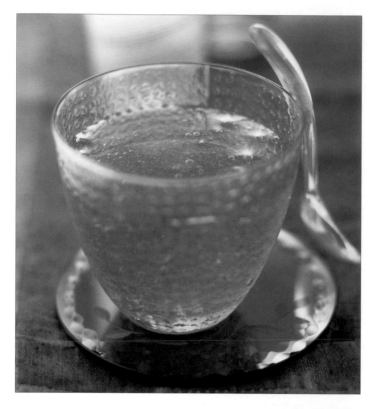

2 Leave the fruit to cool slightly,
then pour into a scalded jelly bag
suspended over a non-metallic
bowl and leave to drain overnight.

3 Measure the strained juice into
a preserving pan. Add 450g/1lb/
2¼ cups warmed sugar for every
600ml/1 pint/2½ cups juice.

4 Heat, stirring, over a low heat
until the sugar has completely
dissolved. Increase the heat and
boil rapidly, without stirring, for
5–10 minutes or until the jelly
reaches setting point (105°C/220°F).

Makes about 900g/2lb

INGREDIENTS

1kg/2¼lb quinces, washed and coarsely
 chopped with skins and cores intact

15ml/1 tbsp coriander seeds

juice and pips (seeds) of 2 large lemons

900ml/1½ pints/3¾ cups water

about 900g/2lb/4½ cups preserving
 or granulated (white) sugar, warmed

5 Remove the pan from the heat
and skim off any scum from the
surface using a slotted spoon.
Ladle into warmed sterilized jars,
cover and seal. When cold, label
and store in a cool, dark place.

COOK'S TIP

Jellies can look very pretty served in
decorative glasses. Bottle the jelly in
jars as above, then, when ready to
serve, gently heat the jelly in a pan
with a very small amount of water until
melted. Pour the jelly into a heatproof
glass and leave to set before serving.

VARIATION

If you don't have enough quinces, you
can make up the quantity with apples.
The flavour won't be quite the same
but the jelly will still be delicious.

1 Put the quinces in a pan with
the coriander seeds, lemon juice
and pips, and the water. Bring to
the boil, cover and simmer gently
for about 1½ hours.

Energy 3678kcal/15687kJ; Protein 5.5g; Carbohydrate 973.5g, of which sugars 973.5g; Fat 0.3g, of which saturates 0g; Cholesterol 0mg; Calcium 513mg; Fibre 7.3g; Sodium 64mg.

geranium and pear jelly

This jelly uses the leaves of scented geranium to give an aromatic lift to the pears. Use rose-scented leaves if you have them, otherwise add a couple of drops of rose water to the strained juice.

Makes about 900g/2lb

INGREDIENTS

900g/2lb Comice pears, washed and coarsely chopped with skins and cores intact

7 rose-scented geranium leaves, plus extra for storing

juice and pips (seeds) of 1 lemon

60ml/4 tbsp clear honey

900ml/1½ pints/3¾ cups water

about 900g/2lb/4½ cups preserving or granulated (white) sugar, warmed

1 Put the pears, geranium leaves, lemon juice, honey and water in a large pan. Bring to the boil, then cover and simmer for 1 hour.

2 Remove the pan from the heat and leave to cool slightly. Pour the fruit into a scalded jelly bag suspended over a non-metallic bowl and leave to drain overnight.

3 Measure the strained juice into a preserving pan. Add 450g/1lb/2¼ cups warmed sugar for every 600ml/1 pint/2½ cups juice.

4 Heat, stirring, over a low heat until the sugar has dissolved. Increase the heat and boil rapidly, without stirring, for 10 minutes, or to setting point (105°C/220°F).

5 Remove the pan from the heat and skim off any scum using a slotted spoon. Place a blanched geranium leaf into each warmed sterilized jar, Then ladle in the jelly. Cover and seal, then label.

Energy 3851kcal/16424kJ; Protein 5.7g; Carbohydrate 1019.3g, of which sugars 1019.3g; Fat 0.3g, of which saturates 0g; Cholesterol 0mg; Calcium 516mg; Fibre 7.3g; Sodium 71mg.

clementine and lemon balm jelly

This sweet, aromatic jelly make a delicious alternative to marmalade at breakfast.

Makes about 900g/2lb

INGREDIENTS

900g/2lb clementines, washed and
coarsely chopped

450g/1lb tart cooking apples,
coarsely chopped, with skins
and cores intact

2 large sprigs of lemon balm or
1 lemon grass stalk, crushed

900ml/1½ pints/3¾ cups water

about 900g/2lb/4½ cups preserving
or granulated (white) sugar, warmed

COOK'S TIP

To prepare the lemon grass, you only
need to crush the bulbous end of the
stalk. Using the end of a rolling pin,
gently bash the bulbous end of the
stalk, then add to the pan. This helps
to release its fragrant, zesty flavour
into the jelly.

1 Put the fruit, lemon balm or
lemon grass and water in a pan.
Bring to the boil, cover and
simmer for 1 hour until the fruit is
soft. Cool slightly, then pour into
a scalded jelly bag over a bowl and
leave to drain overnight.

2 Measure the juice into a pan.
Add 450g/1lb/2¼ cups sugar for
every 600ml/1 pint/2½ cups juice.

3 Heat gently, stirring until the
sugar has dissolved. Increase the
heat and boil, without stirring, for
5–10 minutes, or until the jelly
reaches setting point (105°C/220°F).

4 Remove the pan from the heat
and skim off any scum using a
slotted spoon. Pour into warmed
sterilized jars, cover and seal.
Label and store in a cool place.

Energy 3721kcal/15877kJ; Protein 7.9g; Carbohydrate 982.6g, of which sugars 982.6g; Fat 0.5g, of which saturates 0g; Cholesterol 0mg; Calcium 585mg; Fibre 6.4g; Sodium 70mg.

muscat grape jelly

The perfumed flavour of Muscat grapes produces a unique fragrant, scented jelly.

Makes about 900g/2lb

INGREDIENTS

900g/2lb/6 cups Muscat grapes,
washed and halved

juice and pips (seeds) of 2 lemons

600ml/1 pint/2½ cups water

30ml/2 tbsp elderflower cordial

about 900g/2lb/4½ cups preserving
or granulated (white) sugar, warmed

1 Place the grapes in a pan with
the lemon juice and pips, and
water. Bring to the boil, cover and
simmer for 1½ hours. Cool slightly.

2 Mash the grapes, then pour the
mixture into a scalded jelly bag
suspended over a non-metallic
bowl and leave to drain overnight.

3 Measure the juice into a pan and
pour in the elderflower cordial.
Add 450g/1lb/2¼ cups sugar for
every 600ml/1 pint/2½ cups juice.
Heat gently, stirring, until the sugar
has dissolved. Increase the heat
and boil, without stirring, for
5–10 minutes, or until the jelly
reaches setting point (105°C/220°F).

4 Remove the pan from the heat
and skim off any scum. Ladle into
warmed sterilized jars. Cover, seal
and label. Store in a cool place.

Energy 3778kcal/16121kJ; Protein 5.9g; Carbohydrate 1000.3g, of which sugars 1000.3g; Fat 0.3g, of which saturates 0g; Cholesterol 0mg; Calcium 523mg; Fibre 2.3g; Sodium 63mg.

pineapple and passion fruit jelly

This exotic jelly has a wonderful warming glow to its taste and appearance. For the best-flavoured jelly, use a tart-tasting, not too ripe pineapple rather than a very ripe, sweet one.

Makes about 900g/2lb

INGREDIENTS

1 large pineapple, peeled, topped and tailed and coarsely chopped

4 passion fruit, halved, with seeds and pulp scooped out

900ml/1½ pints/3¾ cups water

about 900g/2lb/4½ cups preserving or granulated (white) sugar, warmed

COOK'S TIP

For the best flavour, choose passion fruit with dark, wrinkled skins.

1 Place the pineapple and the passion fruit seeds and pulp in a large pan with the water.

2 Bring the mixture to the boil, cover and simmer for 1½ hours. Remove from the heat and leave to cool slightly. Transfer the fruit to a food processor and process briefly.

3 Tip the fruit pulp and any juices from the pan, into a scalded jelly bag suspended over a non-metallic bowl and leave to drain overnight.

4 Measure the strained juice into a preserving pan and add 450g/1lb/2¼ cups warmed sugar for every 600ml/1 pint/2½ cups juice.

5 Heat gently, stirring, until the sugar has dissolved. Increase the heat and boil rapidly, without stirring, for 10–15 minutes or to setting point (105°C/220°F).

6 Remove the pan from the heat and skim off any scum using a slotted spoon. Ladle the jelly into warmed sterilized jars, cover and seal. When cool, label and store in a cool, dark place.

Energy 3633kcal/15504kJ; Protein 5.7g; Carbohydrate 961.6g, of which sugars 961.6g; Fat 0.5g, of which saturates 0g; Cholesterol 0mg; Calcium 515mg; Fibre 2.9g; Sodium 61mg.

pomegranate and grenadine jelly

The slightly tart flavoured, jewel-like flesh of the pomegranate makes the most wonderful jelly. Be careful though, because pomegranate juice can stain indelibly when spilt on clothing.

Makes about 900g/2lb

INGREDIENTS

6 ripe red pomegranates, peeled and
  seeds removed from membranes

120ml/4fl oz/½ cup grenadine syrup

juice and pips (seeds) of 2 oranges

300ml/½ pint/1¼ cups water

about 900g/2lb/4½ cups preserving
  or granulated (white) sugar, warmed

1 Put the pomegranate seeds in bowl and crush to release their juice. Transfer them to a pan and add the grenadine, orange juice, pips and water.

2 Bring the mixture to the boil, cover and simmer for 1½ hours. Mash the fruit and leave to cool slightly, then pour into a scalded jelly bag suspended over a bowl and leave to drain overnight.

3 Measure the juice into a pan and add 450g/1lb/2¼ cups sugar for every 600ml/1 pint/2½ cups juice.

4 Heat, stirring, over a low heat until the sugar has dissolved. Increase the heat and boil rapidly, without stirring, for 5–10 minutes, or until the jelly reaches setting point (105°C/220°F).

5 Remove the pan from the heat and skim off any scum. Ladle into warmed sterilized jars, cover, seal and label. Store in a cool place.

Energy 3776kcal/16114kJ; Protein 5.5g; Carbohydrate 1000.5g, of which sugars 1000.5g; Fat 0.2g, of which saturates 0g; Cholesterol 0mg; Calcium 511mg; Fibre 0.8g; Sodium 76mg.

jams, marmalades and butters

Glistening with fine shreds or rind, or lusciously smooth, these classic preserves cannot be matched by anything the commercial world has to offer. Combinations of citrus and berries, spices and soft fruit, seeds and nuts are all here to enjoy. They can be lavished on breads and pancakes, used as fillings for cakes, or used to flavour delicious dessert sauces. You can also add them in small quantities to savoury sauces, marinades and dressings.

seedless raspberry and passion fruit jam

The pips in raspberry jam can often put people off this wonderful preserve. This version has none of the pips and all of the flavour, and is enhanced by the tangy addition of passion fruit.

Makes about 1.3kg/3lb

INGREDIENTS

1.6kg/3½lb/14 cups raspberries

4 passion fruit, halved

1.3kg/3lb/6½ cups preserving sugar
with pectin, warmed

juice of 1 lemon

COOK'S TIPS

• Check the instructions on the sugar
packet for details of the boiling time.

• If you cannot find preserving sugar
with pectin, use the same quantity of
regular sugar and add powdered or
liquid pectin. Check the instructions
on the packet for quantities.

1 Place the raspberries in a large pan, then scoop out the passion fruit seeds and pulp and add to the raspberries. Cover and cook over a low heat for 20 minutes, or until the juices begin to run.

2 Remove the pan from the heat and leave to cool slightly, then, using the back of a spoon, press the fruit through a coarse sieve into a preserving pan.

3 Add the sugar and lemon juice to the pan and stir over a low heat until the sugar has dissolved. Bring to the boil and cook for 4 minutes, or until the jam reaches setting point (105°C/220°F).

4 Remove the pan from the heat and skim off any scum. Leave to cool slightly, then pour into warmed sterilized jars. Seal and label, then store in a cool place.

Energy 5544kcal/23688kJ; Protein 30.5g; Carbohydrate 1435.6g, of which sugars 1435.6g; Fat 5g, of which saturates 1.7g; Cholesterol 0mg; Calcium 1096mg; Fibre 42g; Sodium 137mg.

wild strawberry and rose petal conserve

This fragrant jam is ideal served with summer cream teas. Rose water complements the strawberries beautifully, but only add a few drops because the flavour can easily become over-powering.

Makes about 900g/2lb

INGREDIENTS

900g/2lb/8 cups wild Alpine strawberries

450g/1lb/4 cups strawberries, hulled and mashed

2 dark pink rose buds, petals only

juice of 2 lemons

1.3kg/3lb/6½ cups granulated (white) sugar, warmed

a few drops of rose water

1 Put all the strawberries in a non-metallic bowl with the rose petals, lemon juice and warmed sugar. Cover and leave overnight.

2 The next day, tip the fruit into a preserving pan and heat gently, stirring, until all the sugar has dissolved. Boil for 10–15 minutes, or to setting point (105°C/220°F).

3 Stir the rose water into the jam, then remove the pan from the heat. Skim off any scum and leave to cool for 5 minutes, then stir and pour into warmed sterilized jars. Seal and label, then store.

COOK'S TIPS

• If you are unable to find wild berries, use ordinary strawberries instead. Leave the smaller berries whole but mash any large ones.

• To make plain strawberry jam, make in the same way but leave out the rose petals and rose water.

Energy 5487kcal/23379kJ; Protein 17.3g; Carbohydrate 1439.5g, of which sugars 1439.5g; Fat 1.4g, of which saturates 0g; Cholesterol 0mg; Calcium 905mg; Fibre 14.9g; Sodium 159mg.

cherry-berry conserve

Tart cranberries enliven the taste of cherries and also add an essential dose of pectin to this pretty conserve, which is fabulous spread on crumpets or toast. It is also delicious stirred into meaty gravies and sauces served with roast duck, poultry or pork.

2 Add the water to the pan. Cover and bring to the boil, then simmer for 20–30 minutes, or until the cranberries are very tender.

3 Add the sugar to the pan and heat gently, stirring, until the sugar has dissolved. Bring to the boil, then cook for 10 minutes, or to setting point (105°C/220°F).

4 Remove the pan from the heat and skim off any scum using a slotted spoon. Leave to cool for 10 minutes, then stir gently and pour into warmed sterilized jars. Seal, label and store.

Makes about 1.3kg/3lb

INGREDIENTS

350g/12oz/3 cups fresh cranberries

1kg/2¼lb/5½ cups cherries, pitted

120ml/4fl oz/½ cup blackcurrant or raspberry syrup

juice of 2 lemons

250ml/8fl oz/1 cup water

1.3kg/3lb/6½ cups preserving or granulated (white) sugar, warmed

COOK'S TIP

The cranberries must be cooked until very tender before the sugar is added, otherwise they will become tough.

1 Put the cranberries in a food processor and process until coarsely chopped. Scrape into a pan and add the cherries, fruit syrup and lemon juice.

Energy 5859kcal/24986kJ; Protein 16.7g; Carbohydrate 1540.4g, of which sugars 1540.4g; Fat 1.4g, of which saturates 0g; Cholesterol 0mg; Calcium 844mg; Fibre 14.6g; Sodium 105mg.

summer berry and juniper jam

In late summer, there is a moment when all the different varieties of berries suddenly seem to be ripe at the same time. Combine them in jam as the flavours work well together, particularly when blended with juniper, which produces a taste reminiscent of gin.

Makes about 1.3kg/3lb

INGREDIENTS

675g/1½lb/6 cups raspberries
675g/1½lb/6 cups blackberries
10ml/2 tsp juniper berries, crushed
300ml/½ pint/1¼ cups water
1.3kg/3lb/6½ cups granulated (white) sugar, warmed
juice of 2 lemons

COOK'S TIP

Juniper berries are quite soft and are easily broken down into coarsely crushed pieces. Put the berries in a mortar and crush with a pestle.

1 Put the raspberries, blackberries and juniper berries in a large heavy pan with the water. Set over a low heat, cover and cook gently for about 15 minutes, or until the juices begin to run.

2 Add the sugar and lemon juice to the pan and cook over a low heat, stirring frequently, until the sugar has dissolved. (Be careful not to break up the berries too much.)

3 Bring to the boil and cook for 5–10 minutes, or until the jam reaches setting point (105°C/220°F). Remove the pan from the heat and skim off any scum from the surface using a slotted spoon. Leave to cool for about 5 minutes, then stir gently and pour into warmed sterilized jars. Seal and label, then store in a cool, dark place.

Energy 5460kcal/23325kJ; Protein 25.4g; Carbohydrate 1420.6g, of which sugars 1420.6g; Fat 4g, of which saturates 1.4g; Cholesterol 0mg; Calcium 1027mg; Fibre 33.8g; Sodium 119mg.

blueberry and lime jam

The subtle yet fragrant flavour of blueberries can be illusive on its own. Adding a generous quantity of tangy lime juice enhances their flavour and gives this jam a wonderful zesty taste.

Makes about 1.3kg/3lb

INGREDIENTS

1.3kg/3lb/12 cups blueberries

finely pared rind and juice
of 4 limes

1kg/2¼lb/5 cups preserving sugar
with pectin

COOK'S TIP

Blueberries are not naturally high in pectin, so extra pectin is needed for a good set. If you prefer, used granulated sugar and add pectin according to the instruction on the packet in place of the preserving sugar with pectin.

1 Put the blueberries, lime juice and half the sugar in a large, non-metallic bowl and lightly crush the berries using a potato masher. Set aside for about 4 hours.

2 Tip the crushed berry mixture into a pan and stir in the finely pared lime rind and the remaining preserving sugar. Heat slowly, stirring continuously, until the sugar has completely dissolved.

3 Increase the heat and bring to the boil. Boil rapidly for about 4 minutes, or until the jam reaches setting point (105°C/220°F).

4 Remove the pan from the heat and set aside for 5 minutes. Stir the jam gently, then pour into warmed sterilized jars. Seal the jars, then label when completely cool. Store in a cool, dark place.

Energy 4265kcal/18162kJ; Protein 16.7g; Carbohydrate 1111.3g, of which sugars 1111.3g; Fat 2.6g, of which saturates 0g; Cholesterol 0mg; Calcium 1063mg; Fibre 40.3g; Sodium 86mg.

blackcurrant jam

This jam has a rich, fruity flavour and a wonderfully strong dark colour. It is punchy and delicious with scones for tea or spread on croissants for a continental-style breakfast.

Makes about 1.3kg/3lb

INGREDIENTS

1.3kg/3lb/12 cups blackcurrants

grated rind and juice of 1 orange

475ml/16fl oz/2 cups water

1.3kg/3lb/6½ cups granulated (white) sugar, warmed

30ml/2 tbsp cassis (optional)

1 Place the blackcurrants, orange rind and juice and water in a large heavy pan. Bring to the boil, reduce the heat and simmer for 30 minutes.

2 Add the warmed sugar to the pan and stir over a low heat until the sugar has dissolved.

3 Bring the mixture to the boil and cook for about 8 minutes, or until the jam reaches setting point (105°C/220°F).

4 Remove the pan from the heat and skim off any scum from the surface using a slotted spoon. Leave to cool for 5 minutes, then stir in the cassis, if using.

5 Pour the jam into warmed sterilized jars and seal. Leave the jars to cool completely, then label and store in a cool, dark place.

Energy 5504kcal/23503kJ; Protein 18.4g; Carbohydrate 1448.7g, of which sugars 1448.7g; Fat 0.1g, of which saturates 0g; Cholesterol 0mg; Calcium 1474mg; Fibre 46.8g; Sodium 122mg.

dried apricot jam

This richly flavoured jam can be made at any time of year, so even if you miss the short apricot season, you can still enjoy the delicious taste of sweet, tangy apricot jam all year round.

Makes about 2kg/4½lb

INGREDIENTS

675g/1½lb dried apricots

900ml/1½ pints/3¾ cups apple juice

juice and grated rind of
 2 unwaxed lemons

675g/1½lb/scant 3½ cups preserving
 or granulated (white) sugar, warmed

50g/2oz/½ cup blanched almonds,
 coarsely chopped

COOK'S TIP

Use the best quality traditional dried apricots to make this jam. They have a more suitable texture than the soft ready-to-eat dried apricots and will produce a better end result.

1 Put the apricots in a bowl, pour over the apple juice and leave to soak overnight.

2 Pour the soaked apricots and juice into a preserving pan and add the lemon juice and rind. Bring to the boil, then lower the heat and simmer for 15–20 minutes until the apricots are soft.

3 Add the warmed sugar to the pan and bring to the boil, stirring until the sugar has completely dissolved. Boil for 15–20 minutes, or until setting point is reached (105°C/220°F).

4 Stir the chopped almonds into the jam and leave to stand for about 15 minutes, then pour the jam into warmed, sterilized jars. Seal, then leave to cool completely before labelling. Store in a cool, dark place.

Energy 4032kcal/17163kJ; Protein 40.9g; Carbohydrate 955.2g, of which sugars 953.9g; Fat 31.9g, of which saturates 2.2g; Cholesterol 0mg; Calcium 971mg; Fibre 46.2g; Sodium 142mg.

peach and amaretto jam

Adding amaretto (almond liqueur) produces a luxurious jam that's perfect served on warm buttered toast or English muffins. You can use peach schnapps in place of the amaretto if you prefer.

Makes about 1.3kg/3lb

INGREDIENTS

1.3kg/3lb peaches
250ml/8fl oz/1 cup water
juice of 2 lemons
1.3kg/3lb/6½ cups granulated (white) sugar, warmed
45ml/3 tbsp amaretto liqueur

1 Carefully peel the peaches using a vegetable peeler, or blanch briefly in boiling water, then peel with a knife. Reserve the skins.

2 Halve and stone the fruit, dice the flesh and put in a pan with the water. Place the peach skins in a small pan with water to cover. Boil until the liquid is reduced to 30ml/2 tbsp. Press the skins and liquid through a sieve into the peaches. Cover and simmer for 20 minutes, or until soft.

3 Add the lemon juice and sugar to the pan. Heat, stirring, until the sugar has dissolved completely. Bring to the boil and cook for 10–15 minutes, or to setting point (105°C/220°F). Remove from the heat and skim off any scum from the surface using a slotted spoon.

4 Leave the jam to cool for about 10 minutes, then stir in the amaretto and pour into warmed sterilized jars. Seal, then leave to cool completely before labelling. Store in a cool, dark place.

Energy 5669kcal/24194kJ; Protein 19.5g; Carbohydrate 1472.1g, of which sugars 1472.1g; Fat 1.3g, of which saturates 0g; Cholesterol 0mg; Calcium 782mg; Fibre 19.5g; Sodium 96mg.

gooseberry and elderflower jam

Pale green gooseberries and fragrant elderflowers make perfect partners in this aromatic jam.

Makes about 2kg/4½lb

INGREDIENTS

1.3kg/3lb/12 cups firm gooseberries, topped and tailed

300ml/½ pint/1¼ cups water

1.3kg/3lb/6½ cups granulated (white) sugar, warmed

juice of 1 lemon

2 handfuls of elderflowers removed from their stalks

COOK'S TIP

The time taken to reach setting point will vary depending on the ripeness of the gooseberries. The riper the fruit, the longer the jam will need to be cooked to reach setting point.

1 Put the gooseberries into a large preserving pan, add the water and bring the mixture to the boil.

2 Cover the pan with a lid and simmer gently for 20 minutes until the fruit is soft. Using a potato masher, gently mash the fruit to crush it lightly.

3 Add the sugar, lemon juice and elderflowers to the pan and stir over a low heat until the sugar has dissolved. Boil for 10 minutes, or to setting point (105°C/220°F). Remove from the heat, skim off any scum and cool for 5 minutes, then stir. Pot and seal, then leave to cool before labelling.

Energy 5369kcal/22906kJ; Protein 20.8g; Carbohydrate 1397.5g, of which sugars 1397.5g; Fat 5.2g, of which saturates 0g; Cholesterol 0mg; Calcium 1053mg; Fibre 31.2g; Sodium 104mg.

damson jam

Dark, plump damsons produce a deeply coloured and richly flavoured jam that makes a delicious treat spread on toasted English muffins or warm crumpets at tea time.

Makes about 2kg/4½lb

INGREDIENTS

1kg/2¼lb damsons or wild plums

1.4 litres/2½ pints/6 cups water

1kg/2¼lb/5 cups preserving or granulated (white) sugar, warmed

COOK'S TIP

It is important to seal the jars as soon as you have filled them to ensure the jam remains sterile. However, you should then leave the jars to cool completely before labelling and storing them to avoid the risk of burns.

1 Put the damsons in a preserving pan and pour in the water. Bring to the boil. Reduce the heat and simmer gently until the damsons are soft, then stir in the sugar.

2 Bring the mixture to the boil, skimming off stones as they rise. Boil to setting point (105°C/220°F). Leave to cool for 10 minutes, then pot. Seal, then label and store when cool.

Energy 4320kcal/18430kJ; Protein 10g; Carbohydrate 1141g, of which sugars 1141g; Fat 0g, of which saturates 0g; Cholesterol 0mg; Calcium 770mg; Fibre 18g; Sodium 80mg.

greengage and almond jam

This is the perfect preserve to make when greengages are readily available in stores, or if you find you have a glut of the fruit. It has a gloriously rich, golden honey colour and a smooth texture that contrasts wonderfully with the little slivers of almond.

Makes about 1.3kg/3lb

INGREDIENTS

1.3kg/3lb greengages, stoned (pitted)

350ml/12fl oz/1½ cups water

juice of 1 lemon

50g/2oz/½ cup blanched almonds,
cut into thin slivers

1.3kg/3lb/6½ cups granulated (white)
sugar, warmed

COOK'S TIP

Greengages look like unripened plums. However, despite their appearance, they have a wonderfully aromatic flavour that is captured perfectly in this delicious jam.

1 Put the greengages and water in a preserving pan with the lemon juice and almond slivers. Bring to the boil, then cover and simmer for 15–20 minutes, or until the greengages are really soft.

2 Add the sugar to the pan and stir over a low heat until the sugar has dissolved. Bring to the boil and cook for 10–15 minutes, or until the jam reaches setting point (105°C/220°F).

3 Remove the pan from the heat and skim off any scum from the surface using a slotted spoon.

4 Leave to cool for 10 minutes, then stir gently and pour into warmed sterilized jars. Seal, then leave to cool completely before labelling. Store in a cool place.

Energy 5896kcal/25135kJ; Protein 24.9g; Carbohydrate 1476.3g, of which sugars 1475g; Fat 29.2g, of which saturates 2.2g; Cholesterol 0mg; Calcium 978mg; Fibre 24.5g; Sodium 111mg.

rhubarb and ginger jam

Late summer is the time to make this preserve, when rhubarb leaves are enormous and the stalks thick and green. It has a wonderfully tart, tangy flavour and is delicious spooned over plain cake, or used as a filling with whipped cream.

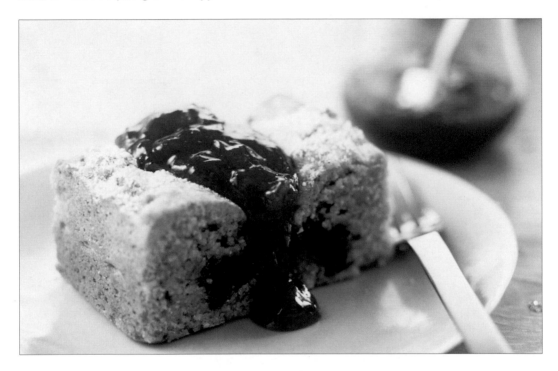

Makes about 2kg/4½lb

INGREDIENTS

1kg/2¼lb rhubarb

1kg/2¼lb/5 cups preserving
  or granulated (white) sugar

25g/1oz fresh root ginger, bruised

115g/4oz crystallized ginger

50g/2oz/¼ cup candied orange
  peel, chopped

COOK'S TIP

The young, slender rhubarb stems that are available in the spring are more suitable for making tarts and pies. Their delicate flavour does not shine through in preserves, so it is worth waiting until later in the season for mature rhubarb.

1 Cut the rhubarb into short pieces and layer with the sugar in a glass bowl. Leave to stand overnight.

2 The next day, scrape the rhubarb and sugar mixture into a large, heavy preserving pan.

3 Tie the bruised ginger root in a piece of muslin (cheesecloth) and add it to the rhubarb. Cook gently for 30 minutes, or until the rhubarb has softened.

4 Remove the root ginger from the pan and stir in the crystallized ginger and candied orange peel.

5 Bring the mixture to the boil, then cook over a high heat until setting point is reached (105°C/220°F). Leave to cool for a few minutes, then pour into warmed sterilized jars and seal. When completely cool, label and store.

Energy 4135kcal/17664kJ; Protein 14.9g; Carbohydrate 1083.8g, of which sugars 1083.8g; Fat 1.7g, of which saturates 0g; Cholesterol 0mg; Calcium 1582mg; Fibre 17.9g; Sodium 314mg.

papaya and apricot jam

Apricots and papaya make perfect partners in this tantalizing jam. However, if you prefer plain apricot jam, simply replace the papaya with the same weight of apricots.

2 Slice the apricots and place in a preserving pan with the kernels, papaya, grated lemon rind and juice and the water. Bring to the boil then cover and simmer for 20–30 minutes, or until the fruit is really tender.

3 Add the sugar to the pan and stir continuously over a low heat until the sugar has dissolved. Bring to the boil and cook for about 15 minutes, or until the jam reaches setting point (105°C/220°F).

Makes about 1.3kg/3lb

INGREDIENTS

900g/2lb stoned (pitted) apricots, 6 stones (pits) reserved

450g/1lb papaya, peeled, seeded and cut into small chunks

grated rind and juice of 2 lemons

250ml/8fl oz/1 cup water

1.3kg/3lb/6½ cups granulated (white) sugar, warmed

COOK'S TIP

The bitter kernels from apricot stones (pits) contribute an almond-like flavour to the jam. Only a few should be used as they have a strong flavour. They are blanched to remove natural toxins.

1 Using a nut cracker or wooden mallet, crack the reserved apricot stones and remove the kernels inside. Put the kernels in a pan, pour over boiling water and cook for 2 minutes, then drain and slide off their skins.

4 Remove the pan from the heat and skim off any scum from the surface using a slotted spoon. Cool for 5 minutes, then stir gently and pour into warmed sterilized jars and seal. When cool, label the jars, then store in a cool, dark place.

Energy 5599kcal/23901kJ; Protein 17.4g; Carbohydrate 1471.7g, of which sugars 1471.7g; Fat 1.5g, of which saturates 0g; Cholesterol 0mg; Calcium 938mg; Fibre 25.3g; Sodium 129mg.

melon and star anise jam

The delicate flavour of melon is brought out by spicy ginger and perfectly complemented by aromatic star anise. Once opened, store this delicious jam in the refrigerator.

Makes about 1.3kg/3lb

INGREDIENTS

2 Charentais or cantaloupe melons, peeled and seeded

450g/1lb/2¼ cups granulated (white) sugar

2 star anise

4 pieces preserved stem ginger in syrup, drained and finely chopped

finely grated rind and juice of 2 lemons

2 Tip the melon and sugar mixture into a large pan and add the star anise, chopped ginger, lemon rind and juice and stir to combine.

3 Bring the mixture to the boil, then lower the heat. Simmer for 25 minutes, or until the melon has become transparent and the setting point reached (105°C/220°F).

4 Spoon the jam into hot sterilized jars and seal. Leave to cool, then label and store in a cool, dark place.

COOK'S TIP

To test for the set, spoon a little jam on to a chilled plate. It should wrinkle when pushed with a finger.

1 Cut the melons into small cubes and layer with the granulated sugar in a large non-metallic bowl. Cover with clear film (plastic wrap) and leave overnight, or until the melons release their juices.

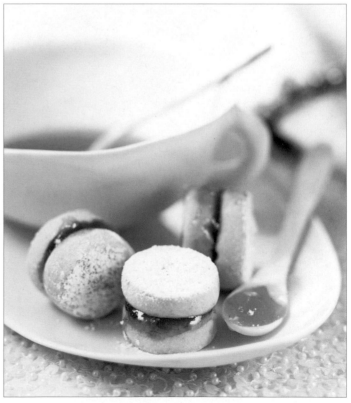

Energy 2133kcal/9095kJ; Protein 9.8g; Carbohydrate 554.3g, of which sugars 554.3g; Fat 1.5g, of which saturates 0g; Cholesterol 0mg; Calcium 434mg; Fibre 6g; Sodium 492mg.

oxford marmalade

The characteristic caramel colour and rich flavour of a traditional Oxford marmalade is obtained by cutting the fruit coarsely and cooking it for several hours before adding the sugar.

Makes about 2.25kg/5lb

INGREDIENTS

900g/2lb Seville (Temple) oranges
1.75 litres/3 pints/7½ cups water
1.3kg/3lb/6½ cups granulated
    (white) sugar, warmed

COOK'S TIP

Traditionalists say that only bitter oranges such as Seville (Temple) should be used to make marmalade. Although this isn't always true, it is certainly the case when making Oxford marmalade.

1 Scrub the orange skins, then remove the rind using a vegetable peeler. Thickly slice the rind and put in a large pan.

2 Chop the fruit, reserving the pips (seeds), and add to the rind in the pan, along with the water. Tie the orange pips in a piece of muslin (cheesecloth) and add to the pan. Bring to the boil, then cover and simmer for 2 hours. Add more water during cooking to maintain the same volume. Remove the pan from the heat and leave overnight.

3 The next day, remove the muslin bag from the oranges, squeezing well, and return the pan to the heat. Bring to the boil, then cover and simmer for 1 hour.

4 Add the warmed sugar to the pan, then slowly bring the mixture to the boil, stirring until the sugar has dissolved completely. Increase the heat and boil rapidly for about 15 minutes, or until setting point is reached (105°C/220°F).

5 Remove the pan from the heat and skim off any scum from the surface. Leave to cool for about 5 minutes, stir, then pour into warmed sterilized jars and seal. When cold, label, then store in a cool, dark place.

Energy 5455kcal/23275kJ; Protein 16.4g; Carbohydrate 1435g, of which sugars 1435g; Fat 0.9g, of which saturates 0g; Cholesterol 0mg; Calcium 1112mg; Fibre 15.3g; Sodium 123mg.

st clement's marmalade

This classic preserve made from oranges and lemons has a lovely citrus tang. It has a light, refreshing flavour and is perfect for serving for breakfast, spread on freshly toasted bread.

Makes about 2.25kg/5lb

INGREDIENTS

450g/1lb Seville (Temple) oranges
450g/1lb sweet oranges
4 lemons
1.5 litres/2½ pints/6¼ cups water
1.2kg/2½lb/5½ cups granulated (white) sugar, warmed

1 Wash the oranges and lemons, then halve and squeeze the juice into a large pan. Tie the pips (seeds) and membranes in a muslin (cheesecloth) bag, shred the orange and lemon rind and add to the pan.

2 Add the water to the pan, bring to the boil, then cover and simmer for 2 hours. Remove the muslin bag, leave to cool, then squeeze any liquid back into the pan.

3 Add the warmed sugar to the pan and stir over a low heat until completely dissolved. Bring to the boil and boil rapidly for about 15 minutes or until the marmalade reaches setting point (105°C/220°F).

4 Remove the pan from the heat and skim off any scum from the surface. Leave to cool for about 5 minutes, stir, then pour into warmed sterilized jars and seal. When cold, label, then store in a cool, dark place.

Energy 5061kcal/21594kJ; Protein 15.9g; Carbohydrate 1330.5g, of which sugars 1330.5g; Fat 0.9g, of which saturates 0g; Cholesterol 0mg; Calcium 1059mg; Fibre 15.3g; Sodium 117mg.

pink grapefruit and cranberry marmalade

Cranberries give this glorious marmalade an extra tartness and a full fruit flavour, as well as an inimitable vibrant colour. The resulting preserve makes a lively choice for breakfast or a brilliant accompaniment for cold roast turkey during the festive season.

2 Tie the grapefruit and lemon pips in a muslin (cheesecloth) bag and place in a large pan with the grapefruit slices and lemon juice.

3 Add the water and bring to the boil. Cover and simmer gently for 1½–2 hours, or until the grapefruit rind is very tender. Remove the muslin bag, leave to cool, then squeeze over the pan.

4 Add the cranberries to the pan, then bring to the boil. Simmer for 15–20 minutes, or until the berries have popped and softened.

Makes about 2.25kg/5lb

INGREDIENTS

675g/1½lb pink grapefruit
juice and pips (seeds) of 2 lemons
900ml/1½ pints/3¾ cups water
225g/8oz/2 cups cranberries
1.3kg/3lb/6½ cups granulated (white), sugar, warmed

5 Add the sugar to the pan and stir over a low heat until the sugar has completely dissolved. Bring to the boil and boil rapidly for about 10 minutes, or until setting point is reached (105°C/220°F).

6 Remove the pan from the heat and skim off any scum from the surface using a slotted spoon. Leave to cool for 5–10 minutes, then stir and pour into warmed sterilized jars. Seal, then label when the marmalade is cold.

COOK'S TIP

You can use fresh or frozen cranberries to make this marmalade. Either gives equally good results.

1 Wash, halve and quarter the grapefruit, then slice them thinly, reserving the pips (seeds) and any juice that runs out.

Energy 5403kcal/23043kJ; Protein 12.6g; Carbohydrate 1424.4g, of which sugars 1424.4g; Fat 0.9g, of which saturates 0g; Cholesterol 0mg; Calcium 853mg; Fibre 12.4g; Sodium 103mg.

ruby red grapefruit marmalade

If you prefer a really tangy marmalade, grapefruit is the perfect choice. To achieve a wonderfully red-blushed preserve, look for the red variety rather than pink. They have a lovely flavour and make a really delicious, sweet, jewel-coloured preserve.

Makes about 1.8kg/4lb

INGREDIENTS

900g/2lb ruby red grapefruit
1 lemon
1.2 litres/2 pints/5 cups water
1.3kg/3lb/6½ cups granulated (white) sugar, warmed

4 Add the water to the pan and bring to the boil. Cover and simmer for 2 hours, or until the rind is very tender.

5 Remove the muslin bag from the pan, leave to cool, then squeeze it over the pan. Add the sugar and stir over a low heat until it has dissolved. Bring to the boil, then boil rapidly for 10–15 minutes, or to setting point (105°C/220°F).

6 Remove the pan from the heat and skim off any scum using a slotted spoon. Leave to cool for about 10 minutes, then stir and pour into warmed sterilized jars. Seal, then label when cold.

1 Wash the grapefruit and lemon and remove the rind in thick pieces using a vegetable peeler. Cut the fruit in half and squeeze the juice into a preserving pan, reserving all the pips (seeds).

2 Put the pips and membranes from the fruit in a muslin (cheesecloth) bag and add to the pan. Discard the grapefruit and lemon shells.

3 Using a sharp knife, cut the grapefruit and lemon rind into thin or coarse shreds, as preferred, and place in the pan.

COOK'S TIP

Although you can use yellow grapefruit to make this marmalade, it tends to give a very pale result with more tang than the ruby red variety, but a much less fruity flavour.

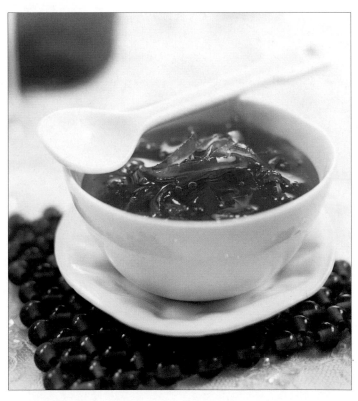

Energy 5392kcal/22987kJ; Protein 13.7g; Carbohydrate 1419.7g, of which sugars 1419.7g; Fat 0.9g, of which saturates 0g; Cholesterol 0mg; Calcium 896mg; Fibre 11.7g; Sodium 105mg.

lemon and ginger marmalade

This zesty marmalade makes an excellent basis for meat glazes. Simply mix a few spoonfuls with a little soy sauce and brush over the meat before grilling.

Makes about 1.8kg/4lb

INGREDIENTS

1.2kg/2½lb lemons

150g/5oz fresh root ginger, peeled and finely grated

1.2 litres/2 pints/5 cups water

900g/2lb/4½ cups granulated (white) sugar, warmed

COOK'S TIP

When choosing fresh root ginger, select young, firm, fine-skinned pieces. For the best results, grate only the tender, juicy parts of the root and discard any tough, hairy parts.

1 Quarter and slice the lemons. Tie the pips (seeds) in a muslin (cheesecloth) bag and place in a preserving pan with the lemons, ginger and water. Bring to the boil, cover with a lid and simmer for 2 hours, or until the fruit is tender.

2 Remove the muslin bag from the pan, leave to cool then squeeze over the pan to release all the juice and pectin. Stir in the sugar over a low heat until dissolved, then increase the heat and boil for 5–10 minutes, or until setting point is reached (105°C/220°F).

3 Remove the pan from the heat and skim off any scum from the surface using a slotted spoon.

4 Leave to cool for 5 minutes, stir, then pour into warmed sterilized jars and seal. When cold, label and store in a cool place.

Energy 3785kcal/16122kJ; Protein 17.3g; Carbohydrate 980.3g, of which sugars 980.3g; Fat 3.9g, of which saturates 1.2g; Cholesterol 0mg; Calcium 1559mg; Fibre 1.6g; Sodium 204mg.

orange and coriander marmalade

This marmalade made with bitter Seville oranges has the added zing of warm, spicy coriander.

Makes about 1.8kg/4lb

INGREDIENTS

675g/1½lb Seville (Temple) oranges

2 lemons

15ml/1 tbsp crushed coriander seeds

1.5 litres/2½ pints/6¼ cups water

900g/2lb/4½ cups granulated (white) sugar, warmed

1 Cut the oranges and lemons in half and squeeze out all the juice. Place the orange and lemon pips (seeds) in a muslin (cheesecloth) bag. Using a sharp knife, cut the rind into shreds and place in a preserving pan with the juice.

2 Put the coriander seeds in the muslin bag with the pips and place in the pan. Add the water and bring to the boil. Cover and simmer for 2 hours, or until the mixture has reduced by half and the peel is soft.

3 Remove the muslin bag from the pan. Set it aside to cool, then squeeze it over the pan to release all the juices and pectin.

4 Add the sugar to the pan and stir over a low heat until it has dissolved. Bring to the boil and boil rapidly for 5–10 minutes, or to setting point (105°C/220°F).

5 Remove the pan from the heat and skim off any scum from the surface using a slotted spoon. Leave to cool for 5 minutes, stir then pour into warmed sterilized jars. Seal, then label when cold.

Energy 3807kcal/16244kJ; Protein 12.4g; Carbohydrate 999.2g, of which sugars 997.9g; Fat 1.2g, of which saturates 0g; Cholesterol 0mg; Calcium 826mg; Fibre 12.6g; Sodium 110mg.

orange and whisky marmalade

Adding whisky to orange marmalade gives it a fantastic warmth and flavour. The whisky is stirred in after the marmalade is cooked, to retain its strength and slightly bitter edge, which would be lost if boiled. Whisky marmalade is great spooned over a steamed sponge pudding.

3 Remove the muslin bag from the pan, leave to cool, then squeeze it over the pan to release any juice and pectin. Add the sugar, then stir over a low heat until the sugar has dissolved. Increase the heat and boil for 5–10 minutes until setting point is reached (105°C/220°F).

4 Remove the pan from the heat and skim off any scum from the surface using a slotted spoon. Stir in the whisky, then leave to cool for 5 minutes. Stir and pour the marmalade into warmed sterilized jars. Seal, then label when cold. Store in a cool dark place.

Makes about 2.25kg/5lb

INGREDIENTS

900g/2lb Seville (Temple) oranges
juice and pips (seeds) of 1 large lemon
1.2 litres/2 pints/5 cups water
1.5kg/3lb 6oz/7½ cups granulated (white) sugar, warmed
60ml/4 tbsp whisky

1 Scrub the oranges and cut in half. Squeeze the juice into a large pan, reserving the pips (seeds) and any membranes. Place these in a muslin (cheesecloth) bag with the lemon pips and add to the juice.

2 Using a sharp knife, thinly slice the orange rind and put in the pan along with the water. Bring to the boil, then cover and simmer for 1½–2 hours, or until the citrus rind is very tender.

Energy 5588kcal/23826kJ; Protein 16.4g; Carbohydrate 1435g, of which sugars 1435g; Fat 0.9g, of which saturates 0g; Cholesterol 0mg; Calcium 1112mg; Fibre 15.3g; Sodium 123mg.

fine lime shred marmalade

There is something about lime marmalade that really captures the flavour and essence of the fruit. It is important to cut the slices very finely though, because lime skins tend to be tougher than those on any other citrus fruit and can result in a chewy marmalade if cut thickly.

Makes about 2.25kg/5lb

INGREDIENTS

12 limes

4 kaffir lime leaves

1.2 litres/2 pints/5 cups water

1.3kg/3lb/6½ cups granulated (white) sugar, warmed

1 Halve the limes lengthways, then slice thinly, reserving any pips (seeds). Tie the pips and lime leaves in a muslin (cheesecloth) bag and place the bag in a large pan with the sliced fruit.

2 Add the water to the pan and bring to the boil. Cover and simmer gently for 1½–2 hours, or until the rind is very soft. Remove the muslin bag, leave to cool, then squeeze it over the pan to release any juice and pectin.

COOK'S TIP

To check whether the rind is cooked, remove a piece from the pan (before the sugar is added) and leave it to cool briefly. When cool enough to handle, press the rind between finger and thumb – it should be very soft.

3 Add the sugar to the pan, and stir over a low heat until the sugar has dissolved. Bring to the boil, then boil rapidly for 15 minutes, stirring occasionally, until setting point is reached (105°C/220°F).

4 Remove the pan from the heat and skim off any scum. Leave to cool for 5 minutes, stir, then pour into warmed sterilized jars. Seal, then label when cold. Store in a cool, dark place.

COOK'S TIPS

• To check for setting, spoon a little marmalade on to a chilled saucer and chill for 2 minutes. Push the surface with your finger; if wrinkles form, the marmalade is ready to bottle.

• Stirring marmalade after standing and before potting distributes the fruit rind evenly as the preserve begins to set.

Energy 5250kcal/22386kJ; Protein 13.3g; Carbohydrate 1380.1g, of which sugars 1380.1g; Fat 2g, of which saturates 0.7g; Cholesterol 0mg; Calcium 1263mg; Fibre 0g; Sodium 112mg.

spiced pumpkin marmalade

The bright orange colour and warm flavour of this marmalade is guaranteed to banish the winter blues. The addition of pumpkin gives the preserve more body and a lovely, satisfying texture. It is perfect for spreading on hot buttered toast or serving with warm croissants.

Makes about 2.75kg/6lb

INGREDIENTS

900g/2lb Seville (Temple) oranges, washed and halved

450g/1lb lemons, halved and thinly sliced, pips (seeds) reserved

2 cinnamon sticks

2.5cm/1in piece fresh root ginger, peeled and thinly sliced

1.5ml/¼ tsp grated nutmeg

1.75 litres/3 pints/7½ cups water

800g/1¾lb squash or pumpkin, peeled, seeds (pips) removed and thinly sliced

1.3kg/3lb/6½ cups granulated (white) sugar, warmed

1 Squeeze the juice from the oranges and pour into a preserving pan. Remove the white membranes and reserve with the pips.

2 Thinly slice the orange rind and place in the pan, along with the sliced lemons. Tie the orange and lemon pips and membranes in a muslin (cheesecloth) bag with the spices and add to the pan with the water. Bring to the boil, then cover and simmer for 1 hour.

3 Add the pumpkin to the pan and continue cooking for 1–1½ hours. Remove the muslin bag, leave to cool, then squeeze over the pan.

4 Stir in the sugar over a low heat until completely dissolved. Bring to the boil, then boil rapidly for 15 minutes, or until the marmalade becomes thick and reaches setting point (105°C/220°F). Stir once or twice to ensure the marmalade does not stick to the pan.

5 Remove the pan from the heat and skim off any scum. Leave to cool for 5 minutes, then stir and pour into warmed sterilized jars. Cover the surface of the preserve with wax discs, then seal. Label when the marmalade is cold and store in a cool, dark place.

Energy 5645kcal/24071kJ; Protein 26.5g; Carbohydrate 1467g, of which sugars 1463g; Fat 3.9g, of which saturates 1.3g; Cholesterol 0mg; Calcium 1727mg; Fibre 23.3g; Sodium 146mg.

clementine and liqueur marmalade

Small, tart clementines make a particularly full-flavoured preserve, which can be put to a wide variety of culinary uses. Stir it into yogurt or warm it with a little water to make a zesty sauce for pancakes or crêpes. It is also superlative served with smooth ripe brie and crisp crackers.

Makes about 1.8kg/4lb

INGREDIENTS

900g/2lb clementines, washed and halved

juice and pips (seeds) of 2 lemons

900ml/1½ pints/3¾ cups water

900g/2lb/4½ cups granulated (white) sugar, warmed

60ml/4 tbsp Grand Marnier or Cointreau

COOK'S TIP

Any member of the mandarin family can be used to make this preserve, but clementines give the best result.

1 Slice the clementines, reserving any pips. Tie the pips in a muslin (cheesecloth) bag with the lemon pips and place in a large pan with the sliced fruit.

2 Add the lemon juice and water to the pan and bring to the boil, then cover and simmer for about 1½ hours, or until the rind is very tender. Remove the muslin bag, cool, then squeeze over the pan.

3 Stir in the sugar over a low heat until dissolved, then bring to the boil and cook 5–10 minutes, or to setting point (105°C/220°F).

4 Remove the pan from the heat and skim off any scum. Cool for 5 minutes, then stir in the liqueur and pour into warmed sterilized jars. Seal, then label when cold.

Energy 4036kcal/17210kJ; Protein 12.6g; Carbohydrate 1038.5g, of which sugars 1038.5g; Fat 0.9g, of which saturates 0g; Cholesterol 0mg; Calcium 759mg; Fibre 10.8g; Sodium 97mg.

tangerine and lemon grass marmalade

The subtle flavours of lemon grass and kaffir lime leaves add an exotic edge to this marmalade. You can also stir in thinly shredded lime leaf before bottling, which gives a very pretty result.

2 Tie all the pips, lemon grass and lime leaves in a piece of muslin (cheesecloth) and add to the pan. Boil, then simmer for 1½–2 hours, or until the tangerine rind is soft. Remove the bag, leave to cool, then squeeze over the pan.

3 Stir in the sugar over a low heat until completely dissolved, then boil for 5–10 minutes, or to setting point (105°C/220°F).

4 Remove the pan from the heat and skim off any scum. Leave to cool for 5 minutes, then stir and pour into warmed sterilized jars. Seal, then label when cold.

Makes about 1.8kg/4lb

INGREDIENTS

900g/2lb tangerines, washed and halved

juice and pips (seeds) of 2 Seville (Temple) oranges

900ml/1½ pints/3¾ cups water

2 lemon grass sticks, halved and crushed

3 kaffir lime leaves

900g/2lb/4½ cups granulated (white) sugar, warmed

COOK'S TIP

If you can't find kaffir lime leaves, you can substitute the finely pared rind of one lime.

1 Using a sharp knife, slice the tangerines thinly, reserving the pips. Place the sliced fruit in a preserving pan, along with juice from the Seville oranges and the measured water.

Energy 3935kcal/16768kJ; Protein 14.8g; Carbohydrate 1029.5g, of which sugars 1029.5g; Fat 1.1g, of which saturates 0g; Cholesterol 0mg; Calcium 949mg; Fibre 15.1g; Sodium 82mg.

pomelo and pineapple marmalade

Slightly larger than a grapefruit, pomelos have lime-green skin and a sharp, refreshing flavour and are delicious combined with tangy pineapple. Serve as a spread or spoon over desserts.

Makes about 2.75kg/6lb

INGREDIENTS

2 pomelos

900ml/1½ pints/3¾ cups water

2 x 432g/14¼oz cans crushed pineapple in fruit juice

900g/2lb/4½ cups granulated (white) sugar, warmed

2 Cover the pan and simmer for 1½–2 hours, stirring occasionally, or until the fruit is soft. Add the pineapple and juice and simmer for a further 30 minutes.

3 Remove the muslin bag from the pan, leave to cool, then squeeze over the pan. Add the sugar and stir over a low heat until it has dissolved. Increase the heat and boil for 10 minutes, or to setting point (105°C/220°F).

4 Remove the pan from the heat and skim off any scum from the surface using a slotted spoon. Leave to cool for 10 minutes, then stir and pour into warmed sterilized jars. Seal, then label the jars when they are cold.

1 Wash and halve the pomelos. Squeeze out the juice, reserving any pips (seeds), and pour into a large pan. Remove the membranes and any excess pith and tie in muslin (cheesecloth) with the pips. Slice the peel thinly and add to the pan along with the muslin bag and water. Bring to the boil.

Energy 4042kcal/17233kJ; Protein 10.1g; Carbohydrate 1065.3g, of which sugars 1065.3g; Fat 0.4g, of which saturates 0g; Cholesterol 0mg; Calcium 633mg; Fibre 9.2g; Sodium 74mg.

peach and kumquat marmalade

Combined with sweet, scented peaches, kumquats make a wonderful, fresh-tasting preserve.

Makes about 1.8kg/4lb

INGREDIENTS

675g/1½lb kumquats, sliced thinly, pips (seeds) and juice reserved

juice and pips (seeds) of 1 lime

900g/2lb peaches, skinned and thinly sliced, skins reserved

900ml/1½ pints/3¾ cups water

900g/2lb/4½ cups granulated (white) sugar, warmed

1 Tie the pips and the peach skins in a muslin (cheesecloth) bag and put in a pan with the kumquats, juices and water. Bring to the boil, then cover and simmer for 50 minutes.

2 Add the peaches to the pan, bring to the boil, then simmer for 40–50 minutes, or until the fruit has become very soft. Remove the muslin bag, leave to cool, then squeeze over the pan.

3 Add the sugar to the pan and stir over a low heat until it has dissolved. Bring the mixture to the boil, then boil rapidly for about 15 minutes, stirring occasionally, to setting point (105°C/220°F).

4 Remove the pan from the heat and skim off any scum from the surface using a slotted spoon.

5 Leave to cool for 5–10 minutes, then stir and pour into warmed sterilized jars. Seal, then label when the jars are cold. Store in a cool, dark place.

Energy 4093kcal/17474kJ; Protein 19.6g; Carbohydrate 1067.6g, of which sugars 1067.6g; Fat 1.6g, of which saturates 0g; Cholesterol 0mg; Calcium 749mg; Fibre 21.6g; Sodium 90mg.

apricot and orange marmalade

This combination of oranges and rich-tasting apricots is a winner with strong coffee.

Makes about 1.5kg/3lb 6oz

INGREDIENTS

2 Seville (Temple) oranges, washed and quartered

1 lemon, washed and quartered,

1.2 litres/2 pints/5 cups water

900g/2lb apricots, stoned (pitted) and thinly sliced

900g/2lb/4½ cups granulated (white) sugar, warmed

COOK'S TIP

It is important to use a food processor to chop the oranges and lemon for this recipe. Chopping them this finely igves the marmalade its wonderful consistency. Preparing the fruits by hand will not give the same result.

1 Remove the pips (seeds) from the citrus fruit and tie in a muslin (cheesecloth) bag. Finely chop the oranges and lemons in a food processor and put in a large pan with the muslin bag and water.

2 Bring the mixture to the boil, then simmer, covered, for 1 hour.

3 Add the apricots to the pan, bring to the boil, then simmer for 30–40 minutes, or until the fruits are very tender.

4 Add the sugar to the pan and stir over a low heat until the sugar has dissolved. Bring to the boil, then boil rapidly for 15 minutes, stirring occasionally, until setting point is reached (105°C/220°F).

5 Remove the pan from the heat and skim off any scum using a slotted spoon. Leave to cool for about 5 minutes, then stir and pour into warmed sterilized jars. Seal, then label when cold and store in a cool, dry place.

Energy 3936kcal/16809kJ; Protein 15.9g; Carbohydrate 1030.8g, of which sugars 1030.8g; Fat 1.2g, of which saturates 0g; Cholesterol 0mg; Calcium 753mg; Fibre 20.4g; Sodium 87mg.

lemon curd

This classic tangy, creamy curd is still one of the most popular of all the curds. It is delicious spread thickly over freshly baked white bread or served with American-style pancakes, and also makes a wonderfully rich, zesty sauce spooned over fresh fruit tarts.

Makes about 450g/1lb

INGREDIENTS

3 lemons

200g/7oz/1 cup caster (superfine) sugar

115g/4oz/8 tbsp unsalted (sweet) butter, diced

2 large (US extra large) eggs

2 large (US extra large) egg yolks

1 Wash the lemons, then finely grate the rind and place in a large heatproof bowl. Using a sharp knife, halve the lemons and squeeze the juice into the bowl. Set over a pan of gently simmering water and add the sugar and butter. Stir until the sugar has dissolved and the butter melted.

2 Put the eggs and yolks in a bowl and beat together with a fork. Pour the eggs through a sieve into the lemon mixture, and whisk well until thoroughly combined.

3 Stir the mixture constantly over the heat until the lemon curd thickens and lightly coats the back of a wooden spoon.

4 Remove the pan from the heat and pour the curd into small, warmed sterilized jars. Cover, seal and label. Store in a cool, dark place, ideally in the refrigerator. Use within 3 months. (Once opened, store in the refrigerator.)

COOK'S TIP

If you are really impatient when it comes to cooking, it is possible to cook the curd in a heavy pan directly over a low heat. However, you really need to watch it like a hawk to avoid the mixture curdling. If the curd looks as though it's beginning to curdle, plunge the base of the pan in cold water and beat vigorously.

Energy 1942kcal/8119kJ; Protein 22.5g; Carbohydrate 209.7g, of which sugars 209.7g; Fat 118.8g, of which saturates 66.8g; Cholesterol 1105mg; Calcium 242mg; Fibre 0g; Sodium 895mg.

seville orange curd

Using flavoursome Seville oranges gives this curd a fantastic orange flavour and a real citrus tang. It is perfect for spreading on toast for breakfast or at tea time, and is also superlative folded into whipped cream and used as a filling for cakes, roulades and scones.

Makes about 450g/1lb

INGREDIENTS

2 Seville (Temple) oranges

115g/4oz/8 tbsp unsalted (sweet) butter, diced

200g/7oz/1 cup caster (superfine) sugar

2 large (US extra large) eggs

2 large (US extra large) egg yolks

1 Wash the oranges, then finely grate the rind and place in a large heatproof bowl. Halve the oranges and squeeze the juice into the bowl with the rind.

2 Place the bowl over a pan of gently simmering water and add the butter and sugar. Stir until the sugar has completely dissolved and the butter melted.

3 Put the eggs and yolks in a small bowl and lightly whisk, then pour into the orange mixture through a sieve. Whisk them together until thoroughly combined.

4 Stir the orange and egg mixture constantly over the heat until the mixture thickens and lightly coats the back of a wooden spoon.

5 Pour the orange curd into small, warmed sterilized jars, cover and seal. Store in a cool, dark place, preferably in the refrigerator.

WATCHPOINTS

• The very young, the elderly, pregnant women, and those with a compromised immune system are advised against eating raw eggs or food containing raw eggs. Although the eggs in fruit curds are lightly cooked, they may still be unsuitable for these groups of people.

• Fruit curds do not have the shelf-life of many other preserves and should be used within 3 months of making.

• Once opened, always store fruit curds in the refrigerator.

Energy 2053kcal/8593kJ; Protein 25.8g; Carbohydrate 235.2g, of which sugars 235.2g; Fat 119.1g, of which saturates 66.8g; Cholesterol 1105mg; Calcium 383mg; Fibre 5.1g; Sodium 910mg.

grapefruit curd

If you favour tangy and refreshing preserves, this grapefruit curd is the one to try. Really fresh free-range eggs give the best results and flavour when making curd.

Makes about 675g/1½lb

INGREDIENTS

finely grated rind and juice of 1 grapefruit

115g/4oz/8 tbsp unsalted (sweet)
  butter, diced

200g/7oz/1 cup caster (superfine) sugar

4 large (US extra large) eggs,
  lightly beaten

1 Put the grapefruit rind and juice in a large heatproof bowl with the butter and sugar, and set over a pan of gently simmering water. Heat the mixture, stirring occasionally, until the sugar has dissolved and the butter melted.

2 Add the beaten eggs to the fruit mixture, straining them through a sieve. Whisk together, then stir constantly over the heat until the mixture thickens and lightly coats the back of a wooden spoon.

3 Pour the curd into small, warmed sterilized jars, cover and seal. Once the jars are cold you can label and store them in a cool, dark place, preferably in the refrigerator. They should be used within 3 months. (Once opened, store the curd in the refrigerator.)

VARIATION

Tangy grapefruit and sweet orange marry particularly well in creamy fruit curds. Add the grated rind of a small orange to this grapefruit recipe for an extra zingy, zesty alternative.

Energy 1971kcal/8244kJ; Protein 27.1g; Carbohydrate 218g, of which sugars 218g; Fat 116.8g, of which saturates 66.1g; Cholesterol 1006mg; Calcium 255mg; Fibre 0g; Sodium 996mg.

passion fruit curd

The tropical flavour and aroma of passion fruit fills this curd with a gloriously sunny character. It is perfect spread on toasted English muffins or little American pancakes.

Makes about 675g/1½lb

INGREDIENTS

grated rind and juice of 2 lemons

115g/4oz/8 tbsp unsalted (sweet) butter, diced

275g/10oz/1⅓ cups caster (superfine) sugar

4 passion fruit

4 eggs

2 egg yolks

1 Place the lemon rind and juice in a large heatproof bowl and add the butter and sugar.

2 Halve the passion fruit and scoop the seeds into a sieve set over the bowl. Press out all the juice and discard the seeds.

3 Place the bowl over a pan of gently simmering water and stir occasionally until the sugar has dissolved and the butter melted.

4 Beat the eggs and yolks together and add to the bowl, pouring them through a sieve, then whisk well to combine. Stir constantly until the mixture thickens and lightly coats the back of a spoon.

5 Pour the curd into small, warmed sterilized jars, cover and seal. Store in a cool, dark place, preferably in the refrigerator and use within 3 months. (Once opened, store in the refrigerator.)

Energy 2377kcal/9961kJ; Protein 34.4g; Carbohydrate 291.5g, of which sugars 291.5g; Fat 128g, of which saturates 69.3g; Cholesterol 1409mg; Calcium 334mg; Fibre 2g; Sodium 1023mg.

apple and cinnamon butter

Fans of apple pies and crumbles will love this luscious apple butter. Serve on toast or with warmed brioche for a breakfast treat or with pancakes and cream for tea.

Makes about 1.8kg/4lb

INGREDIENTS

475ml/16fl oz/2 cups dry (hard) cider

450g/1lb tart cooking apples, peeled, cored and sliced

450g/1lb eating apples, peeled, cored and sliced

grated rind and juice of 1 lemon

675g/1½lb/scant 3½ cups granulated (white) sugar, warmed

5ml/1 tsp ground cinnamon

COOK'S TIP

Leaving the butter to stand for 2 days give the flavours a chance to develop.

1 Pour the cider into a large pan and bring to the boil. Boil hard until the volume is reduced by half, then add the apples and lemon rind and juice.

2 Cover the pan and cook for 10 minutes. Uncover and continue cooking for 20–30 minutes, or until the apples are very soft.

3 Leave the mixture to cool slightly, then pour into a food processor or blender and blend to a purée. Press through a fine sieve into a bowl.

4 Measure the purée into a large heavy pan, adding 275g/10oz/ 1⅓ cups warmed sugar for every 600ml/1 pint/2½ cups of purée. Add the ground cinnamon and stir well to combine.

5 Gently heat the mixture, stirring continuously, until the sugar has completely dissolved. Increase the heat and boil steadily for about 20 minutes, stirring frequently, until the mixture forms a thick purée that hold its shape when spooned on to a cold plate.

6 Spoon the apple and cinnamon butter into warmed sterilized jars. Seal and label, then store in a cool, dark place for 2 days to allow the flavours to develop before serving.

Energy 3146kcal/13428kJ]; Protein 6.1g; Carbohydrate 797.8g, of which sugars 797.8g; Fat 0.9g, of which saturates 0g; Cholesterol 0mg; Calcium 432mg; Fibre 14.4g; Sodium 92mg.

pear and vanilla butter

The delicate flavour of pears is enhanced by vanilla in this butter that really captures the essence of the fruit. It is well worth allowing it to mature for a few days before eating.

Makes about 675g/1½lb

INGREDIENTS

900g/2lb pears, peeled, cored
and chopped

juice of 3 lemons

300ml/½ pint/1¼ cups water

1 vanilla pod (bean), split

675g/1½lb/scant 3½ cups granulated
(white) sugar, warmed

1 Place the pears in a large pan with the lemon juice, water and vanilla pod. Bring to the boil, then cover and simmer for 10 minutes. Uncover the pan and continue cooking for a further 15–20 minutes, or until the pears are very soft.

2 Remove the vanilla pod from the pan, then carefully scrape the seeds into the fruit mixture using the tip of a knife.

3 Tip the fruit and juices into a food processor or blender and blend to a purée. Press the purée through a fine sieve into a bowl.

4 Measure the purée into a large heavy pan, adding 275g/10oz/1⅓ cups warmed sugar for every 600ml/1 pint/2½ cups of purée.

5 Stir the mixture over a low heat until the sugar dissolves. Increase the heat and boil for 15 minutes, stirring, until the mixture forms a thick purée that holds its shape when spooned on to a cold plate.

6 Spoon the pear butter into small, warmed sterilized jars. Seal, label and store in a cool, dark place for at least 2 days before serving.

COOK'S TIPS

• Fruit butters have a soft spreading consistency – thicker than fruit curds, but softer than fruit cheeses. They make an excellent tea time preserve.

• Fruit butters keep well in sealed jars and can be stored for up to 3 months. Once opened, they should be stored in the refrigerator.

Energy 3020kcal/12868kJ; Protein 6.1g; Carbohydrate 795.4g, of which sugars 795.4g; Fat 0.9g, of which saturates 0g; Cholesterol 0mg; Calcium 457mg; Fibre 19.8g; Sodium 68mg.

plum butter

Simmering plums down creates a preserve with a rich, red colour and a smooth texture.

Makes about 900g/2lb

INGREDIENTS

900g/2lb red plums, stoned (pitted)
grated rind and juice of 1 orange
150ml/¼ pint/⅔ cup water
450g/1lb/2¼ cups granulated (white)
  sugar, warmed

1 Place the plums in a large, heavy pan with the orange rind and juice and the water. Bring to the boil, then cover with a lid and cook for 20–30 minutes, or until the plums are very soft. Set aside to cool.

2 Press the fruit through a fine sieve. Measure the purée into a pan and add 350g/12oz/1¾ cups sugar for every 600ml/1 pint/2½ cups purée. Gently heat, stirring.

3 When the sugar has dissolved, increase the heat and boil for 10–15 minutes, stirring frequently, until the mixture holds its shape when spooned on to a cold plate.

4 Spoon the mixture into warmed sterilized jars. Seal and label, then store in a cool, dark place for 2 days to mature before serving.

COOK'S TIP
Serve the plum butter on toasted walnut and raisin bread for a delicious breakfast, at tea time or just as a snack.

Energy 2115kcal/9036kJ; Protein 7.9g; Carbohydrate 553.9g, of which sugars 553.9g; Fat 1g, of which saturates 0g; Cholesterol 0mg; Calcium 361mg; Fibre 14.5g; Sodium 50mg.

golden peach butter

The rich, dark golden colour and delicate, spicy flavour of this butter makes it a real treat.

Makes about 2.25kg/5lb

INGREDIENTS

1.3kg/3lb ripe peaches, stoned (pitted)
600ml/1 pint/2½ cups water
675g/1½lb/scant 3½ cups granulated
  (white) sugar, warmed
grated rind and juice of 1 lemon
2.5ml/½ tsp ground cinnamon
2.5ml/½ tsp ground nutmeg

1 Slice the peaches and place in a large pan with the water. Bring to the boil, then cover and simmer for about 10 minutes.

2 Remove the lid from the pan and simmer gently for a further 45 minutes, or until the peaches are quite soft.

3 Leave the fruit mixture to cool slightly, then transfer to a food processor or blender and process to a purée. Press the purée through a fine sieve into a bowl.

4 Measure the purée into a large heavy pan, adding 275g/10oz/1⅓ cups warmed sugar for every 600ml/1 pint/2½ cups of purée.

5 Add the lemon rind and juice and spices to the pan and stir to combine. Gently heat, stirring, until the sugar has dissolved.

6 Bring the mixture to the boil and cook for 15–20 minutes, stirring frequently, until the mixture forms a thick purée that holds its shape when spooned on to a cold plate.

7 Spoon the butter into small, warmed sterilized jars and seal and label, then store in a cool, dark place for 2 days before eating.

COOK'S TIP
For a really special treat, spoon this sweet, fragrant butter into tiny tart cases or on to bite-size brioches.

Energy 3089kcal/13193kJ; Protein 16.4g; Carbohydrate 804.2g, of which sugars 804.2g; Fat 1.3g, of which saturates 0g; Cholesterol 0mg; Calcium 449mg; Fibre 19.5g; Sodium 54mg.

pumpkin and maple butter

This all-American butter has a lovely bright, autumnal colour and flavour. It is perfect served spread on little pancakes fresh from the griddle, or used as a filling or topping for cakes.

Makes about 675g/1½lb

INGREDIENTS

1.2kg/2½lb pumpkin or butternut
   squash, peeled, seeded
   and chopped
450ml/¾ pint/scant 2 cups water
grated rind and juice of 1 orange
5ml/1 tsp ground cinnamon
120ml/4fl oz/½ cup maple syrup
675g/1½lb/scant 3½ cups granulated
   (white) sugar, warmed

VARIATION

This butter is also delicious made with
clear honey instead of maple syrup.
It adds a distinct flavour.

1 Put the pumpkin or squash in the pan with the water and cook for 30–40 minutes, or until it is very tender. Drain and, using the back of a spoon, press the cooked pumpkin or squash through a fine sieve into a bowl.

2 Stir the orange rind and juice, cinnamon and maple syrup into the purée, then measure the purée into a large pan, adding 275g/10oz/1⅓ cups warmed sugar for every 600ml/1 pint/2½ cups purée.

3 Gently heat the purée, stirring, until the sugar has dissolved. Increase the heat and boil for 10–20 minutes, stirring frequently, until the mixture forms a thick purée that holds its shape when spooned on to a cold plate.

4 Spoon the butter into small, warmed sterilized jars. Seal and label, then store in a cool, dark place for 2 days before eating.

Energy 3191kcal/13606kJ; Protein 12.4g; Carbohydrate 831g, of which sugars 825g; Fat 2.4g, of which saturates 1.2g; Cholesterol 0mg; Calcium 730mg; Fibre 12.1g; Sodium 370mg.

mango and cardamom butter

You need to use really ripe mangoes for this recipe. If the mangoes are not ripe enough, they will need much longer cooking and will not produce such a richly flavoured butter.

Makes about 675g/1½lb

INGREDIENTS

900g/2lb ripe mangoes, peeled

6 green cardamom pods, split

120ml/4fl oz/½ cup freshly squeezed lemon juice

120ml/4fl oz/½ cup freshly squeezed orange juice

50ml/2fl oz/¼ cup water

675g/1½lb/scant 3½ cups granulated (white) sugar, warmed

1 Cut the mango flesh away from the stones and chop, then place it in a pan with the cardamom pods, fruit juices and water.

2 Cover and simmer for 10 minutes. Remove the lid and simmer for a further 25 minutes, or until the mangoes are very soft and there is very little liquid left in the pan.

3 Remove the cardamom pods from the pan and discard. Transfer the fruit to a food processor and blend to a purée. Press the purée through a fine sieve into a bowl.

4 Measure the purée into a large, heavy pan, adding 275g/10oz/ 1⅓ cups warmed sugar for every 600ml/1 pint/2½ cups purée. Gently heat, stirring, until the sugar has dissolved. Increase the heat and boil for 10–20 minutes, stirring, until a thick butter forms that holds its shape when spooned on to a cold plate.

5 Spoon the mango and cardamom butter into small, warmed sterilized jars. Seal and label, then store in a cool, dark place for at least 2 days before eating. (The butter can be stored for up to 3 months.)

Energy 3216kcal/13735kJ; Protein 10.3g; Carbohydrate 842.8g, of which sugars 840.1g; Fat 1.9g, of which saturates 0.9g; Cholesterol 0mg; Calcium 478mg; Fibre 23.5g; Sodium 71mg.

damson and vanilla cheese

This cheese is good with roast lamb, duck and game, or semi-soft cheese.

Makes about 900g/2lb

INGREDIENTS

1.5kg/3lb 6oz damsons
1 vanilla pod (bean), split
800g/1¾lb/4 cups granulated (white)
  sugar, warmed

COOK'S TIPS

• When the cheese is ready, you
should be able to see the base of the
pan when a wooden spoon is drawn
through the mixture. To test the set,
spoon a small amount of the damson
mixture on to a chilled plate; it should
form a firm jelly.
• To make cheese shapes, spoon the
mixture into greased moulds, and leave
to set before turning out and serving.

1 Wash the damsons and place in
a large pan with the vanilla pod
and pour in enough water to come
halfway up the fruit. Cover and
simmer for 30 minutes.

2 Remove the vanilla pod from the
pan and scrape the seeds back into
the pan using the point of a knife.

3 Press the fruit and juices
through a sieve into a bowl.
Measure the purée into a large,
heavy pan, adding 400g/14oz/
2 cups sugar for every 600ml/
1 pint/2½ cups purée.

4 Gently heat the purée, stirring,
until the sugar has dissolved.
Increase the heat slightly and cook
for about 45 minutes, stirring
frequently with a wooden spoon,
until very thick.

5 Spoon the damson cheese into
warmed, sterilized jars. Seal and
label, then store in a cool, dark
place for 2–3 months to dry out
slightly before eating.

Energy 3722kcal/15878kJ; Protein 11.5g; Carbohydrate 980g, of which sugars 980g; Fat 0g, of which saturates 0g; Cholesterol 0mg; Calcium 784mg; Fibre 27g; Sodium 78mg.

quince cheese

This wonderfully fragrant fruit cheese is particularly good served as a sweetmeat.

Makes about 900g/2lb

INGREDIENTS

1.3kg/3lb quinces
800g/1¾lb/4 cups granulated (white)
  sugar, warmed
caster (superfine) sugar, for dusting

COOK'S TIP

Rather than setting the cheese and
cutting it into squares, simply
spoon the mixture into warmed,
sterilized, straight-sided jars. Seal
and label, then store in a cool,
dark place for 2–3 months to dry
out slightly before eating.

1 Wash the quinces, then chop
and place in a large pan. Pour in
enough water to nearly cover the
fruit, then cover with a lid and
simmer for 45 minutes, or until the
fruit is very tender. Cool slightly.

2 Press the mixture through a fine
sieve into a bowl. Measure the
purée into a large, heavy pan,
adding 400g/14oz/2 cups sugar for
every 600ml/1 pint/2½ cups purée.
Heat gently, stirring, until the sugar
has dissolved. Increase the heat and
cook for 40–50 minutes, stirring
frequently, until very thick (see
Cook's Tip left).

3 Pour the mixture into a small
oiled baking tin (pan) and leave
to set for 24 hours. Cut into small
squares, dust with sugar and store
in an airtight container.

Energy 3672kcal/15645kJ; Protein 7.9g; Carbohydrate 966g, of which sugars 966g; Fat 1.3g, of which saturates 0g; Cholesterol 0mg; Calcium 567mg; Fibre 28.6g; Sodium 87mg.

spiced cherry cheese

For the best results, try to use cherries that have a good tart flavour and dark red flesh.
Serve as an accompaniment to strong cheese, or sliced with roast duck or pork.

Makes about 900g/2lb

INGREDIENTS

1.5kg/3lb 6oz/8¼ cups cherries,
  stoned (pitted)

2 cinnamon sticks

800g/1¾lb/4 cups granulated (white)
  sugar, warmed

COOK'S TIPS

• Store the cheese in a cool, dark
place for 2–3 months before eating.
• To serve a fruit cheese in slices, turn
it out of its container and slice using a
sharp knife. The slices may be cut into
smaller portions. Try to use a straight-
sided container so that the cheese can
slide out easily.

1 Place the cherries in a large pan
with the cinnamon sticks. Pour in
enough water to almost cover the
fruit. Bring to the boil, then cover
and simmer for 20–30 minutes, or
until the cherries are very tender.
Remove the cinnamon sticks from
the pan and discard.

2 Tip the fruit into a sieve and
press into a bowl, using the back
of a spoon. Measure the purée into
a large, heavy pan, adding 350g/
12oz/1¾ cups warmed sugar for
every 600ml/1 pint/2½ cups purée.

3 Gently heat the purée, stirring,
until the sugar dissolves. Increase
the heat and cook for 45 minutes,
stirring frequently, until very thick.
To test, spoon a little of the cheese
on to a cold plate; it should form
a firm jelly.

4 Spoon into warmed, sterilized
jars or oiled moulds. Seal, label,
and store in a cool, dark place.

Energy 3872kcal/16493kJ; Protein 17.5g; Carbohydrate 1008.5g, of which sugars 1008.5g; Fat 1.5g, of which saturates 0g; Cholesterol 0mg; Calcium 619mg; Fibre 13.5g; Sodium 63mg.

blackberry and apple cheese

This rich, dark preserve has an incredibly intense flavour and fabulous colour. For a fragrant twist, add a few raspberries – or even strawberries – in place of some of the blackberries.

Makes about 900g/2lb

INGREDIENTS

900g/2lb/8 cups blackberries

450g/1lb tart cooking apples, cut into chunks, with skins and cores intact

grated rind and juice of 1 lemon

800g/1¾lb/4 cups granulated (white) sugar, warmed

1 Put the blackberries, apples and lemon rind and juice in a pan and pour in enough water to come halfway up the fruit. Bring to the boil, then uncover and simmer for 15–20 minutes or until the fruit is very soft.

2 Leave the fruit to cool slightly, then tip the mixture into a sieve and press into a bowl, using the back of a spoon. Measure the purée into a large, heavy pan, adding 400g/14oz/2 cups warmed sugar for every 600ml/1 pint/ 2½ cups purée.

3 Gently heat the purée, stirring, until the sugar dissolves. Increase the heat slightly and cook for 40–50 minutes, stirring frequently, until very thick (see Cook's Tip).

4 Spoon the blackberry and apple cheese into warmed, sterilized straight-sided jars or oiled moulds. Seal and label the jars or moulds, then store in a cool, dark place for 2–3 months to dry out slightly.

COOK'S TIP

When the cheese is ready, you should be able to see the base of the pan when a wooden spoon is drawn through the mixture. Spoon a small amount of the mixture on to a chilled plate; it should form a firm jelly.

Energy 3535kcal/15064kJ; Protein 13.4g; Carbohydrate 921.9g, of which sugars 921.9g; Fat 2.3g, of which saturates 0g; Cholesterol 0mg; Calcium 811mg; Fibre 35.1g; Sodium 75mg.

INDEX